"For Me to Live Is Christ"

"For Me to Live Is Christ"
FROM GENESIS TO REVELATION

Joel R. Beeke

Reformation Heritage Books
Grand Rapids, Michigan

"For Me to Live Is Christ"
© 2025 by Joel R. Beeke

All rights reserved. No part of this book may be used or reproduced in any manner whatsoever without written permission except in the case of brief quotations embodied in critical articles and reviews. Direct your requests to the publisher at the following addresses:

Reformation Heritage Books
3070 29th St. SE
Grand Rapids, MI 49512
616-977-0889
orders@heritagebooks.org
www.heritagebooks.org

Printed in the United States of America
25 26 27 28 29 30/10 9 8 7 6 5 4 3 2

ISBN 979-8-88686-199-0 (hardcover)
ISBN 979-8-88686-200-3 (e-pub)

For the beloved flock,

**The Heritage Reformed Congregation
of Grand Rapids,**

With love for you and appreciation
for your listening well to my sermons.

And for the beloved students and alumni of

**Puritan Reformed Theological Seminary
of Grand Rapids,**

With love for you and appreciation for
listening well to my lectures.

---

*I love you all in Christ far more than you know.
It has been a great joy to know and to serve you.*

Contents

Foreword ix
Preface xi

1. The Creation of the Woman (Genesis 2:18–24)............ 1
2. Advent and the First Gospel Promise (Genesis 3:15)...... 15
3. Joseph and His Brothers (Genesis 45:3–4)................ 27
4. Seeing God's Glory (Exodus 33:18)....................... 41
5. Following God Fully (Numbers 14:24).................... 53
6. National Repentance Needed: Ezra's Example
   (Ezra 9:4)... 69
7. Why Do the Nations Rage? (Psalm 2)..................... 79
8. The Satisfying and Nourishing Word of God
   (Psalm 19)... 95
9. The Shepherd's Gift of Rest (Psalm 23:2a).............. 109
10. God's Holiness (Isaiah 6)............................. 125
11. The Tenth Anniversary of 9/11: The Lord Questions Us
    (Jeremiah 2:31)....................................... 143
12. Our Nation Laid in the Balances (Jeremiah 9:9)........ 157
13. Daniel's Separation from the World (Daniel 1:8, 14, 21) ... 167
14. Matchless Mercy for God's Heritage (Micah 7:18–19).... 183
15. The Spirit of Grace and Supplication (Zechariah 12:10) ... 195
16. The Glory of God as Father: Undue Anxiety Out of
    Order for Adopted Believers (Matthew 6:25–34)......... 213
17. Christ Forsaken! (Matthew 27:33–50)................... 229
18. Fighting Unbelief (Mark 9:24)......................... 247
19. Jesus Touches the Open Coffin (Luke 7:14)............. 267
20. Christ's Tears Over Jerusalem (Luke 19:41–42)......... 283

21. Like Father, Like Son (John 1:12–13) 297
22. Empty Grave Clothes (John 20:5–9) 317
23. Pentecost: The Outpouring of the Holy Spirit
    (Acts 2:1–4) 331
24. Crying Out to the God of Providence (Acts 4:23–37) 347
25. Felix Under the Preaching of the Word of God
    (Acts 24:24–25) 363
26. Our Reformation Heritage: The Just Living by Faith
    (Romans 1:16–17) 377
27. All Things Working Together for Good for God's People
    (Romans 8:28) 391
28. The Only Way to Live and Die (Philippians 1:21) 405
29. The Glory of the Son's Purchase: The Privilege
    and Right of Adoption (Ephesians 1:3–6) 419
30. Zero Tolerance for Lust (Ephesians 5:3–4) 435
31. Using, Not Abusing the World (1 Timothy 4:1–8) 449
32. Holding Fast to Christ Who Holds Fast to You
    (Hebrews 4:14–16) 467
33. Precious Blood (1 Peter 1:18–19) 489
34. Worldliness (1 John 2:15–17) 507
35. God Is Love (1 John 4:7) 527
36. Seals Five and Six: The Persecuted Church
    (Revelation 6:9–17) 543

Foreword

I consider it a great privilege to recommend the reading of this collection of Dr. Beeke's sermons. Our spiritual friendship spans a period of fifty-six years and began during our teen years when it pleased the Lord to lead us to a saving knowledge of the Christ who is the preeminent theme of these sermons.

During these fifty-six years, we have been privileged to co-labor in the service of our Lord Jesus Christ on multiple levels. This includes being trained for gospel ministry by him during the embryonic days of Puritan Reformed Theological Seminary (1995–1998) and being ordained by him as a minister of the gospel (1998).

As a result of our lengthy friendship, I have become thoroughly familiar with the preaching of my beloved brother. The sermons in this volume are an excellent representation of his preaching ministry that spans a period of nearly fifty years—a period marked by remarkable growth in my brother's grasp of the gospel he so passionately preaches.

As you prayerfully read these sermons, you will discover what many would affirm who have been privileged to be at the receiving end of my brother's preaching, namely, that his sermons

- are consistently Christ-centered and Christ-exalting;
- give evidence of careful textual exegesis and exposition;
- exemplify the experiential emphasis he has been consistently promoting throughout his entire ministry;
- are discriminatory in the rich Puritan tradition he so passionately promotes;
- are filled with helpful and compelling applications that are extracted from the text.

In short, given his lengthy tenure as homiletics professor, Dr. Beeke practices what he preaches!

May God, therefore, richly bless the reading of these sermons—sermons that affirm that also of my brother it is true that he ceases "not to preach and teach Jesus Christ" (Acts 5:42).

Thus, may this book, with the Holy Spirit's blessing, fulfill the mandate of all gospel ministry: "Comfort ye, comfort ye my people, saith your God. Speak ye comfortably to Jerusalem, and cry unto her, that her warfare is accomplished, that her iniquity is pardoned: for she hath received of the LORD's hand double for all her sins" (Isa. 40:1–2). May the fruit be that we would wholeheartedly echo the theme of this book, "For me to live is Christ!" That, after all, is the bottom line of Spirit-wrought, experiential Christianity.

—Bartel Elshout
Pastor of Kalamazoo
Reformed Church

Preface

For the last quarter of a century, I have had the privilege of serving the Gospel Trumpet ministry sponsored by the Heritage Reformed Congregations (HRC) of North America as its radio preacher for several stations around the country. To edify God's people and to assist fundraising for the radio ministry, I helped establish a printed sermon ministry that has sent tens of thousands of sermons to believers throughout the English-speaking world. Twice a year we (the HRC Gospel Trumpet Committee) print three sermons from Heritage Reformed pastors in a booklet, and then send out these sermon booklets to a growing mailing list of thousands of people. By God's grace, incoming donations from these booklets, combined with church collections, supply the needed funds for the radio ministry. One of my joyous tasks is to serve as final editor for these booklets, as well as usually contributing one or two of the sermons in these booklets myself.

The book you hold in your hand, *"For Me to Live is Christ,"* is a selection of these Gospel Trumpet sermons that I have written in the last few decades. They are placed in the order of the Scriptures themselves and stand independently of each other. Since they are all sermons preached in the Heritage Reformed Congregation of Grand Rapids at some point, I trust you will excuse me for having not given full footnote citations for every quotation from a forefather. I do wish to thank my beloved flock for listening well to these and other sermons and for their love for sound preaching. I wish to dedicate this book to them as I complete 38 years among them, and to our seminary students and alumni as we complete 30 years of training men for the ministry at Puritan Reformed Theological Seminary. I thank Dr. Paul M. Smalley for his able research assistance on sermons 10, 16, 24, 28, 30, 31, and 35; Dr. Maarten Kuivenhoven for co-authoring sermon 27 with me; Fraser Jones and Gary den Hollander for carefully editing this volume; Irene VandenBerg for proofreading it; and Linda den Hollander for meticulously typesetting it.

Though books of sermons do not tend to sell well today—unlike in Puritan times when nearly all their books were repackaged sermons—the reading of edifying sermons can still be a great blessing to God's children today. Believers today would be greatly edified, I believe, by reading one sermon—or even half a sermon—a day. I have a friend who for decades grew his spiritual life by reading one of Charles Spurgeon's sermons each day! It is my earnest and humble prayer that believers will also find the sermons in this volume to be spiritually beneficial, so that they would grow in spiritual maturation to the glory of the triune God.

There is one grand theme that I trust runs through these sermons, namely, Jesus Christ and how to live in Him, by Him, and out of Him. Hence the title for this volume, which are the opening words of one of my favorite sermons to preach in this book: "For me to live is Christ" (Phil. 1:21—sermon no. 28). Like Paul, the goal of every faithful preacher is to proclaim nothing but Jesus Christ and Him crucified (1 Cor. 2:2). I can wholeheartedly identify with Samuel Rutherford who said that his two favorite things in life were to know Christ and to preach Christ.

Recently, a dear believer in my own flock shook my hand at the church exit after I preached, and said, "You know, after preaching for us for so many years I have finally figured out that you actually are bringing us the same message every week—it is simply Jesus Christ!" She then paused, and sighed, "But you know, we need to hear Him preached all over again every week because He is really all that we have and all that we need!" To this, I could only reply: "Amen, may it be so; *soli Deo gloria!*"

I still remember with fondness Dr. Sinclair Ferguson saying to us PhD students at Westminster Seminary in Philadelphia back in the early 1980s, "Dear brothers, I urge you to save the best energies of your life for preparing to preach Christ and for preaching Him." To that, again, I can only say, "Amen, may it be so."

I pray God that you will find Christ in this volume of sermons, and grow in Him. He is so worthy of being read about, meditated upon, cherished, worshiped, and loved. May God grant that by the time you turn the last page of this book, you might be able to say, with heartfelt conviction, "For me to live is Christ, and to die is gain"—because, by grace, I am in Christ and He is in me.

—JRB

Chapter 1

The Creation of the Woman

And the LORD God said, It is not good that the man should be alone; I will make him an help meet for him. And out of the ground the LORD God formed every beast of the field, and every fowl of the air; and brought them unto Adam to see what he would call them: and whatsoever Adam called every living creature, that was the name thereof. And Adam gave names to all cattle, and to the fowl of the air, and to every beast of the field; but for Adam there was not found an help meet for him. And the LORD God caused a deep sleep to fall upon Adam, and he slept: and he took one of his ribs, and closed up the flesh instead thereof; and the rib, which the LORD God had taken from man, made he a woman, and brought her unto the man. And Adam said, This is now bone of my bones, and flesh of my flesh: she shall be called Woman, because she was taken out of Man. Therefore shall a man leave his father and his mother, and shall cleave unto his wife: and they shall be one flesh. —GENESIS 2:18–24

Genesis 2:18–24 graphically describes God's creation of the first woman. It begins with the Lord God's remarkable statement, "It is not good that man should be alone." The negative, "not good," is emphatic. Until now, God has done everything good; He has pronounced His benediction upon all of His creation. Here, for the first time, we find that something is lacking. Without female companionship and a partner in reproduction, man could not fully realize his humanity. Out of this need comes the creation of the woman who will be Adam's wife and companion.

The creation of woman in Genesis 2 has far-reaching consequences. It sets the foundation for three important areas: the relationship of a husband and a wife within marriage; the relationship of Jesus Christ, the Husband of His church, and the church as Christ's bride; and the function of a man and a woman within the church. In this sermon, I will primarily address the first of these—the relationship of a husband and a wife within marriage. Our text is Genesis 2:18–24.

With God's help, we wish to consider:

The Creation of the Woman
1. The woman made as a helpmeet for the man
2. The woman made by God as His special handiwork
3. The woman made to be one with the man

1. The Woman Made as a Helpmeet for the Man

God's creation of Eve is set within the context of the creation story. The first part of that story is the preparation of the man for the woman's arrival. Adam had been made in God's image. He was filled with God's pristine glory. And yet, God showed Adam that in all the created order, with all its variety, there was no creature suited to be his companion.

God chose a fascinating way to teach Adam this lesson. God had stood side by side with Adam while a great variety of animals passed before Adam. As they passed by—from the ant to the zebra—Adam studied each animal, then named it. That was no arbitrary naming. Adam noted each animal's nature and relationship. In the back of his mind, he must have wondered if one might be suitable as his companion. Yet there was none. As Genesis 2:20 says, "For Adam there was not found an help meet for him."

After he named all the animals, Adam realized that not one had been created in the image of God. Each had a body, and even a personality in some sense. But none had a soul. Adam could not commune with any on a spiritual level. No matter how good Adam's relationship was with an animal, something was missing. Let me illustrate.

Perhaps you have an excellent relationship with your dog. You have a great friendship with him. You share many enjoyable hours with him. You play games with him; you show affection to him. But all your fellowship must be on a dog's level because a dog can only communicate on that level. Adam no doubt realized that if he was to have a companion, the companion would have to be specially created by God in His image, just as Adam himself had been.

So Adam was prepared for a woman, and the woman was now to be prepared for him. She was to be created as his ideal counterpart in the world. Man and woman were made differently, and yet, by God's act of creation, they were to be more alike than anything else in creation.

Eve was created as a perfect woman. What a striking woman she must have been! When commenting on the creation of man, Luther said that Adam must have been an extraordinary being. He thought that Adam must have excelled the animals even in those points in which they excelled; he would have had power greater than a lion's, and eyesight sharper than an eagle's. But if that was true of Adam, what are we to say of Eve? Luther thought that Eve would have been as strong, fast, clear-sighted, and brilliant as Adam. In addition, Luther said, she must have had beauty and grace that excelled him. This much we can say for sure: Eve, too, was created in pristine glory.

In spite of Eve's physical, mental, and moral excellence, verse 18 says she was made "for" the man, "an help meet [suitable] for him." In this perfect pre-fall condition, every woman has a clue to her unique, God-given position in marriage. She is to be a "help meet" for her husband.

Genesis 2:18 greatly angers radical feminists and is sometimes a cause for concern, if not anxiety, for other women as well. To speak of woman being made for man, or of her need to be obedient to the man in marriage, is anathema. Many women and even men—think such ideas outdated, unjust, and prejudiced against women,

Our fallen human nature never likes to surrender its desired independence. Man does not want to be subject to God, and woman does not want to be subject to man. Rev. J. Fraanje once wrote that

"Independency"—today we would perhaps say "autonomy"—is the word written on the inside of the gate that led out of Paradise.

We need clear thinking today on this issue. We must understand, first of all, that the word *help* is not a derogatory term. God created us to serve Him and to help our neighbor. It is an honor for a woman to help her husband, for *help* is a word frequently used in reference to God Himself in the Psalms (10:14; 22:11; 28:7; 46:1; 54:4; 72:12; 86:17; 119:173, 175; 121:1–2). If God is not ashamed to be the help of fallen sinners, why should we look askance on Eve being the "help" of her unfallen husband? Being a helpmeet is not a degrading position. The verb form of this word basically means to aid or supply what an individual cannot provide for himself. The Septuagint translates it with a word that the New Testament uses in the sense of "physician" (Matt. 15:25). It conveys the idea of aiding someone in need, such as the oppressed. Certainly a godly wife delights to meet the needs of her husband.

Meet comes from the Hebrew word meaning "opposite." Literally it is "according to the opposite of him," meaning that a woman will complement and correspond to her husband. She is equal to and adequate for the man.

In what way is she to be equal? We must grapple with this word *equality*, which we hear so much of today. Are men and women truly equal?

Yes and no. There are important ways in which men and women are equal. First, they were both equally created in the image of God. That is what made them fit companions for each other. It explains why animals are not fit companions for us. Second, they were both placed under the moral command of God and thus were given moral responsibility. Third, they were both guilty of disobeying the command of God and were therefore judged by God for their disobedience. Fourth, Paul tells us in Galatians 3:28 that both men and women are equally objects of God's gracious redemption in Jesus Christ. Fifth, as husband and wife, a man and a woman are equally called to leave father and mother, to cleave to each other, and to love each other as one flesh.

In another sense, however, man and woman were not created equal. Because the woman was created for the man, they were not created equal in authority. God has a different structure of authority laid out for husbands than He does for wives. The inequality of that authority structure does not mean that a husband has the advantage over his wife or that one position is better than another, however. Nor does it mean that one position is higher than another. We must purge our minds of that way of thinking, which is all too common in the business world of our day. The higher we are on the corporate business ladder, many think, the better off we are.

That is not what God has in mind with man and woman. In the God-given structure of authority, a husband and wife mutually submit to Christ (Eph. 5:20), then, under Christ, to each other, fulfilling each other's needs. Already in Paradise, there is glory and humility in both the man and the woman. The man's glory is that he is the head; his humility is that he is not complete without the woman. The woman's glory is that only she can give the man fulfillment; her humility is that she is made from man.

Post-fall, these complementary roles are even stronger, especially for husbands and wives who desire to model their marriages in Christ according to God's directions. Paul enlightens us on these roles in Ephesians 5. The husband is to love his wife as Christ loves the church—absolutely (He gave Himself, v. 25b), realistically (Christ realized that the church, in herself, needed cleansing, v. 26), purposely (to make the church holy and blemish-free, v. 27), and sacrificially (to care for the bride as one cares for his own body, vv. 28–29).

In turn, the wife must show her husband reverence and submission, Paul says (vv. 22, 33). Elsewhere, Paul provides four reasons why: because the woman is made from man (1 Cor. 11:3, 8), because the woman was made for man (1 Cor. 11:9), because the man was created first (1 Tim. 2:12–13), and because sin entered the world by the woman (1 Tim. 2:14). As the man is to show loving headship, so the woman is to show loving submission.

Submission is not degrading. It is found even in the relationship between the incarnate Son of God and God the Father. In fact, the submission of wives to their husbands parallels the submission of Christ to the Father. In the Trinity, each person is "the same in substance, equal in power and glory," as the Westminster Shorter

Catechism says. However, when God the Son became a man, for the purposes of His mediatorial work He subjected His humanity to the Father's divine will (Matt. 26:39; John 6:38), even becoming "under the law" of God (Gal. 4:4). Thus, the Son, who is the Lord, became the Servant of the Lord (Isa. 42:1). Having become a man, "he humbled himself, and became obedient unto death, even the death of the cross" (Phil. 2:8). Paul points to the parallel between Christ's human submission and marital submission, when he says, "The head of every man is Christ; and the head of the woman is the man; and the head of Christ is God" (1 Cor. 11:3). Our submissiveness to proper authority—in the home and in every sphere of life—is a manifestation of the beauty of Jesus Christ.

Some feminists respond to such texts by arguing that submission is part of the curse, now abrogated by Christ's atonement. Their argument, however, does not reckon with the fact that the subordinate relationship of wife to husband is found first in Genesis 2, *before* the fall and the curse.

Submission within marriage also has parallels within the church, which is the family of God. Though women may and should exercise caring ministries in the church, Paul makes clear that the headship principle prevents them from bearing office. Moreover, this submission in marriage and in the church is to be voluntary. In short, if a woman cannot be a loving, submissive helper to the man who proposes to her, she should not marry him any more than a man should propose marriage to a woman to whom he does not intend to show loving, self-denying leadership.

2. The Woman Made by God as His Special Handiwork

The woman is not only made for man; she is also made by God as a special act of creation. Both the man and woman were special creations of God. They were created in equal dignity. Genesis 2:21–22 says, "And the LORD God caused a deep sleep to fall upon Adam, and he slept: and he took one of his ribs, and closed up the flesh instead thereof."

God caused a deep sleep to fall on Adam as an initial step in the creation of woman. This "deep sleep" must have been something like anesthesia today, and the operation that God performed much like medical surgery. God took away one of man's ribs and filled the empty place with flesh, closing up the wound.

From the rib, God then "made"—literally, in Hebrew, "built" or "constructed" a woman. God miraculously, meticulously, beautifully, and laboriously, formed woman with His own hands, making her every bit as special as the man he had created before her.

There is something particularly beautiful, even poetic, about this creation. The woman is made for the man and might therefore be thought of as man's servant. But Genesis says nothing of this. Instead, as Matthew Henry put it: "The woman was not made out of the man's head to rule over him, nor out of his feet to be trampled upon by him, but out of his side to be equal with him, under his arm to be protected, and near his heart to be beloved."

Then the loving Father presented the bride that His own hands had carefully formed to the man. He "brought her unto the man" (v. 22b), which is a special phrase in Hebrew that means "presented or conducted her to the man." The word also implies the formal, solemn giving of the woman within the bonds of the marriage covenant, which Proverbs 2:17 calls "the covenant of God." God, as the woman's Creator and Father, brought her to the man, as the Puritans used to say, "as his second self, to be a help meet for him."

In bringing the woman to the man, God established marriage as the first, most basic of all human institutions. Before there were governments, churches, schools, or any other social structures, God established a household based on the mutual respect and love of a husband and wife. All other human institutions derived from that. From the authority of the father came the patriarchal systems of human government, which eventually gave rise to monarchies and democracies. From the responsibility of parents to educate their children came the more formal systems of education that we call schools and colleges. From the need to care for the family's health came physicians and hospitals. From the obligation of parents to train their children in the knowledge of God came temples, synagogues, and churches. All human organizations can be traced back to the home, the family, and ultimately to marriage.

Adam, whom God then awakened, immediately recognized Eve as his companion—the perfect fit for the longing that had been awakened in him. In response, he broke into a kind of wedding song, celebrating his similarity and union with the woman by naming her.

Adam said, "This is now" (v. 23a)—literally "this time" or "now," "at long last," Adam finds what corresponds to him. The close association is emphasized by their names, since she is called "woman" [*ishah*] because she was taken out of man [*ish*]. The Hebrew word for "woman" is formed simply by adding the feminine ending, "-ah," to the word for "man." A parallel difference would be between lion and lioness, or tiger and tigress. So Adam, by divine revelation, realized the woman was taken out of him. His act of naming his wife reinforced his leadership and authority over her, but her name also indicated that he understood her equality with him as his partner.

The divine miracle that Adam witnessed filled him with inexpressible joy, inspiring him to cry out in beautiful poetry, "This is now bone of my bones, and flesh of my flesh: she shall be called Woman, because she was taken out of Man" (v. 23).

Adam and Eve then entered a sinless marriage. "Marriage is honorable," wrote Matthew Henry, "but this surely was the most honorable marriage that ever was, in which God Himself had all along an immediate hand."

To Adam's wedding song, God appends in verse 24 a beautiful, sacred blueprint for marriage, which involves leaving, joining, and oneness: "Therefore shall a man leave his father and his mother, and shall cleave unto his wife: and they shall be one flesh." These are the words of Moses, the inspired author of Genesis, who provides us with this sacred precept that Jesus repeats in Matthew 19 and Paul repeats in Ephesians 5:31–32, saying, "For this cause shall a man leave his father and mother, and shall be joined unto his wife, and they two shall be one flesh. This is a great mystery: but I speak concerning Christ and the church." These three essential traits—leaving, cleaving [or joining], and oneness—still exist post-fall, in Christ, in a good marriage.

3. The Woman Made to be One with the Man

The three parts of God's blueprint for marriage are important marks of a good marriage:

1. *Leaving.* Leaving father and mother is a tremendous adjustment. The intimacy of family unity must yield to a new family unit with a new head. This new unity takes priority over the parent-child relationship. There is a chain of reasoned thought here: One must leave in order to cleave, and two must cleave to become one flesh.

2. *Cleaving.* A newly married couple must join together. The original Greek word can be translated "cemented together." The bridegroom and bride form a new relationship inseparable from each other. The woman becomes part of the man, and vice versa. They become more than each other's intimate companion, best friend, and faithful partner.

3. *Oneness.* The expression *one flesh* is the strongest Hebrew construction to indicate a change of state. This is already implied when God formed Eve out of Adam. The goal of marriage, however, is not just to become one physically, as important and fulfilling as that may be, but in every aspect of the relationship: one in heart, one in love, one in trust, one in purpose, one in thinking, and, above all, one in Christ. A oneness that is no deeper than physical intimacy will soon dissipate and most likely end in an unhappy marriage or in a divorce court. But a marriage that has an overall oneness in heart, mind, and action will have special physical oneness as well. Physical oneness does not produce a great marriage; but a great marriage, in Christ, produces fulfilling physical oneness as well as fulfilling intellectual, emotional, and spiritual oneness.

The great goal of marriage is to be one with God through Christ, then, out of that oneness, to be one with each other. But how can a sinner, who has separated from God, become one with God? Only through the Savior, Jesus Christ, who Himself engaged in a leaving, a joining, and a oneness in wooing and winning His bride. Paul puts it this way, "This is a great mystery, but I speak concerning Christ and the church" (Eph. 5:32). Here is how He did that:

1. Christ left His Father willingly. He left the crown and throne and courts of glory to come into this world, to seek out His bride. He endured heart-wrenching separation from His Father on the cross. He thus paid the dowry price for His bride so that she might become part of His body, His flesh, and His bones.

2. On Calvary's cross, Christ joined Himself to His bride. As He was dying, she was mystically formed out of Him, the Second Adam, just as Eve was formed out of the first Adam while he was in a deep sleep. As the woman came from Adam's side to symbolize their union, so from the wounded, bleeding, dying side of our Savior, the church of God was taken out, as it were, to be born, to live, and to be joined with her Savior. This is a great mystery indeed!

3. The greatest part of this mystery, however, is this: "They shall become one flesh." The church of God, says Paul, makes up the total fullness of Christ as Mediator. He is the Head; the church is the body. "And [the Father] gave him to be the head over all things to the church, which is his body, the fulness of him that filleth all in all" (Eph. 1:22–23). This mystical union will be perfected one day in heaven's ideal, unbreakable union.

When we are born again through the regenerating power of the Holy Spirit, we become personally united with Jesus Christ. We become one "in Christ." That is why Paul never tired of describing a Christian in this way. In his epistles, Paul uses this phrase or a similar phrase—*in Christ, in Christ Jesus,* or *in Him*—at least 164 times. That is Paul's favorite way of describing a Christian,

For example, Paul writes, "If any man be in Christ, he is a new creature," or, as the original has it, "a new creation" (2 Cor. 5:17). By being united with Christ, a person becomes a new creation. He is one in Christ; he is united with Christ. Likewise, in Ephesians 1:3, Paul says, "Blessed be the God and Father of our Lord Jesus Christ, who hath blessed us with all spiritual blessings in heavenly places *in Christ.*"

The believer's union with Christ is profoundly intimate. When Paul speaks of union with Christ, he uses a special prefix in Greek, best translated as "co-," meaning that tie is indissoluble. Literally, he says in Galatians 2:20, "I am co-crucified with Christ." That is, when Christ died, in a sense I also died. In Romans 6:4, Paul speaks of being buried with Christ, in Ephesians 2 of being raised with Christ and of sitting with Him in heavenly places, and in Romans 8 of being glorified together with Christ. Paul is saying that the intimacy of the believer's union with Christ is so great that there is a sense in which, when He was crucified, the believer was also crucified; when He died, the believer also died; when He was buried, the believer was also buried; when He was raised from the dead, the believer was also raised from the dead; when He ascended, the believer also ascended. Who can comprehend this mystical union? One poet said:

> One in the tomb, one when He arose,
> One when He triumphed o'er His foes,
> One when in heaven He took His seat,
> While seraphs sang all hell's defeat.
> With Him our Head we stand or fall,
> Our life, our surety, our all.

Oh, what dignity exists in all this dignity in Eve's creation as a woman, one with her husband, sharing that dignity with him! And now, through faith, dignity in the re-creation of Christ's bride, to be made one with the Bridegroom, to share in His dignity and glory, and to be loved by God with the same love He has for His own Son! Truly, there is no dignity like the dignity of re-creation and becoming the very bride of Jesus Christ.

Closing Applications
What about your marriage—does it reflect oneness in Christ? When it is not what you expect it to be, do you ask: How can I (not my spouse) make a more profound oneness? Do you work toward cultivating greater intimacy in your marriage?

Today, marriage is under attack. Hedonism is rampant. Adultery is gaining widespread acceptance. Unbiblical divorces can now be granted via the internet. The basic structure of society is falling apart. Too often believers fare little better. We desperately need to understand the value of marriage and to work hard at achieving excellence in marriage through the Lord Jesus. We must strive for oneness so that our marriages may be open epistles of God's grace in an ungodly world.

We must not surrender to the self-love that is fostered by our culture. The only way to have a truly successful marriage is to put Christ first, your spouse second, and yourself third. Love of self must be broken at the foot of the cross of Christ. Only when we see ourselves as sinners in rebellion against God and bow before Him for forgiveness and help in pursuing holiness, will love fill our marriages and spill over into all our other relationships. Then we will truly understand that marriage does not exist for self, but for our spouse, our children, and our society, and ultimately for the glory of God.

Are we daily seeking God's glory in our marriages? Husbands, are you striving to be loving heads in your marriage? Wives, are you striving to show loving submission to your husband? There is no room in a biblical marriage for bosses—only for loving headship and loving submission as one man and one woman seek to live out, by God's grace, the Christ-church relationship on earth.

Finally, a word to young people: The oneness that God intends for marriage in Christ means that you must not marry an unbeliever. If you marry someone who has a personal agenda for marriage instead of God's agenda, you will most likely be setting yourself up for years of heartbreak and sorrow. Second Corinthians 6:14 says, "Be not unequally yoked together with unbelievers; for what fellowship hath righteousness with unrighteousness, and what communion hath light with darkness?"

Seek a marriage partner given to you in God's favor and out of His hand. And if you want to be a good marriage partner yourself, wrote Thomas Manton, "Clear up your right and title by Christ." Make your own calling and election sure. If you and your spouse are God-fearing, your marriage will greatly benefit because you will have someone to help you strive to live to God's glory, to live a holy life, to bear the crosses God will send your way, and to confidently approach God through Christ in prayer and worship.

Pray for God's direction, counsel, and blessing as you wait on Him to lead you to a God-fearing spouse who is suitable for you. Ask Him for one who is a help meet for you.

Dear friend, are *you* married to Jesus Christ? Adam and Eve were not ashamed because they were clothed with God-given, original righteousness. Are you, too, not ashamed because you are clothed with the God-given righteousness of Jesus Christ? Remember, this blessed Savior demands your faithfulness. Spiritually speaking, He is jealous for your wedded love. You must not stray from Him.

What do you think of this perfect Bridegroom? Are you married to another lord—to the prince of this world? Satan's promises are lies. His dowry is anguish. His embrace is death. His chamber is darkness. His bed is in flames of fire.

Whatever our case may be, let us flee with all our shortcomings in our natural married life and in our spiritual marriage to the perfect Bridegroom, Jesus Christ. Let us leave the godlessness of this world and cleave to Christ, to be one with Him—now and forever. Amen.

Chapter 2

Advent and the First Gospel Promise

And I will put enmity between thee and the woman, and between thy seed and her seed; it shall bruise thy head, and thou shalt bruise his heel.
—GENESIS 3:15

Around the beginning of December, we enter a new ecclesiastical year. For four weeks before Christmas, the message of Advent sets the tone for the Christian church's festival season which lasts for six months, culminating in Pentecost.

"Advent" is a Latin word which means *coming, arriving,* or *approaching,* and often connotes haste. The church calls its four-week pre-Christmas season *Advent* because of the comings of Jesus Christ. In the fullness of time, He came with haste in Bethlehem's manger (the First Advent). He shall come again upon the clouds with haste to judge the living and the dead when God's time is ripe (the Second Advent).

Advent also contains the idea of waiting for the coming Messiah. Oh, that this Advent season we all may experience something of that true waiting for the Christ-child! True waiting for Jesus is not a task that human nature enjoys. True waiting is hard work. It involves wrestling and looking and expecting. True waiting is very different from passive indifference. To wait by faith requires both confident expectation and holy impatience. The chord of balance between these twin gifts can only be properly struck through the guidance of the blessed Holy Spirit: "Not by might, nor by power, but by my spirit, saith the LORD of hosts" (Zech. 4:6).

Such waiting in dependency upon the Spirit will result in a genuine spiritual breakthrough at Bethlehem's manger. The sinner who learns to cry the authentic advent complaint, "Give me Jesus, else I die," shall not be disappointed in the Christmas time of divine fulfilment. Our prayer for each of you is that you will experience this blessing for the first time or by renewal this very Christmas season.

For God's church, Advent contains profound meaning. Advent memorializes the past. Advent confesses faith for the future. Advent gives expression to present yearnings and hope. Advent preaches that the coming Christ of yesterday and of tomorrow is the "always coming," "always advent" Christ of today. Advent preaches that Christ is always on His way, always near-at-hand, yes, always present. Advent proclaims, "For he hath said, I will never leave thee, nor forsake thee.... Jesus Christ the same yesterday, and today, and forever" (Heb. 13:5, 8).

Today, we want to turn to the first Advent text of Scripture: "And I will put enmity between thee and the woman, and between thy seed and her seed; it shall bruise thy head, and thou shalt bruise his heel" (Gen. 3:15).

With God's help, we wish to consider:

Advent and the First Gospel Promise
1. Enmity announced by God
2. Conflict waged by Satan
3. Victory assured in Christ

First, we will consider the enmity announced by God, "I will put enmity between thee and the woman." Second, we will examine the conflict waged by Satan: "Thou [Satan] shalt bruise his [Christ's] heel." Third, we will see victory assured in Christ: "It [Christ, the Seed of the woman], shall bruise thy [Satan's] head."

1. Enmity Announced by God

Genesis 3 has rightly been called "the black chapter" of Scripture. Our fall in Adam is the blackest reality of human history. Genesis 3 tells us sad truth about ourselves.

Any attempt to exclude ourselves from Genesis 3 is futile. Through the fall of Adam as representative head in the covenant of works, we have all become children of the devil and servants of sin. We have subjected ourselves to the sentence of death, the infinite wrath of God, the curse of the law, and the dominion of Satan. Experientially, we must become Adam before God. The fall must become our fall, our guilt.

Genesis 3 unlocks the secrets of many tragic realities. How did we break God's covenant, scorn His majesty, trample His law underfoot, and challenge His attributes? How did we turn our backs on our worthy Creator? How did we cast away His image in its narrower sense—exchanging ignorance for knowledge, unrighteousness for righteousness, and perversity for holiness? Genesis 3 answers these questions succinctly, graphically, and tragically.

Genesis 3 unveils how we have become what we are by nature: lost, condemnable, rejectable sinners; dead in sins and trespasses; and hell-worthy, fit to be vessels of sovereign and just reprobation. Total depravity, separation from God, slavery to Satan, the origin of sin and evil, the cause of all misery and death, and a stained creation—Genesis 3 explains it all.

A black chapter indeed! Its blackness is beyond human expression. Who can comprehend the depth of our fall and its consequences for our natural hearts and daily lives? "The heart is deceitful above all things, and desperately wicked: who can know it?" (Jer. 17:9).

By nature, we do not know ourselves. Daily, we live out our fall unaware in actions, thoughts, words, motives, and perceptions. We are blind to our blindness. We are such slaves of Satan that this enslaver's hold over us passes us by largely unnoticed. As Rev. L. Ledeboer wrote, "Our greatest misery is that we do not know our misery."

Grace, however, changes all this. For God's people, sin becomes sin. Satan becomes the archenemy. The fall becomes their fall. The burden of original sin experientially becomes ten times greater than the burden of actual sins. Paul expresses this burden well when he exclaims: "For I know that in me (that is, in my flesh,) dwelleth no good thing: for to will is present with me; but how to perform that which is good I find not. For the good that I would I do not: but the evil which I would not, that I do.... O wretched man that I am! Who shall deliver me from the body of this death?" (Rom. 7:18, 19, 24).

Happily, Genesis 3 also speaks about this grace of self-awareness, of self-abasement, as well as the grace of divine intervention and provision. Genesis 3 may also rightly be called "the red chapter" of Scripture, for three reasons. First, on its page the Father's first gospel promise of His coming, blood-shedding Son is unfurled in verse 15 which is our text today. Second, on its page the first exercise of faith in the Father's Advent promise of life is expressed by Adam in the naming of his wife Eve, which means in Hebrew *life* or *living*! We read in verse 20, "And Adam called his wife's name Eve; because she was the mother of all living." Third, on its page, the first sacrificial blood is spilled, pointing to the gospel, when God slew animals to make Adam and Eve coats of skins. We read in verse 21, "Unto Adam also and to his wife did the LORD God make coats of skins, and clothed them."

Against the black backdrop of tragedy in Genesis 3, God paints a red chapter of atonement, and a white chapter of hope. Genesis 3 preaches that God is always ahead of Satan. It preaches amazing, staggering grace to lost sinners. Especially in the first gospel promise of Genesis 3:15, it presents sovereign grace as flowing out of enmity announced by God, conflict waged against Satan, and victory assured in Christ.

Genesis 3:15 is the first advent text of Scripture. Most remarkable is its beginning, "And I will put enmity." In the original Hebrew, which often accents the first word of a sentence, we read: "Enmity will I put...." "Enmity" introduces Scripture's first gospel promise and sets the tone for the entire verse!

For lost, fallen sinners, *deliverance and enmity* are inseparable. Some find this astonishing. Some do not believe it. They say that the gospel should contain nothing but love. Still others do not understand. They ask: *Why does God begin with enmity? Wasn't enmity already present? Didn't Satan show enmity when he tempted Eve? Didn't Eve show enmity when she gave fruit to Adam? Didn't Adam show enmity when he ate forbidden fruit and then blamed God and Eve for his sin? Why would God bring more enmity into a world which only moments prior knew nothing of enmity?*

Enmity itself was not the problem in Paradise. Adam and Eve should have been at holy enmity with, and full of holy hatred toward, the serpent for even suggesting the possibility of eating the forbidden fruit. They knew well that such eating entailed challenging God's authority, calling Him a liar, and breaking His covenant.

Adam and Eve had a *misdirected* enmity. They directed their enmity against God instead of Satan. Mercifully, the Lord came to intervene in the Paradise scene to *redirect* their enmity to its proper focus—to sin and Satan. The Lord said, as it were, "I will place enmity between the serpent and his seed (or Satan and unbelievers) and the woman and her seed (or the elect church). I will reverse your newly acquired values. I will cause you to hate what you now love, and love what you now despise. I will plant new enmity—an enmity which hates sin. I will give you a new heart."

God's surprising intervention in Paradise was not an appeal to the "free will" of man; it was a declaration, an announcement of His irresistible "free grace." "*I* will put enmity." God did not stir up enmity already present. He did not ask Adam and Eve to put enmity into exercise. In fact, He was not even addressing Himself directly to them, for He was speaking to the serpent.

All of this underscores one solemn truth: Fallen man cannot put enmity against sin in his own heart. Only God can do what man cannot do for himself. God takes the initiative. This is our only hope as fallen creatures: divine initiative, sovereign intervention, and amazing grace.

God takes salvation into His own hands, allowing for no uncertainty: "I *will* put enmity." Hence, the new birth always does *and must* bring new enmity, yes, God-planted enmity. This enmity is against sin, the "old-man" nature, Satan, the pride of life, the lusts of the flesh and eye—anything that dishonors the Lord.

Are you experientially acquainted with this sovereign grace: "I will put enmity"? Dear believer, you know that you not only *could* not, but also *would* not have placed enmity in your own heart against sin. Is not sovereign grace your only hope—that grace which does all for a sinner who can do nothing rightly? That grace which turns around those who are rushing to hell, and plants their footsteps in the narrow pathway to heaven? Let us now look at our second thought.

2. Conflict Waged By Satan

The fruit of divine planting will always be conflict. Spiritual life is a struggling, bruising battle. It is holy warfare. Scripture's first gospel promise is plain: "It [Christ, the Seed of the woman], shall bruise thy [Satan's] head, and thou [Satan] shalt bruise his [Christ's] heel."

The Lord never promised His Son or His people an easy way of salvation. How can the enmity He placed between the devil's seed and the woman's seed, between Satan and Christ, between the world and the church, between the wicked and the righteous, between the flesh and the spirit, not lead to conflict?

Where God builds His church on the foundation of the Advent proclamation of His Son, Satan will build His temple next door. To the end of time, Satan will wage war against all that is of God and Christ.

We must not minimize the power of Satan. He never stops nibbling at the heels of the church of God. Though he shall not conquer the living church, he knows that a church "without heels" will be handicapped and severely weakened in battle. As J. C. Philpot noted, "Satan will never keep a child of God out of heaven, but he strives to keep heaven out of a child of God."

Satan is a fallen angel. His powers far supersede our human powers. He is mighty. Under the permission of divine decree, he bruises the heel of the woman's seed. This is the spiritual conflict of all ages: Cain versus Abel, Ishmael versus Isaac, Esau versus Jacob, Egypt versus Israel. Satan's goal is always to wipe out the chosen seed. Consider the command of Pharaoh to destroy all Israel's male children. Consider Egypt's attack at the Red Sea or the plot of Haman.

Consider especially Satan's attacks culminating on Christ. Go to the desert of Judea. There we meet Christ who had stepped away from the water of baptism into the fire of temptation. Satan attacked fiercely for forty days. He raged to bruise the heels of Christ, to get the Advent Seed to fall. He attempted every avenue of attack to subdue Christ's sacred humanity under satanic control.

In Gethsemane, all the powers of hell were unleashed. Crawling as a worm and no man! Bloody sweat! The profound cry and negated answer: "Oh my Father, if it be possible, let this cup pass from me"—oh, what soul-bruisings, heel-nibblings Christ experienced! No wonder He spoke to the satanic forces, "This is your hour, and the power of darkness" (Luke 22:53).

The conflict continues at Gabbatha. The purple robe. The crown of thorns. Scourging. Mockery. Slappings. More internal war and bloody bruisings.

And then Golgotha. Here Genesis 3:15 reaches its apex. The unfathomable cry rings through the darkened realm of nature, "My God, my God, why hast thou forsaken me?" (Matt. 27:46).

Luther once spent an entire morning trying to comprehend this fourth word of Christ from the cross, only to arise from his knees, confessing: "God forsaken of God; who can comprehend it?"

And indeed, it is incomprehensible, eternally incomprehensible, but this much we know: Satan was defeated on the cross, once and for all. "Through death he [Christ] might destroy him that had the power of death, that is, the devil" (Heb. 2:14). The victory belongs to Christ. Nevertheless, Satan will not admit to being a vanquished foe. He continues to nibble at the heels of Christ's church. Throughout all ages, victory comes through a suffering, bruising way in Christ. Consider the book of Acts, the early church's persecution, the Reformation and post-Reformation era, the Great Awakening, and times of revival. The church's most blessed times have also been times of most severe conflict. Tertullian rightly compared the church to a mowed field. He wrote, "The more frequently it is cut, the more it grows." Church history confirms the adage: The blood of the martyrs is the seed of the church.

Today the conflict continues in the breast of each true believer. Bunyan called this conflict "the holy war." Each believer knows the struggle within between the seed of the woman and the seed of the serpent. Oh, what battles between the old and new man, flesh and spirit, nature and grace! Rebecca-like, God's people often feel two seeds within struggling to break forth, causing the cry, "Why am I thus?" The severity of such struggles can better be experienced than expressed. Oh, what struggles do we experience with the triple-headed enemy—Satan, the world, and self! With what doubts, questions, unanswered riddles, unfulfilled promises, and satanic bruisings must the believer contend! No wonder such souls become a mystery to themselves!

By nature, we live largely struggle-free. We do not know holy battle. With God's people it is different. Dear friend, if God becomes God in our life, Satan shall become Satan, that archenemy of God and of grace, that constant "bruiser" who seeks to avenge day and night. Does he not bruise you severely, dear child of God, at such times as these?

- When he injects blasphemous thoughts into your mind
- When he then whispers that you cannot be a child of God and have such thoughts
- When he succeeds to get you to question the truth of the promises of God and of the mercy of that God who has never treated you ill
- When he seeks to persuade you that you have no portion in the matter of salvation, for you have only begun with the Lord and not He with you
- When he argues with you that no child of God could be like you—so weak in faith, so corrupt, such a poor example, so hard and prayerless, so foolish and vain
- When he comes as an accuser on the left hand or as an angel of light on the right hand, seeking to lead you to the extremes of despair or presumption
- When he presents the world to you in fair colors, attempting to move you back into the customs, friendships, and vanities of the world, inch by inch
- When he presses you to indulge, albeit briefly, in the lust of the flesh, the lust of the eyes, and the pride of life.

God's people experience that the greatest enemy in all spiritual conflict is sinful self. Self becomes the chief opponent. On the one hand, the new life desires to live perfectly before God, without sin and blemish; on the other, the old nature is constantly pursuing former paths of living without God, without love, and for self. Oh, what holy battles sometimes wage against self within the renewed heart! Has your own heart ever become your greatest obstacle, your greatest plague in spiritual life? Do you know the heavy burden of both hating sin and not being able to purge yourself from it—that burden which Paul unveils so movingly in Romans 7?

Such bruised warriors often fear that they are fighting a losing war. Repeatedly, they spend all their strength in spiritual struggle only to discover that on *account of themselves* they are sliding down the perishing slope of sin and, if God prevent not, destruction. At such times, spiritual poverty and weakness seem to overcome them. The tempter is following them, bruising and running hard upon their heels. David's cry ascends with groans and pleadings, "I shall one day perish at the hand of Saul." The hand of God is hidden; the brink of hell is visible. Voices within urge the abandoning of all pursuit of God and His grace. Other voices condemn them, and *justly* so. Satan is a liar, but much of what he speaks to their condemnation is all too sadly true. Conscience condemns. The law demands and curses. Divine justice is unsatisfied.

They are bitten by the seed of the serpent—by Satan, the world, and their sinful nature. They cannot walk without heels. They must fall and say farewell to self-help. They must die to self. They must sign their own death sentence that God is just and righteous to cast them away forever. In that signing, not Satan, but self, becomes the greatest culprit. It becomes real: *I have fallen. I am polluted throughout. I have chosen death above life, hell above heaven, Satan above God. I have bitten myself.* All seems fatally bruised—all my righteousness, repentance, prayer, humility, worthiness, yes, even my unworthiness. Death is written across all of self.

And yet, the amazing wonder of the gospel is that precisely in this way, that is, through self-condemning judgment, God makes room for the woman's Seed—for the victorious Advent Christ. Our text concludes, "It [Christ] shall bruise thy head." Let's consider this victory in Christ in our third thought.

3. Victory Assured in Christ

Satan's heel-nibbling is burdensome, but not fatal. God overrules it for the good of His people. Through surrender lies victory in Christ. He gathers the self-condemned in His shepherding arms and opens His gospel victory to them. He says, as it were, "Dear sheep, Satan bruises your heels, but I have bruised his head on your account—in death, in resurrection, and in judgment."

First, Christ bruises Satan's head in His *atoning death*. While Christ's heel—the "lower part" which is symbolic of His human nature—was being bruised on Calvary, He was crushing the head of Satan. The same heel Satan was bruising on Calvary was simultaneously crushing Satan fatally, for on Calvary, Christ was making full payment for all the sins of His elect. Let us listen to Hebrews 2:14 again, "That through death he might destroy him that had the power of death, that is, the devil."

Second, Christ bruises Satan's head in His *victorious resurrection*. Satan could not keep the Victor buried. His body could not see corruption. Christ arose from the grave. He showed Himself alive for forty days and ascended in triumph to His Father, leading captivity captive (Ps. 68:18). He is now in heaven at the right hand of the Father beyond the reach of all the heel-bruising powers of hell. He is in His state of exaltation; He has the keys of death, hell, and grave in His hand. The church is safe in Christ. His resurrection is a pledge of their blessed resurrection. Christ assures victory.

Third, Christ shall bruise Satan's head fatally and finally in His *final judgment*. On the day of judgment, Satan and his seed shall be cast out forever. Never again shall Satan trouble the Seed of the woman. The Victor will come upon the clouds, seize the old serpent, and cast him eternally into the bottomless pit. The bruising of Satan's head shall then be complete and final. The accuser of the brethren shall accuse no more, All heel-nibblings shall be gone forever. The militant church shall become the church triumphant. All Egyptians shall be drowned. The elect shall experience in full: "Fear ye not, stand still, and see the salvation of the LORD, which He will show to you today: for the Egyptians whom ye have seen today, ye shall see them again no more forever. The LORD shall fight for you, and ye shall hold your peace" (Ex. 14:13–14).

Oh, blessed day when corruption shall inherit incorruption (1 Cor. 15:50)! That day shall usher all the elect—beginners and advanced in grace—into the everlasting Elim of a perfect heaven. All good shall be walled in and all evil shall be walled out. Conflict shall be gone forever. The satanic seed shall be left buried in the grave.

Keep courage, dear child of God. Christ's seed shall not perish. Your Victor cannot fail. His cause is sure. His Second Advent is near. He will not forsake the work of His own hands.

On the other hand, dear unconverted friend, Satan's seed must perish with him. Hell means to be *without* God forever, and to be *with* Satan forever. In hell there shall be no relief from his nibblings, from the agonizing worm that dies not, nor from the evil devices of the wicked one. Terrible shall it be in that day to fall into the hands of the living God unprepared to meet Him! "How shall we escape, if we neglect so great salvation?" (Heb. 2:3).

To which seed do you belong? Dear friend, please remember that there is no third seed, no "in-between" seed. You either belong to Christ or to Satan.

Make haste for your life! You are still in the day of grace and the time of salvation. The Seed of the woman is still presented to you; yes, He offers Himself to you. Pray for grace to receive His gracious invitations and to bow under His Word in holy surrender. Pray that the authentic, Spirit-worked Advent cry may become real in your heart, "Give me Jesus, else I die," and that you, by gracious faith, may find salvation—full and free salvation—in Christ alone!

Chapter 3

Joseph and His Brothers[1]

And Joseph said unto his brethren, I am Joseph; doth my father yet live? And his brethren could not answer him; for they were troubled at his presence. And Joseph said unto his brethren, Come near to me, I pray you. And they came near. And he said, I am Joseph your brother, whom ye sold into Egypt.
—GENESIS 45:3–4

With God's help, we wish to consider:

Joseph and His Brothers
1. Betraying Joseph as an enemy
2. Meeting Joseph as a judge
3. Knowing Joseph as a deliverer

I once received a letter from a child who wrote, "Would you please preach a sermon about Joseph and his brothers?" With God's help, I will seek to do that now. But I want to do that in a way, boys and girls, that you may be able to understand it. I know sometimes sermons are difficult for children to understand, but today we will try to make this sermon very simple—especially for you. I hope when you go home after this service that you will tell your mom and your dad what the sermon was about, but above all, boys and girls, that the Lord may bless this sermon to your hearts, because you and I also need the same thing that Joseph's brothers needed. You cannot be too young, dear children, to seek the Lord, even if you are only three or four years

---

1. A sermon especially for children

old. You may still ask the Lord, "Give me a new heart." The Lord is almighty. And I hope, boys and girls, that you are often asking Him, "Lord, teach me how to pray."

1. Betraying Joseph as an Enemy

I think many of you already know the story of Joseph and his brothers quite well, and yet, boys and girls, there is something wonderful about the stories of the Bible. No matter how well we know those stories, there is always something new to learn, not only in our minds but also in our hearts. You will remember, I think, that when Joseph and his brothers were very young, they did not get along so well. Not one of Joseph's brothers liked him. That would be something, wouldn't it? Many of you have brothers and sisters. How would you feel if you didn't have one brother or sister that liked you—if they all hated you? That would be very sad. I hope, boys and girls, that all of you love your brothers and sisters, and that you don't do bad things or say mean words to your brothers and sisters. You must treat each other with love.

There was a problem in Joseph's family. Joseph's father, whose name as you know was Jacob, kept giving more things to Joseph than he did to the other brothers. That was not very wise of Jacob. That was a mistake. The result was that Joseph's brothers became very envious of Joseph. How would you feel if one of your brothers or sisters received most of the toys and gifts from your mom and dad and you received very little? Jacob, of course, gave something to all of his sons, but he gave special things to Joseph. That is why Joseph's brothers hated him. They were angry with Joseph. They didn't want to have anything to do with him. If Joseph came along and tried to play with them or do something with them, they would send him away. Later, when they became teenagers and young men, they would go out to the fields to work. One day Jacob called Joseph and said, "Joseph, go out to the fields and find out where your brothers are." And what did Joseph say? Did he say, "No, father, I won't do that because my brothers don't like me"? No; he was willing to do what his father commanded. He went out to look for brothers who hated him.

And so Joseph went to the fields. He arrived at one field and his brothers weren't there. A stranger told him, "No, they're not in Shechem anymore; they're in another place called Dothan." So Joseph went to Dothan to look for his brothers. Do you remember, boys and girls, what happened when he got to Dothan? His brothers threw him into a pit. They weren't so easy on Joseph. They sat down to eat, and you can be sure that Joseph was crying in that pit. It hurt to be cast away. It was a very hard time for Joseph, but his brothers all sat down content.

What happened next? Since Joseph's brothers were tired of Joseph's dreams too because he told them that they would bow before him one day, they said to one another, "Let's get rid of this dreamer and his dreams." And so they sold him. They sold him for the cheapest price possible for a slave. In those days, the lowest price for the most worthless slave was twenty shekels of silver, and that's what they sold Joseph for. They sold him as if he were the most worthless person on earth.

And now, boys and girls, you have to listen carefully. In all these things I have been telling you so far, Joseph was a type of the Lord Jesus Christ who comes from all eternity. He was born in Bethlehem's manger to make a long journey, to seek and to save sinners like you and I are. He goes into the field of the church; He comes especially on Sunday to seek sinners in His house. Jesus Christ is the greater Joseph who goes from field to field and city to city to seek His brethren whom God has given to Him from all eternity. Before there was anything in this world, Jesus said to His Father in eternity, "Lo, I come…to do Thy will, O God." He was more willing than Joseph was. There was never anyone so willing as Jesus Christ to do the will of His Father. His whole life was about His Father's work.

When Jesus comes to seek sinners, He is hated—just like Joseph was hated by his brothers. Joseph was hated for his person and his words—for his person because he was the favorite son of his father and for his words because of his dreams. Jesus is hated because He is the God-man, but He is also hated because He says, "I tell you the truth. The world cannot hate you; but me it hateth, because I testify of it, that the works thereof are evil" (John 7:7). When Jesus comes into the life of a sinner, boys and girls, He tells that sinner about his sinful nature, but we don't want to hear that we are sinners. By nature, we are at enmity with Jesus, with God, and with our neighbor. We are no better than Joseph's brothers. Do you remember in the New Testament how many shekels Judas sold Jesus for? Thirty shekels of silver. That was the lowest price for a slave in New Testament times, just as twenty shekels was in Old Testament times. Thus Jesus was that greater Joseph who, like Joseph, was hated by His brothers, was sold for the lowest price, and still went out to seek His brothers. He is the greater Joseph.

But now, boys and girls, the very worst thing of all is that you and I with our lives and sins also sell and crucify the Lord Jesus. No, that doesn't mean that we were physically standing there by the cross, but I mean in our hearts. You know, boys and girls, we can be guilty of something even if we don't do it. If we think bad thoughts, that's sinful too. You see, we grow up not loving God as we should unless the Lord gives us a new heart, but by nature we grow up not desiring God. We are enemies of God. We don't want to admit that we are sinners. We want to sit down like Joseph's brothers, saying, "Away with Him." We want to sit down content, just like Joseph's brothers. How sad it is that Joseph's brothers had so much enmity against him that they could be content to leave Joseph alone while he was in the pit. Similarly, boys and girls, our great problem is that we are content to leave Jesus alone when He is on the cross. Though He still says to us today that He is also willing to be the Savior of sinful boys and girls, we will have nothing to do with Him. We sit down content without a new heart, without Christ. We are content to be without God. We are content to be without a Savior for our soul. What a sad thing! These brothers wanted to sell Joseph. They never wanted to see Joseph again. Never! And what do we want, boys and girls? By nature, if God just keeps giving us food and clothing and all that we need, for the rest we say (and it's terrible to have to say it), "Lord, leave us alone." We want to live our own lives. We don't want to be bothered by the Lord, just like Joseph's brothers didn't want to be bothered with Joseph.

2. Meeting Joseph as a Judge

But now, what God does is wonderful. Joseph was sold, and his brothers were glad. They thought, "Now we will never see Joseph again." But man proposes, and God disposes. In other words, man can do something, but the Lord rules in the heavens. And twenty years later—that's older than all of you, boys and girls, Joseph and his brothers would meet again, but in a very surprising way. In the meantime Jacob was very sad because he thought he had lost his son Joseph. He said, "All these things are against me." What Jacob didn't realize is that all these things were *for* him.

Dear children of God in our midst, what an encouragement it is that God reigns! Once Jacob said, "All these things are against me," but later he said, "It is enough." In the original language it reads, "It is all"; in other words, "I have everything."

The Lord's ways are so far above our ways. That Ishmaelite caravan was God's divine chariot to convey Joseph to the throne of Egypt. But what a hard way it was for Joseph! It was bad enough being in the pit, but now he came to Potiphar's house, and you know, boys and girls, what happened there. He was accused of something he did not do, and that man, Potiphar, believed his ungodly, sinful wife more than he believed godly Joseph. What happened to Joseph then? They cast him into prison. That was his second pit. And then what happened? You will remember that when he was in prison he told the butler and the baker the meaning of their dreams. The butler was restored to his position and the baker died. But the butler was supposed to remember Joseph, wasn't he? He returned to Pharaoh's courts and forgot all about Joseph for two more years. That was another trial for Joseph.

Then Pharaoh had a dream. He told that dream but no one could understand it. Finally the butler said to Pharaoh, "Oh, now I remember, there is a man named Joseph in prison who can interpret dreams." Then Pharaoh called for Joseph and Joseph came in front of Pharaoh. Pharaoh said, "I have heard, Joseph, that you can interpret dreams." And what did Joseph say? Did he say, "Yes I can"? No. Did he say, "Well, king, with the help of the Lord I may be able to"? No. What did he say? He said, "It is not in me: God shall give Pharaoh an answer of peace."

And now, boys and girls, I want you to think about those words; "It is not in me." Do you realize how much Joseph learned in the pit, in prison, and through being forgotten? He learned a lot. When he was younger, he never said, "It is not in me." He said to his brothers, "I have a dream. You shall all bow before me. I will be something, and you will be under me." But when he came into a pit, into prison, and then was forgotten, what was the Lord doing? He was doing just what Joseph needed. He was emptying Joseph of his own self-righteousness, bit by bit, so that there was nothing of Joseph left. Now, even when Joseph had an opportunity to say something good about himself, he said, "It is not in me." That took grace, boys and girls. That took great grace. And then Pharaoh told him his dream and Joseph explained it. There would be seven years of plenty and seven years of famine. Pharaoh then made Joseph the second-in-command (like a vice-president) over the whole country. Thus, people brought grain for seven years and they built up a big supply of grain for people all over the world for the seven years of famine that were to come. In those seven years, people came from all over the world to Joseph to buy grain.

Now Joseph's brothers also had to come, didn't they? Yes, indeed. They ran out of grain too. They came and Joseph said to them, "You are spies." Joseph was known to them by a very long name. Try to remember it. It was Zaphnath-paaneah (Zaf-nath-pay-uh-nee-ah). They didn't realize he was Joseph. Joseph knew them, but they didn't know him. When Joseph came to his brothers and said, "You are spies," they said, "No, we are true men," or in the original language of the Bible, "We are pious men." In other words, "We are religious, God-fearing men." And did Joseph say, "Oh, that's wonderful that you are so pious, religious, and true"? No; Joseph put them into prison for three days—not out of anger, but out of love. "Love?" you say. "Is it loving to put someone in prison?" Boys and girls, Joseph had to teach his brothers that they could not have his heart until they had repented of their sin. We cannot find the Lord and be at peace with God until we know what it means to be lost and to repent from our sins. The world today is filled with people who have Jesus on their lips but they have never confessed Him with their hearts.

If you have a strong disagreement with someone, perhaps your brother or sister, you cannot become one again until you confess. You cannot have reconciliation—that means, you cannot be one again—until you first have confession, until you first say, "I'm sorry." So it is between God and us in spiritual life. We must truly be sorry for our sin shall we be reconciled to the Lord.

Joseph's brothers were finally freed from prison and they went back home, but soon they ran out of grain again. And what did they do the second time? The second time they put all kinds of things together. They had saved their best food for last to bring to Joseph—fruits, balm, honey, spices, myrrh, nuts, and almonds. They also brought double money and, as Joseph had commanded, Benjamin. They came to him with the very best that they had, thinking, "If we give everything to him, Zaphnath-Paaneah won't be so angry and stern with us and be so much like a judge."

Boys and girls, that is just what happens when God works in the heart of a sinner. He makes that person feel he is a sinner and makes him hungry for the Lord. He runs out of grain, so to speak. He has nothing to eat spiritually. He cannot make ends meet with all his works, his prayers, and his tears. He becomes very hungry. He must have the Lord. And so he comes to the Lord. But when he comes to the Lord, the Lord doesn't begin right away with Jesus Christ. Rather, the Lord begins as Joseph began, with rough questions. "Where are you from?" And when the Lord first begins, we say, "Lord, we are true men. We are concerned about our sins and we really want to be saved." But the Lord has to teach us, boys and girls, that there is so much wickedness inside our hearts. We first need to feel that we are unsaved before we can feel saved. We first need to feel that we are lost before we can feel that we are found. Sometimes the Lord will give a little encouragement to seeking souls, and that may be a little food to eat for a while, but the time comes again when they cannot live without the Lord. They have to go back a second time. And the further the Lord leads His child, then that child will experience that he or she will bring his or her very best to God. In other words, we will try to impress the Lord.

3. Knowing Joseph as a Deliverer

Well, what did Joseph do? He sent his brothers to his house and the servant met them there. They were very worried and afraid. They thought, "We don't know why we have to go to his house. This is very scary." But the servant smiled at them and spoke kind words to them. He said, "Peace be to you." But that didn't solve their problem; they had to hear that from Joseph's mouth. It is the same thing, boys and girls, with a lost sinner. It is one thing to have someone else say, "The Lord is working in your heart. Peace be to you." But that's not enough. We must hear it from the Lord through His Word that there is also salvation for us.

The Bible says something very interesting. The brothers were waiting for Joseph to come home, and it says that they made ready the present for Joseph who came at noon. They were working until the very last moment when Joseph came. How surprised they were when Joseph came, because he set them down in the order of their age! He knew all about them, it seemed. He gave them food and was kind to them; he sent them away with money, with food, and with Benjamin, whom they were so worried about. And while they were eating, the Bible says, "They drank, and were merry with him." They thought that everything was well. And in the morning they went home. They had their grain; they paid double for it; nobody was left behind; the ruler had been kind to them. They could hardly wait to tell Jacob. Everything was fine after all.

And yet, boys and girls, everything was not fine. They had still not confessed to Joseph. There are so many people today who are traveling to eternity with a religion that gives them, so to speak, full sacks and double money. They seem to have everything, but if you ask them how they received it and how they were emptied and how they became a lost sinner before God as a holy Judge, their mouth is closed. Oh, boys and girls, we need to know how God saves a sinner! Many times these people who always have their sacks full and can always speak about wonderful things in religion can even make a child of God jealous, but it is nothing to be jealous about. You could better be jealous of those whose sacks are empty and who are poor beggars waiting for a crumb from the Master's table. Joseph's brothers had yet to learn that.

But it was soon to happen. For while they were traveling back to Jacob, they heard a voice behind them. It was Joseph's steward and he was calling them to stop! They stopped and he said, "You have a cup, the silver cup of my lord. Wherefore have ye rewarded my master evil for all his good?" But the brothers were sure the cup was not in their sacks, so they took down all their sacks and opened them—and they found the cup in Benjamin's sack!

Benjamin here, boys and girls, is also pointing us to Christ. The cup of sin was placed upon Christ and He had to bear the price of sin for His people. But there is also another meaning here. We must learn that in our lives, we have rewarded the Lord evil for all His good. Now the Lord is finally beginning to teach these brothers important lessons. Had that happened twenty years ago, the brothers would have sent Benjamin back alone—just as they left Joseph alone. But they all went back with him this time. All the brothers went back to Joseph.

Joseph's brothers returned to him, and Joseph, the Bible says, "was yet there." What a mercy! When sinners come back to God after years of sin, God is still there. On the day of judgment it will be too late to repent. But Joseph was still there. When a poor, lost sinner comes back to the Lord, dear children, he can hardly believe that the Lord would still be there to hear his cries after so many years of sin. That's true if you are seventy years old, but it is also true if you are seven years old. If you are seven years old and the Lord begins to work savingly in you today, you would say, "Lord, how could I have sinned so many years against Thee? If you are seventy years old and you look at that seven-year-old boy or girl, you say, "He or she is so young to be converted, so young in sin," but, boys and girls, if the Lord works savingly in your life you will feel like you have sinned far too long, that you are old in sin, no matter how young you are.

Joseph was still there. This time everything was different. This time Judah stepped forward and said, "God has found out our iniquity." This time all their excuses were lost. This time Judah offered to be a surety for his brother Benjamin. He said, "Spare Benjamin, and condemn me," and that was like sweet music in the ears of Joseph because that was what Joseph had been waiting for all this time, namely, that his brothers would become guilty before him. He was waiting to hear that they were willing to be a surety for Benjamin. Joseph read between the lines of Judah's confession and realized that Judah felt guilty for the sin committed many years ago. Moreover, he saw that all the brothers agreed with Judah.

Then Joseph could hold himself back no longer. He was longing to make himself known to his brothers. He said, "Send all the Egyptians out of the room," and they all left. But that doesn't mean that they were forgiven yet. They didn't know what was happening. Joseph was crying, but tears do not mean forgiveness. They wondered what was happening. They didn't know. They had come back before Joseph as Zaphnath-paaneah, and he was a judge who had every right to condemn them. He was vice-president under Pharaoh. He could kill them.

Finally Joseph opened his mouth and said, "I am Joseph." Joseph? They looked at each other; they were troubled. Do you know why they were troubled? Because in Israel if you sold another Israelite into slavery you would receive a death sentence. If you sold a brother Hebrew into slavery you had to be killed. They had sold Joseph as a slave to the Ishmaelites, so immediately when they heard the words, "I am Joseph," they thought, "That means we have to die, for we have sold our brother into slavery." They were troubled at his presence. They came before him as a judge, and they had to perish.

And now, boys and girls, it is the same way with poor sinners. When they are brought back before the Lord as a Judge, then the Lord is just like Joseph. It seems that the Lord has to condemn them. He is too holy to let them go. It seems they have to die. They have sinned too much and they have no excuses.

But then Joseph said something else. He said, "Come near to me, I pray you…I am Joseph, your brother." Then he poured out his love, and they who betrayed him as an enemy and who came before him as a judge now would come to know him as a great deliverer.

Application

"I am Joseph." Oh, what an amazing thing, boys and girls! "We thought he was Zaphnath-paaneah, and here he is—Joseph!" Those brothers could hardly believe their ears. But then he said, "Come near to me, I pray you," and they saw his tears and felt his love. Their hearts were won over. They could not run away; they first dared not go to him. But when he said, "Come near to me, I pray you," and when he repeated it, "I am Joseph your brother," there was too much love in his words, too many tears on his face, for them to believe that he would kill them. No, it was just the opposite. They suddenly saw love in Joseph instead of judgment. They saw inexpressible love. "I am Joseph your brother." Boys and girls, there was so much love there. Here was a man who was one of the most important men in the whole world, and he said, "I am not ashamed to be called the brother of brothers who have betrayed me and sold me as the lowest person on earth. I will not sell you, my brothers. I will give you love for your hatred, and I will give you food for your selling me into slavery. I will render you good for evil." This is amazing love! "I am Joseph your brother."

Dear boys and girls, this love of Joseph, though it was so great, was not as great as the love of Jesus, the greater Joseph, to His people, for we have all become sinners and we all deserve to be cast away as slaves, but instead we have cast Christ away. But Christ comes back to His people and He draws poor sinners to Himself, saying, as it were, "I am the greater Joseph, your Elder Brother. I am not ashamed to be called your Brother, even though I am the King of kings and the Lord of lords and the whole universe belongs to Me. I am not ashamed to be called an Elder Brother of brothers who have sold Me and crucified Me and would have nothing to do with Me."

In these words, "I am Joseph," the gospel is freely preached. The greater Joseph arose from the dead that He may be the firstborn among many brethren. And when He arose after all His sufferings, He said, "Go tell my brethren and Peter that I will meet them in Galilee." Oh, congregation, is there any love like that love? We have said, "Away with Him, crucify Him!" When Peter said, "I know not the man," Jesus arose from the dead and said, "Go tell my brethren and Peter"—Peter is still a brother—"that I will meet them in Galilee." "I am Joseph your brother, your deliverer, your redeemer. Fear ye not: I am Joseph your brother, whom ye sold into Egypt." Joseph did not overlook their sin—he reminded them of it—but he reminded them of their sin to magnify his grace. And still today, when God comes to remind His people of their sins, He does not do that to punish them, for their punishment is paid by Jesus Christ, but He reminds them of their sins to magnify His grace.

Here was Joseph giving his love to brothers who sold him into Egypt as a type of Jesus Christ who keeps loving those who have betrayed Him and are unworthy of Him. "I *am* Joseph." That word "am" never changes. That is the present tense. It is an eternal present tense. "I shall always be the greater Joseph," Jesus would say. "I shall never be changeable. I will always take care of My people, no matter how they treat Me, no matter how My Peters deny Me, no matter how My children betray Me and sell Me short."

"I am Joseph." It was as if Joseph said to his brothers, "Brothers, no matter how much you did to me, no matter how much you would still do to me, I am still Joseph, your brother. That blood tie cannot be broken." To this day, Jesus Christ remains faithful unto His people, no matter how they treat Him. That's the gospel. The Heidelberg Catechism says in Lord's Day 19, "What comfort is it to thee that 'Christ shall come again to judge the quick and the dead'? That in all my sorrows and persecutions, with uplifted head I look for *the very same Person*, who before offered Himself for my sake, to the tribunal of God, and has removed all curse from me, to come as Judge from heaven: who shall cast all His and my enemies into everlasting condemnation, but shall translate me with all His chosen ones to Himself, into heavenly joys and glory." That "very same Person." "I am what I am. I am the greater Joseph and I cannot change. I am tied with everlasting blood ties of heavenly adoption, from the stillness of the eternal council of peace, to My people, and no matter what they have done, I cannot break those blood ties."

"I am Joseph your brother." That's the hope and the future for God's people. Dear friend, do you know a brother like the Lord Jesus Christ who is faithful in everything?

Now his brothers could truly go home happy. They fell on his neck, they wept, and they kissed him. Now they had reconciliation following confession. Now they realized that before they had never confessed and they never were reconciled. Now they had everything. Now they had a real gospel story to tell Jacob.

Boys and girls, dear congregation, have you ever met the greater Joseph as Judge, but also, have you ever met Him as Savior? Do you know what it means to expect to perish on account of sin, but also, do you know what it means to hear from His mouth, through His Word, by His Spirit, "I am Joseph your Brother"? Then a child of God sees that everything he needs is to be found in Christ. He has done everything. Joseph had everything ready for his brothers—the sacks, the grain, the money—he had everything they needed. Jesus Christ is the greater Joseph who has the greater storehouse. Of that storehouse we read in Luke 15, that in Him there is bread enough and to spare. There is no emptying of the fullness of Christ. He is the perfect and the greater Joseph.

Either we know this greater Joseph or we do not. And if we do not know Him, I appeal to your consciences and beg you for your own soul's sake, allow yourself no rest until you find Him. Can you bring yourself there? No, but you do have knees that you can bend, you do have hands that you can fold, and you do have lips that can speak. Ask the Lord to teach you who this greater Joseph is, and to teach you your sin, that you may need Him, that you cannot live without Him, and that you cannot rest until He is revealed to your heart by the power of the Holy Spirit.

"I am Joseph your brother." Does that mean that Joseph's brothers had no more troubles in their life? No, it doesn't mean that. They were truly happy now. But the doubts would come again. "The doubts?" you say. Yes, the doubts. How do we know that? We know that from Genesis 50. Jacob died, and suddenly Joseph's brothers were worried. They thought to themselves, "Now Joseph will still take revenge." And thus they sent a messenger; they were afraid to come before him. They sent a messenger with this message, "Behold, we be thy servants." And what did Joseph do? He wept again and he called his brothers and they bowed down before him. His dream was fulfilled in the process again. When they bowed before him, they said, "Behold, we be thy servants," he answered, "Fear ye not: I will nourish you" (Gen. 50:21).

Dear child of God, when you have tasted of the riches of Christ and the doubts come in again like a flood, do like Joseph's brothers: Bow before Him and say, "Behold, we be Thy servants." That means slaves, willing servitude—and wait at the gates of His house. He will say—and how sweet it is when you hear Him say it by renewal—"Fear ye not: I will nourish you." He is a rich God to a poor and needy people.

Thus, boys and girls, I want to commend to you the true and living Savior who is like the greater Joseph. In Jesus Christ there is room also for boys and girls to be saved. Seek Him, children, while you are young. Call upon Him while He is near. Repent of all your many sins and believe in Jesus Christ alone for your salvation.

Chapter 4

Seeing God's Glory

And he said, I beseech thee, shew me thy glory.
—EXODUS 33:18

Let me call your attention to the words of Exodus 33:18, "And he [Moses] said, I beseech thee, shew me thy glory." With God's help we wish to consider:

Seeing God's Glory
1. A prayer circumstantially motivated
2. A prayer wonderfully answered

1. A Prayer Circumstantially Motivated

Usually when we meet Moses in Exodus, we see him in his public work as a servant of God. Sometimes he is working miracles. Often he is proclaiming God's word or judging some particular evil. But in Exodus 33, we see Moses in the secret place as the servant of the people, speaking with God face to face in a time of great need. Let me provide some background of the circumstances under which Moses was communing with God.

The people of Israel had sinned heinously in making a golden calf. God was terribly displeased. At first, He threatened to consume them and destroy them all. He proposed to make a new nation of the seed of Moses. "I will make of thee a great nation" (Ex. 32:10). Moses besought the Lord to show pity and turn from such fierce wrath, and to repent of such an evil against the people, for the sake of God's honor in the eyes of the heathen, and the promise made to the fathers (vv. 11–13). So the people were spared. God now commands

Moses and the people to go up unto the land of promise. He promises to send an angel before them, and to drive out the people who now dwell in that land, but He Himself would not go up in the midst of them, "for thou art a stiffnecked people: lest I consume thee in the way" (Ex. 33:1–3).

Moses writes that "when the people heard these evil tidings, they mourned" (Ex. 33:4). As for Moses, he sees that he has more praying to do. To commune with God, Moses pitched a tent outside the camp, calling it "the tabernacle of the congregation," and there he spoke with God.

Attended by his servant, Joshua, Moses went out to the tabernacle to meet with God. Knowing the greatness of Israel's sin, and knowing how justly they deserved God's wrath and curse, the people looked to Moses and his priestly intercession for salvation. So they watched Moses and Joshua exit the camp. They stood in the door of their tents and saw the glory of God coming down as the pillar of cloud, and Moses going into the tabernacle to commune with God, and to plead for the people.

Exodus 33:12–23 relates some of the conversation between Moses and God. Moses declared that he couldn't go on without the Lord: "If thy presence go not with me, carry us not up hence," he said (Ex. 33:15). He yearned for God to be with His people and to be in their midst. Moses would rather die than go on without this sign of God's favor. Then he made the ultimate request: "I beseech thee, shew me thy glory" (Ex. 33:18).

Moses could scarcely have asked for more. No doubt, like Peter on the Mount of Transfiguration, he little knew the magnitude of what he asked. As Charles Spurgeon said, "It was vast faith which enabled Jacob to grasp the angel; it was mighty faith which made Elijah rend the heavens, and fetch down rain; but this prayer contains a greater amount of faith than those prayers combined."

How did Moses dare to ask for such a blessing? I believe that former communion with God encouraged him to ask for greater communion. Had Moses not spent forty days in sweet communion with God? Had not the Lord spoken unto him "face to face, as a man speaketh unto his friend"? Like Jacob, he had wrestled hard with God and, by grace, had prevailed.

Moreover, Moses had come with one petition after another, and God had answered them all. That made him bold. Faith does not retreat but grows bolder with each answered prayer. If it receives two answers, it prays for five more. Faith scales the walls of heaven.

The desire to see God's glory is the essence of Moses's prayer. It is also the highest request of every true believer. Every genuinely converted man and woman, boy and girl, longs to see the glory of God. Moses's example encourages us to be filled with boldness in prayer. It calls us to be in constant fellowship with the Father and with His Son, Jesus Christ. Only intimacy with God can raise us to such levels of boldness to ask, "I beseech thee, shew me thy glory."

Most of us are too hesitant to go to God. We bring Him far too little, and our expectation is far too small. We too seldom realize that seeing the glory of God is the essence of conversion. In conversion, the believer sees the glory of God—not physically but spiritually, by faith. Only a true Christian sees the glory of God. When you see God's glory, you know that you are a Christian.

An unbeliever, of course, sees something of God in creation and acquires some knowledge of God as he moves through life. David says, "The heavens declare the glory of God and the firmament sheweth his handywork" (Ps. 19:1). Paul tells us that the world reveals enough of the power and wisdom of God to leave people without excuse for their unbelief (Rom. 1:18–21). But only a true Christian sees the glory of God in the face of Jesus Christ (2 Cor. 4:6).

Most prayers, including those recorded in the Bible, rise out of circumstances. A good example of that is Jacob wrestling with the angel of God because he is afraid of meeting his brother, Esau (Genesis 32). Jacob prayed to God because of the danger of his circumstances. Consider also Solomon's prayer at the dedication of the temple (1 Kings 8:22–53), Daniel's confession of sin (Dan. 9:3–19); and Paul's prayers for the churches of Ephesus, Philippi, and Colosse (Eph. 1:15–23; 3:14–21; Phil. 1:9–11; Col. 1:9–15). All of those prayers were motivated by circumstances. So also the circumstances of our daily life motivate many of our prayers.

There were at least three circumstances that gave rise to Moses's petition "Shew me thy glory":

1. *He wanted to see more of God.* Moses had seen much of God's glory in his life, and he wanted more. All of Moses's life was one long experience of God revealing His glory to men and nations. When Moses's parents looked at him in the cradle, they knew that he was a special child. By faith, they understood that God had ordained this child to be a great man. At the age of forty, Moses tried to free his captive people in Egypt by slaying an Egyptian, but that didn't work, so Moses had to wait another forty years. That's when he saw the burning bush out of which God spoke to him and commissioned him to speak to Pharaoh and to free the people of Israel from slavery.

The ten plagues followed, then the exodus through the waters of the Red Sea, and then everything that happened on Mount Sinai, including meeting God and receiving the Ten Commandments. In those experiences, Moses saw the glory of God. And the more he saw of God's glory, the more he prayed, "O God, I beseech thee, shew me thy glory."

2. *He wanted assurance of God's forgiveness.* When Moses ascended Mount Sinai to meet with God, Aaron was given the responsibility of leading the people. Sinai was shrouded in smoke and clouds while Moses stayed there, talking with God for forty days and nights. But while one brother was up on the mountain, receiving the Ten Commandments, the other brother was at the foot of the mountain, helping the people break that Law. While Moses was receiving the commandment "Thou shalt not make a graven image," Aaron was melting gold trinkets to make a statue to worship in place of God. He built an altar for it and proclaimed a feast. He had the people offer sacrifices. "The people sat down to eat and to drink, and rose up to play," that is, to dance before the image of the molten calf. He even had them strip off their clothes and go naked "unto their shame" (Ex. 32:25).

Now Moses and Aaron were both great men of God. But there was a great difference between the two. Moses's first concern was the glory of God, and the honor of His name. Aaron, by contrast, could not say "no" to the people, regardless of what they asked. He was more concerned about his popularity than saying "no" to sin. When Moses came down the mountain and saw what the people were doing, he was so angry that he broke the tablets of stone, as a sign that they had broken their covenant with God. Shouting, "Who is on the Lord's side?" he enlisted those who stepped forward to help him slay three thousand Israelites.

On God's behalf, Moses applied the rod of reproof and correction. All this took its toll, however. Witnessing such gross sin and then administering such severe punishment in the name of God exhausted Moses's spirit. He desperately needed the calm refreshment and restoration that can only be found in the presence of God.

So you see the explanation for the prayer, "O God, I beseech thee, shew me thy glory." Moses is asking, "Take my eyes off this world. Put my eyes upon that heavenly One who is the Lord of glory. Take my mind off the sorrows and trials of this present time. Let me be so taken up with heavenly things until I forget the things of earth that vex my spirit. Oh that I might see again that heavenly vision of the glory of the Lord."

3. *He needed strength for the journey.* A long journey lay before Moses and the people, as well as the prospect of a great conflict with the people of the land. In fact, Israel would spend the next forty years in travail, sorrow, and difficulty traveling through the wilderness to the promised land. Moses needed his soul fortified for that great ordeal. He needed the strength and depth of his relationship with God to carry him through.

One thing that worried Moses was how superficial the faith of God's people was at that time. God had taken the people out of Egypt. He had brought them to the foot of Mount Sinai. God had shown His glory on top of the mountain. The Israelites had cowered in terror at the trumpet, the lightning, the thunder, the fire, the smoke, and the voice of God who had commanded them, "Thou shalt not make unto thee any graven image." And yet, only a short time later, the people lost heart when Moses failed to return and said to Aaron, "Up, make us gods, which shall go before us; for as for this Moses, the man that brought us up out of the land of Egypt, we wot [know] not what is become of him" (Ex. 32:1).

Moses's prayer reminds us how shallow and superficial we all are. What we need is not simply the grace of God touching the surface of our lives; we need the grace of God carving its way deep into our souls. Moses longed for depth. He was asking, in effect, "O God, we are so shallow—please do not simply *scratch* Thy grace into our souls but *carve* it down deep. Show us Thy glory."

The church today needs both depth and strength. We desperately need communion with God. We live in a stifling, wicked world. It is difficult to breathe in such an atmosphere, saturated as it is with sin, and still go forward. We need help from above. So let us cry, "Shew me thy glory."

2. A Prayer Wonderfully Answered

To see how God wonderfully answered the prayer of Moses, we must first understand what is meant by the glory of God. The word "glory" in Hebrew signifies weightiness, or something of great value. God is infinitely valuable. There is no God, as it were, so big, so weighty, so invaluable as the triune God of the Scriptures. God's glory is the splendor of His being, what He is absolutely in Himself, infinite, eternal, and unchangeable. God's glory is the radiant beauty, or brightness (Heb. 1:3) of the sum of all His attributes, His wisdom, power, holiness, justice, goodness, and truth. God's glory is the light in which He dwells, "the light which no man can approach unto" (1 Tim. 6:16).

Children, you know that sunlight can be broken into various colors. You take a wedge of glass, called a prism, and place it on a stand. In a darkened room, you shine a jet of pure white light onto the prism. It will break up the light into all the different colors that make up the light: red, orange, yellow, green, blue, indigo, and violet. That's a faint illustration of what God's glory is like. It is the total splendor of His holiness, justice, truth, wisdom, power, grace, and love. Those attributes are inseparable from His glory; they are the source of His glory. What Moses asks now is, "O God, show me what manner of God Thou art. Make me stand in awe at the wonder of Thy being. Portray to my mind and soul all the wondrous truths of who Thou art."

God responds to Moses's prayer in three ways:

1. *He promises to answer it.* He does not shake the mountain in justice, holiness, and wrath. Rather, He promises to come to Moses in the still small voice of the gospel. "I will make all my goodness to pass before thee," God says (v. 19).

God's goodness is the brightest diamond in His crown, for His greatest glory is that He is good. He is goodness itself; it is the essence of His every attribute as well as His every act. As Thomas Boston (1676–1732) wrote, "All the variations of the creatures which He made were so many beams and apparitions of His goodness." He is good in creation, in providence, and above all, in redemption. He is the overflowing fountain of all good. No wonder, then, that when Stephen Charnock wrote the great classic *The Existence and Attributes of God*, he devoted more pages to divine goodness than to any other attribute.

What a promise—"I will make all my goodness pass before thee"! Moses would no doubt witness God's sovereign goodness toward His chosen people. But herein lies the apex of God's goodness. When we see God's redemptive goodness, we see not only His goodness in our regeneration, conversion, justification, and sanctification, but we are also led back to our Savior in Gethesemane, Gabbatha, and Golgotha. From there, God's goodness takes us to eternity past, where we gaze by faith upon our election, then to eternity future, where we, by hope, anticipate dwelling in the eternal goodness of Yahweh.

God's goodness is boundless and timeless. From eternity to eternity, God is "the overflowing fountain of all good," as we read in the Belgic Confession. God "is good and doeth good unto all," as we read in the Westminster Confession. Oh, that we might both hunger and thirst for His goodness, and heed the words of the psalmist, "O taste and see that the LORD is good" (Ps. 34:8). Let us be in constant awe and admiration of God's goodness.

God promises that He will also show Moses the sovereignty of His grace and mercy. "I will be gracious to whom I will be gracious, and will shew mercy on whom I will shew mercy" (v. 19). God's glory is on display when sovereignty accompanies goodness. To see God's sovereign grace and mercy, therefore, is to see God's glory, and to see it more fully. In the gospel, that glory is revealed in Christ as the brightness of God's glory (Heb. 1:3) and the Word made flesh: "And the Word was made flesh, and dwelt among us, (and we beheld his glory, the glory as of the only begotten of the Father,) full of grace and truth" (John 1:14).

2. He gives more than he asked. God goes on to show Moses the entire spectrum of His glorious attributes. We read, "And the LORD passed by before him, and proclaimed, The LORD, The LORD God, merciful and gracious, longsuffering, and abundant in goodness and truth, keeping mercy for thousands, forgiving iniquity and transgression and sin, and that will by no means clear the guilty; visiting the iniquity of the fathers upon the children, and upon the children's children, unto the third and to the fourth generation" (Ex. 34:6–7).

In essence, the answer to Moses's prayer is that the glory of God is the character of God. It is the glory of God to be what He is! Our problem is that we do not know God as He is. The more we know God as He is, the more godly—or "like God"—we will become. The difference between much godliness and little godliness is how much we know the glory of God. Moses longed to know that glory and to possess a degree of godliness.

Sometimes we say that a person is unbalanced. Sadly, we are all unbalanced because sin has spoiled our character. We are prone to extremes. Not so with God! Everything in God is in perfect poise. Justice and holiness on one side are perfectly balanced with grace and love on the other. It is the glory of God's redemptive work that in setting forth Christ Jesus "to be a propitiation through faith in his blood," He is most just in the punishing of sin, but also most gracious as "the justifier of him which believeth in Jesus" (Rom. 3:25–26).

We must strive for grace to be like God and to be balanced in our character. Then, on the one hand, we can uphold a high standard of holiness, righteousness, and justice; and on the other hand, we can show kindness, mercy, and patience to others. Sin and the temptations of an evil world pressure us to lose that balance. We must never forget to look to God's character as the pattern for our own. Let us pray, "Lord, dig deeper; form me in accord with Thy communicable attributes. Help me to reflect Thy balanced character as a husband to my wife (or as a wife to my husband); as a parent to my children; as an office-bearer to the congregation; as an employer to employees—indeed, in every relationship of life."

That is what we need today. If we profess faith in Christ, we must dig deeper into the character of God to understand what He is like, that we might live according to the pattern of His glorious image. God tells Moses, "I will make all my goodness pass before thee." When you and I are in the right place, we will love that picture of God. We will strive to imitate what we see in it so that we may become more like God.

3. *He imposes two conditions.* In order to see God's glory, Moses must yield to two gracious limitations or conditions. God told Moses to hide in the cleft of a rock as God's glory passed by. As Exodus 33:20–23 says, "Behold, there is a place by me, and thou shalt stand upon a rock: and it shall come to pass, while my glory passeth by, that I will put thee in a clift of the rock, and will cover thee with my hand while I pass by: and I will take away mine hand, and thou shalt see my back parts: but my face shall not be seen."

God is willing to show some part of His glory to Moses but Moses is not allowed to see the whole of God's face because "There shall no man see me, and live." Gazing upon the full glory of God is like looking at the light of the sun. If you stare at it for too long, the sun will blind you. Likewise, man cannot look on God. His glory is so intense that the eye of man cannot stand it. So God set a limit, for Moses's sake, and said that he could see only some of the divine glory.

God also put Moses into a safe place—"a clift of the rock," a crack or crevice in the rock that Moses was to stand upon—from which he could observe "the back parts" (or a small part), of God's glory. In doing so, God was teaching Moses the absolute necessity for a Savior and Mediator. He was saying that man in his sinful condition cannot live when God comes near, nor look upon even the least part of His glory, unless he has taken refuge in Christ the Mediator. Outside of Christ, without the protection of His broken body and shed blood, not Moses, and not any of us, can look upon the glory of God and live. So the Christian learns to sing from Psalter 34:

> I love the Lord, His strength is mine;
> He is my God, I trust His grace;
> My fortress high, my shield divine,
> My Savior and my hiding place.

Application

As Augustus Toplady (1740–1778) wrote in his well-known hymn,

> Rock of ages, cleft for me
> Let me hide myself in Thee.

Moses needed that lesson. He said to God, "This people have sinned a great sin." Now he says to God, "Yet now, if thou wilt forgive their sin—; and if not, blot me, I pray thee, out of thy book which thou hast written" (Ex. 32:32). Moses was offering to be the savior of the people. That was a noble sentiment, but it was not enough. No man could bear the wrath of God. Moses offered himself as a substitute, but God refused. "Whosoever hath sinned against me, him will I blot out of my book," was God's answer. God was already preparing Someone far better than Moses to bear the sins of the world. The law would come by Moses, but grace and truth, and the complete remission of all our sins, by Jesus Christ (John 1:17).

It was good that Moses was so zealous for the glory of God. But Moses also needed to learn that the Messiah to come would be the only Rock of refuge, for his own soul as well as for his fellow Israelites.

There is an important lesson here. Every true Christian should desire to see the glory of God (Ps. 63:1–2). We shall see it in the face of Jesus Christ. As Paul says in 2 Corinthians 3:18: "But we all [as Christians], with open face [a reference to Moses going to the tent of meeting] beholding as in a glass the glory of the Lord, are changed into the same image from glory to glory, even as by the Spirit of the Lord."

The "glass" (or mirror) in which we see the glory of the Lord is God's Word and the preaching of God's Word. Scripture is God's witness to Christ: "They are they which testify of me" (John 5:39). Knowing God's Word is essential for salvation, as well as for our sanctification and growth in grace. As we see the face of Christ in Scripture, we behold the glory of God (2 Cor. 4:6). And what happens? We are changed, says Paul. The Word of God changes us "into the same image, from glory to glory, even as by the Spirit of the Lord." That is how sanctification proceeds.

My friends, this is what we need. We must look into this mirror of glory—the Word of God. We must see the glory of God in the face of Jesus Christ. Then we shall be changed "from glory to glory," and come forth from God's presence with a radiant countenance. Men shall know that we have been with God. Is that not what happened in the days of the apostles? The Pharisees scoffed at those ignorant, unschooled men—at first. But those leaders began to think again when they saw the boldness and conviction of men who had been with Jesus and witnessed the glory of God (Acts 4:13). May God therefore move us to pray all our lives, and with all our hearts, "Shew me Thy glory."

Chapter 5

Following God Fully

> *But my servant Caleb, because he had another spirit with him, and hath followed me fully, him will I bring into the land whereinto he went; and his seed shall possess it.*
> —NUMBERS 14:24

With God's help, we wish to consider:

Following God Fully
1. *The meaning* of this expression: what it means that Caleb followed God fully
2. *Its root in grace*: why Caleb could follow God fully
3. *Its reward of grace*: the reward God granted to Caleb because he followed Him fully

Scripture provides many thumbnail biographical sketches for us. Some are examples of people we should not follow, such as Judas Iscariot, Ahab, and Cain; others are great men and women of God whom we should follow as mentors on our journey through this world. Among these great mentors is a godly man, seldom preached about and often ignored, even in sound literature—Caleb the son of Jephunneh. Caleb is an eminent example of godliness, such that God attributed to him great grace, declaring that he followed God fully all the days of his life.

If you are a true believer, I am sure this is your desire. You do not desire to serve God half-heartedly; you desire to love Him with all your heart, your mind, your soul, and your strength. You desire to live a consistent life; you desire to follow God fully. I wish to set before you this great man of God, praying that the Lord may give you and me grace to follow Caleb's example through the Lord Jesus Christ.

Caleb was one of the twelve spies who Moses sent into Canaan to spy out the land and to bring back a report. Caleb and Joshua were the only spies who brought back an encouraging report fueled by faith. With Joshua, Caleb encouraged Israel to fight against the inhabitants of the land because of God's faithfulness and promises. After forty days, when the spies had completed their task and brought back their report, it is remarkable that all twelve agreed on several facts. They all agreed the land Canaan was a good land, flowing with milk and honey. They brought back a huge cluster of grapes from Eshcol. They all agreed that the inhabitants of the land were, for the most part, warlike people. They all agreed there were giants in the land: big men, eight or nine feet tall—"children of Anak" (Num. 13:22). They all agreed that cities were walled about and that they were great strongholds. They all agreed that it would be complicated and difficult to fight against these foes. They all told the true story as far as the *facts* were concerned. However, when it came to the consequences of those facts—when it came to the conclusion, the bottom line, "What shall we do?"—the twelve spies disagreed with one another.

The majority report, presented by ten, was very negative. They said there was no use to try to overcome these enemies; they were too strong and too large to conquer. The task that God had given them was impossible to fulfill, they insisted. They said: "We be not able to go up against the people; for they are stronger than we. And they brought up an evil report of the land which they had searched unto the children of Israel, saying, The land, through which we have gone to search it, is a land that eateth up the inhabitants thereof; and all the people that we saw in it are men of a great stature. And there we saw the giants, the sons of Anak, which come of the giants: and we were in our own sight as grasshoppers, and so we were in their sight" (Num. 13:31–33).

Can you imagine two and a half million people (the population of Israel at the time) hearing this dreadful report: "We were in our own sight as grasshoppers" (Num. 13:33)? "We have come through the wilderness, we have come at last to the Promised Land and now we face giants and walled cities and impossibilities." Fear and unbelief took hold of them. Fear and unbelief are the parents of their conclusion. Fear and unbelief, friends, always bring a negative report. Fear and unbelief can have a right account of the facts but they assess those facts incorrectly.

The ten false spies left out one important fact—they forgot God and His promises! They looked at the circumstances instead of God. They forgot what God had said: "Go in to possess the land, which the Lord your God giveth you to possess it" (Josh. 1:11). You and I are prone to do the same thing, aren't we? Difficulties and troubles enter our lives—personal troubles, domestic trials, trials with our occupation, church troubles. We are prone to look at our circumstances rather than our God. We are prone to respond in unbelief, aren't we? Unbelief measures the walls and tallies up the Amalekites, the Hittites, the Canaanites, and all the giants; and the conclusion is—we simply can't do it!

The people are inclined to follow the majority. What a tragedy: two and a half million people led astray by ten men! What a responsibility every Christian has to lead people rightly, and especially a servant of God. We ministers are, in some senses, spies in the land. Every week we are to search the Scriptures. We are to spy out the truths of God's grace in the Scriptures. We are to report on them the following Sabbath and tell of the wonders and the glory and the might of our God. Every Sabbath we are to tell people about the dangers they face and the way to Zion, about their enemies, about their problems, and the narrow road that leads to salvation. Yet, we are not to overwhelm people with these problems, we must direct them to Jesus Christ and tell them that our God is able: without Christ, we can do nothing, but in Christ we can do all things, for He strengthens us. That is the report we are to bring—our God is able! Look not to circumstances, look to the living God. The ten spies forgot that. They forgot about the God of the Red Sea. They forgot the God who said to them, "Fear ye not, stand still, and see the salvation of the Lord, which he shall shew to you to day" (Ex. 14:13); "The Lord shall fight for you, and ye shall hold your peace" (v. 14).

How dreadful this majority report was! There was no faith in God's sovereignty, no faith in God's omnipotence, and no faith in God's promises. These ten false spies didn't even rise to the level of ungodly Balaam who confessed, "God is not a man, that he should lie; neither the son of man that he should repent: hath he said, and shall he not do it? or hath he spoken, and shall he not make it good?" (Num. 23:19). Unbelief makes our problems big and it makes God small. The tragedy of unbelief is that it drags masses of God's people into the "slough of despond" with it. When they are in their right place, God's Joshuas and God's Calebs have a different spirit—not a contagious, unbelieving spirit that easily persuades people that the giants of Anak are larger than the promises of God, thereby making the promises look weak. For then, the vitals of faith are chipped away at, spiritual growth is stunted, and people stop fearing God. But Joshua and Caleb bring God into the equation. Joshua and Caleb stand up and Caleb stills the people and says, "Let us go up at once, and possess it; for we are well able to overcome it" (Num. 13:30). You see, Joshua and Caleb believe that God is bigger than the largest giant in Canaan. Let us go, they say, and claim the inheritance that God has promised us. All twelve spies use their eyes; all twelve use their minds; but only Joshua and Caleb had a heart for God and for His people. They had a heart to walk the way of faith, dear friends. That is the way you and I are called to walk in this world—the way of faith.

The way of faith is not an easy way. God never promised His people an easy life, did He? The way of faith is a blessed way though not an easy way. It is a sure way though not an easy way. The way of faith urges people to trust God, to believe in His Son, to repent before Him, to walk in His ways, *to follow God fully*. Faith trusts, for that is the nature of faith. Faith believes, trusts, and rests.

Caleb says that the giants shall become dwarfs before the promises of God. He says, "Rebel not ye against the Lord, neither fear ye the people of the land; for they are bread for us: their defence is departed from them, and the Lord is with us: fear them not" (Num. 14:9). So you see, this is the minority report of two who believe in God. This minority report is positive in nature. Caleb and Joshua believe that

God will never go back on His Word. Dear friends, when we believe and live that, by the grace of the Holy Spirit, we honor our God.

Joshua and Caleb dared to stand up against intense pressure; you can imagine the other ten, and the two and a half million people behind them. Two men stand up boldly for the cause of God despite pressure from all their peers. Caleb, in this instance, appears to be the spokesman for the two. God honors his stand, even when the people take stones to stone them: "But all the congregation bade stone them with stones" (Num. 14:10). Caleb doesn't flinch. Caleb doesn't say that maybe he had got it a bit wrong or suggest that they sit down and talk over whether they really should go in to Canaan or send a second group of spies to compare notes. Caleb and Joshua do not suggest any compromise. No, Caleb says, as it were, "Stone me with stones but I will follow the Lord. Do what you must do but I must follow the Lord *fully*." That leads us to our text tonight.

1. Its Meaning by Grace
Notice, first of all, that "following God fully" is God's testimony of Caleb—not Caleb's testimony of himself. There is a big difference, isn't there? If you asked Caleb himself, no doubt he would say, "O, my heart is so wicked! I have been so inconsistent. I have been so faltering. My obedience has been so meager." However, *God* said of Caleb, "My servant...hath followed me fully." That is what counts, friends— not what we say of ourselves, but what God says of us.

God gives a similar testimony of Job. We can't imagine Job saying, "I am thy perfect servant Job." However, God said of Job, "There is none like him in the earth, a perfect and an upright man, one that feareth God, and escheweth evil" (Job 1:8), Caleb was such a man who received the benediction and approbation of his God. That is what we want, friends; that is what we want more than anything in all the world: that God will look down from heaven upon us, in the Lord Jesus Christ, and grant us His divine approbation. We desire that He would say, "This is My child who has followed Me fully."

What does it mean to follow God *fully*? It means at least four things. It means first of all that Caleb followed God all his life. He followed God *persistently*. Turn to Joshua 14:13–14. This is what God's

Word says of Caleb after his forty years in the wilderness, where he was surrounded by unbelieving people: "And Joshua blessed him, and gave unto Caleb the son of Jephunneh Hebron for an inheritance. Hebron therefore became the inheritance of Caleb the son of Jephunneh the Kenezite unto this day, because that he wholly followed the LORD God of Israel" (Josh. 14:13–14). Here you have a testimony about Caleb in his old age that parallels our text. When he was a young man in his forties and when he was an old man in his eighties, God says the same thing of him. This is a man of consistency and persistency. This is a man of godliness. This is a man who did not serve God by fits and starts, as John Warburton used to say. Here is a man who served God habitually, constantly, evenly. All those years he lived in the camp of the Israelites, Caleb refused to yield to the murmuring rebels that surrounded him. He was faithful unto death and God crowned him with a crown of life.

I wonder about you and me, friends. Do we follow the Lord persistently and consistently? Some people follow the Lord only for a season, don't they? They are like flames that rise up, then quickly die away. They seem to have meant well but when persecution comes, their flame of Christianity dies out and the smoke fades away until there is nothing left. Think of Lot's wife. She left Sodom and Gomorrah, but she gave up, looked back, and became a pillar of salt. Think of the Jews in John 6:66; they walked no more with Jesus. Think of the Galatians; Paul says, "Ye did run well" (Gal. 5:7); "O foolish Galatians, who hath bewitched you?" (Gal. 3:1).

Still today, there are many people like that. Years ago, a former church member who was hospitalized seemed to be under great spiritual impressions. I had a strong hope that the Lord was converting this young man. He went back into his family, encountered the peer pressures around him, and all the impressions faded away. Can that be said of you or me? In times of adversity, do we lose our "Christianity"? In times of pressure and persecution, do we fall away? Oh, what a tragedy! In times of persecution and difficulty the world watches us with a penetrating gaze: Is Christianity worth its salt? The world is watching you and me to observe if our Christianity persists in the face of persecution and affliction.

Second, to follow God fully means to follow Him sincerely—not only persistently but also *sincerely*, from the heart. It means to not be a hypocrite, not to be an outward Christian only. Everyone was against Caleb and Joshua. Numbers 14:10 says, "All the congregation"—notice that word *all*—"bade stone them with stones." They endured insults and jeers. Like Moses, they had to bear the reproach of Christ. Yet, Caleb could do nothing else because his heart was sincere before God.

Why were the people so angry that they were ready to stone Caleb? Because he exposed their religion or rather, their lack of religion. He removed all their excuses for not going into Canaan. He took away all their arguments. They were determined to cling to their unbelief, and Caleb reproached them. When you reproach an unbeliever, you will often evoke persecution. "All that will live godly in Christ Jesus shall suffer persecution," 2 Timothy 3:12 says. It will happen, sometimes sooner, sometimes later; sometimes intensely, sometimes minimally. When we walk in the ways of God, we will suffer persecution.

Dear friends, we are called to confess God's name no matter where we are and no matter what the case. I once spoke on a train with a young woman who was an atheist. As I began lovingly to rebuke her because she told me she was going to go live with her boyfriend, she said to me, "You are not going to try to convert me, are you? I don't want to hear that kind of talk." She said, "It is too late in the evening to talk to me about God. Beside, I don't even know if I believe in Him." I asked, "What would you like me to talk to you about?" "Other things," she said. I said, "It seems to me that this is a pretty important thing for you to talk about because if God doesn't exist, then you are not under His command and you can go the way you want to, can't you? However, if God does exist, what do you think He would say about what you are going to do?" "Well," she said, "He would say I was going to live in sin, so I don't want to think about it." That is natural man! We don't want to be confronted. We don't want guilt on our own doorstep. We don't want to face who and what we are. When we biblically and lovingly confront other people with who they are, we will suffer persecution, but we must be willing to pay the price.

Robert Murray M'Cheyne said, "Your best friend is the one who is willing to tell you the most truth about yourself." Scripture says it even better: "Faithful are the wounds of a friend; but the kisses of an enemy are deceitful" (Prov. 27:6). A man who follows God fully, follows God sincerely; he wants to say a word for God wherever he goes.

Martin Luther once said, "Suffering persecution is a mark of the true church." You know the marks of the church: the pure preaching of the Word, the right administration of the sacraments, the exercise of discipline in the church. Well, Luther would have us promote another mark because 2 Timothy 3:12 says: "*All* that will live godly in Christ Jesus shall suffer persecution." A person cannot go to heaven unreproached or unpersecuted. How can you follow a suffering Savior and never have to suffer for His name's sake?

I wonder, congregation, do you ever suffer for the cause and the sake of Jesus Christ? Do you fear God more than man? John Brown wrote, "The fear of God means to esteem the smiles and frowns of God to be of greater weight and greater value than the smiles and frowns of men." That is the way to live. "Oh God, let me live in Thy smile. Let me fear Thy frown. Let me walk in Thy ways. Let me follow Thee *fully*." That doesn't mean, of course, that we may provoke people unnecessarily. It doesn't mean that we are anything other than truly loving to all people. But true love sometimes must say, "No." True love sometimes has to confront. If you really care for someone you want them to come with you, to follow the Lord *fully*.

Thirdly, to follow God fully means to follow God, as an old divine used to say, *indivisibly*, or as Thomas Boston said, "*universally*." That means with all my heart—not only with a sincere heart but also with all my heart. To follow God fully means to say with David, "I will make haste to run in the way of all thy commands" (Ps. 119:32). Some people pick and choose what part of God's will they want to do. They are very consistent in certain areas. Perhaps they are conservative Sabbath-keepers but neglect daily family worship. Perhaps they have very good habits in some areas of their lives but in other areas they say, "I know that this or that is wrong but you can't be perfect. You shouldn't be righteous overmuch. I know it's wrong but I'll just go ahead and do it. I think God will have mercy on me." That is the way some people pick and choose. When a certain commandment comes too close to home, they take refuge in the other commandments that they are supposedly following. Their obedience is partial, halting, and feigned.

Caleb wasn't that way. He said, as it were, "I want the whole fabric of my life to be one pattern. I want to have a seamless, one-track mind when it comes to obedience to God. I want to put blinders on and I want to follow God in the narrow way of salvation all my life. I do not want to turn to the right nor to the left. I want to follow God in everything. I want to follow Him with my thoughts, I want to follow Him with my words, I want to follow Him with my deeds. I want my life to be all of one pattern. I want my life to be an open epistle of the grace of God in Christ Jesus. O God, give me grace to follow Thee *fully*."

That is what we want if we are Christians, isn't it? We want an undivided heart. We don't want to follow God just when it is pleasant to do so. We don't want to be like Mr. Byends in Bunyan's *Pilgrim's Progress* who said of himself and those who lived in the town of Fairspeech, "We are always most zealous when religion goes in its silver slippers." In other words, there are people who walk religiously in the comfort of "silver slippers" so long as everything goes their way. But as soon as something crosses their will, they place their will above God's command. True Christians, however, detest such partiality toward God and His commandments. We want to be men and women and children of God who follow God with an undivided heart.

How is it with us, friends? Are there pockets of our lives where we are engaging even now in any known sin? We must forsake all sin. We must cry for mercy to conquer our so-called bosom or besetting sins. We must pray to the Almighty that we may have strength to pierce every sin with the sword, to put every sin to death. The true child of God who is walking close with God will say, "O God, I wish every sin in me were dead." Can you say that? Are you following God *fully*?

Finally, to follow God fully means to follow God *exclusively*. Not only persistently, sincerely, and indivisibly, but exclusively. That means that we follow no one else whenever and wherever he or she does not follow Christ. It means, like Paul said, to follow Paul only insofar as he followed the Lord Jesus Christ. That is the maxim and the model of the entire Reformation movement to which we are all so greatly indebted. That is what the Reformers did; they followed no man further than that man followed the Lord Jesus Christ. Following God must be the preeminent pursuit of our lives. We must have no other goal in mind, no other desire in mind. Our soul must be consecrated to God. Our entire being must be caught up with this burning passion to walk in the King's highway of holiness.

Our text says, "my *servant* Caleb." A servant obeys his master. A servant yields total consecration; a willing servant is faithful. God says, "Caleb is My servant. He serves Me. He follows no one else." That is what we need, friends. Pray for grace in every trouble and trial that comes your way to follow God persistently, sincerely, indivisibly, and exclusively.

Perhaps you say, "That is so impossible. My heart is a well of iniquity: 'The heart is deceitful above all things and desperately wicked; who can know it?'" (Jer. 17:9). Indeed, that is true, isn't it? How was it possible, then, for Caleb to follow God *fully*? Our text tells us: "because he had another spirit with him and hath followed me fully." Let's consider what that means in our second thought.

2. Its Root in Grace

"Another spirit." These two words obviously contain the secret of how Caleb could follow God fully, but what do they mean? "Another spirit" means that Caleb had a different spirit than did the ten false spies. Theirs was a spirit of unbelief, his a spirit of faith. Theirs was a worldly spirit; his was heavenly. Theirs was a spirit of angry disobedience, his of affectionate obedience; theirs was satanic, his was of God; theirs was lazy, his was active. They wanted the rest without the journey, the reward without the labor, the victory without the warfare. They were led by their own spirits; Caleb was led by the Holy Spirit. He had a noble, courageous, and gentle spirit, a generous and heroic spirit, a self-denying and loyal spirit because he was moved by the Holy Spirit. That is the ultimate cause of the difference between Caleb and the ten false spies. It wasn't Caleb's own strength; it was the Holy Spirit working in him. "Now we have received, not the spirit of the world, but the spirit which is of God; that we might know the things that are freely given to us of God" (1 Cor. 2:12). That is the spirit Caleb had.

Perhaps then you ask, "Why did Caleb have that Holy Spirit and why didn't the ten false spies have that Holy Spirit? What made the difference?" We answer: Only the free and sovereign mercy of God. The Holy Spirit was God's free gift to Caleb and God was pleased for reasons locked up in the secrets of His own heart by His sovereign electing love to have mercy on Caleb and not upon those ten false spies. It pleased God to do so and we cannot go beyond that, can we? We cannot probe beyond the sovereign mysteries of God's eternal love, nor need we do so, for there is nothing beyond that love. For His own reasons, God made Caleb His servant, and gave him His spirit to serve Him. Therefore there was no explanation in Caleb; there was nothing beyond sovereign covenantal mercy and love. Why did Caleb have another spirit? Because of sovereign grace; because God loved him with an everlasting love, therefore, with cords of lovingkindness, He drew him to follow Him *fully*.

Caleb's obedience was first of all the work of the Holy Spirit in him. Caleb was the instrument through which the Spirit worked. Caleb was involved; it didn't happen outside of him, but it was all of grace. Caleb was enabled to follow God fully through the meritorious work of the perfect One, the Lord Jesus Christ—of whom God said, "Behold my servant, whom I uphold; mine elect, in whom my soul delighteth" (Isa. 42:1). Caleb followed God *fully* because of the electing heart of the Father's love, through the meritorious obedience of the Lord Jesus Christ, and by the indwelling of the Holy Spirit.

The triune God is involved. Jesus Christ followed His Father fully: "It is my Father's will"; "I am about my Father's business." He engrafted Caleb into Himself—into the vine—and the sap of Christ flowed into the veins of Caleb. Out of Christ and by the Spirit of Christ, Caleb followed God *fully*.

We need to pray for that spirit. We need to pray that we will be indwelt and governed by the Spirit of Christ so that we receive by true faith and with meekness the engrafted Word that is able to save our soul—so that we follow God *fully*.

Perhaps you have one objection: If Caleb followed God *fully* by grace only, why did God give Caleb a reward? Notice the conclusion of our text: "him will I bring into the land whereinto he went; and his seed shall possess it" (Num. 14:24). That leads us to our third thought, which is to examine God's gracious reward promised to Caleb.

3. Its Reward of Grace

To follow God fully, in the first place, means to follow Him by grace, persistently, sincerely, indivisibly, and exclusively. Second, that following is rooted in grace; that is why Caleb could follow God *fully*. Third, God rewards Caleb for following, out of grace. God's reward to Caleb is not a reward of merit; Caleb did not merit it. It is a reward of grace. What God does in His people by way of sanctification, He really gives to His people and He rewards His own work in them. Let me give you an example. Do you remember the story of the Canaanite woman? Christ worked faith in her. He matured that faith through her trials and then He crowns His own work by stating, "O woman, great is thy faith" (Matt. 15:28). God gives away His graces to His people, including the grace of faith, and then when they by His Spirit act out that faith, God rewards His own work within them with the crownings of grace.

Let me illustrate. When my birthday is approaching, my wife will take the money I have given to her, and tell our children, "Go buy a present for Dad for his birthday." When I receive the present, I don't say to my children, "I really don't need to thank you for this because you spent my money to get it." What a cruel father I would be to respond like that! Rather, I treat the gifts as if my children had earned the money to buy them. I thank them for those gifts with all my heart, and graciously reward them with embraces and kisses and affirming words. You see, God rewards the obedience of His people by His own grace. He gives them grace to follow Him, but is genuinely grateful when they do follow Him, and graciously rewards them.

Article 24 of the Belgic Confession of Faith is a beautiful statement on the doctrine of sanctification. At one point, it affirms that God is not obliged to us for the good works that we do, but we are obliged to Him, because He gives us the grace to do the good works. God's grace leads us to walk by grace, out of grace, to His glory. Therefore, the wonderful promises in Numbers 14:24 are just grace on top of grace. John tells us, "And of his fullness have all we received, and grace for grace" (John 1:16). Literally, this means grace piled up on top of grace. The lives of God's people are like the ocean tide coming in: one wave of grace upon another—in prosperity and through affliction. Prosperity is grace; adversity is grace. Where would you be without adversity and persecution in your life? You would remain spiritually immature and become spoiled, but God gives grace—wave after wave—precisely according to what we need. On top of it all comes His waves of gracious, precious promises. What a wonderful promise He gave to Caleb, crowning His own grace—"him will I bring into the land whereinto he went; and his seed shall possess it" (Num. 14:24).

Actually, there are three promises here, *life*, *land*, and *legacy*. In the first place, God is promising to preserve Caleb's life: "him will I bring into the land whereinto he went." Six hundred thousand men of that generation who were unbelieving, their spouses, and many of their children are all going to die in the wilderness, Caleb is in his forties already and they are going to wander for forty years, but God says, "him will I bring into the land." Caleb and Joshua will outlive them all. Caleb will be an old man in his eighties, nevertheless, "him will I bring into the land." It is a blessing when God promises long life upon obedience.

Second, God promises to give Caleb the land he spied out for an inheritance. That is fulfilled in the book of Joshua in a remarkable way. In Joshua 14:10–11, Caleb says, "And now, behold, the LORD hath kept me alive, as he said, these forty and five years, even since the LORD spake this word unto Moses, while the children of Israel wandered in the wilderness: and now, lo, I am this day fourscore and five years old. As yet I am as strong this day as I was in the day that Moses sent me: as my strength was then, even so is my strength now, for war, both to go out, and to come in." So God gave Caleb remarkable strength and endurance. Joshua then gives Hebron to Caleb and you remember what was in Hebron—the giants: Ahiman, Sheshai and Talmai, the children of Anak. In the next chapter, Joshua 15:14 astonishingly says, "And Caleb drove thence the three sons of Anak, Sheshai, and Ahiman, and Talmai, the children of Anak." Don't forget, Caleb is now eighty-five years old. An eighty-five year old man drove out those very giants before whom two and a half million people trembled and said, "We can't go in." That is what God can do!

One of our deceased ministers said he once saw an old rickety truck going down a road in Nigeria with a crudely painted sign that read, "God plus one = majority." That's what Caleb experienced. "Him will I bring into the land" and him will I bless. God promises so much. He does "exceeding abundantly above all that we ask or think" (Eph. 3:20). Wouldn't it be great, if God did everything we asked? Paul says He will do more. He will do everything you *ask* or *think*. That is truly great. No, Paul says, He will do more; He will do *above* what you ask or think. Even more, He will do *exceeding* above what you ask or think. Paul proceeds yet further; he breaks the boundaries of Greek grammar. He says the same word twice in Greek, which doesn't make grammatical sense, but Paul was carried away with the greatness of God's gracious promises. The King James Bible translates it, "he does *exceeding abundantly*, above all that you ask or think."

Caleb, you are eighty-five; what do you think you are doing going into the land? Caleb believes God; he enters the land and slays the giants. Oh, what a great God! Is your God like that?

I read a wonderful story some months ago of a little boy in Connecticut who was on his deathbed. George Whitefield visited him, and spoke to him about God and His way of salvation in Christ. The boy was converted. Some weeks later, his unbelieving father said to him, "Son, are you not afraid to die?" The boy said, "No, Daddy, I'm not afraid to die." His father said, "Why not?" The little boy said, "Because I am going to Mr. Whitefield's big God."

Whitefield made God look big. So did Caleb. Do you? Do you have a big God? Do you believe in Him—the God of promises? The world never gives what it promises; God never gives less than He promises. And He promises, "Where sin abounded, grace did much more abound" (Rom. 5:20).

Third, God promises to give Caleb a legacy. His descendants will receive the promised land, ultimately symbolizing the heavenly Canaan, to possess; Caleb will have something invaluable to leave behind. He will leave a blessing to his children and those God-fearing children wil become his legacy. We read in Joshua 15 that his children were blessed. The Lord is faithful as the covenant-keeping Yahweh to fulfill His promises "from generation to generation."

The only way to live blessedly is to follow God *fully*. To follow God out of grace, rooted in grace, and rewarded by grace—to follow God unconditionally, trusting in His promises.

Do *you* follow God fully? Do you follow God at all? That is the first question, isn't it? As long as we are unrenewed, we don't follow the Lord at all. We have only one brief lifetime to follow God. Samuel Rutherford said, "If I had a thousand souls, I wouldn't risk one of them outside of Jesus." You have but one soul and are you risking that soul outside of Jesus Christ? Don't do it! Don't destroy yourself; don't play games with God; don't keep on going your own way. Bow before the Most High. Surrender in repentance and faith at the feet of the Lord Jesus Christ. Seek His face. You and I either belong with the unbelieving spies or with the believing spies. By nature, we want to be among the popular majority, but by grace, God brings us into the despised minority. That is a blessed place to be! The God of Caleb still lives; seek grace to follow his example, no matter the cost, even if you are threatened with death. Follow God *fully*!

Remarkably, Caleb was not the one who died. He faced great dangers and great enemies, but God kept him. He lived to be an old man, but what happened to his enemies? The glory of the Lord appeared in the tabernacle of the congregation and that very day God killed all ten false spies. Then, eventually, all the people aged twenty and higher died. Like Caleb, those who follow God fully by gracious faith, will live to see God's promises fulfilled as their exceeding great reward.

Pray for grace every day to follow God fully. God will bring those who follow Him into the heavenly land of Canaan to His glory and their comfort. Don't rest until you are assured, for Christ's sake, that you are among that happy throng.

Chapter 6

National Repentance Needed: Ezra's Example
NATIONAL DAY OF PRAYER

I sat astonied until the evening sacrifice.
—EZRA 9:4

Given the abandonment of scriptural norms in our nation, it is surprising, even humbling, that our government still calls us as citizens to a National Day of Prayer. Sadly, however, few observe this annual day with earnest repentance and heartfelt prayer; still fewer realize that every day in our lawless times ought to be saturated with prayer and repentance. Who among us wrestles with how we are to live lives of prayer and repentance? We wish to consider with you how the godly priest Ezra wrestled for his nation. Our text you can find in Ezra 9:4b, only these words, "I sat astonied until the evening sacrifice." With God's help, our theme will be:

National Repentance Needed: Ezra's Example
1. His great astonishment because of Israel's sins
2. His penitent confession of Israel's sins
3. His acknowledgment of grace despite Israel's sins

1. His Great Astonishment Because of Israel's Sins
In Ezra 9, the priest Ezra serves as a remarkable example for us of how we ought to observe a National Day of Prayer. Ezra lived during the last period of Israel's captivity in Babylon and the beginning of Israel's return from captivity. King Cyrus of Persia had given permission to the Jews to return to their native land, and had even provided money for the rebuilding of Jerusalem's walls. By the time Ezra came to renown as a counselor at the court of the new king of

Persia, Artaxerxes, the temple had already been rebuilt and work was proceeding on rebuilding the walls of Jerusalem, notwithstanding the opposition of many Samaritans.

Some of the God-fearing Jews, however, had remained behind in Babylon to be a witness to the name of the Lord there. One member of this remnant was Ezra. As a descendant of Aaron, Ezra was a priest by birth. He was an educated man of considerable dignity and piety, who also served as a prophet and scribe. The Bible says that he had prepared his heart to seek the Lord and sought to do good to Israel. His heart burned with holy zeal and genuine patriotism.

For some time, Ezra had desired to return to Israel to assist with the rebuilding of Jerusalem. One day he expressed this desire to the king. Artaxerxes not only granted his request, but also gave gold and silver to assist in buying materials for the walls of Jerusalem.

Ezra returned to Jerusalem with several of his fellow Jews. When he saw the people worshiping in the rebuilt temple of Jerusalem, he rejoiced in Yahweh and was deeply humbled. The first thing he did was sacrifice sin-offerings to God—twelve bullocks, twelve male goats, ninety-six rams, and seventy-seven lambs.

After Ezra had finished offering sacrifices, God-fearing rulers of the Jews approached him with sad news. They informed him that many of the Jews, priests, and rulers had married heathen women who lived in the area. The people of God, in direct violation of the express command of God (Ezra 9:1), had mingled with the heathen—not only in trade and conversation, but also through intermarriage.

Ezra informs us of his reaction: "And when I heard this thing, I rent my garment and my mantle, and plucked off the hair of my head and of my beard, and sat down astonied" (Ezra 9:3). Ezra was grieved at heart to hear that a nation called after the name of Jehovah had so grievously violated the law of God. He was grieved that a nation which had encountered so much tribulation had learned so little about the holiness and judgments of God. It was painful to realize that the long Babylonian captivity had not been sanctified to the majority. Moreover, even all the blessings that God had recently bestowed had not brought them to a heartfelt desire and conviction to serve God and walk in His ways.

Ezra was greatly troubled and perplexed. He was astonished at the dishonor done to God and because of the sorrow the people were about to bring upon themselves. Why should that holy God, who did not spare their fathers, spare them when they were committing the identical evil for which their fathers felt the heavy wrath of God and for which they were sent into captivity?

Dear friend, when we consider this once great nation of ours, must we not also sit down astonished?

We have a rich heritage and peculiar privileges, Among America's early settlers, the Pilgrims and Puritans were, for the most part, godly men and women. They fled to the New World, motivated to live according to Scripture and with freedom from government-controlled state churches. They yearned for freedom to worship without persecution. Before leaving ship, the Pilgrim leaders compiled the well-known Mayflower Compact in which they confessed that their primary purpose in settling in this new land was "for the glory of God and the advancement of the Christian faith."

The Colonies developed to such a degree that many settlers were attracted to the New World's promise of riches and freedom from political oppression. The pervasive influence of the godly began to wane and the government increasingly fell into the hands of those who were not moved by the biblical principle of God's glory.

Matters moved from bad to worse in the 1700s, with the exception of seasons of remarkable revival, especially in the 1730s and 1740s. The age of Enlightenment and the skepticism of the Frenchmen Voltaire and Rousseau helped to propagate the naturalism and deism that permeated England and spread to the Colonies. Political ambition, greed, and the natural result of loose, unbiblical living had a disastrous effect on the morals of Western civilization.

Today we face the outgrowth of the Enlightenment, that is, pragmatic, atheistic humanism. Humanism has permeated our public square, our public schools, and our courtrooms; it destroys our inheritance and our moral character.

Morality has dropped to an all-time low in our nation. Uncleanness and licentiousness abound on every hand. Adultery has become socially acceptable providing there are two mutually agreeing parties.

Perverted sexual relationships that God calls an abomination are increasingly gaining "rights" with the government. Transgenderism, woke culture, critical race theory, and a host of unbiblical -isms parade themselves throughout our land unashamed.

Passion for wealth, properly called materialism, is regarded as prudence. Materialism feeds our quest for pleasure and gratification. We endorse gambling and lotteries for pragmatic reasons. Covetousness, the mother of so much sin, is encouraged through high-pressure advertising. Pride and selfishness are promoted as virtues rather than vices. For the most part, we use God's generosity for ourselves rather than for His glory. God's curse pronounced against Israel in Malachi 3:9 applies equally to us: "Ye are cursed with a curse: for ye have robbed me, even this whole nation."

Violence has overwhelmed our civility. Crime threatens the personal safety of millions, Teenagers, even young children, imitate the murders they watch on television and in movies. Drugs are rampant nearly everywhere. Excessive drinking is considered an innocent pastime.

The baby-killing practice of abortion remains commonplace. Since 1973, when this nation legalized abortion, we have killed some sixty million babies, more than the population of the entire nation of Canada. The blood of unborn millions is on our hands.

Euthanasia, the deliberate taking of a human life, is proceeding apace. Sabbath desecration is the norm rather than the exception. The majority of our citizens no longer attend any church on a regular basis.

Neglect and contempt of God through swearing and taking His name in vain have become socially acceptable. We pretend to live as if there is no God, as if we have never fallen in Paradise, as if there is no approaching day of death and judgment. We live as if we are gods, daring to oppose the Lord's revealed will and Word.

Divorces on unbiblical grounds are a stench in God's nostrils, crippling our families and nation. Parental rights are increasingly denied.

Politicians appear more concerned about reelection than spiritual, moral, and fiscal responsibility. National debt is multiplying exponentially. Contrary to Scripture, national alliances are made with nations which do not fear God (Isa. 8:12; Ezra 9:14).

Worldliness—that spirit in which every man does what is right in his own eyes—is rampant. Self-centeredness, self-gratification, and self-love are the order of the day. The lust of the flesh, the lust of the eyes, and the pride of life are promoted. Worldly music, worldly partying, worldly friendships, and worldly media abounds.

The power of the modern media, be it through television, ungodly music, or an illegitimate use of technology, bodes ill for our future. Through the media, we worship at the shrine of professional organized sports without shame. We pay our sports heroes more for six weeks of play than we do our president for a full term of service for four years.

Scriptural integrity and submission to authority are considered outdated and abhorrent, Prayer, church attendance, and religious duties are performed in a perfunctory manner, if at all. Parental biblical instruction, family worship, private devotions, and conscientious catechizing are all on the wane. There is little esteem for the gospel and its privileges. The blessed Savior and the freely offered gospel are despised and slighted. Christ's blood is counted an unclean thing by millions.

Millions more rest in outward forms of worship or a shallow profession of Christianity. Millions build on the sands of false security, "easy believism," claiming forgiveness without repentance and salvation and without ever becoming sinners before God. For the most part, Christianity has merged with materialism, humanism, and secularism. The result is that in America, Christianity is three thousand miles wide, fifteen hundred miles tall, and less than one inch deep.

We are backslidden. Iniquity abounds in all levels of society. The lives of the vast majority evidence little more than a pursuit after the carnal pleasures of this world. The corrective adversities that God sends seem to profit us little; the blessings of prosperity only move us further from our great Benefactor.

When neither blessing nor cursing can do a nation any good, we must fear that we have been given over to ourselves. May not God say of us what He said of Ephraim, "Ephraim is joined to idols: let him alone" (Hos. 4:17)?

Sin is no longer sin because our spiritual foundations are gone. As Senator Hatfield noted, "We witness a country torn apart by division and lacking the spiritual foundations which would restore its vision and purpose."

We too must sit down astonished beside Ezra. Like him, we must be filled with dismay, with holy anger, with earnest repentance.

The Bible says that Ezra sat astonished until the evening sacrifice. Until that time, we do not even read that he prayed. It appeared that the case of those for whom he grieved was beyond hope and repair.

But at the time of the evening sacrifice, Ezra received fresh hope, as we will see in our second thought when we consider:

2. Ezra's Penitent Confession of Israel's Sins

The evening sacrifice was offered daily at 3:00 p.m. on the brazen altar as an offering of atonement, pointing especially to the Messiah to come who would sacrifice Himself in the place of sinners on the cross of Calvary. In the evening of the world, in the fullness of time, the Son of God would sacrifice Himself as a lamb without spot or blemish to atone for sin and to reconcile sinners to Himself. Many Jews gathered together at that time for an hour of prayer, beseeching God that as their prayers ascended with the smoke of the evening sacrifice to the heavens, the Lord Himself might hear and answer their petitions for the sake of the Messiah.

Now when the evening sacrifice was offered on this particular day of grief, and Ezra saw how the lamb was offered in the place of sinners, he recovered sufficiently from his astonishment to fall upon his knees. He placed himself in the posture of a penitent petitioner begging for mercy, and spread out his hands to God. He reached out as one who desired to reach God, to touch the hem of His garment. With an eye to God as a God of mercy who desires to reconcile sinners unto Himself by means of His Son's sacrifice, Ezra confessed Israel's transgressions and pleaded for mercy and pardon.

Dear friend, this is what you need also. If the Holy Spirit may enter your life and convict you of sin, righteousness, and judgment, you too will be struck dumb and not be able to rise up from your astonishment so long as your eyes are not opened to God's great evening sacrifice, Jesus Christ, who gave Himself on Calvary as the divinely approved sacrifice for sinners. But if the Holy Spirit opens your eyes to "behold the Lamb of God, which taketh away the sins of the world," and you receive grace to repent before Him and believe on Him as your only hope and refuge of salvation, then you too will be able to rise up from your heaviness. Then you too will stretch out your hands to touch the hem of the garment of the Lamb of God. Then you will be enabled to look away from your misery and guilt to see that though there is great power in your sins to condemn you, there is even more power in the blood of Jesus to save you.

Ezra's bonds were broken; his lips were opened. By faith he made confession, as it were, with his hands upon the evening sacrifice (Ezra 9:6–7). Two critical elements mark his confession. First, he took upon himself the guilt of Israel's sins. He spoke of "our iniquities" and "our trespass." He didn't lift himself above his people or nation, but realized that he was intimately involved in the nation's sins. And second, he was enabled to transfer at God's altar all those sins to Christ, placing them by faith upon the head of the evening sacrifice.

Only in this way can we make true confession before God. All Christless confession is ineffectual confession. Judas Iscariot also made confession, but without placing his hand by faith upon the head of the evening sacrifice. He had no eye for mercy, no heart for the Lamb of God. Without this faith in Christ, we cannot truly unburden ourselves before God and confess sin in His sight. Outside of Christ, God can only be a holy, consuming fire.

Oh, what a blessed, sweet reality confession is when it may be done at God's altar with an eye to Calvary's cross! Have you ever made confession in such a way? Have you ever experienced the sweetness of making confession at the foot of the cross of Calvary? Dear friend, there is no better place to be in all the earth than to confess sin at the feet of the merciful Savior.

There would be real hope for our nation and the entire world if true Christians throughout this land would come by faith to God's altar, confessing our national and personal sins with our hand upon the evening sacrifice. In fact, the opening verses of Ezra 10 teach us that this one man's blessed example reaped repentance and reformation throughout Jerusalem.

3. Ezra's Acknowledgment of Grace Despite Israel's Sins

Our nation desperately needs to return to God. After all, what makes a country blessed? Geographical beauty? Military prowess? Unparalleled prosperity? Huge metropolises? Psalm 33:12 tells us: "Blessed is the nation whose God is the LORD; and the people whom he hath chosen for his own inheritance."

What does a country do with God and His Word? This is the critical question; everything else is secondary.

If this nation, yes, we ourselves, do not become Ezras before God—repenting, pleading upon His Word, and fleeing to Christ—sin will ultimately reap divine destruction. The day or year of divine visitation shall come. God's patience will have an end. He has justly sworn that sinners and nations continuing in sin will not see His kingdom. He will not break His Word; His vengeance is unimpeachable.

We have squandered our rich heritage. We have multiplied our national debt materially, morally, and spiritually. We have lost the greatest weapon of our armory, the weapon of prayer. We have turned our backs on God, His Word, and the fear of His Name. We have spoiled what our forefathers have struggled to provide—a solid biblical foundation on which to build a nation. Dark clouds righteously hang above us.

Our only hope lies in the intervening, sovereign grace of God blessing the means that He has called us to use. What are those means? What does God call us to do?

First, God calls us to seek the grace of repentance that Ezra received. Our nation needs neither more unbelievers nor more Pharisees. We need more men like Ezra. Blessed is the nation in whose midst are many who take the guilt of the sins of the nation upon themselves and who learn to bring that guilt to the cross of Calvary. If you desire to do a favor to your nation, church, family, and yourself, seek grace to bring the sins of nation, church, family, and yourself to the New Testament evening sacrifice, the cross of Calvary.

Second, God calls us to pray earnestly for reformation and revival, to pray in the spirit of 2 Chronicles 7:14, "If my people, which are called by my name, shall humble themselves, and pray, and seek my face, and turn from their wicked ways; then will I hear from heaven, and will forgive their sin, and will heal their land." With idolatry, perversion, and lawlessness flooding our land, let us earnestly intercede and pray that conviction of sin, repentance, the fear and truth of God, and the centrality of Christ and His cross may be restored. Pray that men and women, teens and children, may be turned from vain pursuits and entertainments to the living triune God. Pray for the saving work of the Holy Spirit to be poured out upon many through the preaching and teaching of godly men qualified to lead churches in the way of truth. Pray for the revival of the historic Reformed faith, which insists that Christianity move beyond church walls to embrace a distinctively Christian worldview and lifestyle in all areas of life, including education, politics, and business.

Third, be more active in alerting our political leaders to the evils of our day. We must admonish ourselves, each other, and them, in the spirit of Isaiah 8:20, "To the law and to the testimony: if they speak not according to this word, it is because there is no light in them."

Finally, let us be active in our local neighborhoods and at work by speaking and embodying the truth in every area of our lives. Communicate with others as opportunities arise about the need for prayer, revival, repentance, and truth. Pass out Bibles, tracts, and other biblical literature, bearing in mind the truth of an early American adage: "The pen is mightier than the sword." If you claim to be a Christian, be assured that many are carefully watching you. Pray daily for grace to be salt in the earth and light on the hill.

Let us ask ourselves: Am I contributing to the swelling of our large debt of rational sin? Dear friend, we must all be born again and flee to God's proffered mercy in Jesus Christ. May God grant that we may all search and try our ways and turn to the Lord against whom we have so deeply rebelled. He is able and willing to make us genuine disciples of Jesus Christ—disciples who will not be part of the problem but part of the solution.

"Seek ye the LORD while he may be found, call ye upon him while he is near: Let the wicked forsake his way, and the unrighteous man his thoughts: and let him return unto the LORD, and he will have mercy upon him; and to our God, for he will abundantly pardon" (Isa. 55:6–7).

Chapter 7

Why Do the Nations Rage?

Why do the heathen rage, and the people imagine a vain thing? The kings of the earth set themselves, and the rulers take counsel together, against the LORD, *and against his anointed, saying, Let us break their bands asunder, and cast away their cords from us. He that sitteth in the heavens shall laugh: the Lord shall have them in derision. Then shall he speak unto them in his wrath, and vex them in his sore displeasure. Yet have I set my king upon my holy hill of Zion. I will declare the decree: the* LORD *hath said unto me, Thou art my Son; this day have I begotten thee. Ask of me, and I shall give thee the heathen for thine inheritance, and the uttermost parts of the earth for thy possession. Thou shalt break them with a rod of iron; thou shalt dash them in pieces like a potter's vessel. Be wise now therefore, O ye kings: be instructed, ye judges of the earth. Serve the* LORD *with fear, and rejoice with trembling. Kiss the Son, lest he be angry, and ye perish from the way, when his wrath is kindled but a little. Blessed are all they that put their trust in him.*

—PSALM 2

Jesus is the King. God the Father says that He has set His King, as we read in Psalm 2, upon His holy hill of Zion. We read in Zechariah 9:9, "Rejoice greatly, O daughter of Zion; shout, O daughter of Jerusalem: behold, thy King cometh unto thee." And Gabriel said to Mary, "The Lord God shall give unto him the throne of his father David: and he shall reign over the house of Jacob for ever" (Luke 1:32–33).

Christ is the supreme King. He will have dominion over land and sea. To Him are the kingdom, the power, and the glory forever. Of His kingdom, there is no end. And He is King over all creation. He is King over His people; He is the King of grace, the King of glory. He is King in the inward life, and He is King over the outward life. He is King of kings and Lord of lords. Every kingdom of this earth has been brought to naught—the Assyrian kingdom, the Persian kingdom, the Roman kingdom, the Egyptian kingdom, the Greek kingdom. One day, the present kingdom of the United States of America as a world power shall come to an end. But of this King and of this kingdom we read it shall never end.

Thus, it is of this King that you and I must be made willing subjects in the day of His power. We must learn what it means to bow before Him because His kingdom has eternal consequences for every one of us. This King invites and calls us to enter into His great kingdom. This King tells us the way of entrance: "Ye must be born again" (John 3:7). This King calls us to seek Him while He is yet able to be found, to call upon Him while He is yet near. He commands us to believe in Him and to bow before Him. This King tells us that if we reject His work, His person, His invitation, we reject Him and we reject His salvation.

However, though no one can avoid this King, mankind does not receive Him. Though He made the world, the world does not know Him (John 1:10). The human race is on a collision course with their rightful Sovereign, and if we do not repent of our treason, His justice will crush us. But if we put our trust in Him, then we will be blessed by God and happy forever. In Psalm 2, we learn the gospel, or good news, of the kingdom, which raises the thematic question, "Why do the nations rage?" Under this theme, we will see that Psalm 2 tells us about *man's rebellion, Christ's reign,* and *the sinner's refuge.*

1. Man's Rebellion

Consider verses 1–3: "Why do the heathen rage, and the people imagine a vain thing? The kings of the earth set themselves, and the rulers take counsel together, against the LORD, and against his anointed, saying, Let us break their bands asunder, and cast away their cords from us." "Heathen" means the nations of this world. God's "anointed" is His chosen king from the family line of David (Ps. 18:50). Therefore, Psalm 2 is teaching us that all the nations of this world reject the Lord and rebel against His anointed King. It is not a matter of bad behavior, but of the thoughts and purposes of their hearts. Whereas the blessed man of Psalm 1 delights in God's law and meditates on how he can obey it, the accursed nations hate God's law and meditate on how they can overthrow it.[1] In other words, mankind hates God and Christ.

The apostle Paul wrote the following about all people who lack the Holy Spirit: "The carnal mind is enmity against God: for it is not subject to the law of God, neither indeed can be. So then they that are in the flesh cannot please God" (Rom. 8:7–8). Sin is a "turning aside from the law of God," as William Ames said, whether in who we are or what we do.[2] Our inner desires and will have become corrupted by Adam's fall so that "spiritual and true goods taste bad," and "evil things...seem the most gratifying."[3] At its core, sin is hatred ("enmity" is the attitude of an enemy) against God rooted in a refusal to believe His Word.

If this conclusion seems rather extreme, remember that it is the teaching of Jesus Christ. He said in John 15:18, 23, "If the world hate you, ye know that it hated me before it hated you.... He that hateth me hateth my Father also." Men, women, and children love the darkness of sin and hate the holy light of Christ—until God works salvation in them (John 3:19–21).

Christ not only revealed the world's hatred for God, but Christ also experienced it personally. In Acts 4:24–27, the early church quoted man's rebellion in Psalm 2 and applied it to how "both Herod, and Pontius Pilate, with the Gentiles, and the people of Israel" treated Jesus Christ. If you ever wonder how the world views God, consider

---

1. The same Hebrew word (*hagah*) for "meditate" (Ps. 1:2) is used for "imagine" (Ps. 2:1).
2. William Ames, *The Marrow of Theology*, ed. and trans. John Eusden (Grand Rapids: Baker, 1968), 13.2; 14.2 (120–21).
3. William Ames, *A Sketch of the Christian's Catechism*, trans. Todd M. Rester, Classic Reformed Theology 1 (Grand Rapids: Reformation Heritage Books, 2008), 18.

how it handled His Son. When God became a man and lived among us, we crucified Him and mocked Him as He died.

We should not be shocked, then, when we see the world rebelling against God's good and righteous laws, wallowing in moral filth, bowing before ridiculous idols, attacking Christ's holy church, and destroying human life in every way. Man's rejection of God spawns a host of evils: sexual immorality, pornography, homosexuality, malice, greed, envy, murder, lies, gossip, pride, boasting, disobedience to parents, cruelty—and all this while cheering others on in their sins though we know that God outlaws it all (Rom. 1:21–32). We should marvel that God's common grace holds back so much of this evil so that civil society can continue to exist and so that the gospel can go forth in some measure of peace.

Oh, what need we have to really see and know ourselves—to know that we hate God! Those are strong words, but apart from saving grace, we have a strong, evil heart. Are not these words really true? When it comes to a test between God and yourself, who do you pick? Do you not pick yourself? Is that not hating God? When God's providence cuts across your hopes and ambitions, how do you respond? Is it not with resentment? Is that not hatred against God? We are haters, enemies of God. The bent of our nature is to hatred. Only grace makes it different. The bent of our nature is always to say, "Lord, let *my* will be done," not "*Thy* will."

The unfathomable truth is that for such corrupt enemies and rebels God still sends His gospel of love, grace, and mercy. But as He sends the gospel, He usually probes our hearts with the law. He comes and asks each one of us, "Is your heart set against God? Are your thoughts and purposes striving after a vain and empty thing? Do you love God's Word, or regard it as a chain that enslaves you to a tyrant? Are you yet a sinner in need of salvation?"

Who is this King that the world so hates? Who is this ruler that the world thinks is worthy of no obedience whatsoever? Is it some evil beast that commits moral atrocities against his people? No. This hated King is none other than Jesus Christ, the Lord's anointed.

2. Christ's Reign

Jesus Christ is the King of the world. We see Christ's reign in the heart of verses 4–9. The first part of this section speaks of God's absolute sovereignty, victorious wrath, and appointed King. The second part of this section speaks of God's promises to His Son.

The King Appointed by the Absolute Lord

Look first at verses 4–6: "He that sitteth in the heavens shall laugh: the LORD shall have them in derision. Then shall he speak unto them in his wrath, and vex them in his sore displeasure. Yet have I set my king upon my holy hill of Zion." For God to sit enthroned in the heavens means that He is the supreme and sovereign Lord over all. God is not anxious, though the whole world rages against Him, but laughs at His puny enemies. The words "vex them in his sore displeasure" can be translated, "terrify them in his wrath."

God does not worry about polls. He is not concerned when the world is against Him. His mere rebuke can shake the powers of this age. Therefore, let God's people not fear the face of man. Certainly, we must honor civil authorities and not mock them, for we are not the sovereign Judge, but mere men under the institutions that God ordained (Rom. 13:1–7). However, though we honor authority, let us never think too highly of man, whose breath is in his nostrils, for on the day of the Lord all the pride of man will be cast down (Isa. 2:12–22).

This text reminds us of God's omnipotence. "Omnipotence" comes from the words "omni," which means "all," and "potent," which means "power." Thus, "omnipotence" means *all-powerful*. God creates all things by the free act of His omnipotent will so that not only we but all creation came into existence through the sovereign will of God. He speaks and it is; He commands and it stands firm (Ps. 33:9). By that same omnipotent power, God's plans never fail and He frustrates the evil schemes of sinners (vv. 10, 11). If you stop and think about this, it is an awesome thought that every movement we make, every thought we think, every moment of health we have, every breath we take, is God's powerful act of upholding and ruling His creation. There is nothing that happens by chance.

The omnipotent God overthrows the wicked plots of mankind by appointing His own King to rule the world: "Yet have I set my king upon my holy hill of Zion" (Ps. 2:6). Zion represents the holy presence and mighty kingdom of God. God has entrusted to Jesus Christ the right as Mediator to rule, defend, and advance God's kingdom in every respect. Though individual churches and Christian organizations may fail and nations may fall under God's judgment, Christ's kingdom cannot fail. This can give us great confidence as we serve Him.

Our Reformed forefathers used to speak of three dimensions of Christ's kingship. They spoke of His *kingdom of power*, for when He rose again and was about to ascend on high, He said, "All power is given unto me in heaven and in earth" (Matt. 28:18). He rules over the whole universe as King of power—over heaven, over earth, and yes, even over hell. Theodorus VanderGroe explained, "He therefore governs all His and His people's enemies, including Satan, the world, and sin. He so completely controls and governs them by His hand that, apart from His divine power and will, they cannot make even a single move."[4] This is His kingdom of power.

Second, they spoke of a *kingdom of grace*. That is His special rule over the lives of His dear children whom He serves out of His mediatorial office of mercy and compassion. Christ rules in the hearts of believers by the saving work of the Holy Spirit.

Third, they spoke of His *kingdom of glory* through which He prepares heavenly places for a people He will prepare on earth and who He will bring to their everlasting God of glory.

Thus, how critical it is that you and I know Him not only in His kingdom of power, as we all shall know Him—for every knee shall bow and every tongue shall confess that He is Lord—but that we know Him internally in the kingdom of grace through faith in Him! Only then, when we are in His kingdom of grace, can we be assured that we will participate in His kingdom of glory. Otherwise, the very sound of Christ's voice—the voice of the Lord is full of majesty—will terrify us when He comes again as Judge.

---

4. Theodorus VanderGroe, *The Christian's Only Comfort in Life and Death: An Exposition of the Heidelberg Catechism*, ed. Joel R. Beeke, trans. Bartel Elshout (Grand Rapids: Reformation Heritage Books, 2016), 1:391.

Do you see that everything hinges upon who Jesus is? Martyn Lloyd-Jones said, "It is clear that if He is not who He claims to be, there is no need to listen to Him. If He is, then we are bound to listen to Him and to do whatever He may tell us to do. My own happiness is not the criterion. If He allows me to go on being ill or in trouble—whatever He says, I will answer, 'Yes, Lord.' I will do so because He is the Lord."[5] We may be sure that Christ is King because of God's Word. God made a solemn covenant with this King (Ps. 110:1–4), and here we find some of God's promises. This is very precious, for God's promises to Christ are promises to all who belong to Christ's kingdom.

The Promises Made to God's Appointed King
Look now at verses 7–9: "I will declare the decree: the LORD hath said unto me, Thou art my Son; this day have I begotten thee. Ask of me, and I shall give thee the heathen for thine inheritance, and the uttermost parts of the earth for thy possession. Thou shalt break them with a rod of iron; thou shalt dash them in pieces like a potter's vessel." The Lord promised, first, *the glory belonging to God's Son*. We must remember at this point what the rest of the Bible teaches us. Christ is eternal, without beginning or end (John 1:1; Heb. 1:10–12). He has always been the Son of the Father, even "before the world was" (John 17:5). Yet in the fullness of time, God's Son became a man and was born of a woman (Gal. 4:4). Though equal to God the Father, God the Son took the nature of a servant and humbled Himself by becoming obedient—even to death on the cross (Phil. 2:6–8). Therefore, God has exalted and honored His Son to the highest place as Lord of all (Phil. 2:9–11).

When Psalm 2:7 records God's decree, "Thou art my Son; this day have I begotten thee," it refers to Christ's exaltation and enthronement as the risen Lord. The apostle Paul preaches this in Acts 13:33: "He hath raised up Jesus again; as it is also written in the second psalm, Thou art my Son, this day have I begotten thee." Though Christ has been God's Son from the beginning (Heb. 1:2), God promised that His humbled and lowly Son would be "declared to be the Son of God with power, according to the spirit of holiness, by the resurrection from the

---

5. D. Martyn Lloyd-Jones, *Authority* (Edinburgh: Banner of Truth, 1984), 21.

dead" (Rom. 1:4). Once put to shame on the cross, Christ was lifted up over the angels (Heb. 1:4–5).

We need never fear that the name of Jesus Christ will be disgraced. Though men and women may rage against Him, God will see to it that His beloved Son is honored. Christ's kingdom will be established in justice without end, for "the zeal of the Lord of hosts will perform this" (Isa. 9:7). God's love for His Son guarantees that His kingdom cannot fail. John Owen said, "Though our persons fall, our cause shall be as truly, certainly, and infallibly victorious, as that Christ sits at the right hand of God.... The cause in which we are engaged shall surely conquer as Christ is alive and shall prevail at last.... The gospel shall be victorious."[6]

Second, God promised Christ *a worldwide inheritance of people*. The Father covenanted with His Son, "Ask of me, and I shall give thee the heathen for thine inheritance." This is a remarkable statement, for God's "inheritance" (*nakhalat*) was the nation of Israel.[7] Here, Christ's inheritance, the covenant people given to Him by God, includes the Gentile nations (Isa. 19:25). God promises not only that Christ will own this people, but that God will make them willing to be owned. Psalm 110:3 says to the One seated at God's right hand, "Thy people shall be willing in the day of thy power." The salvation of each soul is a work of Christ's power, a work of the conquering King of grace. It must be so, for the forces of sin and Satan fight to retain their dominion. John Flavel said, "Christ obtains a throne in the hearts of men... by conquest, for though the souls of the elect are his by donation and right of redemption (the Father gave them to him, and he died for them), yet Satan hath the first possession."[8]

The Lord Jesus makes Himself that King of grace when He enters the heart of a sinner in the moment of regeneration. He is then that King of kings who comes with irresistible power to gain a heavenly conquest in the heart of a sinner. He rides His white horse, John tells

---

6. John Owen, "The Use of Faith, If Popery Should Return upon Us," in *The Works of John Owen* (1850–1853; repr., Edinburgh: Banner of Truth, 1965), 9:507–8.

7. See Deut. 4:20; 9:26, 29; 32:9; 1 Kings 8:51; Pss. 28:9; 33:12; 78:62; 94:5; 106:5, 40.

8. John Flavel, *Fountain of Life*, in *The Works of John Flavel* (1820; repr., Edinburgh: Banner of Truth, 1968), 1:201.

us, and He shoots with His bow the sharp arrows of His Word into the hearts of sinners and causes them to be convicted and to cry out, "Take me out of the battle, for I am sore wounded!" He strips sinners of all their power and all their methods of salvation and draws them to find salvation in Christ alone. He sets up His throne of grace in the heart of a sinner. He causes grace to reign. He causes sin to no longer have dominion. "This is the regeneration," we read in the Canons of Dort, "so highly celebrated in Scripture and denominated a new creation: a resurrection from the dead, a making alive, which God works in us without our aid."[9]

Christ not only begins with His Word and Spirit as King of kings, but He also governs His people by that same Word and Spirit. He leads them in the way of salvation. He keeps them. He reigns. He watches over them in every respect. He is King over all the spiritual battles of their souls. He understands their thoughts afar off. Oh, what a precious governor Christ is! Not that He governs the way *we* want Him to; His thoughts are above our thoughts and His ways are above our ways. But as King of kings He governs His people in the way that is best for them.

The living church is in the hands of Christ, and that is their great comfort. Is it *your* comfort? Are you in the hands of Christ? Do you know what it means to bow under His kingship? Is He your King by grace? Have you learned to know Him as that wise King who makes no mistakes, who directs your whole life in such a way that you have to say later on, "Lord, Thou hast done all things well"? Is He a wooing King for you who woos you and wins you to His love so that you learn to trust Him and to say with your whole heart, "Thy will be done"? We don't learn that in a day, and we need to relearn it again and again. But the more we are acquainted with the kingship of Christ, the more we learn to trust Him and His will rather than ourselves and our will.

Third, God promised to Christ a *crushing victory over His enemies*. The Father said, "Thou shalt break them with a rod of iron; thou shalt dash them in pieces like a potter's vessel." The picture is

---

9. The Canons of Dort (Heads 3 and 4, Art. 12), in *The Three Forms of Unity* (Vestavia Hills, Ala.: Solid Ground Christian Books, 2010), 144.

vivid, bloody, and frightening: the warrior goes forth with an iron club and crushes his enemies like fragile pottery. Already Christ rules the world with "a rod of iron," using His supreme power to fight against the wicked forces of evil (Rev. 12:5). Though He is the Lamb that was slain for our sins to redeem sinners for God, He is also the Lord who holds the scroll of God in His hand and unleashes God's judgments upon the nations so that the gospel may go forth on the white horse of victory (Revelation 5–6).

Christ is the defender of His people. He will keep an eye upon His people and He will defend them from every enemy. What a blessing! He will keep them from sin's dominion and will protect them from its damning power. He will deliver them from Satan and all his devices, assaults, and temptations. He delivers from the world with all its enticements, with all its drawing power. He will keep His people *in* the world but be sure that they do not become *of* the world. He will protect from heretical doctrine. He will keep the feet of His saints in the pathway of His truth.

Jesus will protect us from ourselves, which is the greatest wonder of all, that we may not re-enslave ourselves to sin or self-righteousness. He will protect from unbelief. He will protect us even in death. He will protect us not from physical dying, but from the sting of death, from the punishment of death, from the spiritual and eternal forms of death. He will protect as the great King, as a King who is mightier than Satan, the world, self, and death combined. He is almighty. Asa cried unto God, "Lord, it is nothing with thee to help, whether with many, or with them that have no power" (2 Chron. 14:11).

This promise of "a rod of iron" will find its ultimate fulfillment when Christ returns on the day of judgment. Revelation 19 presents the vision of the Rider on a white horse who comes to wage war, and says in verses 15–16, "And out of his mouth goeth a sharp sword, that with it he should smite the nations: and he shall rule them with a rod of iron: and he treadeth the winepress of the fierceness and wrath of Almighty God. And he hath on his vesture and on his thigh a name written, King Of Kings, And Lord Of Lords."

The day of judgment will be ushered in with a glorious coming of the Son of God on the clouds of heaven. He shall come "in the glory of his Father" (Matt. 16:27). In that day, the glory of His Father will radiate from Jesus Christ as He comes in solemn majesty with divine authority. The glory of the Father with which Christ will appear is Christ's own glory (Matt. 25:31), for God's Son is "the brightness of his glory, and the express image of his person" (Heb. 1:3). Thomas Manton told us that "this glory must be exceeding great," for it is the glory of the "God-man"—infinitely more majestic than all created persons in heaven and earth; it is the glory of "the judge of the world, who now cometh to appear upon the throne to be seen by all"; and it is the glory of a great work "on the one side, to gather together, to convince, to judge, and punish creatures opposite and rebellious; and to honour and reward his servants, on the other."[10] So much glory of God shall shine forth at His coming and shall fill the heavens and the earth that the ungodly shall cry out, "Mountains and rocks, fall on us, and hide us from the face of him that sitteth on the throne, and from the wrath of the Lamb" (Rev. 6:16).

Jesus's coming will be sudden. We don't know when He will return. We know that we are living in the last days. We know that it may be soon. We know it will be unexpected, coming as a thief in the night (1 Thess. 5:2; 2 Peter 3:10). He will come when few are expecting Him.

When He comes, it will be the day of resurrection and judgment. All mankind will hear His voice and come out of their graves to receive either life or damnation (John 5:28–29). And in that day, there will be no more mockers who will challenge the promises of God. In that day all the ungodly will have their knees knock together in fear. In that day all that is truly real will become real. Christ will become real, eternity will become real, the fact that I have a soul will become real. Yet it will be too late to repent.

When we are brought to give an account before God in that day, nothing will escape the Lord. Every thought, every word, every action will be accounted for. The Lord is not in a hurry on the day of judgment. The day of judgment is a day in which everyone will give an account. And if we are not ready to meet God in that day, if we are

---

10. Thomas Manton, "Sermons upon Matthew XXV," in *The Complete Works of Thomas Manton* (London: James Nisbet, 1872), 10:23–24.

not washed by the blood of Jesus in that day, our entire lives will have been a miserable failure. You can be successful in your job in the eyes of men; you can have a happy family; you can have a relatively easy life; you can have a cheerful and positive disposition; but if in that day you are not under the cleansing power of the blood of the Son of God, your entire life will have been a miserable, eternal failure.

Are you ready for the day of the Lord? If Jesus were to come today, would you be ready to meet Him? Do you have a new heart? Are you born again? Have you learned to hate sin? Have you learned to love the Lord? Is your faith in Christ alone? Are you ready for the great day which is the only thing that we know for sure is coming in our lives? You don't know if you will be able to realize your plans for tomorrow, but this you know: Jesus is coming. This we know, you and I—if you are four years old, if you are eighty-four years old—Jesus is coming. You must be *ready*. You *must* be ready. *You* must be ready.

3. The Sinner's Refuge
Next, in verses 10–12, we see the sinner's refuge or hiding place: "Be wise now therefore, O ye kings: be instructed, ye judges of the earth. Serve the LORD with fear, and rejoice with trembling. Kiss the Son, lest he be angry, and ye perish from the way, when his wrath is kindled but a little. Blessed are all they that put their trust in him."

The Lord can terrify the rebels with His word of judgment, but now He speaks to them with His word of grace. They must stop being so foolish as to "imagine a vain thing" (v. 1), and instead "be wise" and receive God's correction. The day of wrath and revelation of the righteous judgment of God has not yet arrived. There is still time for mercy; we live in the day of grace.

God calls rebellious men, women, and children, and even kings and high officials of the government, to repent of their rebellion against Him. Repentance is not just an improvement in behavior, but a completely new direction for the heart. The Scripture says, "Serve the LORD with fear, and rejoice with trembling." You have despised God; you have treated Him like a little ant upon which you may put your foot. You must now see Him and reverence Him as the omnipotent Lord who holds you in His hand. You have hated God;

you have turned away from Him like a hateful enemy. You must now know Him and love Him as the supreme Good who is the giver of all good gifts. This combination of fear and joy arises from a true faith. Wilhelmus à Brakel said, "Such a soul exalts Him above all, has a high esteem for His majesty, which is delightful and awe-inspiring, and stirs up in him extraordinary reverence."[11]

To honor God, we must honor God's King. To honor the Father, we must honor the Son (John 5:23). "Kiss the Son," the Bible says. In the ancient Near East and in some cultures today, a kiss was a common way to say hello. However, a kiss could also be a sign of submission to authority or even an act of worship.[12] In today's language, we would say, "Bow down to the Son." Bow not just your body, but bow your heart because Jesus is Lord. If you continue in your rebellion, Christ's anger will come upon you like a burning fire. If you will trust in Him, then His love will bless you forever.

What a blessed King! He is the great Physician. Sometimes a doctor says, "I will take no new patients. I am booked full." But this Physician is never booked full—not until He comes again on the clouds. Then it will be too late to seek Him. Still today He receives new patients who have nothing to offer Him but putrefying sores and deadly bruises from head to toe. Still today, He receives children, young people, parents, grandparents. Some physicians specialize. Some only see children; some only do one or two particular tasks. But this physician does every task, and this physician sees all kinds of patients—all kinds of races, all kinds of classes, all kinds of people. There is no one who has sinned too much; there is no heart too hard; there are no hopeless cases with Him. He never needs to send anyone home, saying, "There is nothing I can do for you." And besides all this, He does all His work freely. He has paid the price Himself. He has earned as High Priest to do what He does as King.

Do you see no beauty in Him to desire Him? Can you be your own king? Can you rescue yourself from Satan and sin and evil? Are you so strong, my friend, that you can stand up to the powers of evil without

---

11. Wilhelmus à Brakel, *The Christian's Reasonable Service*, ed. Joel R. Beeke, trans. Bartel Elshout (Grand Rapids: Reformation Heritage Books, 1992), 1:570.
12. See 1 Sam. 10:1; 1 Kings 19:18; Job 31:26–27; Hos. 13:2.

the power of Jesus? Do you not yet know your own heart at all? I urge you to bow before this King, take refuge in Him, and be made a subject of Him. The subjects of this King are the only truly joyful people on the face of this earth. I know there are many people who do a lot more laughing and they have more worldly fun, but I am speaking of true joy, deep joy in the heart, the joy of knowing God, the joy of being safe in the hands of Christ, the joy of being a willing subject of a worthy King of kings! That is a joy that the world does not know, and that joy is yet available. Bow, sinner; bow before it is forever too late!

How do you bow your heart? You bow by believing in Him. There is a wonderful specificity to the last sentence of Psalm 2: "Blessed are all they that put their trust in him." We are saved by faith in Christ alone. Saving faith, or saving believing, believes something. Saving faith is not the kind of faith that so many people make it out to be today when they say, "It really doesn't make too much difference what you believe. As long as you are sincere, as long as you believe, it's okay. You will go to heaven, no matter what you believe—just as long as you are sure that you really believe what you believe." That doctrine is from the pit of hell. We do not believe that we can be saved by a faith without content. Faith believes something. By faith you depend on someone outside of yourself to be and to do what you cannot be or do.

Faith is expressed by the idea of leaning your weight upon something. Proverbs 3:5 says, "Trust in the LORD with all thine heart; and lean not unto thine own understanding." The Scottish missionary John Paton related how he discovered how to translate faith in the native language of the Pacific islanders of the New Hebrides. One day, he was sitting in a chair and he had an idea. He asked a native woman, "What am I doing?" She said, "You are sitting down." He then pulled up his feet off the floor so that his weight rested entirely on the chair and repeated the question. She answered, "You are leaning wholly," using a term in their language for depending entirely upon one thing for support. Paton knew that this was the term he must use for faith. He would now tell the islanders they must be "leaning on Jesus" for eternal life.[13] Are you leaning on Jesus? Have you rested the weight of your sins and your guilt before God, your future hope and happiness, entirely upon Christ? You must do so in order to be saved.

Another way to express faith is the idea of taking refuge or hiding in something. That is the term used in Psalm 2:12: "put their trust in him" is literally "take refuge" (*khasah*) or "hide themselves in him." King Jesus can be your hiding place. David prays in Psalm 18:2, "The LORD is my rock, and my fortress, and my deliverer; my God, my strength, in whom I will trust; my buckler, and the horn of my salvation, and my high tower." When sin and Satan, death and hell, and the wicked people of this world surround you, hide in Jesus Christ. If you take refuge in God's King, then you will find yourself "blessed" by God (Ps. 2:12).

Blessed means granted by God everything necessary for life and happiness. Thus, God teaches here where true enjoyment is to be found, namely, in willing subjection to the King of kings. Hiding in the shadow of His wings, Christ's people drink from the river of His delights (Ps. 36:7–8). They are enabled to praise God even in their sleepless nights, in the days of warfare and strife, for the Lord's hand upholds them (Ps. 63:3–9).

However, the blessedness spoken of here goes far beyond our present communion with Christ. God's people will see the King in His beauty. This King prepares a place for them in glory and He makes them homesick for that glory. He preserves them for the full enjoyment of that salvation He has purchased for them. They shall enter a land of enjoyment of which Scripture says, "Eye hath not seen, nor ear heard, neither have entered into the heart of man, the things which God hath prepared for them that love him" (1 Cor. 2:9). In that day, there will be no more sin. There will be no more Satan, no more world, no more influences from my own evil heart, and no more death. Oh, to be preserved forever, preserved to enjoy the Father through the Son by the Spirit; to enjoy the company of the

---

13. A. K. Langridge and Frank H. L. Paton, *John G. Paton: Later Years and Farewell* (New York: Hodder and Stoughton, 1910), 56.

redeemed, the saints made perfect, and the legions of holy angels! The Lord will be the glory of heaven (Zech. 2:5).

Thus, the Christian life is a life that knows true enjoyment, a joy that would not be traded for all the pleasures of this world (Ps. 4:7). That is why we read in Nehemiah 8:10, "The joy of the LORD is your strength." Is that your strength, my friend, the joy of the Lord? Is that your strength? Do you know both the sorrow of sin and the joy of divine fellowship?

The Westminster Shorter Catechism opens so beautifully: "What is the chief end of man?" What is the chief purpose of your life? "To glorify God and to enjoy him forever."[14] *Forever.* This is a kingdom that does not end with death or the grave. This King went through death and through the grave to conquer them both so that death may have no sting, so that the grave may be a pillow for His people, and so that they may arise one day with soul and body reunited, and with the whole man may glorify God and enjoy Him forever. This is the end result of the kingship of Jesus.

Oh, happy is that people who has the God of Jacob, King Jesus, for their help, whose hope is in the Lord their God. One day, dear child of God, you will be fully delivered from all evil. You will fully enjoy the gracious, glorious presence of your faithful King. And then your greatest happiness will be to praise Him; your greatest freedom shall be to serve Him; your greatest honor will be to obey Him; and your greatest peace will be to dwell with Him. Everything then will be focused for you upon this King of kings. All our hearts will go back out to the King of kings, and we will say, "Not unto us, O King of kings, be honor, and glory, and dominion, but unto Thee, O King immortal, to Thee be all honor, glory, and dominion." Truly, "blessed are all they that put their trust in him" (Ps. 2:12).

---

14. Westminster Shorter Catechism (Q. 1), in James T. Dennison Jr., comp., *Reformed Confessions of the 16th and 17th Centuries in English Translation: Volume 4, 1600–1693* (Grand Rapids: Reformation Heritage Books, 2014), 353.

Chapter 8

The Satisfying and Nourishing Word of God

The heavens declare the glory of God; and the firmament sheweth his handywork. Day unto day uttereth speech, and night unto night sheweth knowledge. There is no speech nor language, where their voice is not heard. Their line is gone out through all the earth, and their words to the end of the world. In them hath he set a tabernacle for the sun, which is as a bridegroom coming out of his chamber, and rejoiceth as a strong man to run a race. His going forth is from the end of the heaven, and his circuit unto the ends of it: and there is nothing hid from the heat thereof. The law of the LORD *is perfect, converting the soul: the testimony of the* LORD *is sure, making wise the simple. The statutes of the* LORD *are right, rejoicing the heart: the commandment of the* LORD *is pure, enlightening the eyes. The fear of the* LORD *is clean, enduring for ever: the judgments of the* LORD *are true and righteous altogether. More to be desired are they than gold, yea, than much fine gold: sweeter also than honey and the honeycomb. Moreover by them is thy servant warned: and in keeping of them there is great reward. Who can understand his errors? cleanse thou me from secret faults. Keep back thy servant also from presumptuous sins; let them not have dominion over me: then shall I be upright, and I shall be innocent from the great transgression. Let the words of my mouth, and the meditation of my heart, be acceptable in thy sight, O* LORD, *my strength, and my redeemer.* —PSALM 19

Hunger is an all-consuming passion. When a baby is hungry, you can give him toys, play with him, change his diaper, rock him, lay him down to sleep, and sing to him, but he will be restless and unhappy—and likely let you know it in the loudest of ways—until you satisfy his hunger. Babies grow up into men and women with more self-control, but when people are hungry, they are not happy and have trouble concentrating on anything except food. When people are desperately hungry and their bodies are starving, they will do almost anything to get food.

Therefore, it is hard to imagine the experience of our Lord Jesus Christ when He went for forty days and forty nights without food. He was not fasting in a comfortable place surrounded by friends, but alone in the wilderness of Judea, an area known for its hot, dry climate. If He had continued to fast much longer, it seems likely that He would have begun to die of starvation.[1] Yet Christ chose to do this. Why? It was not because Jesus was an ascetic who thought the pleasures of this life are inherently sinful. Christ chose to endure the hunger of the body for a time because He had a far greater hunger. As He Himself said, "Man shall not live by bread alone, but by every word that proceedeth out of the mouth of God" (Matt. 4:4). Christ hungered for the truth, life, and power of God's Word.

God's Word reveals that Christ must be the last (or second) Adam and defeat the devil's temptations through the power of faith and the suffering of obedience. Christ must succeed where the first Adam failed in trusting and obeying the Word of God. And Christ did succeed, because He hungered and thirsted for God's revelation of saving, sustaining truth more than for life itself. He told His disciples

---

1. Although the effects of fasting vary depending on health and hydration, severe starvation generally sets in after thirty-five to forty days, during which the body consumes the protein of its own muscles and organs to survive, leading to death after anywhere from forty-five to sixty days of no nutrition, occasionally longer. Peter Janiszewski, "The Science of Starvation: How Long Can Humans Survive Without Food or Water," *Plos Blogs*, May 13, 2011, http://blogs.plos.org/obesitypanacea/2011/05/13/the-science-of-starvation-how-long-can-humans-survive-without-food-or-water/; Thomas C. Weiss, "The Phases of Starvation—What Happens When We Starve," *Disabled World*, February 1, 2016, rev. January 18, 2018, https://www.disabled-world.com/fitness/starving.php.

in John 4:34, "My meat is to do the will of him that sent me, and to finish his work." In order that "the scripture might be fulfilled," Christ endured wracking, unquenched thirst upon the cross as He suffered for hell-worthy sinners like us and completed the work of redemption (John 19:28–30).

Although Christ's calling to obey and suffer for the salvation of His people was a unique calling, His hunger for the Word is a model for us all. In the wilderness of Judea, Christ quoted Moses's words concerning how God had led Israel through the wilderness of Sinai. Moses said that the Lord had humbled them and trained them to live in absolute dependence and obedience to God's Word: "that he might make thee know that man doth not live by bread only, but by every word that proceedeth out of the mouth of the LORD doth man live" (Deut. 8:3). This is a lesson that God the Father is teaching His children in all times through their many trials. The Word of God, as the great object of our dependence and obedience, must be our greatest hunger, our persistent appetite, and our most savory delight. It is our blessed duty (and privilege!) to feed upon the Word all our lives.

With God's help, I wish to consider, based on Psalm 19:7–14:

The Satisfying and Nourishing Word of God
1. Our delight in God's nourishing Word
2. Our duty toward God's nourishing Word

1. Our Delight in God's Nourishing Word
The Holy Scriptures abound with testimony that God's Word is the satisfying and nourishing food of our souls. Psalm 119:103 says, "How sweet are thy words unto my taste! Yea, sweeter than honey to my mouth!" In Proverbs 8–9, God's Wisdom invites all people to come and enjoy the bread of understanding and the wine of knowledge (Prov. 8:1–11; 9:1–5). Jeremiah had a very difficult ministry, but he declares in Jeremiah 15:16, "Thy words were found, and I did eat them; and thy word was unto me the joy and rejoicing of mine heart: for I am called by thy name, O LORD God of hosts." God said to Ezekiel, "Open thy mouth, and eat [what] I give thee," and the prophet

ate God's Word and said, "It was in my mouth as honey for sweetness" (Ezek. 2:8; 3:3).

Why is God's Word such savory and nutritious food for our souls? David explains in Psalm 19:7–9 that it is because of the Bible's attributes and operations as the inspired Word of God:

> The law of the LORD is perfect, converting the soul:
> The testimony of the LORD is sure, making wise the simple.
> The statutes of the LORD are right, rejoicing the heart:
> The commandment of the LORD is pure, enlightening the eyes.
> The fear of the LORD is clean, enduring for ever:
> The judgments of the LORD are true and righteous altogether.

Mark these attributes of God's Word: it is perfect, sure, right, pure, clean, true, and righteous. Although the very heavens above us declare the glory of God, as David said earlier in this psalm, only God's Word brings the knowledge of God and His will into such sharp focus and fullness of detail so that we can know Him personally as our Rock and Redeemer. Mark as well the effects and operations of God's Word: it is the Holy Spirit's effectual means of salvation and sanctification. John Calvin said, "Since God in vain calls all peoples to himself by the contemplation of heaven and earth, this [God's Word] is the very school of God's children."[2]

The Bible is divinely designed for effective application (2 Tim. 3:16). It is not a textbook for mere intellectual theology, but doctrine for life, "truth in order to goodness," as the Old Princeton divines saw it. This is one reason for the great variety of ways or forms in which its books are written. William Ames said that the Holy Scripture reveals God and His will "by stories, examples, precepts, exhortations, admonitions, and promises. This style best fits the common usage of all sorts of men and also greatly affects the will by stirring up pious motives, which is the chief end of theology."[3]

At every point, Psalm 19 tells us that God's Word is the answer to

---

2. John Calvin, *Institutes of the Christian Religion*, ed. John T. McNeill, trans. Ford Lewis Battles (Philadelphia: Westminster, 1960), 1.6.4.

3. William Ames, *The Marrow of Theology*, ed. and trans. John Dykstra Eusden (Grand Rapids: Baker, 1968), 1.34.19 (187–88).

our fallen condition in Adam, for the Word reveals Jesus Christ, "the bread of life" (John 6:35).[4]

- First, the Word nourishes us by "converting the soul" (Ps. 19:7), which may be translated as "restoring the soul" (KJV mg.). The phrase is used elsewhere in the Bible for reviving or restoring someone's life by giving food to the hungry (Lam. 1:11, 19). Adam and Eve fell into disobedience to God's Word by lusting after forbidden food (Gen. 3:1–6), but God's Word is the spiritual food that gives life to sinners.

- Second, the Word nourishes us by "making wise the simple" (Ps. 19:7). Satan enticed Adam and Eve with the lie that disobedience would make them "as gods, knowing good and evil," so that they would be "wise" (Gen. 3:5–6). But, "professing themselves to be wise, they became fools" (Rom. 1:22). God's Word is "able to make thee wise unto salvation through faith which is in Christ Jesus" (2 Tim. 3:15).

- Third, the Word nourishes us by "rejoicing the heart" (Ps. 19:8). Eve coveted the forbidden fruit because Satan deceived her into thinking it was "good," "pleasant," and "to be desired" (Gen. 3:6). Instead of joy, our first parents tasted death. God's Word brings us back into fellowship with the triune God and with each other, so that our joy may be full (1 John 1:3–4).

- Fourth, the Word nourishes us by "enlightening the eyes" (Ps. 19:8). When Adam and Eve ate the fruit, "the eyes of them both were opened," but only to a new experience of shame and fear as God's enemies (Gen. 3:7–8). Man's heart became darkened by sin and idolatry (Rom. 1:21–23). God's Word illuminates us so that we walk in knowledge, hope, life, and power as God's forgiven and adopted children (Eph. 1:17–19).

- Fifth, the Word nourishes us by "enduring for ever" (Ps. 19:9). Because Adam dishonored God by not listening to His Word, God gave mankind over to death (Gen. 2:17; 3:19). We have become shadows on the earth (Job 8:9), and our lives are but

---

4. For what follows, see D. J. A. Clines, "The Tree of Knowledge and the Law of Yahweh (Psalm XIX)," *Vetus Testamentum* 24, no. 1 (1974): 9–13; Peter C. Craigie, *Psalm 1–50*, Word Biblical Commentary 19, 2nd ed. (Nashville: Thomas Nelson, 2004), 182–83.

a vapor that quickly passes away (James 4:14). But the Word of the Lord "abideth for ever," and by it God's Spirit causes us to be "born again" to eternal life (1 Peter 1:22–23). This living and abiding Word is the incorruptible seed of eternal life in Christ (1 Peter 1:23–25).

- Sixth, the Word nourishes us by being "true and righteous altogether" (Ps. 19:9). Adam's fall corrupted our entire being with sin so that every purpose of our hearts became evil (Gen. 6:5; 8:21). God's Word is the seed of the righteous God, which when planted in us, sends down roots into our innermost being, and produces the good fruit of new obedience to His commands (Mark 4:8).

- Seventh, the Word nourishes us in all these ways because it is the Word of "the LORD." Psalm 19:7–9 repeats the name of "the LORD" six times. This is God's covenant name, Jehovah, by which He revealed Himself to Israel as the ever-living God, the faithful Redeemer and the sovereign King. He has promised salvation to His people, and all who trust in Jesus Christ will inherit it. This is the secret of God's Word: it is not merely a collection of human words, but the Word of the covenant Lord, and in it we meet the living God who speaks to us both of judgment and salvation. God's Word is the means by which God establishes a covenant relationship between Himself and us through Jesus Christ.

Have you opened your mouth and eaten the Word of God? That is to say, have you received the Holy Scriptures as the bread and wine of your soul? Do you believe that this Book is the Word of God, not just man's word about God but God's Word to man? Have you experienced its life-giving, life-changing, life-sustaining effects?

If the Bible is just dead letters on a page to you, that is because you lack the Holy Spirit of God. As John Calvin said, it is by "the secret energy of the Spirit" that "we come to enjoy Christ and all his benefits."[5] The Holy Spirit is "the inner teacher by whose effort the promise of salvation penetrates into our minds, a promise that would

---

5. Calvin, *Institutes*, 3.1.1.

otherwise only strike the air or beat upon our ears."[6] If you are blind to the beauty and glory of God's Word, then you do not have the power to heal yourself. But you may be like blind Bartimaeus when he heard that Jesus was passing by. Cry out, "Jesus, thou Son of David, have mercy on me," and do not stop your crying until Christ opens your eyes by faith in His Word (cf. Mark 10:46–52).

If you know, believe, and have experienced that the Bible is the Word of life, then give all glory to God through Jesus Christ, who by His Holy Spirit has made the Word to be life and salvation unto you. Cherish the Word. Feed upon the Word. Beware of anything that would draw you away from the Word, which is exactly what Satan and this world labor to do. Be faithful to carry out your duty toward the Word.

2. Our Duty toward God's Nourishing Word

God's Word does not work automatically apart from our minds and wills, but calls for a response from us—indeed, it *demands* a response. Just as we must ingest, chew, swallow, and digest our food for it to strengthen our bodies, so we must receive God's Word, hearing it with faith in our hearts, and hiding it in our hearts, for it to save and sanctify our souls. The Lord says in Isaiah 55:1, "Ho, every one that thirsteth, come ye to the waters, and he that hath no money; come ye, buy, and eat; yea, come, buy wine and milk without money and without price." What is this feast God offers for free? Verse 3 says it is the hearing of God's Word: "Incline your ear, and come unto me: hear, and your soul shall live." Paul tells us, "Faith cometh by hearing, and hearing by the word of God" (Rom. 10:17). Such faith is likewise nourished and sustained by the Word. Peter says to all believers, "As newborn babes, desire the sincere milk of the word, that ye may grow thereby" (1 Peter 2:2).

Again, we find a model of a proper response to God's Word in Psalm 19, especially verses 10–14:

---

6. Calvin, *Institutes*, 3.1.4.

> More to be desired are they than gold,
>   yea, than much fine gold:
>   sweeter also than honey and the honeycomb.
> Moreover by them is thy servant warned:
>   and in keeping of them there is great reward.
> Who can understand his errors?
>   cleanse thou me from secret faults.
> Keep back thy servant also from presumptuous sins;
>   let them not have dominion over me:
>   then shall I be upright,
>   and I shall be innocent from the great transgression.
> Let the words of my mouth, and the meditation of
>   my heart,
>   be acceptable in thy sight, O LORD, my strength,
>   and my redeemer.

These words both describe the response of a true believer to God's Word, and prescribe to us our duty that we must obediently follow in order to walk with God more and more:

- First, we must love God's Word, treasuring it more "than gold, yea, than much fine gold," and delighting in it as "sweeter also than honey" (Ps. 19:10). Such love springs from faith in the gospel for salvation. Psalm 119:174 says, "I have longed for thy salvation, O LORD; and thy law is my delight." If we long for Christ, then we must long also to become like Christ in obedience to God's laws. Paul wrote in Romans 7:12, 22, "Wherefore the law is holy, and the commandment holy, and just, and good.... For I delight in the law of God after the inward man." An inward pleasure or relish in the holiness of keeping God's commandments shows that we are truly converted. John wrote in 1 John 2:3, "And hereby we do know that we know him, if we keep his commandments." When obedience is born of love, then it is a delight: "For this is the love of God, that we keep his commandments: and his commandments are not grievous" (1 John 5:3). Charles Bridges wrote, "Duties become privileges when Christ is their source and life."[7]

---

7. Charles Bridges, *An Exposition of Psalm 119* (1827; repr., Edinburgh: Banner of Truth, 1974), 471.

- Second, we must listen to God's Word as God's servants so that by it we may be warned of what displeases our Lord and instructed in how to obtain God's "great reward" (Ps. 19:11). Strive to possess the attitude expressed by young Samuel: "Speak, LORD, for thy servant heareth" (1 Sam. 3:9). Every time we open the Bible, we must remember and, if we are in Christ, look forward to that day when God will open the books of judgment and call us to account for all that we have said and done. Ecclesiastes 12:13–14 sums up the matter: "Fear God, and keep his commandments: for this is the whole duty of man. For God shall bring every work into judgment, with every secret thing, whether it be good, or whether it be evil." Therefore, listen with a profound sense that you need God to teach you His ways. Psalm 25:4–5 says, "Shew me thy ways, O LORD; teach me thy paths. Lead me in thy truth, and teach me: for thou art the God of my salvation; on thee do I wait all the day." When you open the Bible, do you do so with an attitude that says, "Lord, show me Thy ways"? Approach the Bible saying, "O LORD, truly I am thy servant" (Ps. 116:16).

- Third, we must look to God's saving grace promised in His Word. David confesses the deceitful depth of his sins ("Who can understand his errors?"), and seeks grace for justification or acquittal from his guilt: "cleanse thou me from secret faults" (Ps. 19:12).[8] He seeks grace for sanctification: "Keep back thy servant also from presumptuous sins; let them not have dominion over me: then shall I be upright, and I shall be innocent from the great transgression" (v. 13). If we do not cultivate this kind of dependence upon God's justifying and sanctifying grace, we will either neglect or turn away from God's Word or we will become Pharisees who distort it to maintain our external self-righteousness.

- Fourth, we must long to please God by meditating on His Word, obeying His Word, and speaking His Word to others. David teaches us to pray, "Let the words of my mouth, and the meditation of my heart, be acceptable in thy sight" (Ps. 19:14). Meditation is the chewing, swallowing, and inward digesting of

---

8. The verb translated "cleanse" (*naqah*) means to be acquitted, free from guilt or punishment. See Gen. 24:8, 41; Ex. 20:7; 21:19; 34:7; Num. 5:19, 31; 14:18; Deut. 5:11.

our spiritual food by continuing to think about what God says and how it applies to our lives. William Greenhill explained, "Digest the truths thou hearest, by serious meditation, and by faith that they may become thy nutriment, and thou mayst feel the power and efficacy of them in thy heart, and act accordingly."[9] We must meditate on God's Word not only as servants, but also as sons and daughters who love their heavenly Father and desire more than anything to please Him. This is the heartbeat of the fear of the Lord. Anthony Burgess said, "There is nothing done in secret, but thy Father seeth it. There is no heart-pride, no heart-earthliness, but thy Father seeth it. There is never a time thou prayest, hearest the word, but thy Father seeth with what form of spirit it is. Oh therefore if thou art a son of God, thou wilt discover it in thy whole carriage [show it in your whole course of life]: a son feareth the frowns of his father; I dare not do this; my father will be offended."[10]

- Fifth, we must lean, more and more, on the Savior revealed in God's Word. David concludes his psalm by praying, "O LORD, my strength [literally, "my rock"], and my redeemer" (Ps. 19:14). These are words of trust (Ps. 18:2), a personal confession of faith, indicating that our greatest duty toward God's Word is faith in Christ. Here we find the seventh use of God's name ("LORD") in this psalm, showing that God's Word calls us to rest our hearts upon the faithful Savior and only Mediator of the covenant of grace. Christ is the center of the Bible's message from beginning to end. Let us never fall into the grave error of searching the Scriptures to find the way of eternal life while turning a blind eye to the fact that they all, with one accord, testify of Christ, and Christ alone as the way, the truth, and the life (John 5:39; 14:6).

It is important to note that the third, fourth, and fifth duties I have mentioned all appear in Psalm 19 in the form of prayers. Prayer is faith taking hold of the Word of God, and seeking all that God promises to us in His Word. Douglas Kelly writes that all true

---

9. William Greenhill, *An Exposition of the Prophet Ezekiel*, ed. James Sherman (Edinburgh: James Nichol, 1864), 96.

10. Anthony Burgess, *Spiritual Refining: or, A Treatise of Grace and Assurance* (London: Thomas Underhill, 1652), 239.

knowledge of God "lives and breathes in an atmosphere of prayer."[11] John Owen said he who studies the Scriptures must "abide in fervent supplications, in and by Jesus Christ, for supplies of the Spirit of grace, to lead him into all truth." Owen warned that any man who undertakes to interpret any portion of Scripture without praying to God for the Holy Spirit to instruct him greatly provokes God, for that man acts in pride and ignorance.[12] Therefore, pray every time you open the Bible in your devotions or family worship. Pray for the preachers of God's Word in preparation for public worship. Pray for missionaries and Bible teachers around the world. Ask God for illumination to understand the Bible and sanctifying grace to believe and obey it. And thank God for every drop of blessing you receive through the Word.

One reason why we must pray is that we need supernatural strength to think clearly and act boldly against this wicked world. To delight in God's Word, it is necessary that we do not walk in the counsel of the ungodly, nor stand in the way "of sinners," nor sit in the "seat of the scornful" (Ps. 1:1–2). It's not easy being different. Greenhill said the "example of others is like a mighty torrent that carries down all before it."[13] Flood waters have immense force to move boulders, uproot trees, and destroy buildings and bridges. Just six inches of rapidly moving flood water can knock an adult over.[14] When we try to stand against popular tastes, prejudices, preferences, or practices, we are like people trying to wade upstream through a flood. But Christ is sufficient. Greenhill imagined how Christ might answer our fears about proclaiming the truth in the face of opposition. We might say, "Lord, if I do this I will lose my friends," but Christ answers, "I am your friend, your best friend." We might say, "I will alienate my family

---

11. Douglas F. Kelly, *Systematic Theology: Grounded in Holy Scripture and Understood in the Light of the Church, Volume 1, The God Who Is: The Holy Trinity* (Fearn, Ross-shire, Scotland: Christian Focus, 2008), 48.

12. John Owen, *The Causes, Ways, and Means of Understanding the Mind of God as Revealed in His Word*, in *The Works of John Owen*, ed. William H. Goold (1850–1853; repr., Edinburgh: Banner of Truth, 1967), 4:204–5.

13. Greenhill, *An Exposition of the Prophet Ezekiel*, 93.

14. National Weather Service, "Turn Around Don't Drown," accessed April 11, 2024, https://www.weather.gov/safety/flood-turn-around-dont-drown.

from me," but Christ replies, "I am your brother, for I took your very nature to suffer for you and make you a child of God." We might say, "Great and powerful men will become my enemies," but Christ says, "I am greater than they, and my throne is above all thrones." Therefore, Greenhill said, "Do not make the manners of the world the rule of your life, nor the worship of the world the rule of your worship, but look higher."[15]

The Westminster divines summed up our duties toward God's nourishing Word by saying, "The holy scriptures are to be read with an high and reverent esteem of them; with a firm persuasion that they are the very word of God, and that he only can enable us to understand them; with desire to know, believe, and obey the will of God revealed in them; with diligence, and attention to the matter and scope of them; with meditation, application, self-denial, and prayer."[16] Furthermore, if you are a preacher of God's Word, then stand in awe of your calling and let nothing distract you from the ministry of the Word. As William Perkins wrote in the flyleaf of his books, "Thou art a minister of the Word; mind thy business."[17]

Conclusion

What an unspeakable blessing we receive when we do our duty and feed upon God's Word in a regular, humble, diligent, faithful manner! In the Word, we find Christ, the Bread of life, who alone can satisfy us forever. And in Christ, the Mediator, we find God, who is the fountain of life and the fullness of joy.

Perhaps you do not have a regular time to read the Bible and pray. If that's the case, then start now. Resolve that by God's grace you will not let another day of your life pass without reading and meditating on God's Word. Get a Bible reading plan, choose a particular time when you can concentrate, and begin immediately. If you are

---

15. Greenhill, *An Exposition of the Prophet Ezekiel*, 93.
16. Westminster Larger Catechism (Q. 157), in *Reformed Confessions of the 16th and 17th Centuries in English Translation: Volume 4, 1600–1693*, comp. James T. Dennison Jr. (Grand Rapids: Reformation Heritage Books, 2014), 340–41.
17. As cited in Ian Breward, "The Life and Theology of William Perkins, 1558–1602" (PhD diss., University of Manchester, 1963), 35.

a child, talk to your parents about how they can help you to do this all-important duty.

It is crucial that you approach the reading and hearing of God's Word with a right attitude in your heart. Do not do it resentfully, as a duty or chore that you must fulfill but inwardly dislike. Do not do it like a Pharisee, abusing God's Word as if it were a way for you to feel that you are better than other people. Instead, do it with hunger, as someone who knows that it is his necessary and nutritious food. If you do not have a good appetite for God's Word, then be warned that you are not spiritually healthy, and you may be yet dead in your sins. Pray to the Lord to give you a heart that hungers and thirsts for righteousness.

Have the mindset present in this poem, titled, "Of the Incomparable Treasure of the Holy Scriptures," that appears in the front matter of the 1599 edition of the Geneva Bible.

> Here is the spring where waters flow,
>   to quench our heart of sin.
> Here is the tree where truth doth grow,
>   to lead our lives therein.
> Here is the judge that stints the strife,
>   when men's devices fail.
> Here is the bread that feeds the life,
>   that death cannot assail.
>
> The tidings of salvation dear,
>   comes to our ears from hence.
> The fortress of our faith is here,
>   and shield of our defense.
>
> Then be not like the hog that hath
>   a pearl at his desire,
> And takes more pleasure in the trough
>   and wallowing in the mire.
> Read not this book in any case,
>   but with a single eye.
> Read not but first desire God's grace,
>   to understand thereby.

> Pray still in faith with this respect,
> >   to fructify therein,
> > That knowledge may bring this effect,
> >   to mortify thy sin.
>
> Then happy thou in all thy life,
> >   what so to thee befalls,
> > Yea, double happy shalt thou be,
> >   when God by death thee calls.[18]

May God grant you the happiness, yes, the double happiness, of feasting on His Word throughout your life, and one day entering heaven to behold the glory of the eternal Word, Jesus Christ.

---

18. *The Bible* (London: Christopher Barker, 1599), no pagination.

Chapter 9

The Shepherd's Gift of Rest

He maketh me to lie down in green pastures.
—PSALM 23:2a

A flock of sheep feeding and resting in rich, green pastures by a cooling stream is a pleasant sight in any country.[1] But green pastures are a rare feast for sheep in Israel. Not only are the sheep grazed in the wilderness instead of cultivated fields, but lack of rain allows for verdant grass only two or three months per year.[2] Such a pastoral scene understandably becomes a vivid symbol of spiritual rest and contentment, and David used this symbol in saying: the Lord "maketh me to lie down in green pastures."

Some people are quick to interpret the blessings of Psalm 23 as natural benefits. We will not deny, of course, that everyone needs physical rest. There must be pauses and parentheses in every life, for our hand cannot always be laboring, nor our brain always given to intense thought. Pleasure and relaxation are part of enjoying God's good gifts. But if we apply the Shepherd's benefits of Psalm 23 only in a natural way, we soon forget the spiritual benefits enjoyed by God's people in addressing their deepest spiritual needs.

Due to our fall in Adam, we lost God and His image as well as true, spiritual rest. Augustine rightly said, "Thou hast formed us for

---

1. This sermon is largely drawn from "The Shepherd's Gift of Divine Rest," in Joel R. Beeke, *The Lord Shepherding His Sheep: Psalm 23* (Welwyn Garden City, UK: EP, 2015), 75–91.
2. Kenneth E. Bailey, *The Good Shepherd: A Thousand-Year Journey from Psalm 23 to the New Testament* (Downers Grove, Ill.: IVP Academic, 2014), 40.

Thyself, and our hearts are restless until they find rest in Thee."[3] To fill the void within, we grasp for the world's promises of satisfaction. Even though the world around us and within us is but a land of deserts, we still pursue its elusive promise of rest. We live as if we were the first people in the history of mankind to find true contentment apart from our Creator. "The wicked are like the troubled sea, when it cannot rest, whose waters cast up mire and dirt" (Isa. 57:20).

Today's generation is living proof of this truth in its restlessness, dissatisfaction, and unhappiness. Millions immerse themselves in senseless forms of entertainment. Millions more grasp illegal drugs, alcohol, and prescription medications to lift their moods. Flashing advertisements constantly promise peace, popularity, and pleasure for a price. Our society is one mass of restless people, continually returning empty-handed from selfish pursuits.

True rest is to be found by grace in God alone. There is true rest only in the Jehovah-Shepherd. This rest is reserved only for His people and is granted only by sovereign grace. This rest makes a lost sheep willing to follow the Shepherd in the day of divine power, for He alone can lead to rest. The Lord "maketh me to lie down in green pastures."

1. The Shepherd Provides the Conditions for Rest

It would seem easy to get a sheep to lie down and rest. A shepherd, however, knows better. Kenneth Bailey writes, "A dog can be trained to sit and lie down. Not so a sheep."[4] Sheep will only rest when certain conditions have been met. Just as an earthly shepherd will labor diligently to provide the necessary conditions to grant his sheep natural rest, so the heavenly Shepherd will labor to provide the necessary conditions for His flock's spiritual rest.

The Rest of Safety

Freedom from fear and a sense of safety is something a shepherd must provide his flock for them to feel free to lie down and rest. Phillip

---

3. Augustine, *Confessions*, 1.1, in *A Select Library of the Nicene and Post-Nicene Fathers of the Christian Church*, ed. Philip Schaff (Buffalo: Christian Literature Co., 1886), 1:45.
4. Bailey, *The Good Shepherd*, 39–40.

Keller writes, "Sheep are so timid and easily panicked that even a stray jackrabbit suddenly bounding from behind a bush can stampede a whole flock. When one startled sheep runs in flight a dozen others will bolt with it in blind fear, not waiting to see what frightened them."[5]

Sheep need a sense of security in order to rest. Keller explains, "As long as there is even the slightest suspicion of danger from dogs, coyotes, cougars, bears or other enemies the sheep stand up ready to flee for their lives. They have little or no means of self-defense. They are helpless, timid, feeble creatures whose only recourse is to run."[6] Indeed, a single predator can kill several, even dozens, of sheep in one night.

How does a shepherd quiet his flock's fears so that they may lie down and rest? Certainly, he seeks to remove as many causes of their fear as he possibly can. Yet nothing brings more of a sense of safety to the flock than the presence of the shepherd himself. Simply seeing him in their midst puts their fears to rest.

Such is also the condition of Jesus Christ's spiritual flock. Due to their helplessness and vulnerability, they are a timid flock with many things to fear. When the Lord begins His saving work in their souls, they learn that they have no strength in themselves to fight against spiritual predators.

First, Christ's sheep come to fear *sin*. The guilt, penalty, power, pollution, and consequences of sin press upon their consciences. They also fear the *law*. Its demand for perfection allows them no rest, but drives them like an Egyptian slave-master to make bricks without straw. They also fear *Satan*. Where can they find rest when they are continually confronted with this roaring lion's fearful attacks of temptation and accusation? They also fear *death and judgment*. How can they rest if their everlasting destiny lies in the balance and is found wanting?

Only the presence of the Shepherd can dispel the fears of Christ's sheep. His blood has brought reconciliation and peace in the midst of all that threatens them (Col. 1:20). His presence makes them calm

---

5. Phillip Keller, *A Shepherd Looks at Psalm 23* (Grand Rapids: Zondervan, 1970), 36.
6. Keller, *A Shepherd Looks at Psalm 23*, 36.

as the Shepherd stands with them and leads them in the strength of the Lord. He is their peace (Mic. 5:4–5). The Lord Jesus said, "I will not leave you comfortless: I will come to you" (John 14:18). Literally, His promise is, "I will not leave you *orphans*." By the indwelling Spirit (v. 16), Christ and the Father dwell in the believer, are always present (v. 20), and are "a very present help in trouble" (Ps. 46:1).

The Shepherd stands by His flock and grants them the faith to behold Him and to believe that He is looking on them in His favor. They are thus free to lay all their fears at His feet and to place all their trust and confidence in Him as the Great Shepherd. By protecting the sheep from the things they fear, but especially by staying close to them and enabling them to behold His presence, Jehovah-Shepherd provides His flock with the first condition necessary to make room for spiritual rest.

The Rest of Harmony
Sheep must also be at peace with one another to rest. Keller writes, "The second source of fear from which the sheepman delivers his sheep is that of tension, rivalry, and cruel competition within the flock itself."[7] Like other animals, sheep fight among themselves, creating strife and tension within the flock. The stronger attack the weaker and claim the best pasture for themselves. As a result, the flock cannot lie down and rest.

Is it any different with Christ's flock spiritually? Did you ever find one of God's children at rest spiritually while striving to be "top sheep"? Do not the head butting and shoving among God's children sometimes cause so much disorder that the entire congregation becomes edgy and tense? Paul's advice in Philippians 2:3 is necessary among believers today: "In lowliness of mind let each esteem [the] other better than themselves."

The Good Shepherd responds to fighting in the flock in justice, wisdom, and love. He disciplines the strong for pushing around the weaker sheep. In Ezekiel 34:21–22, He says, "Because ye have thrust with side and with shoulder, and pushed all the diseased with your

---

7. Keller, *A Shepherd Looks at Psalm 23*, 39.

horns, till ye have scattered them abroad; therefore will I save my flock, and they shall no more be a prey."

The Shepherd also makes known His presence in the flock as Lord and Son of David. Ezekiel 34:23–24 says, "And I will set up one shepherd over them, and he shall feed them, even my servant David; he shall feed them, and he shall be their shepherd. And I the LORD will be their God, and my servant David a prince among them; I the LORD have spoken it." Just as the presence of the shepherd often causes sheep to stop fighting, so the presence of the Lord silences bickering and promotes humility and peace among all who are truly His.[8]

Furthermore, the Good Shepherd shows special compassion for the weaker sheep. Isaiah 40:11 says, "He shall feed his flock like a shepherd: he shall gather the lambs with his arm, and carry them in his bosom, and shall gently lead those that are with young." The Shepherd shows His sheep that the greatest advantages come not from striving to dominate others but from being the servant of all. "God resisteth the proud, but giveth grace unto the humble" (James 4:6).

Then, instead of a *butting order* the sheep respond with a *bowing order*. The Lord's sheep cannot come low enough. Are you seeking grace to become one of the lowliest sheep of God? Have you learned that the closer you are to the bottom the closer you are to the Shepherd? Let this be your prayer: "Lord, give me grace to come down, for I cannot bring myself there. Make room for spiritual rest by bringing me before Thee as one of the lowest sheep. I am glad to rest there, if only I may be part of *Thy* flock."

The Rest of Tranquility

A third thing that prevents sheep from lying down to rest is the painful bite of insects. Keller writes, "Sheep, especially in the summer, can be driven to absolute distraction by nasal flies, bot flies, warble flies and ticks. When tormented by these pests it is literally impossible for them to lie down and rest. Instead they are up and on their feet, stamping their legs, shaking their heads, ready to rush off into

---

8. Keller, *A Shepherd Looks at Psalm 23*, 40, 42.

the bush for relief from the pests."⁹ The shepherd must help ward off these insects by applying oil to the sheep's head.¹⁰

Jehovah's sheep are also preyed on by pests that prevent spiritual rest. Although true believers strive against worldliness, the world often comes back to live within them, much to their annoyance. It encroaches upon their souls through many disguises. Like Lot, the sheep can become entangled with the world even as its filth vexes their righteous souls (2 Peter 2:7). Various temptations can be such spiritual pests that the sheep cannot lie down to rest. Some of God's sheep struggle with doubts concerning doctrinal truths, while others battle the temptation of a particular sin or fear that they will one day commit a gross sin. The greatest pest, however, is *self*. Like the apostle Paul, God's sheep often discover that "what I hate, that do I," so that they cry out, "O wretched man that I am! who shall deliver me?" (Rom. 7:15, 24).

The divine Shepherd provides something far better than insect repellent for relief from tormentors. He dips His flock in *the oil of the Spirit,* who cleanses, sanctifies, heals, comforts, and transforms the flock, working faith in their souls and uniting them to the Great Shepherd. Christ shares with His sheep the oil of gladness and joy that God has poured out on Him through the Spirit (Ps. 45:7; Isa. 61:1–3). The Spirit's work gives them relief, especially when He takes the things of Christ and shows them to the flock (John 16:13–14). That allows them by faith to place their feet on the neck of the world, on temptations, and even on self. In this way too, the way is opened to true spiritual rest.

The Rest of Sufficiency
Finally, sheep will not lie down to rest if they are hungry. Keller writes, "A hungry, ill-fed sheep is ever on its feet, on the move, searching for another scanty mouthful of forage to try and satisfy its gnawing hunger. Such sheep are not contented, they do not thrive."¹¹ Only when sheep have sufficient food to fill their hungry bellies can they lie down to rest.

---

9. Keller, *A Shepherd Looks at Psalm 23*, 43.
10. Keller, *A Shepherd Looks at Psalm 23*, 116.
11. Keller, *A Shepherd Looks at Psalm 23*, 46.

Given the semi-arid climate of Israel, it is challenging for a shepherd to find good pasture for his flock. It demands careful forethought and constant effort. Bailey recounts how he was near the summit of Jabal Sannin (8,600 ft.) in Lebanon, where, he says, "I had an interesting conversation with an experienced shepherd (with his large flock) who described to me in fascinating detail the various options and the numerous decisions he was obliged to make each day as he sought forage and water for his more than one hundred sheep."[12]

The Good Shepherd leads His sheep to good pasture. He is the door through which they enter into salvation and go out to find the pasture of life, even abundant life (John 10:1–11). Jesus Christ is Himself the pasture of His people, for He is *the living Word of God*. To provide that cost Him more than planning and hard labor—it cost Him the bloody sweat of crucifixion and death. He is the pasture land of eternal satisfaction for His own. As the true meat and drink of life eternal, Christ feeds and nourishes hungry and thirsty souls with His crucified body and shed blood. His sheep find in Him everything they need for time and eternity. He is the Bread of Life (John 6:35). He is the Father's house in which there is bread enough and to spare. He is the focus, the centerpiece, the delight, and the all-in-all of His flock.

He also gives *the written Word of God* as pasture for His flock. The living Word (Christ) and the written Word (the Bible) are inseparably associated with each other. Christ is the great message of all the Holy Scriptures (Luke 24:27, 44; Acts 3:18, 21; 2 Tim. 3:14–16). The Scriptures reveal Jesus Christ as the righteousness of sinners and the Lord and Savior of all who call upon His name (Rom. 1:16–17; 10:12–15).

God's people love Scripture and honor it as the Word of God (Ps. 119:97), for it is their life, their food, their pasture. It is their bread when they are hungry (Isa. 55:1–3, 10), their honey when they are faint (Ps. 19:10), their milk when they are babes (1 Cor. 3:2), and their strong meat when they are men (Heb. 5:12–14). They are brought by faith and through grace to "receive with meekness the engrafted

---

12. Bailey, *The Good Shepherd*, 41.

word" (James 1:21), to keep this Word (John 17:6), and to continue in this Word (John 8:31).

God's house becomes their home where they feed in the green pastures of the Word of God with its ordinances for the worship of God. In the Old Testament, God gave Himself to His people in His special presence in the temple, though He also heard every prayer whispered in the Israelites' private homes. Psalm 87:2–3 says, "The LORD loveth the gates of Zion more than all the dwellings of Jacob. Glorious things are spoken of thee, O city of God." In the New Testament, Christ indwelt every believer by the Holy Spirit, but promised His special presence whenever the church gathers in His name (Matt. 18:20). In the congregation, the sheep hear their Shepherd's voice speaking to them through the reading and the preaching of the Word.

In addition to the Holy Spirit, the ministry of the Word is the principal benefit or gift of the Great Shepherd's ascension (Eph. 4:10–11). It is a standing pledge to the church that Christ is now "in the presence of God for us" (Heb. 9:24). Therefore it pleases Him to put special honor upon the preaching of "Christ crucified, unto the Jews a stumbling block, and unto the Greeks foolishness; but unto them which are called, both Jews and Greeks, Christ the power of God, and the wisdom of God" (1 Cor. 1:23–24). Oh, what a blessing it is to find rest for the soul in God's preached Word! In the house of God, Jehovah's flock meets their God and shepherding King. There Christ rests and dwells, "for the LORD hath chosen Zion; he hath desired it for his habitation." He promises to "abundantly bless her provision" and to "satisfy her poor with bread…and her saints shall shout aloud for joy" (Ps. 132:13, 15, 16).

There, like sheep lying down in green pastures, the Lord's flock experiences divine rest. There the Shepherd provides spiritual *safety* from the predatory fears of sin, Satan, death, and judgment. He gives them spiritual *harmony* with one another so that they dwell together in humility and peace. He blesses them with spiritual *tranquility* as the oil of the Spirit soothes the pricking irritations of temptation and self. He feeds them with the spiritual *sufficiency* of His own fullness offered in His Word, the Holy Scriptures. Have you experienced this rest?

Arise, O Lord, our God, arise
And enter now into Thy rest
O let this house be Thy abode,
Forever with Thy presence blest.

I will abundantly provide
For Zion's good, the Lord hath said;
I will supply her daily need
And satisfy her poor with bread.

Salvation shall adorn her priests,
Her saints shall shout with joy divine,
Messiah's pow'r shall be revealed,
His glory in His Church shall shine.[13]

2. Enjoying Divine Rest by Faith

Jesus Christ is not only the Redeemer who purchases salvation for His flock, but He is also the King who applies that salvation to His flock. "He maketh me to lie down," David says. Jehovah provides salvation based on Christ's objective work of grace for His sheep. However, the Shepherd also works subjectively in His sheep, and this work appears in their experience and activity. *God* did the work, but *David* needed to lie down.

Likewise, we must experience not only how the Lord provides the four conditions necessary for spiritual rest, but also the application of true rest to our souls. If we are one of Jehovah's sheep, the divine means that are instrumental to embrace spiritual rest must be exercised within our souls, enabling us to confess, "He maketh me to lie down in green pastures." This is the exercise of true, saving faith.

True faith is *of* the Lord and its only object *is* the Lord. Faith is essential for every aspect of spiritual life. It is the captain of all spiritual graces. George Swinnock (1627–1673) wrote, "Call forth that commander-in-chief; and then the private soldiers, the other graces, will all follow."[14] Christ honors faith the most, because faith honors

---

13. *The Psalter: with Doctrinal Standards, Liturgy, Church Order, and Added Chorale Section* (Grand Rapids: Eerdmans, 1965), no. 368 [based on Psalm 132].

14. George Swinnock, *The Christian Man's Calling*, in *The Works of George Swinnock* (1868; repr., Edinburgh: Banner of Truth, 1992), 1:202.

Christ the most. Faith focuses upon Christ, believes in Him, trusts Him, and leans upon Him. True faith lies down in the finished work of Christ, confessing by its very exercise both self-deficiency and divine sufficiency. Oh, for grace to *abide* in the pastures of the living and written Word by faith!

In the exercise of faith the Holy Spirit offers to meet all the needs of His people in the Lamb of God, applying to them the written Word of God so that they are enabled to rest in the living Word. Through faith, they come to see that Christ is the answer to all the problems that burden their souls.

Are they *sinners*? Christ became sin for His people to redeem them from it (2 Cor. 5:21).

Are they *law-breakers*? Christ is the law-keeper (Matt. 5:17).

Are they *separated from God*? Christ was forsaken of His Father as Judge so that they might never be forsaken of Him (Matt. 27:46).

Are they *unrighteous*? Christ is the all-righteous One, having a perfect robe of righteousness through His active and passive obedience to the will of God (Isa. 61:10).

Are they *cursed*? Christ died the accursed death as curse-bearer of His elect (Gal. 3:13).

Are they under divine *wrath*? Christ is the peacemaker (Isa. 53:5).

Are they *enemies of God*? In Christ "mercy and truth are met together; righteousness and peace have kissed each other" (Ps. 85:10).

Are they *foolish*? Christ is wisdom (Proverbs 8).

Are they *filthy*? Christ is "holy, harmless, undefiled" (Heb. 7:26).

Are they *tempted*? Christ was "in all points tempted like as we are, yet without sin" (Heb. 4:15).

Are they spiritually *poor*? Christ, who was rich, became poor so that through His poverty they might become rich (2 Cor. 8:9).

Are they in spiritual *bondage*? In Christ there is liberty, for "if the Son therefore shall make you free, ye shall be free indeed" (John 8:36).

Are they *weak*? Christ is their strength (1 Sam. 15:29).

Are they *in need of prayer*? Christ is the praying High Priest, sitting at the right hand of the Father, who never ceases to make intercession for His people (Rom. 8:34).

Are they *restless*? Christ, who by Himself purged our sins, is now sitting on His throne of rest, causing His people to rest in Him as the Priest who has paid everything, as the Prophet who teaches everything they need to learn, and as the King who rules over everything on their behalf.

There is no end to it. The green pastures of God's living and written Word can never become parched or overgrazed as long as we receive this Word in faith. The Word of God reveals Christ's person, natures, states, and offices as a medicine cabinet out of which the Holy Spirit administers healing for every disease that may afflict Jehovah's sheep.

By teaching that faith is the instrument through which God provides these rich spiritual blessings for His flock, we do not imply that the life of faith is easy or can have everything it desires. Far from it, for true faith can only receive what God gives. Faith does not labor to deserve anything from God. Faith is only the hand by which we receive God's gift in Jesus Christ. Christ's merit alone saves sinners.

Ever since the fall of mankind, we have fought to be our own shepherds, to find our own rest, and to be our own Lord. God's grace breaks this stubborn pride, making us dependent upon Him. Only then can we find true rest. By faith, we come to Christ and learn the reality of His promise: "Come unto me, all ye that labour and are heavy laden, and I will give you rest. Take my yoke upon you, and learn of me; for I am meek and lowly in heart: and ye shall find rest unto your souls. For my yoke is easy, and my burden is light" (Matt. 11:28–30).

The Holy Spirit works this rest in the souls of God's people. This rest increases in God and decreases in self-righteousness, self-reliance, and self-idolatry. It is spiritual rest, not a rest dependent on earthly circumstances or goods. As Luther said, the Spirit gives the believer "spiritual eyes" so that he knows "what is the best and noblest thing on earth," not visible splendor, power, and wealth, but "that the Lord is his Shepherd and that he is in His pasture and in His care, that is, that he has God's Word."[15] This rest leads them to sing in hope,

---

15. Martin Luther, "Psalm 23," in *Luther's Works*, ed. Jaroslav Pelikan (Saint Louis: Concordia, 1958), 12:161.

> Thou wilt stretch forth Thy mighty arm
> To save me when my foes alarm;
> The work Thou hast for me begun
> Shall by Thy grace be fully done;
> Forever mercy dwells with Thee;
> O Lord, my Maker, think on me.[16]

As the faith of God's people increases, it flowers and bears fruit in full assurance of faith. The Spirit applies the work of Christ deeply to the conscience. There is a difference between justification by faith, and the assurance of grace and salvation.[17] The first is an objective reality for all believers; the latter is a rich privilege which we must seek in growing experience.

United to Christ, believers can say with Asa even in days of conflict, "Help us, O LORD our God; for we rest on thee" (2 Chron. 14:11). Yet this rest can attain greater stability and personal application. It has been said, "The heart of religion lies in its personal pronouns."[18] God's sheep thus learn to say, "*I* know whom *I* have believed" (2 Tim. 1:12); "*My* redeemer liveth" (Job 19:25); "*I* live by the faith of the Son of God, who loved *me*, and gave himself for *me*" (Gal. 2:20).

Spiritual rest in God becomes the flock's rich possession only as a fruit of justification. "Being justified by faith we have peace with God through our Lord Jesus Christ" (Rom. 5:1). The guilt of sin is removed in its condemning power. The law of God no longer curses us with its impossible demand for perfection, for Christ has fulfilled its precepts and carried its curse (Gal. 3:13; 4:4). Conscience, once accusing, now rests quietly in Christ. "There is therefore now no condemnation to them which are in Christ Jesus" (Rom. 8:1).

In Christ, God becomes a glorious resting ground instead of a cause for terror. Has God's *justice* become your strong fortress, knowing that Christ satisfied justice for you? Do you rest in God's *eternal*

---

16. *The Psalter*, no. 381 [based on Psalm 138].
17. See The Westminster Confession of Faith (11.4 and 18.2–4) in James T. Dennison, Jr., comp., *Reformed Confessions of the 16th and 17th Centuries in English Translation: Volume 4, 1600–1693* (Grand Rapids: Reformation Heritage Books, 2014), 248, §54–55.
18. The saying is attributed to Martin Luther.

truthfulness, praying, "Fulfill this word unto Thy servant upon which Thou hast caused me to hope; O Lord, do as Thou hast said"? Are you conscious of your sin and are you being led to rest in the *mercy* of God which alone can blot it out? Burdened with guilt, have you found a resting place in sovereign, divine *grace?* Overwhelmed with affliction, have you been brought to rest in the *omnipotence* of Jehovah? Bound up with your own foolishness, do you rest in the *wisdom* of God? Has the Lord enabled you to rest in His *immutability* as a sure anchor in the troubled sea of life? Despite your unfaithfulness, are you resting in God's *faithfulness* whose promise is as good as His fulfillment?

The gospel gives us rest from our enemies. Satan's accusing head is crushed in Christ. The believer receives courage in Christ as his crucified, exalted King to resist the devil and put him to flight. Having died with Christ and raised with Him, the Christian finds some rest even from self; the old nature can no longer have the upper hand, though the conflict continues until death.

At peace with God and in victory over his enemies, the redeemed sinner gains new strength to submit to the will of God, praying, "Thy will be done." Whatever the Lord does is best. The assured Christian wants to do God's will because it is *His* will. This gives believers great liberty in prayer. The Lord does not hesitate to hand them the keys of the storehouse of divine grace, saying to them what He did to the Canaanite woman: "O woman, great is thy faith; be it unto thee even as thou wilt" (Matt. 15:28). Indeed, they may then experience more rest in the furnace of affliction than with the king in his palace (Dan. 3:24), knowing that "many are the afflictions of the righteous, but the LORD delivereth him out of them all" (Ps. 34:19). They learn the secrets of Psalm 37:7, "Rest in the LORD and wait patiently for Him."

All the lions that once terrified them are chained. They see Jesus holding the keys to death and hell (Rev. 1:18). They commit themselves to His hands for time and eternity. Sin itself is defeated and has lost its power to dominate them.

Oh, blessed is the rest that a sinner experiences in salvation! Secure in the possession of everlasting good, he may say, "'Return unto thy rest, O my soul, for the LORD hath dealt bountifully with thee'" (Ps. 116:7). He maketh me to lie down in green pastures. Till the pastures of God wither and the river of life fails, my soul cannot lack anything, for the LORD is my Shepherd." This is a blessed foretaste of heaven.

3. Resting in the Love of the Triune God

The exercise of faith in Christ brings God's sheep to "boldness and access of confidence" (Eph. 3:12) to the triune God. After describing the peacemaking work of Christ, Paul writes, "For through him we both have access by one Spirit unto the Father" (Eph. 2:18). There is an experiential resting in God by coming to know Him personally in His three divine persons. Paul desired this blessing for all believers: "The grace of the Lord Jesus Christ, and the love of God, and the communion of the Holy Ghost, be with you all" (2 Cor. 13:14). Augustine taught that the Trinity is the true object of our enjoyment beyond anything that this world can offer.[19] By grace, we come to know the love and grace of each divine person, and in return our love and joy overflow.

The child of God has the privilege of knowing the second person of the Holy Trinity as his Elder Brother (Rom. 8:29), as a merciful and faithful High Priest (Heb. 4:15–16), and as his Advocate with the Father (1 John 2:1). The believer can become personally acquainted with Immanuel Himself. He can know Christ as "a friend that sticketh closer than a brother" (Prov. 18:24). Christ's gifts and benefits are wonderful, but His person is "altogether lovely" (Song 5:16). Blessed are they who cannot only say, "He gave me peace," but also "He *is* my peace." This conviction strengthened the early Christians as they faced martyrdom; they inscribed on the walls of the catacombs, "In Christ, in peace."

What a wonder it is to be admitted into the circle of Christ's personal friends! He brings us to rest in Himself with the very rest which He enjoys with His Father. He rests in grateful submission in the Father's sovereign decree of electing love. He rests in the blessed contemplation of all that is delivered unto Him by the Father as the

---

19. Augustine, *On Christian Doctrine*, trans. J. F. Shaw, 1.5, in *The Works of Aurelius Augustine*, ed. Marcus Dods (Edinburgh: T&T Clark, 1892), 9:10.

fruit of His work as Mediator. He rests in the completion of His work that the Father gave Him to do in this world (Heb. 4:10). He rests in the full knowledge that He has of the Father and the Father of Him, and in the incomprehensible love between them. He rests in the very heart of His Father as the only-begotten Son (John 1:18). As we come to know Him better, we increasingly rest in His rest.

To know the Son is also to know the Father (John 14:9). Christ brings His friends and brothers to know the first person of the Holy Trinity. He opens up for them the experiential enjoyment of their adoption into the household of God. The Father makes their adoption real by the Spirit of the Son, who witnesses with their spirits that they are children of God, leading them to cry out, "Abba, Father!" (Rom. 8:15; Gal. 4:6). Through the last Adam, the Father restores the relationship they lost in the first Adam. Justification removes condemnation from a sinner and places him in a status of righteousness in God's courtroom. However, adoption goes further; it brings him to the table of God's household as one of His dear children.

Blessed are the prodigals who experience not only repentance and confession but are also received into the arms of a loving Father. In mercy, the Father sees them a great way off, has compassion on them, runs to them, embraces them, and kisses them (Luke 15:20). Instead of being servants, they are restored to sonship; instead of filthy rags, they are given the best robe, a ring for their fingers, and shoes for their feet; and instead of the death they deserve, they partake of the feast of the fattened calf. Blessed are they who know what it means to rest in the green pastures of God's fatherly heart. They have access to His throne of grace, which is the richest blessing in the whole world. They may tell the Father everything. No need is too small. No sin is too great. When they ask for bread, He will not give them a stone. "As a father pitieth his children, so the LORD pitieth them that fear him" (Ps. 103:13).

Finally, true children of God may rest in the Holy Spirit, the third person of the Trinity. At Pentecost, the disciples were allowed to embrace and rest in the triune God. Through Christ, they received reconciliation with God and adoption by the Father. As the "promise of the Father," they also received an experiential knowledge of the Holy Spirit. Jesus became their Elder Brother, God became their

Father, and the Holy Ghost came to dwell with them and work in them, in His offices as comforter, sealer, and intercessor (John 14:16; Eph. 1:13; Rom. 8:26). By the Spirit's indwelling, Christ's resurrection life dwelled in them, and the Father and the Son made their home with them (John 14:17, 19, 23). Richard Sibbes wrote that the Spirit "knits us to the Father and the Son...because all the communion we have with God is by the Holy Ghost."[20] Resting in the Spirit, we find ourselves resting with the Son in the heart of the Father.

Yet all resting this side of the grave is a mere shadow of the perfect, eternal, and heavenly rest to come. Moments of rest that are "unspeakable and full of glory" here on earth (1 Peter 1:8) are but a foretaste of the river of pleasure flowing out of the throne of God (Rev. 22:1). Rest on earth from the guilt and dominion of sin foreshadows eternal rest from the pollution of sin. Here on earth, children of God are pilgrims passing through a wilderness, but soon they will arrive at the Father's house, where all their sorrows shall cease and they shall enter eternal rest.

In the mountains of Scotland, a steep trail finally leads to a breathtaking mountain pass called Glencoe. At the top of the pass a stone is engraved with these words, "Rest, and be thankful." Sheep of the Lord's flock, the summit of the narrow way will be won. Here, though we are not weary *of* our Shepherd's service, we are often weary *in* His service. But the day will come when we will look back at the way of life with true thankfulness as we view the wisdom of every little winding turn in the steep ascent by which we were led. Here in this world our sense of rest in God is feeble at best, but "when that which is perfect is come, then that which is in part shall be done away...then shall I know even as also I am known" (1 Cor. 13:10, 12). Finally, we will know perfect, eternal rest!

---

20. Richard Sibbes, *A Description of Christ*, in *The Works of Richard Sibbes* (1862–1864; repr., Edinburgh: Banner of Truth, 1973), 1:17.

Chapter 10

God's Holiness

> *In the year that king Uzziah died I saw also the Lord sitting upon a throne, high and lifted up, and his train filled the temple. Above it stood the seraphims: each one had six wings; with twain he covered his face, and with twain he covered his feet, and with twain he did fly. And one cried unto another, and said, Holy, holy, holy, is the LORD of hosts: the whole earth is full of his glory. And the posts of the door moved at the voice of him that cried, and the house was filled with smoke. Then said I, Woe is me! for I am undone; because I am a man of unclean lips, and I dwell in the midst of a people of unclean lips: for mine eyes have seen the King, the LORD of hosts. Then flew one of the seraphims unto me, having a live coal in his hand, which he had taken with the tongs from off the altar: and he laid it upon my mouth, and said, Lo, this hath touched thy lips; and thine iniquity is taken away, and thy sin purged.* —ISAIAH 6:1–7

The greatest need of the church today is an encounter with the holiness of God. Proverbs 9:10 says, "The fear of the LORD is the beginning of wisdom: and the knowledge of the holy [One] is understanding." A cold, dispassionate analysis of God's holiness might fascinate our minds, but it won't benefit our souls unless our study of God is done in the pursuit of our personal and saving knowledge of Him in His holiness. What we desperately need is not only a renewed understanding of His holiness but an actual *reckoning* with Him in the majesty, purity, and grace of His holiness.

The various dimensions of God's holiness are recognized by many theologians. A. A. Hodge said, "The holiness of God is not to be conceived of as one attribute among others; it is rather a general term representing the conception of his consummate perfection and total glory." Thus, Hodge said, the Scriptures speak of God's holiness as "his transcendently august and venerable majesty" and his "moral purity."[1] This accords with the biblical testimony, which portrays God's holiness as His transcendence as well as His moral perfection.

Both of these aspects can be seen in Isaiah 6. Using this passage as our textual guide, let's peer into the prophet's encounter with the holiness of God in its majesty, purity, and grace:

1. God's majestic holiness
2. God's moral holiness
3. God's gracious holiness

1. God's Majestic Holiness

The climactic Old Testament revelation of God's holiness appears in Isaiah's vision. Isaiah 6:1–3 reads, "In the year that king Uzziah died I saw also the Lord sitting upon a throne, high and lifted up, and his train filled the temple. Above it stood the seraphims: each one had six wings; with twain he covered his face, and with twain he covered his feet, and with twain he did fly. And one cried unto another, and said, Holy, holy, holy, is the LORD of hosts: the whole earth is full of his glory."

Isaiah saw the Lord on an exalted throne, transcendent in regal majesty. He reigns supreme over the affairs of men and is worshiped by the hosts of heaven. The emphasis of Isaiah's vision falls upon God's sovereignty and greatness. Note the titles used of God in verses 1, 3, and 5: "the Lord," (Adonai) "the LORD (*YHWH*) of hosts," and "the King." In verse 1, where Isaiah says, "I saw the Lord," the Hebrew title is *Adonai*, which means Ruler, Master, Sovereign, Exalted One. The vision vividly depicts God's supremacy over angelic powers and

---

1. A. A. Hodge, *Outlines of Theology* (Edinburgh: Banner of Truth, 1983), 163.

earthly kings. The greatest of men still die, but the Lord remains forever; "thy throne [is] from generation to generation" (Lam. 5:19). Thomas Goodwin said, "He is separate and alone in his holiness, as he is alone in his being.... Now of all that could have been said or attributed to him, this sets up God the highest, and as most sovereign. And this, of all others, layeth us low, both as we are creatures and as we are sinners," for God's holiness "separates him from the creatures."[2] In other words, the holiness of God exalts Him without equal and casts down human pride into the dust.

Holiness is the peculiar glory of His divine nature. Edward Leigh said that God's essential holiness "is the incommunicable eminency of the divine Majesty, exalted above all."[3] Herman Bavinck wrote, "He is rather called holy in a comprehensive sense in connection with every revelation that impresses humans with his deity."[4] R. C. Sproul wrote that God's holiness "signifies everything about God that sets Him apart from us and makes Him an object of awe, adoration, and dread to us."[5]

God's holiness reminds us that His difference from us is not merely quantitative, as if God were better than we are just because He has a longer list of things He knows, actions He can do, and places where He is present. It is not simply that He is 'more holy' than His saints, but that He is qualitatively different from us. He is in a category by Himself (*sui generis*). In Revelation 15:4, the sinless saints sing, "Thou only art holy." God's holiness, as Thomas Goodwin noted, implies that we should never treat God as if He were first on a list of beings, but, as the Holy One, He is *unicus*, the Only One who "stands apart by himself" from all our categories.[6] Another writer put it well

---

2. Thomas Goodwin, *Of the Creatures, and the Condition of Their State by Creation*, in Thomas Goodwin, *The Works of Thomas Goodwin* (1861–1866; repr., Eureka, Calif.: Tanski, 1996), 7:15.

3. Edward Leigh, *A Treatise of Divinity*, book 2 (London: William Lee, 1647), 102.

4. Herman Bavinck, *Reformed Dogmatics, Volume 2: God and Creation*, ed. John Bolt, trans. John Vriend (Grand Rapids: Baker Academic, 2003), 220.

5. R. C. Sproul, ed., *The Reformation Study Bible*, (Orlando, Fla.: Reformation Trust, 2015), 168.

6. Goodwin, *Of the Creatures*, in *Works*, 7:20.

when he said, "There is a terrifying unfamiliarity in the things that God says about Himself."[7]

The seraphim cover themselves in God's presence, crying out "holy, holy, holy," thus ascribing to God a holiness that even they fall short of—not because they have sinned, but because even sinless, immortal spirits are overwhelmed by God's holiness and unapproachable light. Stephen Charnock said,

> Holiness is the substance of God, but a quality and accident in a creature. God is infinitely holy, creatures finitely holy. He is holy from himself, creatures are holy by derivation from him.... Though God hath crowned the angels with an unspotted sanctity, and placed them in a habitation of glory, yet as illustrious as they are, they have an unworthiness in their own nature to appear before the throne of so holy a God. Their holiness grows dim and pale in his presence; it is but a weak shadow of that divine parity, whose light is so glorious that it makes them cover their faces out of weakness to behold it, and cover their feet out of shame in themselves.[8]

The Scriptures hail the holiness of God as His crowning attribute. Thomas Watson said, "Holiness is the most sparkling jewel of [God's] diadem."[9] Yes, God is love, and He is just, wise, and good, and every attribute He possesses is one with His nature, identical and coextensive with His entire being, consubstantial within the simplicity of the divine essence. But it is especially God's holiness that radiates through all His attributes and makes each one shine with a peculiar splendor. John Gill noted, "It has been thought to be not so much a particular and distinct attribute of itself, as the lustre, glory, and harmony of all the rest; and this is what is called 'the beauty of the Lord' (Ps. 27:4)."[10]

---

7. Donald Macleod, *Behold Your God* (Fearn, Ross-shire, Scotland: Christian Focus, 1995), 108.

8. Stephen Charnock, *Discourse on the Existence and Attributes of God*, in *The Complete Works of Stephen Charnock* (Edinburgh: James Nichol, 1864), 2:195–96.

9. Thomas Watson, *Puritan Gems; or, Wise and Holy Sayings of the Rev. Thomas Watson*, ed. John Adey (London: J. Snow, and Ward and Co., 1850), 66.

10. John Gill, *A Complete Body of Doctrinal and Practical Divinity* (Paris, Ark.: Baptist Standard Bearer, 1987), 1:104.

God's glory is the outshining, the brilliant display, of His holiness.[11] Just think of the most beautiful thing you could imagine. What would it be? Majestic mountains, a renaissance painting, a symphony, a Caribbean sunset over crystal blue waters? Compared to the beauty of divine holiness, all those things are profane and base. The most ravishing things on earth are but faint reflections or dull images of God's beautiful holiness which shines in unapproachable, radiant splendor. We were made to contemplate this glory, and, as Augustine said, our hearts will be restless until they find their rest in beholding God in His superlative, soul-satisfying beauty.

All throughout the Scriptures, holiness correlates with both *glory* and *beauty*. The psalmist declared, "Honour and majesty are before him: strength and beauty are in his sanctuary [Holy Place]" (Ps. 96:6). David thirsted "to see thy power and thy glory, so as I have seen thee in the sanctuary" (Ps. 63:2). The "one thing" he desired of God was to dwell in His temple "to behold the beauty of the Lord" (Ps. 27:4). Isaiah promised, "Thine eyes shall see the king in his beauty" (Isa. 33:17). When we view the holiness of God in His "brilliant splendor," we feel compelled to cover our faces, as it were, crying out, "Holy, holy, holy, is the LORD of hosts!" Seeing His beauty causes us to be irresistibly attracted to holiness so that we desire, above all, to reflect His image "in true righteousness and holiness" (Eph. 4:24).[12]

It has been said by many theologians that the highest task of theology is the contemplation of God—to gaze upon Him through His own self-revelation in the Scriptures and to be beautified by this contemplation. A true view of God ushers us beyond the speculative into the transformative, because the true knowledge of God brings us into an encounter with His holy presence through the atoning blood of Christ. As His holiness shines into our hearts through the Word, it illuminates us, humbles us, convicts us, enlivens us, purifies us,

---

11. "His glory (*câbod*) is His manifested holiness…just as, on the other hand, His holiness is His veiled or hidden glory." Carl Friedrich Keil and Franz Delitzsch, *Commentary on the Old Testament*, trans. James Martin (Grand Rapids: Eerdmans, 1986), 7:125.

12. Brakel, *The Christian's Reasonable Service*, 1:135.

and beautifies our souls. Are you, dear believer, being beautified continually by beholding the beauty of God's holiness in the Scriptures? There is no substitute for this. Secondhand knowledge of God will not suffice. You must know and encounter the triune God as "the Holy One," or else you must perish from His presence as an unholy thing.

Holiness demands our worship of God and is central to it. God's holiness stirs "awe and dread," but at the same time His people are "fascinated" and "entranced" by the Holy One.[13] The seraphim in Isaiah's vision both covered their faces and sang God's praises, evidencing *dread and delight*. A high view of God leads to a high esteem for worship. If we lose sight of God's holiness, we will lose fervor and fear in our worship. Joseph Pipa says, "We worship Him because of who He is.... One of the reasons, therefore, our worship totters on the edge of irrelevance is because we do not come into God's presence aware of who He is."[14] Jeremiah Burroughs (c. 1600–1646) wrote, "The great reason why people come and worship God in a slight way is because they do not see God in His glory." On the other hand, when we encounter God in His holiness, it either propels us into glad worship or threatens to destroy us for dishonoring His holy name.

Let us, therefore, give our fervent, heartfelt worship to our triune God. When we adore Him, earth offers up a faint echo of heaven's thunder. The seraphim Isaiah speaks of are angelic creatures created for worship. The word *seraph* in the Hebrew literally means "burning one"—lit aflame with the fire of God. Psalm 104:4 says that God makes His angels "a flaming fire." They burn with holy fire, burning with zeal to worship God in the splendor of His holiness. Their entire being is lit ablaze and taken up with the act of worship, purest worship. And if we get a glimpse, just a small glimpse, of the greatness of our God, we will find that we too are impelled to worship Him with all our mind, heart, soul, and strength. Our apathetic prayers,

---

13. Robert L. Reymond, *"What Is God?" An Investigation of the Perfections of God's Nature* (Fearn, Ross-shire, Scotland: Christian Focus, 2007), 183–84. Reymond summarized the thesis of Rudolf Otto, *The Idea of the Holy: An Inquiry into the Non-Rational Factor in the Idea of the Divine and Its Relation to the Rational*, trans. John W. Harvey, 2nd ed. (New York: Oxford University Press, 1950), 12–40.

14. Joseph Pipa, *The Worship of God: Reformed Concepts of Biblical Worship* (Fearn, Ross-shire, Scotland: Christian Focus, 2005), 63, 65.

half-hearted devotions, sluggishness in service, irreverence in worship, will be transformed into fervent activities set ablaze by the fire of God's holiness, radiating with reverent delight that beautifies all that we do in the service of the King.

2. God's Moral Holiness

That God is holy has massive moral implications, beginning with the righteous character of God Himself and reaching to the moral character and conduct of all angels and men. The holiness of God is somewhat like the sun. Its massive presence exerts pervasive force so that all things within the solar system must revolve around its brilliant glory. However, God's presence is infinitely more pervasive. Nothing in creation lies beyond or outside of the influence of His holiness. God's holiness in its moral dimensions can be best appreciated if we consider its relationship to three things.

First, consider its relationship to God's glory. The Lord's holiness entails His purpose to glorify Himself in all that He does, for He alone is the glorious God. If He is supremely sacred, then He must honor Himself as such and require others to do the same, or He would deny Himself. The angels cried, "Holy, holy, holy, is the LORD of hosts: the whole earth is full of his glory" (Isa. 6:3). Thomas Goodwin concluded, "Holiness is that whereby God aims at his own glory."[15] James Ussher said that God's holiness means that "he most justly loveth, liketh, and preferreth himself above all."[16] Edward Leigh wrote, "God's holiness is that excellency of his nature, by which he gives himself (as I may say) unto himself, doing all for himself, and in all, and by all, and above all, aiming at his own pleasure and glory."[17] The Lord commands us to love Him with all our hearts, all our souls, and all our strength (Deut. 6:5), but God alone is able to love Himself with an infinite love, and thus He alone is infinitely holy.[18]

---

15. Goodwin, *Of the Creatures*, in *Works*, 7:15.
16. James Ussher, *A Body of Divinity: or The Sum and Substance of Christian Religion* (Birmingham, Ala.: Solid Ground Christian Books, 2007), 3rd head (52).
17. Leigh, *A Treatise of Divinity*, 2:102.
18. Charnock, *The Existence and Attributes of God*, 2:115, 117.

Therefore, we may speak of God's moral holiness not as a separate attribute from God's majestic holiness but as another dimension of the one divine holiness. This is the aspect of God's holiness that the Christian tradition has emphasized historically: holiness as the virtue or perfection of God's nature.[19] Holiness is defined more narrowly as God's moral purity and settled opposition to all impurity.[20] He is the "Holy One" who is "of purer eyes than to behold evil" and cannot "look on iniquity" with approval and pleasure (Hab. 1:12–13).

In the moral realm, as well, God's holiness denotes His separation and supremacy. The moral holiness of God is the absolute righteousness of His whole nature. It sanctifies all that God does and puts divine glory in all His works. Without holiness, God would be a terror to us. Leigh said, "Holiness is the beauty of all God's attributes, without which his wisdom would be but subtlety, his justice cruelty, his sovereignty tyranny, his mercy foolish pity."[21] With holiness, however, all of God's attributes shine with amazing loveliness.

Second, consider God's moral holiness in relationship to our sin. Isaiah understood this truth with painful clarity. The divine vision broke him and threatened to destroy him. In verse 5, he recalls his sinfulness and the sinfulness of the people he is associated with: "I am a man of unclean lips, and I dwell in the midst of a people of unclean lips." We swim in sin like fish swim in water. But when Isaiah was taken up into the atmosphere of heaven, he was like a fish out of water. The sights were terrifying, the sounds were sublime, the very air was dense with the luminescent smoke of the divine presence.

But why did he confess this about his *lips*? Why does he confess the impurity of his lips of all things? It is because of the praises of the seraphim. Isaiah's unclean lips stand in contrast to the purity and power of the praises of the heavenly hosts. Their worship was

---

19. William Ames, *The Marrow of Theology*, ed. John D. Eusden (Grand Rapids: Baker, 1997), 1.4.63 (87); Johannes Polyander, Antonius Walaeus, Antoine Thysius, and André Rivetus, *Synopsis Purioris Theologiae/Synopsis of a Purer Theology: Latin Text and English Translation: Volume 1, Disputations 1–23*, eds., Dolfe te Velde and Rein Ferwerda, trans. Riemer A. Faber, (Leiden: Brill, 2014), 6.39 (1:177).

20. Polyander, Walaeus, Thysius, and Rivetus, *Synopsis Purioris Theologiae*, 6.40 (1:179); Leigh, *A Treatise of Divinity*, 2:102.

21. Leigh, *A Treatise of Divinity*, 2:104.

untainted and unhindered by sin, and they could not cease to praise God nonstop, so overwhelmed were they at the sight of His glory. So thunderous was their praise that the very posts of the door were shaken by the reverberation of the sound (v. 4). That magnificent sound shook and jolted Isaiah to the core of his being.

Isaiah recognized that he, in comparison to the seraphim, had little regard for God. He had never praised Him as He ought. The weight of God's holy glory so penetrated his being that it *constrained* praise from him, but he could not praise because he was so overcome with a sense of his unworthiness. He saw himself as unworthy to even speak a word to God's praise, so the only recourse left in the light of such weighty, overwhelming glory was *simply to die*! So he cries out, "Woe is me!"

Notice what he confesses; not just his profane speech, not just the words that he did and did not say, but the *lips* that make utterance. He traces the sin of his speech to its root in his very being. "I am a *man* of unclean lips"—a *man* of profane speech. He is saying, "My person, my humanity, is characterized by inherent taintedness and fallenness and corruption. My sinful actions by sinful words betray my sinful nature, revealing the plague of my own heart."

This all seems so awful, so awesome, so dreadful! It reminds us of Isaiah 8:13, where the prophet said, "Sanctify the LORD of hosts himself; and let him be your fear, and let him be your dread." But this is precisely what proximity to God will necessarily elicit from sinners. This is also how a genuine work of grace normally functions in its beginnings. In the beginning of the creation God said, "Let there be light: and there was light" (Gen. 1:3). When God begins to make us a new creation by grace, the first thing He does is say, "Let there be light in their hearts." He shines the light of His holiness into our hearts to awaken us to the knowledge of Himself and the knowledge of ourselves, and He bombards our understanding with a sense of His holiness.

When the conviction of the Spirit works in the heart of a sinner, the conscience is awakened from its slumber and sins come to mind and come to light. As Moses said, "Thou hast set our iniquities before thee, our secret sins in the light of thy countenance" (Ps. 90:8). Sins that we once saw as small become grave transgressions. Little peccadillos become monstrous atrocities in the light of God's infinite holiness and worthiness. We say with David, "I acknowledge my transgressions: and my sin is ever before me" (Ps. 51:3). We cease to justify and rationalize our sin, and instead we confess it, we abhor it, we forsake it, if only we can get its burden off our conscience. We cry out for "truth in the inward parts" (Ps. 51:6). The gravity of our transgressions becomes commensurate with our sense of the enormity of God's holiness and glory.

So we should ask ourselves: Do I know anything of this humbling work of the Spirit? Have I ever caught a glimpse of God's holy glory? Has my heart ever been pierced and cut asunder by His penetrating purity? I'm not just talking about the disturbings of natural conscience but the piercings of the Spirit's sword into the very joints and marrow, to expose the thoughts and intentions of the heart in all their impurity in the light of God's holiness. If you have indeed experienced such conviction, then the question is this: What did you do with it? Conviction alone is not salvation or sanctification. God convicts us to lead us to a recognition of our guilt and misery, so that we would hunger and thirst for His righteousness, so that we would long for His grace and goodness in salvation and set our hearts on seeking Him (see Matt. 5:6).

Third, consider the relationship between God's moral holiness and our holiness. The moral excellence of God's holiness blazes forth in His law, which itself is "holy, and just, and good" (Rom. 7:12). God's perfection is the standard for our moral character and one of our most important motivations for our religious practice. God's entire moral code flows out of His holiness. Human holiness is wholeminded and wholehearted obedience to God's law. The "law of the LORD of hosts" is "the word of the Holy One of Israel," so we must not despise it (Isa. 5:24). Therefore, Christians must live "as obedient children" who do their Father's will, heeding the call, "Be ye holy; for I am holy" (1 Peter 1:14–16; cf. Lev. 11:45; 19:2). Thomas Watson said that our holiness consists "in our suitableness to God's nature, and in our subjection to his will."[22]

---

22. Thomas Watson, *A Body of Divinity* (Edinburgh: Banner of Truth, 2000), 85.

Personal holiness is possible only because God's "holy calling" has powerfully gripped us, "not according to our works, but according to his own purpose and grace, which was given us in Christ Jesus before the world began" (2 Tim. 1:9). God is saving his chosen ones "through sanctification of the Spirit and belief of the truth" (2 Thess. 2:13). If we are His children, the Father wisely disciplines us through painful trials "that we might be partakers of his holiness," that is, that we might have "the peaceable fruit of righteousness" (Heb. 12:10–11). We must pursue holiness because without it no one will see the Lord (v. 14).

J. C. Ryle describes true practical holiness: "Holiness is the habit of being of one mind with God…hating what He hates—loving what He loves—and measuring everything in this world by the standard of His Word." A holy person will "endeavour to shun every known sin, and to keep every known commandment." He will "strive to be like our Lord Jesus Christ." He will pursue meekness, patience, gentleness, self-control in word and deed, self-denial, love, kindness, mercy, purity of heart, fear of God, humility, and faithfulness in all his responsibilities. A holy person "will endeavour to set his affections entirely on things above, and to hold things on earth with a very loose hand."[23] This is the character of the holy Lord Jesus, and it will increasingly become the character of all who are united to Him by a living faith, especially as they follow Him, growing in conformity to Him by diligence and suffering under God's gracious hand.

It is well to remember that, unlike our justification, our sanctification in this life is always a work in progress and never complete, since, as the Heidelberg Catechism states, "Even the holiest men, while in this life, have only a small beginning of such obedience, yet so that with earnest purpose they begin to live not only according to some, but according to all the Commandments of God." Yet this small beginning gives us hope that we shall "attain the goal of perfection after this life," through Jesus Christ.[24] Thanks be to God that in

---

23. J. C. Ryle, *Holiness: Its Nature, Hindrances, Difficulties, and Roots* (Cambridge: James Clarke, 1977), 34–38.
24. The Heidelberg Catechism (LD 44, Q. 114–15), in James T. Dennison, Jr., comp., *Reformed Confessions of the 16th and 17th Centuries in English Translation: Volume 2, 1552–1566* (Grand Rapids: Reformation Heritage Books, 2010), 796.

Christ He has made provision for us to become by grace what we are not by nature.

3. God's Gracious Holiness

The moral excellence of God's holiness appears both in His judgments and His acts of grace and mercy. Rev. G. H. Kersten said, "The attribute of God's holiness is a terror to the wicked, to whom He is a devouring fire and everlasting burning, so that the wicked shall not dwell with Him. On the other hand it is a source of comfort and salvation for those who fear Him, and out of love to His perfection, seek to flee from sin, and to perfect their holiness in the fear of God."[25]

Grace is an important aspect of divine holiness for Christ's sake. The Lord said, "For thus saith the high and lofty One that inhabiteth eternity, whose name is Holy; I dwell in the high and holy place, with him also that is of a contrite and humble spirit, to revive the spirit of the humble, and to revive the heart of the contrite ones" (Isa. 57:15). This is the wonder of holiness: it both exalts God infinitely above all creation in eternal transcendence and brings Him near to those broken over their sins so that He tenderly renews them. God's very holiness is the reason why He will not destroy His covenant people but will redeem them (Isa. 41:14; Hos. 11:9).[26]

In Isaiah 6:6–7, we read, "Then flew one of the seraphims unto me, having a live coal in his hand, which he had taken with the tongs from off the altar: and he laid it upon my mouth, and said, Lo, this hath touched thy lips; and thine iniquity is taken away, and thy sin purged." Upon beholding the sovereign majesty and glorious holiness of God, and upon being penetrated to the core of his being with the light of God's purity, and crying out in abhorrence of sin, Isaiah receives three wonderful and astonishing *gracious* blessings.

The first is the pardon of his sin. "Thine iniquity is taken away." It is gone! Removed! This was free forgiveness by the sheer mercy

---

25. G. H. Kersten, *Reformed Dogmatics: A Systematic Treatment of Reformed Doctrine* (Sioux Center, Iowa: Netherlands Reformed Book and Publishing Committee), 1:86.

26. John Frame, *The Doctrine of God: A Theology of Lordship*, 2 (Phillipsburg, N.J.: P&R, 2002), 29.

and grace of God. Isaiah did not merit it, and he certainly did not deserve it. He didn't try to bribe God or coerce God's favor through self-concocted works of righteousness. He didn't promise to make amends; he didn't make a vow that he would try to do better in the future. He simply *confessed* and *received*. He deprecated himself and his sin and he had nowhere else to look but to God's pure grace. When you see God's holiness for what it is, you realize that all your works are as "filthy rags" (Isa. 64:6). You realize that you have the sentence of death in yourself, and you realize that your only hope is in the God who pardons by His sovereign mercy alone (Rom. 9:15).

Yet the meaning of the text goes deeper than that. When the seraph says to Isaiah, "Thy sin [is] purged," the Hebrew word that is used here, in the passive voice, can literally be rendered, "atoned for."[27] The word is associated with blood atonement in Numbers 35:33. You may be familiar with Leviticus 16, which speaks of the Day of Atonement. The Jews have a name for this even to this day. They call it Yom Kippur, the Day (*yom*) of Atonement (*kippur*). Our text has that same word in its verbal form. It is saying, Your sin is *atoned for*!

Now if we know anything about how atonement and pardon work, we know that the Bible teaches that the atonement for the life or soul of the sinner can only be accomplished through the shedding of blood. Leviticus 17:11 says, "For the life of the flesh is in the blood: and I have given it to you upon the altar to make atonement for your souls: for it is the blood that maketh an atonement for the soul." But where is the blood in Isaiah's vision?

The answer is in the symbolism of the burning coal. This was a coal from the altar of burnt offering. In the outer court of the temple, there was a bronze altar. And upon that altar, the priests of Israel would burn the animals that they had previously killed by letting out their blood. So, the altar burned with fire day and night; it was to never go out, symbolizing the blazing purity of the Lord, whose holiness is like an all-consuming fire (Deut. 4:24). The animals, after shedding their blood, would be burnt on this altar to make atonement

---

27. William L. Holladay, *A Concise Hebrew and Aramaic Lexicon of the Old Testament: Based upon the Lexical Work of Ludwig Koehler and Walter Baumgartner* (Grand Rapids: Eerdmans, 1988), 163.

every day. The fire of judgment would consume the victims as substitutes for the people, and the people would receive God's blessing and not be consumed with the fire of His wrath. The burning coal in Isaiah's vision is a prophetic symbol—it bears the symbolism and significance of the altar on which atonement was made. Alec Motyer comments, "The live coal thus encapsulates the ideas of atonement, propitiation, satisfaction, forgiveness, cleansing and reconciliation."[28] So when the coal is touched to Isaiah's lips, it is understood that all of this redemptive significance comes with it.

Isaiah's atonement ultimately did not come from the earthly temple altar, however, but from the heavenly altar in the heavenly temple. In his vision, he is seeing the archetypal temple in glory that the book of Hebrews describes (chapters 8–9). The temple on earth was but a picture of heavenly reality. It bore sacramental, symbolic significance of eternal salvation truths. The book of Hebrews tells us that the heavenly temple is all about Jesus Christ and His work of redemption. So, Isaiah's sin was atoned for ultimately by the One he wrote about—by the Suffering Servant led as a lamb to the slaughter, who was crushed for Isaiah's iniquities on the cross (Isaiah 53). Jesus Christ was consumed with the fire of God's fury and He went through hell on the cross to save us from the all-consuming fire of God's blazing holiness in eternity.

When Christ was forsaken by God upon the cross for our sins, He was especially conscious of God's holiness. In Psalm 22, which He quoted on the cross, after crying out, "My God, my God, why hast thou forsaken me?" the psalm follows that with the declaration, "But thou art holy" (v. 3). The eyes of the Holy One cannot look with favor upon iniquity (Hab. 1:12–13). Thomas Boston said, "There is nothing wherein the divine holiness and hatred of sin is so manifest as in the sufferings of his own dear Son. This was a greater demonstration thereof than if all men and angels had suffered for it eternally in hellfire."[29] Yet it was precisely God's holiness that evoked Christ's trust that God would faithfully save Him and all His people (Ps. 22:3–5).

---

28. J. Alec Motyer, *Isaiah: An Introduction and Commentary*, Tyndale Old Testament Commentaries, 20 (Downers Grove, Ill.: InterVarsity, 1993), 82.

29. Thomas Boston, *An Illustration of the Doctrines of the Christian Religion*, in

Christ's death satisfied God's holiness, for on the cross He "sanctified" (*hagiazō*) His people (Heb. 10:10, 14; 13:12). From beginning to end, Christ's obedient sufferings were engraved, as it were, with the words engraved on the golden plate of the high priest, "Holiness unto the LORD."

The second thing Isaiah received was cleansing, purging, purification. The coal symbolized the atonement made on the altar, but it was also a "live" coal, a *burning* coal. Fire purifies, and this symbolized the cleansing effect of God's grace in application. Isaiah 4:4 talks about purging away the filth of the daughters of Zion "by the spirit of judgment, and by the spirit of burning." In salvation, the Holy Spirit comes like a purifying fire of judgment upon our sin, purging our pollution and sanctifying us by the communication of His holiness to us so that we would live in holiness unto Him.

That is how salvation works, dear friends. It brings pardon and purification, justification and sanctification, forgiveness and cleansing. There is no forgiveness of sin without also experiencing cleansing from it. We cannot remain filthy and unclean as a people of unclean lips. God sanctifies our lips to His praise. He sanctifies our hearts to His devotion. He sanctifies our hands to His service. The proof that you've been justified is that you are being sanctified. Without evidence of sanctification in our lives, there is no reliable way to prove that we have been justified. To receive the benefits of Christ's justifying work is inseparable from receiving the grace of the Spirit's sanctifying influence.

God's moral and gracious holiness pervades the Trinity revealed in the gospel. Jesus Christ is "the Holy One and the Just" (Acts 3:14), who perfectly fulfilled God's law and deserved no punishment. We may trust Him entirely, for He is holy and true (Rev. 3:7). The name "Holy Spirit" sets the third person of the Trinity apart from every unclean spirit (Mark 3:29–30) and distinguishes Him as the divine agent to sanctify those people in whom He dwells so that they live for God's glory (1 Cor. 6:19–20). The gospel is a message of the triune

---

The Complete Works of the Late Rev. Thomas Boston, Ettrick, ed. Samuel McMillan (Stoke-on-Trent, U.K.: Tentmaker, 2002), 1:102–3.

God's holiness: holiness in judging sinners, holiness in redeeming sinners, and holiness in sanctifying sinners. How sweet, then, is the holiness of God when we encounter it through faith in Christ!

Finally, the third thing Isaiah received is the assurance of pardon. The seraph assures him that his "iniquity is taken away." He assures him of pardon and peace with God. God made Isaiah to know the joy of His salvation. The dread and despair left, and peace and assurance flooded his soul with a sense of relief. Gratitude for such a great salvation animated his resolve to offer himself as his Lord's servant. So Isaiah cried out, "Here am I! Send me!" When we realize how great and glorious salvation is, our gratitude moves us to offer ourselves as living sacrifices for the sake of His cause. When we see the holiness of God, not in despair but in faith, it fills us with zeal to join our song with the seraphim and to pray, "May the whole earth be full of Thy glory, Lord! I long to see that day, and I will do whatever I can to hasten that day!"

In Christ, the searing holiness of God has become our salvation. Although God remains a "consuming fire" who requires our "reverence and godly fear" (Heb. 12:28–29), by faith we may boldly "enter into the holiest by the blood of Jesus" (Heb. 10:19). The God who sent Christ to give eternal life to sinners is our "holy Father" (John 17:11). God's holiness guarantees His sworn promise that the kingdom of Christ, the Son of David, will not fail (Ps. 89:33–35). In swearing by His holiness, God has sworn by Himself, and He would cease to be God if He did not completely save those "who have fled for refuge" to this great High Priest (Heb. 6:13–20). In Jesus Christ, Christians can fulfill Psalm 99:5: "Exalt ye the Lord our God, and worship at his footstool; for he is holy." Yet their freedom to approach God's holy presence does not make Him any less holy, "for great is the Holy One of Israel in the midst of thee" (Isa. 12:6).

Dear friends, Isaiah's encounter with the Holy One was a paradigm for what God wanted the nation of Judah to experience. It is a paradigm for what He wants us all to experience as well—not through direct prophetic revelation, but through the illumination and application of the Spirit as we are exposed to the holiness of God in the Holy Scriptures.

Conclusion

The right human response to God's holiness is the fear of God. He is "glorious in holiness, fearful in praises" (Ex. 15:11). David prayed, "In thy fear will I worship toward thy holy temple" (Ps. 5:7). God's Word aims to move people to "fear this glorious and fearful name, THE LORD THY GOD" (Deut. 28:58), for "holy and reverend [awe-inspiring] is his name" (Ps. 111:9). This fear arises not merely from a dread of God's holy judgment but from an experience of God's holy salvation. The Lord said that when He restored Israel, "they shall sanctify my name, and sanctify the Holy One of Jacob, and shall fear the God of Israel" (Isa. 29:23). Bavinck said, "To sanctify him is to fear him."[30]

Sinful fear of God drives people away from Him, but godly fear of God attracts us to Him. The fear of God must beautify and vivify our theology. Too often, man distorts the doctrine of God to create a god in his own image. The result is a banal but comfortable theology for sinners—marked by doctrinal error and practical irreverence. Martin Luther said to Desiderius Erasmus, "Your thoughts of God are all too human."[31] Let us follow the Holy Scriptures to an awe-inspiring view of "the high and lofty One that inhabiteth eternity, whose name is Holy" (Isa. 57:15).

The general decline of godly fear among professing Christians today is directly related to an ignorance of God's holiness. John Murray said that the core of the fear of God is "the controlling sense of the majesty and holiness of God."[32] Wilhelmus à Brakel said that God's holiness is "the brightness of all His perfections," and God "reveals Himself as holy, in order that the heart of man may continually be filled with deep awe and reverence."[33] Mary's adoration of her Savior led her to say, "Holy is his name" (Luke 1:49). John Calvin commented, "The name of God is called *holy* because it is entitled to the

---

30. Bavinck, *Reformed Dogmatics*, 2:220.
31. Martin Luther, *The Bondage of the Will*, trans. Philip S. Watson in *Luther's Works*, ed. Helmut T. Lehmann, Volume 33: Career of the Reformer, ed. Philip S. Watson (Philadelphia: Fortress Press, 1958), 47.
32. John Murray, *Principles of Conduct: Aspects of Biblical Ethics* (Grand Rapids: Eerdmans, 1957), 237.
33. Brakel, *The Christian's Reasonable Service*, 1:121–22.

highest reverence; and whenever the name of God is mentioned, it ought immediately to remind us of his adorable majesty."[34]

We dare not neglect God's holiness or the reverence that it inspires, for the fear of God is essential to Christ-centered spirituality (Isa. 11:2–3; Acts 9:31). John Murray wrote, "The church walks in the fear of the Lord because the Spirit of Christ indwells, fills, directs, and rests upon the church and the Spirit of Christ is the Spirit of the fear of the Lord."[35] The fear of the Lord is the very life breath of God-centered obedience (Eccl. 12:13). It teaches us to value the smiles and frowns of God more than the smiles and frowns of people. It declares God to be big and people to be small. It is "a fountain of life," pouring out energy for the Christian to do his duty. Murray said, "The fear of God is the soul of godliness."[36] It esteems the smiles and frowns of God to be of greater value than the smiles and frowns of people.

Is your worship sluggish? Is your obedience half-hearted? Do you find yourself easily distracted by worldly desires and anxieties? Have you shrunk back from opportunities to speak up as a witness for the Lord? Seek a renewed sight of God's holiness in the Word. Pray, "Unite my heart to fear thy name" (Ps. 86:11). "Sanctify the LORD of hosts himself; and let him be your fear, and let him be your dread. And he shall be for a sanctuary" (Isa. 8:13–14). When by grace you honor God's holiness, you will find that His holiness is and will be your hiding place. Praise God for His majestic, moral, and gracious holiness!

---

34. John Calvin, *Commentary on a Harmony of the Evangelists, Matthew, Mark, and Luke*, trans. William Pringle, vol. 16, *Calvin's Commentaries* (1845; repr., Grand Rapids: Baker, 1996), 56 [on Luke 1:49], emphasis original.
35. Murray, *Principles of Conduct*, 230.
36. Murray, *Principles of Conduct*, 229.

Chapter 11

The Tenth Anniversary of 9/11: The Lord Questions Us

O generation, see ye the word of the LORD. Have I been a wilderness unto Israel? a land of darkness? wherefore say my people, We are lords; we will come no more unto thee?
—JEREMIAH 2:31

Our nation has experienced the Lord's hand of discipline. Ten years ago wicked men flew three large jet aircraft full of fuel into the World Trade Center in New York and the Pentagon in Virginia. A fourth plane aimed at a similar diabolical purpose but fell short, thanks to the sacrificial courage of its passengers and crew. Thousands of people died in these conflagrations. One of the greatest symbols of our nation's financial prosperity fell to the ground in a heap of dust and wreckage. The very headquarters of our armed forces was pierced and ignited in flame. We were stunned, shocked, horrified, and scarcely knew what to do. We had perceived ourselves as untouchable, shielded by two wide oceans and the might of our military from such dangers. But after September 11, 2001, we could never feel untouchable again. While God viewed the actions of these terrorists with hatred and detestation, nevertheless we remember Lamentations 3:37–38, "Who is he that saith, and it cometh to pass, when the Lord commandeth it not? Out of the mouth of the most High proceedeth not evil and good?" Yes, both good and evil are ordained by the Most High. These evil men could not have accomplished anything unless the Lord had decreed it in His righteousness and wisdom.

But this is not all. Six years ago in early September, the people of Mississippi and Louisiana were starting to pick up the pieces after the devastation of Hurricane Katrina (August 2005). Much of the city of New Orleans was under water. Refugees streamed north and west, desperately seeking shelter and aid. Many trace this disaster to human hands, and no doubt human wickedness and incompetency greatly aggravated the situation. But again we remember from the Scriptures that God rules over life and death. Psalm 107:25 reminds us that the winds and the waves of the sea still obey His voice, "For he commandeth, and raiseth the stormy wind, which lifteth up the waves thereof." Katrina did what God ordained for it to do.

Three years ago, the housing bubble collapsed (August 2008) and the value of the real estate market fell dramatically. Banks and lenders staggered under the defaults of millions of homeowners, and massive bailouts by the federal government have not renewed the economy. Unemployment is at about nine percent. The national debt is ballooning at an alarming rate. Again, we could trace these effects to human greed and foolishness. But over all is the hand of the Lord. Moses warned Israel in Deuteronomy 8, "Lest when thou hast eaten and art full, and hast built goodly houses, and dwelt therein; and when thy herds and thy flocks multiply, and thy silver and thy gold is multiplied, and all that thou hast is multiplied; then thine heart be lifted up, and thou forget the LORD thy God...and thou say in thine heart, My power and the might of mine hand hath gotten me this wealth. But thou shalt remember the LORD thy God: for it is he that giveth thee power to get wealth" (vv. 12–14, 17–18).

Why does God send such judgments upon the land? Our Lord Jesus explained that disasters call each of us to repentance. Luke 13:2–5 says, "And Jesus answering said unto them, Suppose ye that these Galilaeans were sinners above all the Galilaeans, because they suffered such things? I tell you, Nay: but, except ye repent, ye shall all likewise perish. Or those eighteen, upon whom the tower in Siloam fell, and slew them, think ye that they were sinners above all men that dwelt in Jerusalem? I tell you, Nay: but, except ye repent, ye shall all likewise perish."

We dare not look down upon New York City, Washington DC, or New Orleans, and say, "We thank Thee, Lord, that we are not sinners like these men whom Thou hast judged." God forbid! These disasters call to each of us, especially to the visible church, "Repent, repent!" These are but the lightest touches of the Day of the Lord upon our world. What will it be when the hammer of divine justice falls? When the towers fell, the United States of America should have fallen to its knees in true repentance for its national and individual sins.

But did we fall down? Well, there was a brief surge in church attendance and prayer. No doubt some individuals turned from sin to Christ, by the drawing power of the Father. But where is the fruit of repentance in our society as a whole? Our national culture has accelerated in its downward plunge into immorality and false teaching.

Perhaps most abominable in the eyes of God is the condition of His own church in our land. Prayerlessness reduces our impact to an anemic shadow of what it might be. Millions build their assurance on the sands of easy-believism, claiming salvation without repentance. Pluralism, relativism, and so-called "tolerance" have made us gutless, spineless, and voiceless in the face of great errors and evils. Family worship and the catechizing of our children are neglected in some circles, and practically forgotten in others. Doctrine is either ignored as irrelevant and divisive, or idolized by dead orthodoxy without a matching experience of the glory of God. False teaching for which our forefathers would not have given the time of day now abounds as a popular alternative within evangelical Protestantism. Public worship has become the playground of fallen man's imagination where anything that attracts a crowd is legitimate, instead of a reverent and glad submission to bring to the King all and only what He commands in Scripture. Submission to proper authority in the home, the church, the school, and the community is scorned as outdated and oppressive instead of the law of liberty.

In sum, American religion is a paper-thin veneer of faith barely covering the American idols of materialism, hedonism, secular humanism, and religious pluralism. The church drinks up worldliness like water, claiming it can act like the world but still follow the One whom the world crucified. All around are prophets proclaiming, "Peace, peace," and claiming, "The temple of the Lord, the temple of the Lord," while God's glory withdraws and His judgment draws near.

To be sure, there are renewal movements and pockets of faithfulness among American churches. We are grateful for the resurgence of Reformed doctrine and the call in some circles for a deeper experience of the joy and fear of the Lord. But even among the faithful, we grieve that God's glory elicits so little love from our hearts, our neighbors' needs provoke so little compassion, and sin so easily lulls us into complacency. Too often we walk with Christ as if slogging through waist-deep snow in bitter cold, hardly making progress and feeling dangerously sleepy. We know that we need repentance, but we scarcely even pray for it.

It is precisely in this situation that the prophet Jeremiah speaks so powerfully to the American church. Jeremiah ministered in the last decades of the kingdom of Judah. God's covenant people had already seen the northern kingdom of Israel wiped away by Assyria. The throne of David's seed had survived the Assyrian incursions, but now Babylon had arisen as the regional superpower. Again and again the Lord chastised His people through the hands of men. But they would not hear the prophets. Indeed, they hated the true preachers of God's Word. They were satisfied with an outward form of religion as long as they could live as they pleased. So the Lord exclaimed against them in Jeremiah 2:30, "In vain have I smitten your children; they received no correction: your own sword hath devoured your prophets, like a destroying lion." All the discipline, all the prophetic warnings—but where was the repentance?

Judgment begins in the house of the Lord (1 Peter 4:17). Yet it is a judgment designed by mercy. Just as He did with Adam in the garden, before coming to pronounce the curse upon sin, the Lord comes to us with questions, searching questions. He seeks the lost. When Jeremiah prophesied, he did so with weeping, sighing, and suffering—a picture of our Prophet Jesus in His compassionate calling of sinners to repentance. In Jeremiah 2:31 we see that *the Lord questions His church for her lack of repentance*. As we consider verse 31 we see two questions—one that is humiliating and one that is revealing.

1. The Lord Asks Us a Humiliating Question

The Lord came so plainly and simply to Israel, using pictures of the common things from ordinary life. He desires to speak to us plainly and simply today. God says, "Have I been a wilderness unto Israel? a land of darkness?"

A wilderness is a barren place full of dangers. Lions prowl seeking prey, and pits wait for the unwary traveler to slip and fall to his death. The wilderness is the place of banishment, away from friends. It is an uncultivated and unfruitful place. Darkness even today can stir our fears, even if we are inside our homes with a light switch at our fingertips. For Israel, darkness was a time of real danger. It was the time when the wild animals hunted and killed. Crimes are most often committed in darkness.

Therefore the Lord asks us, "Have I been such a God to you? Have I withheld light and life from you? Have I done nothing for you? Have you invested your time and energy into Me and found Me to be unfruitful?"

One glance at the history of Israel shows how untrue this is. God multiplied the Israelites in Egypt until they were a mighty people. He showed His wonders and miracles. He preserved them from death by the blood of the Passover lamb. He led them out through the Red Sea with a mighty hand, treading the floor of the sea as on dry ground though no man had ever walked on it before. He brought them forth loaded with the riches of Egypt, gold and silver and beautiful cloth. Even when they journeyed long in the wilderness, God was not a wilderness to them but provided them their daily bread and saw to it that their clothing did not wear out. He made the bitter waters sweet and drew out water from the rock so they could drink in abundance.

The Lord God led them into the land of Canaan. He toppled the walls of Jericho. He gave the kings and armies of the land into their hands. Even when they proved unfaithful He heard their cries and gave them judges. When they did not want judges but wanted a king, He gave them kings. He bore with them patiently but they hardened their hearts against Him. When they turned to other gods, He remembered His covenant with David. Even when God chastised them and warned them, He did it for their good, that He might bless them if they repented.

So the Lord said to them in all righteousness, "Tell me, O Israel, how have I wronged you? How have I failed you? Have I not followed you all your days with goodness?" As He said in Micah 6:3, "O my people, what have I done unto thee? and wherein have I wearied thee? testify against me."

How much more does this question ring in our ears now that Christ has come in the flesh and made atonement for sin. Did God wrong us by making a covenant from all eternity to save those who sinned against Him? Was God stingy when He gave His only begotten Son, so that whoever believes in Him should not perish but have eternal life? Did Christ turn His back on us when He gave His back to the whip and the scourge, then carried on His back the cruel cross? Indeed the cross was a light burden compared to the spiritual weight that Christ needed to bear. Isaiah 53:6 says, "The LORD hath laid on him the iniquity of us all." Galatians 3:13 teaches us that Christ bore the very curse of the living God so that His elect people would get the blessing. Has God failed us by providing a full and rich salvation in Christ, sufficient to save the chief of sinners? Do we have any right to complain against God? Do we have any justification for not turning to Him with all our hearts?

The Lord asks this question of us, as well. Look back as far as you can. Look back to the beginning of our nation. When those early colonists arrived in New England, did not God preserve them through great famines and dangers? Has He not granted us over the years an abundance of harvests to feed our bodies, while other nations have suffered terrible famines? God's blessings have rested in such abundance upon our land that millions of people made the arduous journey to immigrate here from their homelands, including our own forefathers.

Hasn't the Lord also provided food for our souls? Many of the first fathers of our land came with Bibles under their arms and ministers at their sides. While so many nations toiled in spiritual darkness, did not God grant this nation the truth of His Word from its very inception in the preaching of men like John Cotton, Thomas Hooker, and Thomas Shepard? When our dullness threatened to engulf the land in darkness, did not God send the light again through the preaching of men like Theodorus Frelinghuysen, Jonathan Edwards, and George Whitefield? Has not the Lord preserved in this nation His truth through faithful men like Charles Hodge, B. B. Warfield, and even many today? Surely we can say of the American church what the Lord said of Israel in Isaiah 5:4, "What could have been done more to my vineyard, that I have not done in it? wherefore, when I looked that it should bring forth grapes, brought it forth wild grapes?"

Look back in your own life too. From the moment you were conceived, God cared for you. He formed you in your mother's womb. Has the Lord not provided food and clothing for you all your life? Whatever education you received, was it not His gift to you? Has not the Lord provided for the education of your soul? While multitudes perish in their sins without knowledge of salvation in Christ alone by grace alone, you are privileged to hear the call of the gospel. In Isaiah 45:19 God says, "I have not spoken in secret, in a dark place of the earth: I said not unto the seed of Jacob, Seek ye me in vain: I the LORD speak righteousness, I declare things that are right." Furthermore, is it not a singular grace of God that you worship in a church that preaches Reformed experiential truth, the riches of Christ for us and the riches of His Spirit in us?

The Lord says, "Have I been a wilderness unto Israel? a land of darkness?" No, no, a thousand times no! God has been a garden of delicious fruit for us, and a land full of light.

But now, if that is true, the Lord asks, then why does not your gratitude answer to My mercies? Why do you treat Me as if I were a wilderness and land of darkness? Why do you not seek Me earnestly in prayer? Why do you not seek Me in the keeping of My commands? The Lord demands an answer. If I am no wilderness to you, then why have you been a wilderness to Me? Why do you give more of your time and more of your heart to the idols of this world—which profit nothing—than to using the means of grace to draw near to Me? Why do you not desire Me, desire to know Me, or desire to have My wisdom and salvation? Though I have planted among you the seed of My Word, why do you not produce the fruit of righteousness for My pleasure?

The Lord questions His church for her lack of repentance. What answer will you give to the Lord? It is not a mere man who asks you this question. It is not your neighbor. It is the Word of the Lord, the voice of God addressing your heart. What answer do you give to the Lord in the secret place of your heart?

This is a humiliating question. It aims at the humiliation of our souls. When God says, "Have I been a wilderness unto Israel? a land of darkness?" the question presses us to see that we have no excuse for the way we have forgotten the Lord. It's not His fault. He has multiplied His blessings, His words, and His warnings to us. There is nothing else to do but to humble ourselves to the dust and say, "It is I, O Lord. I am the problem. I am the sinner." Like Nehemiah, we must review all the disasters which God has brought upon us and still confess, "Howbeit thou art just in all that is brought upon us; for thou hast done right, but we have done wickedly" (Neh. 9:33).

We must say, "Thou hast sent the light, but I turned mine eyes away. Thou hast granted water, but I refused to drink. Thou hast told me to call Thy Sabbath a delight, but I have counted it a wearisome thing to worship Thee. Thou hast commanded me to speak of Thee to my friends, but I have hidden Thee like an object of shame. Thou hast called me to Thyself, the fountain of living water, but I have clung to broken cisterns which cannot hold water. O my idols! O my wicked trust in man! O God, have mercy on this stubborn sinner!"

But God not only asks a humiliating question. There is another question which Jeremiah records, another question which searches our hearts yet deeper.

2. The Lord Asks a Revealing Question

The Lord will become more specific. This is His way. He desires to pinpoint the exact problem. This is always what He does through His prophets. It is not sufficient to know that we have sinned in a general way. The prophets addressed specific sins. This is what made people hate them. When we deal with sin in a general way, it is easy for us to look at others. So God brings it home to us. Dear congregation, when will we ever look at ourselves?

The Lord says in Jeremiah 2:31, "Wherefore say my people, We are lords; we will come no more unto thee?" "We are lords," literally, "we reign." Here is the problem: pride—spiritual pride. We insist on being lords, masters, rulers of our own affairs. Our hearts say, "We will not bow before Thee. We will make it if we do it ourselves. Life is better our way. We will take all Thy blessings, but we refuse to bow before Thee."

What sad and proud language! It is the language of the fallen children of Adam. It is the language which springs from the mouth of Satan, "Ye shall be as gods" (Gen. 3:5). Instead of our rightful place under God, we chose and still choose daily to be above God. We would take God off the throne and put ourselves on it. Indeed, we foolishly insist that we are already on the throne. "We are lords." The word can be translated, "We have broken loose," or, "We are free." This is exactly what we thought we were doing in the garden when we broke God's law. As Rev. Fraanje said, Satan wrote "independence" above the gate leading out of Paradise. In the secrecy of our hearts, fallen man breathes the same spirit as William Henley, who wrote defiantly:

> It matters not how strait the gate,
> How charged with punishments the scroll,
> I am the master of my fate:
> I am the captain of my soul.

And so rather than accept the laws which God puts upon us, we would claim to be nothing less than the "I Am," declaring, "I will be what I will to be." We ignore our callings to be faithful children and faithful parents, faithful church members and faithful office-bearers, faithful citizens and faithful governors. We act as though we have the right to define our own destiny regardless of what God says or does. We throw His warnings to the side and go on blindly in our own ways. "We are lords."

Israel always lived in the midst of enemies, the nations surrounding them. But do you know who their greatest enemy was? The greatest danger they faced was themselves: the enemy within, the heart of fallen man. "We are lords. Who is the Lord that I should obey Him? Who is Christ? Let us break their bands asunder, and cast away their cords from us. Who is this Shepherd? We all like sheep will go our own way."

Such is the idle boast of us all by nature. But oh, what a serious question this is because none can escape God's control or God's judgment. "Wherefore say my people, We are lords?" Why do men say this, when there is only one Lord? Every knee will bow to Him. Everyone shall give an account to Him for what they have done. He is our only hope, the only Judge and only Savior. The Lord says in Hosea 13:9, "O Israel, thou hast destroyed thyself; but in me is thine help." He calls out in Isaiah 45:22, "Look unto me, and be ye saved, all the ends of the earth: for I am God, and there is none else."

But Israel would not. They would trust in their own prosperity and resources. Deuteronomy 32:15 says, "But Jeshurun waxed fat, and kicked: thou art waxen fat, thou art grown thick, thou art covered with fatness; then he forsook God which made him, and lightly esteemed the Rock of his salvation." They would trust in Egypt or Assyria—anyone but the Lord. Isaiah 31:1 says, "Woe to them that go down to Egypt for help; and stay on horses, and trust in chariots, because they are many; and in horsemen, because they are very strong; but they look not unto the Holy One of Israel, neither seek the LORD!" We too are determined to find our help in the strength of man, and so resolved to fight against the Lord. We know it from our own experience. The Lord is the last place we are prone to go. Many of us know that the things we are doing are wrong but we refuse to give in. We refuse to bow down. We hug our sins. We fight against the Lord. Why? Because we say, "We are lords."

We have chosen the most dangerous fight. The Lord can destroy us in a single moment. The Lord can also give us up to our own lordship, give us up to what we desire. He can remove His gracious restraints and let us run headlong toward our sinful desires. That would be the most terrifying punishment of all.

Notice too in this question the sobering words "my people": "Wherefore say my people, We are lords?" The Lord is not asking this question of the pagans, the heathen who openly worship other gods. The Lord asks this question of the visible church, those who outwardly separate themselves from the world and are marked by the sacraments. They have been brought up in the truth. They know something about the way of salvation. But to them too God says, "Why do they say, We are lords?" God is probing His church, revealing the deep roots of pride underneath our refusal to repent.

Then come the awful words, "We will come no more to thee." What does this mean, for God's visible people to come to the Lord? It is written in 2 Chronicles 7:14, "If my people, which are called by my name, shall humble themselves, and pray, and seek my face, and turn from their wicked ways; then will I hear from heaven, and will forgive their sin, and will heal their land." So this coming involves first humbling ourselves for our sins, confessing sin, grieving over sin, bowing before God's just punishment of our sin. Second, we come to the Lord through seeking His grace in private and public worship, crying out for mercy with an eye upon His promises and atonement for sin in Christ. Prayer is the panting of faith after mercy. Third, we come to the Lord through true repentance, turning from our wicked thoughts, words, and deeds and returning to the Lord as our Lord. This is the threefold work of the Holy Spirit.

How tragic then these words, "We will come no more to thee." We will not humble ourselves for our sins. We will not pursue grace in faith. We will not repent of our wickedness. Perhaps such people will go through the outward motions of piety, but they will merely honor God with their lips while their hearts are far from Him.

How these words will ring in the ears of the damned: "We will come no more to thee," no more, no more! How about *you*? Will you, too, choose to be forever separated from the Lord? Will you choose to serve His archenemy forever? Remember, in rejecting the prophet of the Lord you reject the Word of the Lord, and in rejecting the Word you reject the Lord Himself. How can we embrace the Lord while we insist on being lords ourselves?

This is the ultimate motivation behind our stubborn refusal to repent. It is not that sin satisfies us. Sin against God cannot satisfy anyone created by God in the image of God. It is not that God's terms of submission are unreasonable. They are most gracious and kind. The deepest reason why we refuse to turn back to God is that in our hearts we say, "We are lords," and therefore, "We will come no more to thee." If the church is ever going to move beyond a superficial repentance, it must come to grips with our insistent demand to be lords.

The Lord questions His church for her lack of repentance. God's humiliating question leads us to acknowledge that He is not the problem. We are the problem. God's revealing question shows us the heart of the problem: we think we are lords, so we will not come to Him—indeed, we *cannot* come to Him apart from His drawing grace. May God grant that we may feel our own lordship as a painful, crushing burden. May the Spirit move us so that we cry out to the Lord Jesus to save us from our own lordship.

Conclusion: See the Word of the Lord

As people visit the 9/11 Memorial in New York, and stand looking at the waterfalls and pools located where the bases of the Twin Towers once stood, many questions will no doubt flood their minds. Some of those questions will be directed to God. What we need to realize is that ten years after 9/11, God has questions for us. After such a massive reminder of our vulnerability and mortality, why haven't we repented? Why hasn't the spiritual condition of the American church evidenced a dramatic turn-around? Why haven't we received correction? Has God been a wilderness to the church? Why do we, His professing people, say in our hearts that we are lords, when in fact we are poor and blind and naked? Why don't we come to Him for the gold and eye-salve and white garments of Christ?

The Lord Jesus has been knocking on the door of His church. Sometimes His knocks are quiet and subtle. Sometimes they make the ground shake. But we fear that by-and-large in the United States the doors of the churches remain closed to their Lord. It would be just for the glory of the Lord to depart from His temple, leaving behind the empty shell of an outward form of religion without the power. Christ could very well send a famine to our land, not a famine of bread or water, but a famine of hearing the Word of the Lord, so that people might wander from the East Coast to the West Coast seeking the Word of the Lord, but not finding it (Amos 8:11).

Our nation is ripe for judgment. These events of 9/11 and Hurricane Katrina and our economic woes caused much suffering, but they cannot begin to compare to the judgment which our nation deserves. We do not know how long the door of the ark will remain open before the Lord shuts it and the floods of God's wrath wash away all who remain outside.

By the mercy and longsuffering of God, we are not there yet. God's voice is still heard in our nation. Jeremiah 2:31 begins, "O generation, see ye the word of the LORD." Though God's humiliating and revealing questions should cause us to despair in ourselves, the very fact that God is speaking to us should move us to hope in the Lord.

"O generation, *see* ye the word of the Lord." You have heard the word often enough. But do you see it? In other words, have you taken it to heart so that it has become as real to you as what you see with your eyes? Do you see and embrace by faith the merciful Redeemer, the suffering Savior, the exalted Lord, as your Redeemer, your Savior, your Lord? Do you see everything you need in God's living Word, the Lord Jesus Christ—in His humiliation to pay for your sins; in His perfect obedience to the law, to earn you the right to eternal life? Do you see in His person and states and offices everything you need for this life and a better future life? "O generation, *see—see ye—by faith*—the Word, the living Word of the Lord—in the person of Jesus Christ."

God is still warning us of our sins and pride. God is still inviting us and calling us to repent. But is it to you nothing more than a fantasy, like an interesting story or entertaining song that you hear but makes no impact on your life? Or has it gripped you with a conviction of the reality of God, the reality of sin, the reality of Christ, the reality of heaven and hell? Psalm 95:7–8 warns, "Today if ye will hear his voice, harden not your heart." Rev. G. H. Kersten said, "Oh that the Lord's complaints of love might yet break your heart and you might learn to make supplication to your Judge while it is still called today."

People of God, we have heard the Lord asking us humiliating questions and revealing questions, but we must remember that these are merciful questions. They are indeed the complaints of love, the calls of love, and the convictions of love. Let His love draw you to Jesus Christ, crying, "Thou art a garden of delights. I have been a wilderness. Thou art light. I have been a land of darkness. Thou art the only Lord. I have pretended to be lord. Thou art my only hope. But I have refused to come to Thee. But now, O Lord, have mercy upon me. Make me a fruitful branch on the vine of Christ. Make me a glowing light by the illumination of Thy Spirit. Take me as Thine own, demolish my petty throne, and establish Thy throne in my heart. Draw me to Christ, and I will come, and—joy of joys—He will certainly not cast out any who come to Him."

Chapter 12

Our Nation Laid in the Balances
NATIONAL DAY OF PRAYER

Shall I not visit them for these things? saith the L*ORD*:
shall not my soul be avenged on such a nation as this?
—JEREMIAH 9:9

Dear congregation, it is good that we have an opportunity to come together for an annual National Day of Prayer service. Today we are called to consider the moral and spiritual fiber of our nation and of ourselves as citizens who either contribute to or detract from the well-being of our country. When we are called upon to examine our nation in the light of Scripture, we shall find, as you well know, that as a people we are laid in the balances and found wanting. Moreover, we must bear in mind that we are not mere spectators looking upon this nation. Every sin which cripples this land has its beginning in our natural, corrupt, fallen hearts. We are involved; we are part of the problem. And only by grace can we ever become part of the solution.

Our nation is at a critical juncture. We are on the verge of spiritual, moral, and financial collapse. Only the intervening grace of God can help us and deliver us, and so we turn to the living God as our only hope. We want to consider not only the plague that is upon us, but also the only cure of that dreadful plague.

With God's help, we will consider:

Our Nation Laid in the Balances
1. The sad condition of our nation
2. The impending judgment upon our nation
3. The only hope for our nation

1. The Sad Condition of Our Nation

In English grammar there is such a thing that we call a *rhetorical question*. A rhetorical question is a question one asks that does not need an answer because the question *implies* the answer. Our text is a rhetorical question. Jeremiah has listed in eight or nine verses the great and gross sins of the people of Israel. The conclusion can only be judgment if there is no national repentance. So when the Lord asks this question in our text, we do not need to wonder what the answer is. The answer is in the question: "Shall not my soul be avenged on such a nation as this?"

God says as it were "This nation—the nation that I have delivered from Egypt with an outstretched arm; the nation for whom I have divided the Red Sea and led them through the wilderness by a cloud and a pillar of fire; this nation that I fed with manna and gave water from a rock to drink, and planted in a good land; this nation that has often rebelled and I have been merciful again and again to them; this nation which is now worshiping Baalim—shall I not be avenged upon such a nation as this?"

God fulfilled this rhetorical question. Israel did not listen to Jeremiah. She filled her cup of iniquity and God sent Nebuchadnezzar to conquer the land, to destroy the temple and city of Jerusalem. The temple was burned, the land was desolate, and most of the citizens were killed. Survivors were led as captives to a distant land. God was avenged of such a nation as this.

We must consider, dear congregation, that the parallels that our nation has with Old Testament Israel are both striking and disturbing. We are also a highly favored nation. Even today we are the envy of most nations, but like Israel, we are a sinful, ungrateful, immoral people in the midst of prosperity. We are an ungodly people despite the godly roots our forefathers have established when they landed on the shores of this nation. They wrote in their *Mayflower Compact*: "The primary purpose of settling in this new land is for the glory of God and the advancement of the Christian faith." Should we not be filled with both sorrow and joy today—joy that we had such a rich beginning; sorrow over where we are at now? Today, we have judges who have decided that the Ten Commandments cannot be placed on the classroom walls of a public school because some children might be offended by their contents. We have caved to pluralism; we have surrendered our Christian moorings so that most historians now speak of our age as post-Christian America.

Things have gone from bad to worse. Our beginnings were good. Godly laymen like John Winthrop, as well as godly preachers like Thomas Shepard, Thomas Hooker, John Cotton, Peter Bulkeley, and Thomas Cobbett had a great impact on the morality of the people. It was not long, however, before the so-called "Enlightenment" blew over from France and took deep root in this land. It gave birth to humanism; humanism in turn fostered pluralism and pragmatism, such that God, His law, and His Word are excluded from the classroom and the courtroom.

Today we have the full outgrowth of secular humanism. Morality is at an all time low. I read only yesterday that sixty-two percent of children born to black women are illegitimate. Thirty years ago it was twenty-one percent. It has tripled in just thirty years. But the same article said that among white women thirty years ago, illegitimacy was at seven percent, but today it is at twenty-one percent—also a triple jump. Among whites it is exactly where it was at thirty years ago among blacks. If immorality continues to proceed at this pace, most children born in this country will be born illegitimately. Financially, our nation is a disaster. We are tens of trillions of dollars in debt.

Spiritually, we are faring no better. A few weeks ago, when I was flying out to Iowa, I happened to sit next to a minister who is involved in Reformed radio ministry. He told me that there were sixteen thousand "Christian" radio stations in North America, of which less than one hundred ever present anything which resembles the Reformed faith. The vast majority of them proclaim one form of Arminianism or another. So this nation is being inundated with Arminianism—man can accept Jesus; man has a free will. Arminianism was practically foreign to our soil until the 1820s, when Charles Finney arrived on the scene and developed a man-structured, man-organized revivalism. Since that day, America has no longer seen any major Spirit-filled revivals. The 1730s, 1740s, and the early 1800s, sometimes called the First and Second Awakenings, were the bright spots, but they all happened in the context of Calvinism, not Arminianism. The greatest missionaries of this land's history and the greatest fruits upon preaching have been the result of solid, biblical, Calvinistic exposition, not Arminian exposition. What does that say to us? Well, that says that there is a tremendous burden resting upon all of us; a tremendous responsibility to swim against the stream and to declare a God of sovereign grace. We desperately need biblical Calvinistic preachers in this land to proclaim to young and old through preaching, the printed word, and on radio, that God is the living God, that man is depraved, but that God is able and willing to save the greatest of sinners out of free and sovereign grace.

The consequences of the baby holocaust we call abortion will come back to haunt us, if the Lord tarries. Soon there will be more older people who need help than we know how to cope with, and not enough young ones to care for them, and it will be our own fault. And yet we go on. God shouts with a megaphone through a variety of national judgments, and yet we continue to rush headlong into sin. We have become a national Sodom and Gomorrah. We go on flirting with euthanasia. We go on blatantly in Sabbath desecration, pursuing our own desires on the Lord's Day. In the last decade, for the first time in the history of America, the majority of our citizens no longer attend any church on a regular basis. God's Word is joked about, even among people who name the name of Christ. Worldliness abounds in the lust of the eyes, the lust of the flesh, and the pride of life.

We have lost our sense of scriptural integrity. We submit to no authority. The means of grace are abandoned; religious duties are neglected; prayer is something done for a few minutes a day at best. Ninety-six percent of Americans today are convinced that they will not go to hell.

We are a nation just like Israel. We are living in the midst of deceit. We are deceiving ourselves financially, morally, and spiritually. We are saying to ourselves, "Peace, peace, when there is no peace."

Where are the fathers who are busy instructing their children in the Scriptures? Where are the homes that engage in daily, conscientious family worship? Where are the people, even in our midst, who genuinely wrestle in the inner closet for our nation? So much is disappearing. Our own congregations have seen encouraging increases of spiritual life on the one hand, but discouraging developments on the other—discouraging when some take their Christianity so lightly, and do not live it out in daily life; discouraging when our talk and our dress and our walk do not reflect the sobriety with which God's Word calls us to walk through this Mesech here below; discouraging when some among us continue to persist in habitually involving themselves in various forms of ungodly entertainment.

Today, Christianity by-and-large has baptized itself into materialism and humanism and "selfism." Many do not come to church as a family any more. They do not grieve with those who grieve, nor rejoice with those who rejoice, but they come to church saying, "What's in it for *me*?" There is little bearing of each others' burdens, whereby we fulfill the law of Christ. Christianity in America today is three thousand miles wide, fifteen hundred miles high, but only one inch deep. We are shallow, we are backslidden, and God can say of us as citizens of this nation: "Hear, O heavens, and give ear, O earth: for the LORD hath spoken, I have nourished and brought up my children, and they have rebelled against me. The ox knows his owner, and the ass his master's crib: but Israel doth not know, my people doth not consider. Ah sinful nation, a people laden with iniquity, a seed of evildoers, children that are corrupters: they have forsaken the LORD, they have provoked the Holy One of Israel to anger, they are gone away backward. Why should ye be stricken any more? ye will revolt more and more: the whole head is sick, and the whole heart is faint" (Isa. 1:2–5).

2. Impending Judgment for our Nation

Decay is everywhere; we have forgotten the Lord God. Why should not the Lord be avenged on such a nation as ours? Is it not a rhetorical question? Is not the Lord already on His way with divine judgment? God's patience will come to an end. Ecclesiastes 8:11 says, "Because sentence against an evil work is not executed speedily, therefore the heart of the sons of men is fully set in them to do evil." That is the picture of our nation, but it will not be its picture much longer because we are destroying ourselves. The pattern of nations almost always follows a fivestep process. There is the *infancy* time where the nation bands together in organization; then there is the *growth* period; then the time of *maturity and prosperity*; then the time of *decay*; and finally the time of *destruction*. That was the pattern of the world's mighty empires—Assyria, Persia, Macedonia, and Rome. Our nation appears to be at the end of the fourth step. We do not need to be prophets to observe that; it is obvious. We are filled with decay, we are on the verge of destruction, and the Lord is asking in our text for us to lay before ourselves this question: "How shall I spare you for your sins, United States of America? Would it be consistent with the nature and the glory of My Name and My government to spare such a nation? Do not the holiness of My nature, the honor of My government, the rectitude of My law, and the truth of My Word compel Me to destroy such a nation as this?" Ought not every mouth in the United States of America—yours and mine also—be stopped, and the whole country be united in declaring that God would be righteous and just to abandon us altogether, to destroy us as a people, to let all the crops rot in the field this year, and to let us have our financial, moral, and spiritual debts collapse upon our heads? We have asked for divine destruction.

Perhaps you ask: Is there then no hope? There is no hope in this nation nor in ourselves—only in the grace of God.

3. The Only Hope for our Nation

We have squandered our rich heritage, we have spoiled what our forebears have striven for, and now we must say in the words of Lamentations 5:16, "The crown is fallen from our head: woe unto us, that we have sinned!" We have turned our backs to God and clouds of darkness hang above us. Everything seems to be on the verge of collapse; the future seems to be hopeless. And if you look at our text, that is what you must think.

Is there then nothing in our text that gives any hope? Look again, congregation. "Shall I not visit them for these things? saith the LORD." Notice that God uses His covenant name Yahweh, the special name of the living God who will remain faithful and true to His covenant. There is still hope. Our only hope is in the name of the Almighty God, that God who still says to us as we are about to slip into destruction, "Only acknowledge your iniquities and turn back to the Lord your

God for I will yet have mercy upon you." I am convinced, congregation, that if this nation would cry mightily to God as we read in 2 Chronicles 7:14, repent of our sins, take upon ourselves moral and financial and spiritual responsibility, and beg for mercy, that this land could yet be restored. It is our fault, but there is hope *in the Lord God*, in His covenant name, the LORD. There is hope if God visits us with covenantal judgments; there is hope if He visits us with covenantal mercies; there is hope as long as that covenant-keeping God does not stop dealing altogether with such a nation as we are. That is what God said to Israel in Deuteronomy, did He not? He said as it were: The greatest punishment that I can ever bring upon you as a people or as a nation is when I stop sending you both My mercies and My judgments, and leave you to yourselves. The greatest judgment that God can bring upon a nation is to stop visiting that nation. Will God stop visiting us altogether this year? Next year? Are His present judgments an open testimony that He is giving us one or two final calls to repent, and then He will let us be? "Turn ye, turn ye, O house of Israel—oh congregation, oh America—for why will ye die?"

Dear friend, it is a serious thing to be a human being; a serious thing to have a soul; to have time on our hands; to be journeying to eternity—especially to be journeying to eternity without our sins having been washed away by the blood of Jesus Christ. If our sins are not washed away, I tremble to say it but I must say it, then we are but adding to the large debt of national sin! Oh, I call to you in the name of God, repent, sinner, before the vengeance of God descends upon you and your family as well. Hear the call of God before it is too late. You must be born again!

But there is still hope! Hope for the unsaved? Yes. In what? In God, in the overtures of His gospel grace, and in His open declarations that He is willing to save lost sinners! It is not man's word that says, "Seek ye the Lord," but it is God's Word! God says, "Seek *ye* the LORD while he may be found, call *ye* upon him (not just God's people) while he is near: let the wicked forsake his way, and the unrighteous man his thoughts: and let him *return* unto the LORD, and he will have mercy upon him; and to our God, for he will abundantly pardon" (Isa. 55:6–7). What we need today is national repentance; we need thousands upon thousands to bow in individual repentance in their own homes. We need fathers to call their children to repentance. We need mothers to bow in the dust in the presence of Almighty God. We need husbands and wives to repent before God together in secret and individually. We need children to call out to God, "O God be merciful to me a sinner."

The solution to all our problems lies only in the God of grace granting true and godly repentance. Our duty is to get on our knees like the people of Nineveh, to believe that the time is short and that judgment is ripe, and to put our hope in the Lord God. The prayers of God's people can only stay the hand of God so long. There came a time when there were not enough petitioners in Sodom and Gomorrah to keep back the judgment. And God said in Jeremiah 15:1, "Then said the LORD unto me, Though Moses and Samuel stood before me, yet my mind could not be toward this people: cast them out of my sight, and let them go forth." Is that day coming, when intercessors like Moses and Samuel in this land—those who are still interceding between the porch and the temple for Almighty God and for the glory of His Name in the midst of this nation, become so few and far between and the population so large that God would say, "I will not spare this nation any more"? God calls us to pray to Him as the almighty, faithful, covenant-keeping God.

What must we then pray for? We must pray in the first place that God may send godly preachers, for not only does judgment begin at the house of God, but revival also begins at the house of God. Revival in church history began with those who fear the Lord being aroused in their own spiritual life, and storming the kingdom of heaven and taking it by violence. That is the pattern of revival. Revival begins with the children of God, particularly with bold and courageous servants of God who dare to declare death in Adam and life in Christ, and the need for repentance. We need godly preachers. We need to pray for revival—revival of the historic biblical, Reformed, experiential faith. The books we sell and read are needed throughout this whole land. We need to get them out. We need to pray for open doors to reach the millions of the lost—those in our own families, in our churches, but also in our city, our state, our nation—with the message of the gospel. We need to pray for godly politicians, for godly business people, for godly educators, for godly physicians and nurses. We need to pray for missionaries, for mission workers, for evangelists—yes, for gatekeepers who are willing to lay down their lives, to labor for the gospel's sake, to make a difference in this world in which so many are just padding their bank accounts and abandoning the spiritual needs of their fellow man. We need to pray for the outpouring of the Holy Spirit. We need to pray for revival of truth—not only the outward shell of the doctrines of the Bible but the inward living essence. We need to pray that sinners may experience sound and true conversions that evidence the marks and fruits of grace which Scripture expounds.

We need to *pray*. Prayer is the *greatest weapon* at our disposal. "Prayer," said Octavius Winslow, "is the pulse of the renewed soul, and the constancy of its beat is the test and measure of spiritual life." As the poet William Cowper wrote:

> Restraining prayer we cease to fight;
> Prayer makes the Christian's armour bright;
> And Satan trembles when he sees
> The weakest saint upon his knees.

But we need more than prayer. The boat must be rowed with two oars—*prayer and work*: work, not in our own strength, but work that is mixed with prayer; work under God, work in obedience to God. We do not have much to say about the way things are in our nation if we never sit down and write letters to our political leaders on the moral issues of the day. We do not have much to say as citizens who contribute to this nation, do we, if we have never done anything in our local neighborhood to promote the gospel and biblical morality. We do not have much to say if we never speak about the one thing needful to those with whom we work, or have never given away any tracts or books.

Let me ask you this question: *What difference would it make in the world today if you were not here, and if I were not here?* How many people would not hear the gospel? How many people would not be lovingly—I stress *lovingly*—confronted with their sin? What difference would it make if you were not here? We must *work*. And work does not always mean *talking*; work also means *walking*, being examples. Do you realize that the world is watching every one of us who profess the name of Christ?

Finally, let me say to you, dear child of God: To you belongs the future. Even in wars and rumors of wars, to you belongs the future. "And ye shall hear of wars and rumours of wars: see that ye be not troubled: for all these things must come to pass, but the end is not yet" (Matt. 24:6). Today the end is not yet, but ask God, dear believer, that the rest of your life may be wholly consecrated to God, for the cause and the sake of the gospel. Pray that God may make you useful; that He may bless you and let you be a blessing, because that is what this land desperately needs—children of God who do not belong to themselves but to the faithful Savior, Jesus Christ, and who lay down their lives in adversity and in prosperity for the glorious coming of the kingdom of God in the church and in the world.

May God have mercy upon us—you and me—and upon this land. "To us belongeth confusion of face. To the Lord our God belong mercies and forgivenesses, though we have rebelled against him" (Dan. 9:8–9). "Oh that thou wouldest rend the heavens, that thou wouldest come down, that the mountains might flow down at thy presence" (Isa. 64:1).

Chapter 13

Daniel's Separation from the World

But Daniel purposed in his heart that he would not defile himself with the portion of the king's meat, nor with the wine which he drank: therefore he requested of the prince of the eunuchs that he might not defile himself.... So he consented to them in this matter, and proved them ten days.... And Daniel continued even unto the first year of king Cyrus....

—DANIEL 1:8, 14, 21

With God's help, we wish to consider:
Daniel's Separation from the World
1. How to resist temptation
2. How to go through trial
3. How to live

1. How to Resist Temptation

Perhaps you've heard the children's song many times, "Dare to be a Daniel, dare to stand alone." Most of the time when we hear this, we think of Daniel in the lions' den, but "dare to be a Daniel" also applies to the first chapter of the book of Daniel, which is too often a forgotten chapter. Today, I want to consider with you Daniel in Daniel 1.

As the book of Daniel opens, we meet Daniel in the college of Babylon. He was probably about fifteen years old. He and three of his Israelite friends were forced to go to a college in a city where they did not want to be. They were carried away captive by Nebuchadnezzar to the large city and college of Babylon, far from home and the temple where they had worshiped God.

Babylon was a worldly city full of temptations. It was the capital of the vast kingdom over which Nebuchadnezzar was reigning. It was a city with walls as high as towers and so thick that four chariots could safely ride abreast on top of them. Inside, all was luxury. It was the richest city in the world. Hanging gardens, supported by pillars, were sprinkled throughout Babylon.

Babylon was filled with pride, lust, and sin. Daniel and his friends were brought to the two most magnificent buildings in the very heart of Babylon—the king's palace and the temple of Bel, the supreme god of Babylon.

No doubt the Babylonian college was particularly full of temptations. Immediately Daniel was confronted with a whole new way of life. According to the king's commandments, courtiers were appointed to train these young men (as well as other young men from various conquered countries) so that after three years all the captives were supposed to be true Babylonians—both outwardly in behavior and inwardly in heart.

Everything needed to change to meet the goal and demands of the proud Nebuchadnezzar. Daniel and his friends needed to learn the language of Babylon. Only Babylonian clothing could be worn. Their names needed to be changed. Instead of being named after the God of Israel they were named after the gods of Babylon. Daniel, which means, "God is my judge," was changed to Belteshazzar, or "keeper of the hid treasures of Bel." Hananiah, "the grace of God," was changed to Shadrach, or "inspiration of the sun"—which the Babylonians also worshiped as a god. Mishael, "the Lord is a strong God," became Meshach—"devoted to the goddess Shach," the goddess of their feasts. Azariah, meaning "the Lord is a help," was given the name Abednego—"servant of Nebo," the god of fire.

The food and drink of these young Israelite men were changed. No longer could they eat their simple Jewish diet, but now rich foods and wine, both of which had been previously consecrated to idols through the performing of sacrificial rites, were placed before them.

They were instructed in Babylonian education which was filled with heathenism. Babylonian literature, sciences, music, superstition, astrology, soothsaying, sorcery, and religion were the "classes" they were required to take.

After three years of thorough indoctrination, Daniel and his friends were to appear before the king as true Babylonians, having forgotten their former life, morals, education, and especially, *the God of Israel*.

Today, we would call this brainwashing, especially when you consider that Daniel could have almost anything a natural heart could want. He and his friends could live like princes. Nebuchadnezzar would spoil them into forgetfulness of their past and into allegiance to himself.

Dear friends, is the situation really any different today in the world? Babylon rightly became a symbol of the world. Perhaps the world today does not tempt you in precisely the same way, but are not its current temptations, albeit somewhat less direct, just as powerful as in Daniel's day?

Consider worldly *language*. Is not this Babylonian world full of it? Profanity abounds. Secular humanism is even more commonly revealed in the speech of millions. Of the billions of words spoken every day, how many honor God? Of the words that proceed from your mouth each day, how many of them glorify God?

Are matters better with *clothing*? Let us be honest—much immodest, Babylonian clothing is worn nearly everywhere in society today. Our clothing conveys a message. What message are you conveying?

With *food and drink* some of us fare no better. Many eat like heathens, refusing to acknowledge God as the Giver of all that we receive. Are we among them? Do we quickly say a prayer without concentrating upon the great God whom we are acknowledging?

"Babylon" is alive and prosperous today in *education*. All around us today we are taught either that God does not exist at all or an attempt is made to portray Him as a God who loves everyone. devil- and spirit-worship abound around the world. In fact, the devil has his visible classroom in many homes through today's media. He uses media as an effective tool to teach principles contrary to the Ten

Commandments hundreds of times every day. He uses television, radio, social media, magazines, books, movies—all to educate our minds in worldly, unbiblical ways.

Babylon is still here. The temptations are great and many, especially for young people. The pride of life, the lust of the flesh, and the lust of the eye increase ten times faster than inflation.

We are all guilty. We are in grave danger of being overcome by the flood of worldliness that sweeps over us and lives within us. Dear friend, has worldliness ever become sin for you? Do you realize how deeply you are prone to drink in the world's philosophy and its sins? Do you feel its dangers? Are you afraid of your own worldly hearts?

Yes, perhaps you will say, but did not Daniel need to go along with it? It was not his choice; he was in Babylon, was he not? After all, was he not in the land of the enemy, and is it not true, "when in Rome we must do as the Romans"? If Daniel objected, the king would not hesitate to take his life—surely then he had better compromise somewhat, hadn't he? Otherwise, he would lose his honorable position and perhaps even his life. And besides, aren't such things as clothing, food, names, and language rather small things to protest about?

This was precisely Daniel's temptation. It is still our temptation today. Many go right along with the world while professing to be Christians. They pray, attend church, and read the Bible faithfully. For the rest, however, they think and act as the world thinks and acts, not wanting to be viewed as being different.

Young people, you understand this kind of peer pressure, don't you? When in school or at work, do you easily go along with "the crowd" or do you pray for strength to reject and resist sin? Mixing Christianity and worldliness, Babylon and Jerusalem, keeping a form of religion but doing away with a separated and godly lifestyle—this is your temptation every day.

Part of this temptation is a mixed lifestyle which appears to make daily living so much easier. Little self-denial is needed. It is a lifestyle that can always be positive, can always say "yes"—"yes" to the church and "yes" to the world. How few realize that they are then saying "no" to God! God will not have a mixed, half-hearted people.

Dear young friends, what is your life? Is your talk Babylonian? Are you worshiping worldly idols—the idol of entertainment, of riches, of ease, yes, of sinful self? Are you leading a life of "compromise"?

Compromise—that is one of Satan's favorite words when sin is involved. He likes to take us one step at a time down the slippery slope of iniquity. Gradually, he aims to lead us into what has been rightly called "practical atheism"—living as if there were no God.

The first step down this slippery slope begins with abandoning secret prayer. Then the Bible is increasingly neglected. Searching of the Scriptures stops. We reason, "There are more things to do—I am so busy. Besides, we can't always be so strict—I would not care to have others see me so. It is wrong to be righteous overmuch, I won't let happen what Jesus said must happen: 'The world must hate you.' After all, don't I have to be kind to everyone?"

Such are Satan's reasonings and devices. More and more conscience is overstepped. Compromise. Babylon. Worldliness. It is a never-ending cycle. Eventually, the slippery slope may lead to a whole variety of sins. And all the while, Satan is whispering, "Try it—how do you know what it is like unless you eat with the Babylonians and share their food? You will soon be used to it. It is not so bad. Experiment! You're old enough."

What a seemingly easy life Daniel could have had if he had only been willing to compromise! He could still have kept his own religion privately, couldn't he? All he needed to do was go along with these customs and not take them so seriously. Are you such a compromiser?

By grace, however, Daniel could not compromise. The fear of the Lord was planted in his young heart. He could not be at home in the world. He could not defile himself.

"But Daniel purposed in his heart that he would not defile himself with the portion of the king's meat, nor with the wine which he drank." Here lies the secret: "Daniel purposed in his heart." Not because of parents, church, or any person, but because it was the desire of his heart. It was not legalism. It was not fear of God's punishment. It was out of love for the Lord who is so worthy to be feared that "Daniel purposed in his heart" to say "no" to the world.

Daniel desired to walk before the Lord, to live to His honor and glory. He knew from experience: "Man does not live by bread alone but by every word that proceeds from the mouth of God." Young people, can you say from the heart that you agree with Daniel? Do you dare to be a Daniel, dare to flee the world, dare to stand alone? Is the divine pressure of God's Word more weighty for you than the peer pressure of your friends?

There is still another reason "Daniel purposed in his heart" not to defile himself—*jealousy*. He was jealous for the Lord's name, so he would not eat what was offered in the name of other gods, But he was also jealous over his own heart. He knew the power of temptation, of the world, and of Satan. He knew his own heart. He knew how quickly his conscience could be dulled, how soon secret prayer could suffer, how quickly communion with God could be broken. Therefore "Daniel purposed in his heart."

By grace Daniel was more afraid of the snares of the devil and the pollutions of sin than of losing his own life. He would rather die than sin. That is not legalism. That is not being "righteous overmuch." Rather, that is love, God-given love, which he is returning to the God who gave it.

Daniel received the courage to say "no" to sin from his heart as a gracious fruit of the Lord Jesus Christ who purposed in His heart from eternity to say "no" to sin for His entire life on earth. He gave His heart and life to the death of the cross in behalf of His Daniels who were by nature enemies of God but were made to fear and love His Name. May the Lord make us jealous of such Daniels. We often purpose in our minds or conscience, but how different that is from purposing through faith in our hearts!

This is real life, real living, real purpose. "Daniel purposed in his heart not to defile himself." Let us pray for grace to reject the world's selfish lifestyles and to seek first the kingdom of God and His righteousness!

With such laudable, God-glorifying motives we would be quick to think, "The Lord will now hurry to make everything well for Daniel. Now everything will go easy for him."

But no. The trial was yet to come. Let's focus on this trial in our second thought.

2. How to Go through Trial

Daniel received grace to persevere with his rejection of worldly Babylon and its food offered to idols. He did all in his power to resist the temptation himself. He did not say, "Now that I have purposed in my heart not to eat with the Babylonians, I shall sit back and wait for the Lord to find a way to have me excused from their presence at mealtimes." Rather, he used means, praying that the Lord might bless them: "Therefore Daniel requested the prince of the eunuchs that he might not defile himself" (v. 8b).

Daniel went to his superior, Ashpenaz, to request what he had purposed in his heart. He was not ashamed to confess his belief—not even to his employer. Can that also be said of us?

Dear friend, when you say "no" to worldliness—even outwardly—you will experience at times in your life the Lord's favor upon your steadfastness. In Daniel's case, this is already evident in the following verse: "Now God had brought Daniel into favour and tender love with the prince of the eunuchs" (v. 9).

Did you read this verse carefully? God brought Daniel into favor—thus the Lord had already gone before him. He was already making all things well. It seemed He was already paving the way for Daniel to live out his convictions.

No doubt Daniel himself had hoped his request would be quite easily granted. After all, "if God be for us who can be against us?" (Rom. 8:31). But Ashpenaz's answer was a grave disappointment: "And the prince of the eunuchs said unto Daniel, I fear my lord the king, who hath appointed your meat and your drink: for why should he see your faces worse liking than the children which are of your sort? then shall ye make me endanger my head to the king" (v. 10).

What a trial! What a mystery! Had not Daniel's request been a matter of prayer? Had it not been motivated by a sincere and earnest desire to avoid sin? Had not God Himself helped Daniel quite pointedly by bringing him into favor with Ashpenaz? And now the answer was "no"!

Daniel's "no" to the spirit of the world received a "no" from the Lord who had seemed to say "yes" before. What now? Must he give up? Must he give in? Our fleshly nature would be prone to say: "Now I can fully indulge; otherwise God would have changed the mind of the prince. I must have been too strict, too religious, too narrow minded, too intolerant."

Do you not think that Satan was also active in planting seeds of doubt within Daniel? "Daniel, it was all only pride—religious pride, stubbornness, and legalism. The Lord was not in it. It was only you. You are in Babylon now. Here the God of Israel won't answer your prayers. Here you must compromise with the gods and customs of Babylon."

Are you acquainted with such inner wrestlings of soul? You can believe that Daniel, the young man of prayer, was brought back to prayer through such a disappointment! Do you know times when God's mysterious providences and afflictions sweep over you, such that your soul cries out, "Lord, why? Oh God, did I not beg of Thee not to let me go my own way? Now what must I do? Lord, show me Thy will before I succumb to the snares of unbelief."

Do you know something of being driven back to prayer—time and again? You cannot be there too much. Usually, we are far too little in prayer. And when we do pray, how seldom we are brought to truly pray in our prayers!

I believe that there on his knees, looking and praying toward Jerusalem, Daniel received insight from the Lord to know what to do. The Lord directed him to try again—only this time he went to the prince's subordinate, Melzar.

"Then said Daniel to Melzar…prove thy servants I beseech thee, ten days; and let them give us pulse to eat, and water to drink. Then let our countenances be looked upon before thee, and the countenance of the children that eat of the portion of the king's meat: and as thou seest, deal with thy servants" (vv. 11–13).

The first time it was Daniel's plan. This time it was the Lord's. Therefore he received courage to ask for a miraculous ten-day plan in which his life could be at stake if a difference were not to be seen on these four young men after eating common vegetable food for ten days. "As thou seest" after ten days, "deal with thy servants."

"So he consented to them in this matter" (v. 14a). The Lord showed His favor and power in prospering this plan.

Melzar consented! No doubt Daniel was so glad at that moment with what the Lord had done that he forgot about the ten-day trial he was entering. "And he proved them ten days" (v. 14b).

Now the trial began in earnest. A trial of waiting. What would happen? Would the Lord fulfill His promise? Would He be true to His own Word? Would they all be killed if they did not appear more healthy than the others after ten days?

A ten-day, waiting trial. God's people often experience "waiting trials." Waiting times can become double trials for them when an unfulfilled promise of God is involved. Oh, to be waiting with a divine promise without seeing any signs of fulfillment—what a trial this can be! When God's promises are first received by faith, they are unspeakably precious, but a time can arrive—a time between promise and fulfillment—when these promises can be a burden rather than a joy.

Ten days. Ten is often used in Scripture as the number of God's perfect purpose. It is no accident that Daniel needed to endure this trial for ten days—not nine or eleven. His "ten-day" trial here serves as a type of the "ten-day trials" that God's people often encounter in the pathway to heaven. When God reaches His perfect purposes with His people in their trials, then the trial is taken away, but not before. Sometimes that calls for trials of only minutes or hours; at other times, it means trials of years or even for the rest of their lives.

The Lord knows best. He makes no mistakes. His trials are always of perfect quantity and quality to serve His eternal and blessed purposes.

In these trials, Daniel and all of God's people must be come to that blessed place where they die to themselves and their own righteousness. Together with Daniel, we must come to that place in our trials where the Lord would be righteous and just if there would be no difference after ten days. At that place we confess, "Oh Lord, I am unworthy that Thou shouldest make a difference where there is no difference by nature between myself and the worst of all the Babylonians in Satan's service!"

No doubt Daniel came to truly learn the meaning of his name during those ten days. The name "Daniel" means "God is my judge." Daniel needed to learn that man (think of Ashpenaz) and self could not be trusted. Hoping against hope, he cast himself and his trial upon the Lord. The Lord was free to judge both his case and himself. The Lord could do with Daniel what He desired.

Dear friend, this dying to self, this surrender to God and His will, is both trying and sweet. There, God's Daniels are cut off from everything of themselves. There, all comes to a standstill, and nothing remains but to sigh, "Lord, remember me in Thy mercy; I am unworthy; if I perish, I perish, but then I will perish in prayer to Thee. I will not let Thee go."

How many times Daniel and his three friends—Shadrach, Meshech, and Abednego—prayed during those ten days I can't tell you. No doubt they often encouraged and admonished one another to persevere in the way of obedience no matter what Ashpenaz, Melzar, or any courtier would say. But that too must be cut off—the Lord alone can help; the Lord alone is free and sovereign. In the end, the case was between the Lord and Daniel—yes, even Daniel needed to fall out of it. It was between the Lord and His Son. It was the Lord's case.

"He proved them." Dear friends, I cannot express in human vocabulary everything contained in this simple yet profound word, "proved." In the final analysis, the Lord Himself was the One being tried, for Daniel was His child and belonged to His family.

The Lord will never disappoint His Son nor His people. The Lord made the difference: "And at the end of ten days their countenances appeared fairer and fatter in flesh than all the children which did eat the portion of the king's meat. Thus Melzar took away the portion of their meat, and the wine that they should drink; and gave them pulse" (vv. 15–16).

The Lord is faithful! By this special providence, He miraculously caused a clear distinction in the physical beauty and strength of Daniel and his three friends.

Matters are no different in spiritual life. God's people have food to eat of which worldly people do not know or understand. Ten days of spiritual food will do much for the spiritual beauty and strength of God's people. Too often they are lean and unhealthy, and then have nothing to say. It is all their own fault.

But the Lord comes back. He is the faithful God who plants faith, gives strength to walk in faith, tries faith, and fulfills His own Word in 1 John 5:4, "For whatsoever is born of God overcometh the world: and this is the victory that overcometh the world, even our faith."

Daniel's life was not easy, but it was blessed. Let us pray for that kind of life—especially you, young people. Pray for a life that remains separate from worldly influences not only in temptation, but also through trial. In trial it takes special grace not to return to the world, but to choose, like Moses, rather "to suffer affliction with the people of God than to enjoy the pleasures of sin for a season" (Heb. 11:25). May the Lord grant this good choice to you out of free grace.

Never forget: The Lord does not promise His people an easy life, but He does promise them a blessed life. He will fulfill Romans 8:28 for them through all their trials: "And we know that all things work together for good to them that love God, to them who are the called according to his purpose."

Oh, dear young friend, ask the Lord to come against your natural, fleshly inclinations, in order to teach you the great blessedness of His service! All that is worldly is vanity and temporary; all that is of the Lord is invaluable and shall endure forever.

"Happy is that people, that is in such a case; yea, happy is that people, whose God is the LORD" (Ps. 144:15). "Seek ye the LORD while he may be found, call ye upon him while he is near" (Isa. 55:6).

3. How to Live

We read in the closing verse of Daniel 1: "And Daniel continued even unto the first year of king Cyrus" (v. 21). The first year of King Cyrus was 539 B.C.—nearly seventy years after Daniel was first taken captive. For seventy years Daniel continued to live separately from Babylonian worldliness. Amid all the honor of his exalted position as the king's counsellor, Daniel continued. Despite all the jealousy toward a foreign captive in a coveted office, Daniel continued. Through the insanity of one king and the murder of three of his successors, Daniel continued.

Daniel continued. For seventy long years Daniel walked by faith in a foreign land, placed only below the king in authority. During the reigns of four earthly kings he continued to trust the King of kings—believing, obeying, and knowing that He who gave the commandment to remain separate would also supply the grace. "He shall never suffer the righteous to be moved" (Ps. 55:22).

Do you ever read once in the book of Daniel that this great prophet who dared to stand alone regretted his separate lifestyle? The answer is obvious: of course not. But the deeper question must then be asked: Are you, my friend, following his example by grace?

Sometimes when a person lives to be very old you read in the newspaper that he is asked the secret of reaching such an age. Most of the time a foolish, humanistic answer is given. I once read of a man who was asked on his 107th birthday if he ever thought about death.

"No," he replied, "I have a brother who turned 120."

Such is the foolishness of man. How seldom we realize that every day of our life we are totally dependent on the longsuffering forbearance of God!

If you could have asked Daniel what the secret was of his becoming nearly ninety years old while still walking a God-fearing life in the midst of a heathen country, he would have had a much different answer. He would have said, "Grace. Free, sovereign grace."

You can read this answer between the lines in Daniel 9. Over fifteen times in this one chapter Daniel confesses his sins and unworthiness.

That Daniel *continued* a separate lifestyle was entirely because of grace. Grace is God's unmerited favor to unworthy sinners, granted for Christ's sake.

Grace was Daniel's secret from beginning to end. *Preventing grace* kept him from falling into temptations, *accompanying grace* brought him safely and profitably through trials, and *following grace* pursued him all the days of his life (Ps. 23:6). For over seventy years Daniel experienced God's comforting declaration to His children: "My grace is sufficient for thee" (2 Cor. 12:9).

The gracious, eternal love of a triune God—that was everything for Daniel. He tasted the *drawing love* of the Father who chose him from eternity. This eternal love enabled Jesus to say of His Father's chosen Daniels: "No one shall pluck them out of My Father's hand."

But Daniel also experienced the *sustaining love* of the Son, who "ever liveth to make intercession for [His people]" (Heb. 7:25). Daniel was also intimately acquainted with the *applying love* of the eternal Spirit, who enables believers to sing by faith:

> Lord, though I walk 'mid troubles sore,
> Thou wilt restore my faltering spirit;
> Though angry foes my soul alarm,
> Thy mighty arm will save and cheer it.
> Yea, Thou wilt finish perfectly
> What Thou for me hast undertaken;
> May not Thy works, in mercy wrought,
> E'er come to naught, or be forsaken.

"And Daniel continued"—solely because of the triune Jehovah. He is the great "I AM THAT I AM," who abides eternally the same. Therefore the burning bush which Moses saw was burned with fire but not consumed. As Father, the unchangeable Jehovah lit the burning bush of salvation already from eternity in the counsel of peace. The Son fulfilled all the requirements of salvation for the hell-worthy in time by obeying the law perfectly and by enduring the agonies of death—all the while burning with love for His Father and His people. The Holy Spirit works savingly in the elect, thereby guaranteeing that there shall be a living, burning, but not-consumed church even until the end of the world.

It was not Daniel, not his free will nor his good works, which enabled him to persevere in a God-fearing lifestyle. If God's people, as branches of the living Vine, were the fuel upon which the continuance of the flame depended, the living church would have been consumed long ago. The tender branches would have withered and died from the heat of God's wrath in a moment. But the Lord Jesus Christ took all the heat upon Himself—the heat of God's wrath, of hellish powers, and of the sins of His people—so that His church could walk in the midst of the fire and not have a hair of their heads singed. Christ walks with His people in the midst of all their burning, fiery furnaces.

In a word, Daniel continued with God because the triune God continued with Daniel. His name is Yahweh. He is the Unchangeable

One: "For I am the LORD, I change not; therefore ye sons of Jacob are not consumed" (Mal. 3:6).

I would say it even stronger: Daniel continued with God because God cannot but continue with His people. God's continuation with His people is inseparable from His Name, His cause, and His glory. God's people and God's church belong to God. Oh, what comfort lies in this for all of God's persecuted Daniels! No matter how stoked the fiery furnace of Nebuchadnezzar may be, and no matter how deep and closed the den of lions may become, the Lord maintains His church and His people.

This was not always easy for Daniel to believe. No doubt there were times when Daniel cried out to the Lord, "Shall I ever continue to the end with all these temptations surrounding me and within me? Oh Lord, I have forfeited everything—also that Thou wouldest continue with me—but Thou canst do it for Thine own Name's sake. Lord, continue with me, though I have made myself unworthy a thousand times."

"And Daniel continued"—it could not be any different. Not one child of God will be lost.

God was good to Daniel—so good that he was spared to see better days when God's promises were fulfilled. When King Cyrus conquered Babylon, he allowed the people to return to Jerusalem. He allowed Daniel to see Israel's deliverance from captivity before he died.

Young people, there are many lessons to learn from the first chapter of Daniel for all of us, but especially for you. Before we close this service, let me summarize a few of them for you:

First, ask for grace to live Daniel's kind of life, a life of separation from the world and in the fear of God. Perhaps you will respond, "But this would be so hard. My friends will despise me. I will be considered old-fashioned and strange. I will be persecuted to no end."

That may all be true. But remember, friends who seek to lead you into the world and away from God are no friends at all. In fact, they are your enemies. And remember too, that the loudest mockers often have the deepest respect underneath. Often they will even show you their respect later in private. "When a man's ways please the LORD, he maketh even his enemies to be at peace with him" (Prov. 16:7).

Second, ask for grace to have a higher regard for what the Lord thinks about you than for what people think of you. Daniel continued in honor with those from whom he had separated himself and in honor with God's people, but most importantly, he continued in the favor of the Lord. "In His favour is life" (Ps. 30:5).

Third, ask for grace to be faithful, also in little things. "He that is faithful in that which is least is faithful also in much: and he that is unjust in the least is unjust also in much" (Luke 16:10).

Fourth, ask for grace to be courageous, to stand firm for biblical principles. Ask the Lord to give you what you need to dare to be a Daniel—to dare to stand alone. That is what the future of the church desperately needs—Joshuas and Daniels who dare to say "no" to sin and "yes" to God.

Fifth, ask the Lord to grant you friends who also dare to say "no"— friends like Shadrach, Meshach, and Abednego. When looking for a mate for life, do not look for one who always says "yes." Pray that God may guide you to a partner who has a deep respect for the truth, and yearns to know and walk in the fear of the Lord.

Sixth, ask the Lord for a praying life. Bring all your needs to Him. You cannot come too often, nor stay too long at the throne of grace. The Lord says to you, "Acknowledge Me in all thy ways and I shall direct thy paths" (cf. Prov. 3:6). Pray above all for true conversion; do not rest short of a personal, saving acquaintance with Jesus Christ, the only Savior.

Seventh, ask for grace to refrain from sin. Don't think you can stand in your own strength. Bow your knees every morning and pray, "Lord, give me what I need to avoid temptation as much as possible, but also to remain firm when in the midst of it."

Eighth, like Daniel, avoid as much as possible those people, places, and customs which place temptation in your pathway. Instead of the attitude, "How far may I go and still not sin?", ask, "How may I stay as far as possible from sin?"

Ninth, search the Word of God. Pray that the Lord might grant you David's precious testimony: "Thy word have I hid in mine heart that I might not sin against thee" (Ps. 119:11).

All of us, young or old, stand on one side or the other. We are ruled either by the childlike fear of God or by the slavish fear of man and self. Are you standing on Daniel's side? Is your life an example like Joseph in the house of Potiphar and Moses in the courts of Pharaoh? Do you know what it is by grace to "fight the good fight of faith" (1 Tim. 6:12), to "endure hardness as a good soldier of Jesus Christ" (2 Tim. 2:3), and to put on "the whole armour of God that ye may be able to withstand in the evil day" (Eph. 6:13)?

Or are you pursuing a lifestyle of compromise with sin—a life of "halting between two opinions" (1 Kings 18:21), of trying to give God half a heart? Are you trying to live a somewhat religious life while avoiding Christ's command, "If any man will come after me, let him deny himself, and take up his cross, and follow me" (Matt. 16:24)?

Perhaps matters are even worse. Perhaps you are siding totally with the Babylonians. Do you never pick persecution and worldly loss above God's displeasure and a wounded conscience?

Do not forget: Both the compromisers and those who are altogether worldly are on the Babylonian side.

Dear friend, there is no third side—a half-and-half life is the devil's side.

On which side are you standing—the side of Babylon or the side of Daniel? Daniel's side is the only life worth living. May God grant us to live such a life by His grace and for His glory, for Christ's sake in whom alone we can do so.

Chapter 14

Matchless Mercy for God's Heritage

> *Who is a God like unto thee, that pardoneth iniquity, and passeth by the transgression of the remnant of his heritage? he retaineth not his anger for ever, because he delighteth in mercy. He will turn again, he will have compassion upon us; he will subdue our iniquities; and thou wilt cast all their sins into the depths of the sea.*
>
> —MICAH 7:18–19

The young denomination's name in which I am privileged to serve as an ordained minister includes the significant word, "heritage" (Heritage Reformed Congregations). Heritage is a biblical name; it occurs some thirty times in the Scriptures. Sometimes it refers to God as the heritage of His people, but more often it refers to believers as God's heritage. At times, it also refers to an inheritance, or to the riches that God's children possess in Jesus Christ.

In our case, the name *Heritage* was chosen for at least three reasons. First, it was chosen to direct our attention to the heritage most of our members have known which finds its roots in the Dutch Further Reformation in the writings of such notable divines as Willem Teellinck, Wilhelmus à Brakel, Gijsbertus Voetius, and Alexander Comrie, as well as in the Reformation proper, in men such as John Calvin, Heinrich Bullinger, and John Knox. In the North American context, that heritage is also rooted both in English Puritanism, via William Perkins, John Bunyan, John Owen, and many others, and in American Puritanism, represented by Thomas Shepard, Thomas

Hooker, and John Cotton. We desire to be true to this rich heritage insofar as it is true to the Word and Son of God.

Second, and more importantly, the name *Heritage* was selected, I trust, because deep within us we feel a great need to return to the founding watchword of the Reformation, *sola Scriptura* (Scripture alone). Scripture is the real foundation of our heritage; indeed, Scripture itself is our best heritage. Its inspiration, inerrancy, and authority must ever be our mainstay. What is not in accord with Scripture must be explicitly rejected.

The bare affirmation of Scripture's infallibility, inerrancy, and authority, however, is not enough for us. God gives us His Word as both a Word of truth and a Word of power. As a Word of truth, we must trust in and rest everything upon Scripture for time and eternity. We must also look to Scripture as the source of the transforming powers used by the Spirit of God to renew us from within. That power must be manifested in our lives, our homes, our churches, and our communities. Other books may inform or reform us, but only one Book, the Holy Bible, can and does transform us, for through it, the Holy Spirit conforms us to the image of Christ.

Finally, and most importantly, let us never forget that even Scripture is not an end in itself, but points us to *the* heritage of every true believer, Jesus Christ, and through Him, the triune God. God Himself, in Christ, is ultimately who we have in mind when we ascribe the title "*Heritage*" to our churches. Our heritage is not so much a "what," as it is a "who"—the ever-blessed Father, Son, and Holy Spirit. Psalm 16:5–6 says, "The LORD is the portion of mine inheritance and of my cup: thou maintainest my lot. The lines are fallen unto me in pleasant places; yea, I have a goodly heritage."

Now, this blessed triune God will have a heritage in His living church. But how is this possible, when all have sinned and come short of His glory, when sinners are by nature under the curse of the law and the wrath of God? How is it possible when everyone has a bad record, and worse, a bad heart? It is only possible, dear friends, because of the heart of God. God's heart is a heart of mercy; He delights in mercy—yes, matchless mercy. Let's look at that from Micah 7:18–19, which says, "Who is a God like unto thee, that pardoneth iniquity, and passeth by the transgression of the remnant of his heritage? he retaineth not his anger for ever, because he delighteth in mercy. He will turn again, he will have compassion upon us; he will subdue our iniquities; and thou wilt cast all their sins into the depths of the sea."

This marvelous text speaks of "Matchless Mercy for God's Heritage." We will consider this theme through three questions: Who is God's heritage? What is their inheritance? Who is like God?

1. Who Is God's Heritage?
God delights in all His attributes, such as His love, holiness, truth, grace, omniscience, and omnipotence. God and His attributes are inseparable. He preserves all His attributes untarnished; nevertheless, our text tells us that God takes special delight in His mercy. God "delighteth in mercy," Micah says.

Micah implies—and other texts in Scripture state even more explicitly—that God does not delight in executing justice as much as in manifesting mercy. God does not rejoice over the destruction of a sinner as He does over the salvation of the lost. His saving compassion moves toward the vessels of mercy, not toward the unbelieving and impenitent. As the Puritans often said, mercy is God's darling attribute. Mercy is God's Benjamin—the son of His right hand and the son of His sorrow, for mercy cost Him the sorrows of the Son of God.

Thomas Watson put it so beautifully: "The Scripture represents God in white robes of mercy more often than with garments rolled in blood; with His golden sceptre more often than His iron rod. The bee naturally gives honey, it stings only when it is provoked, so God does not punish till He can bear no longer. Mercy is God's right hand that He is most used to; inflicting punishment is called His strange work (Isa. 28:21)."

What a person delights in, he usually becomes proficient in. That is certainly the case with God. God is proficient in showing mercy to all men in a general way through His beneficent nature, but He particularly excels in showing mercy in a saving way, says Micah, toward "the remnant of his heritage" in passing by their transgression and pardoning their iniquity.

What, then, is the saving mercy of God? God's saving mercy is His sovereign, gracious pardon toward guilty sinners and compassion toward miserable sinners. Mercy makes things right for sinners through justification, and keeps things right within them by sanctification. Mercy pities them in misery, relieves in affliction, comforts in distress, and counsels in difficulties.

On whom, then, does God exercise His saving mercy? He exercises the "darling attribute" of mercy toward believers in salvation. God's mercy flows from His own heart to every sinner who comes to Jesus by faith (John 3:36). That faith, of course, is itself a receptive gift of God and not a meritorious work of man (Eph. 2:8–10). There is no competition in Scripture between *sola fide* (faith alone) and *sola gratia* (grace alone). God views mercy in contrast to all merits and works. Mercy is the free gift of God.

Those believers are elect believers. God's mercy showers on all the elect, for only the elect come to Jesus by saving faith. Indeed, God's mercy cannot fail for His people, for it is ratified from eternity in the Trinity's counsel of peace, or covenant of redemption. The Father's covenant is sure; the Son's blood is sure; the Spirit's application is sure—therefore, mercy is sure.

God's free mercy and His electing love are best friends. The doctrine of election declares that God delights in mercy. God thought of mercy from eternity. He planned mercy before anyone needed mercy; He chose fit objects for mercy from eternity. He selected them entirely out of His own good pleasure without any merit in them. The heart of mercy is that God will have mercy on whom He will have mercy (Rom. 9:15). If God had sent into the world a gospel full of conditions and human merit, it would have been no gospel to anyone, for no one but Christ can fulfill the conditions of God's justice.

Those believers are also needy believers. Sinners who, like the publican, cannot live without mercy are the recipients of mercy (Luke 18:9–14). Sinners who can find no reason in themselves to be recipients of mercy but yet cry out, "Give me Jesus, else I die," shall never perish. God's mercy is always overflowing to every needy believer. His vial of wrath drips, but His fountain of mercy runs. His anger lasts a moment, but His mercy endures forever. Believers shall bathe themselves eternally in God's ocean of mercy, without ever diminishing its abundance.

Dear friend, are you, too, by grace, a believer and a recipient of mercy? Have you experienced that God delights in mercy, and that therefore everything that transpires in your life has mercy at its core? As Thomas Watson wrote, "There is no condition, but we may spy mercy in it. In all afflictions we may see some sunshine of mercy. That outward and inward troubles do not come together is mercy. Mercy sweetens all God's other attributes; it makes His Godhead appear amiable and lovely. His mercy in election makes Him justify, adopt, glorify; one act of mercy engages God to more."

Truly, God gives His people a vast inheritance of mercy. Our text richly opens up that inheritance for us.

2. What Is Their Inheritance?
Micah tells us that the heritage or inheritance of believers is *justifying* mercy, *sanctifying* mercy, and *eternal* mercy. We will briefly consider each of these.

1. *Justifying mercy* is expressed in two ways in verse 18. First, God is a God "that pardoneth iniquity." That expression in Hebrew literally means that God "lifts up" iniquity. He lifts it up by lifting it off our shoulders and placing it upon the shoulders of Christ. As Isaiah says, "Surely he hath borne our griefs, and carried our sorrows" (Isa. 53:4). By carrying our sins as the sinless Savior, Christ takes our sins away, pardons them, and buries them. He is the scapegoat for us, who takes our sins upon Himself, and pays their full price, delivering and forgiving us. Through Christ, Numbers 14:18 is fulfilled for us: "The LORD is longsuffering, and of great mercy, forgiving iniquity and transgression."

Dear friend, is Jesus also your scapegoat? Have you experienced, by faith, His justifying mercy for your own unworthy soul?

Second, Micah tells us that God "passeth by the transgression of the remnant of his heritage." The expression "passeth by," or literally "passeth over," signifies movement. The same word is used in Exodus 12:23 of Israel's deliverance from Egypt: "For the LORD will pass through to smite the Egyptians; and when he seeth the blood upon the lintel, and on the two side posts, the LORD will pass over [or 'pass by'] the door, and will not suffer the destroyer to come in unto your houses to smite you." How can God do this—how can He pass over sin? God passes by His people's transgressions because divine justice did not pass by Christ, but fixed and poured itself upon Him. For Christ's sake, God has justifying mercy upon every believer, graciously pardoning iniquity and passing by transgression.

2. *Sanctifying mercy* is expressed in three ways in our text. First, "he retaineth not his anger for ever, because he delighteth in mercy." Literally, Micah says, "God does not make strong His anger for ever." God is justly angry with the sins of His people; He hates their sins with perfect hatred. Sin is so contrary to His holy nature that He cannot but show indignation against it. And yet, because that indignation is poured out upon Christ and borne by Him, God does not retain His anger against believers—not in the area of sanctification and personal experience, either.

Dear believer, when you slip or backslide and bring guilt upon your own conscience, fly directly to Christ with all your sin and the sense of divine anger you feel. Confess your sin, forsake it, and seek forgiveness only in Christ, for God delights to show mercy in Christ. As you trust Christ and God's promises in Him, you will experience that God does not retain His anger but will enable you to experience daily, sanctifying cleansing, so that you can say with Isaiah: "O Lord, I will praise thee; though thou wast angry with me, thine anger is turned away, and thou comfortedst me" (Isa. 12:1).

Second, Micah says, God "will turn again, he will have compassion [literally, pity] upon us." We often feel that we have sinned against the Lord too often to remain recipients of mercy, but Micah says that God so delights in mercy that He will turn again. God will turn once more to you, repenting believer; He will grant you one more look of love; one more glimpse of the way of salvation through the blood of Christ; one more promise from His Word, convincing you of His peace that passes all understanding. He will turn His reconciled countenance in Christ Jesus to you, and you, like Peter, will weep bitterly that you have so sinned against Him and yet weep in joy for His awesome forgiveness.

Blessed be God that He turns again! If He did not turn again, you and I would only grow harder and colder. Because He turns again, our hearts may again be broken, healed, and comforted. Because He turns again, His work in you shall never fail, never die. Because He turns again, your repentance is intensified, your hope is encouraged, your love is enflamed, and you receive inward strength to persevere in faith.

Because He turns again, you experience His compassion and pity, for Christ's sake. You experience, "Like as a father pitieth his children, so the LORD pitieth them that fear him" (Ps. 103:13). As Christ had compassion upon the fainting multitude, upon Jairus, upon lepers, and upon the handicapped and blind, so God has compassion upon all those who mourn over their souls' pitiable condition and take refuge in His Son with all their sins, confessing their unworthiness before Him, and resting upon His mercy alone.

Third, Micah says, "he will subdue [literally, trample or suppress] our iniquities." He will take away the tyranny of sin; he will sanctify us and renew us. This is sanctification indeed! Sin *subdued* is the next greatest blessing to sin *pardoned*. Wherever God pardons sin, He will also subdue sin—here on earth, partially; in heaven, perfectly. The same grace that casts sin behind God's back puts its foot upon the corruption of the believer and tramples sin in the dust.

But what a struggle the battle between the flesh and the spirit ignites! The flesh will seize every opportunity to reestablish its dominion in the soul. Flesh wants grace out of the way; it wants to rule the heart and have sin carry the day as before. Flesh blinds our eyes to the reality of sin; it deadens our conscience; it dulls our spiritual affection. We need the sovereign grace of God every bit as much to subdue our sins as we need it to pardon our sins.

3. Finally, Micah speaks of *eternal mercy*: "And thou wilt cast all their sins into the depths of the sea." The Dutch annotations say, "Our sins shall not be looked upon by God, but shall be put in everlasting oblivion, covered, unregarded, and sunk away for ever." Those

who have sins forgiven and subdued while they live, shall have them drowned when they die. God promises, "I, even I, am he that blotteth out thy transgressions for mine own sake, and will not remember thy sins" (Isa. 43:25).

Blessed, eternal mercy: forgiveness of all your sins, dear believer! What an inheritance! Were there one sin left between God and your soul, you could never enter into God's presence with eternal joy.

Let us never rest when there are any sins between God and us. Let us press on, every day seeking fresh applications of this mercy of mercies—the forgiveness of all our sins.

Forgiveness is matchless mercy—necessary, great, sure, free, and eternal mercy, and leads believers to cry out with amazement, like Micah, "Who is like God?"

3. Who Is Like God?

Micah becomes bold. He challenges the false gods of heathen lands all around. "Who is like God?" he asks. "What other god lifts up the burden of sin, passes by transgression, turns again to unworthy sinners, tramples upon sin, and casts sin behind His back forever, burying it in the bottomless ocean of His grace? Where is there a god like this God—a God who takes care of His heritage so that they will never perish, a God who loves them so profoundly because of His eternal, purchasing, preserving grace? Where is there another god who sees and sympathizes with every sorrow and care of His children?"

How applicable Micah's exclamation is yet today: "Who is like unto God?" The question is rhetorical. There is not, of course, any other like unto God, not Moloch, Baal, or Ashteroth; not the god of self-righteousness, the god of materialism, or the god of this world (cf. Isa. 40:18). What can any god other than Micah's God do for us in that hour when flesh and heart fail?

If there is no God so merciful as Micah's living God, why should we not bring all our sins to Him? Why should we not, like the prodigal, arise and return to our Creator-Father? Dear believer, should we not cry out, "Let this ever be our God—the God whom we believe in, the God whom we know and worship, adore, and love! "Whom have I in heaven but thee? And there is none upon earth that I desire beside thee" (Ps. 73:25).

Let's close with a few applications. Dear believer:

First, consider the greatness of God's mercy in showing saving mercy to such a person as you. Were you the most virtuous, the most gifted, the most honest, the most worthy? Oh, wonder of wonders! The Lord laid hold of you, stopped and turned you, and brought you to know His mercy in Christ. He lays hold of the polluted publican; He singles out the wandering prodigal. He regenerates, and brings them to repentance and faith in Christ. He lifts the poor out of the dunghill, and sets him among princes. If you consider that the accumulated guilt of our souls would be enough to sink an entire world into perdition, is it not clear that our salvation is a vivid proof that God delights in mercy? *"Who is like God?"*

Second, consider the greatness of God's ongoing mercy by meditating on how you have been toward the Lord after first tasting His mercy. How unbelieving, how proud, how fainthearted, how selfish, how ungrateful, and how unfaithful have we been! Should we not be ashamed? Have we not sinned against the merciful heart of the Father, against the merciful blood of Christ, against the precious comforts of the Holy Spirit, and yet, has the Lord ever spewed us out of His mouth? Have we ever been disowned by Christ? Has not the mercy which once flowed to us in the early hours of our new birth continued to flow ever since like a surging, ever-widening river, bursting its banks? Why? Because God delights in mercy; and what He delights in must come to pass. Nothing and no one can stop His hand of mercy, or say unto Him, "What doest Thou?" *"Who is like God?"*

Does the mercy of God work within us a great love to God, and admiring, reverential thoughts of Him? Does it confirm for us that true religion resides exclusively in mercy? Does it provide fresh strength and encouragement for new obedience?

Third, let mercy be your delight. If God delights in mercy, and you are His child, shouldn't you delight in mercy as well? Shouldn't you be merciful to the guilty, the poor, the ignorant, the lonely? Do not be the first to cast a stone at the adulterous woman, for your Master did not condemn her. *"Who is like God?"* Are you like Him in mercy?

Mercy ought to run through your entire character since you are an heir of mercy. Never say of another, "I can't or won't forgive," for in so saying, you condemn yourself. If you don't forgive your brother his trespasses, neither will your heavenly Father forgive you. How can we, with one hand stretched out against our brother, lift our other hand to God and pray the publican's prayer?

Are you not yet a true believer in Christ? If so, I'm afraid that you don't truly believe that God delights in mercy. In fact, you probably have many objections against His mercy. You perhaps ask questions like these:

If God is merciful, why do so many go lost? Remember this: The fact that God delights in mercy does not tarnish His justice. Those who persevere in rejecting the gospel and living impenitently shall justly be lost. Of all the lost that shall throng the corridors of hell, not one has received more than the due reward of his deeds (Luke 23:42).

If God is merciful, why is there an unpardonable sin? Let's turn that question around: If we grasp even a small portion of the heinousness of sin, the wonder is that there is only one sin that is unpardonable! God could have made a long list of unpardonable sins; instead, He reduced that list to one: waging war against the Holy Spirit and completely searing one's conscience so that it makes it impossible for him to seek for pardon. Don't misinterpret God's mercy—no one has ever sincerely cried for mercy in vain.

If God is merciful, why do I feel that God can't have mercy upon me? That could be due to any number of reasons, such as a faulty view of God; fears you've sinned too much in the past; fears you're still sinning too much in the present; a conviction that there simply is nothing special about you for God to notice you and save you, and so on. At any rate, your feelings in this matter are not to be trusted. God's Word is better than your feelings. You may be a filthy sinner, but God declares that He delights to wash and dine with polluted sinners. You may have repeatedly offended Him for fifty, sixty, or even eighty years, but His arm is still not shortened that He cannot save. He has strength for the weak, wisdom for the foolish, and righteousness for the unrighteous.

Are you a lost sheep bleating on the mountains of your sins? The Good Shepherd hears you and will reach you. Don't allow your thoughts to run contrary to the gospel—indeed, to the declarations of heaven. God is able and willing even to save rebellious sheep such as you are—sheep who have nothing left but the publican's prayer: "God be merciful (literally, be "full of mercy") to me, the sinner."

I must proclaim most freely that God delights in mercy. His mercy endureth for ever! I would let this pulpit ring with mercy! No heart is too hard for God to reach; no beggar too bankrupt; no sinner too steeped in iniquity. *Who is like God*?

Friend, the very fact that you and I are still alive after all we've done to provoke God is irrefutable proof that God is a merciful God. Why do you still keep your distance from Him? However grossly you have offended Him, He is ready to forgive. He will hear your prayers, even when they are feeble and broken. He says to you still: "Look unto me, and be ye saved, all the ends of the earth: for I am God, and there is none else" (Isa. 45:22).

Finally, let us admonish each other not to abuse God's delight in mercy. We must never fall into the antinomian spirit which abuses mercy by saying that if we let sin abound, grace will abound the more. Sin is never a trifle with God. It is always deadly fire. Calvary is a sacred place—a place that we must never abuse. How shall we minimize sin when our Savior died to save us from it? Do not trifle with sin because God is merciful. Rather, because God is merciful, let us flee from sin and flee to Calvary. There is no other place of divine mercy on the face of the earth. There, at Calvary, cling to the horns of God's altar that are dripping with the blood of Immanuel—the blood in which mercy and justice meet and kiss each other. As John Newton wrote,

> If Thou hadst bid Thy thunders roll,
> And lightning's flash to blast my soul,
> I still had stubborn been;
> But *mercy* has my heart subdued,
> A bleeding Savior I have viewed,
> And now I hate my sin.

God has nailed every other door closed, but the door of Calvary and of the empty tomb. The dying, living Immanuel is our only and sufficient hope. The open door of the gospel proclaimed to you is sprinkled with the blood of Jesus on every side—on the lintel and the two side posts. And written on that door, you can find: "Whosoever believeth in the Lord Jesus Christ shall never perish, but have everlasting life."

Yes, there is another door—a bloodless door, a door that leads to death. On that door is written, "He that believeth not shall be condemned." To be without Christ is to be without mercy.

"Seek ye the LORD while he may be found, call ye upon him while he is near" (Isa. 55:6). Don't be discouraged as you seek God and the graces of repentance and faith. There is not one word in the entire Bible to discourage poor, guilty, coming, repenting, believing sinners. God's throne of grace is open; God's house is open; God's heart is open. He delights in mercy—matchless mercy. "*Who is like God?*" This is the heritage of sinners who trust exclusively in Christ for salvation. May it be the heritage of every one of us—now, in future decades and generations, and forever.

Chapter 15

The Spirit of Grace and Supplication

> *And I will pour upon the house of David, and upon the inhabitants of Jerusalem, the spirit of grace and of supplications: and they shall look upon me whom they have pierced, and they shall mourn for him, as one mourneth for his only son, and shall be in bitterness for him, as one that is in bitterness for his firstborn.*
> —ZECHARIAH 12:10

After the murder of Caesar by Brutus, a Roman senator tried to provoke the people to revenge the death of the late emperor by bringing out his bloody robe. He held up the robe for all the people to see, and cried, "Here is the robe of your late emperor." When the rebellious people saw it, they repented of their sins, and took revenge upon the murderers of their emperor. Similarly, in the preaching of the gospel, when the bloody robe of Christ is lifted up, and the message is proclaimed, "Behold what sin has cost Jesus," the Holy Spirit causes us, if we are believers, to repent and to take revenge upon our sins.

We wish to consider this blessed work of the Spirit, flowing out of Christ's suffering and death, based on Zechariah 12:10: "I will pour upon the house of David, and upon the inhabitants of Jerusalem, the spirit of grace and of supplications: and they shall look upon me whom they have pierced, and they shall mourn for him, as one mourneth for his only son, and shall be in bitterness for him, as one that is in bitterness for his firstborn."

With God's help, we wish to consider:

The Spirit of Grace and Supplication
1. The Spirit's given name
2. The Spirit's saving work
3. The Spirit's personal application

1. The Spirit's Given Name

Zechariah was a post-exilic prophet—that is, he prophesied to Israel after the Babylonian exile. A minority of the Jewish people—about forty-two thousand—had returned to Judah from Babylon. No doubt this minority hoped that they would be only the first wave of many so that national life would be renewed in Israel. God commanded the people to rebuild the temple and reinstate His worship. Fortifying their souls with God's promises, this minority were longing for the day when all the nations of the earth would gather themselves together in Jerusalem to worship the Lord in His temple.

But soon a harsh, painful reality set in. After a difficult time of drought and local resistance, the people became despondent. Soon they abandoned God's commands, and everyone began to think only about themselves and their own families. They settled on the land and enlarged their homes and fields. They neglected the worship of God, forgot the importance of the temple, and abandoned the quest for reestablishing their national identity. Spiritual lethargy abounded. Even idol worship began to rear its head.

It is still the same today, isn't it? If we're not involved with God and His work and truth, we backslide rather than progress. We grow distant from that spiritual life we once craved and enjoyed. Our spiritual aspirations wither.

God then sends Zechariah to the remnant who remained on the land—now shrunk almost in half to about twenty-two thousand people. Zechariah brings to a despondent, despairing people a striking message. God looks at His sinful people and determines to transform them: "I will pour upon the house of David, and upon the inhabitants of Jerusalem, the spirit of grace and of supplications" (Zech. 12:10). This is a striking contrast to the previous verse: "It shall come to pass in that day, that I will seek to destroy all the nations that come against

Jerusalem" (12:9). God says that He will pour out His just fury on the nations, even as He promises to pour out His Spirit upon the inhabitants of Jerusalem. God will turn to His people in mercy. When God does so, His mercy begins with the outpouring of His Spirit of grace and supplication.

God will pour out His Spirit upon the house of David—the princes and rulers of Israel—and upon the inhabitants of Jerusalem, the common people. He will pour out His Spirit upon all of Israel combined—upon a guilty nation; upon a guilty David, who committed adultery and murder; upon Jerusalem, the city that would crucify the Lord of glory. The effect will be that "they shall look upon me whom they have pierced, and they shall mourn for him, as one mourneth for his only son, and shall be in bitterness for him, as one that is in bitterness for his firstborn" (12:10).

When we read this text, we immediately think about what happened on the day of Pentecost. Zechariah 12:10 was literally fulfilled on that glorious day when Peter preached the gospel to the Jews, accusing them of crucifying their Messiah. Three thousand were pricked in their hearts. They cried out, "Men and brethren, what shall we do?" (Acts 2:37). They mourned over the Savior whom they had pierced.

Zechariah 12:10 is a fulfilled prophecy. We bring this prophecy before you again because we believe that God continues to fulfill this prophecy until the end of time; the Spirit is still being poured out today. Sinners are still brought to mourn for the Messiah whom they have pierced.

The Spirit of Grace
The first question we must ask is: Who is the Spirit that the Lord promises to pour out? He is the *Spirit of grace and supplication*. The Holy Spirit is here called a Spirit of grace. The Holy Spirit is a Spirit of grace because of the mediatorial work of the Lord Jesus Christ. We must never forget that the Holy Spirit, like the Father and the Son, was also provoked by the sin of man. The Holy Spirit was also angry with man for transgressing God's law and breaking His covenant. When we fell in Adam, the Holy Spirit withdrew Himself and His blessed

influences from fallen man. Man was left void of all spiritual good. Man was left behind, dead in trespasses and sins.

The Bible teaches us that nothing is to be feared so much as the breath of the Almighty. Isaiah 11:4, speaking of God's wrath, says that the breath (literally, "the Spirit") of the Lord shall slay the wicked. That breath is symbolic of the Holy Spirit. The Spirit is angry with the sins of the wicked.

But Christ's mediatorial work in dying for sinners opened the way for the Spirit to be a Spirit of grace, mercy, love, and compassion. That's why Christ said to the disciples, "It is expedient for you that I go away; for if I go not away, the Comforter will not come unto you" (John 16:7). Christ first needed to complete His meritorious mediatorial work. He needed to complete the mission assigned to Him by His Father and return to His Father—and then He would pour out the Holy Spirit and His gracious influences. The Spirit's outpouring was dependent on the birth, death, resurrection, and ascension of Jesus Christ. This outpouring was a fruit of the accomplishment of Jesus's mission. Because of Christ's work, the Bible can call the Holy Spirit this beautiful name, *the Spirit of grace*.

The Spirit is also called the Spirit of grace because He authors all spiritual graces in sinners. He is the author of all genuine conviction of sin. He authors the grace of repentance, the grace of faith, the grace of sanctification, the grace of perseverance, and the graces of love and humility.

The Spirit is the author of all spiritual life. What sap is to a tree to make it bear fruit, what electricity is to a lightbulb to cause it to produce light, what air is to a musical instrument to make it play, so the Holy Spirit is to all spiritual life. He is the author of all spiritual grace.

God's people experience the truth of this doctrine. They experience as a living reality that the Holy Spirit is the author of all grace. Have you also experienced this reality?

Without the Holy Spirit, we remain dead in trespasses and sins, impenitent, and unbelieving. Just as Jesus said, "Without me ye can do nothing" (John 15:5), so the believer experiences that, after being born again, "Without the Spirit of Christ, I can perform nothing acceptable to God. I cannot give myself one spiritual grace. I cannot give myself faith. I cannot give myself hands to receive Jesus or arms to embrace Jesus. I cannot retain what has been given. I cannot endure to the end without the Spirit of grace. I am utterly dependent on Jesus Christ and His Spirit." Praise God that the Holy Spirit is the Spirit of grace.

The Spirit of Supplication
The Holy Spirit is not only the Spirit of grace. He is also the *Spirit of supplication*. He is the ultimate author of all true prayer. When we were little children, our parents taught us to pray. That is good, necessary, and unforgettable. But we need another teacher—we need the Holy Spirit to teach us to pray. He is the Spirit of supplication. As soon as He takes up residence in the heart of a sinner, the result is, "Behold, that sinner prayeth" (see Acts 9:11).

When the Holy Spirit begins His saving work, Jeremiah says that such sinners will come to the Lord with weeping and supplication (Jer. 31:29). The Holy Spirit teaches us to cry for mercy and to beg for pardon. Without the Spirit's groaning within us, our prayer is little more than lip-work.

Grace and supplication are inseparable. When there is grace, there is supplication. Where there is much grace, there is much supplication. Where there is no grace, there is no genuine supplication.

Supplication here means *pleading*—pleading out of shame and desperation. It is akin to the groaning we read of in Romans 8:26: "Likewise the Spirit also helpeth our infirmities: for we know not what we should pray for as we ought: but the Spirit itself maketh intercession for us with groanings which cannot be uttered."

There are two intercessors for the Christian. We have an intercessor *within the veil*—Jesus Christ; He is objectively interceding for us. But then we have a second intercessor *within our hearts*. He is subjectively interceding for us; that is, the Spirit of God is touching the wellsprings of our affections. He is inciting prayer, He is provoking prayer, He is stirring us up to prayer.

Let me illustrate. Imagine that you are attending an organ concert, where beautiful and reverent music is being played. You see the organist take her place at the organ, and watch her skillful fingers, that have practiced for years, fly up and down the keyboard; you marvel at the beautiful sound that is made. So the Spirit of God touches the strings of a believer's heart and creates a sort of music of the soul, and the consequence is that we cannot but pour out our desires to God. And when we do so, God recognizes that this is the work of His Spirit within us.

"We know not what we should pray for as we ought," but the Spirit teaches us. This is the extraordinary thing about prayer. Sometimes you go on your knees and you feel as dead as a piece of wood. You have had that experience many times, and so have I. At times, I have said to myself, "How am I going to get through even a few minutes on my knees of addressing God?" You begin, but it doesn't work; it is terrible. You try again, and it is just as difficult. You struggle on. You pray that you may pray. Perhaps you are just about to give up when you say, "I'll try a bit longer," and then all of a sudden the Spirit of God fills your heart and it becomes easy to pray, even to pray at some length. You then arise from your knees and say, "Oh, that I had more time to pray. This is heaven upon earth; this is a heaven before heaven; this is the enjoyment of God!" Then you brush away your tears and you say to yourself, "What a glorious, beautiful thing it is to lay hold of God in prayer, to enjoy communion with the living God!" Well, that is because it is the Spirit helping us. We are not on our own. Christ is helping us at the throne and the Spirit is helping us here below in the depths of our minds and souls. So the doctrine here is that we should strive to pray in the Spirit.

Do you know the difference between merely *praying* and *praying in the Spirit*? Paul does not simply tell us to pray; he says we are to pray in the Spirit. In Ephesians 6:18 he says, "Praying always with all prayer and supplication in the Spirit." So there is a difference between prayer and *prayer*. And here is a good test for your spiritual progress. Do you know the difference between prayer and *prayer*? Would you know the difference between praying, and praying *in the Spirit*? Now, this is not an absolute distinction, of course, but it is a relative one. In other words, sometimes when people pray, they receive help. Occasionally they receive *extraordinary help*. Too often we feel as though we are struggling more or less on our own as we pray. But we are always desiring to get through that striving to the point where we receive that spiritual help. That is precisely what we should look for and wait upon God to give us. Whether it be relative help or extraordinary help, it is the "Spirit [who] helpeth our infirmities" (Rom. 8:26).

But how exactly does the Holy Spirit help us in praying? What does this term "helpeth" mean here: "the Spirit also helpeth our infirmities"? Commenting on this word *helpeth*, Charles Hodge says, "This word means to take hold of any thing with another. To take part of his burden or work."[1] John Calvin puts it this way: "The Spirit takes on himself a part of the burden, by which our weakness is oppressed [weighed down]."[2]

Let me illustrate what Paul, Calvin, and Hodge are saying. Imagine there is a large piece of wood, like a plank. Suppose a young boy, about seven, sees this plank, and wants to try out his own strength, even though his father is right behind him. "Let me do it, Dad," he says. This is a common thing, isn't it? Most boys that are growing in strength like to try out their vigor. So the boy picks up one end of the plank, and he can lift it six or so inches off the ground, maybe a foot. His father smiles and, realizing what the boy is up to, he comes behind him and says, "Now son, you take that end and I will take the other end, and between us we will carry it out through the door." So the boy is delighted and he lifts it with all his strength. But the father skillfully, concealing somewhat what he is doing, puts both his hands under the plank near the center, so as to take ninety percent of the weight, and the boy, of course, thinks he is carrying a considerable portion, helping his father through the door with the plank. Now that is what this word *helpeth* means.

Prayer can be a great burden. The work of prayer is really too great for us. We are like children. Our strength is not up to it. "But," says Paul, "Someone is helping our infirmities." Someone is there—the gracious Holy Spirit of supplication is there to help. We are not on

---

1. Charles Hodge, *Commentary of the Epistle to the Romans* (Philadelphia: William S. & Alfred Marten, 1864), 437.
2. John Calvin, *Commentaries on the Epistle of Paul the Apostle to the Romans*, ed. and trans. John Owen, vol. 19, *Calvin's Commentaries* (1849; repr., Grand Rapids: Baker, 1996), 311 [on Rom. 8:26].

our own with this burden. His mighty arms are underneath the burden, and we go forward carrying out our little end. The Spirit carries the bulk of the weight—in true prayer we are mostly following Him. In the work of praying, there are two persons with one burden. The burden is the cause of Christ upon the earth and the manifestation of the glory of God in the world.

A true Christian is one who can't be content without the Spirit of grace and supplication. He or she can't be content with prayerless praying. To be content with prayerless praying is like a sailor being content without any wind after he hoists the sail of his boat. You can't sail when there's no wind. Pray much for the wind of the Spirit. By all means, do set sail; do use the means. Do show the Lord His own handwriting; plead on His own promises. But remember, only the Spirit can empower prayer to move the soul. Without the Spirit's movement, the sails of prayer will hang limp.

A true Christian seeks grace to maintain the priority of prayer in everything he does. He strives to live out the advice of John Bunyan: "You can do more than pray after you have prayed, but you cannot do more than pray until you have prayed."

Now this blessed Spirit of grace and supplication will be poured out, Zechariah says, and the result will be: "They shall look upon me whom they have pierced, and they shall mourn for him, as one mourneth for his only son." Zechariah is speaking here of the Spirit's work in producing evangelical repentance.

2. The Spirit's Saving Work

The great end in view of all the operations of the Holy Spirit is to glorify Christ. Christ Himself said, "He will glorify me" (John 16:14). That is what our text says here. The Holy Spirit will be poured out, and the result will be that Christ will be glorified. He will teach sinners to look upon Christ. Our text says, "They shall look upon me whom they have pierced" (Zech. 12:10). The Holy Spirit will make a sinner look to Christ—but, says our text, a Christ whom that sinner has pierced. Usually, the Holy Spirit does not get us to look first to Christ as our Redeemer and Savior, but as one whom we have rejected; one whom we have despised; one whose blood we have counted as an unclean thing; one whom we have crucified.

Our text is powerful: "They shall look upon me whom they have pierced, and they shall mourn for him, as one mourneth for his only son, and shall be in bitterness for him, as one that is in bitterness for his firstborn" (Zech. 12:10). This prophecy was literally fulfilled on the day of Pentecost. The multitude listened intently to Peter's sermon. When Peter proved from the prophets that Jesus of Nazareth was the promised Messiah, their amazement gave way to perplexity, then to conviction and sorrow. When the multitude heard Peter's terrible charge against them, "Jesus, being delivered by the determinate counsel and foreknowledge of God, *ye* have taken and by wicked hands have crucified and slain"—they stood crushed before the bar of God and the bar of their own conscience. Then they cried, "Men and brethren, what shall we do?" This prophecy was then fulfilled literally, "They shall look on me whom they have pierced."

Those Jews began to look on Christ. They had despised and rejected Jesus. They didn't even think Him worthy to be looked upon. They didn't want to look upon Him. They didn't want to think about the possibility that He could be the Messiah. But now, they began to reflect on what had happened with Christ. They began to see that their sins pierced Christ. The Holy Spirit persuaded them that the One against whom they had cried, "Away with him; crucify him," was, in fact, the Messiah of God!

Those repentant Jerusalem sinners mourned as one mourns for his only son. Their hearts were wounded, broken with sorrow and shame. The reality was crushing—"We are murderers of the promised Messiah!" The verse after our text, Zechariah 12:11, became an experiential reality. There was "a great mourning in Jerusalem." This was from the powerful, convicting, and blessed effect of the Spirit's outpouring.

Do you think that this prophecy is only applicable to the Jews because they were the ones who rejected and crucified Christ? Dear friends, we are guilty of the same crime. What the Jews did literally, we are inclined to do spiritually when we live under the preaching of the gospel and do not embrace the Messiah by faith. We reject Christ every time we hear the gospel and do not repent and believe in the Son of God. We crucify Jesus Christ with our unbelief.

What is unbelief? Unbelief is enmity against God. Unbelief is refusing to believe the record that God gave of His only-begotten Son. Unbelief is disobedience to the Word of God. We reject and crucify Christ when we cleave to our sins and idols. We crucify Christ by cleaving to our self-righteousness; by refusing to bow under Christ as our Lord and Master, by refusing to take His yoke upon us as His disciples.

When Christ preached on earth, many were displeased. They were displeased because His sermons condemned them. His messages condemned their self-righteousness and worldliness. Christ preached, "Wide is the gate, and broad is the way, that leadeth to destruction, and many there be which go in threat: Because strait is the gate, and narrow is the way, which leadeth unto life, and few there be that find it" (Matt. 7:13). Christ said, "For I say unto you, That except your righteousness shall exceed the righteousness of the scribes and Pharisees, ye shall in no case enter the kingdom of God" (Matt. 5:20).

Many picked up stones to kill Christ when He spoke such things because His preaching condemned them. And we do the same thing by nature. But we do not see this; nor do we believe this. In our foolishness, we say, "If I had been living when Jesus was on earth, I surely would have been one of His disciples."

Unbelief is the reigning and damning sin of the outward Christian world. And yet, the Christian world is not aware of the tragedy of unbelief.

I'm afraid some of you scarcely think about these things. Some of you don't even realize the seriousness of being unconverted. You don't see it as a sin. You don't realize the damning nature of your unbelief. You never stop to consider that it is your unbelief that will bring you to hell. You never weep over your unbelief. You never despise its cursed nature. You never bemoan it.

Unbelief is the crowning sin we commit against that God to whom we owe everything that we are and everything that we have.

Many unconverted people think of themselves as victims of Satan, as people who are to be pitied, rather than as criminals. You think of yourselves as people who are to be *excused* rather than *accused* for being unbelievers. You say within yourselves, "It is not my fault; I can't help it. What can I do about it? I can't convert myself. I can't bring myself to the right place." How few think of being unconverted as a sin—as a terrible crime!

Some of you think that you're not so bad. Perhaps you're outwardly moral. You live a decent life. You attend a conservative, Christian church faithfully. You believe in the truths of the Bible.

My friend, that is not enough. I fear that the devils believe in the Bible more than some of you. The devil believes more of Christ than you do. Of the devils it is written that they believe and tremble (James 2:19)—and that is more than some among us do. The truth is, my unconverted friend, you are an unbeliever. That means that you are unwilling to believe the testimony of God concerning yourself and concerning God. An unbeliever is an enemy of God and Christ.

Do you know what it is to be an unbeliever? Let me explain by way of illustration. Think of a sick man who has a particular disease that only one medicine, with God's help, can be used to cure him. What would you think if that man refused to take the only possible medicine that could cure him? That is an unbeliever. An unbeliever pushes away the only medicine that can save him from destruction— the shed blood and righteousness of Jesus Christ.

My friend, be honest with yourself. You are unconverted because you do not want God to be King over you. When Christ says, "Ye will not come unto me that ye may have life" (John 5:40), He also says of you. Deep down in your soul, you know that is true. You are not desiring Christ, you are not looking to Christ. You are not willing to forsake sin and surrender your idols. You are not willing to crucify your flesh and renounce your self-righteousness. You are not willing to be saved as a poor sinner trusting exclusively in Jesus's blood and righteousness.

But you do not see it—or, perhaps, more accurately, you do not want to see it. By nature, we hate to hear the truth about ourselves. Therefore, when Christ taught the Pharisees that they were in bondage, that the devil was their master, and that they needed to be delivered by Him, they took up stones to stone Him. Christ said, "Do you want to stone me, because I have told you the truth?" (see John 10:32). He told them the truth about themselves, and therefore they hated Him.

It is no different today. People still don't want the truth to be told about themselves. By nature, they still cry out, "Away with Him! We don't want all our righteousness to be grounded in Jesus Christ alone." By nature, we are like those pious Jews who had come from afar to Jerusalem to celebrate the Feast of the Passover and the Feast of Tabernacles. They thought of themselves as pious and strict people, believers in Jehovah, lovers of God's law, keepers of His ordinances, travelers to heaven. But then the Holy Spirit was poured out. They began to look upon Christ, they began to see the truth about themselves and what they had done. They saw that they had rejected and crucified the Messiah, the only divine remedy for all their sins. They realized the enormity of their crime.

When the Holy Spirit teaches us the truth about ourselves, and our rejection of Jesus Christ, we see the exceeding sinfulness of sin in our own hearts and lives. Then we see that we have sinned against a holy and good God—against a God who has sent "His only begotten Son into the world, that whosoever believeth in Him should not perish but have everlasting life" (John 3:16).

When the Holy Spirit is poured out upon us, it becomes our sorrow that we have sinned against such a God. Then we confess, "How have I dared to sin against such a God? How have I dared to reject the Savior whom He has sent—a merciful, gracious Savior? Woe is me, I have despised the blood of the New Testament! I have rejected the merciful invitations of the gospel! My sins have nailed the promised Messiah to the tree. My sins are the cause of the suffering and death of the Lord Jesus. I have repeated the crime of the Jews against the cross. Oh, it rings in my ears: 'whom *ye* have crucified.'"

Zechariah says that the bitterness of this mourning and true repentance is like two sad occurrences. First, this bitterness is like the grief a parent feels upon the loss of a firstborn or of an only son. Our text says, "They shall mourn for him, as one mourneth for his only son, and shall be in bitterness for him, as one that is in bitterness for his firstborn." According to Jewish custom, this grief would be the greatest sorrow that God could lay upon a family. Jeremiah speaks of this mourning in Jeremiah 6:26 as a "most bitter lamentation."

Second, this bitterness is like the grief that the Israelites felt when the God-fearing Josiah was slain in battle by the Egyptians. We read in the verse following our text, "In that day shall there be a great mourning in Jerusalem, as the mourning of Hadadrimmon in the valley of Megiddon" (Zech. 12:11). When Josiah was slain at Hadadrimmon, a town in the valley of Megiddon, there was profound lamentation in Judah and Israel (2 Chron. 35:24–25). Jeremiah wrote a book called Lamentations, in which he tells us that all of Judah and Israel mourned the loss of this God-fearing king. So, says Zechariah, a sinner who sees that he has pierced Christ with his sins, may be compared with these two events.

This sorrow is bitter and sincere because it sorrows over sin as sin. Then we do not sorrow only over sin's *consequences*—for the harm it does to us. But we sorrow for sin *as sin* because we see the dishonor and wrong that sin does to a holy and merciful God. Sin always has a Godward thrust. Sin is a grave matter. He who gives us our breath has so humbled Himself that, though He is the Creator of heaven and earth, He is affected by our deeds. Sin, as it were, pierces the Son of God.

Sin especially becomes sin when we see our sins in the light of Christ's sufferings. When we view our sins as the cause of the *red glass* of Christ's sufferings, as Thomas Watson put it, then we will mourn "for him as one mourneth for his only son."

The sufferings of Christ have been called God's commentaries on sin—commentaries which the penitent sinner reads with sorrow. There is no better commentary on the subject of sin than the sufferings and death of Christ. To know what sin is, you must read this commentary on sin. You must see sin in the face of Christ's agony. When our fathers tried to expound the sinfulness of sin in the Form for the Celebration of the Lord's Supper, they place sin in the context of Golgotha: "The wrath of God against sin is so great," they say, "that rather than that God would let sin go unpunished, He has punished sin in the bitter and shameful death of His Son on the cross."

When Peter saw his sins against Christ in the light of Christ's sufferings and love, he went out and wept bitterly. There is nothing so humbling as to see that my sins have nailed Christ to the tree. My sins have pierced the merciful Savior. When the rock of the heart is struck by the rod of the gospel, then the waters gush out.

Brokenness of heart and contrition of spirit is what God calls for in the context of Golgotha. This godly sorrow, which works "repentance not to be repented of" (2 Cor. 7:10), is the result of the outpouring of the Holy Spirit.

The glorious promise unveiled at the beginning of the next chapter is designed especially for such mourners: "In that day there shall be a fountain opened to the house of David and to the inhabitants of Jerusalem for sin and for uncleanness" (Zech. 13:1).

A fountain opened for sin and uncleanness! Plentiful cleansing—more than you could ever need—enough, as Luther said, for a thousand worlds. This fountain is a tremendous illustration of God's utter ability and willingness to save.

Zechariah is one of several prophets who often draws us back to certain portions of the Old Testament by using rare Hebrew words, sometimes, as in this case, using technical terms. The terms, *sin and uncleanness*, when used together in Hebrew, describe a particularly difficult and heinous state of defilement. In Numbers 19, we have the account of the red heifer, the most awesome of all the rites of purification that the people of Israel had, apart from the great Day of Atonement. A red heifer or cow was taken out of the camp, slaughtered, and burnt. Its ashes were gathered together and used in combination with water as a rite of purification. So thoroughly sacred was this rite that anyone who came into the slightest contact with the red heifer and its ashes was regarded as unclean. This rite was used to cleanse people from every kind of defilement.

That is precisely what Zechariah is telling us: even sin and uncleanness can be cleansed—not by a little sprinkling of water with ashes from a red heifer, but by "a fountain opened to the house of David and the inhabitants of Jerusalem." It is an everlasting, ever-present, everflowing fountain that is able to cleanse the chief sinner. It should remind us of Romans 5:6: "For when we were yet without strength, in due time Christ died for the ungodly."

This fountain is God's pure, sovereign grace. We need a thousand tongues to sing our great Redeemer's praise for this open fountain of blood that invites everyone to come to Jesus just as they are and be saved by drinking from its fullness.

Sinners who have pierced Christ will look upon Christ as being crucified *for* their sins. First they look upon Him whom they have pierced, rejected, and despised—and see with horror that their sins were the cause of His suffering. But now they may look upon Him who loved them and did not reject them. Now they see that His sufferings are the cause of their salvation from sin. Now they embrace with experiential reality the fact that "he was wounded for our transgressions; bruised for our iniquities" (Isa. 53:5).

Did you notice that Zechariah 13:1 says that this open fountain is for the very same people: "to the house of David and to the inhabitants of Jerusalem"? Oh, what a wonder His grace is! God turns our sorrow into joy when we may see by faith that this fountain is opened, when we are led to the fountain of Jesus's blood. We know unspeakable joy when we embrace Him as our Substitute. Then we begin to understand, as the Form for the Lord's Supper in our Reformed liturgy says: that "whereas you would otherwise have suffered eternal death, I have given my body and shed my blood for you—even unto death."[3]

The Holy Spirit teaches proper communicants to look upon Christ: to look upon Christ crucified—Christ crucified *by* us and Christ crucified *for* us. Such lookers are welcome, yes, commanded, to come and show forth the death of the Lord till He comes again (Heb. 9:28).

3. The Spirit's Personal Application

Zechariah 12 describes the conversion of Jews—of religious people—of people who have lived under the means of grace. When a thief is converted, he will mourn over his theft; when an adulterer is converted, he will mourn over his adultery. But when a gospel-despiser is converted, he will mourn over despising the gospel.

---

3. *The Psalter: With Doctrinal Standards, Liturgy, Church Order, and Added Chorale Section* (Grand Rapids: Eerdmans, 2015), 138.

What is your sin? Theft? Adultery? Yes, in the heart—but most likely not in practice. Your sin in practice—the sin of the religious world—is the rejection of Jesus Christ as the exclusive Messiah. Peter tells the religious Jews in Acts 4 that they have killed God's holy Child, Jesus. So wicked, and so full of enmity is a religious heart against the gospel.

Perhaps you think you're not guilty of that crime. You have many excuses for why you're not converted—even after hearing gospel sermons for decades. You say you *cannot* convert yourself, but you don't admit the deeper problem: you *will not* be converted. You *cannot* because you *will not*. Your unwillingness is an active sin against God and His gospel. You need to see that and become guilty under that truth. The sooner you stop excusing yourself, my friend, the better. We can answer all your excuses, with the words of an old divine: "Save all your objections for the judgment day, and you will see what remains of them."

Have you ever looked upon Christ as being pierced by your sin? Such a sight kills all our self-righteousness, destroys all our so-called goodness. It makes us true penitents at the foot of the cross.

All evangelical repentance has a supernatural spring. The Spirit of grace and supplication authors it. Joseph Hart wrote,

> True religion is more than notion,
> Something must be known and felt.

If you do not look upon Christ now, whom you have pierced, the day is coming when Revelation 1:7 will be fulfilled: "Every eye shall see him, and they also which pierced him." One day you will be compelled to look upon Jesus Christ. But on that day, there will no longer be any time for mourning; God's fountain will be shut. Our hearts must be broken here by evangelical repentance; if it is not, be assured, our hearts will be broken by eternal judgment hereafter.

Friend, you must begin *now* to reflect upon Him whom you have pierced; if you don't, you will begin *hereafter* to reflect upon Him when it shall be eternally too late to be saved.

Dear believer, by grace the Holy Spirit has made you one who looks to Christ here, and at times you long to behold Him hereafter.

You long at times for the fulfillment of Hebrews 9:28: "Christ was once offered to bear the sins of many; and unto them that look for him shall he appear the second time without sin unto salvation." One day you will gaze on Him forever without any more mourning. Sorrow and sighing shall flee away; you shall be comforted with the oil of gladness. Forever you shall praise Christ, as you gaze upon the Lamb who sits in the midst of the throne. Forever, you shall take the crown from your own head and cast it at His feet, saying, "Not unto us, O LORD, not unto us, but unto thy name give glory, for thy mercy, and for thy truth's sake" (Ps. 115:1).

Ask God for grace to encamp your soul at Calvary every day. Bring your sorrow for sin to Him and cling to His open fountain of blood and salvation. He has given you this imperative: "Ye believe in God, believe also in me" (John 14:1). Drink deeply from that fountain. One day you will experience with all the redeemed the reality that "they shall hunger no more, neither thirst any more; neither shall the sun light on them, nor any heat. For the Lamb which is in the midst of the throne shall feed them, and shall lead them unto living fountains of waters: and God shall wipe away all tears from their eyes" (Rev. 7:16–17).

Chapter 16

The Glory of God as Father: Undue Anxiety Out of Order for Adopted Believers

Therefore I say unto you, Take no thought for your life, what ye shall eat, or what ye shall drink; nor yet for your body, what ye shall put on. Is not the life more than meat, and the body than raiment? Behold the fowls of the air: for they sow not, neither do they reap, nor gather into barns; yet your heavenly Father feedeth them. Are ye not much better than they? Which of you by taking thought can add one cubit unto his stature? And why take ye thought for raiment? Consider the lilies of the field, how they grow; they toil not, neither do they spin: and yet I say unto you, That even Solomon in all his glory was not arrayed like one of these. Wherefore, if God so clothe the grass of the field, which today is, and tomorrow is cast into the oven, shall he not much more clothe you, O ye of little faith? Therefore take no thought, saying, What shall we eat? or, What shall we drink: or, Wherewithal shall we be clothed? (For after all these things do the Gentiles seek): for your heavenly Father knoweth that ye have need of all these things. But seek ye first the kingdom of God, and his righteousness; and all these things shall be added unto you. Take therefore no thought for the morrow: for the morrow shall take thought for the things of itself. Sufficient unto the day is the evil thereof.

—MATTHEW 6:25–34

With God's help, our theme for this message is: *The Glory of God as Father*, with this subtitle: *Undue Anxiety Out of Order for Adopted Believers.*

Setting the Context

Although Matthew 5–7 is commonly referred to as the Sermon on the Mount, a more accurate title might be "Jesus's Discourse on Discipleship."[1] Jesus began the Sermon on the Mount by describing the relationship between God the Father and His disciples. From the start, Jesus was explicit that those who are in fellowship with God are very different from people who are not in fellowship with God (Matt. 5:3–12). Jesus said that people are blessed who are poor in spirit (v. 3), who mourn (v. 4), who are meek (v. 5), who hunger and thirst after righteousness (v. 6), who are merciful (v. 7), who are pure in heart (v. 8), who are peacemakers (v. 9), and who are persecuted for the sake of righteousness (vv. 10–12). Such traits are not natural in people; rather, they are the distinguishing marks of God's children. They are kingdom virtues. That's one reason why Dr. Martyn Lloyd-Jones suggests that the Sermon on the Mount is a character sketch of a true believer, "not a code of ethics or of morals."[2]

James Boice says, "Left to ourselves, our natural beatitudes would go something like this: Blessed are the rich, for they have it all and have it all now; blessed are the happy, for they are content with themselves and don't need others; blessed are the arrogant, for people defer to them; blessed are those who fight for the good things in life, for they will get them; blessed are the sophisticated, for they will have a good time."[3]

Jesus explained the heart of the law in Matthew 5:17–48. In chapter 6, he instructed the disciples *how* to pray and *for what*. However, before he reached the climax of the sermon in Matthew 6:33, which is, "But seek ye first the kingdom of God, and his righteousness; and all these things shall be added unto you," Jesus dealt with

---

1. R. T. France, *The Gospel of Matthew* (Grand Rapids: Eerdmans, 2007), 153.
2. Martyn Lloyd-Jones, *Studies in the Sermon on the Mount* (Grand Rapids: Eerdmans, 1979), 28.
3. James Montgomery Boice, *The Gospel of Matthew* (Grand Rapids: Baker, 2001), 1:74.

genuine Christian piety (vv. 1–18) and the problem of covetousness (vv. 19–24). In our text He then offered the cure for undue anxiety, which is to trust God as our heavenly Father. This teaching strikes at the very root of covetousness by exposing our natural, inordinate care for the things of this life (vv. 25–34).

Basically, our text teaches that undue anxiety is out of order for adopted believers. Undue anxiety is a grave sin, an act of wicked unbelief that doubts God's love in Christ to us as believers. At the same time, we must understand that Jesus did not say all concern or anxiety is sin. To maintain that would be an exaggerated position.

When we compare Scripture with Scripture, we see that there are two kinds of concern or worry: a godly, circumspect, and moderate concern; and a distrustful, inordinate, and overwhelming concern. God commands us in Proverbs 6:6, 2 Corinthians 12:14, and 1 Timothy 5:8 to be concerned about properly providing for our future and that of our family. "Taking no thought" for earthly things does not negate this concern; rather, it means that we are not to be overly anxious about temporal matters. We must not go beyond due bounds in caring for our physical and temporal needs but must always subject the needs of the body to the higher and deeper needs of our souls. Temporal matters must not distract us from spiritual matters. To be tormented by anxious thoughts about future physical needs is not worthy of our Father's glory and our adoption as God's children. It reveals sinful self-centeredness and a lack of confidence in our Father. It is out of order for a child of the heavenly Father to be unduly anxious about the future.

Let me illustrate. My oldest brother loves to shop for books. When we go into a Christian bookstore, I start with the top shelf of the first bookcase in the store and work my way methodically through the store. My brother walks through the store very rapidly, searching a bit anxiously for any valuable antiquarian work. He then rushes back to me with any special volume he finds so that I won't miss it. I have assured him many times that he should trust me; since I move through the store thoroughly, I will not bypass any special book. Then we joke about the situation. When my brother even approaches me with a book, I say, "Stop worrying. Stop going ahead of me. You are out of order!"

Likewise, we often run ahead of the Lord. We try to discover God's ways for our future, pulling works off shelves that we think will be good for us and bringing them to God. We then almost dictate to Him how He should rule our lives instead of letting Him govern our lives from moment to moment. This undue anxiety is out of order! Our heavenly Father will provide everything that we need at the right time and in the right way.

Jesus warns us against undue anxiety because of the negative way it impacts the glory of God our Father. Such anxiety is inexcusable for the following six reasons.

1. Our Father Values Us (vv. 25b, 26b)

Jesus says in verse 25, "*Therefore*, I say unto you." He uses the word *therefore* three times in this section of Scripture. He uses it the first time in verse 25 in response to the argument in verse 24: "No man can serve two masters: for either he will hate the one, and love the other; or else he will hold to the one, and despise the other. Ye cannot serve God and mammon."

"*Therefore*," He says, "take no thought (literally, do not worry or become unduly anxious) about your life, what you shall eat or drink; or about your body, what you will wear." Jesus is warning believers against committing the same sin mentioned in verses 19–24,[4] of loving material possessions more than fearing God. That command is followed by various reasons not to worry about physical needs because worry is an offense to our Father in heaven who values and cares for us.

If we are believers, the first cure for undue anxiety is to believe that our heavenly Father values us. In verse 25b, Jesus asks this question: "Is not the life more than meat, and the body more than raiment?" In other words, focusing one's attention on the necessities of life is wrong. If we are obliged to trust God for life itself, why should we be anxious about food or clothing? Isn't our life itself worth more than what we eat

---

4. Herman Ridderbos, *Matthew*, trans. Ray Togtman, Bible Students' Commentary (Grand Rapids: Zondervan, 1987), 139.

or put on? Moreover, if we have been called of God and regenerated by the Holy Spirit, are we not children of our Father in heaven? Doesn't that imply that He values us enough to take care of us?

The second argument in verse 26 for our Father's valuing us is an *a fortiori* argument—it argues from the lesser to the greater. If our heavenly Father provides for the birds of the air, Jesus says, how much more will He provide for us, for "are ye not much better [or 'of much more value'] than they?"

Our Father is glorified in valuing us who are made in His image as His children. We rob Him of that glory when we do not believe that He values us.

2. Our Father Governs Us (v. 27)

As Jesus asks in verse 27, which of you by being anxious can add one "cubit" to your "stature." Jesus asks in verse 27. Many commentators suggest that the King James translation is not quite accurate here, and the verse should be translated as, "Who among you is able, by being anxious, to add (even) one cubit to his lifespan?"[5] The Greek word for stature here may mean height, but it may also refer to a length or span of time. The point of Jesus's argument is this: "Although we try to extend our lives in many ways, we cannot add even one breath to our life." Jesus has just leveled the playing field, for the wealthy executive on Wall Street has no earthly advantage over the average Joe on Main Street. In the end, our good and gracious God governs the length of everyone's life.

Undue anxiety about longevity, therefore, accomplishes nothing. A.W. Pink says anxiety is *needless* because the bounty of God assures supplies; it is *senseless* because of the providence of God over inferior creatures; and it is *useless* because of the impotency of man. We cannot add one cubit to our stature. That leaves us with one conclusion: Since you and I are completely dependent on our Father, why should we not fully trust Him?

---

5. William Hendriksen, *Exposition of the Gospel according to Matthew*, New Testament Commentary (Grand Rapids: Baker, 2007), 351. See also Lloyd-Jones, *Studies in the Sermon on the Mount*, 121; Daniel M. Doriani, *Matthew, Volume 1: Chapters 1–13*, Reformed Expository Commentary (Phillipsburg, N.J.: P&R, 2005), 260.

Do you believe these words of Christ? Do they encourage you? Do you truly believe that our Father counsels and directs us? The Puritan Samuel Willard says, "Believers are tender and foolish in themselves, they have not wisdom enough of their own to order and direct their way; and are therefore easily seduced and cheated by the adversary, who is subtle, and watcheth [for] all advantages against [them]: but God is always giving them his fatherly advice, warning them of their danger, showing them a way how to escape it. They have the voice of his Spirit behind them, telling them this is the way (Isa. 30:21); they have the guidance of his most wise counsel to keep them in the right way unto glory (Ps. 74:24)."

3. Our Father Feeds and Clothes Us (vv. 26, 28–31)

Jesus uses *a fortiori* reasoning again in verses 28–31, arguing from the lesser to the greater. Here, He asks us to observe nature. We are told to "consider the flowers of the field" to see "how they grow." They neither toil nor spin, Jesus says. Without any care or cultivation by people, these natural beauties look more glorious than King Solomon himself.

Jesus is arguing here that trusting the heavenly Father is at the heart of true discipleship. At the end of verse 30, Jesus asks, "Shall he not much more clothe you, O ye of little faith?" The phrase *O ye of little faith* is Jesus's reprimand of those who minimize God's promises and are overly anxious about the necessities of life. The phrase *of little faith* comes from the Greek word *oligopistoi*, which Matthew uses four times: in Matthew 6:30 (our text), Matthew 8:26, Matthew 14:31, and Matthew 16:8. In each case, the disciples are rebuked for having too little faith. William Hendriksen explains, "It would seem that...those so characterized were not sufficiently *taking to heart* the comfort they should have derived from the presence, promises, power, and love of Christ."[6]

This rebuke is for us as well. How many times have we failed to trust the fullness of the promises of our Father in Christ and instead settled for meager scraps produced by our own efforts? Though we may offer thanks for past blessings, we too often fail to trust our

---

6. Hendriksen, *Exposition of the Gospel according to Matthew*, 353, italics mine.

Father for future graces. As John Piper says, "Faith in future grace, not gratitude, is the source of radical, risk-taking, kingdom obedience."[7] Only when we recognize the grandeur of almighty God as our heavenly Father in Christ will we begin to trust Him for all things, both great and small, in the present as well as in the future.

Why do we presume upon our Father's bounty by seeking to gather and take comfort in earthly possessions? Should we not first be busy seeking the kingdom of God and His righteousness? Will He not provide us with all of life's necessities? Daniel Doriani writes, "We set out on a desperate, hopeless quest when we search for fulfillment where it cannot be found."[8]

Christ also tells us to look at the birds around us, which neither sow nor reap, nor fill barns with food for tomorrow; yet, as Christ says, "your heavenly Father feedeth them."

Dear friends, do not let the Lord's teaching here rush in one ear and out the other. Let it sink into the depths of your souls. As Herman Ridderbos says, "It is God's open hand, not human effort that makes life possible."[9] The question each of us must ask is this: "Am I living by faith, trusting in God, the Father, and Christ, His Son; or am I living as a practical atheist by fearing that if I do not take charge of my life, all may be lost?" The old Princeton divine, B. B. Warfield, asks: "Is it true that He [the heavenly Father] has provided salvation for us at the tremendous cost of the death of His Son, and will not provide food for us to eat and clothes for us to wear at the cost of the directive word that speaks and it is done?"[10]

The words of Christ in our text expose our unbelief. Warfield goes on to say: "What a rebuke these lessons are to our practical atheism, which says, in effect, that we cannot trust God for our earthly prosperity but must bid Him wait until we make good our earthly fortunes before we can afford to turn to Him."[11]

---

7. John Piper, *The Purifying Power of Living by Faith*, in *Future Grace* (Sisters, Ore.: Multnomah, 1995), 43.
8. Doriani, *Matthew*, 259.
9. Ridderbos, *Matthew*, 140.
10. Benjamin B. Warfield, *Faith and Life* (Edinburgh: Banner of Truth, 1974), 45.
11. Warfield, *Faith and Life*, 46.

Do you know God as your heavenly Father? Does your heart drive you to trust Him? Can you say with the old hymnwriter, "Give me a calm, a thankful heart, from every murmur free; the blessings of Thy grace impart, and let me live to Thee"?[12]

In verse 31, Jesus summarizes His lesson by referring to the sin and senselessness of undue anxiety regarding food and clothing.[13] He says that since our heavenly Father cares for creation, He will surely provide the daily necessities of His children.

Therefore, dear believer, when you are tempted to be over-anxious, take to heart these words of Scripture: "Commit thy way unto the LORD: trust also in him, and he shall bring it to pass" (Ps. 37:5); "Cast thy burden upon the LORD, and he shall sustain thee" (Ps. 55:22), "for he careth for you" (1 Peter 5:7).

4. Our Father Knows and Meets Every Need in His Son (v. 32)

Jesus's focus shifts in verse 32 from lessons in nature to people who live as though God does not exist. He says that unbelievers spend their lives groping after material possessions. The preposition "for" in verse 32 is directive—"For after all these things do the Gentiles seek." Unbelievers focus all of their efforts on obtaining food, drink, and material wealth. By contrast, the children of God are assured, "Your heavenly Father knoweth that ye have need of all these things." Therefore, we are to live an anxiety-free life, believing that our loving heavenly Father knows all of our needs and promises to provide for them.

In other words, Jesus says, do not chase after things as the Gentiles do, for two reasons: first, because it is worldly—even heathenish—to focus on such things as food and clothing, for these are the gods of heathens. The original Greek of this text is more emphatic, saying that Gentiles "set themselves to seek" such things. They seek things with all their might. They find life in things rather than in the living, holy Father of heaven and earth.

---

12. Anne Steele, "Father, Whate'er of Earthly Bliss," in *Christian Hymns* (Bridgend: Evangelical Movement of Wales, 1977), no. 570.

13. Hendriksen, *Exposition of the Gospel according to Matthew*, 353.

Second, we must not chase after the things of this life because our heavenly Father—in contrast to the impotent gods of the heathen—will give food, clothing, and other such things to us, anyway. He knows what you need and will not deny it to you, dear believer. Jesus says later in Matthew 7:11, "If ye then, being evil, know how to give good gifts unto your children, how much more shall your Father which is in heaven give good things to them that ask him?"

Lloyd-Jones comments on this verse, "The question I now ask myself is, Does that Christian faith of mine affect my whole detailed view of life? Is it always determining my reaction and my response to the particular things that happen? Or, we can put it like this. Is it clear and obvious to myself and to everybody else that my whole approach to life, my essential view of life in general and in particular, is altogether different from that of the non-Christian? It should be.... If, then, we are different essentially, we must be different in our view of, and in our reaction to, everything."[14]

Don Carson puts it this way: "When the Christian faces the pressure of examinations, does he sound like the pagan in the next room? When he is short of money, even for the essentials, does he complain with the same tone, the same words, the same attitude as those around him? Away with secular thinking. The follower of Jesus will be concerned to have a distinctive lifestyle, one that is characterized by values and perspectives so un-pagan that his life and conduct are, as it were, stamped all over with the words: *Made in the kingdom of God.*"[15]

As Christians, we differ from pagans in our views and reactions to everything because we see that in Christ our Father provides everything we need as His children, both physically and spiritually. Moreover, He will protect us from all harm. He will defend us against enemies such as Satan, the world, and our own flesh. He will right us when we are wronged. He will assist and strengthen us, carrying us through every difficulty and temptation (2 Tim. 4:17). We may thus safely entrust everything to His fatherly hands, knowing that He will never leave us nor forsake us (Heb. 13:5–6). We are under our Father's

---

14. Lloyd-Jones, *Studies in the Sermon on the Mount*, 139–40.
15. Don Carson, *Jesus's Sermon on the Mount and His Confrontation with the World* (Grand Rapids: Baker, 1978), 92.

special inspection and care (1 Peter 5:7) during all of our earthly pilgrimage, "sealed to the day of redemption" in glory,[16] when we will be beyond all danger (Rev. 21:25).

All of this is only possible in Christ Jesus, who gave His life so that God could be our Father. As John Flavel writes:

> He spared not his own Son, but delivered him up for us all; how shall he not with him freely give us all things? (Rom. 8:32).... Surely if he would not spare his own Son one stroke, one tear, one groan, one sigh, one circumstance of misery, it can never be imagined that ever he should, after this, deny or withhold from his people, for whose sakes all this was suffered, any mercies, and comforts, any privilege, spiritual or temporal, which is good for them.[17]

This does not mean that we should sit back and let God do everything for us. We are not to lack action and motivation in this life. Rather, it means that we are to live in the assurance that our heavenly Father cares for us and will provide everything we need for *life and godliness* (2 Peter 1:3). We as Christians must primarily be focused on pursuing a life of holiness. That includes studying God's Word, praying in accordance with the Word, contemplating what it means to live in and under the dominion of God, and seeking to bring all things in subjection to the rule and reign of Christ. That is our chief end in life.

5. Our Father Commands and Promises Us (v. 33)

In verse 33, Jesus identifies what His disciples should seek after. Since the Father will provide His children with the things that the Gentiles (or unbelievers) seek after, the Christian should seek after the kingdom of God and His righteousness. In other words, we must be resolved to live life under our Father's direction and control, aiming for our Father's glory.[18] Our paramount concern must be God and His righteousness.

---

16. See The Westminster Confession of Faith (chap. 12) in James T. Dennison, Jr., *Reformed Confessions of the 16th and 17th Centuries in English Translation: Volume 4, 1600–1693* (Grand Rapids: Reformation Heritage Books, 2014), 249.

17. *The Works of John Flavel* (Edinburgh: Banner of Truth, reprint 1988), 4:418.

18. France, *The Gospel of Matthew*, 271.

We glorify our Father when He becomes number one in our life. We glorify Him when we become a new creation and operate under "the impulse power of a new affection," as Thomas Chalmers says. We will no longer serve two masters, for our affections will be set upon God and the things that are above.

Seeking after the kingdom of God and His righteousness is a command. We are commanded to be children of God's kingdom everywhere: in creation, providence, and redemption; in privacy, in our families, at work and school and play. We are to be children of God's kingdom in our eternal state through regeneration and in our present condition through sanctification. Our lives should manifest God's own Word, for, as Psalm 103:19 says, "The LORD hath prepared his throne in the heavens, and his kingdom ruleth over all."

When we seek God's kingdom, we also seek His righteousness. We seek His imputed righteousness in Christ, which justifies us; His imparted righteousness through Christ, which sanctifies us; and His moral righteousness, which makes the world livable by His common grace. If the Gentiles seek gods that are no gods, how much more should Christians seek their living God and Father and His righteousness! We must seek the kingdom of God and His righteousness above all else in this world.

By nature, we do not obey this command, for we are born outside of God's kingdom. In our unregenerate state, we are under the power of Satan and are members of his kingdom of darkness. Jesus commands us to flee from Satan and his kingdom and to seek after the triune God and His kingdom.

How do we find this kingdom? We must turn to God's Word, which Matthew 13:19 calls "the word of the kingdom." We must pursue its truth in corporate, family, and private worship. We must exercise the spiritual disciplines that are connected to this Word and flow from it. And we must pray for true regeneration, repentance, and faith, so that we may enter into this kingdom to possess it, in part in this life, and in full in the life to come.

In response to our obedience to the command to seek after God and His righteousness, Jesus promises, "all these things shall be added unto you." In the original Greek, this phrase referred to a custom in which goods were sold by measure. The seller would add a little extra to the required amount to ensure a good weight and to foster goodwill. So the Lord here promises to those who seek after His kingdom and righteousness that He will throw in for good measure all the temporal things they need in this life.

Christ strengthens our faith through such generosity and good will. How precious such promises are to us as God's adopted children! As the Puritan Thomas Watson writes, "If we are adopted, then we have an interest in all the promises: the promises are children's bread." Or, as William Spurstowe says, God's promises are like a bag of coins that He pours out at the feet of His adopted children, saying, "Take what you will."

Are you living to the glory of God by resting in His goodness? Are you looking for the Father's care through His Son, Jesus Christ? All the promises of God to His children are yea and amen in Christ Jesus (2 Cor. 1:20).

6. Our Father Cares for Us Every Day (v. 34)

Our Father knows exactly how much affliction to send our way. In saying "sufficient unto the day is the evil thereof" (v. 34), Jesus tells us that God will give us the right amount of trials each day for our own good and the right amount of grace to cope with them.

Jesus is implying two things here. First, He is very practical in saying that since each day has a sufficient number of trials, we should not worry about what may happen the next day. We should seek to live to God's glory today, and God will give us fresh grace to handle the troubles of tomorrow. We must trust our Father to help us through today, for He will care for us in all the tomorrows that stretch before us. He will care for us every day.

Second, Jesus is implying that we need each day's troubles to keep us close to Him, for our Father uses such troubles to correct and chasten us for our sanctification. Hebrews 12 tells us that our Father chastens "every son whom he receiveth" (Heb. 12:6). The Father uses all of our troubles for our welfare and as occasions to disciple us (Rom. 8:28; 2 Cor. 12:7). John Owen says that all our sufferings are "for our education and instruction in his family." Samuel Willard says: "All our afflictions are helps toward heaven" and contribute to the "increase of their eternal glory: every reproach and injury doth but add weight to their crown." We foolishly think that God chastens us to destroy us, for 1 Corinthians 11:32 teaches us that the Lord chastens us so that we will not be condemned with the world. God's chastenings are badges of our adoption as God's children and of His fatherly love (Heb. 12:3–11). Once we understand that, we may be comforted by the afflictions our Father gives us. The Heidelberg Catechism summarizes all of this beautifully:

> That the eternal Father of our Lord Jesus Christ, who of nothing made heaven and earth with all that in them is, who likewise upholds, and governs the same by His eternal counsel and providence, is for the sake of Christ, His Son, my God and my Father, in whom I so trust as to have no doubt that He will provide me with all things necessary for body and soul; and further, that whatever evil He sends upon me in this troubled life, He will turn to my good; for He is able to do it, being Almighty God, and willing also, being a faithful Father.[19]

What if we cannot feel the powerful love of our Father when we suffer daily afflictions? What if such troubles make us question the Father's love to us and our adoption by Him? Thomas Shepard responds, "Is thy son not thy child, because while it is young it knows not the father that begot it, or because thou art sometimes departed from it, and hast it not always in thine own arms?"

How precious the love of the heavenly Father is toward His children! Jeremiah Burroughs writes, "God, who is the infinite glorious first-being, embraces them with an entire fatherly love. All the love that ever was in any parents towards children is but as one drop of the infinite ocean of fatherly love that there is in God unto his people."

In verse 34, Jesus says worldly minded people mainly consist of two groups. The first group enslaves itself to material possessions, seeking to amass as much as life will allow. The second group never seems to have enough and is constantly fretting over its neediness. The problem is the same for both groups: instead of trusting God as

---

19. The Heidelberg Catechism (LD 9, Q. 26), in Dennison, *Reformed Confessions of the 16th and 17th Centuries in English Translation: Volume 2, 1552–1566* (Grand Rapids: Reformation Heritage Books, 2010), 775–76.

their Father through Jesus Christ, these people measure themselves by what they have or do not have.

For both groups, tomorrow's cares are knocking at their doors today. Jesus commands His disciples not to be stuck in such worry. That does not suggest that tomorrow may be free of trouble. Rather, we are to limit ourselves to handling the troubles that come our way each day. Jesus says that we are to live every moment of every day with our eyes on the Father. For His own glory's sake, we are to trust Him.

Let me offer an example. My Dad was really happy on family vacation. During that time he was willing to give us his undivided attention. He was also generous in spending his hard-earned money. Just as Dad found satisfaction in supplying his family's temporal and financial needs while on vacation, I want to care for the needs of my family rather than seeing them worry about them. I want to show them my generosity. I feel honored when my family comes to me and asks for things, and when they are thankful when I supply them.

Likewise our Father in heaven is delighted when we come to Him with our every need. We honor Him when we come to Him boldly, cast our cares upon Him, appeal to His generosity, and are grateful when He shows His goodness to us.

If you have never known God as your Father through Jesus Christ, you have much to be anxious about. If God is not your Father, then Satan is your father, and if that does not change, you will spend eternity in hell with him.

The gospel offer still comes to you. Fly to the throne of grace and plead for forgiveness from God through the blood of His Son, Jesus Christ. Ask for grace to experience what Paul writes in Romans 8:14–15: "For as many as are led by the Spirit of God, they are the sons of God. For ye have not received the spirit of bondage again to fear; but ye have received the Spirit of adoption, whereby we cry, Abba, Father."

If God has performed a work of grace in your life but you struggle with trusting Him for today and tomorrow, think of what Jesus said in John 17:9: "I pray not for the world, but for them which thou hast given me; for they are thine." Later, He asks the Father to sanctify His disciples and those who come to faith through their testimony (vv. 17–20). Those who come to faith are believers in all ages.

If you have an intimate relationship with Jesus Christ, take comfort, for the Father's only-begotten Son has pleaded your case in the heavenly court, and the Father will withhold nothing from you. Entrust all of your cares to Him who values you, governs you, feeds and clothes you, knows your every need, commands you, gives promises to you, and cares for you every day and through all eternity.

Concluding Applications: Responding to My Father
You may now ask, "How should I respond to my Father so that I truly glorify Him?" In closing, let me offer six practical ways to do this:

1. *Trust your Father for every need.* Behave as a child of your heavenly Father by living above slavish fear and the anxieties of this world. Do not be dejected when you lack much of this world's comforts and toys. You will lack no needful thing, and every trial will work for your good.

2. *Show childlike reverence, love, and zeal for your Father in everything.* Reflect often upon your Father's great glory and majesty. Stand in awe of Him; render Him praise and thanksgiving in all things.

3. *Submit to your Father in every providence.* When He visits you with the rod, do not resist or murmur. Do not immediately respond by saying, "I am so afflicted that God cannot possibly be my Father." Rather, say with gratitude, "My Father is dealing with me again."

4. *Obey and imitate your Father.* Strive to be like Him. Be holy as He is holy; be loving as He is loving. Imitate your Father (Eph. 5:1) to show that you bear the family likeness.

5. *Engage in your Father's work.* Like a true son, do your Father's will and engage in His work. Discipline yourself and channel your energy into profitable use for God's church and kingdom. Turn your anxiety into ministry for your Father's cause. Like Christ, your Elder Brother, be about your Father's business, remembering that the night is coming when no man can work (John 9:4).

6. *Rejoice in your Father's presence.* Delight in communing with your Father in private, family, and corporate worship. Above all, long for

heaven, where your adoption will be perfected. As a child of God, wait eagerly for your full inheritance when the triune God will be your all in all.

All glory be to our Father who never fails us but always cares for us. *Soli Deo gloria* to Him who never makes one mistake in His paternal care on our behalf!

Chapter 17

Christ Forsaken!

> *And about the ninth hour Jesus cried with a loud voice, saying, Eli, Eli, lama sabachthani? that is to say, My God, my God, why has thou forsaken me?* —MATTHEW 27:46

With God's help, we wish to consider one of Scripture's most solemn and immense texts, Matthew 27:46:

Christ Forsaken!
1. The profundity of Christ's sufferings
2. The purpose that lay behind Christ's sufferings
3. The love that pervaded Christ's sufferings

1. The Profundity of Christ's Sufferings

It is twelve o'clock. Jesus has been on the cross for three pain-filled hours. Three times He has spoken from the cursed tree, focusing on the well-being of others: He has lovingly prayed for His enemies, promised salvation to a thief, and made arrangements for His mother's care. Many in the tumultuous crowd have scarcely heard the words that Jesus has said. Many who, five days earlier, waved palm branches before Him and cried, "Hosanna!" are now making abominable accusations against Christ.

Then, at noon, something unusual happens. Something quiets the noise and clamor at the place of execution. It suddenly becomes strangely dark at Calvary, and "over all the land." This darkness is no natural phenomenon; it is more than a thunderstorm and more than an eclipse. By a miraculous act of Almighty God, midday becomes midnight.

This supernatural darkness, which lasts for three hours, is a symbol of God's judgment on sin. God is light and in Him is no darkness at all, Scripture tells us. The Bible often associates sin with darkness and holiness with light. So the physical darkness that covers Calvary signals a deeper and more fearsome darkness that Christ Himself has described as "outer darkness," or the darkness of hell, where there is "weeping and gnashing of teeth."

The sun withholds its light as thick, heavy darkness descends on Golgotha, and the great High Priest enters Golgotha's holy of holies. The curtain is drawn, excluding friends and enemies. The Son of God is left alone. At Christ's birth, the bright light of God's glory and a multitude of angels fill the heavens. When Christ dies, the heavens go black because God is forsaking His Son. It is night within Jesus, for the God of light is letting go of Him. God does not look upon His suffering Servant. Forsaken of God and forsaken of people, Jesus confronts a dark end.

In His first three hours on the cross, Jesus has suffered intense physical and internal pain; in His last three hours, He suffers such incredible internal pain that it induces darkness to descend on Calvary. From noon to 3:00 p.m. that Friday, the Lord Jesus Christ is cast out of God's presence into utter darkness. What the Savior endures in those final three hours on the cross defies our imagination. No film maker can begin to picture it.

A plague of darkness preceded the slaying of the Passover lamb in Exodus 12. Here on the cross, the great Passover Lamb is being sacrificed in a much more profound darkness. The thick darkness over the land is intensified in the darkness within the soul of Jesus Christ. For three long hours, Christ wrestles with the powers of darkness. He is in the midst of natural darkness as spiritual darkness descends into the depths of His being. We read of no word during these three hours by Christ or anyone in the crowd around the cross. It is an awesome, eerie, unforgettable scene of silence.

Hear the silence and feel the darkness, then tell me that Jesus doesn't understand your darkness. He *does* understand. He is a Friend who can sympathize with your darkest moments, your deepest fears, your most indescribable agony. He comes alongside you when you cry out with tears, saying, "Heaven is silent!" His response is: "I understand; I have been there and I know what it is like. I can get you through this. Your weeping may endure for a night, but joy will come in the morning." When you walk in darkness, Jesus is there, for He has endured midnight at midday.

Christ has endured most of His physical suffering in silence. He has not responded to the spitting and scourging at Gabbatha; He has been silent as He has carried the cross, as He has been lifted on it, and as nails have torn at His flesh. But as He experiences the full brunt of His Father's wrath, Jesus cannot remain silent. Though invisible in the darkness, He cries out: "My God, my God, why hast thou forsaken me?"

This fourth word from the cross represents the nadir, the lowest point, of Jesus's sufferings. Here Jesus descends, figuratively speaking, into the essence of hell in the most extreme suffering anyone has ever experienced. It is a time of incredible destiny and density—a time so compacted, so infinite, so horrendous as to be incomprehensible and seemingly unsustainable. To begin to grasp a little of the profundity of this amazing cry from the cross, let us look at five things that this word from the cross do *not* reveal, then at four things that it *does* reveal.

First, Jesus's cry, "My God, my God, why hast thou forsaken me?", does not in any way *diminish His deity*. Jesus does not cease being God before, during, or after this moment of utter anguish. He was and is both God and man.

Second, Jesus's cry does not *divide His human nature from His divine person*. His person is not split so that the union between His natures is broken. These two—God and man—never cease to be united. Furthermore, Christ does not experience desertion in His divine nature, but only in His human nature. Nor is this desertion mutual. The Father temporarily deserts Christ, but Christ does not desert His Father.

Third, Jesus's cry does not *destroy the Trinity*. It does not reveal a crack in the Trinity so that the Father and Son fall apart. God the Father cannot forsake His Son as God. Father and Son are still one in their being and one in all their attributes. The three Persons have not become two Persons. The Father, Son, and Holy Spirit remain three Persons in one Godhead, but the awesome fellowship of delight has been temporarily severed between the Father and His Son, the God-man. Thomas Goodwin writes, "The Godhead was not separated, though the operation of comfort from the Godhead was sequestered."

Fourth, Jesus's cry does not *detach Him from the Holy Spirit*. He does not cease to be filled with the Holy Spirit without measure. The Son lacks the *comforts* of the Spirit, but He does not lose the *holiness* of the Spirit. The Spirit is still in Him without measure.

Finally, Jesus's cry does not cause Him to *disavow His mission*. Both the Father and Son have known from all eternity that Jesus will become the Lamb of God who will take away the sin of the world. Acts 15:18 says, "Known unto God are all his works from the beginning of the world." Jesus has been walking with destiny to this very moment, and the hour of laying down His life has finally come. Now He will accomplish the redemption of sinners by becoming a sacrifice for their sin.

It is unthinkable that the Son of God might question what is happening on the cross or be perplexed about why His Father's loving presence departs. Jesus has refused wine mixed with myrrh at the very start of crucifixion so that He will be alert to the end. All His feelings serve this redemptive end.

Taken together, these five principles teach us that even when—indeed, *especially* when—Christ is deserted by His Father, we must bow down and worship Christ. If Christ had ceased to be God when His Father left Him, our worship of the Son would be idolatry, for we would be worshiping a mere creature. Surely, if we are Christians, *the ultimate reason* for worship is the moment when we hear Jesus cry out to God. Instinctively, we feel the need to fall down in worship and say, "My Lord and my God!"

First, Jesus is expressing the *agony of unanswered supplication*. The words Jesus says echo what is said in Psalm 22:1–2, "My God, my God, why hast thou forsaken me? why art thou so far from helping me, and from the words of my roaring? O my God, I cry in the daytime, but thou hearest not; and in the night season, and am not silent." Precisely what Jesus is praying for is not clear. Is He once more asking for the cup of suffering to pass? Is He begging for a token of

His Father's light—a smile or benediction? Whatever it is, He receives no answer except the echo of His own voice and the cruel taunts of hell. The heavens are as brass before Him.

Unanswered, Jesus feels forgotten of God although He is not really forgotten. You too, dear believer, know a little of that sorrow. And yet, in your most "forgotten moments," you are not truly forgotten by God either. A mother would sooner forget her nursing baby than your Father in heaven, for the forgotten Savior's sake, would forget you (Isa. 49:14–17).

Second, Jesus is expressing *the agony of unbearable stress*. Stress and distress so overwhelm Jesus that He cries with a loud voice, the kind of "roaring" mentioned in Psalm 22. The famous painting titled "The Scream" depicts a person with a huge mouth uttering an awful scream. It represents humanity under so much stress that it utters a primal scream. But even this horrific figure pales in comparison to the roaring cry of the Lord Jesus. His cry pierces the darkness. It is the roar of desperate agony without rebellion. John Flavel writes, "It is as much as if Christ had said, O my God, no words can express my anguish: I will not speak, but roar, howl out my complaint; pour it out in vollies of groans: I roar as a lion." It is similar to the cry that is uttered in hell when the wrath of God overwhelms the damned. This cry is heart-piercing, heaven-piercing, and hell-piercing! What agony!

Children, how do you feel when you fall and hurt yourself, then run to your father for help, only to find that your father is not there? You are so anxious that you begin to scream, "Dad, Dad, where are you? My dad is gone!" That anxiety is nothing compared to Jesus's excruciating distress in the absence of His Father. What do the angels think when they hear Jesus cry and witness the Father's silence as He turns His back on His own beloved Son?

In this moment, as in none other, the Son knows the full measure of His Father's wrath. That anger deluges the Son with no restraint. All of divine justice crashes upon Him, wave after wave. Never has He been such an object of wrath!

Yet, at the same time, the Son remains the supreme object of His Father's pleasure. The Father loves His Son because His Son lays down

His life for His enemies. Never has the Father approved and admired His Son so much, though the Son temporarily feels no comfort of it.

If you are not a believer, does this cry of Jesus not frighten you? Does not this cry of hell disturb you and make you tremble? Jesus's words about being forsaken by God will be your words if you remain unrepentant. If you do not believe, you will experience unbearable stress, wrath, abandonment, forsakenness—not for three hours, but forever. Do you not need this Savior for your soul? Will you not embrace Him, believe in Him, trust in Him, and be saved?

Third, Jesus is expressing the *agony of unmitigated sin*. All the sins of the elect of all ages, and the hell that they deserve for eternity, are laid upon Christ on the cross. Without the support of His deity, Jesus could never have sustained the burden. Because His deity and humanity are combined in one infinite person, His sufferings carry infinite value in the presence of an infinitely holy God. That is how Christ can bear our justly deserved eternal hell in such a short time.

I once saw a picture of a man standing in front of the Sears Tower in Chicago. He held two large boulders in his hands. The caption beneath the picture said that some stars are so dense in weight compared to their size that the two boulders the man held could weigh as much as the Sears Tower. That is a faint suggestion of how God compresses on His Son all the agonies of sin in a short period of time.

Jesus's cry includes such a profound sense of sin that, temporarily, His sense of Sonship seems to recede. That does not mean, of course, that Jesus doubts His own divine Sonship or loses a sense of it altogether. That would amount to a failure to receive in faith the Scripture's testimony about His very identity. Jesus is fully conscious of His divine identity and often cites Scriptures that testify to it. So it would not be compatible with Jesus's impeccable faith in the Word of God to think that He doubted His divine identity.

Let me explain. Though Christ has a divine consciousness and a human consciousness, He has only one self-consciousness that belongs to His divine person. His divine personhood is the foundation on which His theanthropic (or "God-man") constitution is erected. Though He experiences change and development in His human consciousness so that He can pass into deeper sorrow when He enters

Gethsemane, Jesus's self-consciousness never changes because it was an aspect of His personhood, and that personhood is divine.

That being the case, how can He cease to be conscious of Himself in His identity as the eternal Son of the Father? Would that not suggest a self-consciousness seated in His humanity rather than in His divine personhood? In His human mind, Jesus is conscious of human experience, and, in His divine mind, He is conscious of realities that His human mind cannot comprehend. But when He reflects on His individual identity, Jesus at all times knows but one self, the self who is the "I Am That I Am," who is with the Father before the creation of the world, and who is sent by the Father to come into the world as a man.

Nevertheless, in these moments, a sense of sin dominates Jesus's consciousness to a frightening degree. In Gethsemane and in the first and last words on the cross, Jesus has called on God as His Father. But now He cries, "Eli, eli," or "Eloi, eloi"—"my God, my God." He is aware of God: the goodness of God, the justice and holiness of God. But that awful moment, in His self-image, He feels sin more intensely than His Sonship, although His Sonship is by no means obliterated.

Christ here is feeling your and my sin, dear believer. Paul says that God the Father "made him to be sin for us, who knew no sin" (2 Cor. 5:21). In His self-image, Jesus feels at this moment not so much that He is the Beloved in whom God is well-pleased, but rather that He is the cursed one who is vile, foul, and repulsive. That is the essence of what God thinks of sin—the essence of the price the God-man needed to pay for sin.

Yet, in the midst of this agony, Jesus exercises unassailable faith. He cries, "Eli, Eli" (which is Hebrew), or "Eloi, Eloi" (which is Aramaic)—the *El* meaning "strong one." His feelings are saying, "No God," but His faith says, "*My* God." His feelings are saying, "No strength, no strong one," but His faith says, "*My* strong One." He is appealing to the One who has always supported Him in His troubles. His feelings are saying, "You have been left alone," yet His faith says, "No matter what my feelings tell me, or what providence tells me, or what taunts are thrown in my face, He is my Lord and my God." Calvin says of Christ in this moment, "Still in His heart faith remained firm, by which He beheld the presence of God, of whose absence He complains."

In these words, "Eli, Eli," Jesus exemplifies how we must abandon our feelings when our feelings say, "God has abandoned me." Too often as Christians and as pastors we are governed by our feelings rather than our faith. We need to model for others how to live by faith in the midst of our darkest hours and our deepest trials. At such times, people are watching us more closely than ever to see how our faith holds up under suffering.

Then, too, we see Christ's faith in the question "Why hast thou forsaken me?" Jesus is not asking this question in a spirit of boldness or impudence or rebellion. Nor is He asking with a sense of bewilderment, as if wondering, "What am I doing here?" Rather, Jesus is asking "Why?" in the spirit of submissive faith. He is asking the Father of heaven to make known in a vivid way why God is abandoning Him. He knows why, but He wants the reasons to be stated again so that He can hold onto them for sustenance in these hours of darkness. He is saying, "Father, remind Me why this is necessary. Oh, yes, it is necessary for Me to be God-forsaken so that God-forsakers may know union with God." And now, look at the end—is it not glorious? This is what the Lord is doing; He is asking in faith that His human nature might be strengthened as He is reminded of the reasons for His suffering and the end to which they serve. Here again is a wonderful example for us to follow.

Finally, Jesus is expressing here the *agony of unassisted solitariness*. Jesus is asking His Father, "Why hast thou forsaken, deserted, and abandoned me?" Before coming to earth, Jesus has been the eternal Son of God in heaven. The Father's love has been lavished generously and continuously upon Him. As Proverbs 8 says, "I was daily his delight, rejoicing always before him."

Jesus also has experienced His Father's love on earth. Jesus has known continuously the Father's love and support and nearness. He has felt one with the Father. There never has been a sweeter Father, and there never has been a more loving Son. They have gone up from Bethlehem to Calvary together, like Abraham and Isaac going up the mount in Genesis 22. In such moments of trouble and sorrow, God has sent help. In John 12, the Father has affirmed the Son, saying,

"This is my beloved Son." In the garden of Gethsemane, God has sent an angel to strengthen His Son.

But now, in His hour of greatest need, Christ experiences a pain unlike anything He has ever experienced—His Father's abandonment. When Jesus most needs encouragement, no voice cries from heaven, "This is my beloved Son." When He most needs reassurance, no one says, "I am well pleased." No dove descends from heaven to symbolize peace; no angel is sent to strengthen Him; no "well done, thou good and faithful servant" resounds in His ears. He is in a far country, a strange country, hanging in the flame of His Father's wrath. The women who have supported Him so often are silent. The disciples, cowardly and terrified, are far away. Feeling disowned by all, Jesus walks the way of suffering alone in pitch-black darkness.

The Father does not permit one beam of sunlight to shine down upon Him. God is present only in displeasure, bearing down upon Christ in anger. Instead of love, there is wrath. Instead of affection, there is coldness. Instead of support, there is opposition. Instead of nearness, there is distance for three long, agonizing hours. The Son's cries do not bring the Father back. There is no change in the Father's demeanor until He is so far away that He eventually disappears. The Son cries out one last time, "My God—why?" That is what we have here. The Son is pursuing the Father as He distances Himself even further. There is an indescribable pursuit going on here, and yet the Father purposefully retreats. No amount of pursuing will catch up with the Father, and eventually there is nothing left but abandonment. Jesus is alone. Deserted. Forsaken.

Please don't misunderstand me. Jesus does not pity Himself. He does not cry out with the rich man, "I am tormented in this flame." But Jesus cries out for God.

Every detail of this abandonment shouts to you and me, "This is what God thinks of your and my sin!" Every detail declares the irrationality, the heinousness, the dreadfulness of sin.

The fourth word that Jesus utters from the cross should take our breath away. We can understand how David can utter this heart-rending cry in Psalm 22, but we find it impossible to understand how those same words can be uttered by Jesus Christ, the Son of God.

How can He endure unanswered prayer, the fading of filial consciousness, and then the abandonment of His Father, when He too is God of God? How can God forsake Christ as though He is Cain and not Christ? How can God the Father forsake God the Son?

Martin Luther exclaimed, "God forsaken of God! Who can comprehend it?" What this abandonment meant for Christ cannot be adequately explained, even by Christ Himself. Although He uttered these words in human language, they reflect an experience of which human beings are strangers. No son of Adam has ever gone through what Christ endured. Many people have felt forsaken of God, but no human being, not even reprobates, are completely forsaken by God while still in this life.

Outside an emergency room in a California hospital is a drop-off box for unwanted babies. The thought of abandoning one's baby like dropping mail in a mailbox makes us shudder. Yet, when believers feel forsaken, it is like that: a feeling that does not correspond with reality. They lose the sense of God's presence, but not this presence itself. With Christ this loss was both feeling and fact. He felt forsaken because He was forsaken. He endured the essence of abandonment; believers endure only the shadows of it, even though those shadows can be so fearsome.

2. The Purpose That Lay behind Christ's Sufferings

Why was Christ forsaken by God? We cannot hope to find a completely satisfying answer to this question. If even Christ Himself asked, "Why?" and received no answer, how shall we find a solution to this terrible darkness, this appalling situation, this unfathomable depth of suffering?

But Scripture does not leave us completely ignorant of why Christ was forsaken. Isaiah 53 offers part of the answer by telling us in verse 10, "It pleased the LORD to bruise him." In His love for this evil world, God the Father offered up His own Son.

But why? Why did God deal this way with His own divine Son, whom He loved? Why did God bruise Him and place Him under His own wrath and curse? Christ was sinless; He was divine; yet He was accursed by God. Why? There are only four possible explanations of such actions of God the Father.

The first possibility is *capriciousness*—the idea that the Father, out of a simple change of mind, anathematized His Son. Such an answer, of course, is blasphemous and unthinkable. God could never bruise and desert His Son out of mere arbitrary sovereignty. He knows no mood changes. He is not capricious. His love is steady; it is *agape* love.

The second possibility is that God the Father bruised His Son out of *malice*—that Jehovah crushed and bruised and extinguished the life of His own Son because of the evil that was part of His nature. This is also unthinkable, for it would be criminal on the part of God. If you saw a father bruising and murdering his son, you would not conclude that this father loved his son, but quite the contrary. Yet many who have no understanding of the atonement stand before the cross and foolishly say, "This is no proof of the love of God!"

The third possibility is *didactic*—that the Father wanted to teach the Son profound lessons about suffering so He laid harsh judgment, especially the judgment of desertion, upon Him. This approach is drawn from how God treats His people at times by bruising them with painful desertions. He appears to leave His people from time to time, although He doesn't actually do so, just as He never actually left Jesus. The Christian can have a sense of God's presence sometimes, but at other times have no sense of it at all.

Sometimes God withdraws His presence as a disciplinary measure because we have offended Him. Sometimes He withdraws Himself as a precautionary measure. He sees us heading into dangerous territory, and He withdraws to make us aware of the direction we are heading. Sometimes He withdraws as a test, not because we have done wrong, but just to ask, "Will you stay with Me if I take away the sense of My presence from you?" But God had no reason to teach His Son such lessons. His Son was already perfect. The Father had no need to bruise His Son as a test, a discipline, or a precaution.

Finally, the Father's real cause of bruising His Son is *penal*. In other words, the righteousness of God is the source of the sufferings of Jesus. The righteousness of God demands that sin be punished.

The Father's bruising was judicial wrath. It was a just infliction of punishment for the sin that Christ carried for His people.

The logic of this judicial substitution is clearly stated in 2 Corinthians 5:21: "For he hath made him to be sin for us, who knew no sin; that we might be made the righteousness of God in him." The logic of Calvary is that Christ was made sin for us. He died for us; He bore our sin; He became a curse for us; He gave His life a ransom for many. When all the anomalies and mysteries of salvation pile on top of one another, this little word *for* demolishes them all. In this *for*, darkness is illuminated; this small word unites Jesus Christ and sinners. In other words, there is only one thing that can explain why God inflicted punishment on His own Son, and that is that His Son stood in an intimate connection with sin and sinners. If Christ did not connect with sin and sinners, then Calvary was the darkest moment this world has ever known. But we are joined with Christ to sin and to sinners by the word *for*!

So in what sense was Christ *for* His people? First of all, Christ was acting on behalf of His people for their benefit. He was acting as their representative; He was acting in their interest. Christ is the Representative, the Advocate, the One who acts in the place of His people. He intercedes for His people, pleads for them, and looks after their interests. But Jesus Christ is more than a representative.

Second, He suffered on behalf of His clients. He is not only the Priest interceding and pleading for His people, but He became the sacrifice in their place. He not only acts for the client, but He assumes the liabilities and responsibilities of the client.

As our substitute, Jesus bore our sin in our place and obeyed the law in our place so that God's justice can be satisfied and that God can be the justifier of those who believe in Jesus (Rom. 3:26). As our substitute, Christ assumed the guilt of His people and justified God in treating Him as His people deserve to be treated on account of their sin.

Dear believer, do you understand how Christ is anathema because He is your substitute? Because He paid for your sin, God bruised His Son and did not spare Him. He was made a curse for you to redeem you from the curse. He is your condemnation so that there is no condemnation for you. He is the Son of God crucified, Son of God anathema, Son of God desolate, Son of God forsaken, because He is the Son of Man who must suffer many things. And that "must" is not rooted in human conventions nor in theological contrivances, but in the great truth that God delights in mercy (Mic. 7:18) and therefore is in the business of saving sinners.

God loves to forgive sin. He loves to multiply pardon and to make it abound. But He condones nothing. God Himself must bear the sin of the elect. The God who forgives, who bears, and who exacts is the God who demands atonement. But wonder of wonders, the God who *provides* the atonement *became* the atonement. God is the Lamb. God has found the Lamb in His own flock, in His own bosom. This, surely, is the greatest reality in the Christian faith: that Jesus Christ became the sacrifice, the scapegoat.

No one at the foot of the cross could answer Christ's profound question. Even the angels had no answer. But in Psalm 22:3, Jesus answers His own question: "But thou art holy, O thou that inhabitest the praises of Israel." Why did God forsake Jesus? Because God is holy. God's love is a pure, sin-hating love. As the prophet Habakkuk says, "Thou art of purer eyes than to behold evil, and canst not look upon iniquity" (Hab. 1:13). This was also true at the cross. God could not behold evil, even when that evil was found on His own Son. He could not look upon the iniquity that His all-seeing eye detected on Christ.

Jesus had no personal sins for which to atone, but as the representative of sinners, He bore much sin. When He took upon Himself His people's sins, God treated Him as the sin-bearer, holding Him responsible for the payment of their sins. That is why God forsook Jesus.

Christ also received the wages of sin, which is death. Death means more than physical death; it also involves spiritual and eternal death—the complete separation between God and man. Adam brought that death upon himself and his descendants. So Christ, having taken Adam's sin upon Himself, also needed to bear Adam's punishment. He descended into the essence of hell, the place of total loneliness and abandonment, where He cried out, "My God, my God, why hast thou forsaken me?"

The answer to that question is this: "Thou art holy, Thou art just in demanding satisfaction for sin at My hand. I know that I must answer for all the sins of My people. Therefore I cannot but justify Thee, O my God. Let Thy sword awake against the Man that is Thy fellow!" (cf. Zech. 13:7).

Christ's penal suffering, therefore, is vicarious—that is, He suffered on our behalf, dear believers. He did not simply share our forsakenness or take the brunt of it, but He saved us from it. He endured it *for* us, not *with* us. You, dear believer, are immune to condemnation (Rom. 8:1) and to God's anathema (Gal. 3:13) because Christ bore it for you in that outer darkness. As interceding High Priest, Christ sympathizes with you, but what Golgotha secured for you was immunity rather than sympathy.

Because Christ died on the tree, there is no longer the slightest need for one grain of penal suffering to be visited on any of His people. He endured all the torments and relational distance from God that we deserve as sinners. The Savior was once abandoned for me so that I will never be abandoned. "Christ also hath once suffered for sins, the just for the unjust, that he might bring us to God" (1 Peter 3:18). Golgotha will achieve all that God intended it to accomplish. Every lost sheep will be brought home to God.

This, then, is the only explanation for the three hours of darkness and for the roar of dereliction. God's people still experience the confirmation of this truth today when the Holy Spirit brings them to the cross in dreadful darkness, before the tribunal of the Judge of heaven and earth, only for them to experience, as the darkness subsides, that they are not consumed for Christ's sake. They come out of the darkness, confessing, "Because Immanuel has descended into the lowest hell for us, God is with us in the darkness, under the darkness, and through the darkness—and we are not consumed!"

3. The Love That Pervaded Christ's Sufferings

I would like to leave you with three applications relating to the triune God's love in Christ's forsakenness.

First, Christ's being forsaken by God reveals the stupendous *love of Christ*. If Samuel Rutherford could say, "God incarnate is nothing but love covered with flesh," how much more vivid is Christ's love displayed in His cry of dereliction. "My God, my God, why hast thou forsaken me?" was the cry of the incarnate God whose soul was sinking ever deeper into the bottomless pit of divine wrath. Believers cannot possibly fathom the love of the One who saved them from perdition. As one hymn writer put it:

> But none of the ransomed ever knew
> How deep were the waters crossed,
> Nor how dark was the night that the Lord passed through,
> Ere He found His sheep that was lost.

As followers of Christ, Christians must expect suffering and persecution. Paul writes, "All that will live godly in Christ Jesus shall suffer persecution" (2 Tim. 3:12). In Philippians 2:5–8, the apostle tells us to let the mind of Christ Jesus dwell in us. The Philippians were claiming their own rights rather than surrendering them; they wanted to be praised for the service they gave the Lord. They wanted their gifts to be acknowledged and honored. Paul responds, "If you are complaining that you are not being honored for what you do, look to the Lord of glory. Although He was God, He did not grasp at equality with God. Jesus did not insist on coming to this earth in all His regalia. He did not protect His dignity by refusing to be born in a stable." Paul cautions the Philippians—and us—to abandon all pretentions of glory.

Is Christ's mind in you, dear friend? What practical, profound teaching lies in the fourth word that Jesus spoke from the cross! If we worship Jesus, we will relinquish every form of unresolved bitterness against anyone. How can we nurse bitterness against someone who treats us far less poorly than we have treated the Lord of glory? Let us abandon our petty rights, our mundane complaints, at the foot of the cross. Let us quit trivializing. How do we dare to trivialize at the foot of the cross?

Second, Christ's being forsaken by God reveals the stupendous *love of the Father*. You ask, "Where is the love? There seems to be nothing but wrath here!" Look again and remember John 3:16: "For God so loved the world, that he gave his only begotten Son." True, God needed to turn His face away from Jesus because He found sin on Him. But this was all according to His plan. Remember, Jesus was made sin by God so that we might be made the righteousness of God in Him. Jesus was forsaken so that we might be accepted of God and never be forsaken of Him.

In the gospel, the Father loves sinners lavishly. He gives everything He has and holds nothing back. When the Father gave His only-begotten Son, His bosom Friend from eternity, He took the best He had and gave Him for the worst He could find—sinners like you and me—sending His Son to experience the worst imaginable humiliation and suffering. He spared not His own Son but gave the supreme commitment of His heart.

Christ's forsakenness by the Father makes plain that the Father held nothing in reserve but was extravagant in His overflowing love to sinners who were at enmity with Him. Dear believer, the fourth word from the cross preaches God's unchangeable love for you. You are caught up in a love that has broken down all the prejudices of your evil mind and heart. That love has brought you into its own domain and caused you to swim in its infinity. The love of the Father flows from His very heart and being. Who can stop such love? No one has ever loved this way. And this love is made transparent at the cross in the cry of dereliction. Amazing grace! God is willing to turn a deaf ear to His Son's agony to listen to your needs as a poor sinner.

Reverently speaking, such extravagant love appears to be almost foolish. When we learn how sinful we are, we are prone to cry out, "O God, how foolish Thou art to love such a creature as I am! Lord, depart from me, for I am a sinful man." The wisdom of men is foolishness with God, Paul says, but "the foolishness of God is wiser than men; and the weakness of God is stronger than men" (1 Cor. 1:25). The foolishness of God's amazing love is incomprehensible to us. Had others treated us the way we treated God, we would offer them no hope, no mercy, no forgiveness. We would refuse to cast our pearls before such swine, but God put the Pearl of great price in the pathway of the likes of us wretched sinners. In His infinite wisdom, God decided to bring glory to Himself and the Son of His love by making His Son the Mediator and Savior of a great multitude that no man can number.

Finally, Christ's being forsaken by God reveals the stupendous *love of the Spirit*. After Christ drank the cup of His Father's wrath, Mark

15:37–39 tells us that three veils were rent. The Father tore the veil in the temple (v. 38), the Son tore the veil of His flesh (v. 37), and the Holy Spirit tore the veil of the human heart (v. 39). The Spirit so convinced a Roman centurion of the true identity of Jesus that he could not help crying out in the midst of a Christ-despising crowd, "Truly this man was the Son of God" (v. 39). The Holy Spirit used Christ's last words and His loud cry of victory in death to persuade the centurion that Jesus Christ was the Messiah.

The Spirit still shows His incredible love in working patiently yet irresistibly in the hearts of sinners, applying to us the wonderful truths of the cross. He lovingly and persuasively shows us that Christ was forsaken of the Father that we might never be forsaken of the Triune God. He convinces us that all our sufferings, including feeling forsaken, are the fruit of merely walking in His shadow and are a far cry from the reality of forsakenness that Christ endured. In response, our hearts so overflow with love that we cry out, "We love him, because he first loved us" (1 John 4:19).

If you are a believer, meditate on this love the next time you feel forsaken of God. Think of what your Savior experienced. No matter how terrible your affliction is, remember that Jesus has been there before you so He understands your feelings. He can sympathize with your fears and anxieties, for He, too, has experienced them. Do not conclude that because you feel forsaken you cannot be a child of God.

A minister was standing by the deathbed of one of his members who suffered from deep depression. The pastor tried to find something to say that might comfort this man who had given evidence of being a Christian. But no matter what he said, the reply was, "It's no use." Suddenly the pastor said, "What became of that Man who died whom God did really forsake? Where is He now?" The dying man clung to that thought and said, "He is in glory, and I shall be with Him where He is!" Light finally came to this dying man.

In Christ's cry of dereliction, there is true hope for discouraged believers. If you feel abandoned and forsaken and wonder where God is, take heart. Your feeling of spiritual abandonment is only a feeling; it is not a fact. Flee to the once-forsaken but never-forsaking Savior, cast yourself upon Him, and you will experience the truth of Hebrews

13:5, perhaps best translated as "He will never, no never, no never forsake you."

Praise be to God, we will never be abandoned because Christ has suffered that abandonment for us. We will worship the Father perfectly, and say, "My Father," and He will respond: "My child, I cannot leave you or forsake you. You are too precious to Me because the Lamb of God has earned the right to make you Mine forever." Experiencing this, we can say, "I live; yet not I, but Christ liveth in me: and the life which I now live in the flesh I live by the faith of the Son of God, who loved me, and gave himself for me" (Gal. 2:20).

We can feel sorry for needy children of God who are thirsting for God and His communion, but at the same time we can rejoice because such people will not perish. They will see God's gracious countenance. But we must be gravely concerned about the self-deceived who profess to know the Lord and yet do not have close communion with Him and who do not seem to know the difference between His presence and His absence. What else can this mean than that they are still strangers to God and His grace?

My friend, if you can live without a sense of the Lord's presence and are satisfied with mere outward Christianity, you are still lost in your sins. The wrath of Almighty God rests on you. If you die like that, you will be forever where Christ was in essence for those three terrible hours on the cross. Hell is utter forsakenness by the favorable presence of God.

Whether you are self-deceived or knowingly unsaved, the fourth word from the cross warns you to flee from the wrath to come. You must be born again. Repent from your sin, believe in Christ alone for salvation, and submit to the Savior's lordship with your entire being. Do not rest until you, too, believe in Him who was forsaken in wrath that you might be accepted in mercy. Receive the admonition of Hebrews 2:2–3: "For if the word spoken by angels was stedfast, and every transgression and disobedience received a just recompense of reward; how shall we escape, if we neglect so great salvation?" May the Lord be pleased to save many through this glorious gospel, for Jesus's sake.

Chapter 18

Fighting Unbelief

And straightway the father of the child cried out, and said with tears, Lord, I believe; help thou mine unbelief.
—MARK 9:24

It is unfortunate that the inexpressible wonder of Christ's incarnation often gets attention only once per year on Christmas. We can hardly comprehend that great change of scene which took place when Jesus Christ willingly left His crown, throne, and glory in heaven above, and came into this sin-sick world to live in the presence of sinners and in the smoke of sin by assuming our human nature out of the virgin Mary. God's people will spend eternity glorying in that wonder of wonders.

Indeed, the Christmas story is not the only place where the Bible displays for us the wonder of that great change of scene from heavenly glory to earthly darkness. In Mark 9 we find Jesus's transition from the mount of His transfiguration and glory to the plain of human distress and confusion.

What a blessed time it must have been for Christ on the mountain of transfiguration. On that mountain He experienced the fullness, communion, and approval of His Father in an inexpressible degree. On that mountain also, Peter, James, and John must have had a blessed experience, even though they did not yet understand its full significance. Peter, for one, wanted to remain there, and desired that a tabernacle be built there for the Lord Jesus.

What a blessing, however, that such a tabernacle was not built. Jesus did not stay on that mountain. If He had, salvation would have been lost forever. Then He never would have given His life as a ransom for His people. If Peter received his wish for a tabernacle to be built, although the church would have been one step from heaven, she never would have entered into heaven.

The time soon came when Jesus needed to go back down the mountain to fulfill His mission. He needed to return to the earthly confusion. The people who had gathered on the plain below did not come up the mountain. Rather, Jesus went down, which illustrates the effect of man's deep fall from Paradise. Man is not able to take one step toward his salvation or toward God, but the great and the necessary blessing is the coming of Jesus.

The first blessing was that Jesus *came*, the second was that He came *down*, and the third was that He came down *just in time*. And so it is always when He comes with salvation. He does not come when His people think they are ready, but He comes to them just in time—when all is hopeless and cut off from their side. He comes when He is absolutely needed.

And how needed Jesus was when He came down from the mount of transfiguration! What an awful scene met His eyes! Here was a physically agonized boy, a deeply distressed father, a band of nine baffled disciples who were unable to give relief, and a group of mocking scribes, who were trying to convince the gathered crowd that the inability of the disciples implied the inability of their Master.

What an awful contrast between the mountain and the plains! What a great change of scene Jesus now experienced! He came from the voice and presence of God above to the work and presence of the devil below. He came from heavenly glory to earthly misery—from peace to agony, from heavenly tranquility to earthly confusion, from holiness to sinfulness.

Yet, how things changed when He came! What a difference it makes when Jesus comes. What an eternal difference—a difference of salvation—it made as He came to Bethlehem's stable for His people, and what a difference it made when He came to this plain.

His presence came as a great surprise. Scripture says, "All the people…were greatly amazed" (Mark 9:15). They were amazed, in the first place, *that* He came, when it seemed as if He were nowhere to be found, and they were amazed, in the second place, *how* He came, showing forth His divine authority as the exceeding brightness of the transfiguration still lingered upon His countenance, as it did when Moses came down the mountain with the law in his hands. And so it is, spiritually speaking, for God's people. We are amazed when Jesus comes—amazed that He comes to such wretches as we are, and amazed how He comes with His salvation in spite of our sinfulness.

What a blessing that may be! There may be moments when some believers experience Jesus placing them on the mount, granting them a foretaste of heaven and a vision of glory. But such times are often brief and infrequent. As a rule, more time is spent by Jesus preparing believers for glory than in their experience of that glory. More time is often spent in the plain—in the midst of weakness, struggles, conflict, and sorrow. God's people must return time and again to a struggling faith here below. In our efforts to pursue holiness by the Spirit's grace, let us consider how to overcome our unbelief through a distressed father's struggling cry of faith in Mark 9:24: "And straightway the father of the child cried out, and said with tears, Lord, I believe; help thou mine unbelief."

When Jesus Helps Us See the Deeper Issue

The father in Mark 9 had a son who was in a very pitiful condition. In the first place, his son had epilepsy. All the conditions of epilepsy were present, as can be gathered from Matthew, Mark, and Luke together, including seizures, convulsions, falling to the ground, foaming at the mouth, grinding teeth, and rigidity. But to this we must immediately add that this was not simply an ordinary case of epilepsy. Second, this son was also deaf and mute: he could not speak and he could not hear. Third, and worst of all, this child was a demoniac: he was possessed by an evil spirit who knocked him down time and again. He was not only *influenced* by that evil spirit, but he was in its *possession*.

This father had no doubt tried everything possible to cure his son. Like the woman with the bloody issue, he must have gone from physician to physician. He must have tried all kinds of remedies, but no remedy, no person, nothing, could help. All physicians were of no value in this apparently hopeless case.

Not even the disciples of Jesus Christ could heal this pitiable man's son. This father might have heard of other occasions when Jesus had worked miracles by means of His disciples. But now, coming to Christ's disciples, he found their healing energy depleted in the case of his son. The disciples tried to cast out the evil spirit in vain.

What a trial for the father! It is difficult to imagine the struggle that must have waged within him in those moments. Surely it must have been a struggle for him in the first place to come to the disciples in front of a large number of people. Wouldn't the people just mock him and say, "Your son has been in such a condition since he was a small boy; his case is hopeless."

Yet the father still came. Hoping against hope he brought his son, and the outcome was clear: there was still no relief. The disciples were unable to cast out the demon. The devil was rejoicing. Inside the father, the voice of the evil one whispered: "I told you so. You were foolish to bring your son in the first place. You have only made a fool of yourself."

As the father now stood in this helpless condition, there was nothing left for him to do but to return home, and yet he could not. Even though it was only logical to conclude that there was no hope, and that even if Jesus Christ were present, He could not heal His son since His own disciples could not; yet this father, seeing no solution, could not leave. He could not return home and he could scarcely stay. He was at his wit's end. It became a lost cause for him and his son.

And now Jesus came! Perhaps we would say, "Why didn't He come sooner? Why did He let His disciples become so ridiculed? Why did He permit the father's agony to escalate to such a seemingly hopeless point?

The answer can be put simply: Jesus is all-knowing. He knew, moment by moment, exactly what was happening in the plain below. He waited until everything else was eliminated as a source of help outside of Himself. Jesus had great and deep lessons to teach this father. He did not come only to heal the physical infirmity of the son, but above all, the spiritual infirmity of the father. In such a way, Jesus also teaches all His people. He leads them to that place where everything is cut off—even the very disciples of Jesus. In other words, everyone—self, God's people, including ministers—must be completely lost as a cure for their deadly spiritual disease. Has that ever taken place in a spiritual sense in our lives? Have we ever stood in that father's place?

Jesus came when the father could not leave and yet could not believe or see how his son could possibly be healed. Then He came—just as He also comes to His people at that time when they cannot leave the Lord alone, even though they cannot believe or see how the Lord will or can have mercy on such a sinful and helpless case as they are. They also come to realize that they are afflicted with an incurable disease, a deadly disease, and yet they cannot leave the Lord. He is their only hope, though it only be a faint one.

How surprised that father must have been when Jesus suddenly came! Could the father then immediately believe? No. Even though Jesus rebuked them all—including the crowd, the scribes, the disciples, and the father himself—by saying, "Oh faithless generation," yet the father could not fully believe.

At most, he received a little encouragement, a little hope, when Jesus commanded, "Bring him to me." The father poured out his heart and spread out his case before Jesus, and now Jesus answered, "Bring him to me." "Oh, perhaps," the agonized father must have thought, "perhaps something can yet be done."

And yet, his son would not yet be healed. It was one thing to bring him to Jesus and quite another if he was healed by Jesus. Such is also the experience of believers. When they may be brought closer to Jesus Christ and when they may receive some encouragement from Him such as in a text of Scripture, an answered prayer, an application under the preaching of the Word, or a remarkable incident in God's providence—then they may receive a little hope. But yet, to be brought near to God and to feel a deep love for Him and His mercy is not necessarily being healed by Him yet. Did we ever feel that difference experientially—that to be brought to Jesus is not yet to be healed by Jesus?

The situation needed to become even more hopeless. Perhaps you will ask, "How is that possible? Was it not hopeless already?" Yes, it was. But it had to become hopeless to the superlative degree. We may have experienced this as Christians, that often when we think our situation is hopeless—when we've reached the proverbial "bottom of the barrel"—the Lord often lets our trials go to even greater depths before He intervenes.

Mark 9:20 says, "And they brought him unto him [Jesus]: and when he saw him, straightway the spirit tare him; and he fell on the ground, and wallowed foaming." While the child was being brought to Jesus things got worse, not better! In those last moments before healing, Satan unleashed all his power with fury to prevent the work of Jesus.

The trial for that man went to even greater depths. First the disciples could not heal him, and now it seemed as if Jesus could not heal him.

Jesus's question did not help either. He asked the father, "How long is it ago since this came unto him?" (v. 21). Once more the father was reminded of the hopelessness of the whole situation. The hopelessness was overwhelming.

"Oh," the father cried out, "If thou canst do anything, have compassion on us, and help us" (v. 22). The father was saying, as it were, "You can see for yourself the impossibility of the circumstances. It is hopeless. But if there is anything you can do—oh, even if you can make my son half better—if there is anything at all, then please help and have compassion."

After the father cried "If thou canst," "Jesus said unto him, If thou canst believe, all things are possible to him that believeth." In the original Greek Jesus literally says, "As to that 'if thou canst,' all things are possible to him that believeth" (v. 23).

Jesus turned the father's attention from his child to himself. It was as if He said to that man, "You say, 'if I can,' but I tell you in response to your 'if thou canst' that anything is possible with me. Do you believe that?"

Why did Jesus say this? Did He say this to get this father to exercise his free will? Did He mean by this that faith is the condition of healing? Did He mean to say that the healing of his son was really dependent on the father's faith?

Rather, Jesus said this to show this father where the fault really laid. The father had implied it was the disciples' fault and even the fault of the Lord Jesus by saying "if," but now he needed to see that the fault was in himself. He needed to see not only the awful condition of his son, but above all, the awful condition of his own heart. He needed to become a sinner. He needed to see that he was an unbeliever within himself.

The Needy Cry for Faith unto Christ
The Lord Jesus took the focus off of the son and placed it on the father. He took it off the physical infirmity of the child and placed it on the spiritual infirmity of the father.

What a change these few words brought! The Lord Jesus spoke these words with divine power to the soul of that father. In those moments he saw that the valley was full of confusion not only because of his son, but now he saw the valley of sin and confusion in his own heart. Immediately, suddenly, irresistibly the Lord Jesus showed the father his need, and the fruit of it was the father's expression of this great need when he cried with tears, "Lord, help thou mine unbelief" (v. 24). A needy cry for faith came from the heart of this father unto Christ. In one moment this father was drawn from his self-made darkness into God's marvelous light, which made him see his sin—"mine unbelief"—for the first time in his life.

Initially, the father cried "help my child," but now, his greatest need became, "help my unbelief." The father saw himself as an even greater problem then his child. The circumstances were no longer the greatest problem, but he himself was. In those moments he became a needy, unbelieving sinner in himself, and therefore his hard heart became a greater problem than the epileptic body of his son.

Can we say the same thing of ourselves? Has our hard heart ever become our greatest problem in life—a problem greater than all external circumstances and afflictions? Has it ever been our cry, "Lord, help thou mine unbelief?"

In a moment the father was led deeply by the Lord Jesus. He was not only led to see his sins of commission but also of omission. He was led to the mother sin—the sin of unbelief. The Holy

Spirit uncovered that father to himself. He showed him his sin and his unbelief, and that immediately became an unbearable burden by grace, so he cried out in desperation, "Lord, help thou mine unbelief."

If we are honest with ourselves, we may think of a time in our lives when we cried to the Lord, "O God, give me true, saving faith. Work irresistibly so that I must believe. Lord, help thou mine unbelief."

For God's people, unbelief becomes their great problem. They cannot rest in historical, temporary, or miraculous faith. They cannot rest in unbelief. Can we rest without a saving knowledge of Jesus Christ and Him crucified worked in our hearts by the Holy Spirit? Can we live without saving faith? Is it enough for us to come to church, to hear the Word of God, and to believe it with our minds?

Historical faith is necessary but it is insufficient by itself. We need true, saving faith; if we can rest without it, then the devil is also resting by us. If we are strangers to that struggling cry, "Lord, help Thou mine unbelief," then we are on good terms with Satan, for we live as if there is no God and as if there is no devil, too.

But if, on the other hand, we have come into that good fight of faith, then we also know something of Satan and his attacks. God's people discover that he is both an attacker as well as an angel of light who will not give them rest night or day as long as they by grace refuse to rest without true faith. As long as we must cry out, "Lord, help thou mine unbelief," Satan will also be at our side trying to persuade us that it is a foolish request which will never be granted us anyway, or alternatively that we already have it, and do not need to struggle anymore for faith.

For the father in Mark 9, faith became a necessity, and he could no longer blame anyone else for his lack of faith anymore; he owned his transgression—*mine* unbelief—for himself.

Has that also happened with us? Has faith become a necessity? Has faith cost us tears? Have we ever owned our unbelief before the Lord? Have we ever taken full blame?

True Christians are led to see that the fault of unbelief lies at their own door—not God's, not Adam's, not man's, nor anyone else's. At moments in their life they must own it for themselves. They begin to see unbelief in everything they do, say, and think. They can trace every sin back to it. Unbelief is the cause of their leaning on false foundations and the cause of their anxiety over materialistic, earthly things that are of no value. Unbelief is the reason their religious duties are so poor, the reason their prayers are so haphazard and halfhearted, and the reason that they are so impatient to wait upon the Lord for mercy. The great problem of who they are—is all traceable to *unbelief*.

Unbelief becomes their great problem. It spoils their religious activities. It hinders their praying, reading, and worship—private worship, family worship, and public worship. It gives more power to Satan's temptations, for faith is the soul's greatest shield against temptation (Eph. 4:16). Above all, it becomes unbearable because it is such a great dishonor to God who is Truth itself and cannot lie.

Oh, that cursed unbelief! How many tears it costs God's people! How many times they have wished they could cast it out of their heart, that they could trample it to death, that they could stamp it out forever. But they must discover that, try what they might, the root of sin and unbelief remains. They must lose all strength from their side to fight it and depend on Christ alone: "Help *thou* mine unbelief."

The father saw his inability and the hopelessness from his side, and he saw that the cause of it was himself. Therefore, he did not say, "Lord, help me to help my unbelief." Nor did he say, "Lord, I will try to do my part if Thou wilt do the rest." No, but rather, in that one word, "thou"—"Lord, help *thou* mine unbelief"—the father confessed death upon all self-help. At the same time that he realized his great problem of unbelief, he also realized God's great exclusivity as the only One who could help.

Now why was it so necessary for that father to have faith? Did he cry "Help my unbelief" because he saw faith as being of merit or worthiness or the condition of God's acceptance? No, faith itself can never save us, but Christ Himself saves us through the instrument or means of true faith which lays hold of Christ. Salvation is applied by faith. Jesus Christ and Him crucified is the object of faith that God's people are ultimately seeking. Faith is like the pitcher with which the sinner draws the living water; faith is the only way through which we are made partakers of salvation. Faith is the hand of the beggar reaching for alms.

To that end we need faith—faith to believe in Him, faith to trust upon Him, faith to lean on Him, faith to give over to Him, faith to see Him in His person and benefits. Therefore, we cry, "Lord, help thou mine unbelief, because I cannot help myself and yet I must be saved."

The Lord will never deny such a cry, for that cry of true need itself reveals His own work, proving that the principle of faith is already planted in the heart by the Holy Spirit. Mourning over unbelief is a sign of true faith, and if we have never mourned then we may be assured that we are still missing faith. The two cannot be separated. The needy cry is a cry of confession at the same time.

The Confessing Cry of Faith in Christ
This father received a great blessing. He not only said through tears, "Help thou mine unbelief," but also through tears, "Lord, I believe." Through tears of sorrow and tears of joy he cried out, "Lord, I believe; help thou mine unbelief."

Truly, it was a God-given confession that came from the heart of the father in the midst of trial. Against all odds, all common sense, and all natural reason he cried out, "Lord, I believe." In spite of the fact that the disciples were unable, that his son had this disease for years, and that even as he confessed it his son was crying out, foaming at the mouth, being torn by the devil, and getting worse instead of better at Jesus's feet—yet the father cried, "Lord, I believe."

The confession of the father "Lord, I believe" was a gift from above, from the God who graciously gives us all that He demands of us. Faith is always the gift of God, whether it be the first time or by renewal, worked by the Holy Spirit, as Ephesians 2:8 teaches us.

Through that Spirit-worked, Christ-applied, God-given faith this father triumphed over all difficulties and impossibilities. He could say even before his son was healed, "Lord, I believe."

But *what* did he believe? Did he only believe that his son would be healed or that all things are possible with Christ? No. These things are included, but ultimately he believed in Jesus Christ Himself in those moments. It was as if he said, "Lord, I believe not in myself, nor in any other man, but I believe in Thee. Lord, Thou art the object of my faith. Lord, I believe in Thee!"

What a great and inexpressible blessing this father received to believe in Jesus Himself. With this confession, he gave himself over unconditionally to the Lord Jesus. All self-trust had sunken away. He could not even trust his own faith: "help mine unbelief." In short, there was only one thing that this father could truly believe in anymore, and that was Jesus Christ: "Lord, I believe in Thee." It was as if in one word he confessed his faith in the Lord Jesus Christ. "Lord, I believe in Thy ability. I believe in Thy willingness. I believe in Thy benefits and in Thy person. Lord, I believe in Thee."

Oh, to believe in the Lord Jesus Christ—has this ever become our portion? Could we ever confess, "Lord, I believe?" Did Jesus's imperative ever become reality in our soul—"Ye believe in God, believe also in me" (John 14:1)? Was He Himself ever the only One that we could truly believe in?

By nature, we are strangers to this confession. Inside us, it is just the opposite of "Lord, I believe," for we will believe in everything and everybody but Jesus—and above all we tend to believe in self.

What is it that we believe in? What do we trust and lean upon? What are we placing above Jesus Christ? Are we believing in ourselves, or our possessions, or our fellow man? Are we leaning upon our religion—our tears, our prayers, our humility, or our repentance?

Anything we believe in as a foundation for salvation outside of Jesus Christ is entirely wrong, false, and futile. Our religion and our experiences can never save us. Blessed are they who lose all such foundations, and who know this simple, tearful confession, "Lord, I believe in Thee."

When a poor and afflicted people may be allowed to believe in that Savior for the first time or by renewal so that this confession—"Lord, I believe"—may come from their heart, then it cannot but be tearful. Outward and inward tears are not, and can never be, a ground of our faith or our salvation, but one thing is sure—confession cannot go without tears either. When that living way is now opened before a dying people who are given grace to believe in Jesus alone for salvation, how can there not be tears? Oh, that precious, deep joy in believing in Him! Do you know that joy by experience—that joy that produces tears of joy?

Mark 9:24 says, "And straightway the father of the child cried out, and said with tears, Lord, I believe." That father's joy was so great that it brought tears—not only because of whom he was allowed to believe in, but also because that faith was made personal. Those two realities coalesced in his heart with profound joy.

"I believe"—that same *I* who is so sinful, so corrupt, so unbelieving—*I* believe. "O Lord, I cannot comprehend it, but yet I cannot deny it. In spite of *what* I am, in spite of *who* I am, yet I, by grace, believe."

Do you know that same confession? Have you experienced the wonder of crying out, "Lord, I believe. In spite of myself, I believe. Thou hast made me believe. Thou hast shown me that the righteousness of Jesus Christ even goes beyond my sinfulness. Lord, I cannot but believe. I believe that Thy power goes beyond my unbelief. Lord, I believe."

What a great blessing when we may be personally made believers. We have come to see that others personally believe. Seeing that is a blessing in itself. But now, it is a greater blessing when the Lord shows us that it also possible for us to be saved despite our monstrous sinfulness and unbelief. Then the Lord reveals to His people that through Christ "He is able to save to the uttermost" (Heb. 7:25). It is that word "uttermost" which is so precious to our souls. He is not only able to save, but to save to the uttermost. How low that comes! That reaches to the bottom of a pile of sinners—to the uttermost. Then we may also become those who make that confession, "Lord, I believe."

The Victorious Cry through Faith by Christ
The tearful confession of the father in our text is not only a needy and a confessing cry; it is also the cry of victory through faith by Christ.

Modern Christendom would not see this as a victorious cry at all. If this man were brought into the counseling rooms after today's evangelistic messages to the masses, then he would be told that his faith was too weak. He would be rejected because of his unbelief. He would be told, "You must believe. You must accept. You must overcome unbelief in your own power, by your force of decision, and then you will be saved. You must allow Jesus to come in."

Scripture makes plain that the struggle of faith versus unbelief remains in the life of God's people until their death. A faith that never doubts and struggles is not true faith. It may be historical or temporary or miraculous faith. True faith is often called to holy war. Many believers feel like their faith is more often fighting in the plain than rejoicing on the mountain.

And yet, whether faith is in the plain or on the mountain, true faith *is* and *remains* true faith. Therefore, the father's cry is a cry of victory—because it is the cry of true saving faith, which can never be taken away. As long as that principle of faith is there, though it be small, the principle of victory is also there. In the activity of faith itself there is no doubt. That is impossible. The very nature of faith excludes doubt. Certainty cannot be separated from faith.

And therefore, by Christ, through this true faith, the cry of faith versus unbelief is a victorious cry. The apostle John writes, "Whatsoever is born of God overcometh the world: and this is the victory that overcometh the world, even our faith" (1 John 5:4).

Through faith, by Christ, God's people have victory. And what a blessing it is when they realize the victory of their faith. Just as Israel shouted with joyous faith before the walls of Jericho fell, so they may cry out by faith like the father of our text did before his son was healed: "Lord, I believe."

What a great blessing—in all the poverty of God's people, victory is yet sure in the great Victor who came to bruise the head of the serpent! Victory is assured to them through faith by King Jesus. He will not fail. We see it also in this case. Jesus calmly, quickly, miraculously, and powerfully cured this child in one moment. "Thou deaf and dumb spirit, I charge thee, come out of him, and enter no more into him" (Mark 9:25). That is, Jesus commanded the demon to come out of the boy and stay out.

In that moment, the victorious cry, "Lord, I believe; help thou mine unbelief" found its fulfillment. The devil was cast out of the child. What a divine power! A father came with his diseased child, and Jesus healed them both.

How full of joy that father must have been when he returned home with his healed son. Now he could talk with his son, and his son could talk back. Oh, how he must have talked with his son about Jesus Christ along the way; about the unspeakable victory of Jesus Christ! He must have told his son about how he was possessed with an evil spirit for so many years, about how he took him from place to place and physician to physician, and that Jesus Christ was the only one who had absolute power over Satan. What inexpressible joy—the joy of victory through faith by Christ—must have filled the heart of that father as he told of the wonderful deeds of Christ to his son. What a blessing that this father was privileged to share it with his own son. Parents, do you know such times when you could talk from your heart to your children of such things? Have you had occasion to tell your children of your hope that the victory you cherish would become their victory as well?

The Daily Cry against Remaining Unbelief
On that journey home there was one thing we can be sure that the father forgot about: his unbelief. If he had looked for it then, he surely would not have been able to find it. Perhaps he even thought to himself—like many of us do—that he would never need to pray that petition again, "Help thou mine unbelief." Like him we may have thought in such moments, "How could we ever possibly doubt again?"

And yet we are mistaken. Although unbelief hides, it will come back. You can read that so beautifully described in John Bunyan's *Holy War*. Unbelief sometimes could not be found in the city of Mansoul, but he never could be killed either. Unbelief is that plaguing and recurring sin that God's people cannot rid themselves of completely in this life no matter how hard they fight the good fight of faith. Unbelief is that captain that they desire to see trodden down and killed in the gates of the city of their soul.

Later, the father must have experienced that a warfare with unbelief remained within. He found out why the disciples themselves needed to pray, "Lord, increase our faith." He would have needed to come back to that needy, confessing, victorious cry time and again in his life, "Lord, I believe; help thou mine unbelief."

And so it goes in the life of God's people. When they may look upon Christ then they may say with the father, "Lord, I believe," but when they look upon themselves and their circumstances, then they must also cry with that same father, "Help thou mine unbelief."

Therefore, that Christianity which says that the children of God go beyond unbelief and that this man's faith here was so weak is a religion which God's true people do not find in their souls. Time and again they cry out, "Help Thou mine unbelief."

We often discover, like the disciples, how little faith we have. How often we feel included in Jesus's words, "O faithless and perverse generation." If only we could be delivered from that faithlessness and perverseness inside! If only we could believe once and for all! We wish that we could always say in triumph, "Lord, I believe," and we long for the day when we will not need to add, "help thou mine unbelief."

But we must also be honest with ourselves. We need daily grace to believe. Although we were delivered from the state of unbelief forever in the moment of regeneration, yet time and again we slip into the condition of unbelief, which, we confess, is always our own fault. The gates of heaven are never shut because of Jesus Christ's merited righteousness, but we are too often shutting them from our side.

Believers often feel they are people of "little faith." When John Newton preached about growth in grace, relating it to three different stages—first the blade, then the ear, then the full corn in the ear—he later received a letter from a person who wrote that he felt he was in the last mature stage of faith. Newton wrote back that there was one thing he forgot to say in his sermon, and that was that those who are in the last stage of being the full corn in the ear seldom realize it!

In other words, God's people do not think so highly of their own faith. They do not think that they are souls that have great faith. Some people today think they are led so far and have so much faith, but then it is only "great faith in a little God" whereas God's people may have that better portion of a "little faith in a great God."

"But isn't doubt sin?" we may ask. Yes, it is. It is bitter sin and it costs us bitter tears. Yet, at the same time it is an inevitable sin because of our own corrupt hearts. Unbelief so quickly arises from within. It begins the moment we think we are independent from the Lord. The moment we think we can begin to make it on our own and don't need the Lord so much in daily life also—then unbelief rears its ugly head.

Unbelief begins when self begins. Like Israel, puffed up with fall of Jericho, we are ready to say to ourselves, "Do not weary all the people there, for the people of Ai are few"—feeling we need God little even after receiving grace (Josh. 7:3).

Thus, God's people live a paradoxical life. On the one hand, they are learning that "without me ye can do nothing" (John 15:5), and on the other hand, they discover that they still too often try to help themselves on earth and leave Christ in heaven. In short, the more they believe, the more they see the power of unbelief.

Unbelief is an awful sin. And yet those who can always believe *and* those who can never believe are both wrong. Unbelief remains, but it must become our great grief that we need the Lord so much yet believe in Him so little. God's people cannot deny faith altogether, yet they often feel weak in faith. They experience that they not only crucified the Lord Jesus on Calvary's cross with their sins, but that they are also rending Him afresh by feeling their need of Him so little even after receiving grace.

This becomes their deepest sorrow. "O Lord," they must cry, "help me to truly need Thee more, to believe in Thee more, and to be exercised with Thee more."

Continuing with Christ from Where We Are
Where do you stand with respect to that needy, confessing, victorious, and persistent cry, "Lord, I believe; help thou mine unbelief?" Where do you stand with respect to faith and unbelief?

Open Unbelievers
Are you an *open unbeliever*? Do you openly reject God's Word? Do you have no desire to believe in Christ? Perhaps you do not even want to hear His Word. Do you come to God's house out of custom, or, even worse, out of obligation?

Then you are truly in a sad condition, and how awful it would be if you died that way. Did you ever think about it—what it means to die as an unbeliever? It means that you will ultimately be forced to believe when it is forever too late. Then you will discover that awful fulfillment of God's own Word: "He that believeth on the Son hath everlasting life: and he that believeth not the Son shall not see life; but the wrath of God abideth on Him" (John 3:36). How awful it will be to fall into the hands of the living God unprepared! Oh, that God might stop you upon your unbelieving way, and enlighten your mind. Do you ever think about Him and eternity?

Do you ever realize that nothing is so sure in this life as death? Ecclesiastes 3 speaks of a time to be born, and a time to die: nothing separates the two but a comma, and so is our life—nothing but a short comma which is soon passed by and then comes the meeting with our Maker for a never-ending eternity. Are we prepared to meet Him?

Historical Believers
Are you a *historical believer* only? Perhaps you will say, "I am not an open unbeliever. I believe that I am a sinner. I believe that Jesus Christ came into the world for His people. I believe the Word of God."

Is that all you believe—in a Christ outside of you but not within you? Is it only a head-belief and not a heart-belief? I hope that we all realize that the Word of God which we profess we believe thoroughly condemns us. Historical faith is necessary but it is insufficient. We must not only have faith *concerning* the triune God, but we must believe *in* Him. The Lord must make that faith a reality in our souls so that it shall be well for time and eternity.

Doubting Believers
Are you a *doubting believer*? Must you confess, "I do not know if I am a true believer or not. Sometimes I hope that the Lord is beginning with me, but at other times it seems absolutely impossible to even consider it. I don't think I could ever say yet, 'Lord, I believe,' as that father did, but I think I know something of his cry from the depths, 'Have mercy and compassion on us.'"

Is this truly your condition? Do you really desire to know if you have true faith or not? Then you may find five marks in the confession of our text by which you may examine yourself.

First, faith made the father's heart melt and become tender. It made him cry out with tears. And why? Because he could not remain cold under the thought of free grace to such a vile creature as he was.

Do you know something of such tenderness and melting-of-heart before the Lord?

Second, faith gave him a deep sense of his remaining unbelief. "Lord, I believe; help Thou mine unbelief." Is it so also with you? Are you a stranger to unbelief? Then you are also a stranger to faith.

Third, faith brought him into a holy war. Faith was pulling at one end and unbelief at the other. Do you also know that struggle and that pulling within? Do you know that cry of Paul, "O wretched man that I am," since the things he wanted to do he found himself not doing, and those things he had no desire for he found himself doing (cf. Rom. 7:14-25)?

Fourth, faith made him hunger and thirst after more faith. It made the disciples cry out, "Lord, increase our faith." Is that also your desire and your prayer?

Finally, faith brought him to Christ with prayers and with cries. That is the question which you must ask yourself above all. If there is true faith within, where does it bring me? Does it bring me to that only foundation, Jesus Christ? Does it make Christ more necessary, more suitable, more precious to me? Does it lead me away from Him or does it bring me closer to Him? True faith takes away every foundation of hope outside of Christ. Do we know that work of the Holy Spirit in our life to cut off all other "helps" and "hopes" but Him?

If we know something of these marks, then we may be encouraged, for the Lord will not break the bruised reed or quench the smoking flax. True faith is saving faith be it small or great. True faith can never be taken away, since it is the Lord's own work.

Hoping Believers

Are you a *hoping believer*? God's people are hoping believers. "By hope ye are saved." They find out that their hope often goes in the reverse of what they imagine. They expect things to get better with their faith, to grow daily in faith—and now they discover that to grow in faith means also to become less and less about self. In means that self-hope must be stripped away more thoroughly and more frequently so that divine-hope would be more valued and more precious. God's people remain "hopers against hope" all their lives.

The dynamics of the believer's struggle with unbelief mirror his struggle for sanctification. Growing in holiness so often involves going backward in order to progress forward: knowing more deeply our unbelief before being able to say afresh "I believe"; coming more and more to feel our unholiness as God helps us grow in holiness. As faith grows, holiness grows; but this growth is often attended by shocking realizations of how full we are of unbelief and unholiness. Growth of faith is attended by an increase of awareness of our own unbelief; growth in holiness is accompanied by an increasing sense of our unholiness. Growth in faith and growth in holiness are not genuine if not attended by new discoveries of our deep poverty of both.

Do we know something of this true faith? God's people discover that all true faith is from God, and all unbelief is always from themselves. The Lord is faithful. He gives them no cause to distrust Him. Despite their unfaithfulness, He will be faithful to His hoping people even to the end, fulfilling their desires by bringing them one day to those mansions he has prepared for them—even for those who are so weak in themselves that they needed to pray all their life long, "Lord, I believe; help thou mine unbelief," and yet who, in that glorious day, will be made perfect in holiness forever in Christ Jesus! May the Lord make us such men and women, for Jesus's sake.

Chapter 19

Jesus Touches the Open Coffin

And he came and touched the bier.
—LUKE 7:14

Our text today is Luke 7:14a, *"And he came and touched the bier."* With God's help, we wish to consider the following theme and points:

Jesus Touches the Open Coffin
1. To show His compassion
2. To declare His willingness
3. To proclaim His gospel

1. To Show His Compassion

The first three gospels of the New Testament provide many details of the life of the Lord Jesus Christ, particularly of the last three years of His public ministry. The most outstanding fact in the life of Jesus was, no doubt, His suffering. Jesus suffered not only in the last few days of His life on earth but throughout His entire life on earth—all of which He voluntarily took upon Himself. This truth is emphasized in the words of our text where we read, in relation to the history of the young man of Nain, "And he came and touched the bier."

Jesus has departed from Capernaum, with several of His disciples. After some hours of walking, they arrive at the village of Nain, probably the present Nain, a small village of two hundred people situated about six miles southeast of Nazareth. There Jesus and His procession meet another procession—another group of people. Verse 12 says, "Behold"—pay special attention: A funeral procession, lamenting loudly, is walking through the gates of the city to the cemetery outside of the city. A young man who has died is about to be buried. His body is being carried out of the city on a bier—a kind of bed or stretcher on which his wrapped body was lying. The bier consisted of two long poles with bands of material across it that was much like a stretcher today. The wrapped body was then borne up by the pallbearers' hands and shoulders. In front of the bier was the funeral orator, who was to proclaim the good deeds of the dead, followed by hired mourning women, who wailed for the deceased. Behind the bier walked the young man's mother, friends, and a sympathizing multitude. The entire procession was moved; many were weeping. The young man's mother was sobbing as the funeral procession moved inexorably to the burial ground; after burial, she would enter a period of profound mourning for thirty days.

The young man's mother has good reason to weep, doesn't she? After all, her husband has already been taken from her side; she is a widow. And now her son, her only son, is taken away as well. This woman has every reason to be weeping, every reason to be filled with sorrow. Death is a harbinger of sorrow; death violates ties of blood and friendship; death strikes down young as well as old. And so, this young man dies, to the great sorrow of his widowed mother.

Remember also that this young man died in his youth. Dying at an early age was considered in Israel to be a particular punishment, something to be expected by the wicked. The Bible says, "Bloody and deceitful men shall not live out half their days." Must this poor widow now conclude that her son was a wicked young man, and because of his wickedness he lost his life prematurely? Sadness and grief fill this mother's wounded heart. Old memories surface; old scars are torn open. All of this makes her load heavier. Her situation is tragic. No doubt, new questions arise in her heart that seriously challenge her faith: Can I trust the Word of God? Has God forgotten His promises? Where is His covenant faithfulness? The Lord has promised that He is the Husband and the Judge of the widow, and the Father of the fatherless. But now it appears that the Lord doesn't verify His Word. He plunges this woman from one misery into another misery. But if these words of the Lord are not true, then what words of the Lord can you put your trust in? What is reliable? This problem of seemingly unfulfilled promises and unreliable words merges with her heavy grief. Behind the bier walks a suffering mother, a suffering widow with great struggles in her soul and mind. Today, as she buries her only son, it seems that she has nothing left. She is bereft of her husband, her son, and, seemingly, her God.

There seems to be no consolation for this woman. There is no hope; her life is immersed in the culture of death; there is death on every side. What future does she have?

Sorrow is washing over this woman like waves. Her final source of protection—her son—is gone. Her hope of perpetuating the family line is gone; the Messiah will never come from her family line. Every hope for the future has perished. She is mourning, she is weeping for her only begotten son. And it was said in Israel that there was no sorrow like the sorrow of burying an only begotten son, the firstborn son.

This is also a blow for the people of Nain. What they are doing is actually tragic. They are going to the cemetery to make space for the body of one of their fellow citizens. Death came into their city and broke the life of one of their own. Death causes sorrow; it violates ties of blood and friendship. It is sad when death comes and destroys life—especially in a case like this, for this young man is struck down by death in the prime of life. The death of a young person usually stirs more emotions of sorrow than the death of someone who has already grown old. The death of a young man is normally more heartbreaking than the death of someone who, after a well-spent life, having many infirmities of old age, becomes feebler and because of physical weakness, finally dies. Of course, that is serious enough, for death is the wages of sin. But the age of the person who dies certainly makes a difference.

There is something very sad about the funeral of a young person, isn't there? And there are so many of them. Just walk through any cemetery and you will see it on the tombstone dates of birth and death. And yet it is so unnatural to bury one's children. I once asked a funeral director, while riding in the car with him to the cemetery: "When you have charge of so many funerals every month, can you still feel the sorrow of death?" I will never forget his answer: "When the person is young, you can and you do feel great sorrow." In other words, he was saying that he became accustomed to elderly people dying, but young people dying is always very moving.

Well, in God's meticulous providence, our text says, "Behold"—pay special attention, Jesus arrives! Jesus and His disciples arrive at Nain at just the right moment, the moment in which they may witness this very sad and tragic event. Now of course that is not a coincidence; it is God's doing, and it is marvelous in our eyes. There are no coincidental happenings with God. God's timing is always perfect. God knows how to bring the Savior and the spiritually dead together. All throughout the Bible, and especially in the book of Luke, such cases abound. Twelve chapters after our text, Luke 19:1–2 says, "And Jesus entered and passed through Jericho. And, behold, there was a man named Zacchaeus." Zacchaeus ran ahead, climbed into a tree, and, when Jesus came to "the place," the right moment at the right place, He looked up and saw Zacchaeus, called him down, saved his soul, and blessed him in his house that night.

Something similar happens here, for here, too, we read this special word, "Behold!" Pay attention; Jesus comes! Jesus comes to Nain, and as verse 13 says, "the Lord [sees] her." There are many people with her there. Many neighbors are there, but the Lord sees *her*. Notice that the Holy Spirit does not say "Jesus" but "the Lord." He uses *Lord* here because the Savior is going to reveal Himself as the Lord and Master over all, even over death.

We are told that there are many people in this funeral procession—all feeling grieved, all mourning and weeping—but the Lord sees this woman in particular. He feels the heavy burden of her grief. Right at that moment when Jesus sees this funeral procession, Jesus suffers. The Lord experiences deeply and painfully in His soul that death is powerful, so powerful that it can even cut off a young life. Jesus experiences grief in His own heart, just as He would later experience when He stood at the grave of His friend, Lazarus. Then, when Jesus perceives the decomposing powers of death, He weeps at the grave. What an affliction this was to Jesus that death causes so much destruction, that death ruins what God has created good and beautiful. Jesus suffers because death breaks the happiness which God has given to man. Jesus is not an unmoved spectator at this funeral. He cannot remain without emotion at the sight of so much destruction and of so many ruinous powers that flow out of sin. His tender soul reacts to everything happening around Him. He feels pain; He experiences grief. Inwardly, He is seized by the solemnity of death.

But at the same moment, Jesus's pure soul, which sees and feels everything, sees and feels something else behind this death—the wrath of God. He sees and feels the curse of God which came upon the human race because of sin. Death is not a natural thing that belongs to our earthly existence, but it is the wages of sin. Death has come as a punishment of God because of man's transgressions against the commandments of God. Death is a judgment of God because man has been disobedient. Jesus also experiences these things when He sees this funeral in Nain. The judgment of the Lord, the wrath and vengeance of God, still hasn't been alleviated. And so, the death of this young man of Nain preaches to Jesus that He who came to earth to perform the work of salvation must continue His way of suffering, and He Himself, being on that way, will meet death personally. Jesus's life also will come to an end. What He sees here at the gate of Nain, when these people are going to bury their dead, is to Jesus a powerful sermon of what He Himself must expect. He will also be buried. For only then, when He, the pure and holy One, bows Himself under the power of death, can the wrath of God be alleviated. Only then, when He Himself dies and is laid in the grave, can the violence of death and the grave be defeated. He must remove sin—the cause of all misery and death.

In this messianic awareness, and with such thoughts and feelings, the Savior suffers. But He also accepts this suffering voluntarily. He says to the widow, "Weep not," brings the funeral procession to a standstill, and then goes to the open coffin being carried, and touches it. The Bible says, movingly, "and he came and touched the bier" (v. 14).

Why does Jesus bring the people to a standstill? And why does He act in this particular way of touching the coffin?

Luke says in verse 13 that Jesus "had compassion on her." The word "compassion" here carries profound meaning. The Greek word is related to the word "bowels," referring to the Greek understanding of the Hebrew sense of "the seat of the affections." The Greek literally means: "Jesus was inwardly moved with compassion." In His inner core being, something begins to move. His heart is moved with tender pity; His heart goes out to her.

"Weep not!" He says to her. Literally, "Stop weeping!" or "Stop sobbing!" Those first words spoken by Jesus must have sounded strange to the crowd of mourners. If any occasion called for weeping, this was surely it. Weren't mourners hired for this very purpose, to increase the weeping? Why did this stranger, whose very demeanor, body language, and tone of voice were full of tender pity, say, "Stop crying"? This is a sensible command, of course, only if the One who spoke these words would remove the cause of the widow's tears, which, of course, is what Jesus was about to do. So, His command and His compassion harmonize well with each other, although the people do not yet understand.

Yes, the Lord Himself feels inwardly moved to show compassion to this sorrowful woman. When He sees her grief, He inwardly yearns to give relief and comfort. This is the kind of Savior Jesus is. Do you know Him as such? Do you see Him in our text as a Priest who feels pity for the grief and misery of others? Do you rejoice in this great High Priest who shows mercy? Does He dry up your tears with His compassion? When He helps, He does so as only He can, not just by speaking words of comfort and by demonstrating sympathy through a warm greeting; rather, He helps by taking the needs of this widow and this funeral procession upon Himself; and so He does for believers still today. If we look closely, that is what is revealed in the words, "He touched the bier"—that is, the coffin.

It was not necessary for Jesus to touch the coffin. The Lord could have stopped the procession by saying to the pallbearers, "Stand still." Or He could have requested them kindly to stand to one side. He could have given an order, and they would have obeyed.

Must we conclude, then, that Jesus's touching the coffin was superfluous? Of course not. The Lord never does superfluous things. He touches the coffin intentionally. He doesn't approach the bearers and touch one of their shoulders, asking them to stand still. No, Jesus puts His hand upon the coffin where the dead young man lies. This reveals Jesus's readiness to take suffering upon Himself and to enter into the misery of the life of sinners.

2. To Declare His Willingness

Perhaps you ask: But how do you get all this out of Jesus simply touching the coffin? Remember what the Old Testament says about dead people and about the things on which a dead person lies. God said clearly and repeatedly that both the body of a dead person, as well as the bed or coffin upon which he lies, is unclean. The Lord prescribed that whoever touches a dead body should be reckoned unclean for seven days. Numbers 19:14 goes even further, "This is the law, when a man dieth in a tent: all that come into the tent, and all that is in the tent, shall be unclean seven days."

Remember, death is ultimately the result of sin (Rom. 6:23); in death, the Lord punishes sin. Precepts concerning death have been given because Israel may not go near sin. Touching a dead body, therefore, makes a person unclean and thus unsuitable for the service of God. So these precepts are lessons; through them Israel knows that God hates sin, and therefore they must hate sin as well. These precepts are the reverse side of the statement, "Be ye holy, for I the Lord thy God am holy" (cf. 1 Peter 1:15–16).

Referring back to our text, then, yes, Jesus could have stopped the procession in some other way, but He chose this particular way of touching the coffin. He took the initiative Himself to become regarded as an unclean One, for we must not forget that He is also under the law of God. As a member of Israel and as a child of the covenant, He was required to obey the precepts of the covenant. So, by touching the coffin, He too, according to law, has been defiled. Here the Lord Jesus meets death, which has come to the young man of Nain and will also come to Jesus Himself. And in meeting death, Jesus, by touching the coffin, testifies, "Lo I come; I delight to do Thy will, O my God; yea, thy law is within my heart" (Ps. 40:7–8); I come to take upon me voluntarily all suffering, and all unrighteousness, and all impurity, and all uncleanness.

When God the Father brings Jesus face to face with death at Nain, Jesus doesn't shrink from His task, fearing those things that will soon come upon Him. Rather, He is completely willing to accept all the consequences of the suffering that awaits Him. Why? When God in heaven, by His divine providence, leads His Son to this meeting with death, Jesus sees not only the dead young man, but His eyes also rest upon the mother, the widow, with all her grief and misery. If Jesus had seen only the death, that could have been by itself a moment of terror, just as in the garden of Gethsemane, where He prays, "Oh my Father, if it be possible, let this cup pass from me." But here the eyes of Jesus are directed to the woman at the same moment He meets the dead. And then Jesus is moved in the core of His inner being. Here then is the point: because of the misery of sinners and of the need in their broken life, Jesus is completely willing and ready to take part in that misery and to take upon Himself the uncleanness and the heavy burden of sin.

"And he touched the bier." That means that Jesus said to His Father, as it were, "Father, I understand what Thou hast told me today. I understand why Thou hast led me to this point, and why I needed to meet this funeral procession. And I fully agree, O God, to let all iniquity be laid upon me. I delight to do Thy will."

Jesus knows what He is doing when He touches the coffin. He knows it better than anyone realizes. He knows the Lord's precepts. He knows that by doing this He becomes unclean, and that He, from this moment, is declared by the law to be unfit for the service of God. And even though He knows all this, He still touches the coffin; He takes upon Himself the uncleanness of death and accepts it. He accepts voluntarily all the suffering, even the bitter suffering on the cross where He must taste the reality and essence of hell, and where He must experience that He must be shut out from communion with God because the Lord forsakes Him. By touching the coffin, Jesus declares that He is willing to take upon Himself all uncleanness and all unrighteousness, all the power of death and the devil—yes, everything that must be borne to give true salvation and deliverance to poor sinners. Jesus is a willing Mediator. He is the Lamb that is ready to be brought to the slaughter.

To the people in Nain, Jesus is a stranger. The dead young man is not a relative or acquaintance of Jesus. He really doesn't need to make Himself unclean; He could have kept at a distance from the funeral. There was no reason to take part in the funeral; He can keep Himself clean. Yes, He can, but He doesn't *desire* to do so. By touching the coffin, He speaks to the mourning people, "I want to be one of you voluntarily, even though I am a stranger. I want to take part in your need and in your sadness. And even more, I want to take part in your uncleanness, for I am the Savior, and I am willing to be the Deliverer. I come to render help by taking upon Me your physical and spiritual needs."

3. To Proclaim His Gospel

By touching the coffin, Jesus was also proclaiming the gospel and revealing Himself as the Messiah. Yes, He really is different from all the priests in Jerusalem. The people in Israel never saw a priest touching a coffin or entering into a house where there was a dead body. Priests always stood at a distance. In fact, God's precepts were even stricter with regard to priests. The Lord had spoken to the priests, "There shall none be defiled for the dead among his people." Uncleanness resulting from touching a dead person made a priest altogether unfit for the Lord's service. And what a tragedy it would be if a priest were no longer able to perform his work as a servant of God! That is why the Jews never saw a priest attending a funeral ceremony.

But here, the people of Nain see that Christ is completely different. He wants to be one of them, to become involved in their need and misery—oh, surely, must He not be the Savior? So, this deed of Jesus preaches the gospel for those who have eyes to see. On this day of sadness, the people of Nain receive glad tidings: the Savior is in our midst! Yes indeed, Jesus is a Priest. His compassion for the woman shows that He has the heart of a priest. But what good is all this, you ask, when this Priest is defiled with death? Then He cannot stand in the service of the Lord! Well—and this is really the secret of His being the Messiah—we can read in Hebrews, "For such an high priest became us who is holy, harmless, undefiled, separate from sinners." Yes, we can see that. But now Jesus is no longer undefiled and no longer in the position to serve God and to commune with God. So in what way can the service of reconciliation continue, when the High Priest is no longer what He ought to be?

Well, this is just the messianic secret, for by touching the coffin, this Priest actually consecrates Himself to the Lord. This Priest becomes the sacrifice; He becomes unclean. And to unclean and defiled sinners, a sacrifice is necessary. So Christ is really saying here, "Here I am, Lord; I am the Lamb of God; I am the sacrifice." He accepts the obligation to offer His own life as a priest. He accepts becoming defiled. But at the same time, He will bring His own soul as an offering to God.

Do you see in our text the willingness and the readiness of the Lord Jesus to suffer? That is the gospel that God has given to this world. The widow in this story profits immensely from the willingness of Christ to identify with her. And the people of Nain have sung of this merciful deed of Christ. After Jesus raised the young man to life, we read in verse 16, "There came a great fear on all: and they glorified God, saying, That a great prophet is risen up among us; and, That God hath visited his people."

How much the people understood at this moment is difficult to determine, but their testimony is true. God indeed has visited His people. He has visited them by sending this willing Savior, this Jesus who touches the coffin. This is the gospel of God for those who must die because they are sinners. And who can save himself from the grave? Who can deliver himself? Who can undo the chains of death? All the people of Nain together were powerless to raise the young man from the dead. They could mourn and weep, they could feel pity for the poor mother, but they couldn't bring the dead man back to life. No one is able to overcome death, for no one is able to overcome sin! You can weep and burst into tears when you stand at the deathbed of your loved one, but it will not stop death as a mighty intruder upon our lives and our plans. You can clench your fists in rebellion against death when death prevails, but that will not help you. There is only One who can undo the price of death, and to deliver, and that One is Jesus! He gives deliverance to all of them who acknowledge before Him that they are justly subject to death, who confess that the cause of death lies in the sin that permeates their lives, and who with pain and grief in their hearts learn to supplicate for mercy. Jesus comes into our lives when we are so needy and miserable because of the continuous threat of death that flows out of our sins and because our lives are one long string of uncleanness. Yes, Jesus enters into our lost lives. Our text says, "He came." He takes the initiative; He steps forward, He makes His way to us as a mourning people and He stands in our midst. Yes, He touches the coffin that signifies uncleanness and unrighteousness. Oh, the beauty and the fullness of His free, sovereign grace!

Jesus wants to touch our coffins, not only to take our death upon Himself but also in order *to deliver us from death*. The history of our text tells us that the young man is raised. Jesus speaks to the dead young man as if he were only asleep, and as if he could hear and obey. His voice rings with authority, "Young man, I say unto thee, Arise." The young man comes to life as if he had merely been sleeping; he sits up and begins to speak, and Jesus delivers him to his mother. It all happens so calmly. There is no protracted struggle, no arduous wrestling, as in the case of Elijah and Elisha, whom God also used to raise children from the dead. With one simple sovereign word of command—"Arise!"—the young man is brought back to life. The simple reason for the difference is that Jesus is God. His victory over death is immediate and complete; He is the calmly victorious Savior and Lord.

"Behold!" Behold, Jesus comes. Behold what happens when the widow of death meets the Prince of life, when the results of sin meet the Savior from sin, when the culture of death meets the culture of life! The king of destruction, death, meets the King of life, Jesus! The king of death, which is so strong and so powerful that everyone falls prey to death—for you and I will also die—meets the King who rightly calls Himself the resurrection and the life. He is far more powerful than death. Death and life meet at the gates of Nain and the Prince of life gloriously, easily prevails. That is the beauty, that is the glory, that is the hope and the wonder of this history.

Behold, the Way of Life triumphs over the way of death; the Second Adam's merits and power counter the tragic fruits of the first Adam. With a touch of His hand and a word from His mouth, Jesus arrests and reverses the chariot of death; the spoil is taken from the mighty, and the lawful captive is delivered. Death flies defeated from the gates of the city.

What a lesson this is for all of us! If Christ can do such mighty works with but a word from His mouth, why should anyone here ever despair of salvation? Where is the heart that is too dead for Christ to break?

By being the willing Savior who does all that must be done, Jesus brings true happiness to this small family—the widow and her son—in the midst of the people of Nain. This is the way that Jesus brings salvation. He takes upon His shoulders all unrighteousness and all uncleanness. And by bearing death and the cause of death—sin—He gives life. When all iniquity is laid upon Him, there is, at the same time, life and deliverance for all who trust in Him and who look for their salvation in Him alone.

What a change there is in Nain, especially for the widow and her son! The day that started so sad and dark ends in happiness. The Savior was there, the willing Savior. Never will the people of Nain forget the glorious moment when the young man sat up and began to speak. They will never forget the moment that Jesus spoke the mighty words, "Young man, arise." Oh, how happy they are that Jesus arrived at that moment in their city. All the people glorified God. They said, "God hath visited his people" (v. 16)—literally, "God has come to look after his people."

Conclusion: What Is Your Response to the Messiah?

Dear friend, there must be a response to God's dealings with us—including this very sermon. God waits for our response. How do you respond tonight to the word of the living God?

1. *Do you respond by glorifying the Lord and resting in His Son for both compassion and salvation?* God has visited His people, not only in first century Judea but also today. The Lord has visited us with the gospel, the blessed message of the Savior, Jesus Christ. Did you listen? Did you see the Savior? Did you see His miracle? Did you see His willingness to be the true Savior? These words are the most important

words in the story, that Jesus touched the coffin. In these words lies the secret of salvation. No, we cannot be saved by a Savior who only performs miracles. We cannot be saved even when we have a Savior who raises one from the dead and who, by His might, performs all kinds of wonders. We can only be saved by a Savior who has compassion and who, because of that compassion, comes into our need, touches the coffin, and takes upon Himself our death, impurity, sin, and guilt. We must know Him as the Savior who willingly bore all our uncleanness and unrighteousness. It is not enough to know *about* a Savior who keeps death from us and who heals us in days of sickness. For the most part, we fear, based on such passages as Luke 9:18–19, that the crowd failed to see the true greatness of the Prophet and Priest among them. Although they glorified God to some degree, they underestimated the majesty and divinity of Jesus and did not worship Him in spirit and truth. They saw Him as a great prophet but not a divine High Priest who saves our souls from all our sin.

We can only find salvation in a Savior who, first of all, takes all uncleanness upon Himself and then overcomes death. Uncleanness because of sin is the first thing that must be removed. When we have discovered by the teaching of the Spirit that we have departed from God and have listened to the devil, when we become aware of the manifold sins and impurities in our life, then we understand, first, that a solution for our sins is necessary. Yes, then we need a Savior who truly reconciles us with God. And that, thanks be to God, is precisely Christ's work: *He* touched the coffin. Oh, friend, have you ever seen by faith His willingness and readiness to take upon Himself all uncleanness and sin, and all the power of death? Has that sight ever moved you to surrender all to this precious Savior?

2. *Do you respond, young people, by consciously rejecting the Savior of sinners, or by receiving Him?* This miracle occurred in the life of a young man, so it has special significance for you, young people. Some of you, spiritually, are like the young man when he was dead. You are dead in your trespasses and sins. You don't see your dangerous plight. Your relatives—parents, brothers, sisters—weep over you, but it doesn't affect you. You don't understand their grief, don't understand

their secret prayers: "Lord, it would be better for my son, my daughter, to never have been born than to turn away from Thee!" Nor do you understand that Jesus is able to raise sinners from the dead. You don't hear the message of life, you don't realize that Jesus speaks to the spiritually dead and the impenitent, just like you, with authority, even now, saying, "Young man, I say unto thee, Arise." *Will you not hear His voice? Will you hear Him before it is forever too late?*

The pallbearers were on their way to bury this young man. It was apparently too late for any possible change, but at the last moment, the King of kings intervened! I warn you, dear friend—and especially you, dear *young* friend—your time may well be running out. You have no idea how long you will live. You can also die young, like many other young people. Don't fritter away your time. Today is the best day of your life to seek the Lord, to repent from your sins, to surrender your sinful heart and life into the hands of the willing and almighty Savior. Remember, as this miracle clearly shows, that God delights to heal sinners just like you. He delights to save sinners; He is in the business of saving sinners; He has decreed to save sinners. It brings Him great glory and great satisfaction to save sinners! Oh, that you would cry out, "Draw me, O Lord, and I will run after Thee!"

On the other hand, are you already saved, and do you respond by resolving to be more like Christ—to show more Christlike compassion and Christlike willingness to assist fellow sinners and to proclaim the gospel to them? Is your sympathy sincere—like the sympathy of Jesus, flowing from your heart—not artificial, like so many in this world? Then you are greatly blessed indeed, and I pray God that your light may shine more and more unto the perfect day.

3. *Dear friends, young and old, do you respond by not responding?* That is what Israel did in 1 Kings 18:21 when Elijah said to them on the top of Mount Carmel, "How long halt ye between two opinions? If the Lord be God, follow him: but if Baal, then follow him." And then we read these tragic words: "And the people answered him not a word" (v. 21b)—not a single word! They responded by not responding! Is that what you will do today? Will you walk out of this church building and talk together outside the church about some secular thing,

perhaps about the score of some ballgame this past week, with the casualness of a worldling, as if Jesus did not offer you His grace today, in this very sermon, to raise you from spiritual death to everlasting life?

Will you once again—like thousands of sermons before this—offer no response to God's overtures to you? Will you once again turn a deaf ear to Jesus—to His compassion, to His willingness, to His gospel? Can you find any fault with this willing Savior? You say, "Oh no, I can't." But why then don't you repent before Him and really believe in Him alone for salvation? What kind of objections do you have against believing in Him? Has He not done enough? Oh, look to Him; consider how He raises the dead young man, and delivers him to his mother. See how He brings happiness in Nain.

But consider especially and be challenged and exhorted and encouraged with this message, this particular point, that He touches the coffin. If He did this for a young man, why can He not also do it for you in all your spiritual deadness? He is able and willing to save the hardest of hearts—and that upon His own initiative. Ask Him to do this also for you. He will show you that He is still today a great, compassionate, and willing Priest-King who triumphs even over sin and death. He can meet and conquer death within you, too, and carry away His helpless prey. To Him be the glory forever.

Chapter 20

Christ's Tears Over Jerusalem

And when he was come near, he beheld the city, and wept over it, saying, If thou hadst known, even thou, at least in this thy day, the things which belong unto thy peace! but now they are hid from thine eyes.
—LUKE 19:41–42

Our text today is from Luke 19:41–42: "And when he was come near, he beheld the city, and wept over it, saying, If thou hadst known, even thou, at least in this thy day, the things which belong unto thy peace! but now they are hid from thine eyes."

With God's help we want to consider with you:

Christ's Tears Over Jerusalem
1. Christ's love manifested in these tears
2. Christ's peace revealed through these tears
3. Christ's judgment pronounced during these tears

1. Christ's Love Manifested in These Tears

We read, dear congregation, in John 1:11 that Jesus "came unto his own, and his own received him not." That was true already at the beginning of His sufferings, in Bethlehem; it was true in the continuation of His sufferings, in Nazareth; and it would again be true at the end of His sufferings, particularly on Palm Sunday as He drew near to Jerusalem, where He would give His life as a ransom for sinners. It was true from the beginning to the end of His life: "He came unto his own, and his own received him not."

The day that Jesus entered the final week of His life and sufferings on earth is often called Palm Sunday. He had arrived in Bethany on Friday, one week before He died. He probably spent a quiet day on Saturday at the home of Martha, Mary, and Lazarus, but on Sunday morning He entered for the last time into Jerusalem triumphantly yet weeping. Jesus was going to celebrate the Passover, but He was also going in order to die. He had told His disciples before what things were going to happen to Him: "Then he took unto him the twelve, and said unto them, Behold, we go up to Jerusalem, and all things that are written by the prophets concerning the Son of man shall be accomplished. For he shall be delivered unto the Gentiles, and shall be mocked, and spitefully entreated, and spitted on: and they shall scourge him, and put him to death" (Luke 18:31–33).

So, on that Sunday morning, knowing everything that would come upon Him, having loved His own and determined to love them to the end, Jesus went forward to face the great suffering that was awaiting Him in Jerusalem. His foreknowledge of His sufferings must have greatly increased His sufferings. For example, if you were to look back over your entire life, and think of the possibility that as a child, you would have already known all the sufferings that would come upon you in God's providence, would you not acknowledge that it would have been too much for you to bear? But "Jesus...knowing all things that were to come upon him, *went forth*" (John 18:4). He, the innocent one, went forth to suffer, to agonize, and to die. He went forth on a lowly colt, the foal of an ass, not only to fulfill the prophecy of Zechariah 9:9, but also because a colt was associated with the pursuit of peace rather than with the activity of war.

Most of the people missed the rich symbolism of Jesus's coming on a colt, an animal of peace, not to establish an *earthly* kingdom by way of war and victory, but a *heavenly* kingdom of eternal peace. Being moved by Jesus's miracles, they began to cry out as He came closer to Jerusalem, "Blessed be the King that cometh in the name of the Lord: peace in heaven, and glory in the highest" (Luke 19:38).

No doubt there were some in the multitude who were confessing these truths from the heart, and were looking more for a sin-bearing Mediator than a political deliverer, but the majority were looking for deliverance from the Roman yoke. Thus, they took off their coats, cast them in the road before Jesus, and carpeted the road with their outer garments. Others cut down palm branches and cast them before Him, paving His way. Still others waved large palm tree leaves. Even the children shouted, "Hosanna." *Hosanna* means "save now" or "save we pray Thee." Hosanna is a word of supplication and adoration; it mingles both prayer and praise. The children said, "Hosanna: Blessed be the King that cometh in the name of the Lord."

At first glance, it appears they finally recognized Him as the Messiah, but then we read something astonishing. In the midst of all this praise and acknowledgment of Christ as Messiah, Jesus burst into weeping. The Greek word literally means that he *sobbed aloud*. He sobbed, as it were, *uncontrollably*; He broke into profuse weeping. What a remarkable scene: a shouting, praising multitude, side by side with a weeping, sobbing Jesus!

Three times in the Bible we read of Jesus weeping. We read of Him, as you know, weeping at the grave of Lazarus. We read in Hebrews 5:7 of His weeping: "He...offered up prayers and supplications with strong crying and tears." And we read of His weeping in our text as He came around the Mount of Olives, descending toward the city. About two-thirds of the way down, when He came in full view of Jerusalem, which was spread at His feet across the valley, He broke into loud weeping.

Today a chapel, called "Chapel of the Tear," is erected on the place where Jesus wept. The entire chapel is in the shape of a tear. I have stood in that chapel; it is a remarkable view as you come around the Mount of Olives, right to that place where all Jerusalem is spread out before you in its beautiful splendor and with its ancient walls. Jesus saw Jerusalem with its magnificent temple. He knew the altar of God was there. He knew the mercy seat was there. He knew that Jerusalem had possessed unique opportunities to be saved and to serve God. He knew that the very people who were crying out "Hosanna" early on this Sunday morning would be crying out by Friday, "Away with Him; crucify Him, crucify Him." Jesus also knew the cruelty, the stubbornness, and the pride of the inhabitants of Jerusalem. He wept; He sobbed because He loved the city. He loved the people and He knew that many of them were delaying, and hardening their hearts, refusing to be converted, and would die in their impenitence. While they were shouting and crying out, "Hosanna," He came near the city, beheld it, and wept over it.

Jerusalem was (and still is) a unique city. It had been a city particularly favored by God. It was called the "city of David," the "city of God," and the "city of the Lord." Jerusalem was the city to which the Lord had sent more warnings, more invitations, more prophets, and upon which He had bestowed more labor than any other city on the face of the earth. He had established His temple there. The altars of God were there, and yet that same city had slain His prophets with the sword, had stoned the messengers He had sent to them, and was now ready to crucify the Messiah, the Son of God. Is it any wonder that Jesus wept? We might well imagine that Jesus would weep when He came to Jerusalem, because of His own impending, unparalleled sufferings that would soon take place there. But that is not what our text says. He wept, not over Himself, but over it—over the city; over the souls of the people of the city. He wept tears over His enemies; He wept tears over lost souls. Oh congregation, what love is manifested in the tears of Jesus! He wept over a city whose people would crucify Him; He pitied a people who would not pity themselves; He wept over souls that would not weep for themselves! He wept over Jerusalem.

2. Christ's Peace Revealed through These Tears

When God comes to us with His Word today, dear friends, He comes with invitations; He comes with warnings; He comes with sovereign grace truth; He comes weeping over our souls. And must *you* not need to acknowledge, must *I* not need to confess, that He has more pity upon us than we have upon ourselves; that He weeps more over us and labors more upon us than we weep for ourselves and our children? Oh, do you not feel the love of God in bringing His Word into your homes, on the pulpit, and into Christian schools? The Lord is taking pains with us, congregation. He is taking pains with you, my friend. He is calling you through His Word; He is weeping over you. "[Oh, that] thou hadst known...the things which belong unto thy peace!" Jesus wept, and as He wept, His words expressed what His tears contained. He said, "If thou hadst known," oh Jerusalem, "even thou, at least in this thy day, the things which belong unto thy peace!" Oh, if only you had known; if only your blind eyes were open; if only you could see what you are doing, Jerusalem, in rejecting the Messiah and spurning the gospel! Jesus's tears and words are full of reality and sincerity. These were no artificial tears, dear congregation. Jesus's heart was burning within Him. He sobbed over Jerusalem. He longed for Jerusalem's peace; not so much for peace from the Roman yoke which was secondary, but for *peace with God*, the inward peace of reconciliation through the blood He was about to shed.

John Calvin wrote that the word *peace* here means all that is essential to true happiness. And oh, dear congregation, when the Lord labors with us by whatever means He does so, the same call goes out to us and says as it were, "Oh that thou hadst known, that thou couldst see the things that belong to thy peace!" Peace does not consist of comfortable platitudes. Rather, peace first begins with realizing that though we were created in a state of peace, we have chosen in Paradise to declare war against God. Shall we ever be brought back to peace with God, we must first come to realize that we are in a state of war with Him. "The carnal mind," said Paul, "is enmity against God: for it is not subject to the law of God, neither indeed can be" (Rom. 8:7).

But Jerusalem would not see that in the gospel of Jesus God was coming to them, a warring, rebellious people, with love, with thoughts of peace and not of evil. Yes, and to us as well—to wretched, fallen sinners He proclaims His marvelous peace. Through Isaiah He offers peace to them that are afar off, and to them that are near; He proclaims peace through the cross. In the preaching of the gospel, God declares to every hearer, "Say unto them, As I live, saith the Lord GOD, I have no pleasure in the death of the wicked; but that the wicked turn from his way and live: turn ye, turn ye from your evil ways; for why will ye die, O house of Israel?" (Ezek. 33:11).

God declares a gospel of peace. That peace, however, is not a peace upon our terms, but a peace upon *God's* terms. And what are God's terms? God's terms involve repentance and surrender. God's way of peace is the way of faith in a crucified Savior. But how can a sinner find peace when the sword of rebellion is still in his hand? This is possible only when the Holy Spirit comes and strikes the sword of rebellion out of a sinner's hand. He finds the sinner in a state of enmity with God; He shows the sinner his iniquity; He exposes his sin until the sinner confesses, "Yes, I have been saying all my life to God, 'Depart from me for I have no pleasure in the knowledge of thy ways.'"

But then God overpowers all that enmity. The sinner's sword is cast from his hand, and he bows in evangelical repentance, in contriteness and complete surrender. He flees as a poor sinner to the Lord, asking, "Lord what wilt thou have me to do?" And then that sinner begins to realize what things belong to his peace—surrender to Christ, faith in Christ, and repentance before Christ. His eyes are opened to see his sin in God's sight; along with David in Psalm 51 he confesses, "Against thee, thee only, have I sinned." He laments his misery; he flees to God for pardon; he pleads for grace. God the Holy Spirit reveals to him that there is a Prince of Peace who came on a lowly colt, who came meek and lowly to pay the price of sin.

When the sinner's eyes are opened to that precious, lowly colt-riding Jesus; when a sinner sees what Jesus has done in Gethsemane, Gabbatha, and Golgotha, and the Holy Spirit reveals to him that the things that belong to his peace are in Jesus, then a door opens wide in the Valley of Achor, in the valley of his misery. He then hears the voice of God, "Come now, and let us reason together, saith the LORD: though your sins be as scarlet, they shall be as white as snow; though they be red like crimson, they shall be as wool" (Isa. 1:18). Then the message of the gospel—sometimes suddenly, sometimes more gradually—warms that soul. All forms of self-righteousness are relinquished; the sinner sinks away as poor and needy at the foot of Calvary. Then he longs to hear in every sermon of the way of blood, the way of peace, the way of redemption, yes, to hear in the apostle's words, Christ "is our peace." And what joy the sinner then has when the Lord Jesus, by His Spirit, speaks to him with divine power and authority, "Come unto me, all ye that labour and are heavy laden, and I will give you rest"! It is a wonderful experience to see Jesus displayed before the eye of faith, through the power of the Word of God, and received by gracious faith through the work of the Holy Spirit. Then that wounded soul gazes upon his wounded Savior and experiences in that moment that the law has lost its curse, Satan has lost his rights, and justice has lost its power of condemnation. The soul may believe and truly experience in that moment that there is indeed a peace which passes all understanding. Then there can be such an amazing degree of peace that it seems that even all of nature is in harmony with God.

And yet, the sense of that revealed peace may not be abiding. For some, it may well be. For some, when Christ is revealed, He may also be immediately applied. For others, when Christ is revealed, their joy is great, but when the conscious nearness of the Lord diminishes, they fear that though the way of the purging of guilt has been opened, guilt itself has not yet been discharged. They learn to cry for a fresh application of that blood upon the doorpost of their consciences. The blood has been revealed, but the peace treaty must be signed and must be sealed to their consciences. To that end, the Lord leads His children back to Paradise to show them how they had willfully broken His covenant, how they had become full of sin, yes, that their whole being is therefore corrupt. And there at the scene of crime—where they have spilt, as it were, their blood in breaking the covenant of works—there God shows them that there is no hope of peace in anything of them. There He reveals to them the blood of the covenant of grace so that *Christ's* blood becomes their salvation. All their own sinful efforts are washed away by the powerful cleansing blood of Jesus Christ.

In a word, God enters into a peace treaty with a sinner. The Holy Spirit imprints God's forgiveness upon the soul. He takes a gospel promise, whichever one it may be, and dips that promise, as it were, in the precious blood of Jesus, applies that promise to the soul, and seals that sinner free in accord with a pronouncement of God the Father as holy Judge for the sake and righteousness of Jesus. This sinner experiences that the Father declares on grounds of satisfied justice that He will no longer be angry nor wroth with him. Divine rebuke is cast behind the Father's back, fear and anxiety disappear, and the believer confesses with Paul in Romans 8:1, "I have heard Him speak through His Word, that 'there is…now no condemnation to them which are in Christ Jesus.'" Oh, what a blessing to know the things that belong to our peace, to know the application of the finished, atoning work of Jesus! That is something that every sinner must covet. Blessed are they who know the power of that blood.

But Jesus must conclude with tears: These things "are hid from [Jerusalem's] eyes." The people saw the miracles and received the bread, but they did not see with the eyes of faith the Prince of Peace, the way of peace, the beauty of peace, the fullness of peace, nor the glory of peace. They were blinded because they would not see that they were at war with God. They never acknowledged their need for peace with God through Jesus Christ. Since they did not see their malady, they felt no need for the remedy. And that is exactly our dreadful state by nature. When we are unconverted, our greatest obstacle is not our past, actual sins, but our greatest obstacle is our blindness to our misery and our unbelief, our refusal to believe in Jesus Christ. Our greatest obstacle is precisely that we think that our own merits are the foundation of our peace. The unconverted are often convinced that they have peace, but the obstacle is that they are resting upon false peace. That is precisely the misery of our misery—*false peace*.

Dear flock, there is no true peace outside of Jesus Christ and His cleansing blood. If you insist on continuing to embrace false peace and find a foundation apart from Jesus, you will be sorely deceived in the Day of Judgment. Oh, I fear there are many who are standing on the brink of hell thinking that all is well with their soul! But when that Day of days comes, all peace which does not rest upon the blood of Jesus will be eternally shattered. That is what Jesus says in verses 43 and 44: "For the days shall come upon thee, that thine enemies shall cast a trench about thee, and compass thee round, and keep thee in on every side, and shall lay thee even with the ground, and thy children within thee; and they shall not leave in thee one stone upon another; because thou knewest not the time of thy visitation."

3. Christ's Judgment Pronounced during These Tears

Jesus wept over Jerusalem not because of the sufferings that He saw coming upon Him in the next week, but especially because He knew that the consequences of Jerusalem rejecting and crucifying Him as the Lord of glory in that week would bear disastrous eternal results for them. Jesus knew with the eye of divine omniscience what was awaiting Jerusalem in 70 A.D., some thirty to forty years after His crucifixion. He foresaw what is recorded in verses 43 and 44.

We know from Josephus what actually happened in that terrible time, when Titus came to destroy Jerusalem. He surrounded and trapped the city. Six hundred thousand people died of starvation. Some family members even ate one another. In all, over one million died by the time the Romans captured the city. Three hundred thousand were crucified all around the city, so many that Josephus recorded they could scarcely find sufficient wood in the area to make the crosses. Almost one hundred thousand, especially women, were carried into captivity. Jerusalem was left a heap of ruins, a bloodbath. The whole city was leveled except for three towers and part of the Western Wall. There was scarcely one stone left upon another.

Jesus saw this day approaching. He saw that this would be the fulfillment of what His own Jewish people would say later in the coming week: "His blood be on us, and on our children" (Matt. 27:25). Is it any wonder that Jesus wept and that His human nature was sorely oppressed? "He came unto his own, and his own received him not."

Jesus then concludes, "Because thou knewest not the time of thy visitation." What does that mean, boys and girls? The time of God's visiting us is when His offers of mercy are still with us. Jerusalem had a special season of offered mercy. God had sent her more prophets than any other city. He had put His throne and His mercy seat in that city. He had provided them altars dripping with blood that proclaimed the gospel. He had sent them priests who instructed them in the law. Moreover, He sent John the Baptist as a forerunner of Jesus, and ultimately sent the Son of God Himself, the Messiah, to visit Jerusalem and preach to them about the gospel, the good news, and the kingdom of heaven. The greatest miracles the world has ever seen were performed in Jerusalem. The most wonderful preaching that ever transpired was delivered in Jerusalem. The clearest calls to repentance that were ever heard were heard in Jerusalem. "O Jerusalem, Jerusalem…how often would I have gathered thy children… as a hen gathereth her chickens under her wings, and ye would not!" Instead, highly privileged Jerusalem would cry out, "Away with Him; crucify Him." Oh, how solemn are Jesus's words, "Thou knewest not the time of thy visitation."

This is a very deep and mysterious subject; yet it is a clear message in the Bible. There are special seasons when the Lord visits a nation, a church, a family, or an individual with special manifestations of His presence; there are special invitations, special times and places where His grace is peculiarly offered, or times when special warnings and admonitions are given. And eternity will reveal that those who have rejected and neglected such seasons often face turning points in their lives, which, if glossed over, will lead them to ultimate and eternal ruin. Boys and girls, young people, fathers and mothers, there are millions even now in hell who must say, "There were special times in my life when God came near with His Word, when He came close with the overtures of the gospel, when He drew near with serious warnings to my conscience or with serious afflictions in my life, but I pushed them all away, and now those special seasons burn in my agonizing conscience as a fire that cannot be quenched."

Dear friend, rejected times of visitation, rejected overtures of the gospel, of peculiar offers of mercy and privileges from God, will be the heaviest charges of a righteous God which a never-dying soul in hell will bear for all eternity! Oh, what shall it be to confess in hell, "Lord, I must admit that my own soul—by refusing Thy special seasons, Thy special times of offered grace—has provoked Thee to leave me alone forever!" This is what Jesus is weeping about over Jerusalem. Jerusalem had rejected the day of her visitation; she had rejected the prophets, rejected John the Baptist, but most of all, rejected Jesus Himself.

The tears of a weeping Jesus on the lower part of the Mount of Olives will do more to damn the souls of Jerusalem sinners in hell forever than all the threatenings of Mount Sinai. The tears of Jesus have a more condemning power than all the curses of the law. Jesus says as much, doesn't He, when He says, "Because thou knewest not the time of thy visitation"? Oh, what a sight—a weeping Jesus, weeping over sinners who would not weep over themselves! This alone will cause all Jerusalem and every unconverted sinner who has lived under the proclamation of the gospel to say in the Day of days, "Mountains and hills, cover me from the wrath of the Lamb of God!"

Did you hear this, congregation? *The wrath of the Lamb of God—* what a chilling description of coming judgment! In our text, the Lamb is meek and lowly, riding upon a colt, a symbol of peace to proclaim peace to them that are far off and to them that are near. But on the Day of days, upon those who rejected Him and used Him for earthly deliverance, but never needed Him as a spiritual Mediator and Savior, the wrath of the Lamb will fall! The tears of Jesus, the overtures of the gospel, and the special seasons of visitation will be a hell within hell to those who have rejected the unconditional gospel of grace.

And so, my dear friends, I cannot close this sermon without a personal application. Does Jesus weep over you because of your rejection, or by grace, does He rejoice over you because of your surrender? When, in the past, He has come into your life in special seasons, has it led you to repentance? Many say, "There was a time in my life when nothing went right; everything went wrong," and yet they do not turn to God in these special times when He visits them with affliction; rather, they cast away these times of divine visitation. Dear friend, let us never forget that times of great trial, times of great affliction, and times of overwhelming need, are times of divine visitation. They are particular times when God calls us to repentance, to dependency, to take refuge to Him.

Boys and girls and young people, the time of your youth is a time of special visitation. It is a time when God comes to you tenderly, when His rich promises are placed before you, promises that adults do not have. Proverbs 8:17 promises you that "those that seek me early shall find me." When you are a boy or a girl, or a teenager, it is a special time, before you are ensnared with all the cares of the world. Children, teenagers, are you seeking God in this special time, when your hearts are still tender? God draws near to you and in Mark 10:14 says to you, "Suffer the little children [the young children, the tempted teenagers], to come unto me, and forbid them not: for of such is the kingdom of God."

It is a special time, too, when God begins to work in our relatives, when others are being saved around us; when friends and family whom we have known for years begin to surrender to the power of the gospel. God is then drawing near also to us, saying, "I am mighty to save." Dear friend, bow before it is too late.

Again, it is a special season of visitation when God sends an ambassador, a minister, to proclaim death in Adam and life in Christ. No matter who or what or how many faults or sins cling and cleave to that ambassador, the *Word* goes out, congregation, and it is that Word of which you and I must give an account one day. You have been invited from this pulpit to flee to Christ; by present and past servants you have been urged to flee to God while it is still the day of His visitation. Must Jesus still weep over you?

God has done wonders in our midst, also in these past years. We have seen great trials, some self-inflicted. We are unworthy and yet we cannot deny that God has been at work. Some of you have had a father or a mother convicted and converted by the Word. Others of you have had a child who has abandoned worldly ways and is crying after the Lord. Oh congregation, do not cast away the hour of visitation! Do not despise the day of small things. Do not reject the movements of the Holy Spirit in the midst of the flock, but pray to God Almighty, "Oh God, Thou who art working here and working there, come in *my* heart, come in *my* life, and cause me to bow beneath the power and the authority, the warnings and the invitations of Thy Holy Word." Oh, what a question this is, "Does Jesus rejoice over me and because of His work in me, or does He weep over my rejection of Him?"

Maybe there are some who say, "I fear that the time of visitation is past for me. My hair is gray, my years are numbered, my season of privileges is past. In the past, my conscience has spoken loudly. I had times in my life when the Word of God came near to me. But now I fear that I have not remembered and did not know the time of God's visitation. Now all is hard and cold, and the day of grace, I fear, is past." Oh, my dear, elderly friends, what must I say to you? This I will say to you: There were those whose hands were red with the blood of Jesus on Good Friday, but who some weeks later were in the multitude of three thousand who cried out, when they realized what they had done, "Men and brethren, what shall we do?" And Peter, who was commissioned to feed poor lambs, beginners in grace—he did not pick out the elderly in that multitude and say, "Your day of visitation is past." He did not say, "There is nothing to do because the door of mercy is shut." Instead, Peter said, "Repent, and be baptized every one of you in the name of Jesus Christ." He preached the name of Jesus to them, even to hardened, aged, Jerusalem sinners who had counted the blood of Jesus an unclean thing.

And today, I say to Jerusalem sinners in our midst: Perhaps there are deep scars of sin, perhaps secret sins, perhaps tragic sins, but oh, today I declare to you, Jerusalem sinner, you had thought the gospel was too impossible for you, that God could never have mercy upon you, but today I say to you, "It is still, this very hour, the day of your visitation. Even as God spoke to His people in Ezekiel 33:11, still today God declares to you as it were, 'I have as yet, sinner, no pleasure in your death, but that ye should turn from your evil ways and live: for why will you die?'" Oh my elderly friend, do not be a Felix; do not leave this place trembling, saying to God, "Go thy way…when I have a convenient season, I will call for thee," but hear the Word of God, hear the invitation of God, "*Today*, when ye hear His voice, harden not your hearts."

Dear child of God, who has made you to differ? Who has drawn you for the first time and by renewal to the blood of Jesus? What hast thou that thou hast not received, and if thou hast received it, wherefore dost thou boast? Ask that God may turn you into a weeping intercessor, to be like Jesus, to weep over the lost souls around you, in your household, among your friends, in the midst of the congregation, but also in our society. May you feel like the apostle Paul who declared: "I have great heaviness and continual sorrow of heart for my brethren." And like Jeremiah, "Oh that my head were waters, and mine eyes a fountain of tears, that I might weep day and night for the slain of the daughter of my people!" (Jer. 9:1).

Young and old, the Prince of Peace is still willing to save sinners, even chief sinners. You cannot convert yourself; you are dead; you are unable; yes, you are even unwilling. That is all true, but ask God to do for you what you cannot do for yourself. Plead for grace to bow before Him, to flee to Him, to surrender *all* to Him. Strive to enter in at the strait gate, Who can tell? Who can tell if a sovereign electing God might not bless it? Who can tell if God will turn and repent, and turn away from His fierce anger that we perish not?

Chapter 21

Like Father, Like Son

> *But as many as received him, to them gave he power to become the sons of God, even to them that believe on his name: which were born, not of blood, nor of the will of the flesh, nor of the will of man, but of God.*
> —JOHN 1:12–13

There are two ways of becoming part of a family. Some children enter our lives through birth. What an amazing thing God does every time a new baby is conceived! I was so excited when I learned that my wife was pregnant with our first child, and I was very nervous when the day came for him to be born. Childbirth is hard on a mother and can be dangerous, but it is so rewarding to see a tiny newborn with his little hands and feet.

As each of our children grew, my wife and I recognized more and more of our images in each—in the shape of their eyes, the sound of their laughs, and the expressions of their personalities. They are like living reflections of us, and yet each one is unique.

The other way of becoming part of a family is by adoption. Just as birth may be full of wonder and joy, so adoption can be an amazing display of love and grace. Adoption is a free choice to bring a child into your home and your heart. It can be costly in home study fees, legal fees, and transportation costs, especially when adoption crosses national boundaries to bring together people from different backgrounds. It is amazing to see fathers and mothers adopt children to love and nurture as their own. In many cases, they adopt orphans who have lost parents either through circumstances or sinful choices. Such children had no claim on the new parents, but once adopted, they share equal rights, equal love, and equal responsibilities in the family. They may come with disabilities or sorrows, but once they become part of the family, their sorrows and joys mingle with those of all.

Each of us became part of our families either by birth or by adoption, and each means of entering a family has its particular glory. One of the marvels of God's grace is that when God brings someone into His family, He does so both by birth and by adoption. In this way, He makes salvation a truly glorious work, for God grants His elect children both divine birth and divine adoption.

John 1:12–13 teaches that *Christ grants divine adoption to all who receive Him because of divine birth.* The Son of God gives the right to be God's children to everyone who trusts Him with the faith created by God's regenerating work. At the beginning of his Gospel, John reveals to us two of the most glorious truths of our salvation and ties them together in Christ. Verse 12 focuses on *divine adoption*, the gracious grant of our Lord Jesus Christ to those who receive Him by faith. This relates to a new status granted to men. Verse 13 focuses on *divine birth*, the supernatural work of God by which fallen people receive Christ by faith. This pertains to a new nature created in men. Divine birth and divine adoption result in divine likeness—like Father, like son. So, with God's help, we wish to consider:

Like Father, Like Son
1. Gracious adoption
2. Supernatural rebirth
3. Amazing likeness

1. The Gracious Adoption of God's Children

John 1:12 says, according to a literal translation from the Greek text, "But as many as received Him, He gave them authority to become children of God, to those who believe in His name." This verse is about a distinct group in the world, the people of God. They are a contrast to the world in general and even to the majority of the chosen nation of Israel. The text does not present individuals in isolation, but as a group unified by a shared spiritual condition: notice the plurals *them* and *those* and, in verse 14, *we*. So this group stands apart from the world but stands together as the family of God. Scripture describes this people first by their right response to Christ, and second by the great benefit given to them by Christ.

God's People Have Received Christ by Faith
John 1:12 says this people "received him." The word *receive* is a common word in Greek and has no unusual significance. The key to understanding what it means is to recognize that God's people receive a specific person who offers Himself to us in a specific capacity. The text further explains these people are "those who believe in his name." To believe is to trust. In the Bible, the name of the Lord is not just a label but God's revelation of who He is. God is His name. Once we see who He is, we begin to understand what it means to trust Him. We may trust someone as our spouse, as our father, or as our accountant; but of Christ this is much more profoundly true: we trust Him according to His names, titles, works, and especially His offices.

Do you believingly receive Jesus Christ as your chief Prophet to teach you His way of salvation? Do you believingly embrace Jesus Christ as your only High Priest to sacrifice Himself for you and to intercede for and bless you? Do you believingly give allegiance to Jesus Christ as your King to govern, defend, and preserve you by His Word and Spirit? Only if you can humbly answer, "Yes, by the grace of God I have received Jesus Christ as being all this for *me*" have you truly received Christ.

No aspect of the doctrine of conversion is so misunderstood today as what it means to receive Christ. Millions of people think that to receive Christ means to simply say a quick prayer asking Him to come into your heart. That is a distortion of biblical evangelism. The great tragedy is that many people have prayed such a prayer while still trusting in their own wisdom to guide them, or their own good works to make them righteous, or their own power to run their lives. They have asked Jesus into their hearts, but never trusted Him as the Christ! Their lives show their shallow commitment to holiness and the church as well as their self-righteous legalism.

Sometimes a little child gets confused in a superstore or even at church about where her father is. Recently, one of my seminary colleague's daughters, looking for a familiar form at our church, raced to me and threw her arms around my leg. But when she looked up, she soon realized I was not her father, and slunk away. That was an embarrassing and frightening experience for her. But more tragic is the person who thinks that he has gotten hold of salvation only to find that he has not thrown his arms around the real Christ. What shame and horror he will experience on Judgment Day, when God reveals that he has trusted in religious rituals, emotional experiences, or self-help schemes. He will see that his "easy-believism" was a fatal delusion. What will he say when his pretense of being a Christian falls away, and the fires of hell open at his feet to imprison him forever?

Oh, make sure to receive the true Christ! Only in receiving Christ do we become part of the family of God.

Christ Grants Adoption to God's People
John 1:12 says, "But as many as received him, to them gave he power to become children of God, to those who believe in his name." Here the word power signifies a right or authority; Christ extends to all believers the right and honor to be God's children and His brethren. Scripture calls this "the adoption of children" (Eph. 1:5). The benefits of trusting in Christ are many. They include justification and sanctification, of course, but also assurance of God's love, peace of conscience, joy in the Holy Ghost, an increase of grace, and perseverance to the end. Yet, of all these benefits, the Holy Spirit singles out adoption in verse 12, as if adoption encompassed them all. So the Puritan Stephen Marshall (ca. 1594–1655) wrote, "Very frequently in the Scriptures all the believers do obtain from Christ in this world and the world to come, here and to eternity, all is comprehended in this one, that they are made the children of God."

Let us consider what this Scripture teaches us about this precious gift from God.

1. Adoption is *the gracious grant of a new status before God*. Adoption is a gift, our text tells us, for "he *gave* them authority to become children of God." As such, it is a free gift, not a commodity we can purchase, or a reward for our hard work. Samuel Willard (1640–1707)

wrote, "He doth not adopt us, because we were lovely, but that we might be so. God saw as much beauty in others as in us, and that was none at all. And hence, that yet he should adopt us, is a demonstration of his inconceivable grace."

By adoption, God grants us a new status. When we read "to them gave he power," we should understand that the Greek word for power specifically refers to legal right or authority. Do not be confused and think that Christ gives people the ability to save themselves and make themselves into God's children. The apostle John is not referring to the ability or strength to do something; he is speaking of a right or authorization. John Calvin thus said that adoption is not the gift of the power to believe, but Christ's gift to those who already believe.

John does not say that adoption by God brings no new abilities with it—it certainly does, for our adoption is sealed with "the Spirit of adoption, whereby we cry, Abba, Father" (Rom. 8:15; Gal. 4:5–6). But adoption is first of all a new legal status and relationship with God. When a husband and wife adopt a child, that adoption does not consist in providing, nurturing, educating, or disciplining him. Rather, it is the legal transaction granting him a new status as a member of the family.

It is critical that we see adoption as granting a *new* status. Many people today erroneously believe that all human beings are children of God. Protestant liberalism teaches that God is the Father of all, and that all are His children. Indeed, human beings are God's offspring in the sense that they were created by Him (Acts 17:24–28). But long ago, by sin and unbelief, fallen humans cut themselves off from their Creator and from His household of faith. Thus Jesus says in John 8:42 and 44, "If God were your Father, ye would love me…. Ye are of your father the devil, and the lusts of your father ye will do."

We also read in 1 John 3:10, "In this the children of God are manifest, and the children of the devil: whosoever doeth not righteousness is not of God, neither he that loveth not his brother." This refers not to a small minority of people in the world but to the entire world apart from those saved by Christ. So 1 John 5:19 says, "And we know that we are of God, and the whole world lieth in wickedness." We are not born into this world as children of God but as children of the devil, the Evil One.

John 1:12 says, "But as many as received him, he gave them authority to *become* children of God." They do not simply realize that they have always been children of God. No, they *become* children of God—with a new status and a new relationship with God—all by free and sovereign grace.

2. More specifically, adoption grants us the status of *being accounted the sons and heirs of God*. The Westminster Shorter Catechism (Q. 34) says, "Adoption is an act of God's free grace, whereby we are received into the number, and have a right to all the privileges of the sons of God." To appreciate the richness of our adoption, we must realize that adoption is not the same as justification. Justification too is the gift of a new legal status. Our sin was imputed, or counted to Christ on the cross, and His righteousness is counted to us by faith (Rom. 3:21–4:8; 2 Cor. 5:21). Justification gives us legal righteousness under God's justice.

Adoption goes even further, however. It establishes a legal relation between us and God, so that He is our Father and we are His children. Adoption is a legal and binding covenant of sonship between God and His people. This status was foreshadowed in God's covenant with Israel (Ex. 4:22; Deut. 14:1), then in God's covenant with David, when the Lord said, "I will be his father, and he shall be my son" (2 Sam. 7:14). So Christ says of every believer, "I will be his God, and he shall be my son" (Rev. 21:7). Thus the central promise of the covenant, "I will be their God, and they shall be my people," reaches its highest point in adoption, in which the people of God are counted as sons and daughters of God with the right to count Him as their Father (Ps. 87:5, 6; 2 Cor. 6:18). Just as adoptive parents give their name to their adopted child, signaling that he is now part of their family, so the Lord puts His name upon us to mark us as His own (Jer. 14:9; Rev. 3:12).

Wilhelmus à Brakel (1635–1711) said, "From being a child of the devil to becoming a child of God, from being a child of wrath to becoming the object of God's favor, from being a child of condemnation to becoming an heir of all the promises and a possessor of all blessings, and to be exalted from the greatest misery to the highest felicity—this is something which exceeds all comprehension and all adoration."

3. Adoption is *a gift from our Lord Jesus Christ*. When John 1:12 says, "He gave them authority to become children of God," it clearly refers to Christ as the incarnate Word. This may strike you as strange, for we normally speak of God the Father adopting us (Eph. 1:3–5; 1 John 3:1). In this, as in all things, Christ is doing the will of the Father (John 4:34). The Father has chosen us for adoption as His children, but it is the Son who confers this gift. What a sweet thought it is to know that the Lord Jesus personally hands us our adoption papers! Augustine (354–430) observed that typically the only child of a father rejoices that he does not need to share his inheritance with anyone else. But Christ is an only Son who gladly shares His inheritance with us as His adopted brothers, takes us as His inheritance, and makes Himself ours!

Moreover, Christ is the one who confers adoption on us because He purchased it for us with His blood. Human adoption can be very expensive, especially if it involves adopting a child from a foreign country. Such a process can cost tens of thousands of dollars. Yet it was far more costly for Christ to secure our adoption: He needed to descend from heaven to earth, humbling Himself to be "made of a woman, made under the law" (Phil. 2:5–8, Gal. 4:4). He redeemed us by dying under the curse of God (Gal. 3:13; 4:5). John 11:52 indicates that Christ died to "gather together in one the children of God that were scattered abroad." Why are we, people of many nations, gathered into God's family? Because Christ died for us.

James Boice said that our adoption, as authorized by Christ, should give us boldness and great confidence. The same Lord Jesus who has all authority in heaven and on earth has given us authority to be the children of God. Therefore, believers have the sovereign right to claim God as their Father. Our adoption stands on the highest possible legal ground and is rooted in the greatest moral and governmental authority.

Boice told how, on one of Napoleon's military campaigns, the Emperor let go of the reins of his horse to read something. The horse reared up. Before it could throw Napoleon off, however, a lowly corporal ran up, seized the horse's bridle, and brought it under control. Napoleon looked at the corporal and said, "Thank you, *Captain*." The newly promoted soldier said, "Of what company, sir?" The emperor replied, "Of my guards." Immediately, the man laid down his musket, ripped off his corporal stripes, and walked to the army's headquarters.

A staff person asked him what he was doing. "I am a captain of the guards," he answered.

"By whose authority?" a man asked.

"By the authority of the Emperor," said the new captain—and that settled the matter!

Dear believers in Jesus Christ, you are children of the living God. If anyone—angel, devil or man—asks by whose authority you claim to be a child of God, you may respond, "By the authority of the Lord Jesus Christ."

How amazing it is that God would adopt His bitter enemies, children of the devil, into His own family! We should marvel at the words of 1 John 3:1, "Behold, what manner of love the Father hath bestowed upon us, that we should be called the sons of God." And we should be awestruck at the thought that God confers this gift on us by the nail-pierced hand of His Son!

2. The Supernatural Birth of God's Children

Thus far, we have considered the gracious adoption of God's children in Christ. In John 1:12, we saw that God's people receive Christ by faith and are granted adoption by Christ. This brings us to the second half of our Scripture text. John 1:12 ends in the Greek with the phrase, "to them that believe in his name." Such persons are further described in John 1:13, literally translated, as those "who not of bloods nor of the will of flesh nor of the will of a man but of God were born."

This verse answers a very important question: How can anyone receive Christ? How can anyone believe in Him? People tend to think that receiving Christ is easy; but John told us in verses 10–11 that the world did not know or recognize Christ, and Israel did not receive

Him. There is a universal resistance in mankind against faith in Christ. As the true Light, Christ has come into the world, but men will not come to this Light, for they hate it and love the darkness instead, because their deeds are evil (John 3:19–20).

Who then can be saved? Matthew 19:25–26 tells us that God must do a supernatural work to convert us. It is so much a work of new creation that the Bible calls it regeneration, or being born again (John 1:13; 3:3–8; 1 Peter 1:3, 23). Literally, it is a "genesis from above" (John 3:6). Our Lord Jesus declares, "Verily, verily, I say unto thee, Except a man be born again, he cannot see the kingdom of God" (John 3:3).

The first three parts of John 1:13 emphatically deny that this spiritual rebirth is produced by man. The fourth part, by contrast, affirms that it is a miracle of God.

Regeneration Is Not a Birth by Any Human Means

John says that God's believing children have been born "not of blood, nor of the will of the flesh, nor of the will of man." Some commentators say that these three phrases say the same thing in three different ways—in other words, that this rebirth is not a physical birth. But that does not fully explain the meaning of the text. The three phrases refer to three distinct matters: our physical birth, our personal choices, and the choices of our forbears or leaders. Specifically, it means the following:

1. We are not born into the kingdom of God *by physical birth*. It is not a matter of biology or geneology. "Blood" refers to the bodily fluids involved in conception, pregnancy, and natural birth, or possibly to the bloodlines of ancestry. You are not born a Christian. No individual or group can be considered Christian by virtue of family or ethnicity. That was a crucial statement for John to make in view of Jewish national pride, but he does not end there. Whenever a particular people generally embrace the Christian faith, they might assume that their race or nation is God's chosen people, but God's elect were never defined by race (Rom. 9:6–13). Since the coming of Christ, the family of God has expanded into every nation (Matt. 28:19). Family

or national pride and racism have no place in biblical Christianity. No one will get to heaven based on the color of his skin, his ethnic heritage, or the correct last name.

2. We are not born into the kingdom *by our will*, or, in the words of our Scripture, "nor of the will of the flesh." Some scholars say "the will of the flesh" refers to sexual desire. "Flesh" can sometimes refer to the physical body, and "the will of the flesh" can refer to physical desires. If that is the meaning here, this phrase would repeat what was said before, that we are not born again by a physical birth. But John's choice of words suggests that he refers here not to the human body, but to the desires and choices of the fallen human heart.

This is confirmed by the Bible's use of *flesh*. So John 1:14 tells us, "the Word was made flesh"—not just a body, but that Jesus is fully human with body and soul. When the Lord Jesus contrasts flesh and spirit in John 3:6 and 6:63, He is not drawing a contrast between the human body and the human spirit, but between man's inability and the supernatural power of the Holy Spirit. In John 8:15, Jesus rebuked the Pharisees for judging after the flesh, not because they were looking at people's bodies, but because they were thinking in a limited human manner. And in John 17:2, Christ prayed to His Father to give His Son "power over all flesh, that he should give eternal life to as many as thou hast given him." Christ did not merely have sovereignty over human bodies, but sovereignty over all humanity, body and soul, to save His elect. So *flesh* often refers to human nature, body and soul together, in a way that emphasizes our weakness due to the fall.

Therefore, when John says, "not of the will of the flesh," he means that our spiritual birth is not produced by human will, human choices, human motivations, or the inclinations of human nature, for we are radically corrupted by sin. Jesus taught this in John 5:40, saying, "Ye will not come to me, that ye might have life." Literally, He is saying, "You are not willing to come to me." People by nature are *unwilling* to trust in Christ. They are also *unable* to come to Christ. In John 6:44, Christ says, "No man can come to me, except the Father which hath sent me draw him: and I will raise him up at the last day." They cannot even truly hear His Word (John 8:43). People must be born again to receive Christ because, in their fallen condition, they are unwilling and unable to trust Him. In the words of the Heidelberg Catechism, "We are so corrupt that we are wholly incapable of doing any good, and inclined to all wickedness, except we are regenerated by the Spirit of God" (Q. 8).

This should humble us. You cannot receive Christ by an act of your own will. Your duty is to come to Christ because you have a will and you are responsible to use it rightly, but our fallen human nature is so twisted by sin that we will not and cannot trust Christ. Do you say to yourself, "I can receive the Lord Jesus whenever I please"? You cannot take one step toward Him without the supernatural grace of God. You are so wicked, so depraved, and so hostile to God that you will never be willing or able to come to Christ unless God works a miracle in your heart. We are not born into the kingdom by our own will.

3. We are born into the kingdom *not by the will of any other human being,* says John 1:12, "nor of the will of man." There are two words for "man" in Greek. One is more generic, *anthropos,* meaning a human being. The other word, *andros,* is gender-specific, referring to an adult male human being, and that is the word used here. Some people think "the will of a man" refers to the choice of an adult male to beget offspring. In that case, this is just another reference to physical birth, and all three phrases have essentially the same meaning.

Again, I do not believe that this interpretation is adequate because it does not square with the biblical view of God's sovereignty over conception and birth. The Bible repeatedly gives us examples of husbands who wanted to have children, but nothing happened until the Lord opened the wombs of their wives. Any couple who has struggled with infertility understands this well. Children are not conceived and born "of the will of a man" but by the will of God. So it seems unlikely that John would refer to natural birth as "of the will of a man" because even natural conception and birth are not under man's control.

On the other hand, I do not agree with those who collapse this phrase into the one before it as if "not by the will of a man" is another way of saying not by "the will of the flesh." That does not do justice to the gender-specific nuance of this word for man.

It seems best to understand that John is saying that not only your will is unable to regenerate you, but also no "father figure" in your life can do it for you by his will. The Jews would have understood this as a reference to circumcision, so this text is very important in John's evangelization of his fellow Jews. The Jews might say, "Of course no one is part of the kingdom just by birth. Our fathers circumcised us into the covenant with Abraham. Circumcision made us sons of the kingdom." To this John responds, "Not by the will of a man." Today someone might say, "I know I am a Christian because my parents baptized me." To this Scripture responds, "Not by the will of a man." No parent's decision can save his children.

John Gill wrote, "The best of men, as Abraham, David, and others; who though ever so willing and desirous that their children, relations, friends, and servants should be born again, be partakers of the grace of God, and live in his sight, yet cannot effect any thing of this kind: all that they can do for them is to pray for them, give advice, and bring them under the means of grace; but all is ineffectual without a divine energy." Only the Word and the Spirit can save us.

This is a warning to parents. We long to see our children saved. It would be so easy to grasp hold of something that would guarantee that our children go to heaven. Isn't that why some parents are so eager for their children to pray the sinner's prayer? How many of us are relying on infant baptism or Christian education to save our little ones? But beware, dear parents. As we already saw in John 1:12, no prayer, no sacrament, and no amount of education can make your child a child of God. They only are saved who embrace Christ and His benefits with a believing heart. You cannot make your child believe. No minister can save him, and no conference, retreat, or school can guarantee his conversion. Evangelize these children, yes, with all diligence. Pray fervently for their salvation, and then wait humbly on the Lord. Only He, the faithful covenant-keeping God, can save them.

This brings us to the last part of our text's description of the new birth.

Regeneration Is an Act of the Sovereign Will of God
John 1:13 declares that Christ-receiving, gospel-believing children of God, "are born of God." The essence of the gospel is that "salvation belongeth unto the LORD" (Ps. 3:8). If men are to be saved, God must do the saving. "God was in Christ, reconciling the world unto Himself" (2 Cor. 5:19). We must trust in the power and grace of God, who works the miracle of regeneration in His chosen ones. To be born again is to be born of God.

In his heart, every Christian knows that he is saved only because of the grace of God. From beginning to end, salvation is all of God. Charles Spurgeon (1834–1892) wrote,

> I remember sitting one day in the House of God and hearing a sermon as dry as possible and as worthless as all such sermons are, when a thought struck my mind—how came I to be converted? I prayed, thought I. Then I thought, how came I to pray? I was induced to pray by reading the Scriptures. How came I to read the Scriptures? Why did I read them and what led me to them? And then, in a moment, I saw that God was at the bottom of all and that He was the Author of faith!

Concerning this rebirth, or birth from above, we may say that:

1. It is *a birth from God the Father*. John 1:12–13 says that the "children of God" have been born "of God." Through this passage, God the Father is distinguished from His only begotten Son. The believer's rebirth is particularly attributed to God the Father. The apostle John repeatedly speaks of being "born of God the Father" (1 John 3:9; 4:7; 5:1, 4, 18). This might surprise you since Christ also speaks of being born of the Holy Spirit (John 3:5–8). The Holy Spirit is the effective agent of the second birth, but Scripture locates the source of our rebirth in the will of God the Father, who works through the Son and by the Holy Spirit (Titus 3:3–7). James 1:17–18 says, "Every good gift and every perfect gift is from above, and cometh down from the Father of lights, with whom is no variableness, neither shadow of turning. Of his own will begat he us with the word of truth, that we should be a kind of first fruits of his creatures." Notice that we are begotten, not of our will, but of the Father's will. So 1 Peter 1:3

says, "Blessed be the God and Father of our Lord Jesus Christ, which according to his abundant mercy hath begotten us again unto a lively hope by the resurrection of Jesus Christ from the dead."

God extends His fatherly love to us even before He adopts us as His children. This reminds us that our adoption is entirely of God's initiative. It is rooted in "His own purpose and grace, which was given us in Christ before the world began" (2 Tim. 1:9). The Spirit freely and sovereignly effects the new birth because the Father chose us for this very thing in eternity past (Eph. 1:3–5; 1 Peter 1:1–2). We were not yet His children at that time, but He had already set His predestinating and adoptive love upon us and, in His time, brought our adoption to fruition.

Do you know the love of the Father? Have you been born again? If so, your rebirth was the effect of His glorious, eternal, fatherly love for you. How personal is the Father's love for you, that He would bring you out of spiritual death and raise you with Christ into spiritual life (Eph. 2:4–5)! If He chose you and loved you and regenerated you, what good things does He yet have in store for you? Exult in the love of the Father; your regeneration is a birth from God the Father.

2. It is *a birth of God's initiative and power alone*. Surely this is part of what Scripture means when it says that God's people "were born...of God." The verb is passive, indicating that God's people did not birth themselves. God did it to them.

The entire metaphor of birth takes the power and initiative out of our hands and puts it in God's. God brought us to birth, and we only realized it afterward as we experienced our conversion from unbelief to faith in Christ. This birth was not of our will, but of God's will.

Our Lord expressed the same truth when He taught Nicodemus about being born of the Spirit. Jesus said that human flesh cannot produce this birth; only the Spirit of God can do that. Then, in John 3:8, Jesus compared the Spirit to the wind. Using the words for Spirit and wind, which are the same in Greek, Jesus said, "The wind bloweth where it listeth, and thou hearest the sound thereof, but canst not tell whence it cometh, and whither it goeth: so is every one that is born of the Spirit." You cannot control the wind any more than you can control how the heavenly Father breathes upon dead sinners by His Spirit.

3. It is *a birth of a new nature in Christ*. The word for birth implies the arrival of a new person into the world. J. C. Ryle (1816–1900) wrote,

> The birth here spoken of is the new birth, or regeneration, that complete change of heart and nature which takes place in a man when he becomes a real Christian. It is a change so great that no other figure but that of birth can fully express it. It is as when a new being, with new appetites, wants, and desires is brought into the world. A person born of God is "a new creature: old things are passed away; behold, all things are become new" (2 Cor. 5:17).

Fallen human nature is diametrically opposed to God. This rebirth of God is a revolution in the heart, overthrowing natural enmity and opening the way for the truth of the gospel. It is the birth of a new nature, the conquest of a rebellious soul, and the dethroning of sin as our master. Sin still remains like an enemy hiding in the mountains, waging guerrilla warfare against our souls (1 Peter 2:11). If we are not watchful, sin can launch devastating attacks upon us; but the King of Kings has asserted His crown rights over us, and has established His throne in our hearts.

The birth of the new nature is our re-creation in the image of God. This too is clearly implied in John 1. If God the Father begets us in a new spiritual birth, doesn't that imply that He makes us like Himself? "Like father, like son," as the saying goes. Natural begetting and birth produces a child in the image of his parents (Gen. 5:3). By analogy, we expect the same to be true of spiritual begetting and birth. If you are born of God, then you bear the image of the Father, in and through Christ.

3. Putting It Together: Divine Birth unto Divine Adoption unto Divine Likeness

Christ grants divine adoption to all who receive Him because of their divine birth. How wise and good God is! He has given us two gifts that reach us in our great need and lift us into the heavens: *divine adoption* and *divine birth*. By sin, our status is doomed and our nature ruined. But, by divine adoption, God changes our status from disgraced sons of hell to honored children of heaven. He gives us a status above the angels, changing our natures from hateful children of Satan to holy children of God.

God has given us these distinct blessings in one inseparable package, for they come to us in the Lord Jesus Christ. In a sense, God's elect are "in Christ" before the world was created (Eph. 1:4; 2 Tim. 1:9). There is a covenantal union between Christ and His elect from all eternity. Within that covenantal union, Christ died in their place. He intercedes for them, obtains the Spirit of regeneration for them, and writes His Word on their hearts with the Holy Spirit as promised in the new covenant (2 Cor. 3:1–6).

The regenerated soul receives Christ by faith, and the covenantal union then becomes a vital, spiritual union through faith. Paul thus speaks in Romans 16:7 of other Christians who "were in Christ before me." In our conversion, we become united to Christ in a new, living manner. The Spirit of Christ dwells in us and we belong to Christ (Rom. 8:9). Christ Himself dwells in us (Col. 1:27) and does so in increasing measure as the Father strengthens our faith by His Spirit (Eph. 3:16–17). United to the Son of God, we are adopted as God's sons and daughters and grow more and more into the image of Christ so that He may be the firstborn among many brethren (Rom. 8:29). In and through Christ and His work by His Spirit, we then become increasingly like our Father in heaven.

Through adoption, our Father grants us likeness to Himself. He imparts to us a filial heart and disposition that resembles His own. The Puritan Roger Drake writes, "All God's adopted children bear their Father's image, as Gideon's brethren did his (Judg. 8:18). They are like God, in holiness [and] in dignity" (Matt. 5:44–45; Rom. 8:29; Heb. 2:7; 1 John 3:2–3).

"Like Father, like son" is true in another sense, too. As God's children, we have been born in our Father's likeness. Yet we have also been born in the likeness of His Son by a living union with that Son. By grace, we increasingly become like them both. Witsius wrote that as those "born of God…the sons of God by grace bear some resemblance to him who is the Son of God by nature…. We are even transformed into his likeness, and have upon us no contemptible effulgence [or brilliant shining forth] of his most glorious holiness."

Concluding Applications and Questions

The privilege of being made like the Father through adoption places believers under responsibilities to our adopting Father that ought to transform the way we think and live. Let me just mention four of these responsibilities, and then conclude with some questions of self-examination.

First, *obey and imitate your Father, and love His image-bearers.* Strive to be like Him, to be holy as He is holy, to be loving as He is loving. We are to be "imitators of God" (Eph. 5:1) to show that we bear the family likeness.

We are, then, to love the Father's image wherever we see it. We are to live as God's children in mutual love and patience with each other, having the same Father, Elder Brother, and indwelling Spirit.

Second, *show childlike reverence and love for your Father in everything.* Reflect habitually upon your Father's great glory and majesty. Stand in awe of Him; render Him praise and thanksgiving in all things. Let overflowing love to your Father constrain you to employ all the means of grace, to obey His commands, and to work for Him.

Third, *submit to your Father in every providence.* When He visits you with the rod, don't resist or murmur. Don't immediately respond by saying, "'I am not a child of God, God is not my Father, God deals harshly with me; if He were my Father, He would have compassion on me; He would then deliver me from this grievous and especially this sinful cross'—to speak thus does not befit the nature of an upright child," writes Brakel. Rather, "it is fitting for a child to be quiet, to humbly submit, and to say, 'I will bear the indignation of the LORD, because I have sinned against him'" (Mic. 7:9).

Fourth, *rejoice in being in your Father's presence and resist every hindrance that keeps you from relishing your Father's adopting grace.*

Delight in communing with Him and avoid all murmuring against Him. In heaven, this joy will be full; our adoption will then be perfected (Rom. 8:23). We will enter into the Father's presence where we will enjoy, delight in, and praise God forever. Let us wait and long for that day, as children who eagerly anticipate our full inheritance, where the triune God shall be our all in all.

Ask yourself, then, these questions:
First, *have I received Jesus Christ as my Prophet, Priest, and King?* If so, continue to live by faith in Him alone. Colossians 2:6 says, "As ye have therefore received Christ Jesus the Lord, so walk ye in him." You will never grow beyond Christ but only deeper into Him.

Second, *have I been adopted by God as one of His dear children?* Then live as a child of God, and not as an orphan. When trouble comes, lift your eyes to your heavenly Father. Be continually amazed at God's kindness to you in adopting you as His child.

Third, *have I been born of God to become a child of God?* If so, walk by the Spirit in a new and godly life. Romans 8:14 says, "For as many as are led by the Spirit of God, they are the sons of God."

Fourth, *am I counted among the children of God?* Then count them as your brothers and sisters, and love them affectionately and patiently. Be a committed and faithful church member. Care for the saints. Hear the words of Jesus calling to His family at the foot of His cross, "Woman, behold thy son!" and "Behold thy mother!" (John 19:26–27). Look around your church at the older men and say, "These are my fathers." View the older women and say, "These are my mothers." Say of the younger men, "These are my brothers," and of the younger women, "These are my sisters in all purity" (1 Tim. 5:1–2).

Fifth, *ask yourself, am I yet lost?* Are these glorious truths not true of me as yet? Am I still separated from Christ, alienated from the holy people of God, a stranger to the covenant of adoption, and dead in my sins? Then cry out to God for salvation until He makes you a child of God. You are presently far from God, but Christ can bring you near by His blood. Refuse to rest upon anything of yourself and to find any peace anywhere except with God through our Lord Jesus Christ. And may God cause you to be born again unto a living hope in Christ. May Christ grant you the right to be a child of God, even today!

Finally, *am I truly saved and becoming increasingly like my Father in heaven?* If so, then sing! If there is any right response to John 1:12–13, surely it is praise and thanksgiving and the lifting up of our hearts to the Lord. In the great congregation of God's people, at home with your loved ones, or alone with God, sing praise to Him with grace in your heart:

> O how shall I the goodness tell,
> Father, which Thou to me hast showed?
> That I, a child of wrath and hell,
> I should be called a child of God;
> Should know, should feel my sins forgiv'n,
> And taste today the joys of heav'n.

Chapter 22

Empty Grave Clothes

> *And he stooping down, and looking in, saw the linen clothes lying; yet went he not in. Then cometh Simon Peter following him, and went into the sepulchre, and seeth the linen clothes lie, and the napkin, that was about his head, not lying with the linen clothes, but wrapped together in a place by itself. Then went in also that other disciple, which came first to the sepulchre, and he saw, and believed. For as yet they knew not the scripture, that he must rise again from the dead.* —JOHN 20:5–9

Have you ever been to the funeral of a family member? Can you remember all the emotions that you felt?

Imagine the emotions of Jesus's friends and followers as they saw their Savior and Lord taken captive. Imagine how John and Peter must have felt as they witnessed the interrogation of Jesus. Imagine what John experienced as he saw his beloved Master being nailed to the cross, dying a shameful, torturous death. There hung his best friend, his confidant, his Master.

Then it was all over. Jesus breathed His last. He was buried. What waves of sorrow and depression must have washed over these disciples! Their Master was dead. They had hoped He would usher in His new kingdom. They had thought that He would be the One who would redeem Israel. But now, everything was over—their hopes, their aspirations, their ministry with Him—all was history.

Now, try to imagine the disciples' emotions, as they became aware of Christ's resurrection. He is alive again! He is not dead! He is indeed the Messiah!

The reason the disciples were so depressed and fearful after Christ's death is that they did not understand the Scriptures, and they forgot Jesus's testimony that He would rise again from the dead (John 2:22). Therefore, Christ lovingly provided wonderful evidence of His resurrection for them. The grave clothes that Jesus left behind were part of this evidence. Let's focus in this sermon on the instruction that these empty linens provide for us in John 20:5–9.

With God's help, we wish to consider:

Empty Grave Clothes!
1. Resurrection by fact
2. Resurrection by faith
3. Resurrection by foreshadowing

1. Resurrection by Fact

It is early Sunday morning, the third day since Jesus had died so dreadfully on the cross. Mary Magdalene, Joanna, Salome, Mary the mother of James, and other women approach the grave of Jesus. They love Him and want to add some spices to His body. Though it is dark, they notice that the stone has been rolled away from the entrance to the tomb. What has happened? Has someone pillaged the sepulcher? Did someone steal Jesus's body? What should they do?

Gathering courage, the women enter the tomb. In the dim light, they notice that Jesus's body is missing. Probably around this time, Mary Magdalene rushes out to find the disciples. Soon she finds Peter and John. Panting for breath, she blurts out her interpretation of what she has seen: "They have taken away the Lord out of the sepulcher, and we know not where they have laid him."

Peter immediately decides to take a look, and John goes with him. They break out into a run. With such urgent matters to attend to, they cannot remain at a calm walk. There is only one thing on their minds. They must get to the tomb to see what has happened.

What must have gone through their minds as they ran? What had happened to Jesus's body? Could someone have stolen it? Certainly

He could not be alive. They were not gullible enough to get their hopes up. But, how could they be so sure?

John outruns Peter. Why does Peter run slower? Some have thought that Peter was simply older and slower. Others stress that his conscience still troubled him about his recent denial of Christ, and this may have slowed him down. Regardless, the fact that John outran Peter indicates that John also desperately wanted to get to the grave as soon as possible. He did not want to take the time to wait for Peter.

Soon John, panting heavily, arrives at the sepulcher. It is true: the stone is rolled aside! Why? He stoops down to look in. He sees the linen grave clothes, still intact, lying there (v. 5). The Greek word here for seeing (*blepo*) merely indicates that John noticed the clothes. He does not inspect them, but just sees them lying there. Respectfully, he hesitates, no doubt instinctively remembering that those who come in contact with the dead are declared ceremonially unclean. So John does not enter the sepulcher.

John notices that Mary Magdalene's testimony had been wrong. He sees that the body of Jesus has not been taken, for then the linen wrappings would have been taken with the body. This would have made transportation of the body much easier.

But, you say, "The plunderer could have pulled off the grave clothes and taken the body." Surely you would agree that if this were the case, the linen clothes would have been torn and scattered about. In addition, the one hundred pounds of spices, mentioned in chapter 19:39, would have been scattered about. But instead, John sees the linen clothes lying there, with no evidence of any disturbance (v. 5).

Moments later, Peter arrives. As usual, Peter does not hesitate. Brushing by John, he goes right into the tomb. Perhaps he feels his uncleanness so strongly combined with such a longing for Jesus that he does not hesitate to take the risk of becoming ceremonially unclean. As his eyes adjust to the darkness, he sees something quite astonishing. The Greek word here for seeing is (*theoreo*), from which we get the English word "theorize." It implies that Peter scrutinized the grave clothes carefully. Literally, he *observed* them. He observed something unusual that caught his attention. The parallel passage in Luke 24:12 says that after Peter saw the linen clothes "laid by themselves," he left the tomb, "wondering in himself at that which was come to pass."

What does Peter see? Our text says in verses 6–7 that he sees "the linen clothes lie, and the napkin, that was about his head, not lying with the linen clothes, but wrapped together in a place by itself." He observes several things. He sees the linen clothes that had been around Jesus's body; and he sees the napkin, or face cloth, wrapped together separate from the body clothes. No doubt he also sees the blood stains on the grave clothes.

You may be wondering: "Why does the text draw so much attention to the grave clothes and how they are arranged? Does this mean that Jesus, after He pulled off the grave clothes, put them in neat piles?"

If we study the text carefully, we don't get the impression that this is what the text has in view. If John were trying to show that Jesus neatly piled up His clothes after He rose from the dead, you would expect him to mention something about neatness. But neither our text, nor the parallel passage in Luke 24:12, says anything about neatness of organization. What then is the text saying?

To fully understand the significance of the position of Jesus's grave clothes, it helps to know something about Jewish burial practices. Every society has its own distinct mode of burial. Greeks and Romans often cremated the dead. Egyptians often embalmed the dead. Some cultures buried tools, money, and food with the dead in a coffin. Jewish burial was different. How did they do it?

Look with me, first of all, at chapter 19, verses 39–40, where John provides a short description of how Jesus was buried: "And there came also Nicodemus, which at the first came to Jesus by night, and brought a mixture of myrrh and aloes, about an hundred pound weight. [Aloes was a powdered wood that had a pleasant fragrance; myrrh was a fragrant gum that was mixed with the aloes.] Then took they the body of Jesus, and wound it in linen clothes with the spices, as the manner of the Jews is to bury."

The Jews normally wrapped the dead person's body in linen, while they mixed in dry spices. The body was wrapped in this way up to the shoulders, leaving the neck and head bare. Then they separately wrapped the head with a face cloth, somewhat like a turban, but covering the entire head. This is why, when Jesus raised Lazarus from the dead, John 11:44 says, "He that was dead came forth, bound hand and foot with grave clothes: and his face was bound about with a napkin." Once the body was wrapped, the Jews put the dead body face up, without a coffin, in a tomb. The tomb was generally cut from rock in the Judean and Galilean hills. Then a large, flat, round rock was rolled in front of the entrance to seal it. It appears, then, that Joseph of Arimathaea and Nicodemus did this with Jesus's body, late on Friday afternoon.

So what does Peter see in the grave clothes that causes him to gaze with amazing wonder? Peter recognizes that the body of Jesus is gone. Luke says he saw the "linen clothes laid by themselves." The body is gone. How can that be? The clothes are here, but the body is gone! Peter also observes that the grave clothes are essentially undisturbed, that is, except for the head cloth. It seems that the head cloth was still wrapped up, as if it was around a person's head (like an empty cocoon), but was separate from the linen clothes. This is strange! Peter leaves the tomb, marveling and wondering about what has happened.

Peter's mind is still in turmoil. Though he is a believer in Christ, light has not broken into his soul. He does not have clarity to see the wondrous truth of Christ's resurrection—at least not more than its fact. But we know that soon after Peter left the grave, Christ met privately with him in a personal restorative encounter that was too sacred for human words. Then Peter's darkness was dispelled. His burdened conscience was healed with the balm of Gilead.

We can experience something quite similar still today. Though we trust that Christ is the Messiah as a fact and believe in Him, our minds and hearts can be so clouded at times that we cannot embrace the full implications of that reality. The promises of the Word seem unreal and far from us. We remain like this until Christ again comes to us, shines with His glory into our souls through His Word and Spirit, and heals our broken hearts.

So we have here facts that testify of Jesus's resurrection. The grave clothes are still lying undisturbed in the tomb. The only unusual thing is that the body of Jesus is absent. It is as if the body of Jesus has disappeared. The linens that had wrapped the body are still lying there, and the head napkin has fallen apart from the body linens. Jesus is no longer in the grave. This could not have been staged. No one could have taken the body out.

Young people, just imagine for a moment that you were one of the disciples. Your whole world had just fallen apart when your Master died the shameful death of the cross. You are afraid that the authorities are going to round you up and finish you off next. Then you receive news that your Master's grave has been pillaged. You rush over, and see the grave clothes lying, but the body is missing. What would you think?

We have seen the response of Peter. Luke says that he marveled. Now what about John? We see his response in our second point:

2. Resurrection by Faith

Before Peter leaves the tomb, John enters. He too sees what Peter saw. The Greek has a third word here for seeing (*horao*). This word means to perceive and take special notice. It has a focus on intellectual activity and concern. It indicates that John went beyond Peter in contemplating the implications of what he saw.

The text indicates a progression from John first *noticing*, then Peter *observing*, then John *perceiving*. There is an important distinction between these words. This perceiving of John fits perfectly with what accompanies his perceiving. Verse 8 says that when John entered the sepulcher, "he saw, *and believed*." Spiritual light arises in his soul through the gentle, powerful work of the Holy Spirit. As a result, he has spiritual sight to behold with the eye of faith.

What does John believe? He believes that Jesus has risen from the dead. He rightly concludes that Jesus's body has not been stolen. Peter had probably also concluded this. But John perceives more. He believes that Jesus has arisen in a wonderful way. His body has somehow come right out of the grave clothes. It has been transformed in a mysterious way to a new form of existence. Jesus is alive and well. John does not know where Jesus is, but he believes that Jesus is alive and begins to grasp its saving ramifications.

That means that Jesus did not die like a martyr. He must have planned His own death. That is indeed correct—Jesus had said that

He was going to die and rise again. Why hadn't he remembered? But why would Jesus have died and risen again? Ah, yes, hadn't Jesus said that "as Moses lifted up the serpent in the wilderness, even so must the Son of man be lifted up: that whosoever believeth in Him should not perish, but have eternal life"? (John 3:14–15). John begins to perceive what has happened, and he embraces the truth wholeheartedly. He is awestruck as the light of the gospel begins to shine in his mind.

Something similar to this happens when the Spirit sheds light into the soul of a believer, after a time of darkness. The glorious light of the gospel grips our entire being, and thrills us as we perceive and believe it. It may be the truth of the atonement, God's providence, the resurrection, or Christ's intercession. Such light is thrown on gospel truth by the Spirit so that we perceive the truth in a fresh, wonderful, new way. Perhaps it takes our breath away and makes us feel weak. We stand dumbfounded before the truth, basking in the glory of Christ. We perceive and believe the truth, and it makes us free and bold, as it did with the disciples.

But why did John not believe earlier? Verse 9 tells us that: "as yet they knew not the Scripture that he must rise again from the dead." This means that they did not have a good, Spirit-applied, working knowledge of the Old Testament Scriptures that predicted Christ's resurrection.

But where does the Old Testament teach that Christ will rise again? Let me mention just two places. For one, Isaiah 53:10–12 says: "Yet it pleased the LORD to bruise him; he hath put him to grief: when thou shalt make his soul an offering for sin, he shall see his seed, he shall prolong his days, and the pleasure of the LORD shall prosper in his hand. He shall see of the travail of his soul, and shall be satisfied: by his knowledge shall my righteous servant justify many; for he shall bear their iniquities. Therefore will I divide him a portion with the great." This cannot make sense if the Messiah remained dead. Then, too, Psalm 16:10 prophesied, "thou wilt not…suffer thine Holy One to see corruption."

Moreover, many Old Testament stories and types predict or prefigure the resurrection of Christ, such as the bird in Leviticus 14 that was dipped in blood and freed, or two chapters later, the goat that was sent away, or the budding rod of Aaron in Numbers 17, or Jonah's "resurrection" from the fish's belly on the third day (Matt. 12:40).

In addition to the Old Testament Scriptures, Christ plainly told the disciples on several occasions that He would die, and then rise again the third day. In John 2, He declared that He would raise up the temple of His body in three days (vv. 19, 21), and in Matthew 16:21 He tells us that He would be killed and rise again on the third day (Luke 9:22; 18:33).

The disciples had deaf ears regarding Christ's teaching on His resurrection. But now John believes. He believes that Jesus is the real Messiah after all, the Lord of glory, the exalted Son of God, who has come to suffer and die, and to rise again, to save sinners.

Notice that John's belief had its roots in Scripture. The implication of verse 9 is that if he had understood the Scripture about Jesus's resurrection, he would have believed already. And this is ultimately where our faith must rest.

And yet we see from this narrative that the Lord is patient with our slowness to believe. What prompted John's faith? Was it the Old Testament Scriptures? Was it the words of Jesus? No; it was the physical evidence of the empty grave clothes.

Isn't it remarkable that none of the disciples believed until they had physical evidence of Jesus's resurrection? Jesus later said to Thomas: "Blessed are they that have not seen, and yet have believed" (John 20:29). On the other hand, we see the condescension of God in providing abundant evidence for us of the resurrection of Christ. The angel did not need to roll the stone to let Jesus out, but he did so to let the disciples in, so they could see the evidence of His resurrection.

Do you believe in the resurrection of Jesus? You say, "I wish we had some strong evidence like John had." My response is: "We do." We have the testimony of John and Peter to what they saw in the tomb. John says in verse 31 that everything in his gospel was written that we might believe that Jesus is the Christ, the Son of God. We have the evidence of the Old Testament Scriptures as well as the complete New Testament canon.

In addition to the straightforward record of the Scriptures (which is more than sufficient), there is abundant circumstantial evidence for the resurrection of Jesus Christ. Just as John was helped to believe by the grave clothes, we can be helped by circumstantial evidence, such as these thoughts:

1. If Jesus had not risen from the dead, then someone would certainly have produced the body, and Christianity would have died. Instead, the angel beckons, "Come, see the place where the Lord lay" (Matt. 28:6). In other words, "See the empty grave clothes where Jesus's body had been laid."
2. Someone could not have stolen the body because the story that the Jewish leaders concocted is not credible at all. It is a stretch to believe that the entire band of Roman guards was sleeping while the disciples stole the body. If somehow they were sleeping, they would have awoken at the sound of the removal of the gravestone. And if they had continued to sleep, their testimony means nothing, because they were not witnesses. There is no way that Peter and John could have found the tomb with no guards and with the grave clothes essentially undisturbed, if the guards had not been supernaturally scared away.
3. How could the defeated and discouraged disciples, who did not even believe that Jesus would rise again, go about making up a story, and live joyfully to the end of their lives, dying martyred deaths, if Jesus did not really rise from the dead?

These kinds of considerations can sometimes be helpful for us to believe in Christ's resurrection. Of course it does not prove the resurrection, but it can help strengthen our faith.

The truth stands: Jesus arose from the dead. The resurrection is a foundational truth. It is the only hope for mankind. The story has been told of an atheist who called a prominent minister for a private talk. He asked the minister if he really believed in the resurrection. The minister said: "Absolutely." The atheist replied: "Although I don't believe in it, the resurrection of Christ is the only hope for mankind."

If Christ did not rise, then He is a liar. If He is a liar, then the Scriptures are not true. If the Scriptures are not true, then there is no God of the Scriptures. Then there was no supernatural creation; then, we are just a cosmic accident. Life then has no meaning, no purpose, and no fulfillment. But Christ did indeed rise from the dead (cf.

1 Cor. 15:12–20). He is not a liar. His life and death were not for nothing. As He rose, leaving behind the empty grave clothes, all His work of humiliation was over.

Do you believe in Christ's resurrection? Do you believe John's testimony in our text that the grave clothes were empty and that Jesus rose bodily from the dead? Do you believe that Christ rose from the dead not just as *a fact*, but do you put your faith in the risen Lord? Does the truth of Christ's resurrection impact your entire life?

You ask, "How does Christ's resurrection impact my life? How does the testimony of the empty grave clothes impact me?" We see that in our third point:

3. Resurrection by Foreshadowing

The empty grave clothes foreshadows several wonderful truths for God's people. If you're a believer, these foreshadowed truths are significant for you in at least five ways:

1. Jesus's empty grave clothes assures us of His resurrection, which in turn foreshadows *our blessed resurrection*. "For if we believe that Jesus died and rose again, even so them also which sleep in Jesus will God bring with him" (1 Thess. 4:14). The Spirit who raised up Jesus, will also quicken our mortal bodies (Rom. 8:11). Just as Jesus left behind His grave clothes, so we will too; Christ's resurrection is a sure pledge of ours (cf. Rom. 6:5; 2 Cor. 4:14; 1 Peter 1:21).

Empty grave clothes show us Christ's victory over sin, for He came into the world in swaddling clothes, and now symbolically leaves behind the clothes of His humiliation, so that we who are believers might leave all our humiliating sin-clothes behind in the grave and be resurrected in the white-robed righteousness of everlasting glory in Christ Jesus. Being raised in the likeness of Christ, clothed in His white robe of righteousness, we may rejoice that, in the day of our resurrection, sin will be left behind forever.

2. Jesus's empty grave clothes foreshadow *our eternal justification*. Those empty clothes declare that divine justice demanded Christ's release, for He had made perfect satisfaction to His Father for all the

sins of His people, had fulfilled all prophecies (Hebrews 10), and was now raised again "for our justification" (Rom. 4:25). Just as the Father confirmed with an oath in Jesus's resurrection that salvation is complete once and for all, so our resurrection will be the consummate declaration of our justification, for Christ's sake, before our holy Judge.

3. Jesus's empty grave clothes foreshadow *how* we will be raised from the dead. It will be *an instant and deliberate transformation of our bodies*. Our text implies that Christ did not rise slowly, unwrap the linens, and walk out of the grave. He was instantly transformed into His glorious resurrected body. Just as He had been deliberate in all His sufferings and death, so He was deliberate in the instantaneousness of His resurrection, which occurred on the morning of the third day, just as He had said that it would. We too—even if we live until the day of judgment—our bodies will be instantly changed, in a moment, in the twinkling of an eye, at the last trumpet, deliberately and precisely at the time appointed by God (1 Cor. 15:52).

What a comfort this is for us, dear believers! Just as our souls are instantly purified in the moment of our physical death, so our bodies will be instantly purified in the moment of our physical resurrection. The empty grave clothes signify that you, too, will live forever in as perfect a state as Jesus lives, glorifying Him with perfect souls and perfect bodies for all eternity—and that from the exact, deliberate moment appointed by God!

4. Jesus's empty grave clothes foreshadow with *what type of body we will be raised*. Our resurrection will be similar to the resurrection of Jesus. He is the firstfruits of the resurrection. Jesus came right out of the grave clothes, leaving them behind. His resurrection was different from that of Lazarus. Lazarus returned to the same life as before. He later died. Jesus, however, in His new glorious body, disappeared and reappeared anywhere He wished. Similarly, our physical bodies will be transformed into new, glorious bodies governed by the Holy Spirit. Christ will "change our vile body, that it may be fashioned like unto his glorious body" (Phil. 3:21).

What body will we be raised with? Paul anticipated this same question when writing to the Corinthians: "But some man will say, How are the dead raised up? and with what body do they come?" (1 Cor. 15:35). He answers with a comparison. When a farmer plants grain, he sows a bare seed. Over time, the seed is transformed into a wonderful plant. In the same way, though our natural body "is sown in corruption; it is raised in incorruption: it is sown in dishonour; it is raised in glory: it is sown in weakness; it is raised in power: it is sown a natural body; it is raised a spiritual body" (vv. 42–44).

Child of God, just think, the body that you now can touch and feel, though it will soon decay in the grave (if the Lord tarries), will be transformed like Christ's was. There is no need to speculate on which atoms and molecules God will use to recreate your new body. It is enough to know that your body will be transformed, recreated, resurrected. It will exist in a whole new way—different than we experience now, and so it will not need the same materials. Not all the particles of the natural body are needed for the resurrection body. The farmer only plants the seed, but out comes the full plant. The plant takes particles from soil, water, and air. Yet the buried seed is the origin and foundation of the new plant. The identity of the seed passes into the plant. Out of its ugliness and decay springs forth the new plant. So our resurrection bodies will rise out of the seed of our decayed bodies. Even elect children, who die before birth, will rise with glorious resurrection bodies.

But perhaps you have a question. Since Christ rose with what Paul calls a spiritual body, did He not then rise bodily? Yes, He did. His physical body did not remain in the grave clothes. It was transformed into a glorified, yet physical body. He ate food in this new body. The disciples could touch His body. Still today, Christ has a human body and soul in heaven, though he shines with glorious, divine light.

Similarly, our resurrection bodies are not only real material bodies, but also spiritual, or glorified bodies. This new body will be grand, glorious, incorruptible, and will never become weary. Our bodies will be recreated to be able to enjoy the glories of being in God's presence. Our new bodies will know no pain, suffering, or illness. There will be unlimited opportunities for service to our King and Savior. This transformation will happen when Christ returns to earth bodily for the second and final time to judge all men.

There is also a dismal flip-side to this truth for the unbeliever. If you do not wholeheartedly believe in Christ's resurrection, you will still be raised from the dead. You too will be raised with a new body. But the purpose of this resurrection will not enable you to sustain and delight in the glory of God. You will be resurrected in a body that will be designed to survive the torments of hell forever. It is said of criminals on the cross that increasingly they have only one desperate desire—to die. Usually they survived for a day or so on the cross, but eventually died. In hell, you too will desire annihilation but it will never come.

Hell is a real place. Jesus preached more about hell than about heaven. Hell is real because God takes sin seriously. Would He have sent His own Son to die the extremely painful and shameful death of the cross, and poured out His wrath upon His Son, if He did not take sin seriously? Anytime you are tempted to doubt the existence of hell, take another look at the cross of Christ.

Have you ever been to the funeral of a family member or a friend? Did it make you think of your own death? Child of God, our text shows that we need not fear the grave. Are you nearing the end of your life? Do you have one foot in the grave already? Does the look of the cold coffin frighten you? Does the prospect of your body disintegrating in the earth make you tremble? Repent from your sins and trust in the resurrected Savior *today*, and your resurrection will be unto glory and not unto eternal shame and pain.

5. Jesus's empty grave clothes foreshadow the truth that *death and the grave have no more dominion over us*. Let us not forget on this resurrection day, that Christ, our Head, has already passed through the grave. He left His grave clothes behind! His body that was buried is no longer on this earth. He is now in heaven. If the Head of the church, Christ, has risen, the body of Christ—the living church—is sure to follow. In principle, we have already risen with Christ (Col. 3:1). If death no longer has dominion over Him, the Head, we can be sure that it will not have dominion over us who form His body. We are raised up together with Him, sitting in heavenly places in Christ Jesus—here in principle already, and eventually forever in perfection

(Eph. 2:6). Your physical grave is merely a temporary resting-place for your body because Jesus is risen and is alive as the empty grave clothes testify.

Let us then sing with the living church:

> Christ the Lord is ris'n today, Alleluia!
> Sons of men and angels say, Alleluia!
> Raise your joys and triumphs high, Alleluia!
> Sing, ye heav'ns, and earth, reply, Alleluia!
>
> Lives again our glorious King, Alleluia!
> Where, O death, is now thy sting? Alleluia!
> Once He died our souls to save, Alleluia!
> Where thy victory, O grave? Alleluia!
>
> Love's redeeming work is done, Alleluia!
> Fought the fight, the battle won, Alleluia!
> Death in vain forbids His rise, Alleluia!
> Christ hath opened paradise, Alleluia!
>
> Soar we now where Christ hath led, Alleluia!
> Foll'wing our exalted Head, Alleluia!
> Made like Him, like Him we rise, Alleluia!
> Ours the cross, the grave, the skies, Alleluia!
>
> Hail the Lord of earth and heaven, Alleluia!
> Praise to Thee by both be given, Alleluia!
> Thee we greet triumphant now, Alleluia!
> Hail the Resurrection, thou, Alleluia!
>
> King of glory, Soul of bliss, Alleluia!
> Everlasting life is this, Alleluia!
> Thee to know, Thy pow'r to prove, Alleluia!
> Thus to sing, and thus to love, Alleluia![1]

---

1. Charles Wesley, "Christ the Lord is Risen Today," in *Trinity Hymnal: Baptist Edition* (Suwanee, Ga.: Great Commission, 1995), no. 205.

Chapter 23

Pentecost: The Outpouring of the Holy Spirit

> *And when the day of Pentecost was fully come, they were all with one accord in one place. And suddenly there came a sound from heaven as of a rushing mighty wind, and it filled all the house where they were sitting. And there appeared unto them cloven tongues like as of fire, and it sat upon each of them. And they were all filled with the Holy Ghost, and began to speak with other tongues, as the Spirit gave them utterance.*
>
> —ACTS 2:1–4

Dear friends, we wish you and your loved ones a blessed Pentecost, a day in which the Holy Spirit may be poured out in your family. How urgently we need His convicting, converting, and confirming work in our hearts!

Our text is Acts 2:1–4. With God's help, we wish to consider with you:

Pentecost: The Outpouring of the Holy Spirit
1. The time when the Holy Spirit was poured out
2. The manner in which the Holy Spirit was poured out
3. The people in whom the Holy Spirit was poured out

1. The Time

"And when the day of Pentecost was fully come." The word Pentecost literally means "fifty." The number fifty points to fullness, to ripeness, to a time that is ready for something to happen. The meaning of the number fifty developed during Old Testament times in part from three different events. In the first place, the number fifty points to the feasts of Israel. The second major annual feast commanded by the Lord was celebrated fifty days after Passover. There was an intimate relationship between that celebration and Passover fifty days earlier. The Passover commemorated the angel passing by the houses of the Israelites in Egypt because their doors were sprinkled with blood. Fifty days later, at a second feast, the firstfruits of harvest were divinely required to be presented. Thus the second feast was a completion of the first. At the first feast some sheaves were presented, but at the second feast two baked loaves of bread were presented. As the law stipulated, these were waved before the Lord and Israel declared, "Lord, Thine they are, and we received them from Thy hands." Thus, this second Israelite feast, the feast of harvest, was a feast that symbolized completion. It was a feast of ingathering, of reaping, and of joy.

Now, in God's providence, Jesus Christ waited to send His Holy Spirit until fifty days after His resurrection. His resurrection was already the firstfruits of the victory, but the actual ingathering of God's spiritual harvest still was yet to transpire. God chose fifty days later as the time to harvest the full fruits of His glorious gospel grace in the midst of the nations by gathering thousands unto salvation through the convicting and saving work of the Holy Spirit. Thus Pentecost is introduced to us with these words: "And when the day of Pentecost (the day of fifty) was fully come." In this day, when the time was ripe, God determined to gather in His harvest. He determined to enlarge the boundaries of the covenant of grace to make them international and universal. From all nations, men and women were gathered and were savingly wrought upon by the power of the Holy Spirit.

My friends, we still live in the New Testament age. God's harvesting work is still happening. God is still able to take your heart, your Gentile heart—for we are Gentiles by blood—and bring it under the canopy of His internal, saving work. Boys and girls, young people, and adult friends: We need God's time to fully come in our individual lives. We need God to do His harvesting task in our hearts. We need God to gather us unto Himself. Are you praying for this? Perhaps even this morning, as you came to God's house, was it your sigh, "Lord, there have been so many thousands converted on Pentecost almost two thousand years ago; can it be even on this Pentecost that Thou might yet gather me—a corrupt, unworthy sinner? Lord, I have so many fears about my soul for eternity, but oh, could it not be on Pentecost that Thou wouldst break through, that Thou wouldst finally harvest my soul? Oh, may the time fully come! May I hear Thy voice of mercy piercing my heart and feel the power of Thy saving Spirit convicting, making room for Christ, and working the glorious acts of salvation."

Pentecost, as we have said, means "fifty." The number fifty should cause us to reflect on the fifty days between the first and the second great feast—between Passover and Pentecost—but secondly, it also should cause us to reflect on the giving of God's law on Mount Sinai. The law was given fifty days after Israel's deliverance from Egypt. Here is a beautiful token of the graciousness of the law—that the law is not a covenant of works, but flows out of the covenant of grace. The law came for God's people as a gracious rule of gratitude because fifty days after Israel was delivered, the Lord came down with a mediator between Himself and Israel, so that Moses, as we read in Acts 7, might receive the law out of the hands of the Lord Jesus Christ.

Thus the law, though it is a convicting and condemning tool in its first usage, is a rule of life for the delivered and grateful believer in another usage. Of this usage, Jeremiah states that God says, "I will put my law in their inward parts, and write it in their hearts; and will be their God, and they shall by my people" (Jer. 31:33). It is this usage of the law that caused David to say, "Oh, how love I thy law! It is my meditation all the day." Those who are delivered from Egypt need sanctification. Those who are justified and escape from the power of a spiritual Pharaoh, of Satan, need the rule of God's law to assist them to walk in their King's highway of holiness. To be harvested, they must exhibit godliness in the fruits of their lives. They must walk out of gratitude according to the law. Thus this number fifty is also a symbolic number of spiritual fullness through holiness. It speaks of God not only working justification, but also of God gathering His people through sanctification to a godly life.

Third, the number fifty reminds us not only of the feast days and of the giving of the law, but especially of the year of jubilee. When the fiftieth year arrived in Old Testament Israel, the command was given that all that had been lost needed to be restored. Everything needed to be returned to its original owner. If you lost something by poverty or through bad debts, in the fiftieth year you would receive back what you originally possessed. It was a gracious act of God's law.

What a fitting picture this is of the gospel! You and I have lost everything in Paradise, including God Himself. In the fullness of time, however, God comes back to an elect sinner. He gives back everything through Jesus Christ that the sinner has lost in the first Adam. God returns and graciously, freely, gives back everything. That is Pentecost—God returning everything in the fullness of His triune being to a sinner who deserves nothing. The Father had returned already in Paradise to establish His covenant of grace by intercepting Adam and Eve, breaking their covenant with Satan. The Son returned in the fullness of time in Bethlehem and for thirty-three years walked on this earth. But now the Holy Ghost returned, so that the church may receive back a full triune God of grace, and may have everything restored that she lost in Paradise. Thus Pentecost may well be called the feast of jubilee, the feast of God's completed return, the feast where God has given Himself away completely.

"When the day of Pentecost was fully come." You see now, do you not, the special timing of God? Do you now see why the disciples needed to wait ten more days? Forty is the number of testing. They needed to be tested for forty days between the resurrection and the ascension. But the time needed to become ripe for the coming of the Holy Spirit, and the Lord planned that timing with perfection. Christ sent His Holy Spirit on the fiftieth day, the day of Pentecost, the day of the feast, the day of the giving of the law, the day that symbolized the year of jubilee, when that whole Old Testament dispensation pointed to the ripeness of God's time.

My friends, God's timing is always best. We are always impatient, but God is patient. His timing is true and right. He knows what He is doing.

Dear children of God, just as He timed this feast day and all the feast days perfectly, so He knows how to time every event in your life.

He knows exactly *what* you need, *when* you need it, *why* you need it, *how* you need it, and *to what degree* you need it. His timing is perfect.

"When the day of Pentecost was fully come." God waits for fullness, God waits for ripeness. God is wise. Even in natural life, if you eat a piece of fruit before it is ripe, it will not leave a good taste in your mouth. Something is wrong; the fruit is not ripe. God waits for ripeness. The beautiful thing is that He who is God of the feast is the God who also works ripeness for His people. This thought alone could easily make a whole sermon. If you start expanding this thought, you see how God in all areas of life deals with His children by making room, by making ripeness, in order to give the feast days of His grace. He will make room for Christmas, for Good Friday, for Easter, for Ascension, but also for Pentecost.

The trouble with our own hearts and with much of modern Christendom is that we are prone to apply feast days to ourselves before God's time is ripe. We are prone to eat fruit that is not ready to be eaten. We are prone to take things into our own hands that God has not yet provided.

2. The Manner

"When the day of Pentecost was fully come," our text says, "they were all with one accord in one place." There is something special about these words—"all with one accord in one place." It means that there was no division among this missing, waiting people. How is that possible? How could one hundred and twenty people be gathered together in the upper room, missing and waiting, and have no division? That is possible because they were waiting in expectation upon God. You can believe that if they had been waiting in expectation upon men, there would have been much division. There would have been many problems, troubles, talking about one another, comparing their experiences with one another, and asking one another if they thought this one or that one was a genuine disciple and a true waiter.

These one hundred and twenty disciples were God-centered in their waiting. It is a great gift when the church is filled with God-centered people. God-centered people have a dampening influence on all talk about men and a dampening influence on division. And how do they do that? I cannot explain that to you fully, but it is in part by their walk, their example, and their priorities. They will not engage or indulge in frivolous talk about people. For example, if someone comes to them and wants to hinder the accord in a certain place, they will say with love to that person, "Come, let us go to the person you are complaining about," and that puts an end to the unedifying conversation.

That is, of course, the way God calls everyone to act. None of us are called to listen to talk about others. Gossip and Christianity do not mix anymore than do oil and water. You are never called to indulge in division. You are never called to break things down in the church. You are always called to deal in accord with the Matthew 18 principle: If you have anything against your brother, go to that brother in love. As a church body, we are called to love one another and to esteem every other person in our congregation higher than ourselves. We are called to dwell with one accord in this place of worship.

Let us love one another. The fruit of the Spirit is love. Tradition tells us that when the apostle John was old, he was brought from a lengthy sickness back to the church of Ephesus where he had preached several years. There was division there also, because there is often some division wherever God builds His church. When John was carried onto the pulpit, tradition says that all he said to his former congregation was, "Little children, love one another." Support, build up, pray for, and treat one another exactly the way you would want to be treated.

Yet there is something deeper in these words: "They were all with one accord in one place." In addition to having outward respect for each other, these believers possessed a deeper unity. They had a spiritual unity. Their expectation was on God. They were in one accord from the heart. They were waiting for the same Holy Spirit. They were praising and praying to the same triune God. This is the accord that we really need to pray for—the accord of the mind of the Spirit.

While they were there, "suddenly," our text says, "there came a sound from heaven as of a rushing mighty wind, and it filled all the house where they were sitting." What the Lord gives comes from heaven. It comes from heaven to earth. It comes from free, sovereign grace. It comes from the one-sided work of God.

Moreover, what the Lord does from heaven, those who are destined to receive will hear. There is "a sound" from heaven. Their deaf ears will be unstopped. They will receive ears to hear the Word of the Lord. They will receive ears to hear what God has done and is doing. They will receive ears to hear what *sin* is, what *truth* is, what *grace* is, and who *Christ* is. When the Lord begins, then many times—most of the time—it is not long before the sinner says, "Is this really what our church believes, what the Bible says what I am hearing? It is as if I never heard the law before, as if I never heard the gospel before, as if I never heard about the beauty of Christ or about the heinousness of sin. It all seems new." And why? Because that sinner never had ears to hear before. When he picks up the Bible or the writings of our forefathers, he is amazed at what he reads, and says, "I never heard these sounds before." And why not? Because now the sounds are coming from heaven. Now they are not coming from the page, so to speak, but from heaven through the page to the heart, through the preaching to the heart, through prayer to the heart, through the means of grace to the heart. There was a rushing mighty wind, a sound from heaven that filled the house where they were sitting.

That sound came suddenly, our text says. God is often a surprising God. Sometimes He works more gradually. But many times He also works very suddenly. Indeed, where He comes even gradually, there still will be times when the heart is broken down and then the sinner will say, "It was sudden." "Suddenly there came a sound from heaven." Sometimes a person dies very suddenly and everyone is shocked. Sometimes a person's death comes very gradually, and yet, if you speak to the relatives when that person dies, most of the time you will hear them still say, "It was so sudden. We knew it was coming and we were expecting it on one side, but when it actually came, it came in a moment."

That is the way God works. Sometimes very suddenly an entire life is turned around—like these three thousand and everyone is surprised. At other times He is working very gradually in someone's heart and everyone can see it except that person himself. Finally, when the Lord grants some spiritual freedom, that person says that He came so suddenly, while everyone else says, "It has been obvious that the Lord has been working there for years already." Whatever the case may be, when it comes to the sinner, he feels the sudden power of the sound from heaven. He feels God pierce his heart.

Scripture compares this awakening to the sound of a rushing mighty wind, and to "cloven tongues like as of fire." What do wind and fire do? Wind and fire do two things. First of all, wind and fire destroy. A wind can be very strong. Boys and girls, you have heard about hurricanes and tornadoes, and you know how strong wind can be. Wind can blow us over; wind can uproot a tree and cast it far away; wind can take a house right off its foundation. And we all know what fire can do. A fire can destroy a whole house in just a few minutes.

The Holy Spirit, the Bible says, is like wind and fire. In fact, the word "spirit" in the original language means wind or breath—the breath of God, the power of God. The Holy Spirit is a person, but also as a divine person He is the power and breath, the wind of God, to do the work of God. Where there is no wind, everything remains stagnant. But when this wind comes, the power of God destroys the house of self-hope; it uproots all our self-righteousness and flattens our trees of self-hope in a moment. The power of God strips us of all our righteousness, both our natural and our religious righteousness, and in God's holy sight it makes us lost sinners with everything uprooted. The Holy Spirit razes everything to the foundation; He casts everything down. The Holy Spirit is like a mighty, destructive, rushing wind.

My friend, do you know what it means to be made bare, to have the house of your hopes, the tree of your planting, flattened, and that you yourself have lain prostrate before the Lord? There are times and places where God's people have been so flattened in all their hopes that they just cast themselves on the ground out of dire urgency and prostrate themselves before the Lord. They groan and cry with wrestlings that are unutterable for the forgiveness of their sin—out of a holy complaint over their grievous woes and their iniquities, their backslidings and their indifference, and the foolish, filthy raggedness of all their righteousnesses. Oh, when the hellish mess inside becomes true, then they become prostrate before the Lord of hosts and cry out, "Oh God, take me out of the battle, for I am sore wounded!" That is the wind, that is the power of the Spirit, that is this pentecostal Spirit convicting of sin, of righteousness, and of judgment, making sinners bare before God Almighty. They become nothing but needy sinners, nothing but lumps of destruction, nothing but fit objects for reprobation, condemnable and rejectable, full of trespasses and sins, yes, dead in trespasses and sins. Oh my friends, there are no words to express our misery! How profound this wind and fire are! They take from a sinner everything he thought he had. Do you know this painful work? Have you become lost, undone, and guilty?

But the wind also heals and the fire also purifies. Wind and fire destroy, but wind and fire also build up.

The Spirit's work is invisible, like wind. It is mysterious, like wind. It is sovereign, like wind. A tornado can wipe out one house and leave the next one standing. It is free, like wind. Jesus said to Nicodemus, "The wind bloweth where it listeth, and thou hearest the sound thereof, but canst not tell whence it cometh, and whither it goeth: so is every one that is born of the Spirit" (John 3:8). Boys and girls, you can feel the wind, but you cannot see it. You can see what the wind does, but you cannot see the wind itself. That is just like the Holy Spirit. We cannot see Him, but we can see what He does. He makes a sinner poor and, needy. He makes him feel the stench, the sin, and the depravity of his own heart. The Holy Spirit brings everything to a total loss from our side. Sometimes people ask, "How deeply does a person experience his sin and misery before he has freedom to embrace Christ by faith?" Well, generally speaking, the Holy Spirit takes a sinner and leads him to write across everything of self, "Undone, unclean! Everything is a total loss, I have no righteousness." Though the sinner may have glimpses of Christ through the lattice of His Word prior to this, normally he will not be enabled to embrace Christ by faith as His own Savior until self-righteousness is in ruins.

But then the wind does a second thing. Not so long ago there was an old castle in England in which a basement was discovered that had been locked up for many years. No wind could get to it. A keeper of that castle went down into the basement and described the stench of that basement. It was unbearably foul. He needed to find a way to bring in wind to purify and to cleanse it. In a similar way, the wind takes a destroyed sinner who says, "I am a total loss," and it blows with gospel breezes, blows with the grace of Jesus Christ, so that this total destruction turns into a garden and so that the spices of God's grace may flow out. "Awake, O north wind; and come, thou south; blow upon my garden, that the spices thereof may flow out" (Song 4:16). The wind softly, gently, and sometimes powerfully, blows on the hearts of God's people, takes that self-destroyed sinner and shows him that there is a way of salvation in Jesus Christ. The great task of the Spirit is to convict and strip in order to take the things of Christ and show them to the sinner.

Thus, this wind works both purifying and healing, so sinners see that everything they miss and everything that is a stench and everything that is sin—Jesus Christ has come to undo. So Jesus Christ "re-does" what the first Adam has undone. He "re-does" it all. Sinners cannot obey the law; but Christ has obeyed the law perfectly. They cannot bear the curse of God's wrath; He is their Curse-bearer. They cannot satisfy God's justice; He satisfied God's justice. They cannot pay for the punishment of their sins; He paid for the punishment of the sins of His people. They cannot pray rightly; He lives at the right hand of the Father to intercede for them. When the purifying wind comes along, they begin to see that all salvation lies in Christ. And that is the work of the Holy Spirit.

The work of the Holy Spirit is twofold: to uncover our unrighteousness and to discover the righteousness of Jesus Christ. Both usually happen gradually, step-by-step. But oh, how beautiful is this wind that fills the whole house! It fills the whole heart. It fills the believer. It makes him long more and more to know Christ better and fuller. Oh my friends, if we smell the stench and taste the destructive power of our so-called righteousness, then the beauty of the righteousness of Jesus Christ will be so great that we will say, when we have received the purifying, refreshing wind, "Oh, come, blow upon my garden all the days of my life, that I may know more and more of Him who is altogether lovely, who is the chief among ten thousand, who is white and ruddy." Blessed Holy Spirit who reveals the blessed Christ! And so the soul grows up in grace to know the winds of the gospel, to know the still, small voice of the gospel, to hear the message that there is salvation in Jesus Christ for a Manasseh, for a Philippian jailor, for a Bartimaeus, and for those who have lost everything.

A fire does the same thing as wind: it destroys, but it also purifies. Thus, when cloven tongues of fire sat upon the apostles, this too was a symbol of the Holy Spirit removing what they had and giving what God would give them, filling their hearts, filling their mouths, filling their houses with the Holy Ghost. A fire destroys. Boys and girls, we all know what a fire can do. But a fire can also heal and purify. Job said as it were, "When he hath tried me in the furnace of his affliction, I shall come forth as gold" (cf. Job 23:10). Abraham saw the burning lamp and his life was spared. Moses stood before a burning bush and his life was spared. Shadrach, Meshach, and Abednego walked in the fiery furnace. Oh my friends, when the fourth One is there who is the first One, when Jesus Christ is there, then the fiery trials He sends are means of purification—means of warming and enlightening, not means of destruction. Yes, He destroys self-help and self-hope, but He builds up through the warming influences of His grace, so the sinner who has his building destroyed by the fire of God's wrath may sit by the hearth of the grace of God in Jesus Christ and see the fire of His tender mercy, purifying, warming, melting, and moving his soul. The fruit of that is that he may say in his heart with the men of Emmaus, "Did not our heart burn within us, while he talked with us by the way?" (Luke 24:32).

Oh my friends, did your heart ever burn within you with the burning, purifying, warming power of the grace of God in Jesus Christ? Did you ever sense His indwelling power? Was there ever a moment of Pentecost, even if you could not say you knew Him well as a person, that you could still say, "I know something of His work. I have felt His influence; I have felt His power breaking me down; I have felt Him also building me up in Jesus Christ. I know this wind and this fire"?

3. The People

God comes to do this in poor sinners. He came to fill 120 at Pentecost with the Holy Ghost. This wind and this fire were symbols of the Holy Ghost, but they were not only filled with the symbols; they were filled with the essence—filled with the Holy Ghost Himself.

That is the essence of Pentecost. What does that mean? It means in the first place that they were filled with the blessings of the Holy Ghost, with the mighty wind of the Spirit, with the purging fire of the Spirit, with the heavenly dew of the Spirit, and with the sacred oil of the Spirit. They were filled with the blessings of justification and sanctification.

Second, it means that they were filled with the fruits of the Spirit—those we read about in Galatians 5—love, joy, peace, longsuffering, gentleness, goodness, faith, meekness, and self-control.

Third, it means too that they were filled with the special gifts of the Holy Spirit. They "began to speak," says our text, "with other tongues, as the Spirit gave them utterance." The word "utterance" in Greek means clarity and accuracy. They spoke perfectly in strange tongues. The matters were given in their hearts and the language in their mouths. It was a miracle.

They were filled with the *blessings*, the *gifts*, and the *fruits* of the Spirit, but also, fourth, with the *work* of the Spirit—that work we have been speaking about in stripping the sinner down, bringing him to Christ, and showing him the things of the Savior. They were filled with experiential misery, experiential deliverance, and experiential gratitude.

Fifth, and above all, they were filled with the person of the Holy Ghost Himself. They were filled with the truth of Lord's Day 20 of our Heidelberg Catechism: "He is given to me to comfort me and to abide with me forever." In other words, they received more here than applied benefits; they received more here than a revelation of Christ. They were allowed here not only to appropriate and embrace Christ by faith, but even more than that. They were even allowed to do more than to have Immanuel in their arms and to embrace their Savior. They were even allowed to do more than have access to the Father, to see their adoption, and to be able to cry out, "Abba, Father," in the presence of God. For here they also received the Holy Ghost, the third person of the triune God, as their seal and their Sealer. They were filled with the Holy Ghost. They were allowed to embrace a triune God. They were not only reconciled to God, but now they were restored into a full knowledge of His personhood, full in the sense that they knew each person. The fullness of the triune being is never exhausted, not even to eternity, but in that fullness they were sealed into the divine household as children of God. They were sealed with the seal of the Spirit who seals Christ within them and of whom John says in John 6:27, "Him hath God the Father sealed." Thus they experienced the triune seal of Father, Son, and Holy Ghost. They were sealed not only *by* but also *with* the Holy Spirit. The Spirit Himself became their Sealer.

Now they experienced what Jesus said. "If the Son shall make you free, ye shall be free indeed." Jesus sets the captives free by the power of His Spirit—the Spirit of Christ. The disciples here received what it means not only to rest in the mediatorial heart of God the Son, and the fatherly heart of God the Father, but also the sealing heart of God the Holy Ghost. "They were filled with the Holy Ghost." Oh, they could rejoice because Christ went to heaven as their Intercessor and Advocate, but they could now also rejoice because they had an Intercessor and an Advocate in their own hearts. To know comfort is one thing, but to know the Comforter is another. I have told the boys and girls in chapel that if they went back to their classrooms and saw something on their desks—some work of someone whom they did not know—they could admire the work, but they would not know the person who had put the work there. Something would still be missing. Likewise, when we may know the work of the Holy Spirit, that is wonderful and that is what we need. It is all that some of God's people will know all their lifetime, but still something is missing. If we would have that full ripeness and that full Pentecost, we must know the triune God. We must also know the Worker, the Promiser, the Fulfiller, the Sealer, the Comforter, the internal Friend, the Indweller—the Holy Ghost.

Only then, when we know the Holy Spirit, shall we rest in the triune rest wherewith God rests in His own triune being. For we read in Zephaniah, "He rests in his love" (Zeph. 3:17). Only when the sinner comes to know Father, Son, and Holy Ghost, can he find an abiding rest in the love of a triune God. In the steps of grace which lead to that, there are moments of rest and there are periods of rest, but only when we learn to know the triune God Himself is there an abiding sense of rest in the trinitarian boundaries wherewith God has bound

Himself to rest within Himself. Only then may the sinner be set inside of those boundaries and see that he is bound and hemmed in by the love and the rest of God who rests upon His own electing work, His own redeeming work, and His own sanctifying work.

They were filled with the Holy Ghost. They were swallowed up with the love of God. They lost themselves in God. They could experience in those moments, as it were, something of what Paul said, "Whether in the body or out of the body, I can hardly tell, but this I know: it was as if I were in the very heavens, filled with the love of God, filled with the Holy Ghost."

Oh my friends, if still today the Lord comes to one of His children and leads him in these experiential ways, then when he comes to feel the indwelling power of the Holy Ghost, that power is so strong and that presence is so real and the Comforter is so true. When he feels the Holy Ghost, he may at the same time believe that all things are his, that he belongs to Christ, and that Christ belongs to God the Father. Then he may cry out from the bottom of his heart, "This is Pentecost through the sealing Spirit! Christ is my Elder Brother. God is my Father."

Dear children of God, there is so much more to know and to learn of God than we yet know. May you become jealous of Pentecost realized experientially. May your longing be to know not only the work of the triune God, but also His persons—as a friend knows a friend—to know Christ as Elder Brother, God as Father, and the Holy Spirit as Sealer.

Is not the world poor in comparison to this? Seek more to be filled with God and with His work. May it be your prayer, dear friends—young and old—"Lord, teach me first to know the destructive wind in order to know the purifying, cleansing wind, but also teach me to know that process again and again in my life." Even after justification? "Yes, all the days of my life." In the process of sanctification we need constant, strong, and destructive winds. Paul said, "I die daily." We need to die to live. Out of dying comes life. That is the example Jesus used of the seed cast into the ground. It needed to die to live. A sinner needs to die to live. Joseph Irons once wrote, "To live under the habitual anointings of the Holy Spirit, we must be dying daily to the world and following hard after God."

Is that your life—dying daily to the world and following hard after God? That is a pentecostal lifestyle. It is not speaking in tongues; those things have been abolished with the first generation, as Paul wrote to the Corinthians. Away then with the mystical Pentecostalism of our day. But seek the pentecostal anointings of habitual, daily, dying to self, in order to be raised to live and to follow hard after God.

Chapter 24

Crying Out to the God of Providence

And being let go, they went to their own company, and reported all that the chief priests and elders had said unto them. And when they heard that, they lifted up their voice to God with one accord, and said, Lord, thou art God, which hast made heaven, and earth, and the sea, and all that in them is: who by the mouth of thy servant David hast said, Why did the heathen rage, and the people imagine vain things? The kings of the earth stood up, and the rulers were gathered together against the Lord, and against his Christ. For of a truth against thy holy child Jesus, whom thou hast anointed, both Herod, and Pontius Pilate, with the Gentiles, and the people of Israel, were gathered together, for to do whatsoever they hand and thy counsel determined before to be done. And now, Lord, behold their threatenings: and grant unto they servants, that with all boldness they may speak they word, by stretching forth thine hand to heal; and that signs and wonders may be done by the name of thy holy child Jesus. And when they had prayed, the place was shaken where they were assembled together; and they were all filled with the Holy Ghost, and they spake the word of God with boldness. And the multitude of them that believed were of one heart and of one soul: neither said any of them that ought of the things which he possessed was his own; but they had all things common. And with great power gave the apostles witness of the resurrection of the Lord Jesus: and great grace was upon them all. Neither was there any

> *among them that lacked: for as many as were possessors of lands or houses sold them, and brought the prices of the things that were sold, and laid them down at the apostles' feet: and distribution was made unto every man according as he had need. And Joses, who by the apostles was surnamed Barnabas, (which is, being interpreted, The son of consolation,) a Levite, and of the country of Cyprus, having land, sold it, and brought the money, and laid it at the apostles' feet.*
>
> —ACTS 4:23–37

For several decades, our nation has been pushing God, prayer, and righteousness out of the public square. Powerful forces have made Christianity unwelcome in the natural sciences, public schools, and seats of government. This was supposedly done to promote tolerance. But the veneer of that lie is cracking, and underneath we are discovering brutal intolerance for the things of God and the name of Christ.

We now face the very real possibility that as Christians we will be forced to choose between obedience to our God and obedience to our government. We want to be obedient to our government and serve it as good citizens, for the governing powers are ordained by God (Rom. 13:1). But Christians may soon need to choose between remaining silent about the perversions of God's design for marriage and going to jail. Christian preachers may need to choose between proclaiming that Christ is the only way to God and being charged with hate crimes. Christian organizations may need to choose between paying tax dollars for abortions and other services that are contrary to their consciences and paying large fines. When we face such choices, we must say with the apostles, "We ought to obey God rather than men" (Acts 5:29).

We can act with courage because our God is in control. Our God is the God of providence. The Belgic Confession teaches us to believe that "God, after He had created all things, did not forsake them or give them up to fortune or chance, but that He rules and governs them according to His holy will, so that nothing happens in this world without His appointment; nevertheless, God neither is the author of, nor can be charged with the sins which are committed."[1]

Let us consider what the doctrine of divine providence teaches us to do when we are threatened with opposition and suffering for our witness of Christ. What difference does it make for us to know that our God governs the heaven and the earth and all that is in them by His eternal counsel and providence?[2]

The book of Acts tells about the apostolic church in just such a situation. The apostles were carrying out their commission to preach Christ and to work miracles of healing in His name. They healed a man born without the ability to walk, opening a door for them to preach to thousands of people (Acts 3). The priests and rulers had the apostles arrested and brought before them. Peter, filled with the Holy Spirit, boldly declared that all they had done was done in the name of Jesus Christ: "Neither is there salvation in any other: for there is none other name under heaven given among men, whereby we must be saved" (Acts 4:12). The council commanded Peter and John to stop preaching in the name of Christ and threatened them with dire consequences. They were then released, and they returned to report to the church all that had happened that day.

What did the apostolic church do in response to the threats of the authorities? What should we do? Acts 4:23–37 gives us the answer: we must cry out in prayer to the God of providence. Acts 4:24 says of the early believers, "And when they heard that, they lifted up their voice to God with one accord." How did they pray? They prayed with urgency and passion: "they lifted up their voice."[3] They also prayed "with one accord." Calvin said that the apostles met with the church "that they might arm themselves with prayer against the furious threatenings of their enemies; and thus must the children of God do, one must prick

---

1. Belgic Confession (Art. 13), in James T. Dennison, Jr., Comp., *Reformed Confessions of the 16th and 17th Centuries in English Translation: Volume 2, 1552–1556* (Grand Rapids: Reformation Heritage Books, 2010), 431.
2. Heidelberg Catechism (LD 9, Q. 26), in Dennison, *Reformed Confessions*, 2:431.
3. "Lift the voice" (*airō* [or *epairō*] *phōnēn*) appears several times with "and wept" (LXX Judg. 2:4; 21:2; Ruth 1:9, 14; 1 Sam. 24:16; 2 Sam. 3:32; 13:36). It can also describe the roaring of the seas (LXX Ps. 92[93]:3) and the cry of lepers to Jesus for healing (Luke 17:13).

forward another, and they must join hand in hand, that they may vanquish the common adversary fighting under Christ's banner."[4]

What did they pray? First, they offered praise to God. Second, they offered prayers for power. God answered those prayers. Let us go on to see how we must join together to lift our prayers to the God of providence.

1. Prayers of Praise

The apostles and the early church did not begin praying by asking God for anything. They knew they faced the immediate danger of being imprisoned, beaten, robbed of their possessions, and even killed. But they started with praise. They glorified God for who He is and what He has done. They did not rush through a quick or well-worn word of praise to get to what they thought was really important—asking God for help. In fact, over two-thirds of their prayer consists of praise to God! Surely this is one effect of faith in God's providence. We do not need to panic as if God were asleep and cry out, "Carest thou not that we perish?" (Mark 4:38). No, we may pray with the calm assurance that He is very much in control, even in the worst of circumstances.

As we look at their praises in verses 24–28, we see that they focus on God's sovereignty in the universe He has created, His sovereignty in exaltation of His Son, and His sovereignty in the redemption of His people.

Praise of God's Sovereignty as the Creator of All Things

Verse 24 tells us that the church prayed, "Lord, thou art God, which hast made heaven, and earth, and the sea, and all that in them is." "Lord" is not the usual word for God used in Greek but a word (*despota*) that refers to the master of a household who rules over servants and slaves, or a king who rules with absolute power.[5] God's kingdom is nothing less than "heaven, and earth, and the sea, and all that in them is," for he "made" them and rules them with total authority. All creatures are His servants (Pss. 119:90–91; 146:5–6).

---

4. John Calvin, *Commentary upon the Acts of the Apostles*, trans. Henry Beveridge (repr., Grand Rapids: Baker, 2003), 1:181.
5. Greek *despotēs*. Cf. Luke 2:29; 1 Tim. 6:1, 2; 2 Tim. 2:21; Titus 2:9; 1 Peter 2:18.

Calvin said, "If we want our faith to be strong, we must consider God's power when praying and mention the promises which we rely on.... We cannot have confidence in God as we ought unless we are firmly convinced that he disposes all things in accordance with his will so that all creatures are subject to him. That stems from the fact that he created all things."[6]

When men begin to act like dictators and tyrants, threatening God's people with penalties for their fidelity to their God, we must begin by praising the One who is the only true Sovereign over all creation. Even if we are beaten, thrown into prison, and locked up in stocks, we may respond as Paul and Silas did by singing praises to God (Acts 16:25).

The early church constantly sang the Psalms (Eph. 5:19; Col. 3:16), so perhaps they had Psalm 146 in mind when they prayed:

> Put not your trust in princes, nor in the son of man, in whom there is no help. His breath goeth forth, he returneth to his earth; in that very day his thoughts perish. Happy is he that hath the God of Jacob for his help, whose hope is in the LORD his God: which made heaven, and earth, the sea, and all that therein is: which keepeth truth for ever: which executeth judgment for the oppressed: which giveth food to the hungry. The LORD looseth the prisoners (Ps. 146:3–7).

How comforting it is for us to remember that men are mere flesh but God is the eternal Spirit who created all things! What peace we can find in His providence! Truly we can sing,

> Heav'n and earth the Lord created,
> Seas and all that they contain;
> He delivers from oppression,
> Righteousness He will maintain.[7]

Let us therefore lift up our voices in praise of God's sovereignty as the Maker of heaven and earth.

---

6. John Calvin, *Sermons on the Acts of the Apostles, Chapters 1–7*, trans. Rob Roy McGregor (Edinburgh: Banner of Truth, 2008), 163–64.

7. *The Psalter. With Doctrinal Standards, Liturgy, Church Order, and Added Chorale Section*, rev. ed. (Grand Rapids: Eerdmans, 1965), no. 400, verse 4 [Ps. 146].

Praise for God's Sovereignty in the Exaltation of His Incarnate Son
Acts 4:25–26 goes on to tell us that the church quoted Psalm 2, saying, "Who by the mouth of thy servant David hast said, Why did the heathen rage, and the people imagine vain things? The kings of the earth stood up, and the rulers were gathered together against the Lord, and against his Christ." How good to pray the words of Scripture! The Bible is God's own Word, placed in the mouth of His servants who spoke it and wrote it. When we saturate our prayers with God's Word, our minds cannot help but be lifted up to Christ and our prayers are aligned with God's will.

When the apostolic church faced opposition, they turned to Psalm 2, which says that God had long before announced that nations would rage and that kings and rulers would conspire against the Lord and against His Anointed. We should not be surprised, then, when this very thing happens in our time. Rather, we should be profoundly grateful when any earthly authority stands up for what is true and good.

Although the rulers of the world war against God, their efforts are vain, empty, and futile, for, as Psalm 2 tells us, God has established His Christ as the King of kings, and He will reign forever. The Father said to the Son, "Ask of me, and I shall give thee the heathen for thine inheritance, and the uttermost parts of the earth for thy possession. Thou shalt break them with a rod of iron; thou shalt dash them in pieces like a potter's vessel" (Ps. 2:8–9).

God's providence is entirely in the hands of Christ as the Mediator (John 17:2). Calvin said, "God will reign in the person of his Son alone."[8] Therefore we may be assured that Christ will conquer all the enemies of the church, and it will not fail on earth. Jesus Christ has already risen from the dead, ascended into heaven, and sits at God's right hand with all authority in heaven and on earth (Ps. 110:1; Matt. 28:18; Eph. 1:20–21). William Perkins said, "Christ, [as] God and man, after his ascension is advanced to such an estate in which he has fulness of glory, power, majesty, and authority in the presence of

---

8. Calvin, *Commentary upon the Acts of the Apostles*, 1:185; cf. *Sermons on the Acts of the Apostles*, 165.

his Father and all the saints and holy angels." His kingdom "spreadeth itself over heaven and earth."⁹

So, when we pray for God's kingdom to come, we should lift our eyes to Jesus Christ, giving thanks that God has promised to establish the throne and kingdom of His Son over all the earth. When the church faces opposition from powerful enemies, we must take time to meditate on the promises and to lift praises to God. Fixing our eyes upon Jesus and setting our affections upon Him, we will then be able to pray with faith and not with the fear of man. We can pray, "Thy kingdom come" with the confidence that we are simply asking God to do what He promised—to give the nations to His Son as His inheritance.

Praise of God's Sovereignty in the Redemption of His People
The third part of the believers' praises, are, according to verses 27–28, "For of a truth against thy holy child Jesus, whom thou hast anointed, both Herod, and Pontius Pilate, with the Gentiles, and the people of Israel, were gathered together, for to do whatsoever thy hand and thy counsel determined before to be done." In the darkest hours of the church's sufferings in this world, God's will is being done. The counsels and deeds of wicked men were the instruments of God's redemption of His people.

There was no darker hour in the history of God's people than when Jesus died on the cross. It seemed to the disciples that all of God's purposes had failed. The Messiah, anointed by God, had perished at the hands of cruel and wicked men. They had brought Him to trial, condemned Him as a criminal, beat Him, nailed Him to the cross, then mocked Him while He slowly died. If ever there was a time for despair, this was it. The apostles hid themselves in fear that they might be taken next (John 20:19). Christians in many parts of the world today might also be tempted to hide themselves for fear of what is coming next in their country.

---

9. William Perkins, *An Exposition of the Symbole or Creed of the Apostles* (London: John Legatt, 1595), 352.

When Christ rose from the dead, however, He told His disciples that everything had happened according to God's providential decree as revealed in Scripture and Christ's own words (Luke 24:25–27, 44–46). What appeared to be the darkest hour was in truth the most glorious moment in history: God had accomplished the redemption of His people. God's providence ruled over the sins of wicked authorities and caused them "to do whatsoever thy hand and thy counsel determined before to be done." God has predestined even the acts of sinners (1 Peter 2:8). The vicious and ugly murder of God's Son was determined by God before time began (1 Peter 1:19).

The apostolic church took hold of this doctrine in the darkness and turned it into a prayer of praise. They knew that the crucified Christ was not a criminal. Though rejected by men, He was God's holy child whom God had anointed. "Child" is the same Greek word used of David in verse 25 and can also be translated as "servant."[10] It is the same word used in the covenant with David and in reference to the suffering Servant in Isaiah.[11] Jesus's death was not a defeat, but an ushering in of the kingdom promised to David. His death on the cross was God's will for our salvation (Isa. 53:10–11). Derek Thomas said, "The doctrine of God's absolute sovereignty is necessary if we are to understand what occurred at Calvary.... God was the Author of the cross."[12]

Can you praise God at the foot of Christ's cross? You can if you trust that Christ suffered for your sins. But can you also praise God as you take up your cross? You may if your faith grasps the doctrine of divine providence. Calvin wrote, "God doth so govern and guide all things by his secret counsel, that he doth bring to pass those things which he hath determined, even by the wicked."[13] If we believe that, we can stand before wicked men, even wicked rulers, and sing God's

---

10. Greek *pais*.

11. LXX 1 Chron. 17:4, 17, 23, 24, 25, 27; Isa. 41:8–9; 42:1, 19; 43:10; 44:1–2, 21, 26; 45:4; 49:6; 50:10; 52:13.

12. Derek W. H. Thomas, *Acts*, Reformed Expositional Commentary (Phillipsburg, N.J.: P&R, 2011), 110.

13. Calvin, *Commentary upon the Acts of the Apostles*, 1:187.

praises. The worst thing they can do to us is the best thing God has planned for our good (Rom. 8:28).

In Christ we are more than overcomers. Though rejected by men, we are not criminals. We are God's children and God's servants. Our suffering does not mean defeat for the kingdom. It is the very means that God has ordained to advance His kingdom and to cause His eternal weight of glory to be revealed in our lives.

When the powers of this world threaten the church, let us lift our voices in prayer. Let us begin with heartwarming and faith-forming praise. We serve the God of providence; therefore, we can adore Him for His supremacy and sovereignty in His Son. We can sing,

> When the needy seek Him, He will mercy show;
> Yea, the weak and helpless shall His pity know;
> He will surely save them from oppression's might,
> For their lives are precious in His holy sight.
> Christ shall have dominion over land and sea,
> Earth's remotest regions shall His empire be.[14]

2. Prayers for Power

The first response of the church to threats of oppression is to lift up prayers of praise. We have great cause to praise God's sovereignty in creation, in the exaltation of His Son, and in the redemption of His people. We should not stop with praise, however. Acts 4:29 reminds us that we are God's servants—literally His slaves[15]—who live to do His will. We have commandments to keep and a mission to fulfill, and we must not allow the high cost of discipleship to deter us from doing the work that God has given us to do. The apostles told the ruling council, "Whether it be right in the sight of God to hearken unto you more than unto God, judge ye" (Acts 4:19). We must keep on listening to God's Word and doing His will as His servants in the world.

We cannot serve God in our own strength. Nothing reveals how weak and fragile we are as does the opposition of sinners. We must

---
14. *The Psalter*, no. 200, verse 2 [Ps. 72].
15. Greek *doulos*, a different word than that translated "servant" in v. 25.

thus pray for power. The last part of the church's prayer in Acts 4 teaches us how to pray for ourselves.

The early believers began their petitions with a brief request for protection. Acts 4:29 says, "And now, Lord, behold their threatenings." This is the only petition the church makes for protection against persecution. "Behold" here means "look upon our painful situation and act out of Thy compassion and love."[16] It is good and right for us to cry out to God for deliverance from those who would harm us so that He may be glorified (Isa. 37:16–20). Let us not romanticize persecution; it is ugly and evil. The Psalms are full of cries for deliverance from the assaults of the wicked, and God's providence often spares His children from suffering in answer to such prayers. Ultimately God will send His Son to deliver us from all evil.

Note, however, that the church quickly goes on to pray for the display of divine power. Verses 29b–30 say, "and grant unto thy servants, that with all boldness they may speak thy word, by stretching forth thine hand to heal; and that signs and wonders may be done by the name of thy holy child Jesus." The believers prayed for power for the ministry of the Word and power for ministry to the bodies of sinful men. In answer to that prayer, verse 31 tells us, "They were all filled with the Holy Ghost." They had offered praise to the Father, taken hold of the promises made to the Son, and now they obtained the power of the Spirit. Their prayer was truly trinitarian in scope and effect.

The heart of their request was for God to empower them by the Holy Spirit with spiritual gifts. We no longer live in the apostolic age; we are not apostles and do not have the same spiritual gifts that they had. But this text does call the church to ask God for spiritual gifts of *speaking* and *serving*. Let us consider each spiritual gift.

Power for Spiritual Gifts of Speaking
First, the believers prayed for the apostles as ministers of the Word, "that with all boldness they may speak thy word" (Acts 4:29). Our

---

16. The verb "look upon" (*ephoraō*) has a variety of applications, yet sometimes takes the special connotation of responding to trouble with mercy and compassion (LXX Gen. 16:13; Ex. 2:25; Ps. 30:8 [31:7]; 112[113]:6; 137[138]:6; Luke 1:25; cf. 2 Macc. 7:6; 8:2; 3 Macc. 6:3, 12).

ministers today are also mere flesh and blood. They may feel as bold as lions, but like Peter, these leaders may also discover all too quickly how easily they can deny their Lord. Pray for your ministers, so they may boldly preach and witness for Christ.

Ministers also carry God's treasure in earthen vessels and often feel troubled, perplexed, and cast down as they experience the dying of Jesus in their own bodies (2 Cor. 4:7–10). Nonetheless, the Holy Spirit gives them courage to speak, for He is "the Spirit of faith" (2 Cor. 4:13). Luke stresses in verse 8 that the apostle who spoke so boldly to the council was not Peter, the man of flesh, but Peter, "filled with the Holy Ghost." Verse 31 says that God answered their prayer, "and they were all filled with the Holy Ghost, and they spake the word of God with boldness."

Boldness refers to being confident, frank, open, and unashamed.[17] We think of Paul, who said in Romans 1:16, "I am not ashamed of the gospel of Christ: for it is the power of God unto salvation to every one that believeth; to the Jew first, and also to the Greek." But even Paul needed people to pray for him when he faced opposition. He wrote in Ephesians 6:19–20, "And for me, that utterance may be given unto me, that I may open my mouth boldly, to make known the mystery of the gospel, for which I am an ambassador in bonds: that therein I may speak boldly, as I ought to speak."

If we would persevere in serving the Lord, we must also seek power for spiritual gifts of speaking. Pray that your preachers would be "full of the Spirit" and they will preach you full.

Charles Spurgeon preached with such power from the Holy Spirit that several thousand people came out to hear him every Lord's Day for thirty-eight years, and millions have read his sermons ever since. On one occasion, Spurgeon met some enthusiastic visitors to his church and asked them if they wanted to see the church's power plant. They were far more interested in the preaching, but they followed him anyway. So he took them to a large room where believers were gathered for prayer. His church sought the power of God through united

---

17. Greek *parrēsia*.

prayer. Spurgeon recognized this was a notable characteristic of the church, saying,

> When I came to New Park Street Chapel, it was a mere handful of people to whom I first preached, yet I could never forget how earnestly they prayed. Sometimes they seemed to plead as though they could really see the Angel of the Covenant [Christ] present with them, and as if they must have a blessing from him. More than once we were so awe-struck with the solemnity of the [prayer] meeting that we sat silent for some moments while the Lord's Power appeared to overshadow us.[18]

Ministers long to see prayer meetings full of people and full of God's Spirit, for powerful preaching in the church begins with powerful praying by the church. Acts 4:33 says what happened after the apostles prayed for boldness to speak: "And with great power gave the apostles witness of the resurrection of the Lord Jesus: and great grace was upon them all."

Cotton Mather said that Thomas Hooker was a minister of such courage that "while doing his Master's work, he would put a king in his pocket."[19] God can give remarkable power to His preachers. We must seek power for spiritual gifts of speaking so that our ministers may preach boldly, even when under fire.

Power for Spiritual Gifts of Serving

In verse 30, the early church prayed that God would assist the preaching of the Word "by stretching forth thine hand to heal; and that signs and wonders may be done by the name of thy holy child Jesus." The apostles were commissioned by Christ Jesus to work miracles as they preached the kingdom of God.[20] They now prayed for God to empower their spiritual gifts in practical ministry as well in order to heal the sick. They could not heal at will; even apostles depended on God's power to work a miracle (Acts 3:12). Such miracles are called

---

18. Lewis A. Drummond, *Spurgeon: Prince of Preachers* (Grand Rapids: Kregel, 1992), 270–71.
19. Cotton Mather, *Magnalia Christi Americana*, book 3 (London: Thomas Parkhurst, 1702), 64.
20. Luke 9:1–2; Acts 5:12; 2 Cor. 12:12.

"signs and wonders" because God used them to confirm publicly that He had sent the apostles (Acts 14:3; Heb. 2:3–4), just as God worked miracles through His servant Moses (Ex. 7:3, 9; Deut. 4:34). By healing the bodies of men, God visibly showed that His redeeming love had come to heal our accursed world and save us from our sins (Isaiah 35; Luke 7:20–23).

God answered their prayer in an extraordinary manner. Verse 31 tells us that "the place was shaken where they were assembled together." In the Bible, earthquakes were signs that God had come to bless His people with His power.[21] Luke reported that shortly afterward, in answer to this prayer, the Lord struck dead some hypocrites in the church, caused amazing miracles of healing through the apostles, and used an angel to release the apostles from prison (Acts 5:1–20).

However, Acts 4 does not focus on these miracles of healing.[22] Instead, verses 32–37 dwell on the practical ministries of loving and caring for the poor. This makes perfect sense. The apostles had prayed for God to stretch out His hand and heal the hurting. God then filled them with the Spirit, and the believers stretched out their hands to care for the widows, orphans, foreigners, handicapped, and poor among them. The church became the fatherly hand of the God of providence. The apostles established a fund for the church to serve the practical needs of people. This was not some form of communism imposed by a church authority or political party. It was instead the voluntary sharing of property and possessions as each had ability or need.[23]

---

21. Earthquakes appear at Mt. Sinai (Ex. 19:18), the death and resurrection of Jesus (Matt. 27:54; 28:2) and at the Day of the Lord (Ezek. 38:19–20; Rev. 6:12; etc.).

22. The only possible reference to miracles in Acts 4:31–37 would be "power" in v. 33, "with great power gave the apostles witness." It seems more likely that the singular "power" (*dunamis*) does not refer to miracles but to the "power" to convict, convert, and comfort souls through witness (Acts 1:8; Rom. 1:16; 1 Cor. 1:18, 24; 2:4–5; Eph. 1:19; Col. 1:28–29; 1 Thess. 1:5). See Simon J. Kistemaker, *Acts*, New Testament Commentary (Grand Rapids: Baker, 1990), 174. However, miracles are called "powers" (Acts 2:22; 6:8; 8:13; 19:11; Gal. 3:5) or works done by "power" (Acts 3:12; 4:7; 6:8; 8:10; 10:38; 2 Thess. 2:9). So Acts 4:33 could mean that the apostles ministered the Word of Christ accompanied by miracles. Nevertheless, this is not the emphasis of this section.

23. Contrast Qumran, where such community of goods was required. See Kistemaker, *Acts*, 173–74.

We must likewise pray for power to serve today. We are neither apostles nor those on whom the apostles laid their hands. We do not possess miraculous gifts. But many of us have practical gifts. If the church in America faces opposition from wicked rulers, people will suffer. The church must develop a culture of caring for each other. In that way, God's providence will turn persecution into an opportunity to glorify Christ.

Practical works of service are greater signs to the world than raising the dead.[24] Christ said, "Let your light so shine before men, that they may see your good works, and glorify your Father which is in heaven" (Matt. 5:16). "By this shall all men know that ye are my disciples, if ye have love one to another" (John 13:35). The diaconal ministry of the church is the most effective gift we have to confirm the truth of the gospel.

We must also pray for God's power. It takes more supernatural power to produce love and practical service to needy people than it does to work a miracle of healing. Our Lord understood that only supernatural grace can make us love each other sacrificially. He prayed that we would love one another and be one with each other so "that the world may know that thou hast sent me, and hast loved them, as thou hast loved me" (John 17:23).

Join your prayers to Christ's prayer, and lift up constant requests for spiritual gifts of service. Pray that God would cause your love to abound yet more and more (Phil. 1:9). Ask the Lord to make us increase and abound in love toward one another and toward all men (1 Thess. 3:12). Cry out that the Lord would bless our church with rich and practical spiritual gifts for mercy and service. Pray for our deacons as they administer the funds of the church to care for those in need. In all this, pray for God to stretch out His loving hands through our ministries, and to show the world that He has come to set sinful and miserable people free.

---

24. "Great grace" (v. 33) may mean "much favor," in the sense that the larger Jewish community looked upon the church with much favor because of their Spirit-empowered lives (Acts 2:47; 4:21; 5:13). See Kistemaker, *Acts*, 174.

Conclusion

The doctrine of providence teaches us that when the church faces opposition, we must lift up our prayers to the God of providence. We must lift up prayers of praise. Praise glorifies God and strengthens our faith and joy. Praise enthrones the Lord as the true Sovereign, even as wicked leaders try to overthrow the kingdom of Christ. We must also lift up prayers for power. The Holy Spirit can give our ministers amazing power to preach the Word even in the face of enemies. The Holy Spirit can also mobilize the body to serve the poor when the church is oppressed.

To enjoy the Spirit's blessings, we must pray for them. Do you believe that God reigns? Then show it in your prayers. God forbid that it be said of our churches, "Ye have not, because ye ask not" (James 4:2). Rather, may our churches be living proof of Christ's promise, "Ask, and it shall be given you" (Matt. 7:7).

Chapter 25

Felix under the Preaching of the Word of God

And after certain days, when Felix came with his wife Drusilla, which was a Jewess, he sent for Paul, and heard him concerning the faith in Christ. And as he reasoned of righteousness, temperance, and judgment to come, Felix trembled, and answered, Go thy way for this time; when I have a convenient season, I will call for thee.
—ACTS 24:24–25

There is nothing so uncertain in this world as our life and nothing so certain as our death. It is appointed unto man once to die and after that the judgment. It is said in our modern day that eighty-five percent of the things which run through our mind in regard to plans and goals never materialize. Yet you and I spend a great deal of time thinking, planning, worrying, about those things, most of which never transpire. There is one thing, however, that will certainly transpire for every one of us. Death can call for us while we are still young; it can come when we are older. But it is inescapably true, my friends, that death is near.

We must be prepared to die. We must not imitate the rich fool who said, "This will I do: I will pull down my barns, and build greater.... And I will say to my soul, Soul, thou hast much goods laid up for many years; take thine ease, eat, drink, and be merry" (Luke 12:18–19). On the contrary, we must live temperately, soberly, and preparedly. We must seek grace to be prepared to meet God. We must not allow ourselves rest without a right foundation for meeting Him.

Death always comes sooner than we think. The day is coming soon when we will sit under our last sermon, receive our last invitation, hear our last warning. After that it shall be forever too late to seek the Lord. Today I desire to show you the solemn reality of this truth clearly spelled out in the tragic history of Felix.

With God's help, we wish to consider:

Felix under the Preaching of the Word of God
1. Hearing the Word
2. Trembling before the Word
3. Rejecting the Word

1. Hearing the Word

Acts 24 records another phase of the life of the apostle Paul, the world's most famous missionary. The missionary Paul could rightly claim that he had labored more abundantly than any apostle. His life and heart were bound up with the gospel message of death in Adam and life in Christ which he felt called to bring. Paul yearned with an unquenchable passion to proclaim to sinners, young and old, "There is only one name under heaven given among men, whereby we must be saved" (Acts 4:12). Paul was willing to count all loss and dung that he might win Christ and be found in Him. To spread the truth was his calling, his burden, his life.

Many times Paul's calling was tested, especially when his life was threatened, but he needed to press on at all costs. Though frequently stoned, beaten with stripes, and suffering shipwreck, he wrote to the Corinthians, "Woe is unto me, if I preach not the gospel!" Necessity was laid upon him.

In the context of Acts 24, Paul faced a new trial—*house imprisonment*. For two years he was forbidden to publicly proclaim the Word of God. What a trial this was for the apostle! During his lifetime he had brought God's Word before Agrippa, the Sanhedrin, Sergius Paulus, Festus, and even Emperor Nero himself, but was deprived unjustly of proclaiming that precious Word in the churches to souls whom he longed to see saved and built up in the most holy faith. In those difficult two years, no doubt, Paul needed to learn that the Lord could carry on His work without him. But he still must have longed in his heart to proclaim God's Word.

Suddenly, however, Paul unexpectedly received a remarkable invitation to lead a church service in the palace of the Roman governor for the governor and his wife, Felix and Drusilla. "And after certain days, when Felix came with his wife Drusilla, which was a Jewess, he sent for Paul, and heard him concerning the faith in Christ" (Acts 24:24).

To understand how special this invitation was, we should first know something about Felix and Drusilla. Felix was a very corrupt man who had astonished nearly the whole world in his time by acquiring a high position in Roman government through bribery, despite his lack of education. Once in power, Felix astonished many with his brutal injustice, cruel murders, and impure life. Several times Felix almost lost his position as governor, but he repeatedly managed to maintain his position through payoffs. All the while Felix remained a slave of the devil and of sin.

Drusilla was Felix's third wife. At the time of Acts 24, Felix was in his sixties. Drusilla was a young girl of seventeen. She was a daughter of Agrippa I, a sister of Agrippa II, and a granddaughter of Herod the Great. This young woman had also lived wickedly. She was engaged as a very young teenager to Antiochus Epiphanes, a prince of another country. The marriage did not take place because he refused to be circumcised, which was a sign of being converted to the Jewish religion. Thus this young girl had some feeling for religion in an outward way, but did not live godly herself. Later on, when she was sixteen years old, she married Azizus, the King of the Amesenes, a territory in northern Syria. Josephus tells us that she was a remarkably beautiful young woman and Felix desired to have her. With the help of Simon the Sorcerer, Felix influenced her to desert her husband in order to marry him. Thus the elderly Felix and his young bride Drusilla entered into an unlawful marriage to the further ruin of both their lives.

Soon after they were married they took a trip. Today we would call it a honeymoon. They spoke together on this trip about the apostle Paul who was imprisoned under Felix's domain. Drusilla's grandfather Herod had greatly desired to hear John the Baptist. Something of that curiosity, that spirit of inquisitiveness, was in Drusilla as well.

Felix too was a bit curious as to what this man who was preaching the name of Jesus Christ would have to say. Thus Felix and Drusilla determined to hear a sermon from Paul's own mouth.

Upon their return from their honeymoon, they invited Paul to appear before them. Paul accepted their invitation. Even though he knew their motive was impure, that their way of life was wicked, and that this could bring him in great danger, he desired to preach. Paul accepted an invitation to preach in front of a woman whose father had killed the apostle James; whose great uncle, Herod Antipas, had killed John the Baptist; and whose great grandfather, Herod the Great, had murdered all the male infants of Bethlehem. He agreed to preach in that palace, formerly owned by Herod, where many had been murdered. There was a saying in that day that there was not a stone of that building which had not been splattered with blood.

Paul went with unflinching courage, unwearied zeal, and unquenchable hope. He thought, "Perhaps God will savingly work upon Felix and Drusilla, despite their motives." No doubt when Paul meditated of Felix, he thought to himself, "Felix too is a man, and does not the gospel say, 'Glory to God…and on earth peace, good will toward *men*'?" *Men* are pricked in the heart by the gospel. Moreover, Felix was a Roman, and Paul felt a special burden for preaching to the Gentiles, including the Romans. Perhaps this heathen was also lying under the seal of election. Moreover, Felix was a governor and had not Paul, at the time he was converted, received as a calling through the mouth of Ananias, "Go thy way: for he (Saul) is a chosen vessel unto me, to bear my name before the Gentiles, and *kings*"?

Oh, Paul thought, "Maybe this king shall now bow in the dust of self-abasement before the Lord; maybe the Lord will use His Word to dethrone the self-enthroned Felix." But above all, I think Paul reasoned, "Felix is a deeply fallen sinner just like I am, like I was, and like I remain in myself. If it was possible for the Lord to stop me on the way to Damascus as a persecutor, is it not possible for the Lord to stop Felix?" It was this in particular that motivated Paul with unquenchable hope.

You and I are always figuring. We have our expectations of whom we think is going to be converted and of whom we think is not going to be converted. My friends, that is all senseless. The Lord can convert the hardest of hearts. If the Lord converts us, then we will feel something of a burden for souls and of an unquenchable hope and zeal for their salvation. Wherever the Word comes, there is the possibility that it may be the hour in which God may work savingly in the hardest heart and the most unlikely human choice. Do you understand now why Paul couldn't decline this dangerous invitation?

This affords us two applications: First, perhaps there are those among us who fear God will never work in their hearts. You view yourself as an unlikely choice. Oh, my dear friend, God delights to choose the unlikely! Contrary to Eve's expectation, God chose Abel and not Cain. He chose Israel, a small nation, and not the world powers. There is hope for those who feel they are unworthy, unlikely choices.

Second, do you and I possess such an evangelistic heart as the apostle Paul? Would we be willing to bring the gospel to those who might endanger our lives?

With holy boldness Paul "reasoned" with them. He had three points to his sermon—righteousness, temperance, and judgment to come. He used each of these points like a barb to pierce the hearts of Felix and Drusilla. He had one great goal: that the Lord might bless His Word to the saving conviction of this ungodly couple. "He reasoned of righteousness, temperance, and judgment to come."

Paul's first point was *righteousness*—a point most appropriate for Felix who was called to be a righteous judge. Can you not almost hear Paul reasoning with Felix about righteousness in this way: "God is righteous, Felix. He is the just One. He created us righteous and holy. He demands that we too be righteous despite our deep fall in Adam. We have lost that original righteousness. We have plunged ourselves into sin. It is not Adam's fault, but our fault that we reveal daily our unrighteous natures. Look at your hands, Felix. Are they not full of bribery? Look at your feet, Felix. Are they not quick to shed blood? Look at your heart, Felix. Is it not full of injustice? Look at your life, Felix. Is it not filled with cruelty? Felix, you must become righteous before God. That is impossible with man but it is possible with God. There is a way of salvation in the Lord Jesus Christ who has paid the full price of sin on behalf of needy sinners such as we are, though He Himself was fully righteous. He did this, Felix, in order to satisfy God's justice as a substitute for unrighteous sinners, so that they might know His righteousness. Felix, there is a way of salvation for unrighteous, cruel, bribing sinners such as you, who are not motivated by principles of righteousness, but who guide their lives by principles of unrighteousness. Felix, how do you stand before the righteousness of God?"

His second point was temperance. Temperance means self-control, purity, and freedom from what defiles. Temperance means the quality of having one's passions under control. Now the sword became even more pointed. "Felix, are you not an adulterer, an unchaste, unclean man? Is not that young woman beside you an adulteress? Are you not living in shameless lust in an unbiblical marriage? Felix, how will you meet a pure and holy God when you are impure and unholy?"

Third, he preached of *judgment to come*. I can see in my mind's eye Paul coming to the climax of his sermon, reasoning from righteousness and temperance to judgment. "Felix, you are guilty with regard to righteousness and temperance. But you are also guilty with regard to judgment to come. That judgment will be *inevitable*. The Judge stands at the door. It will be a *personal* judgment. Every sin will be accounted for. Nothing will be hidden from the omniscient eye of God. All the books of our lives will be opened. And it is an *eternal* judgment. Of that judgment there is no return. We will enter everlasting joy or everlasting torment, the glory of heaven or the torments of hell. Felix, you are a judge, but this Judge does not operate as you do. This Judge takes no bribes on the great Day of days. This Judge offers no parole. This Judge is straightforward. He is just in His justice. The sentence He pronounces is strictly executed. Felix, how shall you stand before a holy and righteous God? Your future, Felix, if you do not repent, shall be everlasting condemnation. Hell is a place where its inhabitants are ever being consumed and yet never fully consumed, ever dying but never dead, ever burning but never burned up. Hell is a place where there is no communion, no friendship—nothing but the wrath of God poured out without mixture. How will you stand? Felix, you need the Lord Jesus Christ as your only hope."

Dear friends, we are called to reason similarly with ourselves, each other, and our neighbors. Though you and I may not have been as notoriously wicked as Felix, the same principles hold true. How can we pass the tests of righteousness, temperance, and judgment to come without the Son of God? We need the Lord Jesus Christ as the only answer for our sins; otherwise every one of us will perish in hell, condemned eternally with no relief. By nature we don't want to hear this solemn warning. We don't want to face the solemn reality that hell and condemnation will be our portion if we are not brought under saving conviction, if we are not driven unto the Lord Jesus Christ to find in Him everything we need.

My friends, I yearn to reason with you too of righteousness, temperance, and judgment to come: How shall you stand before God without His dear Son? You can't meet Him without the blood of Christ. How can you continue to live unprepared? How can you travel to a certain eternity without seeking the application of the blood of Christ? Common sense tells us that we are fools when we don't seek the Lord. "Awake thou that sleepest, and arise from the dead, and Christ shall give thee light" (Eph. 5:14). Don't delay. Make haste for your life's sake. You must be born again. You need a living, real, personal relationship with the Almighty God in the face of His dear Son.

Felix and Drusilla heard the Word of God. Drusilla responded indifferently. We don't read one word of what happened to Drusilla. We fear that this young woman had nearly seared her conscience already at seventeen years of age. She remained unmoved and unashamed under Paul's searching sermon. Oh, what a solemn thing! Paul powerfully used the two-edged sword of law and gospel, but Drusilla was moved neither by the threatenings of the law nor by the sweet tenors of the gospel. She sat as a stone. Neither law nor gospel produced any guilt.

My friends, we could not ask for a greater punishment in this world than to be abandoned to the hardness of our own hearts. Oh, what a dreadful thing to be left over to ourselves! Then the Lord says of us, "I will strive no more with this sinner forever!"

2. Trembling Before the Word

It was different with Felix. Felix, our text says, not only *heard*, but *trembled*. The Greek word for "trembled" corresponds to the Hebrew word used in Daniel about Belshazzar when his knees smote together out of fear. Felix trembled so much that it became visible physically. How severe it was we don't know, but we do know that he received an open conscience. He felt that everything Paul said was true. He *was* unrighteous; he *was* intemperate; he was *not* ready to meet God. He *was* traveling to eternity unprepared for the judgment to come.

As Felix sat on his throne, it was as if he saw God's "great white throne" (Rev. 20:11) displayed, as if he were standing before the Lord of hosts as the holy Judge. It was as if the books were opened as Paul was preaching; Felix saw that every page of his life was stained with guilt. It became true for him: "I, who am accustomed to self-indulgence and to pleasure, will soon become the victim of a worm that dies not and of a fire that is not quenched. I, who have treated so many others unjustly, will soon be justly judged to eternal torment."

Felix trembled. He was terrified. His knees smote together. His conscience spoke, "Thou art the man." Despite political power, he could not shield his soul from being filled with fear.

Felix trembled. He was placed before eternity, before the great Judge of the heavens and the earth. It was as if Paul brought his whole life into the open, exposing his lustful indulgences, briberies, frauds, and cruelties. To some degree Felix could say, "Truly, here is a man that told me all things that ever I did" (John 4:29). He was standing with an open conscience before an open Judge and an open eternity. He was standing on the border of eternal weal and eternal woe. His conscience was speaking, "Felix, Felix, repent, repent! Are you not only treasuring and heaping up wrath against the day of wrath?"

On the borders of eternity, Felix had one more opportunity to bow before the Lord. There that poor, elderly man sat with an open conscience, restless, shifting his position on his throne, hardly able to remain sitting because it was all so true. Temperance, righteousness, judgment to come—each of Paul's three sermon points condemned him. The Lord gave him one more opportunity to beg for mercy. Jesus of Nazareth was passing by one more time, testifying as it were: "Oh, Felix, will you not cry out like Bartimaeus, 'Son of David, have mercy on me'? Felix, will you not give up the battle? Will you not bow before the Lord while you still have opportunity? Felix, bow and confess! You are already old. It could be the last time you hear the Word of God. Bow, Felix, bow!"

Oh, boys and girls, if we had been there would not we also have urged him to bow? "Felix," we would say, "don't ruin for yourself the rest of your life and all of eternity. Here you are placed before a very solemn opportunity where the Lord Himself in the person of Paul invites you to repent."

My friends, you and I are in the same position. Whether we are boys or girls, teenagers, young men or women, parents or grandparents, the Holy Spirit calls to us through the Word, "Bow, sinner. Repent, before it is forever too late." Under the preaching of the Word of God, we are brought to the borders of everlasting weal and everlasting woe. The Word of God reasons also with us of temperance, righteousness, and judgment to come. What will *you* answer today? What have you answered all your lifetime?

3. Rejecting the Word

What will Felix answer? With an open conscience, shifting uncomfortably upon his throne, Felix spoke most tragically: "Go thy way for this time; when I have a convenient season, I will call for thee." He rejected the Word and the invitation of the living God.

Paul preached; Felix trembled. Paul was at the judgment bar; Felix, on the judgment seat. But in their consciences the positions were reversed. Paul was the free man; Felix, the prisoner. The prisoner became the judge; the prince on the throne became the criminal. The ruler of the country trembled before a tentmaker. That's the power of the Word of God.

My friends, that Word comes to you with power also. I thank God that we do not have many Drusillas. I hope there are none. I hope we still have an open conscience. But it is critical what we do with that open conscience. When we hear the Word of God, do we reject it? Do we respond like Felix?

Felix's solemn rejection of Paul's word has at least four important lessons to teach us. The first is this: If the Word is not an applied Word for us by grace, it is a rejected Word. It is one or the other. The

Word can never leave us "in-between." We never leave God's house as we have come because the Word of God always does something. We can never remain neutral under the Word. The Word either hardens us or humbles us.

Dear friend, every time you stifle your conscience, you stifle convictions; every time you neglect an opportunity, you are left in a worse and more hopeless condition than you were in before the Word came to you in the house of God. That is a serious thing; the Lord will not be mocked. When the Lord speaks His Word, He is coming with a heaven-sent invitation addressed to you to repent and turn to Him before it is forever too late. The Lord wants us, as the Puritans would say, to make "use" of the convictions of our conscience by turning those convictions into petitions. But when we pluck from our breasts the very convictions we feel, push away the Word of God, and say, "I cannot be converted," or, "I will not be converted," and leave church to return to the world, then we give ourselves over to further hardening. It is a tragic thing to disregard God's holy, sincere invitations to turn to Him for mercy. "He, that being often reproved hardeneth his neck, shall suddenly be destroyed, and that without remedy." That's the future of Felix and such of his mentality.

The second important lesson we learn from Felix's rejection is the grave danger of delay with regard to our never-dying souls. Felix said as it were, "Go thy way; I will call for you again, Paul." But he never called again. It was probably the last time that Felix heard the Word of God.

Moreover, Felix was not only sending Paul away by saying, "Go thy way," but in essence he was sending away the One who sent Paul, the Lord Jesus Christ. Paul was but the ambassador of the Lord of lords. In essence, Felix was saying, "Go away, Lord. When I have a convenient season, I will call for Thee." But the Lord cut off that way, saying as it were: "Felix, you have cut off My Word. I will cut off My Word from you."

When we reject God's Word repeatedly, my friends, should we be surprised that the Lord finally rejects us? When we repeatedly stand before an open door in which the Lord invites us to bow and repent, be not surprised when the Lord finally closes the door of His invitations if we constantly use excuses of inability or unwillingness. We will not be able to postpone the great day of God's visitation. In that day, all our excuses will be as nothing before the sight of a holy and righteous God. We think we are doing nothing, but we are mistaken. Rejecting the Word of God is saying "no" to the Lord, and there will come a day when the Lord will say "no" to you if you keep saying "no" to Him year in, year out. His patience is not to be mocked. There comes an end. The danger of delay is very great. Felix was saying "farewell" to God. He was deliberately destroying himself. Felix was choosing the easy way out for flesh and blood for the moment, but it was ultimately the choice we all make by nature—the choice of hell and condemnation.

All the while Felix was deceiving himself, too. He said as it were, "Tomorrow I will seek. I will respond when I have a convenient season." Martin Luther said, "The road to hell is paved with good intentions." There are two words that have slain numerous souls—the word "yesterday" and the word "tomorrow." *The word "yesterday" has slain its thousands.* There are thousands who say, "Why should I seek the Lord? I have sinned too much in my past. All my 'yesterdays' testify against me. I have done nothing worthy of God's merciful attention." Such reasoning sounds pious, but it is straight from hell. The Lord invites you *today*: "Sinner, repent." Anything you use of your past life to assert, "The Lord cannot have mercy on me," is simply wrong and is only a technique to avoid a real search for God. The Lord says, 'The blood of Jesus Christ cleanses from all sin," and what have you done in any one of your "yesterdays" to get beyond the words, "all sin"? My friends, ultimately it is not your "yesterdays" that keep you from the Lord, but your *unwillingness* today to lose your life and bow before Him.

But whereas yesterday has slain its thousands, *the word "tomorrow" has slain its tens of thousands.* "Tomorrow I will seek Him." Maybe this very day you will leave this house of prayer saying, "Yes, I need to be converted, and I will begin seeking Him tomorrow." Tomorrow is too late! Tomorrow's faith is today's unbelief. "Today if ye will hear his voice, harden not your heart." "Behold, now is the accepted time; behold, now is the day of salvation." You never read once in Scripture about seeking the Lord tomorrow. Seek Him today. Seek Him this very hour. Ask Him for grace to show you that you are not different from Felix. Though the notoriety of your sins may be less, the essence of your sin is the same. Pray to Him today, "Lord, Son of David, have mercy on me. I must be born again."

You can't afford to delay anymore, my friend. You think you can afford time for lawful entertainment, for friendships, for legitimate reading. You find time for all kinds of lawful things, do you not? But will you let pass by the one thing you really need? How are you spending your time? You need more than outward impressions. You need to bow. It is not enough to come to church and hear a sermon that warns you. You need the essence of true religion. Do not rest until you know the Lord savingly, until you lose your own life and find it in Him, until you may know the Spirit-worked marks and steps of grace. We need these things! We will miss the whole purpose of our lives if we go to eternity without them.

There is a third lesson we must glean from Felix's rejection: *the danger of resting in common convictions.* In the moment, Felix pacified his conscience with his impressions. He rested in his common convictions, in his slavish fear of God, and in his speaking conscience, but he missed the essential, born-again, childlike fear of God. That's a great danger. Herod rejoiced, Felix trembled, Orpah and Esau wept, Ahab mourned, Saul confessed, Balaam desired to die the death of the righteous, the five foolish virgins all waited for the bridegroom, but they all went to hell. They were resting in their common convictions, resting in slavish fear.

What is the difference between slavish fear and childlike fear? Slavish fear has its roots in the covenant of works; childlike fear, in the covenant of grace. Slavish fear is provoked by the consequences of sin; childlike fear, by the God-dishonoring character of sin. Slavish fear is motivated by legalistic servitude, looking for reward; childlike fear is motivated by voluntary obedience, looking for grace. In slavish fear, the enmity of our heart is not broken; in childlike fear, this enmity is broken. In slavish fear we have hard thoughts of God; in childlike fear we have high thoughts of God. Slavish fear hates punishment; childlike fear hates sin. Slavish fear seeks for self-preservation and self-honor; childlike fear seeks the preservation of the Lord's attributes and honor. Slavish fear produces a convinced sinner; childlike fear, a truly convicted, converted sinner. Slavish fear looks for relief; childlike fear looks for welfare above relief.

Slavish fear is temporary. "It is," as John Warburton said, "religion in fits and starts. It comes and goes." Childlike fear is more steady; it abides more deeply; it grows more profoundly in the soil of the heart. Slavish fear ultimately returns to the world. It clings to sin and is choked by the world. Childlike fear cannot return to the world; it parts from sin, and longs to be with God. Slavish fear never truly humbles the sinner as an unworthy sinner; childlike fear humbles the sinner as the chiefest of transgressors. Slavish fear leaves the eye closed to Christ; childlike fear has its eye fixed upon Christ.

Slavish fear has its own glory as its ultimate goal; it desires only a quieted conscience, peace, and rest. Childlike fear aims for the glory of God; true rest in God is its lofty goal. Slavish fear ends in damnation; childlike fear ends in salvation. Which kind of fear do we possess, my friends—slavish or childlike?

The last lesson we wish to consider from Felix's tragic rejection of the Word is that *the end of a life of sin is terrible.* Felix and Drusilla had one son. Drusilla and that son died three years after hearing Paul preach, when a volcano erupted and destroyed two large cities. Felix was spared but soon became insane. Josephus tells us that Felix, whose name means "happy" in Greek, became terribly unhappy. Some years later, Felix committed suicide in the mountains of Italy. It was a tragic end to a tragic life, but it was a life that had rejected a golden opportunity.

Oh my friends, value the opportunities that you receive to hear the Word of God, but do not rest in those opportunities alone. You need Spirit-worked application. If you will end well, you must be brought into personal, saving communion with the Lord in this life. Delay not. Call upon Him while He is yet to be found. Seek Him while He is yet near. Soon it will be too late to call upon the Lord.

The story is told of an agnostic who said to his friends gathered around his deathbed, "Now I know there is a God, a God before whom I shall appear, a God whom I have tried to deny my whole life.

But now it is too late, for I see Him coming, not as a God of mercy, but as a God of judgment, holiness, and wrath."

Dear friend, the Lord says, "I have called and ye have refused. I have stretched out My hands and no man has regarded." Will that take place again today? Will this very message come back in eternity, and will you see yourself again sitting here on this particular day under this particular message and realize that you have passed by a golden opportunity just like Felix? Shall this very sermon add to your condemnation? Shall you say, "There I was, sitting in that particular pew, in that particular seat, and I heard the invitation that God said also to me, 'Turn, turn, for why will ye die?' But I pushed it away; I rejected the Word of God and I said, 'Lord, tomorrow; go Thy way, and I will call for Thee when a convenient season comes.'"

Oh my friends, our natural hearts never have a convenient season! Seek bowing grace before it is forever too late. Pray for grace to pray against your natural inclinations! Take this serious admonition, lay it before the Lord, and pray, "Lord, conquer my heart against my will. I cannot go on without Thee. Let me not be a Felix, but let me be a crying, begging Bartimaeus."

Finally, dear children of God, what a blessing that when you said, "Go away," the Lord became too strong for you. How will you ever fathom the power of God, His Word, and His grace? None of us is inherently better than Felix, but God makes a difference where there is no difference. "Thou art, O God, our boast, the glory of our power; Thy sovereign grace is e'er our fortress and our tower."

Let us all plead that He may make that difference for us. "Strive to enter in at the strait gate: for many…will seek to enter in, and shall not be able" (Luke 13:24).

"Prepare to meet thy God." "Set thine house in order: for thou shalt die, and not live."

Chapter 26

Our Reformation Heritage: The Just Living by Faith

For I am not ashamed of the gospel of Christ: for it is the power of God unto salvation to everyone that believeth; to the Jew first, and also to the Greek. For therein is the righteousness of God revealed from faith to faith: as it is written, The just shall live by faith. —ROMANS 1:16–17

With God's help we ask your attention for Romans 1:16–17. Our focus today will be on the last part of verse 17, and we wish to consider with you *Our Reformation heritage as the just living by faith*. We will consider the doctrine of the just living by faith:

1. As foundational for the breakthrough of the Reformation
2. As foundational for the continuation of the Reformation
3. As foundational for the present-day revival of Reformation truth

1. As Foundational for the Breakthrough of the Reformation

The last day of October marks another anniversary of the birth of the Reformation. The Reformation is formally dated from October 31, 1517—the day when Martin Luther nailed Ninety-five Theses to the chapel door of the Castle Church in Wittenberg, Germany. These theses were translated within weeks into most European languages, and spread throughout Europe in a few months. The Lord had been ripening Europe for the Reformation, and when these theses were spread abroad, the common people passed them from hand to hand. By the grace of God, the Reformation swept through much of Europe.

Today, we are sons and daughters of the Reformation, at least in terms of our heritage. We must also examine if we are sons and daughters of the Reformation in our beliefs and in the daily practice of our lives. It is critical that we examine what God has done in ages past in the light of His Word, and then ask ourselves, "Are we being true to that biblical Reformed heritage?" Reformation Day is designed to revive within us an appreciation not only for what God has done in the past, but also to examine what He is doing with us, with our families, and with our congregations in the present, as well as to examine what we are doing with His great Reformation truths.

Now, wherein does the greatness of the Reformation principally lie? Simply put, it lies in the restoration of the Holy Scriptures as the sole, inerrant, authoritative guide for the belief and practice of both the church and individual believers. Our Reformation heritage is the heritage of Scripture. With the restoration of Scripture, a great heritage developed that affected the church in many scriptural ways which we take very much for granted today.

The return of Scripture in the first place brought the return of biblical preaching. Expository preaching once again gained primacy in worship services, rather than various complex liturgical practices.

The return of Scripture also promoted sound doctrine. Catechisms and doctrinal standards, rich in content, flowed in the wake of a return to Holy Scripture. In our Dutch tradition, of course, we have learned to value the Heidelberg Catechism, the Belgic Confession, and the Canons of Dort—our doctrinal standards from the continent of Europe. We also embrace the Westminster Standards of the British tradition: the Westminster Confession of Faith, the Shorter Catechism, and the Larger Catechism; and in the Swiss tradition, we value the First Helvetic Confession and the Second Helvetic Confession.

These are all excellent confessions, speaking one mind in returning to the doctrines of Scripture. Thus, the apostolic doctrines of the New Testament and the doctrine of Augustine with regard to salvation came back to the fore with vibrant reality in the lives of people. This occurred as people obtained the Bible, read it, searched it, and discovered the doctrines of grace alone, faith alone, Scripture alone, Christ alone, and the glory of God alone. Thousands embraced these truths by the power of the Spirit; they lived them; and they shed their blood for them. This is our heritage today.

The return of Scripture also resulted in the restructuring of the church. The hierarchy of some fifteen offices invented by the Roman Catholic Church was rejected, and the church returned to a simple biblical organization and to biblical principles of discipline.

The return of Scripture also brought back the renewal of godly living and that on the right foundation of gratitude rather than merit. Good works now came to be viewed as flowing *out of* justification rather than as *leading to* justification.

The return of Scripture also promoted Christian education. Schools were established to teach scriptural truths. Christian educators aimed to teach little children to read the Bible. As Martin Luther once said, "A plow boy armed with a Bible in one hand and my catechism in another would be able to defend the truths of God's Word against prelates and bishops and even the pope himself." Dependency upon the local priest for the interpretation of Scripture was nearly abolished. All this came out of the return of Scripture to the common man, blessed by the Holy Spirit.

Above all, the return of Scripture brought back the glory of God into the midst of His church. The traditions, ornaments, and idols of men gave way for the Word of God. Churches were whitewashed and idols were smashed. God alone was worshiped. Man was abased and God was exalted.

The return of Scripture brought back especially those biblical concepts that lie at the very center of the message of Scripture itself, particularly the doctrine of justification by gracious faith alone. That is what distinguishes the forerunners of the Reformation from the Reformers themselves. We do not call John Wycliffe, John Hus, Peter Waldo, Gregory of Rimini, Thomas Bradwardine, and other forerunners, "Reformers," because they never came to a clear grasp of this doctrine of justification by faith alone. This is what makes a Reformer a Reformer. Every Reformer taught justification by faith alone.

Consequently, it was around 1516, when Martin Luther was in his early thirties, that the Reformation was born in his heart, because then the words of our text, "The just shall live by faith," opened his heart to the gospel and turned upside down his former teaching which stressed that salvation came at least partially through human effort.

This glorious statement from the inspired pen of Paul and ultimately from the prophet Habakkuk—"The just shall live by faith"—is the gospel in a nutshell. Paul says in Romans 1 that it is this that he was anxious to bring to the Christians in Rome, but also to preach this gospel in Rome to Jew and Gentile alike. For years, Paul had wanted to come to the so-called eternal city, the city of Rome, but every time some providence occurred which made it impossible for him to do so. Fearing that the Romans would begin to think that he had no desire to be with them, Paul wrote this remarkable epistle in which, perhaps more than in any other book of the Bible, the doctrines of free and sovereign grace are systematically, judiciously, experientially, and persuasively unfolded step by step, following the order of misery, deliverance, and gratitude. The misery of man is expounded in chapters 1 through 3; deliverance, in chapters 4 through 8; and gratitude, in chapters 9 through 16. The book of Romans, more than any other at the beginning of the Reformation, was read and reread. Numerous commentaries were written upon it. It used to be said, half truthfully, that no one could be a real Reformer if he had not written a commentary on Romans. The book of Romans represents the heart of the gospel, for here we see the glorious truths of the gospel set forth vividly and powerfully.

Paul wrote to the Romans to explain to them the gospel. After a powerful introduction, he writes to them, as it were, "Please do not think that I am trying to avoid you because I am afraid to come to your cultured city; for 'I am not ashamed of the gospel of Christ.' I am not ashamed to bring it anywhere, not also to cultured people at Rome." And of course, by saying he was not ashamed, Paul is using a literary device; he is using a negative to express a positive. He is saying as it were: "I would be glad to bring the gospel to you, for I glory in that gospel, I boast of that gospel. I am ready to preach that gospel everywhere, because it is the best news that the world has ever heard. It is the evangel, the good news, the glorious news of Jesus Christ. It is the power of God unto salvation for Jews and Gentiles. Thus, I am not ashamed of the gospel of God; rather, I boast in it! Dear Romans, that is the kind of gospel you need." Paul goes on to say in Romans 1 that you and I also need the kind of righteousness that this gospel presents—the righteousness of God.

By speaking here of the righteousness of God, Paul does not mean in this particular case the attribute of God's righteousness or justice. That is how Luther understood it at first. When reading Romans 1:16–17 in his monastery cell, Luther became very troubled. The justice of God was a source of great fear for him. God was more of a tyrant than a God of love and mercy. He could not grasp how Paul could say that this was his boast, his glory, his joy, and that he could live out of the righteousness of God—"For therein is the righteousness of God revealed from faith to faith." Luther agonized over what that meant. He struggled and said to himself, "How can I live out of the righteousness of God, when I am spending my whole life trying to avoid the righteousness of God because the righteousness of God must condemn me?"

Luther had spent several years trying to meet the demands of divine righteousness. He had slept on cement for many nights in a row. He had denied himself all kinds of basic privileges of life, hoping that somehow he could satisfy God. He turned to mysticism. He tried confession to a priest. Weary of his endless confessions, the priest finally said to him, "Martin, why don't you go out and commit some real sin for once, and then come to me with your confession!" Luther was being led by the Holy Spirit to see his indwelling sin and did not yet know that the solution for all sin was exclusively in the free grace of God. He thought that the solution needed to involve patching up his life and establishing his own righteousness before a righteous God. And so he came to increasingly dread the righteousness of God.

For the next ten years, Luther struggled with the righteousness of God in the face of his own unrighteousness. He had a spiritual counselor named Johann Staupitz who remained in the Roman Catholic Church, but who himself had been delivered by the blood of Jesus Christ alone. Staupitz often found Luther walking back and forth in his cell, grieving and groaning over his sins. One time he told Luther, "Your vows will never be sufficient. Salvation is only to be found outside of yourself in Jesus Christ." Another time, when Luther was pacing the cell, wringing his hands and confessing, "My sins, my sins, my sins!", Staupitz simply quoted the Apostles' Creed: "I believe in the forgiveness of sins," and walked away. These things made a deep impression upon Luther, but he still could not grasp how a holy and righteous God, who could not look upon sin, could ever look upon him in mercy.

Has this ever been your struggle, dear friend? No, I am not saying that we must experience the ten-year struggle that Martin Luther endured. Luther himself would not say that. He once wrote to his congregation, "I am telling you about my struggles not because I want you to imitate them, but because I want to deliver you from them." Then he went on to say something like this: "If you take me as a pattern, you would be foolish. Flee directly, just as you are, with all your sins and all your needs to the blood-bought righteousness of the Son of God."

Finally, God broke through in our text for Luther. It was as if in one moment the gospel was unveiled before his eyes, and he finally saw that Jesus Christ is the whole of a sinner's righteousness; that He has done everything for a sinner; that He has paid the price of sin, and that He has obeyed the law. Luther later wrote that it was as if his soul "went through the open gates of Paradise." His soul was set at liberty in Christ.

Today, if someone is going to dedicate a statue that has been under cover, there is often a date set for its unveiling as the sculptor nears its completion. An official unveiling ceremony takes place where everyone will be able to see it for the first time. Similarly, when Luther saw that the just shall live by faith and not by works; that faith believes the gospel message that Jesus has done everything for a sinner who can do nothing—when he saw the basic truths of the gospel, and his poor soul was cast upon the righteousness of Christ as his only and sufficient hope for time and eternity, it was as if a sheet or veil was thrown off the gospel. For the first time he saw with clarity the gospel grace of God in the person of Jesus Christ who is all and all for sinners who are nothing at all.

You see, congregation, there are two things that you and I will never be able to do that must be done for us: First, we can never fulfill the law, but we must fulfill the law—either by ourselves or by another doing it for us, because God would not allow into heaven anyone who has transgressed the law and was not forgiven. Second, we can never pay for the punishment of our sins, for they demand everlasting hell. What Luther saw in those moments is that through the righteousness of the gospel, Christ had done those two things. He had obeyed the law perfectly for His people; that is what the Reformers would later call His *active obedience*. And Christ had paid for all the sin of His people; that is what the Reformers would later call His *passive obedience*. Through this perfect double obedience Jesus satisfied the justice of God. Thus, by graciously believing these truths, a poor sinner could find all his righteousness in the righteousness of Jesus Christ, "for therein is the righteousness of God revealed from faith to faith; as it is written, The just shall live by faith." Luther saw that such divine righteousness was available to him—a *complete* righteousness. He saw for the first time what Jesus meant when He said on the cross, "It is finished."

Luther also saw that this righteousness must be received by faith—by Spirit-worked gracious faith. He saw that the righteousness received by faith would be fully acceptable for the whole life of the believer, not only to *make* him right with God, but also to *keep* him right with God. "The just shall live by faith." The just are not only *saved* by faith; they *live* by faith. Luther saw that the only way to be a Christian was to live by faith.

Today we too live in the New Testament dispensation when the veil is taken away; Christ is exposed to all who come under the gospel. But our eyes are blinded by nature; we do not have the faith we need to believe the gospel; we do not see that everything is already accomplished. Consequently, we keep busying ourselves, going about to establish our own righteousness.

By grace, Luther, in his so-called tower experience, embraced the righteousness of Jesus Christ, as he would later say, in its personal pronouns. He could now say, "Jesus Christ is *my* righteousness; salvation has become reality for *me*." Luther saw the righteousness of God with the eye of faith through the Scriptures. He would later write:

Here I was in my tower, reading and praying. I labored diligently and anxiously to understand these words of Paul, "the righteousness of God is revealed in the gospel." I sought long and knocked anxiously, for the expression, *the righteousness of God*, blocked my way. As often as I read this expression, I wished that God had not made the gospel known at all. But then one day when I was meditating in the tower, I saw the difference between law and gospel for the first time in my life. The light broke through, and as I formerly hated the expression, "the righteousness of God," I now regarded it as the most comforting word in all the Bible. In very truth, this language of St. Paul was to me the true gate to Paradise.

Thus Luther experienced two things which lie at the heart of the Reformation—two things which we must know: (1) We must know our unrighteousness uncovered, and (2) we must know the righteousness of Jesus Christ discovered.

"Therein is the righteousness of God revealed from faith to faith.… The just shall live by faith." This became the hallmark of the Reformation which then spread to many other places and people. This doctrine was taken up by Calvin and Zwingli in Switzerland; by Knox in Scotland; and by Bullinger, Beza, Bucer, and many others. This doctrine cost martyrs their lifeblood; hundreds were burned at the stake. This doctrine in turn became the seed of the church.

2. As Foundational for the Continuation of the Reformation

The first generation of the Reformation was a tumultuous time, but it was a blessed time. It was a time when thousands of people could no longer remain in the Roman Catholic Church out of principle, and at the risk of their lives joined the Protestant cause. But it wasn't long before this great breakthrough became a dead doctrine. The second-generation Protestants—the children of many of the great Reformers themselves—became, for the most part, cold and lax. They professed the doctrines, were sound in their orthodoxy, but they did not experience the great doctrines of the Reformation in their hearts. And so, by the 1600s things had become dry and cold and dead in many areas. But God raised up the Puritans in England, the Presbyterians in

Scotland, the Dutch Further Reformation divines in the Netherlands, and New England Puritans in America, to revive this glorious Reformation truth—"the just shall live by faith."

Thus, our text is not only foundational for the breakthrough of the Reformation, but also for the continuation of the Reformation. The Dutch Further Reformation and the Puritan movement were dependent on the Reformation. Many divines realized that things were becoming dry and dead. By the grace of the Holy Spirit, men arose who stormed the throne of grace for a revival in practice of the great and glorious doctrines of which Luther had confessed, "Doctrine is heaven." Under the Spirit's tutelage, Reformation doctrine and holy living of this doctrine were promoted by men like William Ames, John Owen, and John Bunyan in England; Hugh Binning, Thomas Boston, and Samuel Rutherford in Scotland; Thomas Shepard, Thomas Hooker, and John Cotton in America; and William Teellinck, Alexander Comrie, and Theodorus van der Groe in the Netherlands. Revival swept through many areas, as the vitality of this doctrine— *the just shall live by faith*—came to the fore again.

This renewal movement of English and Dutch puritanism lasted for varying lengths of time in different places. It lasted most of the seventeenth century in many places, but by 1700 things had become cold and dry and dead again. Liberalism, the Enlightenment, and humanism began to sweep through Europe and North America. But the Spirit's work came to the fore again—especially in the time of the Great Awakening in the 1740s, and from 1800 to the 1820s, when revival swept through much of America and there was a return to this same doctrine—*the just shall live by faith*.

3. As Foundational for the Present-Day Revival of Reformation Truth

Today, we desperately need another revival of Reformation doctrine. We are grateful to see in many areas an increased spiritual concern to search the Scriptures, to know the truth, and to experience and put into practice the doctrines of grace. Our hearts are encouraged, and yet we are still far from putting these doctrines into practice as we ought. We still have so many remnants of Roman Catholicism which cleave to us and are contrary to the Reformed faith; for example, so many of us are still trying to establish our own righteousness. We are still not seeing the righteousness of God revealed from faith to faith. So many do not know anything of the liberty of the gospel. So many are strangers of faith, and we blame God for it, or we go on with our indifference and do not see the urgency that Reformation truth be bound upon our hearts and lived in our lives. We need Reformation truth to sweep through our congregations. We need Reformation truth to sweep through our families and pierce our own hearts. We need to live and to die by this truth—*the just shall live by faith*. Luther said, "Faith is my life; without faith I cannot live; without faith, I would die."

The just shall live by faith. Can you say that also—that without faith you would die? Do you grieve over how little faith you have? Do you yearn to have more faith in the gospel, in Jesus Christ, and in the truths of God?

Oh congregation, we do not need the dead orthodoxy of a "hard believism" that stifles and brings a soul under bondage, on the one hand; and we do not need the shallow Christendom of "easy believism" on the other hand; but we need the heart experience of "God-believism"—to believe in God and His Son, Jesus Christ, wrought by the Holy Spirit, and received by gracious faith. This believing is indeed impossible with man, but is possible, indeed, sure with God. By the power of God's miraculous grace, we may and must experience and live this great truth—*the just shall live by faith*.

Application

"The just shall live by faith." To live out what he experienced in the tower cost Martin Luther his whole life. In 1517, he posted the Ninety-five Theses; in 1521 he was excommunicated from the church. He was invited to go to the Diet of Worms. At the diet, he was surrounded by several church authorities who, after placing his books on a table in front of him, demanded that he recant his writings. The following day, Luther gave this famous answer:

> Unless I am convicted by Scripture and plain reason, I do not accept the authority of popes and councils, for they have

contradicted each other. My conscience is captive to the Word of God. I cannot and will not recant anything, for to go against conscience is neither right nor safe. Here I stand; I cannot do otherwise. God help me, Amen.

Following this noble confession, Luther was immediately banned. To be banned meant that if anyone found you they had a right to capture and kill you. But Frederick III, the elector of Saxony (a powerful political position), anticipating Luther being banned, had arranged that Luther be kidnapped and brought to the Castle of Wartburg. While there, in one year's time, Luther translated the Scriptures into German. The German Bible translated by Luther is even more widely accepted today in Germany than the King James Version is in North America. God had a purpose for everything He did, also in the life of Luther. Throughout his life, Luther needed to live out of this truth—*the just shall live by faith*. There were times that he could not understand God's ways. There were times that his faith waned and he slipped into despondent periods of unbelief. He once wrote that he had more trouble with the Anabaptists on his left than he ever had with the Roman Catholics on his right.

Luther also faced many seasons of sickness. Some years he was sick most of the year; one year he battled sickness for ten months, and yet went on preaching and writing. Sometimes he could only preach about one-third of the time because he was so sick, but he would keep on writing. He wrote ninety-four volumes, many of them from his bed. Also from his bed he gave directions for the Reformation—how to build; how to go forward—all the while experiencing *the just shall live by faith*.

Sometimes Luther was so overwhelmed by liberals on the left and legalists on the right that he could hardly believe that God was directing all these things. One time he said to his wife, "I am afraid that God is dead; it is not easy to build a church with sinful human beings." His wife pulled all the shades of their house that day, and when Luther came home, he rushed to his wife and said, "Who died today?" She said, "Well, you said this morning that God was dead." This broke the bands of unbelief again. So you see, even though Luther had his depressions and his times of unbelief and doubts and fears, still it was this that kept his soul alive—*the just shall live by faith*. When challenged by popes and emperors to renounce Paul's doctrine of justification by faith alone, without works, he once wrote:

> I see that the devil is continually attacking this very fundamental article of justification by faith alone, and that in this respect he cannot and will not stop or slow down any of his attacks. Well, then I, Dr. Martin Luther, unworthy herald of the gospel of our Lord Jesus Christ, do confess this article, that justification by faith alone, without works, justifies in the sight of God. And I declare that in spite of the Emperor of the Romans, the Emperor of the Turks, the pope, all cardinals, bishops, priests, monks, nuns, kings, princes, nobles, all the world, and all the devils of this world, this truth shall stand forever. And those who persist in opposing this truth will draw down upon their heads the flames of hell. Christ alone takes away sin. We cannot do so by all of our works, nor any of our works, but good works follow redemption as surely as fruit appears on the living tree. This is our doctrine and we will hold fast to it in the name of God until we die.

The just shall live by faith. It is all the gift of God. It is all the work of God. The just live by faith in God, by faith in His righteousness. Oh congregation, take away the righteousness of Jesus Christ and we can close the church doors. There is no purpose in going on without the righteousness of Jesus Christ. There is nothing out of which to live. Dear friends, you must be stripped of your righteousness and you must be brought to Jesus Christ. There is no other way to live and there is no other way to die, but upon Christ's righteousness alone.

The Roman Catholics were not against faith; they were not against grace; they were not against Scripture; and they were not against the glory of God. But they said all these things must be combined with other things. There must be the glory of God and honor to the pope; it must be faith and the works of man; it must be Scripture and tradition. But what we have been trying to lay before you is this truth—that you must lose everything from your side to find everything in Jesus Christ.

Sometimes we are encouraged when we may believe that the Holy Spirit is showing some fruit; other times we are discouraged. Sometimes we hear religious talk and even prayers that scarcely mention Christ or His righteousness. We can be ever so religious, but if we are not stripped of our own righteousness and do not know what it means to live out that struggling warfare of the *just shall live by faith*, we will perish in the flames of hell! There is no other righteousness. Luther said, "We need an alien righteousness," and by that he meant a righteousness outside of us; further yet, we need that righteousness brought home to our hearts. *The just shall live by faith.*

What do we need today? We need to embrace with both mind and heart the truth of justification by faith alone. We must not think or feel that we must just sit back and wait to see if God might do something at some time. In the meantime—well, we come to church and do what we can; we do our best, and we just hope for the best. My friend, with that kind of doctrine you will go to the place of the damned. You must be born again. You must lose all your righteousness and you must find righteousness in Jesus Christ alone. And that righteousness is available. God freely offers it to you. It is presented to you. You are invited to come to God just as you are, as a poor, wretched, miserable sinner, in all your sinfulness to receive by Spirit-worked faith the righteousness of God. My friend, out of whose righteousness are you living?

Are you still living by some righteousness that you produced? I warn you with love for your soul's eternal welfare, it will never work— I repeat, establishing your own righteousness will never, never work. God is too holy and you are too sinful. Luther tried it for ten years. He did many more things than you will ever do. He used to fast three days at a time without one drop of water or one bite to eat, and a voice inside would say, "Have you fasted enough?" He would go without sleep, and the voice inside would say, "Are you sleepless enough?" He would repent and go to the priest and confess, and confess, and confess, and the voice inside would say, "Have you confessed enough?" Our righteousness will never be enough. Indeed, as soon as we think we have enough, we have not become Christians but Pharisees.

But the good news of the gospel, dear friend, is that Jesus Christ's righteousness—not your righteousness—is enough, yes, more than enough. The righteousness of Jesus Christ is bread enough and to spare in the Father's house. The greater Joseph is yet alive, the storehouse is open for sinners, for beggars. Oh, go to the greater Joseph and say: "Lord, I need Thy righteousness. Teach me who I am. Teach me who Thou art, and who Thou art willing to be for poor sinners like I am."

Oh, dear congregation, we love your souls and we long to see your souls saved by the righteousness of Jesus Christ. There is no other name to which we can direct you; there is no other righteousness that we can direct you to than this Name and this righteousness. We want to make crystal clear for you that this righteousness can meet your every need. This righteousness does everything for a sinner; it saves him and it keeps him saved, so that his whole life reflects our text, *the just shall live by faith.*

Seek this righteousness. Do not be content being unconverted. Ask God to go against you in order to save you, to go against your natural heart in order to wean you from your own righteousness and to drive you to Christ's righteousness.

What will it be to be in an orthodox church, to be a son or daughter of the Reformation by inheritance, and yet never in your whole life to have grasped the foundational principles—with your mind and with your heart—of the Reformation itself; and then to be cast into hell because you clung to your own righteousness all your life! The sooner it becomes your fault that you are unconverted, the better. I know that is not easy to hear, but it would be good for you if your inability, your unconverted state, and your distance from God would all become your sin, and drive you to the righteousness of Jesus Christ.

"Seek ye the Lord while he may be found, call ye upon him while he is near: Let the wicked forsake his way, and the unrighteous man his thoughts: and let him return unto the Lord, and he will have mercy upon him; and to our God, for he will abundantly pardon" (Isa. 55:6–7).

Chapter 27

All Things Working Together for Good for God's People

> *And we know that all things work together for good to them that love God, to them who are the called according to his purpose.*
> —ROMANS 8:28

In this sermon, we want to focus on a theme that is full of comfort for God's dear people—how God works even some of the most difficult things in the lives of His own for their real good. You can find our text in Romans 8:28.

Our major theme will be this: *All things working together for good for God's people.* With God's help, we will consider the following points:

1. How God works affliction together for the welfare of His people
2. How God works divine desertion together for the welfare of His people
3. How God causes even sin to serve the welfare of His people

1. How God Works Affliction Together for the Welfare of His People

The life of a true Christian resembles the inner workings of a watch. If you open a watch, what do you see? You see that certain wheels which turn in a counterclockwise direction are attached to other wheels that are working in a clockwise direction. Your first thought may be that the watchmaker is either foolish or confused. But he is neither.

Rather, he has so arranged the internals of this watch and put in a mainspring to govern all its wheels, that when wound, though one wheel turns clockwise and another counterclockwise, all work together to move the hands around the face of the watch at precisely the right speed. Many wheels appear to counteract each other, but they all work together for the identical purpose of displaying the time accurately.

A watch, dear congregation, is somewhat like the lives of God's people. Some wheels in their lives run clockwise, which provides hope that the events of their lives directed by God's providence are good for them, but other acts of God's providence seem to run counterclockwise, that is, they appear to run against them. Only when their eye of faith is fixed on the great Watchmaker, who has planned everything in His all-wise decree, do they see and understand that He has placed the mainspring of free grace within their "watch-life" so that all providential and spiritual wheels work together for their welfare. Yes, dear child of God, though much often seems counterclockwise and against you when you see one wheel of providence work within or against another wheel of grace in various afflictions and riddles, yet your wise God knows exactly what He is doing. He will work all things together to produce a divine and blessed result according to His sovereign good pleasure and eternal counsel.

Paul allows for no exceptions to this radical promise. He writes, "*All things*"—that is, all *good* things and all *evil* things—"shall work together for good." The best things—including the attributes and works of God, the promises and providences of the Father, the person and work of the Son, the graces and labors of the Spirit, the everlasting covenant of grace with all its accompanying benefits of salvation, and all divine ordinances, such as the Word and the sacraments, prayer, and the communion of saints—will all work together for your real good if you are one who genuinely loves the God of the Scriptures. Even the worst things—including divine desertion, sin, Satan, infirmities, temptations, afflictions, persecutions, and humiliations—will all work together for your welfare and God's glory.

No doubt some of us will say, "It is easy to understand how good things will work together for good, and I know that evil things are supposed to serve the spiritual welfare of God's people, but how affliction, divine desertion, and even sin can work together for their good I cannot comprehend."

Today I wish to show you in several ways how even these three things—*affliction, divine desertion, and sin*—work together for the spiritual welfare of God's children, and from this we will be able to safely conclude that "all things work together for good to them that love God." First, let's focus on the good that flows out of affliction for the believer, and then we will focus on how good flows out of even divine desertion and sin for the believer.

No one naturally enjoys affliction. Afflictions can be very heavy and difficult to bear. "If sin is the head of the serpent," Ralph Erskine wrote, "affliction is its tail." And yet, dear believer, do not afflictions also serve as medicine for you in the hands of your great Physician, Jesus Christ? Let's look briefly at several different ways in which in His hands your afflictions serve your spiritual welfare and eternal health.

First, doesn't the Lord humble you deeply through affliction, showing you who you are and what you remain in yourself—nothing but sin and corruption apart from divine grace? Does not the Lord teach you through affliction the same truth that He taught Israel in Deuteronomy 8, "I led thee through the great and terrible wilderness, wherein were fiery serpents, and scorpions, and drought, and I fed thee in the wilderness with manna, that I might humble thee, to prove thee, to do thee good at thy latter end" (v. 2)?

Affliction not only makes a true Christian humble before God, but it keeps him humble. Affliction vacuums away the fuel that feeds his pride. An afflicted believer resembles a fruit-ladened tree; the tree that hangs lowest to the ground is usually the tree that bears the most fruit.

If God uses your afflictions to humble you before Him, do not your afflictions work together for good?

Second, through affliction God's people learn what sin is in its God-dishonoring, defiling, and damning nature. Through affliction they learn, as John Bunyan said, "that sin has the devil for its father, shame for its companion, and death for its wages." They learn through affliction that sin is actually an attack upon the very heart and being and attributes of God. As Bunyan also wrote, "Sin is the daring of God's justice, the rape of His mercy, the jeering of His patience, the slighting of His power, and the contempt of His love." They learn through affliction that sin is both the strength of their death and the death of their strength.

In affliction the believer's soul is, as it were, searched with candles (Zeph. 1:12) for secret and open sins. When affliction is sanctified by the Holy Spirit, sin is dragged out of its hiding place in the heart and set in the light of God's holy and all-searching eye. "Thou hast set our iniquities before thee, our secret sins in the light of thy countenance" (Ps. 90:8). Affliction strips off the Adam-like fig-leaf covering that God's child strives to cling to by nature. "The sins of God's people are like birds' nests," wrote William Bridge. "As long as leaves are on the trees you cannot see them, but in the winter of affliction when all the leaves are off, the bird nests appear plainly." When affliction is sanctified, sin becomes heinous and hated. Sin becomes exceeding sinful in its very nature. It becomes hated more for its nature than for its consequences.

Third, the Holy Spirit uses affliction as a medicine to destroy the deadly disease of sin in the children of God, causing them to bring forth healthy and godly fruit. When sin causes the believer to backslide from his Savior, the Lord Jesus as Good Shepherd must send the rod of affliction to set the crooked believer straight. Affliction is the Shepherd's dog, sent out not to devour the sheep, but to bring them back into the fold again. Sanctified affliction cures sin. "Before I was afflicted I went astray," David confesses, "but now have I kept thy word" (Ps. 119:67).

It is as good for a child of God to be chastised with affliction as it is for a young tree to be pruned (John 15:2), for the pressure of affliction not only presses out the awful stink of sin, but also sends forth the fragrant smells and fruits of divine graces. Do you know that in some countries trees will grow, but will bear no fruit because there is no winter there? The Christian needs winter-times of affliction if he is to experience spring-times of blossoming, summer-times of growing, and autumn-times of harvesting.

The life of God's children is like a bell—the harder it is hit, the better it sounds. They learn more under the rod that strikes them than under the staff that comforts them. No, the Good Shepherd is not drowning His sheep when He washes them nor killing them when He shears them. Rather, His washings are necessary cleanings; His shearings are necessary strippings; His corrections are essential lessons.

Affliction reaps golden fruit. It mines, smelts, refines, and forms the believer until the divine goldsmith can see His reflection in the work of His own hands. Then the child of God experiences with Job, "When he hath tried me, I shall come forth as gold" (Job 23:10). "Affliction," wrote the godly Robert Leighton, "is the diamond dust that heaven polishes its jewels with."

Fourth, the Lord uses affliction as a means to cause His people to seek Him, to bring them back into communion with Himself, and to keep them close by His side. As sheep will stay close by their shepherd in storms, so the Lord said of Israel, "In their affliction they will seek me early" (Hos. 5:15). The storms and stones of affliction only force God's sheep closer to their Shepherd. All the stones that hit Stephen only knocked him closer to the chief cornerstone, Jesus Christ, and opened heaven all the more for his soul. Affliction drove the Canaanite woman to the Son of David; it drove a dying thief to a dying Savior. Not the crown of Manasseh, but his chains were used to bring him to the knowledge that "the Lord was God" (2 Chron. 33:11–13). Even the magnet of God's rich mercy does not bring nor keep His flock so close to the Great Shepherd as do the cords of affliction.

Fifth, the Lord uses afflictions for good to conform His flock to Christ, making them partakers of His suffering and His image. "Christ was chastened for our profit," the author to the Hebrews wrote, "that we might be partakers of his holiness" (12:10). God had but one Son without sin, but none without affliction. His afflicting rod is a pencil to draw Christ's image more fully upon His people. Through the way of suffering to glory they become followers of the Lamb of God who walks before His flock. Every path of affliction they encounter has already been traveled, overcome, and sanctified by their Shepherd whose stream of substitutionary blood, from His circumcision to the cross, is their sure pledge that no affliction or trial will be able to separate them from the love of God in Christ Jesus (Rom. 8:39). Their deserved suffering leads them to Christ's substitutionary suffering, which in turn, makes them exclaim, "His yoke is easy and his burden is light" (Matt. 11:30).

Dear believer, are not the occasions of your sufferings usually the times when you have most communion with Jesus Christ in His sufferings—whose entire life was nothing but a series of sufferings, as you can read in Isaiah 53? Can you then complain for the light crosses you must bear as guilty sinners (2 Cor. 4:17) when you behold the heavy crosses Christ had to bear as the innocent sufferer?

Sixth, spiritual afflictions work for good because the Lord balances them with spiritual comfort and joy. David wrote, "For his anger endureth but a moment; in his favour is life: weeping may endure for a night, but joy cometh in the morning" (Ps. 30:5). "Your sorrow," Christ told His disciples, "shall be turned into joy" (John 16:20). He brings His people into the wilderness to speak comfortably to them (Hos. 2:14). Where godly suffering abounds, godly consolation abounds (2 Cor. 1:4–5). "God gives gifts that we may love Him, and stripes that we may fear Him," George Downame wrote; "yea, oftentimes He mixes His frowns with His favours."

The Shepherd's rod has honey at its end. God's Pauls have their prison-songs. The sweet will follow the bitter. Joy will come in the morning. The Lord turns their water into wine. Samuel Rutherford once wrote, "When I am in the cellar of affliction, I find the Lord's choicest wines." In affliction, God's sheep sometimes may experience sweet raptures of divine joy which lead them, as it were, to the very borders of the heavenly Canaan. At such moments they may confess with Eliphaz the Temanite, "Behold, happy is the man whom God correcteth: therefore despise not thou the chastening of the Almighty: for he maketh sore, and bindeth up: he woundeth and his hands make whole. He shall deliver thee in six troubles: yea, in seven there shall no evil touch thee" (Job 5:17–19).

Seventh, affliction also works for good by keeping God's children walking by faith and not by sight. If God always granted sensible enjoyments to believers in this world, they would begin to love this life and live off of their spiritual provisions instead of the Provider Himself. Therefore, with their sweet meals, the Lord orders some sour sauce to help their digestion, in order that they may live not by sense, but by faith. In prosperity God's people talk of living by faith, and often darken counsel by words without knowledge; but in adversity they come to the experimental knowledge of what it means to live by faith.

Eighth, affliction works for good in weaning Christians away from the world. A dog never bites those who live in its home, but only strangers. Affliction bites God's children so deeply because we are too little at home with the Word and ways of God, and too much at home with the world and ways of man. If we were more often at home with our Master and Shepherd in heavenly places, the afflictions would be far easier to bear. "God," says Thomas Watson, "would have the world hang as a loose tooth which, being twitched away, doth not much trouble us."

Finally, affliction is profitable in preparing God's people for their heavenly inheritance. Affliction elevates their soul heavenward, to look for "a city which hath foundations, whose builder and maker is God" (Heb. 11:10). Affliction paves their way for glory. "For our light affliction, which is but for a moment, worketh for us a far more exceeding and eternal weight of glory" (2 Cor. 4:17). "He that rides to be crowned," John Trapp wrote, "will not think much of a rainy day."

Children of God, is not this enough to convince you that affliction is for your spiritual welfare—that you "shall not want" anything necessary or good for you, both temporally and spiritually? Though the wind of affliction is contrary to your flesh, yet it pleases God to use this crosswind to blow you toward heaven. Your afflictions are tailor-made to fit you with divine precision all the way to glory. As George Downame profoundly observes, "The Lord does not measure out our afflictions according to our faults, but according to our strength, and looks not at what we have deserved, but what we are able to bear." Did you ever think of affliction this way, dear child of God? To think of affliction this way is to think exactly the opposite of Job's friends. Job's friends said, "If you are heavily afflicted, you have heavily sinned." But Downame says—please allow me to repeat this wonderful quotation: "The Lord does not measure out our afflictions according to our faults, but according to our strength, and looks not at what we have deserved, but what we are able to bear."

Therefore, shall not all things, even affliction, work together for the welfare of God's people? And therefore, your duty, dear believer, is to do what Paul calls you to do in 1 Thessalonians 5:18, "In every thing [even in affliction], give thanks: for this is the will of God in Christ Jesus concerning you."

2. How Jesus Works Divine Desertion Together for the Welfare of His People.

I trust you are now persuaded that affliction works for good in the lives of genuine Christians. Now we need to turn our attention to the even deeper questions of how God can overrule divine desertion and even sin itself for good in the lives of His people. Let's first look at divine desertion being overruled by God.

Perhaps you ask: What about the dreadful burden of divine desertion—the burden of feeling that God has withdrawn Himself and become silent in my life? How can the groan of Zion, "The LORD hath forsaken me, and my Lord hath forgotten me" (Isa. 49:14), ever work for good? If Thomas Watson called divine desertion "a short hell" and Samuel Rutherford called God's silence (which lies at the heart of experiencing apparent divine desertion) the most bitter ingredient that the believer must drink in his cup of sorrow—how can such desertion work for good?

Perhaps the best way to persuade you, if you are a true Christian, that even God's apparent desertions of you are intended for your welfare by an ascended Jesus, is to ask you a series of questions:

- Does not divine desertion drive you to prayer to seek after and prize communion with God more than ever, causing you to knock at heaven's gates with unceasing petitions?

- Does not the Lord use divine desertion to cause you to examine your own soul in order to discover, pull, and cast away the accursed weeds of sin which have caused you to desert God and Him to desert you?

- When the Holy Spirit teaches you that the most common cause of divine absence is your own sin, does this not cause you to hate sin with a holy hatred?

- Does not God use His own withdrawals in your life like a rough file to scrape off spiritual rust which all too quickly develops on your faith, hope, love, and other graces of God when they are not used regularly?

- Does not an absent God cause you to value more what heaven has given you in a saving way, so that within your soul special grace does not become common grace, nor common grace become special grace?

- Does not God's desertion serve by the Spirit's secret influences to purge you of remaining infirmities, weaning you from worldly thinking, worldly conversations, and worldly actions?

- Have you not experienced that the Holy Spirit uses the withdrawals of God to cut off your reliance upon anything within you, such as your experiences, your humility, your prayers, your faith, and your conversion, so that you may learn to more fully believe in and rely upon Jesus Christ alone for salvation?

- Has not the Holy Spirit used divine desertion to cut off your relying upon even the gracious benefits God has given you, so that what God gives does not lord over your soul above the Lord Himself?

- Through God's apparent desertions are you not often taught that His delays in your life are not denials, but rather, that at His time and in His way, He will again draw close to commune with you through His Word?

- Does not the Lord sometimes hold Himself back in order to teach you that He would be righteous never to commune with you again on account of your continued sinning against Him?

- Through divine desertion does not God persuade you that He alone must be honored in His presence and His absence?

Dear believer, if you are honest, are not these fruits of divine desertion taught by the Spirit of an ascended Mediator profitable for you even though you often fight against many of them? Can you not see that the Lord brings you into the depths of desertion before you die in order to keep you from the depths of damnation after you die? At times you may even fear that He holds you above hell by desertion, but afterward must you not confess that He does so to keep you from hell for eternity? Your desertions work for your spiritual welfare to prepare you for heaven, and to make heaven all the more heavenly when you finally enter glory. Truly, even when Christ appears to absent Himself from you, He is still secretly present with you at the Father's right hand, as the Heidelberg Catechism says so beautifully, with His Godhead, majesty, grace, and Spirit (Lord's Day 18).

Dear believer, keep courage. God's temporary, apparent desertion of you is just that—temporary and only apparent. As John Flavel wrote:

> Christ's desertion [of God] prevents your final desertion. Because He was forsaken for a time you shall not be forsaken for ever. For He was forsaken for you.... [Moreover,] though God deserted Christ, yet at the same time He powerfully supported Him. His omnipotent arms were under Him, though His pleased face was hid from Him.... So, Christian, just so shall it be with thee. Thy God may turn away His face, [but] He will not pluck away His arm.

Puritan Timothy Cruso put it this way: "He who hath engaged to be our Christ for ever, cannot depart for ever."

3. How Jesus Causes Even Sin to Serve the Welfare of His People

"All things," Paul asserts, "work together for good to them that love God." "All things" includes not only affliction and divine desertion, but even sin. Even sin will work together for good—not for them that love sin, but for them that love God. Rightly, Augustine has written, "God would never permit evil, if He could not bring good out of evil." Here, of course, we tread upon cautious ground, for there is nothing worse than sin; we must do all in our power to discourage, and not encourage, sin.

We must maintain at least three important guidelines when considering how sin works for the good of God's people. First, we have to maintain there is nothing good in sin itself. Sin is the evil of evils; in itself it can work nothing but death and damnation. Thomas Watson wrote, "Sin is like poison, which corrupts the blood, infects the heart, and without a sovereign antidote, brings death."

Second, we must maintain that those who encourage themselves in sin by the argument that good will come out of it, twist the Scriptures to their own damnation. Paul is clear in Romans 3:8 that to do evil that good may come is only to make our damnation just. One of the primary marks of being a Christian is to hate all sin and to love holiness and godliness.

Third, only corrupt human nature can abuse the doctrine of good resulting from sin, for true grace can never play lightly with sin. Sin will work for good only to them that hate sin. It will work for good to them that love God and abhor themselves on account of sin. It will work for good to those who are humbled by sin, who fly to Christ to be saved from it, and who dare not allow themselves the least sin to gain an entire world. It will work for good to those who count the least sin worse than the greatest affliction. It will work for good to those who, knowing their own weakness, fight earnestly against sin, using the Word of God, the blood of Christ, the strength of the Spirit, and fervent prayer to wage holy war against it.

Yet, though sin is worse than hell in its essence, God, through Christ, and by His mighty overruling power, directs even sin to our spiritual welfare if we are true believers. Let me explain four ways in which this is so:

First, God causes the sinfulness of sin to bring us to true self-examination and self-knowledge. Scripture tells us that the Lord permitted Hezekiah to fall to teach him what was in his heart. When we are in our right place before God, we will not shrink from knowing the worst about ourselves, just as a cancer patient requests to know the worst of his sickness. Therefore Job prayed, "Make me to know my transgression" (Job 13:23). By nature, our sins will find us out, but by grace we find our sins out. This leads us by the Spirit to a deep and profitable self-knowledge, causing us to confess with Paul, "I am the chief sinner," or with Martin Luther, "In myself I am not only miserable, but misery itself."

Second, God uses the sinfulness of sin to bring us to genuinely condemn ourselves. True Christians are led to pronounce a sentence of condemnation upon themselves, taking God's side against themselves. Thomas Watson profoundly notes, "When a man has judged himself, Satan is put out of office. When he lays anything to a saint's charge, he is able to retort, 'It is true, Satan, I am guilty of these sins, but I have judged myself already for them; and having condemned myself in the lower court of conscience, God (for the sake of Christ) will acquit me in the upper court of heaven!'" God will never step upon a self-condemning beggar who casts himself exclusively on divine mercy. Rather, the owning of my sin as a child of the first Adam works for good by making room for the righteousness of the second Adam, Jesus Christ. God uses the greatest evil of sin to make room for the greatest good of communion with Himself. He uses condemnation to unlock, as it were, the door to salvation.

Third, the sinfulness of sin works for good in the believer by keeping him engaged in the good fight of faith. The Christian not only leads a wayfaring life, but also a warfaring life. His heart is a castle that is in danger of being assaulted every hour. Daily a heavy duel is fought between two seeds, for "the spirit lusts against the flesh" (Gal. 5:17). "Watch and pray" should be the daily, yes, the hourly motto of our lives as believers.

Fourth, an awareness of the sinfulness of sin can also yield the profitable fruit of spiritual reformation. When God permits His people to fall into sin, His normal design is to break the back of that sin into which they have fallen. Abraham stumbled in faith but became a champion of faith. Moses stumbled in meekness, but was a champion of meekness. Peter stumbled in zeal but became the champion of godly zealousness. God makes His children's maladies their medicines when He gives grace to them not only to find out their sin, but also to drive out their sin.

I cannot conclude without a serious warning. Remember, dear believer, though the Lord directs even sin to end in good, allow me to warn you never to make light of sin, nor to become bold in sinning. Sin will always cost you a high price. Just as grace is always amazing, sin is always dreadful. Remember David. Sin cost him his peace, a broken family, and the terrors of the Almighty. Though the Lord will never damn His child, He will have them taste something of the bitterness of hell in this life when they tamper with sin. He chastises sin by placing them into such bitter agonies and soul-distress that they can sometimes be filled with horror and be drawn to the brink of despair.

Oh, that the dread character of sin, as well as its consequences, might serve as flaming swords to keep you from eating of the forbidden tree of iniquity!

Dear unconverted friend, if you are not born again, no affliction and no sin, yes, nothing will serve your good. Sin can only work death and damnation for you unless you learn to flee to God by faith and in repentance, casting yourself upon His mercy in and through the ascended Mediator, Jesus Christ. By nature, through sin we ask God for the shortest way to hell. We would rather sleep our way into damnation than sweat our way into salvation.

Dear friend, dear teenagers, dear children, do not forget that the damned shall live in hell as long as God Himself shall live in heaven. If you refuse to believe in Christ, you will end in hell one day. There you will be constantly dying without ever being dead. In hell there is no relief, no intermission, and no end to the wrath of God.

Allow me to ask you a final question: Can you answer on one hand with Chrysostom when sent a threatening message from the empress, "Go tell her that I fear nothing but sin," and can you answer on the other hand with a godly forefather when offered promotion by King George III, "Sir, I want nothing but more grace"? For those who hate sin and love grace, God shall fulfil His own promise, notwithstanding affliction, desertion, and sin: "All things work together for good to them that love God."

Chapter 28

The Only Way to Live and Die

For to me to live is Christ, and to die is gain.
—PHILIPPIANS 1:21

The apostle Paul did not have an easy life. He endured many trials for the sake of Jesus Christ. One of those trials was imprisonment. Twice he was imprisoned in Rome. We read of his second and final imprisonment in 2 Timothy, written when he was expecting to soon be executed.

During his first imprisonment in Rome, about A.D. 60, Paul had a certain degree of liberty. He was allowed to live in his own rented house. It is from that house that he wrote the epistle to the Philippians. Paul, who had persecuted the church of Christ for many years, is now a prisoner of the very Savior whose followers he once cast into prison.

Of this Savior he now says in our text, "He is my life." Paul the prisoner has become a free man in Jesus Christ. Jesus Christ has freed him from the law of sin and death. So he writes to Philippi with joy. While he is in prison he writes this epistle, often called *the epistle of joy*. Paul says to them, "Rejoice…and again I say, Rejoice."

The church at Philippi had a special place in Paul's heart. Paul founded this church on his second missionary journey. It began with the conversion of Lydia and the Philippian jailer and his family. So Paul writes this letter full of reminiscence, affection, and gratitude. He thanks the Philippians for ministering to his physical and temporal needs, which was quite remarkable because the Philippians, in terms of earthly treasure, were a rather poor congregation. Yet Paul knows that these gifts show their love for him.

In Philippians 1:18 he speaks of his joy in the Lord and in verse 19 he says, "For I know that this shall turn to my salvation through your prayer." He knows that even his imprisonment must be subservient to his salvation through the Philippians' prayers and the supply of the Spirit of Jesus Christ. He says in effect, my imprisonment will work together for good, for Christ will be magnified even in this, "whether it be by [my] life or by [my] death" (v. 20).

And then he says with great confidence, boldness, and simplicity—and this surely is the apex of this opening chapter of Philippians—"For to me to live…Christ, and to die…gain" (v. 21). Notice the italicized word "is" in the Authorized Version; it is only added to make it a complete sentence since the Greek text has no helping verbs. Paul says, "What is my life? When I look to the future, to the past, and to the present—why am I here? What is my life all about? For me to live," and you can see him pausing here with his pen, and he writes, "*Christ.*" And then he says, "and to die…*gain.*"

That is what we need today and every day as we look to the future. May this be the model for your church and your family. May this be your goal. May this be something you not only post on your refrigerator, but something you know, something you live, something you experience. May this be what all your prosperity and all your adversity looks toward: for me to live—Christ; for me to die—gain! And these two are connected. When for us to live is Christ, then for us to die will be gain, because to die in Christ is to be with Christ forever.

Let's look more closely, then, at the words of our text in Philippians 1:21, "For me to live is Christ, and to die is gain."

The Only Way to Live and Die
1. How Christ can be our life
2. How death can be our gain

1. How Christ Can Be Our Life
What does it mean to be able to say, "To live is Christ"? I would like to suggest four things to you, revolving around the words *link, life, love,* and *likeness.*

We Are Linked with Christ
When Christ is our life, we have a special link with Him. As theologians say, we are united to Him. This union with Christ is foundational. We must be in Christ by faith. In a word, we must have a relationship with Him.

Someone was speaking with me recently and they said about a friend, "I'm connected with him." That is a popular word today. People want to feel connected with other people. When you are in Christ, and when your life is Christ, you are connected with Jesus Christ.

Of course, that had not always been the case with Paul. Originally, as a Pharisee, he persecuted those who were connected with Jesus Christ. For Paul, prior to his conversion, to live was Moses. He did everything right, according to the law, and he would have said, "For me to live is the law," for he gloried in legalism and man-made righteousness.

But on the way to Damascus all that changed (Acts 9). A light shone from heaven; Paul fell to the earth trembling, astonished, blinded, and conquered by God. And you know the story—his friends brought him into Damascus. For three days he could not see, nor did he eat or drink. He could only pray.

And there in "the street which is called Straight" the Holy Spirit showed him who he really was in the mirror of the holy law of God (Acts 9:11). Paul saw that "for me to live is sin." That was something he never learned at the feet of Gamaliel. But now he learned that he was a stranger to God, a stranger to grace, a lost sinner before a holy God. His uncircumcised heart was humbled, and there Paul accepted the punishment of his iniquity.

But there too in the street called Straight the Holy Spirit led this persecuting Pharisee to Jesus Christ. The scales fell from Paul's eyes and he wrote, "It pleased God...to reveal His Son in me that I might preach him among the heathen" (Gal. 1:15–16). His life was henceforth linked to the life of Jesus Christ. He entered into a real and vital relationship with Jesus Christ. He came to love Jesus Christ, and in Christ he was filled with the peace that passes all understanding. Christ became his life.

From that moment on Paul was determined to know nothing

except Jesus Christ and Him crucified (1 Cor. 2:2). Acts 9:20 says that just after Paul was converted and came to know Christ, "Straightway he preached Christ in the synagogues, that he is the Son of God." He says to the Philippians, "What things were gain to me, those I counted loss for Christ. Yea doubtless, and I count all things but loss for the excellency of the knowledge of Christ Jesus my Lord…and do count them but dung, that I might win Christ, and be found in him, not having my own righteousness, which is of the law, but that which is through the faith of Christ" (Phil. 3:7–9). That is the way to live, linked up with Jesus Christ. He is our life. He is our righteousness. He is our foundation.

What is your life? Just fill in the blanks for a moment; think autobiographically about yourself. Don't think of anyone else. For me to live is…what? Is it Christ? The way you are living right now—is Christ your life?

What if you have to say, "For me to live is work"? Or, "for me to live is friends and popularity"? Or money? Or reputation? You fill in the blank. What is the highest point in your life? What is the lowest point? What is the foundation? What is your life? Can you say with John 17:3 that this is life eternal, to know God and Jesus Christ whom He has sent? Could you live without Jesus for a week? A month? A year? Are you linked with Jesus Christ?

We Have Life in Christ
When Christ is our life, we are not only linked to Him but we have life in Him. We are linked to Him and united with Him for our justification, finding atonement and forgiveness in Jesus Christ, but Paul's concern here is the living of our daily life. He is saying, "The aim of my daily life, the means and the content of my daily life is Christ." In other words, Paul is discussing our sanctification.

He wants to know Christ better in His person, better in His natures, better in His offices, and better in communion with Him. "For me to live—Christ," says Paul. "Day by day He is my teaching Prophet, and my sacrificial, interceding High Priest, and my ruling and guiding King. The aim of my life is to commune with Him daily. If I don't have contact with Christ in a day it is an empty day, a sad day. But if I have union with Him, and communion out of that union through His Word, the means of grace, and the pursuit of other spiritual disciplines, I rejoice! For me to live is truly a life in Christ."

For Paul everything outside of Christ is death. Only Christ gives real life. Sin means death for Paul. So Christ and sin are antithetical to each other. That is why Paul is so grieved about his indwelling or remaining sin. It is a sorrow for him. He wages war against it and cries out, "O wretched man that I am!" (Rom. 7:24). He grieves when he sins because he knows that to sin is not to live in Christ.

What about you? Do you see the emptiness of all of life outside of Christ? Do you see death in all that is not Christ? When you look back over the last year is this what you valued? Did you grow in Christ in this past year? Did you commune with Christ? What is all the rest of life if you haven't had communion with Christ? It is empty, isn't it? Empty at best, and it will condemn you at worst. Oh, to live truly is to live in Christ, by Christ, for Christ!

We Have Love for Christ

To live Christ means not only to have a link with Christ and life in Christ, but also to have love for Christ. Paul loved the Lord Jesus Christ. If you love your earthly life partner so much you say, "I love you so much, I can't put it into words. I think you are so special!" That is the way true Christians feel even more about Jesus Christ, and they say, "I love Him so much."

To the Ephesians, Paul says that he yearned for them to know the love of Christ in all its depth, height, and breadth, asserting that it passes all understanding (Eph. 3:17–19). To the Corinthians he writes that the love of Christ constrained him to preach the gospel and to warn against sin (2 Cor. 5:8–15). The love of Jesus Christ was Paul's greatest motivator. It is what made him get out of bed in the morning. It is what made him tick all day long; it is what filled his mouth, filled his heart, and filled his life. It was the engine that moved him to do whatever he did. That is why Christ is everywhere in his letters.

I love what Martin Luther said: "Paul could not keep Christ out of his pen because the Holy Spirit kept Christ in his heart." An old saying is that all roads led to Rome. For Paul, all matters large and small lead to Christ because Christ is all. "For I am determined not to know anything among you, save Jesus Christ, and him crucified" (1 Cor. 2:2). That is Paul's great theme. He said to the Colossians, "Christ is all, and in all" (Col. 3:11). That's it; everything we believe, and have, and are as believers, we believe and have and are in relationship to Jesus Christ. He is our only theme.

What is amazing about Paul is that even in practical areas of daily life, mundane things, or everyday problems, he is always taking us back to Christ. Are there divisions in the church in Corinth? He points them to Christ. He writes, "Is Christ divided; was Paul crucified for you?" (1 Cor. 1:13). If the problem is an immoral man in the assembly, he points to Christ again. "Purge out therefore the old leaven, that ye may be a new lump…for even Christ our Passover is sacrificed for us" (1 Cor. 5:7). If the problem is immoral temptations, Christ crucified is once more the answer: "And such were some of you: but ye are washed, but ye are sanctified, but ye are justified in the name of the Lord Jesus, and by the Spirit of our God" (1 Cor. 6:11).

What about living in the home as Christian wives or husbands? Again, he points to Christ. "Wives, submit yourselves unto your own husbands, as unto the Lord" (Eph. 5:22). "Husbands, love your wives, even as Christ also loved the church, and gave himself for it" (Eph. 5:25). "Children, obey your parents in the Lord: for this is right" (Eph. 6:1).

For every aspect of life, every relationship, everything practical, everything spiritual, Paul takes us to Christ. When he tells us to forgive each other he reminds us of Christ who forgave us (Col. 3:13). When he exhorts us to be generous in our giving he reminds us of Christ who gave so much for us (2 Cor. 8:9). When he exhorts us to humility he says, "Put on the mind of Christ" (Phil. 2:5). When he exhorts us to everyday holiness it is on the ground that we are crucified and risen with Christ (Rom. 6:3–5). Christ is the answer to every human problem. To the lost or to the saved, it is all Christ. He is all I preach. He is the sum and substance of my ministry. For me to live is Christ; I love Him with all my heart, says Paul.

Do you love the Lord Jesus Christ? I know when you compare yourself to Paul you feel that you come up short. But can you say with

Peter this morning, "Lord, although I don't love Thee as I should, Thou knowest all things. Thou knowest that I love Thee. I love the Lord Jesus Christ"?

We Have Likeness to Christ
Finally, when our life is Christ we don't only have a link with Him, and life in Him, and love for Him, but we also have likeness to Him. If we really love someone we start to become more like that person, don't we? It is such an intriguing thing to see an elderly couple who are still ravished with each other, still on their honeymoon, as it were, sixty years after they are married. They are so close to each other. They think together, they speak together, they walk together, they talk together, they pray together, and they read together. They just love each other. They become like each other, even in physical appearance. After a while they almost look like brother and sister.

And so it is in a believer; when his life is Christ he becomes more like Christ. There is a savor of Christ that oozes out of him, says Paul elsewhere (2 Cor. 2:15). The fruits of Christ are the fruit of the Spirit: love, joy, peace, humility, temperance. All those fruits listed in Galatians 5:22–23 are really nothing but a moral profile of the Lord Jesus Christ. The believer begins to exercise these graces more and more. We become more like Christ, so that in the great day we can be fully like Him when we enter into glory and see Him as He is. As John says in 1 John 3:2, "We shall be like him," perfectly like Him on that day.

To become like Christ involves chiefly three things.

First, it involves developing, by God's grace, *a servant heart*, thinking not of myself and what *I* want, and what *I* like, and what *I* wish for, but to think in terms of God and His people, and to think corporately in terms of *we* as believers, and in terms of *we* as God's family, and living a life of service to others in Christ's name.

Second, it involves developing *a loving heart*. Christ had such a loving heart. He was a people person. He loved people. He took up little babies in His arms. He healed the lepers, and dared to touch them although they were unclean. There was nothing that held Christ back from loving people. To be like Christ is to love as Christ loved.

Third, to be like Christ is to have *a humble heart*. He was meek and lowly. The more we are like Christ, the more humble we are. You know the famous story about when someone approached Augustine and asked, "What are the three most important Christian graces we need?" He answered, "Humility, humility, humility."

This is what Paul means then when he says, "For me to live is Christ." It means a link with Christ, life in Christ, love for Christ, and likeness to Christ, all flowing out of knowing and experiencing Christ's love to us.

But then he adds these amazing words: "To die…gain." This brings us to the second part of Philippians 1:21.

2. How Death Can Be Our Gain

Is death gain? Why does Paul tie death to life? Because the two belong together. It reminds us of Question 1 of the Heidelberg Catechism: *What is thy only comfort in life and in death?* The world and our natural hearts try to separate the two. I will live the way I want to; I will live for myself. I'll worry about death later. Paul says no; because I live in Christ, to die in Christ—that shall be gain to me. The two belong together; the one truth implies the other. What an amazing confession—death equals gain.

Death is a heavy loss by nature. We must leave husband, wife, father, mother, and children behind. What a loss! We must leave our work and relationships behind. We must leave behind everything we have acquired and enjoyed. We say to each other, and rightly so, "You have my sympathy in your loss." Paul says, "For me it is not a loss, it is a gain." It is not a loss for the people of God. For me to live is Christ and therefore death is gain, for we both live and die in the Lord.

There are two things we need to look at here if we are to understand this text: what the apostle leaves behind, and what he receives when he dies.

What Paul Leaves Behind

So what will he leave behind? He will leave behind his beloved brethren in the Lord. He will leave communion with the people of God on earth. He must leave behind his beloved son Timothy. He leaves his brother and friend Silas. He leaves all that is on earth behind.

But he also leaves behind the body of sin and death. He leaves behind that earthly state or condition which he frankly acknowledged and lamented: "I am carnal, sold under sin. For that which I do I allow not: for what I would, that I do not; but what I hate, that do I" (Rom. 7:14b–15). He leaves behind the body of sin when he dies.

He also leaves behind a life which at best is only labor and sorrow. He leaves behind a life of afflictions. Twice he was beaten with rods. Once he was stoned. He suffered shipwreck three times. He was in the deep for a night and a day and had been in perils of waters, perils of the city and the wilderness and the sea, perils of false brethren, weariness and painfulness, and hunger and thirst. He endured fastings and suffered cold and nakedness. He leaves it all behind.

He also leaves behind a life of temptation, a buffeting Satan, an enticing world—no more problems with the lust of the eye, with the lust of the flesh, or with the pride of life. He leaves behind that troubling thorn in his flesh. No more unanswered prayers, no more vexing riddles.

Death, dear believer, will be gain for you as well. You will leave behind your sinful heart, the hardships of your difficult life, your temptations, and the thorns in your flesh. Think of it. There will be no more sin, no more Satan, no more worldliness, and no more old nature. All evil is walled out and all good is walled in. No more tears, no more pain, no more night, no more death, no more curse, no more temptation. For me to die is gain because of what I leave behind! But even more, dying is gain because of what we will receive.

What Paul Receives at Death
David Murray has written a wonderful article on "Why do believers have to die?"[1] Consider his list of the benefits that a believer receives in death:

(1) "Dying brings us into communion with Christ's sufferings."

---

1. David Murray, "Why Do Believers Have to Die?" *The Banner of Sovereign Grace Truth* 20, no. 1 (Jan. 2012): 17.

That is a great benefit. Though our death does not pay the penalty for our sin, dying reminds us of how Christ died for us and connects us more deeply and lovingly to Him (Phil. 3:10).

(2) "Dying gives us a unique experience of Christ's all-sufficient grace." Dying can be very difficult, painful, and fearful. Christ will help you through your death hours.

(3) "Dying transforms us into Christ's image." What a glorious thing that is! Death can intensify our sanctification so that as the outer man decays, the inner man is renewed in spiritual growth (2 Cor. 4:16).

(4) "Dying is our last and perhaps greatest opportunity to witness for Christ's glory." The deathbed is a pulpit. It may be our supreme test of faith, and the occasion for us to bear witness that Christ is enough. The Lord has saved many through the testimony of a dying saint. This brings us to the most important point.

(5) "Dying brings us into Christ's presence." That is what you will receive, and that is everything, dear believer. To be in His presence is everything you desire, everything you could hope for. This is the apex. This is heaven's heaven—to be with Christ, to be His bride, to be in perfect communion with Him, to enjoy knowing Him and seeing Him and loving Him and praising Him and communing with Him without interruption! What a life, what a future awaits the people of God! For me to die is gain because I will be with Jesus forever!

Of course, that involves so much more; so much surrounds being with Jesus. Let me unpack some of the blessings of going to be with Christ.

(1) *Dying brings us to perfect eternal life with Christ.* Our death is no satisfaction for our sins, but it is the abolishing of sin and entrance into the fullness of life. The eternal life that begins here on earth at regeneration will now be made perfect. Jesus said, "Because I live, ye shall live also" (John 14:19).

(2) *Dying grants us perfect knowledge of Christ.* Believers know Christ here on earth. But in death that knowledge will be perfected. Now I see through a glass darkly, but then I will see face to face. Here I know in part, but there I will know as I am known (1 Cor. 13:12).

(3) *Dying initiates us into perfect activities.* As the Westminster Shorter Catechism says, "the souls of believers are at their death made

perfect in holiness." We will do all things well as "the spirits of just men made perfect" (Heb. 12:23).

We will worship God perfectly. Believers will "stand on the sea of glass, having the harps of God. And they sing the song of Moses the servant of God, and the song of the Lamb, saying, Great and marvelous are thy works, Lord God Almighty; just and true are thy ways, thou King of saints" (Rev. 15:2–3).

We will serve God perfectly. "Therefore are they before the throne of God, and serve him day and night in his temple: and he that sitteth on the throne shall dwell among them" (Rev. 7:15). We will reign with Christ.

We will have perfect fellowship with the saints in glory. They "shall sit down with Abraham, and Isaac, and Jacob, in the kingdom of heaven" (Matt. 8:11).

(4) *Dying welcomes us into a perfect home.* We will enter into perfect mansions shining with the perfect light of our perfect God. We will perpetually feast with Him at whose right hand are pleasures forevermore (Ps. 16:11).

(5) *Dying ushers us into perfect communion with the triune God in Christ.* We will have more intimate communion with Christ than we have known in our highest peaks of spiritual joy on earth. We will have a clearer vision of Christ's glory than our most lucid insights here. We will forever bask in His smile, bathe in His glory, and feast in His presence.

Death does more for us believers than anything this earthly life can do for us. Death is gain for it brings me to Jesus. Death is gain because it brings more of Christ to Paul and more of Paul to Christ. The whole Christ comes no more through a glass darkly. Every believer will be brought to Christ in heaven to be with Him forever. That is why Samuel Rutherford said that God could make ten thousand heavens full of good and glorious joys, but all of them together could not compare to Christ.[2] To die is gain, when to live is Christ.

---

2. Samuel Rutherford, letter of July 6, 1637, in *Letters of Samuel Rutherford*, ed. Andrew A. Bonar (Edinburgh: Oliphant Anderson & Ferrier, n.d.), 413.

But if Christ is not your life, your death is not gain. Your death is tragedy. Your death means hell. Your death means to live forever apart from God. Your death means being shut out of the favor of God, even the common grace you may have experienced in this life. So what we need to ask is this: Is my life Christ? Because only then when I come to die, will death be gain.

Death can't harm you, dear child of God. Death will only do you good; it will take you higher and farther than the Bible, and prayer, and the sacraments, and worship, and all the means of grace will take you in this life. It will take you right into the presence of Jesus Christ.

So Paul has this dilemma. He wants to remain here for certain reasons, but he also wants to depart to be with Christ. Here, as William Hendricksen observes, we have a "temporary residence," a mere tent; there, "a permanent abode." Here, "suffering mixed with joy"; there, "joy unmixed with suffering." Here, "suffering for a little while"; there, "joy forever." Here, "absent from the Lord"; there, "being at home with the Lord." Here, "the fight"; there, "the feast." Here, "the realm of sin"; there, "the realm of complete deliverance."[3] To die in the Lord is great gain.

Are you ready to die? May I ask you that? Are you really living? That is the question. If you are living in Christ, you are ready; your house is set in order. If you are not living in Christ, you are not ready. Dear friend, you must be ready. You must be born again. There is no other way. The Puritans used to say that the way to get ready to die is to practice dying while you are here—dying to yourself, dying to everything that would draw you away from Jesus Christ.

Charles Spurgeon put it this way:

> No man would find it difficult to die who died every day. He would have practiced it so often, that he would only have to die but once more; like the singer who has been through his rehearsals, and is perfect for his part, and has but to pour forth the notes once for all, and have done. Happy are they who every morning go down to Jordan's brink, and wade into the stream in fellowship with Christ, dying in the Lord's death, being crucified

---

3. William Hendriksen, *Exposition of Philippians*, New Testament Commentary (Grand Rapids: Baker, 1962), 78.

on his cross, and raised in his resurrection. They, when they shall climb their Pisgah, shall behold nothing but what has long been familiar to them, as they have studied the map of death.[4]

I'm afraid that some of you are not ready to die, that some of you are still clinging to empty toys and trinkets of this world. For some of you to live is your possessions, your wealth, or your legalism, or maybe, God forbid, some of you even live for sin, or friendships, even things legitimate in themselves, but you are not living for Christ. You are not ready to die. You are not really living. You could die at any moment!

Rutherford wrote, "Build your nest in no tree here, for God has sold the forest to death."[5] Repent, believe the gospel, and bow before the living God. Don't rest until you too can say, "For me to live is Christ, and to die is gain."

There was an Italian man named Galeacius who was converted during the Reformation. He gave up his estates in Italy and fled to Geneva. His loss was so considerable to the Church of Rome that he was offered a free passage back and restoration of his estates if he gave up his newfound Reformed faith. This is the note he sent back to Rome: "Let their money perish with them, who esteem all the gold in this world worthy to be compared with one hour's communion with Jesus Christ and His Holy Spirit."[6] One hour with Christ is better than a lifetime with this world.

I would also remind you of John Paton who went to the New Hebrides in the late 1850s on the Island of Tanna. He was beset by great difficulties. Cannibals there had never heard the gospel. His wife died after childbirth and his little boy died also. Paton buried his wife and his child, and then sat on the grave to prevent the cannibals from digging up their bodies and eating them. He was left alone. Then his house was burned down by one of the cannibals. He lost everything; he had absolutely nothing. He spent the night hiding in a tree, trying

---

4. C. H. Spurgeon, "Dying Daily," sermon 828, on 1 Cor. 15:31, *Metropolitan Tabernacle Pulpit, Volume 14* (Pasadena, Tex.: Pilgrim, 1976), 491.

5. Rutherford, letter of Jan. 15, 1629, to Lady Kenmure, in *Letters*, 41.

6. Cited in Thomas Watson, *The Duty of Self-Denial* (Morgan, Penn.: Soli Deo Gloria, 1996), 25.

to sleep in that tree. He tells us that in the middle of the night as he sat in that tree the words were as clear to him as if they were written across the sky in large letters of gold, "Lo, I am with you alway, even unto the end of the world."[7] That is the way to live.

For me to live is *Christ*, a Christ who is with me always until the end of the world. And to die is *gain*!

---

7. See John G. Paton, *John G. Paton: Missionary to the New Hebrides* (London: Banner of Truth, 1965).

Chapter 29

The Glory of the Son's Purchase: The Privilege and Right of Adoption

> *Blessed be the God and Father of our Lord Jesus Christ, who hath blessed us with all spiritual blessings in heavenly places in Christ: according as he hath chosen us in him before the foundation of the world, that we should be holy and without blame before him in love: having predestinated us unto the adoption of children by Jesus Christ to himself, according to the good pleasure of his will, to the praise of the glory of his grace, wherein he hath made us accepted in the beloved.*
> —EPHESIANS 1:3–6

The Christians of Ephesus to whom Paul wrote lived in a religiously pluralistic environment. The people could choose from a smorgasbord of gods, religions, and occult practices. The worship of Artemis, or Diana, the goddess of fertility and child-bearing, was a major enterprise in Ephesus. The powers of darkness had a firm grip on this city.

Today, millions of people are also falling prey to eclecticism. They are melding various gods to form their own kind of religion. Witchcraft and occultism abound. Many American cities and towns are gripped by the powers of darkness and secularism.

How should Christians function in such a world? When wickedness is pressing in on every side and discouraging us, how do we keep our focus on Jesus Christ? Scripture teaches us to look beyond the circumstances of this life. In Ephesians 1, Paul advises us to focus on the Father's plan of salvation in Jesus Christ and the wonderful blessings we have in Him through His redemptive and adoptive work. To keep this focus, let us look specifically at Ephesians 1:3–6.

Under the theme "The Glory of the Son's Purchase: The Privilege and Right of Adoption," we will consider the following aspects of adoption: its *author, anchor, ambition, advantage,* and *acclamation.*

Ephesians 1:3–14 is a long sentence that praises God for His trinitarian redemption and the privileges of believers. One of the most important of those privileges is adoption—a privilege that is wonderfully grounded in the electing purposes of God the Father and inextricably tied to the redemptive work of Christ. Paul stresses adoption in these ways because it includes so many of God's purposes in salvation. Adoption encompasses so many aspects of the true believer's walk that it actually functions as a dominant metaphor for our salvation.[1] So, let us focus on adoption, particularly as it is laid out for us in these opening verses of Paul's hymn of praise for the trinitarian plan of salvation.

1. The Author of Adoption: God the Father

"Great is Diana of the Ephesians!" was the cry of Ephesus's citizens when the economic wealth that the worship of the goddess Diana provided was threatened by the gospel. Luke tells us in Acts 19 that the gospel threatened to undo what Satan and his silversmiths had crafted for Diana worship. In verse 27 Demetrius the silversmith complained about the impact that the gospel was making on Diana worship: "Not only this our craft is in danger to be set at nought; but also that the temple of the great goddess Diana should be despised, and her magnificence should be destroyed, whom all Asia and the world worshippeth." It is no wonder that Diana's worshipers hated the gospel and those who preached it.

---

1. Jay T. Collier, "The Prayers of Joint-Heirs Together for Adoption," accessed October 20, 2009, http://www.togetherforadoption.org/wp-content/media/prayers-of-joint-heirs-by-jay-t-collier.pdf. John Calvin also equates election with adoption. In his commentary on this verse he writes, "He [Paul] rises to the first cause, to the fountain,—the eternal election of God, by which, ere we are born, (Rom. 9:11) we are adopted as sons." John Calvin, *Commentary on Ephesians* (Grand Rapids: Baker, 2005), 196.

In Ephesians 1:3, Paul countered the cry of Diana worshipers with his own cry of doxology: "Blessed be the God and Father of our Lord Jesus Christ!" The Ephesians worshiped Diana and regarded her as the author of life, but Paul presented the correct perspective of the children of God. We no longer worship the gods of this world; we worship the God and Father of our Lord Jesus Christ. If we are living in union with Christ, then God is also our God and our Father. That is the first privilege and right that Paul mentions in this passage: God the Father is the author of our adoption. Through the Father's Son, we are made sons and daughters of God.

The worship of Diana was of great significance in Ephesus. Historically and religiously, the relationship between Ephesus and Diana was "forged in terms of a divinely directed covenant relationship."[2] The Ephesians were obligated to serve Diana. The economy, entertainment, and worship of the city centered on this goddess. Christians who lived in the region must have felt great pressure to worship both God and Diana. Paul did not rebuke the believers but encouraged them by reminding them of the blessings they had in Christ. He directed them back to the gospel, to their redemption, and to their adoption as sons and daughters of the Most High God. He reminded them of the wonderful covenant that God had made with them. The covenant with Diana and with the gods and goddesses of this world was a covenant of death, but the covenant of God was a covenant of life and of grace.

Paul referred to the covenant relationship of Christ with His Father by saying, "Blessed be the God and Father of our Lord Jesus Christ." God the Father, who is the author of our adoption, has ratified that adoption in this covenant. It is within this covenant relationship that our adoption was ratified. As Son of God, Christ claimed and enjoyed God as His Father. As the Son of man, Christ was subject to God to fulfill His redemptive mission. This covenantal relationship between God the Father and God the Son was forged in eternity to redeem us from sin and break our covenant of death with sin and the world so

---

2. Clinton E. Arnold, *Zondervan Illustrated Bible Backgrounds Commentary* (Grand Rapids: Zondervan, 2002), 303.

that we could enter a new covenant of grace and be adopted by God as our Father.³

As Paul considered the great gospel privileges and blessings of this covenant, he could not help but praise God for His grace. First, he praised God for His *electing grace in Christ*. Verse 4 says that God has blessed us "according as he [the Father] hath chosen us in him [Jesus Christ] before the foundation of the world." God's electing grace is the foundation of the gospel. Without election there would be no gospel, no redemption, and no adoption. Out of this covenantal relationship between the Father and the Son flows the electing grace of God the Father toward His children. God has chosen us in Christ and is worthy to be praised for His electing grace. Without it, we would not be His children.

Second, Paul praises God the Father because of His *redeeming grace in Christ*. In verse 7, Paul says that we have redemption through Christ's blood "according to the riches of his grace." We who are in Christ enjoy redemption from sin and idol worship. Many people cannot tear themselves away from their narcissistic mirrors of self-idolatry. They have become gods unto themselves. But Paul reminds us here that we do not belong to ourselves. We were bought with a price. Although we live in a culture of idol worship and self-absorption, we have been freed from self to worship the true God because of His redeeming grace in Christ.

Election is the bedrock of redemption, Paul says. God the Father provided the way of suffering and the cross so that Christ might bear our punishment and guilt of sin. In the dark, unknown recesses of eternity, God planned our redemption, and in the fullness of time He brought it to pass. As Galatians 4:4–5 says, "But when the fullness of the time was come, God sent forth his Son, made of a woman, made under the law, to redeem them that were under the law, that we might receive the adoption of sons." We have been redeemed by the precious blood of Christ. God the Father is worthy of worship because

---

3. See also Martyn Lloyd-Jones, *God's Ultimate Purpose: An Exposition of Ephesians 1* (Grand Rapids: Baker, 1978), 53–56.

He planned and executed this redemption through Christ, which has resulted in our adoption by the Father.

Third, Paul praises God the Father for His *adopting grace in Christ*. In verses 5 and 6, he praises God for "having predestinated us unto the adoption of children by Jesus Christ to himself, according to the good pleasure of his will, to the praise of the glory of his grace, wherein he hath made us accepted in the beloved." God not only elected and redeemed us, He has also adopted us as His children. Redemption and adoption are inseparable because, as Walter Elwell and Barry Beitzel write, "In the Bible, adoption and the blessing of sonship are viewed almost exclusively as benefits of redemption, so that only the 'saved' are God's children. The ungodly are called children of the devil."[4] Election and redemption affect our adoption as children of the Most High God. Before we were redeemed, we were children of the devil, but God has now made us partakers of His covenant of grace, not only giving us right standing with Him, but also including us in the warm bonds of His trinitarian love. The Father elected us, the Son redeemed us, and the Spirit indwells us. No wonder, then, that Paul exalts God, first to encourage the Ephesian Christians, and, second, to encourage us as we face a world as bleak and filled with idolatry as Ephesus was. "Blessed be the God and Father of our Lord Jesus Christ!"

God is worthy of our praise because Jesus Christ is our Elder Brother, and in Him we have God as our God and Father. The Spirit of adoption dwells in our hearts so that we can run to God and cry, "Abba, Father." We need not turn to weak and beggarly elements but to the high privilege we have as the children of God. So Thomas Watson says, "We have enough in us to move God to correct us, but nothing to move him to adopt us, therefore exalt free grace, begin the work of angels here; bless him with your praises who hath blessed you in making you his sons and daughters."[5]

It is a great privilege to hear our children call us "father," for it conveys dependence, admiration, and love. But the greatest thing of all is to come to our Father in heaven as His children, crying out to

---

4. Walter A. Elwell and Barry J. Beitzel, *Baker Encyclopedia of the Bible* (Grand Rapids: Baker, 1988), 31.
5. Thomas Watson, *A Body of Divinity* (Edinburgh: Banner of Truth, 2000), 240.

Him, "Abba, Father." When we are hemmed in by evil, assaulted by false teachers, or suffering because of our faith, we should cry out with Paul, "Blessed be the God and Father of our Lord Jesus Christ!" Like a child who boasts, "My dad is stronger than your dad," we as believers ought to cry out to the world, "Our God is stronger than your gods. Blessed be the God and Father of our Lord Jesus Christ!" People around us might know God minimally as Creator and as Judge, but we who have been elected, redeemed, and adopted know God personally as our Father!

We ought, then, to ask ourselves this very important question: Does a eulogy of praise reign in our life since God is the fountain of our salvation and our adoption?

2. The Anchor of Adoption: Our Election

Paul next praises God the Father for *choosing* us in Christ. Verse 4 says, "According as he hath chosen us in him before the foundation of the world." Our adoption is anchored in the electing purposes of the Father. God has not loosely arranged our adoption. He has taken great care in adopting us by taking upon Himself the covenant oath and obligation of His people.

Some people think that election is a difficult doctrine to accept, particularly when thinking of sinners who are eternally lost. But Paul finds great comfort in the doctrine, saying that our election in Christ is the foundation of our salvation and adoption. Thomas Watson writes, "When men adopt, they have only some deed sealed, and the thing is effected; but when God adopts, it puts him to a far greater expense; it sets his wisdom to work to find out a way to adopt us."[6] Watson goes on to describe what happens in God's electing grace, "Our adoption was purchased at a dear rate; for when God was about to make us sons and heirs, he could not seal the deed but by the blood of his own Son. Here is the wonder of God's love in adopting us, that he should be at all this expense to accomplish it."[7] For Watson, the

---

6. Watson, *A Body of Divinity*, 235.
7. Watson, *A Body of Divinity*, 235.

three elements of election, redemption, and adoption are essential to the Christian life, for they are all rooted in Christ.

How does God choose us? Paul has three important things to say here. First, God chooses us "in Christ" (v. 4a). When children play soccer, they choose their best friends or the most skilled for their teammates. God, however, does not work this way. He does not choose us on the basis of any ability in us to believe or to be friends with Him. Rather, we are so vile and wretched that there is nothing in us that should move God to choose us. Every reason that God chooses us is found in Himself. As verse 5 says, He chooses us "according to the good pleasure of his will." God has reasons for choosing us that we will never know. What we can know is that God has chosen us in Christ, reconciled us to Himself in Christ, and adopted us in Christ. Our election is realized in a living faith union with Christ. Outside of Christ there is no comforting election. Because God has elected us, He has sent His Son to purchase us and to unite us to Himself by faith.

Second, God chose us from "before the foundation of the world" (v. 4a), Paul says. While we were yet unknown, God already knew us. He knew that there was no good thing in us, yet He chose us. Before we existed, God was already at work, electing us and laying the foundation of our redemption and our adoption. Can you think of any more powerful comfort than to know that there was never a time that God did not intimately know us? We live in a world of shallow friendships, but God delights in deep and profound relationships with His people—relationships that are rooted in eternity! When you talk to people about their friends and ask, "How long have you known them," they may respond, "For a long time." But God says to us, "I've known you forever. There was not a moment that you were out of my sight or out of my mind. I have been in relationship with you from eternity as your electing Father, redeeming Son, and sanctifying Holy Spirit."

Third, God has "predestinated us unto the adoption of children," Paul says (v. 5a). These words destroy any notion we might have of election being a cold, calculating choice made by an arbitrary God. Instead, it is a great wonder that God chooses any one of us rebellious children to be His children. Our adoption is certified because we have been chosen by God. The word here for adoption means "to formally and legally declare that someone who is not one's own child is henceforth to be treated and cared for as one's own child, including complete rights of inheritance."[8] We who were once alienated from God have now been predestined to be adopted as His children.

In *Sermons on Ephesians,* John Calvin explains the assurance of this adoption when he says, "When he [Paul] says that God has predestinated us by adoption, it is to show that if we be God's children it is not through nature but through his pure grace.... For we have no such status by birth or inheritance, neither does it come of flesh and blood."[9] We are assured that by the grace of God in Jesus Christ we are adopted into the family of God. Therefore, "they whom he calls to salvation ought not to seek the cause of it anywhere else than in this gratuitous adoption."[10] Calvin goes on to say:

> Whosoever then believes is thereby assured that God has worked in him, and faith is, as it were, the duplicate copy that God gives us of the original of our adoption.... It follows then that if we have faith, we are also adopted. For why does God give us faith? Even because he elected us before the creation of the world. This therefore is an infallible order, that insofar as the faithful receive God's grace and embrace his mercy, holding Jesus Christ as their Head, to obtain salvation in this way, they know assuredly that God has adopted them.[11]

Election is like a rearview mirror in which you see the steps God took in electing you. When you look back at the Holy Spirit calling you from darkness to light, it confirms that God has chosen you. When you look back at how you were justified by faith in the righteousness of Jesus Christ, it confirms your election. As we, by God's grace, grow in holiness and purity before God, we are assured that

---

8. Johannes E. Louw and Eugene Nida, eds., *Greek-English Lexicon of the New Testament Based on Semantic Domains,* 2nd ed. (New York: United Bible Societies, 1988–89), 35.53. (1:464-65).

9. John Calvin, *John Calvin's Sermons on Ephesians,* trans. Arthur Golding (Edinburgh: Banner of Truth, 1973), 39.

10. Calvin, *Sermons on Ephesians,* 43.

11. Calvin, *Sermons on Ephesians,* 47.

we are the elect of God. As 1 John repeatedly tells us, when we possess Christ in His Word, desire Him for His own sake, know Him in our souls, yearn for Him in our walk of life, and love those who love Him, we know that we are God's elect and have passed from death to life. Ultimately, then, Christ assures us of election. As Calvin writes, "Christ, then, is the mirror wherein we must, and without self-deception may, contemplate our own election."[12]

In Christ, election is our friend, not our enemy. Election produces humility, not pride; encouragement, not depression; confidence, not fear; assurance, not presumption. Election fills us with joy and praise because it glorifies God and His grace from beginning to end. It moves us to confess with Charles Spurgeon, "I believe the doctrine of election, because I am quite sure that if God had not chosen me I would never have chosen Him; and I am sure He chose me before I was born, or else He never would have chosen me afterward."[13] Or as Sinclair Ferguson says, "Until we have come to the place where we can sing about election with a full heart, we have not grasped the spirit of the New Testament teaching."[14]

3. The Ambition of Adoption: Our Holiness

Holiness is the grand ambition of election. Verse 4 says that we were chosen from eternity "that we should be holy and without blame [or blemish] before him [God] in love." When God pursued us in His love, we were ugly and deformed by sin. Realizing that makes the doctrine of election and adoption even more precious because few people would choose terribly deformed orphans to redeem and make them part of their family. But the infinitely perfect and holy God does just that with terribly deformed sinners! God has chosen not only to redeem us but also to restore us in the image of His Son. He has chosen us to be holy and blameless before Him in love.

---

12. Cf. Fred Klooster, *Calvin's Doctrine of Predestination* (Grand Rapids: Baker, 1961), 29ff.

13. Charles Spurgeon, *C. H. Spurgeon Autobiography, Vol. 1: The Early Years, 1834–1859* (Edinburgh: Banner of Truth, 1962), 166.

14. Quoted in John Blanchard, *The Complete Gathered Gold* (Darlington, England: Evangelical Press, 2006), 163.

Many translators stumble over this phrase *in love*. Some keep the phrase with verse 4, explaining that the pathway to holiness is through love.[15] Others put it with verse 5, explaining that God has predestined us to the adoption of sons *in love*.[16] This phrase can go either way. If we unite it with verse 4, it confirms that we are elect if we are fulfilling the purpose for which God has predestined us. The apostle John speaks of that in 1 John 3:10–16, where he says the basic mark of God's children is that they love one another. Their love reflects that of their heavenly Father, who has loved them from all eternity. This truth is confirmed in Galatians 5:22–23, "But the fruit of the Spirit is love, joy, peace, longsuffering, gentleness, goodness, faith, meekness, temperance: against such there is no law." The first fruit of the Spirit is love, and out of this Spirit-worked love flow all other fruits. We are predestined to produce those fruits of the Spirit, and as we demonstrate those fruits with God's help, we can be assured of our election and salvation.

We have also been predestined to holiness, Paul says in verse 4. Holiness is not just a state or a duty but chiefly a privilege to which we have been called by God. Holiness is what distinguished Israel from the nations surrounding her, for she was to be set apart. God told the Israelites, "And ye shall be holy unto me: for I the LORD am holy, and have severed you from other people, that ye should be mine" (Lev. 20:26). Holiness was God's design for Israel, and it is His design for us today. We have been chosen to mirror the image of God. We have been predestined to be made holy and blameless like our God. What a great and solemn purpose we have been predestined to! Are you living out this privilege? When God elects us and adopts us into His family, we are chosen to the privilege of holiness exercised in love.

---

15. John Piper, "God Predestined Us unto Sonship Through Jesus Christ," Desiring God, accessed October 15, 2009, https://www.desiringgod.org/messages/god-predestined-us-unto-sonship-through-jesus-christ.

16. Most newer translations read this phrase with verse 5. The KJV reads it with verse 4. Most commentators argue theologically for the phrase to go with verse 5, but the argument can be made just as strongly in both cases. Both readings are consistent with how Paul uses the phrase elsewhere. See A.T. Lincoln, *Ephesians: Word Biblical Commentary* (Waco, Tex.: Word, 1990), 17. Lincoln treats both positions but argues for the KJV reading based on grammar and syntax.

Paul here refutes the greatest objection Arminians have to the doctrine of election. "If election is true, people can live as they please, without striving after holiness," Arminians say. But Paul says just the opposite. The very purpose of election is to make us holy (1 Peter 1:2). God's election does not destroy moral effort; rather, as Spurgeon notes, "God's choice makes chosen men choice men."[17]

You may ask how you can be predestinated to holiness and blamelessness when you struggle with sin in yourself. Paul says in Romans 7 that he had the same internal struggle between the old man, his flesh, and the new man. All believers deal with that struggle. Yet, our struggle does not negate our being predestined to holiness because this holiness does not depend on us. Notice how Christ-centered Paul is here. He brings everything back to Christ, who controls the entire Christian life. We have been chosen in Christ, which means that our holiness and blamelessness rest in Him and His righteousness. He has bought us with His precious blood, and He will see our sanctification through to the end. His Spirit of adoption dwells in us as children of God; and by grace, the Spirit intercedes for us and sanctifies us unto holiness.

We live with tension—an "already, not yet" tension—as the children of God with regard to this holiness. As adopted children of God we enjoy holiness in this life, but we also battle ferociously with sin. We experience a measure of progressive holiness in our hearts and lives when we gain the victory over sin through faith in Christ and His obedience, but we also anticipate the day when we will be completely holy, without spot and blemish before God. That will be a great day because God's eternal blessing will then be pronounced on us for the sake of Christ's work in us. We live with tension now because we do not know what we will one day be like. So, Scripture tells us that our mortality shall put on immortality and our corruption, incorruptibility (1 Cor. 15:53). When we finally behold Christ face-to-face, our adoption will be perfected forever. God's work in us will be consummated.

---

17. Quoted in John Blanchard, *The Complete Gathered Gold*, 164.

4. The Advantage of Adoption: Spiritual Blessings

If we have been adopted by God, the Father blesses us with all spiritual blessings in Christ. Union with Christ makes us partakers of a vast spiritual treasury in heavenly places. From the moment of our union with Christ by faith, we were given those blessings to enjoy. In verse 3, Paul tells us that God has blessed us with every spiritual blessing *in Christ*. The verb is in the past tense, showing that these blessings are not only in the future, but have already been given. Outside of Christ there are no blessings, only misery, shame, guilt, and a future of everlasting punishment. These blessings include what Paul is speaking about here and so much more! While they are heavenly blessings, we enjoy them here on earth as the children of God. We enjoy them in Christ, for He is the source of all these blessings. They come to us in Christ our Elder Brother. Hugh Martin summarizes these blessings in this way:

> How rich and glorious, then, is Christ, considered as the treasure-house of all spiritual blessings. In him we find laid up for us election, adoption, acceptance, redemption, inheritance, the Spirit's unction, seal and earnest. He is the Elect, the Son, the Beloved, the Redeemer, the Heir, the Anointed and Sealed of the Spirit.... We are elect in Christ the Elect One, sons in Christ the Son, accepted in the Beloved, redeemed in the Redeemer, heirs in the Elder Brother, anointed and sealed in Christ.[18]

When we are in Christ, no blessing is withheld from us.

Apart from union with Christ in His death and resurrection, we would not enjoy any of these blessings. Christ's redemptive work alone has made us fit to receive them, because prior to the Spirit's regenerating work we were not worthy of them. The reality of our unworthiness is what the prodigal son realized when he said, "I am no more worthy to be called thy son; make me as one of thy hired servants." Nevertheless, the father accepted him as his son, saying, "For this my son was dead, and is alive again; he was lost, and is found"

---

18. Hugh Martin, *Christ for Us* (Edinburgh: Banner of Truth, 1974), 216, 219. Quoted in Richard D. Phillips, *Chosen in Christ: The Glory of Grace in Ephesians 1* (Phillipsburg, NJ: P&R, 2004), 39.

(Luke 15:24). The father's response to his prodigal son is how God deals with us in Christ. Not only does He view us from eternity as His sons in Christ, but He also assures us of this fact when He brings us to our senses and applies the redemption of Christ to our hearts. When God speaks this assuring word, we essentially hear Him say, "This my *son*, this my *daughter,* was dead, and is alive again." Because of Christ, we are not servants but children of God. Out of God's sheer grace to us in Christ, we receive the right not only to be His sons and daughters but also to enjoy the vast treasury of privileges that it provides.

Unfortunately, we often live as though we had no privileges and blessings as the sons and daughters of God. Sinclair Ferguson illustrates how we ought to be living according to the blessings we have received in Christ:

> When I was a boy in Scotland, I occasionally read puzzling notices in the local newspaper, such as: "Will Angus MacDonald please contact McKay, Campbell, and Ross (Solicitors) at 10 Bannockburn Street, where he will learn something to his advantage?" Angus, whoever he was, was a beneficiary of someone's will, and he did not yet know it. Angus had suddenly become a rich man. But what if Angus did not see and respond to this notice? His poverty would continue. If Angus did not pursue his claim to his inheritance, he would not taste its riches. Do not make that mistake! If you are a Christian, then you are rich in Christ; enjoy and share your riches.[19]

Do you claim your privileges in Christ? Are you enjoying what was given to you by the Father through the Son's redemption?

5. The Acclamation of Adoption: Amazing Grace

Finally, let us look at adoption's acclamation. Paul highlights this acclamation in verse 6, "To the praise of the glory of his grace, wherein he hath made us accepted in the beloved." These words tell us that adoption is not first and foremost for our benefit, although great benefits accrue to us. The significance of our adoption is to acclaim the grace of God.

---

19. Sinclair Ferguson, *In Christ Alone: Living the Gospel-Centered Life* (Lake Mary, Fla.: Reformation Trust, 2007), 123.

As parents, we pour our lives into our children. We influence them each day with our thoughts, our teaching, and our examples of character and godliness. The same is true of a child of God. We have been chosen to be adopted as God's children to reflect the image of the Father in righteousness and holiness. We have been chosen to acclaim the grace of God who has impacted our lives for good. It is by the grace of God that we are what we are. Paul says in 1 Corinthians 15:10, "But by the grace of God I am what I am." He attributes his apostleship, his character, and his adoption to the grace of God. The glory of the Son's purchase is that we have been adopted to magnify the grace of God. We have been included in the family of God because of His grace. We have been blessed in the Beloved because of the grace of the Father.

The grace of God puts our adoption in perspective. We were once orphaned through sin, walking in the smoking wreckage that we had made of our lives. Why would God want to adopt sinners like us? Paul gives the answer, "To the praise of the glory of His grace." This is the glorious acclamation of our adoption: to magnify the grace of God in our lives.

Grace changes us completely. We were once fatherless orphans alienated from God, but now we are the sons of God. We were once full of the filth and smut of this world, but now we have been washed clean in the blood of Christ. We did not seek after God before, but now our hearts pant after Him, longing for communion with the One who loved us from before the foundation of the world. Before grace, we tried to renovate ourselves. We tried to gloss over the glaring sins of our lives. But now we wholly submit to God's indictment of us as sinners, and we rest in the finished work of Jesus Christ. Before grace, we were powerless to do anything to reverse our condition, but now God has given us the power to become the children of God. In doing so, He has entirely changed our prospects (John 1:12). Before grace, we attempted to reduce feelings of guilt and shame because of our sin, but now through the redemptive work of Christ, God has done away with all that pollution. Before grace, we worshiped ourselves and other gods, but now we worship the God and Father of our Lord Jesus Christ. Grace has turned us from cursing God to worshiping Him. By grace we live as the children of God.

Paul goes on to say that God has "made us *accepted* in the Beloved." As Spurgeon has pointed out, we are accepted as believers in Christ's person, Christ's heart, Christ's book, Christ's loins, and Christ hands. For Christ's sake, we are accepted in our persons, in our prayers, in our participation in God's kingdom through using our gifts, and in our praises. What wonderful content is contained in this short phrase, "accepted in the Beloved"!

Literally, this phrase could also read, "Wherein he has *blessed* us in the Beloved." Again Paul links adopting grace to the Beloved Son, echoing the Father's approbation of Christ our Elder Brother in Matthew 3:17: "This is my beloved Son in whom I am well pleased." Christ is the ultimate object of the Father's affections and good pleasure. Through Him and in Him we are adopted, which is the essence of grace. The Beloved Son has blessed us richly, redeeming us from destruction and transforming us into His image. He has sent His Spirit of adoption into our hearts to enable us to cry, "Abba, Father." This magnifies His grace and causes us to praise it. The apostle thus makes a full circle of praise. He opens in verse 3 by blessing the Father of our Lord Jesus Christ. He ends this circle of praise in verse 6, "To the praise of the glory of his grace." The entire spectrum of God's redemptive work commands our amazement, our acclamation, and our praise.

We owe everything to God's amazing grace. From election to glorification, grace reigns and triumphs. John 1:16 says we receive "grace for grace," which literally means "grace facing or laminated to grace." Grace follows grace in our lives as waves follow one another to the shore. Grace is the divine principle by which God saves us; it is the divine provision in the person and work of Christ; it is the divine prerogative manifesting itself in election and adoption; and it is the divine power that enables us to freely embrace Christ so that we might live, suffer, and even die for His sake and be preserved in our Elder Brother for eternity.

Are you praising the glory of God's grace? When visiting an elderly friend in a nursing home some time ago, I noticed that she had nothing on her walls except a small index card, upon which she had typed:

GOD'S
RICHES
AT
CHRIST'S
EXPENSE

"That means everything to me because I live only by grace," she said.

Is that true of us as well? Do we consider it a wonder to be the sons and daughters of God (1 John 3:1)? Oh, what a privilege it is to be children of God through the great redemption price paid by Jesus Christ! Truly, the glory of the Son's purchase of us culminates in the privilege and right of adoption for all eternity! How blessed we are to be on our way to heaven where we, together with millions of other elected and adopted brothers and sisters, will share in a concert of praise to our Redeemer and in communication with each other! In that eternal family, heaven will teem with wonderful relationships, first with Christ and the triune God, but also with our spiritually adopted siblings and the holy angels.

Are you living with the consciousness of your inestimable privilege of being a son or daughter of God? Is that realization compelling you to worship and live to God alone for His great plan of salvation?

Or, do you lack all the blessings of adoption because you are still children of the devil? You need not live that way any longer. The Father in heaven is willing to adopt you into His glorious family. He has no pleasure in your death but calls you to repent and believe the gospel. Will you hear His voice and enter into the riches of His adopted family, or will you persist in following your self-destructive path into the homelessness of hell? There you will have no faithful Father, no faithful Elder Brother, and no faithful brothers and sisters to love you.

Flee, then, today, to the Redeemer. Allow yourself no rest until you know the privilege and right of God's adopted children through the glory of the Son.

Chapter 30

Zero Tolerance for Lust

But fornication, and all uncleanness, or covetousness, let it not be once named among you, as becometh saints; Neither filthiness, nor foolish talking, nor jesting, which are not convenient: but rather of giving thanks.
—EPHESIANS 5:3–4

In the last few years, we have heard a lot of talk about possible radioactive contamination from the Japanese nuclear reactor damaged in 2011 by an earthquake and tsunami. But the accident in Japan pales in comparison to the disaster that took place in 1986 in Chernobyl, Ukraine (part of the Soviet Union at the time). Even today, an exclusion zone of a thousand square miles prohibits public access. When the accident happened, many emergency responders rushed to the scene to put out the fire. They thought they were only battling fire and smoke. They did not understand that invisible to their eyes was the radioactive contamination in that smoke. Dozens of workers died within a few months, and hundreds suffered from acute radiation sickness. Downwind of the nuclear reactor, horses, cattle, and even trees died. No one knows how many people in Europe were affected.

Today I am warning you about a kind of spiritual contamination that is invisible to the eye but, just like the smoke of Chernobyl, has the power to bring sickness and death. Many people today scoff at this warning, yet in their souls is a growing cancer that will ultimately destroy them if it is not removed by the great Physician. I am speaking of sexual lust. "What?" someone may say, "Sexual lust is fun and natural. I enjoy it." But like poison that tastes sweet but destroys your life, so sexual lust is candy-coated death.

We must have zero tolerance for lust. Some places and schools have a policy of zero tolerance regarding harassment or drugs. Ephesians 5:3–4 calls upon Christians to have a personal policy of zero tolerance regarding sexual lust. This Scripture speaks of "fornication," which means having a sexual relationship with someone to whom one is not married. It also speaks of "uncleanness." That does not refer to getting dirt on your body but contaminating yourself with things offensive to God and harmful to you, especially sexual sins of various kinds.[1] It also speaks of "covetousness," a super-sized desire for more and more, whether it is a desire for more money or more sexual pleasure.[2] Put these words together and you have worldly lust, especially sexual lust.

When it comes to having zero tolerance for lust, this Scripture answers three questions. How do we have zero tolerance for lust? Why should we have zero tolerance for lust? What should we embrace or "put on" instead of lust? So, with God's help, based on Ephesians 5:3–4, we want to consider the how and the why of *zero tolerance for lust*.

1. How Do We Have Zero Tolerance for Lust?

Ephesians 5:3 teaches us, "Let it not be once named among you." To "name" something in this case means to mention it or talk about it.[3] This does not mean that we can't even say the words "fornication," or "lust," or "immorality." If it did, then we couldn't even read this verse of the Bible aloud. What it means is that sexual sin should be a matter

---

1. On the association of "uncleanness" (*akatharsia*) with sexual sin, see Rom. 1:24; 2 Cor. 12:21; Gal. 5:19; Eph. 4:19; 5:3; Col. 3:5; 1 Thess. 4:7.
2. Charles Hodge interprets "covetousness" (*pleonexia*) here to refer to materialistic greed. Andrew Lincoln interprets it as sexual greed. See Charles Hodge, *Ephesians* (Edinburgh: Banner of Truth, 1991), 205; Andrew T. Lincoln, *Ephesians* (Dallas: Word Books, 1990), 322.
3. See Isa. 19:17 and Jer. 23:36 (LXX), where the same Greek word for "name" (*onomazō*) is used in the sense of to mention or speak of something.

of shame.[4] It is disgraceful. It should be such an unpleasant subject that we don't even want to talk about it if possible. It is like a huge, disgusting sore that you want to cover up so no one can see it. Ephesians 5:12 says, "For it is a shame even to speak of those things which are done of them in secret."

It is truly sad how our society has lost its sense of shame. While we should not seek to cause people inappropriate shame, there is a healthy and good kind. Shame gives us a sense that some things are not normal; they are revolting, horrifying, and wrong. Shame is a voice inside of us that says we should avoid such things. It arises from a sense of the evil of sin. Sin damages us, for we were created in the image of God.

Sex is not a form of private recreation. Sex outside of marriage has huge personal consequences. A single sexual experience can negatively and profoundly affect you for the rest of your life. Fornicators sin against themselves, violating the natural principle of self-love. The Bible warns in 1 Corinthians 6:18, "Flee fornication. Every sin that a man doeth is without the body; but he that committeth fornication sinneth against his own body." Romans 1:24 warns that those given up to "uncleanness through the lusts of their own bodies…dishonour their own bodies."

God created us to be men and women of honor and dignity. He did not make us to grovel in filth like animals, but to walk with Him in holiness and ultimately walk with Him in glory. Our noble calling on earth includes our sexuality. Sex itself, when properly enjoyed within the marital relationship, is beautiful and clean, not dirty or shameful. It is precisely because sex is good and honorable and promotes a good conscience that we should allow no tolerance for sins that twist and pervert God's good gift. Hebrews 13:4 says, "Marriage is honourable in all, and the bed undefiled: but whoremongers and adulterers God will judge." The "bed" (the sexual union of a husband and wife) is inherently precious, honorable, and clean as God's plan and creation. The price of waiting for sexual relations until marriage

---

4. The idea of shame is clear in the Greek text. The term "filthiness" in Eph. 5:4 is literally "shamefulness" (*aischrotēs*), from the same root as "shame" (*aischros*) in v. 12.

is well worth the exercise of self-control to embrace the joy of beautiful marital relations.

Sexual sin and the evil desires that produce it therefore should be viewed as shameful, a kind of ugliness we want to avoid. There was a time in our society when getting pregnant outside of marriage brought immense shame. Now many people think that living together outside of marriage is normal, preferable, and even desirable. Pornography, homosexuality, and having multiple sexual partners[5] are no longer done in secret, but celebrated, promoted, and forced upon us in the public square. Today we even have a president who has persuaded his political party to inscribe into its political platform an unqualified support for homosexual marriage. We are told that it is beautiful and normal and healthy and good for anyone to have sex with anyone as long as all the parties consent. But God, who made us and owns us, does not give His consent.

Having rejected God, our society is seeing the inevitable consequence described in Romans 1:32: "Who knowing the judgment of God, that they which commit such things are worthy of death, not only do the same, but have pleasure in them that do them." In many ways, we are beginning to see North America slide into the same corruptions that wreaked havoc in the Roman Empire, the wicked society where Christianity was born. We see Ephesians 4:19 sadly fulfilled among us, as people are calloused to the evils they commit, "who being past feeling have given themselves over unto lasciviousness, to work all uncleanness with greediness."

It is time for Christians to rise up in holy rebellion against this evil and to show the world what true love looks like. Romans 12:9 says, "Let love be without dissimulation. Abhor that which is evil; cleave to that which is good." Literally, that could be translated, "Love without hypocrisy, hating the evil, clinging to the good." Fake love, hypocritical love, may accept all kinds of evil with a mindless smile. But real

---

5. We can expect to read of increasingly bizarre examples of this in the future. For example, a government official in Brazil recently granted a "civil union" to a trio (one man and two women). See Mariano Castillo, "Unprecedented Civil Union Unites Brazilian Trio," CNN, August 31, 2012, http://www.cnn.com/2012/08/31/world/americas/brazil-polyfaithful-union/index.html.

love, true love, must always include hatred against what is evil just as surely as it rejoices in what is good (1 Cor. 13:5). If we really care about people, then we will hate sin because sin destroys.

How do we show zero tolerance for lust in practical ways? If fornication and uncleanness and covetousness are normal and acceptable in a wicked world, how can we be abnormal and radical in a good and holy way? Romans 13:14 says, "But put ye on the Lord Jesus Christ, and make not provision for the flesh, to fulfil the lusts thereof." Let me unpack that in five ways.

1. No tolerance for lustful talk.
Ephesians 5:4 focuses the issue on how we talk: "neither filthiness, nor foolish talking, nor jesting." Does it surprise you that sexual sin often begins with how we talk? Immorality often begins with smooth, pleasant words (Prov. 6:24; 7:21). It might sound like a compliment about how good your body looks or how much someone likes you and wants to be with you—with sexual overtones that should be reserved for how a husband speaks privately to his wife. It might be a joke. This world is full of sexual innuendo. In fact, much of modern comedy consists of the clever use of words to make you think of sex when talking about other things. In other cases, people openly talk in a vulgar and filthy manner, such as in telling dirty jokes.

What should the Christian's response be to this kind of talk? We must have zero tolerance for it. We must never speak in a way that promotes fornication or uncleanness. If our friends ever talk that way, we should walk away. If they insist on talking that way, we should find better friends.

2. No tolerance for lustful looks.
Christ taught us in Matthew 5:28, "That whosoever looketh on a woman to lust after her hath committed adultery with her already in his heart." You need to take severe action to avoid lustful looks. This is particularly a problem for many men, but women are increasingly falling prey to it. Like Job, you need to make a covenant with your eyes not to look upon someone's body with the intent of sexual desire and enjoyment unless you are married to that person (Job 31:1).

Zero tolerance means you must cut out of your life everything that entices you to lust. If you have pornographic images in your possession, whether in print or stored electronically, destroy them. If you visit or are tempted to visit pornographic websites, establish an accountability partner and install a protection system that works. If a video game, movie, television program, or magazine entices your eyes, get rid of it. If a particular person allures you, find ways to avoid that person.

3. No tolerance for lustful reading.
Just as spoken words are powerful to excite our desires, so are written words. In fact, some women who have little interest in pornographic pictures may be caught up in reading books that excite romantic fantasies that are just as defiling. Furthermore, many science fiction and fantasy books popular among young people depict sexual immorality—sometimes subtly and sometimes scandalously, but always in a positive light without showing its tragic consequences.

Ask yourself, "Does this reading material show the honor and dignity of sexual purity, or does it lift up sin?" Remember the command of Philippians 4:8, "Finally, brethren, whatsoever things are true, whatsoever things are honest, whatsoever things are just, whatsoever things are pure, whatsoever things are lovely, whatsoever things are of good report; if there be any virtue, and if there be any praise, think on these things."

4. No tolerance for lustful dress.
Your actions express your character, and how you dress expresses your heart. If you desire to draw attention to your body, then you dress in a way that accentuates parts of your body to grab the attention and stir the desire of others. If you dress provocatively, the Bible says that your heart is wrong (Prov. 7:10). You will then attract the kind of man to you that would be attracted to a prostitute. Perhaps you are beautiful, but Proverbs 11:22 says that a beautiful person without godly wisdom is like a piece of golden jewelry in the snout of a pig.

I am not suggesting that you should dress in a potato sack. There is nothing wrong with spending a moderate amount of time and money to wear attractive clothing. The Lord Himself showed a concern that people have adequate clothing after the fall of man (Gen. 3:21). But we should dress with modesty and focus on the inward beauty of the heart, not flaunting beauty (1 Tim. 2:9; 1 Peter 3:3–4). Very soon these bodies grow old, die, and return to the earth.

5. No tolerance for lustful touch.
As physical creatures, we were made to touch and be touched. In our culture, people use physical touch, such as a handshake or a hug, to greet and welcome each other (Rom. 16:16), without there being anything sexual about it. However, there is such a thing as a sexual touch (1 Cor. 7:1). In order to bless us with a vibrant sexual life in marriage, God designed our bodies to respond to sexual touching and kissing. In marriage it is a beautiful and delightful thing to communicate our affection, friendship, and sexual desire through touch.

But kissing and touching can lead unmarried couples to lust and fornication (Prov. 7:13). Christians therefore need to exercise wisdom and self-control in how we touch people, especially someone to whom you are attracted but not married. There are some actions that the Bible clearly associates with making love, such as touching each other's private parts (Prov. 5:19–20). These are off limits for single people. And if someone touches you in that way against your will, you need to get away from him, end the relationship, and confide in a close friend or pastor, or, if you are young, tell your father immediately.

With regard to holding hands and kissing in a courting or Christian dating relationship, it would go beyond the Scriptures to lay down laws for all Christians. Each Christian must know himself, be wise, and exercise self-control. Wise is the father who establishes guidelines and rules for his children in these areas for their protection and guidance. Wise is the couple who talks these matters over early on in their relationship and, with God's help, resolves to set firm biblical lines of self-denial for their premarital relationship.

Have zero tolerance for lustful touch. So ask yourself these questions. Does this activity stir sexual desires in me or the person I am with? If someone saw us doing this, would he think that we are likely headed for sexual intercourse? If my parents caught me doing this, would I feel ashamed? Dear friends, let there be not even a hint of sexual immorality among you!

2. Why Should We Have Zero Tolerance for Lust?

Why does love for God and love for people move us to firmly reject sexual sin? What motivates us to view fornication and uncleanness as shameful? Why should we have no tolerance for lustful talk, lustful looks, lustful reading, lustful dress, or lustful touch? Ephesians 5:3–4 and its context give us five reasons.

1. Lust is not love (v. 2).

It is no accident that just before warning us against lust, Paul wrote about true Christian love. Throughout history people have confused lust for love. Like Amnon towards Tamar, they can feel so much desire for someone it makes them feel sick. But their lustful desires have more in common with hatred than love (2 Sam. 13:1–2, 4, 15). No matter how much someone might say he loves you, if he tries to draw you into a sexual relationship before marriage, that is not love. It's probably mostly selfishness and using other people to get what he wants.

Ephesians 5:2 says, "And walk in love, as Christ also hath loved us, and hath given himself for us an offering and a sacrifice to God for a sweetsmelling savour." Notice here that the character of true love is self-sacrifice. Sacrifice is costly. It can be painful to wait until you are married. It's hard to say goodbye in the evening to someone for whom you have strong feelings, and nights can be long and lonely. But love is willing to sacrifice yourself for the good of the other; mutual self-restraint is well worth the price of preserving an unstained wedding day and of avoiding a bad conscience in marriage. Premarital relations have a way of wreaking havoc in the area of intimacy within marriage.

Seducing someone or allowing yourself to be seduced into fornication is the opposite of love; ultimately it is an act of hatred. The Bible says in 1 Thessalonians 4:6 that those who commit fornication "defraud" others. The idea is that you greedily steal something precious from them.[6] For the sake of your own pleasure, you have led

---

6. The term "defraud" (*pleonekteō*) means to take advantage of someone, often

someone to sin against the living God and robbed that person of a good conscience and heavenly reward. You have used that person's body and jeopardized that person's eternal destiny. Furthermore, you have also defrauded that person's parents and family and your own family, bringing shame and dishonor on them and robbing them of the joy of seeing their dear children walk in purity to their wedding day.[7]

Sexual sin also has massive public consequences for a nation. Sexual sin is an act of hatred against society at large. Sex in marriage is the cement that holds together the foundation of our society—the family. Sexual immorality breaks up that foundation by weakening marriages. It spreads painful, embarrassing, and sometimes deadly diseases. Immorality also naturally produces children out of wedlock. Standard contraceptives still fail to prevent pregnancy in 9–15% of cases per year.[8] Among teenagers the contraceptive failure rate is even higher. That means that tens of thousands of children are conceived every year by people using contraceptives. What will happen to these children if their parents are not joined in a loving marriage? How many are aborted? What is happening to our society right now as millions of people have grown up without a stable family? Is this love, to engage in an activity harmful to your friend, family, future children, and nation?

This is one great reason to have zero tolerance for lust: lust is not love.

2. Lust defiles desire (v. 3a).
Lust takes something good, useful, beautiful, and pleasing to God and turns it into evil, a monstrosity that is wasteful, ugly, and displeasing

---

financially but also in other ways (2 Cor. 2:11; 7:2; 12:17–18). Interestingly, it is from the same root as the word "covetousness" (*pleonexia*) in our text.

7. The text in 1 Thess. 4:6 says, "defraud his brother," not "defraud the woman," suggesting that the crime in view is particularly against the father of the woman. Under the Mosaic law (Ex. 22:17), a man who seduces a virgin must pay her father the bride-price even if they do not marry each other.

8. Haishan Fu, Jacqueline E. Darroch, Taylor Haas, and Nalini Ranjit, "Contraceptive Failure Rates: New Estimates From the 1995 National Survey of Family Growth," *Family Planning Perspectives* 31, no. 2 (March/April 1999): 56–63, accessed September 13. 2012, http://www.guttmacher.org/pubs/journals/3105699.html. Failure rate for the Pill was 9% and for the male condom was 15%.

in His eyes. In particular, it deforms our desires and makes them dirty. That is why sexual sin is called "uncleanness" (v. 3). It is like throwing vomit and manure on an expensive painting by a gifted artist; sin casts spiritual dirt and filth upon God's amazing creation of our sexuality.

One way lust does this is by wrapping itself in the lie that sex can be our god. Ephesians 4:22 speaks of "deceitful lusts"—strong desires driven by lies. All sin is at root an attempt to treat God's creations as if they were the Creator instead of trusting Him who alone has never-ending happiness (Rom. 1:25). Sex is good, but it is not God. But when in lust we worship sex as our god, we hope for more than it can deliver.

This is a reason why fornication is connected to "covetousness" or greediness (Eph. 5:3; Col. 3:5). Sinners think that if they will just feed their sin, it will be quiet and satisfied. But the truth is that the more they feed their lust, the more it consumes them and the greedier it gets. In the end, lust will turn you into an empty shell of hunger, always wanting more and never content with what you have. The only answer is not to feed lust but to kill it by the grace of Jesus Christ.

Have zero tolerance for lust because it does not satisfy desire, but defiles it.

3. Lust contradicts our holy calling (v. 3b).
In Ephesians 5:3, Paul reminds us that we must give no place to lust because this "becometh saints." In other words, sexual purity is fitting and proper for those called and consecrated to belong to God. The word "saint" literally means "holy ones."[9] It does not describe some elite class of super-spiritual people; all true Christians are saints by the blood of Christ (Eph. 1:1). Ephesians 5:8 tells us that we were once "darkness" but now are "light in the Lord," so we must walk as people who belong to the light. Lust is what we expect from people who do not know God (1 Thess. 4:5). It simply does not fit with who we are in Christ.

If you are a believer, God is building you, together with other

---

9. Greek *hagioi*.

believers, into His "holy temple" where He lives (Eph. 2:21–22). The temple in the Old Testament was a beautiful building full of sparkling gold. Now the temple is people, and we are beautiful in God's sight with the righteousness of Christ and the holiness of His Spirit. Do you want to paint obscene graffiti on God's temple? That is what lust does. Don't you know that your body is the temple of the Holy Spirit? You are not your own. You were bought at the price of Christ's blood. Therefore glorify God with your body and spirit, which belong to God (1 Cor. 6:19–20). Submit to the Spirit's work and grow into a beautiful and holy temple where God will live forever! We have a holy calling, and lust contradicts that calling.

4. Lust corrupts conversation (v. 4a).
Notice that the sins listed in Ephesians 5:4 revolve around how we talk: "neither filthiness, nor foolish talking, nor jesting, which are not convenient: but rather giving of thanks." Our ability to communicate in verbal language distinguishes us from the animals. Nothing like the complex and profound speech of human beings is found in the animal world. Lust takes the noble gift of human speech and turns your mouth into a sewer. There are some people whose speech is so filthy that even if you love them, you hate being around them.

God gave us our mouths to speak the truth in love (Eph. 4:15). He especially gave us our ability to speak so that we could live to the praise of the glory of His grace (Eph. 1:6). Don't allow lust to pollute the streams of your words with the poison of sin. Keep them clean and clear for the glory of God.

5. Lust damns sinners (vv. 5–6).
Paul's warning against lust and greed ends with these sobering words in Ephesians 5:5–6, "For this ye know, that no whoremonger, nor unclean person, nor covetous man, who is an idolater, hath any inheritance in the kingdom of Christ and of God. Let no man deceive you with vain words: for because of these things cometh the wrath of God upon the children of disobedience."

Dear young people, "Let no man deceive you." Lust is not healthy. Lust is not a joke. If it is not broken by the ruling power of Jesus

Christ, lust will condemn you and your friends to hell forever. If you continue in the path of sexual lust without repentance, then you are a fornicator at heart and you have no place in heaven. Unless you declare war on your sexual sin, you remain at war with God. Will you trifle with a few passing pleasures and provoke the living God to anger? Will you plunge yourself into a sea of fire for the sake of a few drops of gratification? Hell is no party, but the never-ending experience of the burning anger of God.

If, on the other hand, you truly repent of sexual sin committed in the past and forsake it, you may find forgiveness in Jesus Christ, even if the scars of sin may remain. As with the woman caught in the act of adultery, Jesus speaks to penitent sinners who are guilty of sexual sin, "Neither do I condemn thee: go, and sin no more" (John 8:11).

Let us pray for God's grace to conquer this sin so that we have zero tolerance for lust. We must not pamper it. We must not permit it in our lives. We must turn from it in disgust and put on the Lord Jesus Christ.

Conclusion: Turn from Lust to Grace and Gratitude

We must put off sexual lust and covetousness, throwing it away like an article of clothing stained by some repulsive, life-threatening contamination. And what must we put on in its place? Every sin needs to be replaced by some form of righteousness and holiness (Eph. 4:22–24). Paul teaches us that we must replace lust with gratitude, writing in verse 3, "but rather giving of thanks."

We must give thanks for the love of God in Christ. Ephesians 5:1–2 says, "Be ye therefore followers of God, as dear children; and walk in love, as Christ also hath loved us, and hath given himself for us an offering and a sacrifice to God for a sweetsmelling savour." Here is true love! Here is the God who loves sinners and makes them His "dear children," adopting them and embracing them with eternal affection. Here is Jesus Christ, giving His life as a sacrifice for our sins so that instead of the revolting stench of our disobedience, He can perfume us with the sweet smell of His obedience and the Father will be pleased with us.

In some ways, sexual lust is a twisted cry for love, but it seeks love in the wrong ways. But God's love can satisfy you and give you peace and contentment. If your heart is hard and cold, His love can give you a new heart that is soft and warm. If you have defiled your mind or body with uncleanness, here is love that can wash you as white as snow. If you have betrayed God with your sins, perhaps sins that no one else knows about, here is love that will accept the repentant sinner. He will be your shield, your glory, and the lifter of your head.

Revel in the grace of God and cultivate gratitude by trusting in Him, for gratitude will heal what lust has destroyed. Lust is not love, but thanksgiving to God ignites love. We love because we are amazed at how He first loved us. Lust defiles desire, but thanksgiving to God purifies desire. It sets us free to enjoy good things but to let God alone be our God.

Lust contradicts our holy calling, but thanksgiving to God fulfills our holy calling. God calls us to give thanks in all things to our God and Father in the name of Jesus Christ. Lust corrupts conversation, but thanksgiving to God gives honor and dignity to our conversation. Lust damns sinners, but thanksgiving to God springs from salvation by grace.

The ultimate reason why Christians should have no tolerance for lust is that Christians have no need for it; we have a God who loves us as His dear children, a Savior who died for our sins—including lustful sins, and the Spirit who lives closer to our hearts than the most intimate companion. Repent of every known lustful sin, and entrust your soul and body to the Triune God of grace, believing in His Son alone for salvation. Know this God, whom to know in Christ is life eternal (John 17:3), and be satisfied.

Chapter 31

Using, Not Abusing the World

Now the Spirit speaketh expressly, that in the latter times some shall depart from the faith, giving heed to seducing spirits, and doctrines of devils; speaking lies in hypocrisy; having their conscience seared with a hot iron; forbidding to marry, and commanding to abstain from meats, which God hath created to be received with thanksgiving of them which believe and know the truth. For every creature of God is good, and nothing to be refused, if it be received with thanksgiving: For it is sanctified by the word of God and prayer.

If thou put the brethren in remembrance of these things, thou shalt be a good minister of Jesus Christ, nourished up in the words of faith and of good doctrine, whereunto thou has attained. But refuse profane and old wives' fables, and exercise thyself rather unto godliness.

For bodily exercise profiteth little: but godliness is profitable unto all things, having promise of the life that now is, and of that which is to come. —1 TIMOTHY 4:1–8

One of the most fascinating sights on earth is a butterfly emerging from its chrysalis. In the process of metamorphosis, the caterpillar attaches itself to a stable object and forms a shell around itself. For a time, this chrysalis protects the worm while it develops its wings. Yet, once it has become a butterfly, it must break out of this shell, dry and expand its wings, and fly away. In some ways, the butterfly and its chrysalis illustrate the relationship of Christians to the world.

God has provided a place for us in the world to protect us and meet our needs for a time as we change and grow in beauty. And yet, like butterflies, we must not cling to this world but be prepared to fly on to glory. Thus we must learn to use the world rightly, for it is but the chrysalis of the new creation.

My theme is, "Using, Not Abusing the World."[1] So I begin by answering the question, "What do I mean by the world?" In the Bible, sometimes the *world* means humanity in general, but we are not talking about using or abusing other people. The New Testament also speaks of the *world* as the sinful, corrupt system of beliefs, values, relationships, and activities of fallen mankind, but again, I am not, first and foremost, using the word in this way. When I speak of using but not abusing the world, I am referring to the resources and objects around us, such as apple trees and horses, iron and copper in the earth, and the cars and computers formed by man out of them. Psalm 24:1 says, "The earth is the LORD's, and the fulness thereof; the world, and they that dwell therein. For he hath founded it upon the seas, and established it upon the floods."

It is fitting for us to address this topic, because how we relate to the world springs directly from the doctrine of creation. On the one hand, creation tells us that *the world came from God*. It is His creation and therefore it is fundamentally good. Genesis 1 opens and closes with these statements: "In the beginning God created the heaven and the earth.... And God saw every thing that he had made, and, behold, it was very good." Between those verses is the account of the creation of mankind in God's image, with the delegated authority to rule over, use, and enjoy God's world.

On the other hand, the doctrine of creation teaches us that *the world is not God*. Therefore we should not worship creation or confuse God with His creatures or visible images of them. That is precisely the horrible error that mankind has fallen into, as Paul explains in Romans 1. By rejecting the glory of God shining in His creation (Ps. 19:1), we have enslaved ourselves to His creatures by making idols

---

1. This sermon is an expanded version of an address I delivered for the Reformed Families Conference at the Creation Museum in Petersburg, Kentucky, on June 12, 2015.

of them. The very world that God created good has become evil to us, not because it is evil, but because we twist it and elevate it and set our hearts upon it to be our God. That is what we mean by worldliness. We must resist and overcome this abuse in order to participate in the new creation in Christ.

As fallen human beings we live in tension regarding our proper relationship to the world. To explore what it means to use the world as God's gift but not abuse it as if it were God, we will consider each side of the tension: using the world, based on 1 Timothy 4:1–8, and not abusing the world, based on 1 John 2:15–17.

With God's help, we wish to consider:

Using, Not Abusing the World
1. Use the world as God's good gift (1 Timothy 4)
2. Do not abuse the world as if it were God (1 John 2)

1. Use the World as God's Good Gift

The apostle Paul warns that we must guard against denying the goodness of God's creation, and against legalistic or ascetic prohibitions that oppose enjoying God's world. He went so far as to say that legalism and asceticism are from Satan. He wrote in 1 Timothy 4:1–5,

> Now the Spirit speaketh expressly, that in the latter times some shall depart from the faith, giving heed to seducing spirits, and doctrines of devils; speaking lies in hypocrisy; having their conscience seared with a hot iron; forbidding to marry, and commanding to abstain from meats, which God hath created to be received with thanksgiving of them which believe and know the truth. For every creature of God is good, and nothing to be refused, if it be received with thanksgiving: for it is sanctified by the word of God and prayer.

Though people who promote legalistic rules may seem very spiritual and scrupulous, Paul says that their consciences are actually profoundly damaged, "seared with a hot iron," so that they are insensitive to right and wrong. Their teachings are the "doctrines of devils." It is diabolical to forbid people to enjoy the sweet intimacy of marriage or the savory taste of ham or beef because "every creature of God is good." Our Reformed heritage encourages us to acknowledge and rejoice in the beauty and goodness of God's world. When we gaze upon towering mountains, listen to singing birds, and taste bread spread with butter and strawberry jam, we truly can confess, "The LORD is good to all: and his tender mercies are over all his works" (Ps. 145:9).

A stunning truth revealed in the garden of Eden is that God not only created the world to meet our needs but also to give us pleasure. The Lord God did not feed Adam and Eve with dry crusts of bread but surrounded them with luscious fruit, beautiful trees, sparkling rivers, and land containing gold and gemstones (Gen. 2:8–15). Paul thus declares that the living God "giveth us richly all things to enjoy" (1 Tim. 6:17).

John Calvin said, "God provided food…not only to provide for necessity but also for delight and good cheer."[2] He then asked whether God would make flowers so beautiful and fragrant if He did not intend us to enjoy them with our eyes and noses. God also invented the diversity of colors. God also made some materials more precious and beautiful than others, such as gold, silver, ivory, and marble. The French Huguenot Pierre Viret (1511–1571), a friend of Calvin, wrote, "God has not only provided in these things for the necessities of mankind, but also for their desires and pleasures, and has desired to join together an excellent beauty with profit and usefulness."[3]

So, if you are a believer, how are you to use the world as God's good gift? Let me give you three ways:

Use the World with a Heart of Gratitude

Paul's words to Timothy give us practical directions on how we are to use this beautiful, profitable, and pleasurable world. In 1 Timothy 4:4 Paul says, "For every creature of God is good, and nothing to be refused, if it be received with thanksgiving." If we view the world as

---

2. John Calvin, *Institutes of the Christian Religion*, ed. John T. McNeill, trans. Ford Lewis Battles (Philadelphia: Westminster, 1960), 3.10.2.

3. Pierre Viret, *Instruction Chretienne* (1564), cited by Douglas F. Kelly, *Systematic Theology, Volume One, The God Who Is: The Holy Trinity* (Fearn, Ross-shire, Scotland: Christian Focus, 2008), 332.

God's creation, then every good thing is a gift from heaven above (James 1:17). Therefore, we should always look beyond the gift to the Giver. Calvin said, "All things were created for us that we might recognize the Author and give thanks for his kindness toward us."[4] I am not speaking of a superficial "thank you" that we say to be polite and then go off to focus on the gift and ignore the person who gave it. That would fill the mind with various things but stupefy that heart toward God.

Gratitude deems the Giver to be a greater treasure than the gift. We must not use God to get more of what we want; we must use the world to get more of God. Every glimpse of majesty we see in the starry galaxies will then make us say, "O LORD our Lord, how excellent is thy name in all the earth!" (Ps. 8:1). Every drop of honey or maple syrup that we taste will then make us think, "God is so good!"

Psalm 148 calls upon every part of the world to praise the Lord because He made it. The psalmist provides us with a catalog of God's creation: the heights of heaven and the hosts of angels dwelling in them; the sun, moon, stars, and clouds above us in the firmament; sea monsters in ocean depths and the fire, hail, snow, vapors, and storms that sweep over the dry land; mountains and hills, fruit trees and cedars; wild beasts and cattle, creeping things and flying birds; kings, generals, and judges of the earth; young men and maidens, old men and little children. He says, "Let them praise the name of the LORD: for his name alone is excellent; his glory is above the earth and heaven" (v. 13). Creation moves us to praise the Creator because the cause is always greater than the effect. God's glory transcends everything the world can offer us.

Gratitude is love returned for love bestowed. True thankfulness is a childlike response of love to the Father who has so greatly loved us in Jesus Christ. It views all of creation through gospel eyes, seeing the world as the handiwork of the God who "sent his Son to be the propitiation for our sins" (1 John 4:10). We respond by saying, "We love him, because he first loved us" (1 John 4:19). In this, as John Owen (1616–1683) explained, God's children have communion with

---

4. Calvin, *Institutes*, 3.10.3.

their heavenly Father. They receive His gifts by faith in Christ, and "they make suitable returns unto him."[5] They use the world with a heart of gratitude.

Use the World with the Mindset of a Pilgrim
We use the world in a way that is holy and pleasing to God when we do so as directed by the truths revealed in Holy Scripture, or as Paul says, as "sanctified by the word of God" (1 Tim. 4:5). We must not use the things of God's creation to break God's commandments. We must also allow the teachings of the Bible to shape how we think about the world and our activities in it. We have already discussed the doctrine of creation. Without faith in the biblical teaching on God's creation of the world, we cannot think rightly about the world or act rightly toward it.

Another major doctrine of the Word of God that Paul has in mind here is the return of Christ and the end of the age. In verse 1 he refers to "the latter times." In verse 8 he mentions "the life…which is to come." He returns to the theme of using this present world in light of the world to come in chapter 6 (vv. 12, 14–15, and 19). We must always view the things of this world in light of "the appearing of our Lord Jesus Christ" (1 Tim. 6:14).

We must use this world knowing that it is neither our true home nor our lasting treasure (Matt. 6:24–34; Heb. 11:8–10). Calvin said that Christ "teaches us to travel as pilgrims in this world."[6] We will know how to make "the right use of earthly benefits" if we remember that "the present life is for his people as a pilgrimage on which they are hastening toward the Heavenly Kingdom."[7] If you are a student visiting another country, you enjoy your time there but you always have in mind that you will eventually go home. In the world, your goal should not be to accumulate large quantities of possessions. You may use what you need and sample what you like, but you should constantly ask whether this possession or that activity will help you

---

5. John Owen, *Of Communion with God*, in *The Works of John Owen*, ed. William H. Goold (1850–1853; repr., Edinburgh: Banner of Truth, 1965), 2:22.
6. Calvin, *Institutes*, 3.7.3.
7. Calvin, *Institutes*, 3.10.1.

along to heaven, or hinder you. We are not tourists in this world living for pleasure and entertainment, but wanderers banished from Paradise and longing to return. Calvin wrote, "For, if heaven is our homeland, what else is the earth but our place of exile?"[8]

The Puritans picked up Calvin's pilgrimage theme and developed it further. The pilgrim mentality, like a multifaceted diamond, includes at least six facets:

- a biblical outlook for our faith and practice

- a godly outlook that promotes conscientious living in the childlike fear of God in our duty to God, to family, and to country

- a churchly outlook that is concerned preeminently with God's glory and the worship, fellowship, doctrine, government, and discipline of Christ's church

- a warfaring outlook, since the church on earth wages war against indwelling sin (for the remains of our old nature lie dormant within us like a volcano that can burn out of control at any time), and against a beckoning, seducing, yet hostile world that does not agree to ceasefires and does not sign peace treaties

- a methodical outlook that trains the believer to use the spiritual disciplines faithfully and regularly every day; and

- a two-worldly outlook, which enables us to have heaven "in our eye" while we are walking on earth, so that we are willing to deny ourselves anything that would hinder us from running the Christian race with our eyes on Jesus and glory (Heb. 12:1–2)[9]

The same Word of God that teaches us that we are pilgrims also teaches us that all mankind is headed for one of two ultimate destinations. Therefore, a pilgrim mindset is also an evangelistic mindset. We are not to envy the rich and powerful but to pray for their salvation through faith in Jesus Christ (1 Tim. 2:1–5). We are to use the

---

8. Calvin, *Institutes*, 3.9.4.
9. Joel R. Beeke and Mark Jones, *A Puritan Theology: Doctrine for Life* (Grand Rapids: Reformation Heritage Books, 2012), 843–58.

world with one eye on judgment day. This perspective makes us willing to make great sacrifices in this life so that other people will find eternal life. It also reminds us that God will call us to account for how we used the world, and whether we did so in a manner that advanced God's purposes and kingdom.[10]

Use the World with an Attitude of Dependence
Paul says that the creatures of God are "sanctified by the word of God *and prayer*" (emphasis added). We thus honor God by receiving our food with thanksgiving. However, that goes far beyond giving thanks to God at meals. The word *prayer* specifically means appealing to someone in power to take action.[11] It reminds us that since God is the Creator and Lord of this world, we are dependent upon Him and receive all things by His grace alone. We express this dependence in continual prayer for God to supply the needs of His people.

Praying without ceasing involves humility. To lift up your soul to the Lord daily is to take the posture of one who cannot get what he needs and desires by his own strength. Whereas sinners look to the power, riches, and oppressive schemes of men, God tells us that men are lighter than air on His scales, so we must instead trust in the Lord and pour out our hearts before Him (Ps. 62:8–11).

This dependence teaches us contentment, for it is the exact opposite of the entitlement mentality that says, "I deserve these good things. And I deserve better." If God created the world, then He has the right to do with it as He pleases. He is the Lord, and we are His servants, created for His glory and for His pleasure. Calvin said that Christians "should know how to bear poverty peaceably and patiently, as well as to bear abundance moderately."[12]

A heart of gratitude, the mindset of a pilgrim, and an attitude of dependence distinguish a truly Christian use of the world from secular and pagan approaches. In union with Jesus Christ, we know the Creator of the world as our heavenly Father. Do you know Him

---

10. Calvin, *Institutes*, 3.10.5.
11. See *entexuis* and its cognate verb (*entugchanō*) in Acts 25:24; Rom. 8:27, 34; 11:2; 1 Tim. 2:1; 4:5; Heb. 7:25.
12. Calvin, *Institutes*, 3:10.4.

as your loving and forgiving Father through Christ? He gave you life and each breath that you take (Acts 17:28). He commands you to turn away from the false gods and idols to which you have given yourself. Just as surely as He raised Christ from the dead, so He will judge the world through Christ in righteousness. How you have used the world will reveal whether you lived for His glory or your own. By God's grace, come to Jesus Christ, and He will teach you to use the world as His own good gift, and for His glory.

2. Do Not Abuse the World as If It Were God

Although the world was created by God and is good, we have misused and abused the world with our worldliness. John describes worldliness in 1 John 2:15–17: "Love not the world, neither the things that are in the world. If any man love the world, the love of the Father is not in him. For all that is in the world, the lust of the flesh, and the lust of the eyes, and the pride of life, is not of the Father, but is of the world. And the world passeth away, and the lust thereof: but he that doeth the will of God abideth for ever."

Here John does not use *world* to refer to God's created order, but to man's sinful disorder. John is talking about Satan's kingdom of darkness, which includes all people who are under his rule and living according to the standards of this world. He is also referring to all the "things," whether ideas and teachings or material possessions and physical experiences, that the world uses to promote its agenda. Calvin wrote, "By the *world* understand everything connected with the present life, apart from the kingdom of God and the hope of eternal life…. In the world are pleasures, delights, and all those allurements by which man is captivated, so as to withdraw himself from God."[13]

Worldliness is human nature without God. The goal of worldly people is to live horizontally rather than vertically, to move forward rather than to look upward. Worldly people seek material prosperity and despise holiness. They burst with selfish desires and disdain heartfelt supplications. They are controlled by worldly pursuits of

---

13. John Calvin, *Commentaries on the Catholic Epistles*, trans. John Owen, vol. 22, *Calvin's Commentaries* (repr., Grand Rapids: Baker, 1999), 186 [1 John 2:15].

this world's trinity of pleasure, profit, and position. Each of us by nature is worldly. As sinners, we belong to this world; it is our natural habitat. We are born with a worldly mind that is "not subject to the law of God, neither can be" (Rom. 8:7). As much as we were tied to our mothers by an umbilical cord, so we were tied to the world from the time of our conception and birth. Our understanding has been darkened (Eph. 4:18) by the guilt of Adam's sin imputed to us and the pollution of his sin passed on to us (Rom. 5:12–21; Ps. 51:5). We are naturally and thoroughly self-seeking and self-indulgent—without regard for God, yes, even prone to hate God!

That doesn't mean we are not masters at masking our worldliness in our outward behavior. John's teaching shows us that worldliness can be very subtle, for it pertains to what we love in our hearts, not just our outward behavior. Worldliness does not always openly reject God. Worldliness can be in men who speak Christian words or even claim to be Christian leaders (1 John 4:1, 5). Worldliness can coexist with high moral standards and lofty idealism. One can be stained by the world by showing favoritism to the rich, by having a bitterly destructive tongue, by getting into quarrels because he is not getting what he wants, or by taking advantage of his employees and workers (see the epistle of James). A straight-A student who does not go to drinking parties can still be worldly.

Worldliness is not always blatant conformity to popular culture, either. We often tend to think of worldliness as the young woman who shops all the time for the trendiest clothing, and dates one young man after another looking for someone to make her feel good about herself. Or perhaps we think of a young man who is addicted to the latest technology or to sports trivia. In reality, a monk eating vegetables in a hut with no internet connection can be worldly as he lives by man-made rules for spirituality (Col. 2:20–23).

How then does worldliness display itself? Here are three ways worldliness shows itself, so that you can discern it in yourself and in your children.

We Abuse the World with Selfish Greed
Worldliness is human love not ruled by the love of God. John writes

in 1 John 2:15, "Love not the world, neither the things that are in the world. If any man love the world, the love of the Father is not in him." The Bible defines worldliness as self-centered love for people and things in the world, in contrast to love that flows first and foremost to God. It is self-love that has put out its own eyes and gone astray.

As a result, John says in verse 16 that worldliness is love degraded into lust, not just sexual lust but greedy desire of any kind. It uses God and people to satisfy our craving for things that please our sensual natures, surrounding ourselves with beautiful and valuable treasures, or boosting our images among friends. Worldliness is exemplified in a recent advertisement featuring a luxury car emblazoned with the words, "Thou shalt covet," which is a blasphemous perversion of the tenth commandment.

God created man to enjoy all things in creation by receiving God's *grace*, relying on God's *power*, obeying God's *will*, and pursuing God's *glory*. But fallen man has rejected God's love for us and cast love for God out of his heart. He now loves only himself and the things of God's creation with a wrongful and idolatrous love. Even if he affirms the doctrine of creation with his lips, he has rejected its application to his heart. Instead he chooses the world to be his God, and loves it with all his heart. He takes the gift and scorns the Giver.

This form of worldliness often disguises itself as a matter of human *need*. Natural and healthy desires grow into ravenous and roaring lions, demanding satisfaction with the words, "I need it." The more we feed these monsters, the larger and stronger they grow, until they devour our very souls. John contrasts this with our true need to do the will of God. The meat and bread of our souls is to do the will of the God who made us and calls us to glorify Him.

These two loves are incompatible. Jesus said, "No one can serve two masters; for either he will hate the one, and love the other; or else he will hold to the one, and despise the other" (Matt. 6:24). Love of the world will destroy us. Paul says in 1 Timothy 6:10, "For the love of money is the root of all evil: which while some coveted after, they have erred from the faith, and pierced themselves through with many sorrows." One love must rule our lives: a holy passion for God and the things of God. But since the fall of man, our souls have been pulled as by hook and line to abuse the world.

We Abuse the World with a Mindset of Materialism
Worldliness values physical appearance more than the image of God in a person's soul. The lust of the flesh, the lust of the eyes, and the pride of life conspire to make us crave things for the body. Worldliness often manifests itself as a yearning for beautiful, expensive, and pleasant things. We live in a world that schools our children to value possessions and outward appearances. Our children will covet a good-looking girlfriend or boyfriend, expensive cars, in-style clothes, new technology, and many other material things. Our daughters compete to be the most attractive. Our boys want to be the strongest or most successful in sports, school, or work. Ironically, this preoccupation with the physical and the material may be turned upside down into a sinful abuse of our bodies through religious asceticism, cutting oneself, or eating disorders.

Worldliness involves preoccupation with temporal things instead of the eternal kingdom of God. John says, "And the world passeth away, and the lust thereof: but he that doeth the will of God abideth for ever" (1 John 2:17). Few things distract our children from serving God as much as neglecting the spiritual and eternal. Our children often view life through the lens of the present. They have trouble learning lessons from the past, and they fail to see that their decisions and choices will have consequences in the future. Instant gratification rules their ethics and becomes their all. This lack of perspective greatly harms our children. When we and our children only think in terms of the temporal, the earthly, and the fleshly, it is no wonder that the things of the world appear so important. If this life were the only life we all lived for, surely we'd all want to make the most of it (Eccl. 2:24).

But this world's pleasures are temporary. Calvin said, "What is most precious in the world and deemed especially desirable, is nothing but a shadowy phantom."[14] The world is our passage, not our

---
14. Calvin, *Commentaries on the Catholic Epistles*, 188 [1 John 2:17].

portion. God has marked the day of our death on His calendar. What will you gain if you gain the whole world, but lose your own soul? As Spurgeon bluntly put it, you will end up with nothing but a coffin on your back and grave dust in your mouth. But eternal glory awaits the child of God. As believers, we understand that we are only renters here; our real home is in heaven.

We Abuse the World with a Spirit of Pride
Worldliness feeds the pride of life. Pride is a dreadful sin. Other sins flee from God, but pride turns on God, attacks Him, and seeks to usurp His throne. That is the character of pride from our fall in Adam until our dying breath. As George Swinnock (ca. 1627–1673) said, "Pride is the shirt of the soul, put on first and put off last."

Pride comes in all varieties, forms, and shapes. Jonathan Edwards said that pride is like an onion—if you peel off one layer, there is always another layer underneath. Oh, the depth and tragedy of our hearts' pride! No wonder then that of the seven things that God hates, four of them are connected to pride (Prov. 6:16–19).

Pride is not always easy to identify. Our children can be prideful with good grades, and they can be prideful with bad grades. They can be prideful when they are complimented by their parents, and prideful when their parents rebuke them. Children can take pride in the amount of material possessions they have, and they can be prideful about the things they don't have. Pride can be present when our children sin willingly, and pride can be present when our children attempt to do what's good. Man's very nature and essence rests in a prideful estimation of himself. We need to teach our children to be God-centered, which will enable them to be others-centered (Rom. 12:1–16).

Worldly pride wants to please sinful man and not God. This is part of what John means when he says, "If any man love the world, the love of the Father is not in him." We naturally seek to please those whom we love. Christ says in John 5:42, "But I know you, that ye have not the love of God in you." How was that demonstrated? In verse 44, Jesus explains, "How can ye believe, which receive honour one of another, and seek not the honour that cometh from God only?" Men with worldly pride live for the smiles of men rather than the smile of God.

Our children, from their youngest years, will hear the message of people-pleasing preached to them by the world. They will be pressured to be cool, attractive, or fashionable in the eyes of others, such as the boy down the street, or a boss at a part-time job, or a college professor. The world will seek to squeeze our children into its mold by demanding that they please people regardless of how corrupt or deceived those people may be. Worldliness then is the hollow shell of our love for people and things minus the love of God. It is the sad, empty, and blasphemous love of the world.

Conclusion: Overcoming Worldliness in Your Family
Our nation has fallen into gross abuse of the world. Rather than cultivating a heart of gratitude, much of America has a heart of greed. Covetousness and the sense of entitlement prevail. The pursuit of happiness has degenerated into the pursuit of pleasure and affluence. Instead of the mindset of pilgrims on the road to heaven, Americans often have a mindset of materialism in which happiness is defined by dollar signs and possessions. Whereas the doctrine of creation instills a spirit of dependence exhibited in prayer, our nation has lifted itself up in pride and people-pleasing.

But thanks be to God, Jesus Christ still saves sinners. Jesus Christ says in John 15:19, "If ye were of the world, the world would love his own: but because ye are not of the world, but I have chosen you out of the world, therefore the world hateth you." Rejection of worldliness requires more than just head knowledge of biblical doctrine; it requires a new heart via the Holy Spirit. When the love of God enters our lives through the gospel and dwells within us (1 John 4:7–12), we may overcome the world through faith in Christ (1 John 5:4–5). But the warnings in the New Testament against worldliness remind us that we must constantly watch and fight against the world as long as we live in it.

I conclude with some specific directions on how to help your family fight worldliness:

1. *Encourage your children with God's promises in the gospel.* Sometimes we are overwhelmed by the command to stand against the world. But Scripture tells us that greater is Christ who is within us than he who is in the world. Remember the promise of Christ in John 16:33, "These things I have spoken unto you, that in me ye might have peace. In the world ye shall have tribulation: but be of good cheer; I have overcome the world."

Remind your children to focus on Christ's redeeming death on the cross. Teach them that God tells us to deny worldly lusts and live righteously by pointing us to the Savior who gave Himself to redeem and purify His people (Titus 2:12, 14). There is more power in the blood of Christ than in all the temptations of Satan and every wicked person on this planet. Remind your children also of the promise that Christ will come again in glory (Titus 2:13). The world's threats and rewards will seem weak indeed if our children can see them in light of judgment day. Teach your children to seek grace to follow Christ and, if they do, help them to see themselves as citizens of a heavenly realm and as pilgrims who are only passing through this world.

2. *Teach your children how to practice self-denial.* Denying ungodliness and worldly lusts means denying ourselves and putting our sinful desires to death by the Holy Spirit (Rom. 8:13). The world tells us to say, "Me, me, me" in gratifying our desires and passions. The way to combat the pride of worldliness is to help our children live in self-denial. One of the best places to begin is in the home. Help your children see the importance of cheerfully serving their brothers and sisters. Give them jobs around the house and encourage them to serve in their church and community.

3. *Rid your homes of needless temptations.* John said that part of worldliness is the lust of the eyes. What are you allowing to enter the eyes and ears of your child's soul? It is tragic to hear of parents who allow their children to watch inappropriate movies, read lewd and materialistic magazines or blogs, buy music that exploits women, or download evil pictures or text on their cell phones. Guard your children's access to electronic devices. Review the books and music they choose. Most of all, talk to them about these things. Use family

worship to talk about the lust of the eyes—what it is, how to fight it, how to practice purity, and why sex is a joyful part of marriage.

4. *Fill your children's minds and hearts with what is good and true.* Limiting our children's access to electronic media or clothing is not enough to guard them from worldliness, for the world is in their hearts. We must therefore do everything we can to see Colossians 3:16 fulfilled in our homes, "Let the word of Christ dwell in you richly in all wisdom; teaching and admonishing one another in psalms and hymns and spiritual songs, singing with grace in your hearts to the Lord." Instead of providing entertainment that makes them passive consumers, do things together as a family to make them active friends to one another.

5. *Train your children to see that no created thing is neutral ground.* All things exist for God's glory and are only properly used out of love for God. Though the objects are not inherently sinful, the uncleanness within us will make all things unclean unless we wash them in the blood of Christ, use them according to His Word, and devote them for His praise. There is no area of your children's life over which Christ does not claim lordship. Material possessions, personal relationships, families, school work, work, spare time, and entertainment are all tools the devil can use to conquer our children with worldliness. Teach your children how to use everything humbly and in gratitude to God.

6. *Be a model for your children in fighting against the world.* Don't just teach these things to your children; do them yourself. Titus 2:7–8 says, "In all things shewing thyself a pattern of good works: in doctrine shewing uncorruptness, gravity, sincerity, sound speech, that cannot be condemned; that he that is of the contrary part may be ashamed, having no evil thing to say of you." If modeling righteousness is the responsibility of the minister in the church, how much more must fathers and mothers be "a pattern of good works" for their children? Many children struggle with worldliness because their parents have not stopped struggling with it. Many parents live as people-pleasers, regard outward appearance as more important

than internal appearance, love material things, live with a temporal outlook on life, and feed on pride. How then can they expect their children to do otherwise?

The Dutch preacher Willem Teellinck (1579–1629) compared the world to a monster with sharp horns that it uses to attack people. One of those horns, he said, is "wrong yet celebrated and very distinguished role models."[15] The church's defense against this horn is the "examples of pious and godly persons in every age" who "lived undefiled by the world."[16] Which will you be: a horn by which the world pierces your children, or an example of godliness for them to follow?

7. Pray for God to give your family kingdom grace. As we have seen, worldliness is not simply external; it is an issue of the heart. As such, we cannot merely regulate our children's outward behavior. To successfully beat back worldliness, our children need new hearts. Pray earnestly that your children will come to embrace the gospel through faith and to trust in Jesus Christ as their only hope of beating back worldliness. Without prayer and the work of the Holy Spirit, everything we do for our children will ultimately fail. However, we overcome through believing prayer. Although the Heidelberg Catechism says, "our mortal enemies, the devil, the world, and our own flesh, cease not to assault us," it also assures us that the Lord will "preserve and strengthen us by the power of [His] Holy Spirit, that we may not be overcome in this spiritual warfare, but constantly and strenuously may resist our foes till at last we obtain a complete victory."[17]

May God give us grace to live in the tension of using but not abusing the world. May we never fail to acknowledge God's overflowing goodness to us in providing us with the necessities and pleasures of creation. May we learn to depend upon Him for all our needs, constantly praying for His blessings and praising Him for His mercies. May we ever live in such a way that we recognize that there is more

---

15. Willem Teellinck, *The Path of True Godliness*, ed. Joel Beeke, trans. Annemie Godbehere (Grand Rapids: Baker Academic, 2003), 65.
16. Teellinck, *The Path of True Godliness*, 94.
17. Heidelberg Catechism (LD 52, Q. 127), in Joel R. Beeke, Michael P. V. Barrett, Gerald, M. Bilkes, and Paul M. Smalley, eds., *The Reformation Heritage KJV Study Bible* (Grand Rapids: Reformation Heritage Books, 2014), 2006.

evil in the smallest sin than there is in the greatest affliction and that there is more good in the smallest good work than there is in the greatest prosperity.

May we make good use of everything God gives us to help us on our journey to the eternal city, never forgetting that the hundred-dollar bills of this world are not worth the pennies of heaven. Let us also remember the lesson of the muck-rake in part two of *The Pilgrim's Progress*. Bunyan wrote that Christiana was taken into a room where a man held a tool for raking the dirt. Another person stood by him, offering him a beautiful, heavenly crown in exchange for the muck-rake. But the man never looked up at the crown above his head and paid no attention to the offer. Instead, he kept looking down, giving all his attention to gathering up grass, sticks, and dirt. Bunyan said that this man was "a man of this world."[18] May God grant that through our words, example, training, and prayers, our families may look up from the dirt and sticks of this world to see the glory of God in Christ and gladly trade the muck-rake for a crown.

---

18. John Bunyan, *The Pilgrim's Progress* (1895; repr., Edinburgh: Banner of Truth, 1977), 233.

Chapter 32

Holding Fast to Christ Who Holds Fast to You

> *Seeing then that we have a great high priest, that is passed into the heavens, Jesus the Son of God, let us hold fast our profession. For we have not an high priest which cannot be touched with the feelings of our infirmities; but was in all points tempted like as we are, yet without sin. Let us therefore come boldly unto the throne of grace, that we may obtain mercy, and find grace to help in time of need.*
> —HEBREWS 4:14–16

God's Word is like a sharp sword that pierces our hearts, and an X-ray machine that scans our innermost thoughts. Before the searching eyes of the Lord, all things are exposed and laid bare (Heb. 4:12–13). The people chosen by the Father, purchased by the Son, and sealed with the Spirit, know this by experience. Like someone who pulls back a rug to reveal the dirt that has been swept under it, the Holy Spirit uses God's Word to show children how they have sinned against their parents, parents how they have sinned against their children, and all people how they have sinned against God. For a time, many try to form their own religion and righteousness to deliver themselves from their guilt and grief, and for a while it seems to go rather well. However, like Jonah's gourd, what once shielded them from the tepid heat of a guilty conscience withers under God's blast of light. Then they see that they cannot save themselves. The cry arises in their hearts, "Is there no way by which I may escape eternal punishment, and be again received into God's favor?" (Heidelberg Catechism, Q. 12).

The great wonder of God's grace is the truth that God has provided a way. From eternity the divine Trinity planned that Jesus Christ, the incarnate Son of God, should become that way. The Father sent His Son, and the Son came in the power of the Holy Spirit, to accomplish redemption for sinners. The epistle to the Hebrews reveals God's Son as our Prophet to make known the way of salvation, our King to make us bow to salvation, and our Priest to obtain this salvation by His precious blood. It is of this Savior and of His fullness as Prophet, King, and Priest that the Holy Spirit speaks in Hebrews 4:14–16.

Hebrews addresses people who already know the way to God and have professed their faith in Christ, but have become discouraged and are in danger of drifting away from their hope. It warns us against the terrible consequences of falling away from the living God and encourages believers to keep on believing and to stay faithful to the Lord. If today you are still in your sins and not saved by grace through faith in Jesus Christ, then it is my prayer that this message will be a tool in the hand of God to rescue you even now. However, this text of Scripture especially speaks to God's saved people, urging them to "hold fast" or cling firmly to Jesus Christ. In God's Son, their great High Priest, discouraged and doubting Christians can find all that they need to take heart, press on, and persevere in the pathway of obedience.

It may be that you have come to this service deeply discouraged. Your heart is crying out to God, "I believe; help thou mine unbelief!" (Mark 9:24). Maybe, if you were honest, you would need to admit that you are tempted to walk away from Christianity and give up on the faith. Sin seems so strong, you feel so weak, and there is something darkly appealing about sinful ways of life. Perhaps your case is not so dire, but you feel tempted to give up on your calling to bring up your children in the nurture and admonition of the Lord. You never thought that your children would resist instruction so fiercely; you never thought that you would find it so hard to go on teaching them consistently and faithfully. Whatever your case may be, the Word of God is calling you to cling to Christ, and—if you are a Christian—to know that Christ is clinging to you. You can do all things through

Christ who strengthens you, for he is a *great* Priest (Heb. 4:14), a *compassionate* Priest (v. 15), and a *helpful* Priest (v. 16).

1. Cling to the Great High Priest Who Clings to You
Hebrews 4:14 says, "Seeing then that we have a great high priest, that is passed into the heavens, Jesus the Son of God, let us hold fast our profession." The author does not say, "seeing then that we have knowledge," or "a spiritual experience," or "good works," but "that we have a great high priest." He points us away from ourselves to find our hope in Christ alone.

Those engaged in rock climbing are always looking for something on which they can get a grip. That word "great" is like a projection of solid rock for the hand of your faith to grasp and hold tightly so that you don't fall but keep moving upward on Hill Difficulty. There are many people in our world who claim to be priests, but here is the only Priest who has the greatness, in His achievements, past and present, His station, and His person, that we need. Verse 14 considers the greatness of His priestly sacrifice, His heavenly intercession, and His divine person.

The Greatness of His Priestly Sacrifice
As sinners, Jesus Christ is all that we need, for He has offered Himself as the perfect sacrifice to take away the guilt of all our sins and reconcile us to God. The apostle had already written of Christ as our "high priest" in Hebrews 2:17, "Wherefore in all things it behoved him to be made like unto his brethren, that he might be a merciful and faithful high priest in things pertaining to God, to make reconciliation for the sins of the people."

The word translated "make reconciliation" means to conciliate someone who is angry so that rather than punish the person who offended him, he forgives him.[1] The primary work of a priest is to turn away God's anger against sinners and obtain forgiveness by

---

1. See the use of this word (*hilaskomai*) and related forms in the Septuagint translation of Gen. 32:20; Ex. 32:14; 30:15–16; Lev. 1:4; Pss. 25:11; 78:38; Lam. 3:42–43. See Leon Morris, "Hebrews," on Heb. 2:17, in *The Expositor's Bible Commentary*, ed. Frank E. Gaebelein (Grand Rapids: Zondervan, 1981), 12:30.

offering a sacrifice for sins. Hebrews 5:1 says, "For every high priest taken from among men is ordained for men in things pertaining to God, that he may offer both gifts and sacrifices for sins."

In the first place, then, Jesus is great in His priestly work of sacrifice. All the Old Testament priests and sacrifices pointed to this great High Priest and found their fulfillment in Him and His sacrifice. He offered the only sacrifice that could satisfy the Father's justice. The way of reconciliation can only go through the door of a perfect satisfaction to the justice of God and His wrath against sin. There is no other way. Modern man tries to make another way, but to do so he must invent a false god whose love is divorced from holiness and justice, thus cheapening grace. It is not the living God who created the heaven and the earth, the righteous God who loves righteousness. He cannot deny Himself or compromise His justice.

Has that ever become real in your life? Have you ever longed to know that God's anger against your sins is quenched and that you have peace with God? Sadly, we are often so concerned about what other people think of us, and care so little about what God thinks of us. Yet behind all our anxiety and stress lies the unacknowledged fear that God is angry with us. Our conscience may speak with only a whisper, but it still speaks to us of the wrath of God against sinners. I work as an educator and greatly value education, but what good is education if we still lie under the wrath of God? Only by the sacrifice of Jesus Christ can we be set free to serve the Lord.

What did Christ sacrifice? What offering could possibly satisfy the holy justice of God against the infinite offense of our sins? The blood of bulls and goats could never remove the guilt of sin. Jesus Christ sacrificed *Himself*. "He offered up himself" (Heb. 7:27). He was both Priest and Sacrifice. He laid down His life willingly (John 10:18). He gave Himself as a ransom for many (Matt. 20:28). By one offering, which never needs to be repeated, He has perfected forever them that are sanctified, and has delivered His people from eternal condemnation. He brought His people into God's favor. He purchased heaven for them. He hung on the cross in their place so that one day they could sit on the throne with Him in eternal glory.

Do you see the horribleness of sin in Christ's sacrifice? Sin cost the very blood of Christ, and truly, if we can remain unaffected by the love of Jesus Christ in His death, then our hearts are harder than rocks. Oh, to think that He did not die for His friends, but for His enemies! He died for those who, by nature, hate Him and crucify Him. Truly, He is the great High Priest. His sacrifice is perfect, meritorious, beneficial, and comforting for all those who stand in need of His priestly office. He is great because He is able to save and to succor His people no matter how wicked and sinful they may be. His righteousness exceeds their sinfulness. His rights exceed their forfeits. There is a fullness in His death on Calvary which can never be emptied. He gave Himself—a gift of infinite value.

And He did still more. He did not remain in the grave. It is the wonder and the victory of Christ over all His enemies that He arose from the grave and ascended on high. There He continues to perform His priestly office, only now not in the way of sacrifice, but in the way of intercession.

The Greatness of Christ's Heavenly Intercession

Hebrews 4:14 says that our "great high priest...is passed into the heavens." Literally, the original Greek reads, "He has passed *through* the heavens."[2] The author alludes to the Jewish high priest going through the veil once a year into the holy of holies to present the blood of atonement (Leviticus 16; Heb. 6:19–20). Thus, says our text, that Jesus Christ, the greater High Priest, has ascended into heaven on high, into the very presence of His Father. Hebrews 9:24 says, "Christ is not entered into the holy places made with hands, which are the figures of the true; but into heaven itself, now to appear in the presence of God for us."

It is as if the apostle is saying, "It is true, we Christians do not have a high priest on earth, but that is only because Christ has finished His work here. That only points to His greatness, to His superiority. And now, on the basis of that finished work He has passed through the heavens. He has passed through the starry skies. He has passed the

---

2. See the use of this verb (*dierchomai*) in 1 Cor. 10:1; 16:5.

seried ranks of angels. Yes, He, the greatest High Priest, has passed through the visible heavens into the heaven of heavens, not the symbolic Holy of Holies, but into the real Holy of Holies, and there He sits enthroned on high."

And now, exalted in heaven, the great High Priest does not forget any of His sheep. He knows them all by name. As Isaiah 49:16 says, "I have graven thee upon the palms of my hands." Therefore, He will never forget them. He will remember them forever. Not even the smallest in grace will be forgotten by this great High Priest even for one moment. What a great comfort this can be—in times of affliction, in times of spiritual barrenness, in times of backsliding, believers may confess: "I am poor and needy; yet the Lord thinketh upon me" (Ps. 40:17). People of God, no matter how afflicted, how harassed, how tempest-tossed you may be in this life at times, you will never be forgotten. It is His own word: "Yet will I not forget thee" (Isa. 49:15). Upon His heavenly throne, your High Priest, who has passed through the heavens, sees you, knows you, cares for you, prays for you, pleads His own sacrifice for you, and will not permit you to be tempted above what you are able to bear.

But this great High Priest does more. By His bodily presence in heaven, He continually presents to His Father the sacrifice which He once offered, so that the guilt of His elect people will never appear before the judgment bar of God to condemn them. He presents the merit of His blood to the Father, and in virtue of that price which He has paid, He pleads for mercy. The atonement made on the cross for His people is continually kept on the foreground in heaven by Him who offered it up once and for all. That sacrifice is never forgotten for one moment in heaven, because the High Priest Himself is always there, continually presenting it on behalf of His people.

As an Advocate, Christ pleads the case of His people in the courts of heaven, and by His intercession He obtains both an acquittal from all their sins and a grant of eternal life. Speaking metaphorically, He opens the book of debts and over all the sins of His people He writes, "paid in full," on the basis of His obedience and sufferings. Therefore, Paul says, "Who shall lay anything to the charge of God's elect? It is God that justifies, who is he that condemneth? It is Christ that died, yea, rather, that is risen again, who is even at the right hand of God, who also maketh intercession for us" (Rom. 8:33–34). And therefore, what an encouragement it can be for God's people when the terrors of the law, the power of sin, the accusations of Satan, or the pangs of their own conscience assail them, that they are entitled by grace to look up unto Him, and to leave it in His hands, who is always standing ready to answer all accusations brought in against them. In this sense the apostle John calls Him the Advocate of His people: "If any man sin, we have an advocate with the Father, Jesus Christ the righteous" (1 John 2:1).

What a comfort this is to the believer! I hope that you take your needs to brothers and sisters in Christ and experience that they pray for you. It is a great consolation in our trials to have godly saints interceding for us. How much more, then, should it comfort us that Jesus Christ intercedes for us! It is all the sweeter when we consider who it is that is interceding.

The Greatness of His Divine Person
Hebrews 4:14 teaches us that our "great high priest" who has "passed into the heavens" is no one less than "the Son of God." Jesus is God Almighty, the Creator of heaven and earth (Heb. 1:10–12). He assumed humanity, but that did not in any way detract from His eternal deity. Jesus is very God of very God. Therefore, His priesthood is greater than all others, for it is divine as well as human. God's people do not have a son of Aaron, but the Son of God as their High Priest.

The relationship of a son to his father in natural life is only a faint shadow of this relationship between God and Christ. Their relationship is so close that, although they are two persons, yet they are one in essence, as Christ Himself said, "I and my Father are one" (John 10:30). And therefore, what amazing power the Son's intercessions must have with His Father! His prayer is not the petition of the creature to His Creator, but the request of the Son to His Father. If the Father were to deny Him anything He would also deny Himself, or else He would cease to be one with His Son, which is impossible.

Therefore, the intercessory prayer of Jesus, the Son of God, cannot fail. His prayer knows no limits with respect to might and power, and therefore, what a great comfort it can be for poor people who, being burdened with manifold sorrows, feel that they cannot pray any longer, but only sigh and cry unto Him. If their salvation depended upon their prayers, then they know for sure that they would be lost forever. But now, they find themselves leaning more and more upon this great High Priest, so that they must confess, "Without Him I can do nothing. I cannot even pray or thank the Lord rightly. Yet I have a praying High Priest who is the Son of God, and His intercession is always effectual."

Application: Cling to God's Glorious Son
Hebrews 4:14 calls upon us to apply these great truths by a persevering faith: "Seeing then that we have a great high priest, that is passed into the heavens, Jesus the Son of God, let us hold fast our profession." The word "profession" refers to our public confession that we believe in the Lord Jesus Christ as revealed in the gospel.[3] When we speak of clinging to Christ, it begins in the heart, but what is real in the heart overflows in the words of your mouth and the actions of your hands and feet. Clinging to Christ changes how you conduct yourself in all areas of life.

Profession of faith is costly. It can alienate friends and relatives and provoke persecution. Children and young people, are you holding fast this true profession with your friends—not just those at church, but in your neighborhood or at work? Or are you ashamed to confess Christ before others? Are you afraid to pray in front of people to give thanks for your food? Parents, are you weary of speaking to your children about Christ and His Word? Have you grown doubtful that it does any good and started to mute your witness to the children God entrusted to you to raise for Him? Are we ashamed of Jesus Christ? Oh, what fools we are! Shall Jesus Christ confess us before the holy Father and we deny Him before mere men?

There is a blessed people, by grace, who desire to profess Him— not only to others, but also in private upon their knees, in their

---

3. See the use of this term (*homologia*) in 2 Cor. 9:13; 1 Tim. 6:12–13; Heb. 3:1; 4:14; 10:23; and its verbal cognate in Matt. 10:32; Luke 12:9; John 9:22; Rom. 10:9.

meditations, in their Bible reading, in their churchgoing, yes, in everything that they do. They desire that their whole life may be nothing but a profession of their faith in His name, however much they must complain that they find so many weaknesses, so many imperfections and inconsistencies in themselves.

But now, poor, afflicted people of God, the great encouragement of this exhortation is the promise of that same great High Priest. In the midst of all difficulties, He will sustain you, He Himself will cling to you by His heavenly intercession. Therefore, there is always hope in the Lord. You will not perish. His priesthood secures you from shipwreck. Left to yourselves, you would never reach your heavenly home. And therefore, all the glory is unto Him and to Him alone! He is at the right hand of His Father, Jesus, the Son of God. He will not fail you. He is a complete Savior. He gives you the strength to hold fast your profession in the midst of all trials, difficulties, and tribulations, and He will one day give you a crown of eternal life. Then, sinful self, sorrow, sickness, death, and Satan will be done forever, and He will become your All-in-all forevermore.

Cling to this glorious Priest, dear believer, knowing that He clings to you. The hand of your faith may be weak, but the hand of His intercession will never let you go.

2. Cling to a Compassionate Priest Who Clings to You

The danger of looking only at Christ's greatness and glory is that we may doubt that such a high and holy Lord would care for the small and insignificant likes of us. What does the Lord of glory have to do with me, such a bundle of fear, sadness, burdens, disappointment, temptations, sorrows, and worst of all, sins that contradict and offend His holy nature? How can He ever look upon me?

The wonderful answer is that Christ is not only God, but man. He stooped very low to seek and find us where we are. Isaiah 53 tells us that He became "a man of sorrows"; he was "despised and rejected of men" (Isa. 53:3). He has "borne our griefs, and carried our sorrows" (v. 4). Therefore, there is hope, for this Priest is not only highly exalted, but also went so low that He is capable of being full of sympathy and tender compassion towards His people.

This is the message of the next part of our Scripture text. Hebrews 4:15 says, "For we have not an high priest which cannot be touched with the feeling of our infirmities; but was in all points tempted like as we are, yet without sin." He is not so transcendent that you cannot reach Him, nor so distant that you cannot touch Him, for He has been touched by all the sorrows that touch you. Therefore, here we find another reason why you can cling to Jesus Christ, whose sympathy was learned in temptations, guarded by sinlessness, and is exercised toward weakness.

His Sympathy Learned in Temptations

This great High Priest is all that we need, not only because of His exaltation but also because of His humiliation while He was on earth. From His lowly birth in Bethlehem's stable to His shameful death on Calvary's cross, He went through unspeakable temptations and trials for His people. Our text says that He "was in all points tempted like as we are."

As man, Jesus Christ was tempted beyond any other man tempted before or since. He was tempted "in all points." He was tempted during His whole life, though with greater intensity during His years of public ministry and especially during the last few days of His life on earth. Therefore, He said to His disciples, "Ye are they which have continued with me in my temptations" (Luke 22:28). Consider Christ's many temptations.

First, *Christ was tried by Satan's enticements.* The Lord Jesus stepped out of the water of baptism into the fire of temptation (Matt. 4:1–11). He was driven by the Spirit into the wilderness. Satan attacked Him fiercely, thoroughly, and exhaustively for forty days. Christ defeated every temptation with the Word of God. Satan totally failed. Christ never wavered, and emerged from the fires of temptations as pure gold. However, Satan only departed for a season. The demon of hell sought to turn Christ away from going to the cross (Matt. 16:22–23). When that failed, the devil moved Judas to betray Christ and cast God's Son into the greatest test of his life in Gethsemane and Golgotha (Luke 22:3; John 13:27). Yet Christ persevered through it all, obeyed His Father to the end, and crushed the serpent under His holy feet.

Second, *Christ was tried by man's provocations*. His own brothers did not believe in Him, but sought to drag him into their worldliness (Ps. 69:8; John 7:3–7). Crowds impressed with His miracles wanted to make him an earthly king (John 6:15). The Pharisees bitterly opposed Him, and the Sadducees wanted to make a fool of Him (Matt. 22:15–40). False witnesses accused Him and soldiers struck Him unjustly. Worst of all, His apostles abandoned Him, one of them betraying Him and another denying that he knew Him. Many people watched Him suffer and die, but mocked Him without pity. Christ was not stoic or unmoved by the insults of the wicked; the loneliness and disgrace heaped upon Him broke His heart (Ps. 69:19–20). Yet He quietly and meekly received their abuse like a lamb taken to the slaughter (Isa. 53:7).

Third, *Christ was tried by God's testing*. All of Christ's tests came about by the Father's eternal ordination and the Spirit's providential execution (Matt. 4:1). One of Christ's greatest tests was to bear the sins of His people. The heavenly Father set before Christ the accursed cup of death, from which Christ's human nature shrank in horror (Mark 14:34–36). Never was such a demand placed upon a man. To obey His Father, Christ needed not only to embrace the painful, shameful death of the cross (Phil. 2:8), but also to submit to the curse of God's holy law against sinners (Deut. 21:23; Gal. 3:10, 13). He needed to experience the wrath of God and be forsaken for our sins; when darkness came upon the land, Christ fell into the spiritual darkness of hell—the hell of divine dereliction and abandonment (Matt. 27:45–46). Nothing held Christ on the cross except His submission to God's will, and the joy set before Him, on the other side of it.

We so quickly grumble about our trials. We resent things that inconvenience us, and resent those who mistreat us. What are our trials and temptations compared to Christ's? We should put our hands on our mouths in shame over our murmuring. It was our sins that did all that to Christ. He was tempted beyond what all men together could possibly bear, and if not sustained by His Godhead, He never could have endured. Therefore, we may cling to Christ with confidence that He has truly walked in our shoes, through the valley of the shadow of death, and indeed experienced more fully the power of temptation than we ever will—yet He overcame it, by faith in the Word of God, in the power of the Spirit of God.

His Sympathy Guarded by Sinlessness
Hebrews 4:15 says that Jesus "was tempted in all points, like as we are, yet without sin." Our Priest is pure of all wrong, as Hebrews 7:26 says, "holy, harmless, undefiled." If Christ had not been tempted, then we might question whether He was truly human. On the other hand, if Christ had yielded to temptation He could not have saved us from our sins, for He would need salvation for Himself. As it was, Christ could "offer himself without spot to God" (Heb. 9:14). He was a Lamb without blemish, a pleasing and acceptable sacrifice. Since He "knew no sin," He could bear the guilt of our sins, "that we might be made the righteousness of God in him" (2 Cor. 5:21).

Christ was completely without sin. He was without original sin. Conceived by the power of the Holy Spirit, God broke the deadly chain from Adam to his natural descendants so that the Child born of a virgin was "holy" from the beginning (Luke 1:35). Christ was without actual sin. He committed no sin in thought, word, or deed. He could say to His adversaries, "Which of you convinceth me of sin?" (John 8:46). Peter spent years in Christ's company, yet said that Christ was "without blemish and without spot" (1 Peter 1:19).

Christ's sinlessness guards His sympathy from all impurity. There is a wicked sympathy that sinners may have toward one another (Rom. 1:32). They wink at sin, pat other sinners on the back, and say, "It's no big deal." This is not a help to sinners, but greasing the skids to hell. Christ has sympathy for sinners, but never has sympathy for sin. His heart beats with compassion and love for us in our temptations, but also burns with holy zeal that we be delivered from sin. This is the sympathy that we need. Christ is full of mercy to His people, but ruthless toward their sin, and thus He is absolutely committed to helping the saints to become holy.

Indeed, Christ is fully qualified to help us to overcome temptation, for He faced it at every turn, but repelled all its advances. Since Christ has suffered under temptation, "he is able" to help those that are being tempted (Heb. 2:18).

His Sympathy Exercised toward Weakness
Christ's suffering temptation and sinlessness under temptation makes Him the truly compassionate Priest. Hebrews 4:15 says, "For we have not an high priest which cannot be touched with the feeling of our infirmities; but was in all points tempted like as we are, yet without sin." Christ is "touched" with our weaknesses. The word translated "touched" means to have one's heart moved with compassion for someone else's hardships.[4] It is more than just knowledge; it is feeling. It speaks of a unity of heart and spirit as one spiritual family bound together by love and tenderness.[5] When something touches Christ's people, Christ is touched.

Jesus is our brother in adversity, companion in sorrows, friend in affliction, and strength in weakness. Isaiah 63:11 says of the Lord, "In all their affliction he was afflicted." To those who persecute His people, Christ says, "Why do you persecute me?" (cf. Acts 9:4). They are His body, and He is their head, He is sensitive to all that affects His body (Eph. 5:28–30). The Lord said in Zechariah 2:8, "He that toucheth you toucheth the apple of his eye."

Consider too that Christ not only is sympathetic to our sorrows, but, as the text says, to "our infirmities." The word infirmity means weakness or human frailty. The Lord Jesus is wonderfully patient with us in our weaknesses, be it disability in the body, ignorance in the mind, fear in the heart, spiritual immaturity, waywardness, or tendency to stray from the right path (Heb. 5:2). Isaiah 40:11 says, "He shall feed his flock like a shepherd: he shall gather the lambs with his arm, and carry them in his bosom, and shall gently lead those that are with young." When Christ sees us stumbling along in the way of

---

4. The word (*sumpatheō*) appears here and in Heb. 10:34, of the saints' compassion for other Christians in prison for their faith. It is used on parallel with being "companions" or "sharers" (*koinōnos*, v. 33).

5. Compare the use of the cognate noun (*sumpathēs*) in 1 Peter 3:8.

discipleship, He does not respond harshly. Rather, our poverty and neediness stirs greater tenderness in His heart. He accommodates Himself to the needs of His flock, and He will not lose the weakest little lamb—for this is His Father's will (John 6:39; 10:27–29). He guides with His staff, and protects us with His rod.

Application: Cling to God's Compassionate Son
The Lord knows your burdens. He knows your sorrows. He knows your weaknesses and your failures. Yet Christ does not turn away from you in impatience or disgust, child of God. His heart is full of tenderness toward you. He understands how difficult it is to live for God in this dark world.

If you feel frustrated over the difficulty of educating your children, consider how frustrated Jesus Christ could have felt about training the twelve disciples! Even Christ cried out, "How long?" (Mark 9:19). He too knew what it was like to say, "Do you still not understand?" Or worse yet, "Are your hearts still so hardened?" (cf. Mark 8:17). When Christ sees your frustration, He remembers His own experience with His hard-hearted disciples, and His heart goes out to you in compassion and love.

Let us remember that the twelve disciples were not just students, they were also called to be the teachers of others—the apostles of Christ's church. Christ has experience with the foolishness and sins of teachers too. Yet what do we read about Christ's attitude toward His disciples? "Having loved his own which were in the world, he loved them unto the end" (John 13:1). If you are a believer in the Lord Jesus Christ, then He will never leave you or forsake you. The Lord Jesus loves you, forgives you of your sins, and will walk with you through all your trials—always!

Christ is the Prophet of His people, and the supreme and sovereign Educator. Cling to Christ in His tender compassion, and know that He clings to you.

3. Cling to a Helpful Priest Who Clings to You
We have seen that our High Priest is a glorious Savior and a compassionate Friend. There is more. A person may have a high position

and a tender heart, but lack the practical ability to help you in your specific needs. Not so with Christ. Hebrews 4:16 says, "Let us therefore come boldly unto the throne of grace, that we may obtain mercy, and find grace to help in time of need." With Christ enthroned as our Priest, we have an open door to go to God and find the resources that we need.

Nothing is more valuable than access to the king. You know the story of Esther, a Jewish woman raised in exile by Mordecai, who was like a father to her. Esther was chosen to be queen to the pagan king over the Persian empire. Wicked Haman persuaded the king to authorize the slaughter of all Jews in the empire. Mordecai appealed to her to go to the king for help. Esther reminded Mordecai that the king had not called for her for a month, and if someone dared to approach the king's throne without being called by him, that person would be killed—unless the king held out his golden scepter. Not long before, this king had had his first wife killed! However, Queen Esther risked her life by going to the king without an invitation. By God's grace, the king held out the golden scepter. Esther was then able to speak with the king, and obtained help in the time of desperate need. The Jewish people were saved by her boldness in going to the king.

Perhaps you feel like Esther sometimes. You know that you need help. You know that God is able to help you. However, you are afraid to go to the King in prayer and ask. Perhaps your mouth can say the words, but in your heart you have little faith that God will help you.

Hebrews 4:16 says that if you trust in Jesus Christ, then God's golden scepter is always held out for you. The door to His throne is always open. The help that you need is there for the asking. The emperor of Persia was a poor beggar compared to the living God. If Queen Esther could find favor with the king, how much more will the Bride of Christ find favor with God while God's Son sits at His right hand? To encourage you to cling to Christ, let us consider the *throne* of grace, the *invitation* of grace, and the *benefits* of grace.

The Throne of Grace

Hebrews 4:16 speaks of a "throne," a special chair where the king sits. A throne is a symbol of power, authority, greatness, wealth, dominion, dignity, and royalty. Seated upon his throne, a king made sovereign decisions and exercised just judgment. It lifted him up above other people to inspire awe and fear.

Thrones are magnificent. Solomon's throne was made of ivory and overlaid with gold. It had six steps and on both sides of the steps were six carved lions. There was nothing like it in any other kingdom on earth (1 King 10:18–20). Solomon's throne could not compare to God's throne, which John saw in the vision of Revelation, surrounded by a beautiful rainbow and like a storm-cloud from which came forth thunder and lightning (Rev. 4:3–5). The princes of heaven surround it with myriads of angels, all worshiping and adoring the Lord for His holiness, power, riches, wisdom, strength, honor, glory, and blessing (Rev. 4–5).

The Bible tells us that God's throne is also a throne of holiness: "God reigneth over the heathen: God sitteth upon the throne of his holiness" (Ps. 47:8). It is a throne from eternity: "Thy throne is established of old: thou art from everlasting" (Ps. 93:2). It is a throne of righteousness: "Clouds and darkness are round about him: righteousness and judgment are the habitation of his throne" (Ps. 97:2). And it is a throne of sovereignty: "The LORD hath prepared his throne in the heavens; and his kingdom ruleth over all" (Ps. 103:19). Surely, it is a throne that inspires fear.

However, in Hebrews 4:16 God's throne is given a special name: "the throne of grace." The throne of glory is the seat of mercy. This is unfathomable and inexpressible. God's holy, righteous, sovereign throne is a throne of grace. Saving grace is God's purpose and power to rescue sinners from the hell that they deserve and to give them the heaven that they cannot merit or achieve. Grace chose sinners before time began, redeemed sinners by the blood of Christ, calls sinners powerfully by the Spirit so that they are justified by faith and sanctified, and carries sinners through all their trials to glory.

What this means for you and for me is that God's throne of sovereign power is now a fountain of mercy for sinners. John saw in Revelation that grace flows like a great river from the throne of God and the Lamb (Rev. 22:1–3). It is cleansing grace to wash away our sins. It is life-giving grace to make us fruitful for the Lord. It is healing grace to relieve us of every pain and sorrow inflicted by God's curse against our sins. God's throne produces not just a trickle of grace, but a mighty flow of grace because of the love of God and the merit of Jesus Christ. All of our needs can be met and the deepest thirsts of our souls quenched and satisfied by streams of living water that pour down on us from the fountain of life and the throne of grace.

The Invitation of Grace

Our text exhorts us, saying, "Let us therefore come boldly unto the throne of grace." The gospel offers Christ freely to sinners. Revelation 22:17 says, "Let him that is athirst come. And whosoever will, let him take the water of life freely." If you are lost and perishing in your sins, then I say to you, yes even now, come to Jesus Christ and find grace and salvation. However, the invitation here in Hebrews 4:16 is addressed not so much to the lost as to believers in Jesus Christ. Christians still need to come, time and again, day after day, to the throne of grace.

What does it mean to "come…unto the throne of grace"? It is not a motion of the body. There is no physical place that is sacred in the new covenant (John 4:21). The coming in view here is a motion of the heart, coming to God by the exercise of faith in Jesus Christ. Hebrews 10:22 says, "Let us draw near with a true heart in full assurance of faith." Hebrew 11:6 says, "But without faith it is impossible to please him: for he that cometh to God must believe that he is, and that he is a rewarder of them that diligently seek him." You come to the throne of grace by looking to Christ with trust and calling upon the name of the Lord for the help that you need.

Faith draws near to the throne of grace through humble prayer. Backsliding often begins with a neglect of private and public prayer. Prayer is the thermostat of the Christian life, for it both displays our current spiritual temperature and, if used well, engages God's power to bring our temperature to where it should be. How is your prayer life? How often are you praising God; confessing your sins and seeking forgiveness; pouring out your fears before the Lord; petitioning God for what you need; interceding for others; and thanking God for His mercies?

Are you praying with faith in Christ that God's throne is a throne of grace? Notice that our Scripture text says, "Let us therefore come boldly." Boldly means freely, such that you pour out your heart to the Lord. Boldly does not mean casually, presumptuously, or irreverently; we are going to the *throne* of God. We are not telling God what to do or treating God like a mere human being, a sort of bureaucrat on high. However, it does mean we go confidently and cheerfully based upon God's promises to us in Christ. We go with faith that God intends to answer our prayers and bless us with grace. We go believing that God is a loving Father who loves to give good gifts to His children. We go trusting that in Christ all our sins are forgiven. We go with consciences cleansed from dead works, entering the holy place without fear of rejection or dread of judgment. Is this how you pray? If not, get a grip on Christ's gospel, and start to pray boldly.

The Benefits of Grace

Hebrews 4:16 says, "Let us therefore come boldly unto the throne of grace, that we may obtain mercy, and find grace to help in time of need." There are tremendous benefits to praying by faith in our great High Priest. The life of praying is a life of receiving and finding. The words used here echo our Lord's promise, "For every one that asketh receiveth; and he that seeketh findeth" (Matt. 7:8; Luke 11:10).[6] This is not a blanket promise that every prayer will obtain what we ask, but it does indicate that God blesses the praying Christian. Effectual prayers are those that seek from God nothing but what He has promised to give us.

How God answers our prayers appears in the words used in our text. The first is "mercy." Mercy answers to misery. God's merciful heart is His compassion to relieve those in a miserable condition (Matt. 9:27; 15:22; Eph. 2:4). The second is "grace." We also find "grace" when we come to God's throne. Whereas mercy answers to misery, grace answers to guilt. God's gracious heart is His goodness in giving blessings to those who deserve only curses. We have so many reasons to go to God's throne of grace and receive more and more mercy and grace for the forgiveness of our sins (Eph. 1:7), continued protection

---

6. Matt. 7:8, Luke 11:10, and Heb. 4:16 use the same Greek verbs "obtain/receive" (*lambanō*) and "find" (*heuriskō*).

from the dominion of sin (Rom. 6:14), the power to live soberly, righteously, and godly in this world (Titus 2:11–12), and the strength to stand firm in suffering (1 Peter 5:10). No matter how much grace you have received, you still need to "grow in grace" (2 Peter 3:18). Yet you never need to fear that God will run out of grace, for Jesus Christ is "full of grace" (John 1:14).

The last words of verse 16 are, "help in time of need." Christ is able to help those in trials and temptations (Heb. 2:18). His heart is full of kindness and His hands are full of power. Furthermore, His mind is full of wisdom. Literally, we might translate the words, "well-timed help." As we wait on the Lord for answers to prayer, let us remember that God's timing is always perfect. We often feel that we must have an answer now, but God knows when to answer.

What a promise we have in this Scripture! Christian, you can go to the throne of grace and receive help from none other than the Lord of Hosts. Let us, therefore, stop wasting energy worrying and fretting, and instead devote ourselves to prayer and thanksgiving. Hebrews 13:6 says, "The Lord is my helper, and I will not fear what man shall do unto me."

Conclusion

Dear non-Christian, not one of the precious promises I have opened up in this text belongs to you. Whether you are a young child or a gray-haired senior citizen, if you have not turned from your sins and trusted in Christ as Savior, the Lord is not your helper, and there is no throne of grace for you. On the contrary, God is your angry Judge, and His throne burns with wrath against your sins. If you continue in your present state, the Son of God will appear with glory to damn you forever to hell, and the very sight of Him will fill you with dread, horror, and grief.

However, every one of these promises can become yours, if Christ becomes yours. All of God's promises are "yea and Amen" in Jesus Christ (2 Cor. 1:20). You cannot obtain them by religious rituals, good works, or good intentions. You must have Christ. Receive Christ Jesus now as your Lord and Savior by trusting in the gospel alone for salvation. Today could be your first day of enjoying a glorious, compassionate, and helpful High Priest.

Christian, do you see why you must cling to Christ? Who can compare to Jesus? He is the great High Priest and exalted Son of God. He alone has shed His blood for the atonement of sin. He alone is the heavenly Intercessor and Mediator of grace. Where will you find another who is so full of sympathy, compassion, and tender mercy? Christ is the only way to the throne of grace, where you meet with sovereign grace that is sufficient for all your needs.

Therefore, cling to Christ in your temptations for grace to flee from sin. Cling to Christ in times of prosperity, lest ease and success make you proud, cold to God, and harsh with men. Cling to Christ when suffering persecution, whether it is blatant persecution or more subtle slander and rejection, so that you may find grace to persevere. Cling to Christ under the clouds of adversity, so that you may not fall into doubt and discouragement.

Cling to Christ in your schooling. Don't give up when you face discouragement. Hold fast to the Lord, and press on. I was once asked at a conference what my greatest weakness was in parenting. After thinking for a while, I replied that I panicked when our children went through a season when they kept doing wrong and I could not get them to stop. In early elementary school, one of our children got in a habit of exaggerating and lying so much that I began to fear I was raising a pathological liar. However, that child left that bad habit behind and became a truth-teller. When your child sins, stay calm, keep doing what is right, and wait on the Lord. "Cast thy bread upon the waters: for thou shalt find it after many days" (Eccl. 11:1). God's ordinary way is to use training from godly parents for the temporal and eternal wellbeing of the next generation. Cling to Christ, and entrust your children to Him.

Children, you too must cling to Christ. Cling to Christ through all the great changes of life such as growing up, graduation, getting married, having children of your own, watching them grow up, and then suffering the trials of old age. Christ is the same yesterday, today, and forever. Cling to Christ with your last dying breath, for the sustaining of your hope and the glorification of His name. Cling to Christ, I say, every day of your life, for to live is Christ.

And as you cling to Christ, remember that your High Priest clings to you. He is praying for you, even when you are not praying. He is loving you, even when your love is weak. He is working in you by His Spirit so that your repentance and faith will not fail. He is walking with you, though perhaps you cannot sense His presence. Christ is able to save you to the uttermost, for He ever lives to make intercession for His own.

Chapter 33

Precious Blood

> *Forasmuch as ye know that ye were not redeemed with corruptible things, as silver and gold, from your vain conversation received by tradition from your fathers; but with the precious blood of Christ, as of a lamb without blemish and without spot.*
> —1 PETER 1:18–19

One little creature mentioned in Proverbs 30:25–28 is the coney, often called a rock rabbit today. It is a feeble animal, the wise man says. It has no means of self-defense. Hawks and other animals of prey have immediate access to the coney when it leaves its home in the rocks. At the slightest sign of danger, conies flee to the rocks. They burrow into the rocks so deeply that even a snake can scarcely follow them. Similarly, believers are to make their home in the Rock, Christ Jesus, to find safety.

Once, after preaching a sermon on conies, I was in Australia, where I saw conies sitting on a pile of rocks. I reached for my camera, but the conies immediately disappeared. I thought, this is the way we ought to be as Christians. We are defenseless as conies without Jesus, the Rock of our salvation. We should flee to Christ at the slightest sign of danger.

Today let us consider what it means to shelter in Jesus as our Rock of salvation, how we are to do this, and why it is important to do so. Our text is 1 Peter 1:18–19, "Forasmuch as ye know that ye were not redeemed with corruptible things, as silver and gold, from your vain conversation received by tradition from your fathers; but with the precious blood of Christ, as of a lamb without blemish and without spot." We will focus on two words: "precious" and "blood," considering the *centrality, cost,* and *capability* of Christ's blood.

1. The Centrality of Christ's Blood

If something is precious, it is valuable. The Bible uses the word *precious* seventy-five times. It speaks of human life as precious. One of the captains sent to seize Elijah says, "O man of God, I pray thee, let my life, and the life of these fifty thy servants, be *precious* in thy sight" (2 Kings 1:13). The blood and the death of saints are called precious. Psalm 72:14 says, "*Precious* shall their blood be in his sight," and Psalm 116:15 says, "*Precious* in the sight of the LORD is the death of his saints."

The redemption of the soul is also precious, says Psalm 49:8. Proverbs 3:15 says wisdom is more precious than rubies. Psalm 139:17 says the thoughts and loving kindnesses of our God are precious. In 2 Peter 1:1 and 4, the apostle Peter speaks of faith and God's promises as precious, and in 1 Peter 1:7, he describes even our trials as precious, for they refine us as gold. But most of all, the Bible speaks of Jesus as precious. He is precious in His sympathy, precious to those who believe, precious as the cornerstone of our salvation, and precious in shedding His blood. Nothing is more precious than the blood of Jesus Christ.

The Bible speaks of blood 450 times. Blood is precious, for it is the most valuable thing in our bodies. Blood is essential to life. Our bodies may be perfectly framed, but if drained of blood, we die. The life of the flesh is in the blood, the Bible says.

Spiritually, the blood of Jesus Christ received by faith gives us spiritual life. In God's eyes, blood is sacred. Twice Hebrews 9 tells us that God cannot be approached without blood (vv. 7, 18). "Without shedding of blood [there] is no remission" of sin (Heb. 9:22). That is the primary message of the entire Bible. When Adam and Eve fell, God shed blood to clothe them and cover their nakedness (Gen. 3:21). In Genesis 4, God showed He was pleased with Abel's sacrifice, which involved sacrificial blood. Hebrews 11:4 confirms that there can be no approach to God, no fellowship with Him by faith, no enjoyment of His favor, apart from blood.

When Noah was released from the ark, the first thing he did was offer bloody sacrifices of thanksgiving to God. God's establishment of a covenant relationship with Abraham involved the slaughter of animals that were cut in two and laid in two paths. God Himself walked between the carcasses, sealing the covenant with blood. Later, in Genesis 22, Abraham and Isaac went up Mount Moriah to offer a sacrifice. Initially the sacrifice was to be Isaac, but God provided the blood of a ram instead, teaching us the great principle of substitution. As the ram took Isaac's place to appease the wrath of God, so Jesus Christ takes our place by His blood shedding.

Exodus is a blood-soaked book. In it God commanded the Israelites to sprinkle their door frames with the blood of a lamb so that He would pass by their homes without killing their firstborn. Again, life was preserved by means of a substitute. Fifty days later, this lesson was reinforced when Israel reached Sinai. God gave His law out of the covenant of grace to show His people how they should live. To ratify that covenant, sacrificial blood needed to be sprinkled, first on the altar, then on the book of the covenant, representing God's side of the covenant. Then it was sprinkled on the people, with the declaration, "Behold the blood of the covenant" (Exod. 24:8). We can only imagine being in that crowd as the blood of sacrifices falls upon us, and we cry out in response, "All that the LORD hath said will we do, and be obedient" (v. 7).

The foundation and power of God's covenant is in sacrificial blood. Only by blood can God and man be brought into covenant fellowship. That is reinforced by God's prescriptions to Israel on how to worship Him. Blood is central to worship. The first thing visible to an Israelite who approached the tabernacle or temple was the altar of burnt offering. That is where the sprinkling of blood continued without ceasing from morning to evening. The worshiper would see blood upon the altar, on the sides of the altar, and flowing around the altar. When the priest entered the Holy Place, the most conspicuous piece of sacred furniture was the golden altar of incense, which was repeatedly sprinkled with blood.

The Holy of Holies was unapproachable without blood. Once a year, the High Priest entered that sacred place walking backwards, sprinkling blood behind him and then on the altar seven times. He was required to do that before he could finally turn to face the holy God of Israel who dwelt in the *shekinah* cloud above the mercy seat, asking Him to turn away His wrath from the sins of the people. The message is clear: Israel cannot worship God without blood. Blood is at the center of biblical worship.

Wherever you look in the Old Testament—whether at the birth of a child, in the highest festival, or in the deepest repentance—the way to life and fellowship with God is through blood. Genesis 2 and Ezekiel 18:30 indicate the wages of sin are death. Substitutionary, bloody sacrifice is the only way to escape death.

The New Testament also teaches this. When John spoke of Jesus, he said, "Behold the Lamb of God, which taketh away the sin of the world" (John 1:29). When Jesus spoke of Himself, He said that His death on the cross was the reason He came into the world. His bloody death was the necessary condition of the redemption that He came to bring. He linked the salvation of sinners to His own blood shedding. His death gave birth to life. That is what we must focus on when we speak of the precious blood of Christ. The expression "blood of Christ" is not intended to mean something crass or crude but to serve as a synonym for the gospel, for redemption, and for the salvation of sinners. The blood of Jesus is a synonym for His suffering and obedience that satisfied the justice of God so that He could justify those who believe in Jesus.

Jesus repeatedly taught that His blood must be believingly and experientially received if we are to be saved. He said, "Except ye drink my blood, ye have no life in you." "He that drinketh my blood hath everlasting life." "My blood is drink indeed." "He that drinketh my blood dwelleth in me and I in him" (cf. John 6). When He instituted the Lord's Supper, Jesus said, "This cup is the new testament in my blood that is shed for you and for many for the remission of sins. Drink ye all of it" (cf. Matt. 26:28). So Jesus confirmed the teaching of the Old Testament offerings that we can live only through death—in this case the death of the Lord Jesus Christ—and by experientially receiving that death as a substitute for our own.

Paul's epistles underscore the centrality of Christ's blood. Paul repeatedly uses such expressions as "being now justified in his blood," "faith in his blood," "the blood of his cross," "redemption through his blood," and "made nigh by the blood of Christ."

The author of Hebrews repeatedly speaks of Christ's blood. "Neither by the blood of goats and calves, but by his own blood he entered in once into the holy place, having obtained eternal redemption for us" (Heb. 9:12). "How much more shall the blood of Christ, who through the eternal Spirit offered himself without spot to God, purge your conscience from dead works to serve the living God?" (v. 14). Hebrews 12:24 says that you are come "to Jesus the mediator of the new covenant, and to the blood of sprinkling, that speaketh better things than that of Abel."

Peter, too, reminds his readers that they were elect "unto obedience and sprinkling of the blood of Jesus Christ" (1 Peter 1:2). And John declares that "the blood of Jesus Christ [God's] Son cleanseth us from all sin" (1 John 1:7). He even writes of seeing Christ's blood in heaven. He saw a Lamb slain on the throne and heard the elders sing before Him, "Thou art worthy...for thou wast slain, and hast redeemed us to God by thy blood" (Rev. 5:9). John describes the redeemed as those who "have washed their robes, and made them white in the blood of the Lamb" (7:14). He says the redeemed overcame Satan "by the blood of the Lamb" (12:11).

From the beginning of Genesis to the end of Revelation, from the closing of the gates of Eden to the opening of the gates of the heavenly Zion, blood runs through Scripture, uniting all. Substitutionary blood gloriously restores what sin destroyed. Through His blood, the second Adam undid what the first Adam did, and so He reconciles sinners to God.

In Germany, there is one particular church building where a beautiful lamb is carved in stone above its entrance. A man at work on the steeple of the church once lost his footing and plunged to the ground below. A flock of sheep happened to be grazing there, and the fall of the man was broken by a lamb. The lamb was killed, but the man's life was saved. Out of gratitude, he cut into the stone over the doors of the church the lamb that saved his life. So, too, you and I, friends, are fallen in Adam and prone to sin. But if we become believers, we are saved from the penalty of sin and death by Christ, God's lamb, who is without blemish and without spot. He rescues us from danger by interposing His precious blood.

Are you resting upon Christ's atoning blood for salvation? Do you believe that God's justice is satisfied only by means of that blood? Do you value the blood of God's Son as highly as your heavenly Father does? Do you realize that all peace and holiness and hope of heaven are bound up in the atoning blood of Immanuel? Or are you a Christian in name only, taking this blood for granted, seeing little or no beauty in Christ and His atoning sacrifice? You do not meditate about Christ's blood. You do not treasure it. You do not realize, as Octavius Winslow says, that "there is no acceptance for the sinner, no cleansing for the guilty, no pardon for the penitent, no sanctification for the believer, but in the vicarious sacrifice of the Son of God."

Let us pray for grace to know and experience more fully the power of Christ's blood. Ask Christ to open your understanding of the efficacy of His blood, to grasp its necessity, to embrace its satisfaction, and to receive its beauty. Trust Christ to give you deeper insight into His blood, that you may think of His blood as God thinks of it. Trust the eternal High Priest to work out in you the merits of His blood so that you may abide in the sanctuary of God's presence. Ask for grace to draw nearer to God to meditate more on His blood shedding, that His blood may become spirit, life, power, and truth to you.

2. The Cost of Christ's Blood

The Bible speaks not only of the centrality of Christ's blood but also of the cost of His blood. Though salvation is free to us, we must never forget its costliness to God. It cost the Father the death of His own Son. It cost the Son suffering and death. It cost the Spirit the constant work of applying the blood of the Son to sinners.

God had only one Son, and He gave that Son for people who rebelled against Him. He gave the best He had for the worst He could find. Oh, what a price the triune God paid in the blood shedding of

Immanuel! When we think of the blood of Jesus, we should think not only of His circumcision as an infant and His sufferings throughout thirty-three years, but especially of the last days of His life when he endured unspeakable suffering in Gethsemane, Gabbatha, and Golgotha, experiencing the essence of hell.

In Gethsemane, Christ's blood exuded from the pores of His skin as He crawled on the ground like a worm and cried out, "O my Father, if it be possible, let this cup pass from me" (Matt. 26:39). Jesus was torn by the grief of being separated from His three best friends, who slept while He agonized with God. He also began to experience God's abandonment and wrath against sin. The death He began to taste was God's unmitigated hatred of our sins, dear believer. Our sins sank Christ to the ground. Our sins made Him crawl in agony. Our sins made Him cry out, "My soul is exceeding sorrowful, even unto death" (Matt. 26:38). Our sins spilled His blood in Gethsemane.

Gabbatha involved more blood shedding. Christ's enemies crowned Him with thorns, which pierced his skull. When I was in Israel a few years ago, a tour guide let me cut a snippet of a thornbush branch. I put it in my wife's knapsack, but it kept pricking through. Merely touching it drew blood, so we eventually threw the branch away. Imagine making a circlet of these thorns, then smashing it down into our Savior's skull. Blood must have gushed from the top of His head. These thorns were the price of our sins.

Next, soldiers fixed Jesus to a post and began scourging Him with a device we can best describe as a mop intermixed with oxtail bones. They hit Him as many as forty times, each time catching flesh with the bones and leaving wounds that wept rivulets of blood. Bleeding from His head and His back, Jesus then carried His cross to Golgotha—all because of our sins.

At Golgotha, Jesus was put on a cross beam, and nails were pounded into His hands and feet. Our sins, dear believer, put Him there.

The cross was lifted and put into the ground. Reportedly there is no pain worse than when the cross hits the bottom of the dug hole. Pain screeches through the body hung on the cross, the flesh tears, and more blood is shed. Jesus then hung there for six long hours. After three hours of unspeakable pain, He entered the abyss of unanswered prayer (Ps. 22:1–2) and unmitigated shame, when God the Father "made him to be sin for us, who knew no sin; that we might be made the righteousness of God in him" (2 Cor. 5:21).

Jesus experienced something far worse than physical suffering in the last three hours of His life. He felt the agony of being abandoned by His Father. The cry of dereliction, "My God, my God, why hast thou forsaken me?" was pressed from Him in the agony of separation. In the midst of darkness, when His Father turned from Him and when heaven, earth, and hell rejected Him, Jesus Christ suffered alone for your sins and mine. In this hour of horror, Immanuel poured out His soul in the bloody death on the cross.

During these final hours, a sense of sin dominated Jesus's consciousness to a frightening degree. In Gethsemane and in the first and last words on the cross, Jesus called on God as His Father. But then He cried, "Eli, eli"—"my God, my God." In that awful moment, He felt sin even more intensely than His Sonship. Jesus felt less like the Beloved in whom God is well pleased, and more like the chief of sinners who was cursed as vile, foul, and repulsive.

Isaac Ambrose, a great Puritan author, says that we should follow the trail of Christ's blood all the way to the cross and through the next six hours, reminding ourselves wherever we see blood that this was done for *our sins*. Oh, what a price our sins cost the precious Savior! Every sin I still commit is another injury to this precious Savior. How His precious blood ought to teach us to hate sin and never to trivialize grace because it is free. Let us heed Paul's warning not to abound in sin because we are saved by grace. We must remember what our sin cost the Lord Jesus Christ. He had no comfort at Golgotha. When Jesus most needed encouragement at Golgotha, no voice from heaven cried, "This is my beloved Son." When He most needed reassurance, no one said, "I am well pleased." No dove descended from heaven to symbolize peace; no angel was sent to strengthen Him; no "well done, thou good and faithful servant" resounded in His ears. He was in a far country, hanging alone in the naked flame of His Father's wrath.

The women who supported Jesus throughout His ministry were silent. The terrified disciples were a long way off. Jesus walked the way of suffering alone in darkness. Not a ray of light came to Him; only the Father's displeasure. Instead of love, there was wrath. Instead of affection, there was coldness. Instead of support, there was opposition. The Son's cries did not bring the Father back. God the Father so distanced Himself from the Son that eventually the Father disappeared. The Son cried out, "My God—why?" He kept pursuing the Father, yet the Father chose to retreat. No amount of pursuit would catch up with the Father. Jesus was alone. Deserted. Forsaken.

Every detail of this abandonment shouts to us, "This is what God thinks of our sin!" Every detail declares the irrationality, heinousness, and dreadfulness of sin. Jesus's suffering at Golgotha is the essence of what God thinks of sin. It is the price that the God-man needed to pay for sin. Oh, what a costly price is the shedding of His precious blood!

Consider also the value of Christ's precious blood. It does what no one else's blood can do—not the blood of believers, or of animals, or of angels. Christ's blood alone could offer satisfaction for sin. His precious blood is *intrinsically* valuable. The divine Son suffered as perfect man, shedding His blood, which is of infinite value. Christ is the tabernacle of the Deity; in Him dwells all the fullness of the Godhead. He is the perfect image of the Father. His blood is precious to the Father, for He is Jehovah's favorite—His only begotten Son. His blood is precious in the Father's eternal plan, not only because of God's parental affection for His Son, but because the Father views the salvation of His elect as fully and forever secured by that blood. That blood is precious to the Father, precious to every pardoned sinner on earth, and precious to every glorified soul before the throne. There is nothing more precious in this world than Christ's blood.

3. The Capability of Christ's Blood

Jesus's blood is also precious because of what it accomplishes. Christ's blood, dear believers, procures inexpressibly great and precious blessings for us. Consider the following:

1. Christ's blood accomplishes *full-orbed redemption* for us. Peter says that Christ's blood is precious because it redeems us. It buys us back from the way of sin. It is our ransom price. You have been redeemed,

dear believer, not with silver or gold or mere tradition, but with the precious blood of Christ.

- You are redeemed to be set free from the slavery of sin. By Christ's blood, the chains of sin have been broken and have fallen from you. You are set free in the Lord to serve God, free from the meaningless life of the unredeemed, and free from spiritual bondage. You have the spirit of adoption whereby you cry, "Abba, Father!" (Rom. 8:14–16). By Christ's blood, you may kill sin and enter into the very family of God as Christ's brother or sister.

- You are redeemed to be set free from the curse of the law. By His precious blood, "Christ hath redeemed us from the curse of the law, being made a curse for us," says Galatians 3:13. By blood, we are freed from the penalty and dreadful thundering of the law. We can now read the law with gratitude.

- You are redeemed to be set free from the enslaving power of Satan. By His blood and death, Christ destroyed "him that had the power of death, that is, the devil" (Heb. 2:14b).

- You are redeemed to be set free from the bondage of everlasting death. By Christ's blood, we who are believers are set free from the chains that bind us to future doom. Death loses its sting and becomes a passageway to life eternal (Rev. 21:1–9).

  Christ's blood was given to buy us back from sin, the law, Satan, and death. Redemption is a magnificent exhibition of divine glory. By means of Christ's blood, God glorifies His holy attributes in saving the lost. Sin is pardoned, not bypassed. Justice is magnified and iniquity is punished. Mercy and love triumph in harmony with righteousness. God proves He is inexorably just and One who lavishes love upon sinners. Truly, "we have redemption through his blood, the forgiveness of sin, according to the riches of his grace" (Eph. 1:7).

2. Christ's blood accomplishes *complete atonement* for us. By Christ's blood, we become one with God again. Christ gave His blood as our atonement price.

- That atonement covers all kinds of sin. Atoning sacrifices under the law made no provision for willful, reckless, presumptuous sins. But Christ's blood atones for all sins and blasphemies, Scripture says.

- That atonement covers all kinds of sinners. Even chief sinners are covered, says 1 Timothy 1:15. Christ was once offered to bear the sins of many (Heb. 10:11–14). Christ is the propitiation for our sins. "The chastisement of our peace was upon Him, and with His stripes we are healed" (Isa. 53:5).

> Now freed from sin, I walk at large;
> The Savior's blood's my full discharge,
> At His dear feet my soul I'll lay
> *A sinner saved, and homage pay.*

The blood of Christ is precious to us because it is the blood of our great High Priest, Shepherd, Friend, Elder Brother, Kinsman, and Redeemer, in whom all salvation is to be found (Acts 4:12).

3. Christ's blood *justifies and cleanses* us. Paul said to the Romans: "Being now justified by his blood, we shall be saved from wrath through him" (Rom. 5:9). God makes the unjust just through Jesus' blood.

Christ literally died in our place, dear believers. We are justified through His active obedience to the law and His passive obedience in paying for our sin. When we receive this gospel by faith, as the Heidelberg Catechism says, God regards us as never having committed sin (Q. 60).

Christ's blood is precious because unspeakable peace flows out of our justification in Christ (Rom. 5:1). We experience peace with God, peace with Christ, peace with the Holy Spirit, peace with those around us, and even peace with nature. Heaven and earth seem to meet and kiss each other.

John says, "The blood of Jesus Christ his Son cleanseth us from all sin" (1 John 1:7). That may seem strange to us, since blood stains clothing. But instead of staining us with filth, the blood of Christ washes out the stain of sin. Instead of defiling our souls, it washes them white as snow. You who have felt this cleansing power know what I mean. You once felt as black as the outer darkness of hell, but in the moment when Christ's blood was applied to you, your soul felt washed white as heaven. Your soiled life was made clean, for sin disappears as soon as Christ's blood falls on the conscience. Divine pardon purges us of all the stains of accumulated years. You know the truth of the promise: "Though your sins be as scarlet, they shall be as white as snow" (Isa. 1:18).

> There is a fountain filled with blood,
> Drawn from Emmanuel's veins;
> And sinners, plunged beneath that flood,
> Lose all their guilty stains.

4. Christ's blood *sanctifies* us. Through the process of sanctification, we are made holy to serve God. Blood separated the Israelites from the Egyptians. Likewise, Christ's blood calls us to separate from the world's sin, the world's religion, the world's sense of goodness, and the world's vileness. The more we rely on Christ's blood, the more we will be sanctified by the Holy Spirit. Let us pray with Charles Spurgeon, "Oh, Lord Jesus Christ, burn up the love of the world! Let Thy death be the death of my sin. Let Thy life be the life of everything that is gracious, heavenly, eternal!"

- Precious blood provides a *melting power*. Nothing can melt the soul like the blood of Christ. Nothing is so humbling as that He "loved me, and gave himself for me" (Gal. 2:20). When our souls melt by the Spirit's powerful application of Christ's blood, we can understand Zechariah 12:10, "They shall look upon me whom they have pierced, and they shall mourn for him, as one mourneth for his only son." Often we complain that our hearts are hard, but seldom do we realize that nothing can melt them like the blood of Jesus.

> Law and terrors do but harden,
> All the while they work alone,
> But a sense of blood-bought pardon,
> Soon dissolves a heart of stone.

- Precious blood provides *pacifying power*. In *Pilgrim's Progress*, John Bunyan says the law is like a maid sweeping dust in the chamber of the soul until the dust of sin clouds the soul and threatens to choke its spiritual life. Only the precious blood of Christ can remove the dust, clean the room, and quiet the soul. Christ's blood is soothing balm for a sin-distressed conscience.

- Precious blood provides *invigorating power.* Just as the bread and wine of the Lord's Supper provide us with spiritual nourishment, so the blood of Jesus nourishes our faith, offers us hope, gives us joy, and makes us sing. There is no cordial for the heart like the blood of Jesus. "Drink, yea, drink abundantly, O beloved," God says (Song of Sol. 5:1). No wine makes glad the heart so much as that which flows from the sacred cup of Christ's substitution. To meditate on Christ's atoning sacrifice is the surest path to comfort.

5. Christ's blood *preserves and assures us,* and *makes us victorious.*

- Christ's blood provides *confirming power.* Jesus' blood is the blood of the new covenant. The blood of Jesus is like His last will and testament. It is the great seal of His testament. His covenant blood confirms and assures us of our salvation.

- Christ's blood provides *intercessory power.* Christ sprinkles His precious blood within the Holy of Holies in the heaven of heavens.

> The wounds of Christ for us
> Incessantly do plead.

Christ pleads, by His precious blood, with continual, personal intercession. He lives to make intercession for us (Heb. 7:25).

- Christ's blood provides *victorious power.* As Revelation 12:11 says, "They overcame him [Satan] by the blood of the Lamb." Those who cling to the blood of Jesus have a weapon that makes hell tremble, heaven subservient, and earth obedient. Sin dies at the presence of Christ's blood; doubts and fears flee. Heaven opens its gates by that blood. Hell would lose its grip if that blood could operate there. Truly, we are more than conquerors through Him that loved us by giving His own blood.

There is no victory without conflict, but there is true victory through faith in the blood of the Lamb. Oh, what glorious victory we have now and forever through the blood of the Lamb!

6. Christ's blood *opens heaven* for us. By Christ's blood:

- *We are made fit for heaven.* By Christ's blood, we are brought into agreement with His will. We learn to delight in His fellowship, and, through Him, to delight also in fellowship with the saints. Christ's blood binds us together. Speaking of Jew and Gentile, Paul said: "He hath made both one through the blood of Christ." What eternal, worldwide union is possible when we meet at the foot of the cross!

  When we look away from Christ's precious blood, however, we quickly find ourselves in darkness. An elderly minister, Hugh McPhail, was on his deathbed. Unable to look to Christ's blood, he feared that he would die as a castaway. Friends attempted to comfort him in vain. Finally, one night, he had a dream. He heard music and saw the Old Testament saints walking to heaven waving palm branches of victory and singing God's praises. As the gates of heaven opened, McPhail was asked, "Can you go in with Abraham, Jacob, and David—all of whom fell into serious sins?" "No, Lord," McPhail responded, "I am a far greater sinner than they are."

  Next, the New Testament saints passed by. McPhail could not follow Peter, who had denied Christ, and Thomas, who had doubted Christ. The Church Fathers came next, then the Reformers, the Puritans, and the Covenanters. McPhail could not go with any of them. Suddenly, he saw believers from his own congregation approaching. Though he well knew their faults and sins, he couldn't go in with them, either, saying, "I am a greater sinner than them all."

  Finally, he saw a figure walking alone to the celestial gates. "Who is he, Lord?" McPhail cried out. He was told, "This is Manasseh, who filled the streets of Jerusalem with the blood of the saints from one end to the other, but he too is going in by the blood of Jesus. Can't you go in with him?"

  McPhail then awoke from his dream. He realized that he had been looking to himself for fitness rather than to the blood of Christ. He called for his wife and asked her to invite his friends to visit him again so he could tell them, "There is room and fitness in the blood of Jesus also for me to go in to the heavenly gates of glory."

We too must learn that no sinner is too old, too hard, or too sinful to find entrance into heaven by the blood of Jesus Christ. May God teach us to sing:

> And can it be that I should gain
> An interest in the Saviour's blood?
> Died He for me, who caused His pain?
> For me, who Him to death pursued?
> Amazing love! How can it be
> That Thou, my God, shouldst die for me?

- *We enter heaven.* Christ is our only altar, our only sacrifice, and our only entrance into heaven. When He comes again, the trumpet will sound, the dead will rise, and everyone will surround the great white throne. There, where God sees Christ's blood, He will pass by in avenging justice. Sheltered under Christ's blood, believers will be washed from every stain of sin. Not a drop of divine wrath will fall upon them. They will be part of the heavenly choir that sings, "Unto him that loved us, and washed us from our sins in his own blood, and hath made us kings and priests unto God and his Father; to him be glory and dominion for ever and ever" (Rev. 1:5–6). Oh, the joy of that moment when we find Christ to be all in all!

- *We enjoy the benefits of heaven.* Christ's blood is our passport to worship, service, and fellowship in the celestial city, where there will be no more tears, no more pain, no more sorrow, no more night, no more death, no more curse, and, best of all, no more sin.

  Recently, I was preaching in Northern Ireland about how God's people will one day enter into glory with unstained souls and perfect bodies. I said death will be like a wheelchair that will roll us into the presence of our Savior where wheelchairs will no longer be needed. Afterwards, an elderly lady, walking with two canes, approached me. Slowly raising one cane she said, "I won't need this up there." She smiled as she lifted the other cane. "I won't need this one, either," she said. Redeemed from every infirmity by the blood of Christ, we will rejoice in singing the Lamb's praises. Oh, happy day, when our mortality puts on immortality, our corruption incorruption, and we are forever with the Lord!

- *We find subject matter for heaven.* Christ's blood provides the subject matter of praise and song in heaven, even by great sinners, such as Adam, Manasseh, and Saul of Tarsus. As Revelation 5:9–10 says, "And they sung a new song, saying, Thou art worthy to take the book, and to open the seals thereof: for thou wast slain, and hast redeemed us to God by thy blood out of every kindred, and tongue, and people, and nation; and hast made us unto our God kings and priests: and we shall reign on the earth."

Let us finish with three points of application:

1. Let us remember that *Christ's precious blood is all-powerful*. It does not fail to release all whom Christ intends to release. Christ paid the ransom for many slaves. His blood was not a mere deposit or part of the ransom, leaving the sinner to pay the balance. No, He paid it in full, and He always gets what He paid for. Yet, He did not pay for every slave, for if He had, then everyone would be saved. Though He offers His blood to all, He sovereignly and justly passes some by, leaving them in their hell-deserving state.

2. Let us remember that *Christ's precious blood is motivated by love*. Christ's blood is precious not only because it is worth much, but also because He loves much. When you say to a dear one, "my dear, precious daughter," or "my dear, precious spouse," you are reflecting not on the person's *value,* but on *love.* Value Christ's blood for love's sake.

Oh, dear believers, let us stop living below our privileges in Christ's blood. Let us stop hugging the chains of sin. The Lord of glory toiled, bled, and died to tear those chains asunder so that we could know the powerful freedom of being sons and daughters in Christ.

3. Let us remember that *no sin is worse than despising Christ's precious blood.* If you do not know Jesus, you are despising His sacrificial blood. You are missing what life is all about. Oh, stop rejecting this blood, which is still being offered to you today! Hear these words of God: "Of how much sorer punishment, suppose ye, shall he be thought worthy, who hath trodden under foot the Son of God, and hath counted the blood of the covenant, wherewith he was sanctified,

an unholy thing, and hath done despite unto the Spirit of grace?" (Heb. 10:29).

I read recently about a shepherd boy who brought his sheep to a cave one evening because of a ferocious storm. The next morning, he saw that the central viaduct of a bridge was washed away by the storm. Knowing that a train was coming, the boy tore his way through the bushes. Bruised and breathless, he reached the track just in time to wave down the train. The conductor, however, waved the boy away and kept the train going. The boy fell onto the tracks. The conductor hit the brakes just in time to keep the train from falling into the abyss. The people on the train were later dismayed to see the mangled body of the shepherd boy.

One passenger finally broke the silence and said, "That boy died for us. He saved our lives."

Likewise, Jesus Christ throws Himself across the tracks of sinners' lives to save them from sin. Why do you wave away His loving warnings? Why do you reject the only gospel that can save you? Will you rush over a crucified Jesus and once more deny His precious blood?

I do not know the enormity of your sin, but I know you may still be saved by the precious blood of Jesus. Ask for grace to repent of your wretched unbelief. Cast all your sins upon Jesus, believe in Him, and surrender to Him as Lord. Believe that our precious Savior gave His precious blood for even the greatest of sinners that they might be saved.

Let us, by the Spirit's grace, be like the conies and flee to the Rock of Ages. Let us also exhort others to flee to the Rock. Let us rely on Christ's blood and rejoice in it, saying with Joseph Irons:

> What sacred fountain yonder spring
> Up from the throne of God,
> And all new covenant blessings brings?
> 'Tis Jesus's precious blood.
>
> What mighty sum paid all my debt,
> When I a bondman stood,
> And has my soul at freedom set?
> 'Tis Jesus's precious blood.

What stream is that which sweeps away
My sins just like a flood,
Nor lets one guilty blemish stay?
'Tis Jesus's precious blood.

What voice is that which speaks for me
In heaven's high court for good,
And from the curse has set me free?
'Tis Jesus's precious blood.

What theme, my soul, shall best employ
Thy harp before thy God,
And make all heaven to ring with joy?
'Tis Jesus's precious blood.

Chapter 34

Worldliness

> *Love not the world, neither the things that are in the world. If any man love the world, the love of the Father is not in him. For all that is in the world, the lust of the flesh, and the lust of the eyes, and the pride of life, is not of the Father, but is of the world. And the world passeth away, and the lust thereof: but he that doeth the will of God abideth for ever.*
> —1 JOHN 2:15–17

With God's help, we wish to consider the theme of worldliness under four headings:
1. The essence of worldliness
2. The paths of worldliness
3. The curse of worldliness
4. The deliverance from worldliness

1. The Essence of Worldliness

In the passage before us, the apostle John contrasts two loves: *love for the world* and *love for the Father*. These two loves are incompatible. They are mutually exclusive and cannot exist together. Either you love God or you love the world. You cannot love both. Jesus said, "No man can serve two masters: for either he will hate the one, and love the other; or else he will hold to the one, and despise the other" (Matt. 6:24). Today we are confronted with a strong warning from God's authoritative word: "Do not love the world or the things in the world!"

There should be one love that rules our life—one holy passion for God and the things of God. The choice is clear and directions are simple, but the way is not easy. The appeal of the world is strong and the flesh is weak. Jesus said, "Watch and pray, that ye enter not into temptation: the spirit indeed is willing, but the flesh is weak." May God bless our consideration of this text, such that we pray earnestly that He would take away our love for the world and cause us to love only Him. We need God's grace for that; we cannot do that without the power of His Holy Spirit.

But why should we not love the world? John gives two critical reasons why we ought not to love the world nor the things in the world. The first reason why we must not love the world is that the world is opposed to God.

To understand John's reasoning, we need to grasp his use of the word *world*. "World" in the New Testament is usually the Greek word *kosmos*. It is related to a verb that means "to set in order" or "to adorn or decorate," and has six basic meanings in New Testament usage:

- The universe created by God with design and order (Matt. 13:35)
- The planet earth (John 11:9) in contrast with heaven (1 John 3:17)—the world God created in six 24-hour days
- The total of mankind, or of all kinds of people such as both kings and subjects, Jews and Gentiles (Matt. 5:14; 2 Cor. 5:19)
- The total of human existence in this present life, with all of its experiences, possessions, and emotions (Matt. 16:26)
- The elect world of fallen people, who are the object of God's everlasting love and for whom Christ died (1 John 2:2)
- The world order or kingdom that is alienated from God, in rebellion against Him, and condemned by nature through the fall in Paradise and by actual sins in thoughts, words, and actions.

In this passage John is using the word world in the last and most common usage. He is not referring to the physical world in which we live or about the mass of people living on the planet. Rather, he uses the term world to refer to a kingdom, a realm and its inhabitants, that is lost in sin, wholly at odds with anything that is divine or pleasing to God. He is talking about Satan's kingdom of darkness which consists of all unsaved people who live according to the standards of this world. John Calvin defined the world in this sense as "everything connected with the present life, apart from the kingdom of God and the hope of eternal life."

Sometimes the New Testament writers also use the word *aion* for world, which literally means "a segment of time, or an age." The New Testament repeatedly contrasts this age (this *aion*) with the age to come (the *aion* to come). When *aion* is used in terms of worldliness, it refers to this present age as a world immersed in sin and evil, a world separated from God, secularized, and demonized. Galatians 1:4 describes this age as an evil age. Evil is its dominant characteristic and the devil is its dominant agent. This present evil age is ruled by the devil under the rule of God. Paul calls Satan the god of this world—of this present age (2 Cor. 4:4). Therefore, Romans 12:2 tells us, believers are not to be conformed to this present age, but to be transformed by the renewing of their minds.

What then is the world, or worldliness, in the sense that John uses it in our text and as it is predominantly spoken of in the New Testament? When the word world—be it *kosmos* or *aion*—is used in the context of warning or divine judgment or as that from which believers have been delivered, it refers to man, his institutions, his surroundings, his goals, and his principles of thought and action as penetrated and controlled by immoral, malignant, devilish forces. This is the world that John tells us we are not to love.

John thus speaks of world in our text as antithetical to God. *World* here has an ethical and spiritual connotation that contrasts it with Christ and His church. This is the world which knows not God, nor His Son, but crucified the Lord of glory (John 1:10). John is referring to this present, evil world (John 8:23), as opposed to the other world, the heavenly world. This world, made to reflect the glory of God, now lives, post-fall, in sinister rebellion against the heavenly world. This world is now a fallen, disordered world, in the grip of the Evil One, he says in 1 John 5:19. This world, despite its great achievements, is a lost world and is incapable of saving itself and ordering its existence in a meaningful, God-glorifying manner.

The world in this sense is the mass of mankind estranged from God through sin and living after the lusts of the flesh. This "world" is populated by sinful men, women, and children who think primarily of this world and neglect the world to come. Worldly people focus more on their bodies than their souls and more on pleasing men than pleasing God. They fear men more than God. They live more horizontally than vertically. Their motto is "forward," never "upward." Their goal is worldly success rather than divine holiness. They worship the creature rather than the Creator. They lack reverence. They never bow in rapt, silent wonder in the secret place. They burst with selfish desires rather than heartfelt supplications. Such people may not deny God, but they certainly forget or ignore Him.

Worldliness, then, is human activity with God left out. Being of this world means being controlled by what preoccupies the world, the quest for pleasure, profit, and position. Worldliness means yielding to the spirit that animates fallen mankind, the spirit of self-seeking and self-indulgence without regard for God.

Every one of us, by nature, was born as a worldling. We have a native attachment to the world. We live in natural rapport with the spirit of the world. We belong to this evil world, to hell-bent humanity. The world is our native habitat and environment, our order and orbit of existence. We are part of the organized kingdom of the carnal mind which is enmity against God, and which is "not subject to the law of God, neither indeed can be" (Rom. 8:7).

As much as we, after conception, were nourished in our mother's womb through an umbilical cord that attached us to her internal life support system, so we were born with an umbilical cord that tied us to the world's system. That was the womb of our fallen existence. Consequently, our understanding is darkened (Eph. 4:18) as we enter the world. The guilt of Adam's sin is imputed to us and the pollution of his sin is inherited by us. Our minds are blinded by the power of the devil (2 Cor. 4:4). Our baser passions and lusts are activated by the devil (Eph. 2:3). We have cast in our allegiance with the prince of this world. We are the children of our father, the devil. We live under the lordship of satanic powers. Sin lords itself over us; we are sinaholics. We live as slaves of sin (Rom. 6:16) in the service of human passions

(1 Peter 4:2). We give our members as weapons to the service of sin (Rom. 6:15). We are self-affirming, anti-God, Tower of Babel builders, driven by pride, autonomy, and paranoia (Gen. 11:1–9).

We are all dead in sins and trespasses and are children of wrath (Eph. 2:1–2), until God graciously regenerates us and makes us true Christians (John 3:5). Only then are we set apart from the rest of mankind, called out of this sinful world to become living members of the church and kingdom of God. Regeneration, or the new birth, divides the world into the kingdom of God and the kingdom of Satan. Those kingdoms always live in war with each other. They live in antithesis rather than synthesis with each other.

The world is one of the three major enemies of the Christian. The other two enemies are the devil and the flesh. All three enemies work together to oppose God and God's people. If you are a true Christian, then you are at war with these enemies.

The devil is the supreme agent of evil as "the prince of this world" (John 12:31). He is the ultimate enemy of God and of the Christian, but he rarely attacks the believer directly. Instead, the devil works through the allurements of the world. The apostle John writes that "the whole world lieth in wickedness" (1 John 5:19). In other words, it is in the grip of the evil one, Satan. This present evil world of people and things is under his sway and influence, with the sovereign permission of God. The world is a major weapon that the devil uses against believers.

We must not look at the evil world as something separate from the devil. We must learn to recognize that the enemy of our souls is behind the scenes controlling the strings of all his subjects, just as a puppeteer controls his puppets. So he tries to control you and your actions as well.

We need to acknowledge that the world still has an attraction for the Christian. This is due to remaining sin in the believer, which the Bible calls the flesh. So then, while you must keep yourself "unspotted from the world," as James says, you must keep in mind that the sinful flesh is in league with the world. That is why isolation from the world, as was practiced by monks and mystics, does not keep you from sin. The truth is that we who are believers carry around a piece of the world within us. Just like the world, the flesh is completely opposed to God. As a Christian, your flesh is in agreement with the world and loves the world.

With the world, the devil, and the flesh fighting against you, is there any hope for victory? Absolutely, for the victory was won when Jesus defeated Satan on the cross and rose again from the dead. In John 15:19 Jesus said, "Ye are not of the world, but I have chosen you out of the world." Because of His victorious death, and through faith in Him, you, dear believer, have been plucked from the kingdom of this world, and now belong to Christ and the kingdom of heaven. You were once a part of this world. You were born into it. But through Jesus Christ, you have overcome the so-called evil trinity of the world, the flesh, and the devil. The apostle John says, "I write unto you, young men, because ye have overcome the wicked one" (1 John 2:13).

In 1 John 5:4 we read, "For whatsoever is born of God overcometh the world: and this is the victory that overcometh the world, even our faith." In Christ, by the Spirit's grace, you have overcome the world, but you must also fight a daily battle against the threefold temptations of the world. John says that there are three paths along which we are pulled into the ways of the world: the *lust of the flesh*, the *lust of the eyes*, and the *pride of life*. Every one of us is drawn into the world by one or more of these three avenues, as I will show in our second thought.

2. The Paths of Worldliness

John becomes very specific in verse 16, "For all that is in the world, the lust of the flesh, and the lust of the eyes, and the pride of life, is not of the Father, but is of the world." We must be specific, too, as we admonish one another of those evils from which we must separate ourselves. We can group these specifics under the three major paths of worldliness that John sets before us.

First, John warns against the *"lust of the flesh."* Love not a world, he warns, that delights in the lusts of the flesh.

John's prohibition calls us to resist many temptations. We must never indulge in substance abuse, whether in the form of drugs or excessive alcohol consumption. We must not overeat either. The Bible warns repeatedly against gluttony and drunkenness. We must discipline ourselves to control what enters our body, for it is the temple of the Holy Ghost.

Young people, don't befriend those who tempt you to excessively drink or do drugs with them. Older friends, don't let your body and health degenerate because of a lack of diligence and discipline over what you eat. "Whether therefore ye eat, or drink, or whatsoever ye do, do all to the glory of God" (1 Cor. 10:31).

The prohibition against fleshly lusting also forbids sexual immorality in all its forms, whether in premarital, extramarital, or homosexual relationships. It forbids any physical intimacy outside the boundaries of biblical marriage. God has wisely and lovingly placed sexual expression within the special, secure bond of marriage. Premarital sex lacks the purity, exclusiveness, and permanence that God intended sexuality to represent. Here too, gracious self-restraint is needed. Young people, make a commitment with those you court or date, that you will preserve each other's bodies for the beauty and fulfillment of marriage. Don't break God's command by sinning against your own body. Deny yourself and seek the best for the one you love. Remember, true love does not harm or lead another into sin. In this context, to say "no" is to truly love. If any of you are presently engaged in unlawful sexual activity, I warn you to cease immediately, repent of your sin, and turn to God for mercy.

We must also avoid provoking lust with our appearance and dress. Men and women must dress modestly, Fashions exposing or accentuating the shame of our nakedness offend the Lord and arouse fleshly lusts. God reckons the sin of lusting to the account of those who promote it as well as those who engage directly in it.

Worldly parties, unedifying entertainment, nightclubs, and dancing excite the lusts of the flesh. Love not this world, John warns.

That includes worldly music. Hard rock, soft rock, contemporary Christian music, and many other forms of music today, promote the lusts of the flesh—either explicitly by their lyrics or implicitly by their beat. We need to ask of all the music we listen to: Can I pray over this music? Does this music glorify God or ignite fleshly lusts? If it facilitates lust, destroy it. Rid yourself of every CD and every piece of music that leads you away from God. Don't love this present, evil world.

Second, John warns against the *"lust of the eyes."* He warns not to love a world that delights in the lusts of the eyes.

How active Satan is today to engage our eyes, particularly through tempting us to indulge in various forms of sinful and worldly entertainment. Just as he approached our first parents to tempt them to believe that their Creator was a hard, legalistic God, so he approaches us, and particularly you, young people, whispering, "Has God said that you cannot eat from all the trees of modern entertainment? Has He said, 'You can't watch immoral movies or engage in any activity that tempts your eyes to lust'? Doesn't He want you to live a boring life, like David who confessed in Psalm 101, 'I will set no wicked thing before mine eyes'?—and so, isn't He a hard, legalistic God?"

Then Satan whispers, "If you just watch this one immoral movie, you will not die. You will be enlightened; you'll be in the know. You'll be able to speak with your peers as they discuss the latest movie. Remember, if you don't participate, you will miss the fun and excitement others have. Besides, everyone is going to these movies anyway. Go ahead, eat this fruit; you will surely live, you will not die. Try it once and see for yourself. Do you always want to stay under the thumb of your parents or the church? Aren't you old enough to decide for yourself what is right and wrong? You can shake off the evil, can't you? Take charge of your own life now-go ahead, let your eyes lust just once. Be your own god; determine good and evil for yourself!"

Satan has been using such approaches for thousands of years. He still goes about as a roaring lion, seeking to devour you through your eye-gate. He knows his time is short, so he will do anything to move people to look with lust in their eyes at bad fruit hanging on the tree of forbidden entertainment—any evil fruit that looks pleasant to the eyes and is desired to make one wise in this world. Perhaps he'll even use a friend to entice you, as he used Eve to tempt Adam. Satan is a master at hiding himself under the cloak of friendship.

How many have fallen prey to Satan's temptations to attend the theatre to indulge in the lusting of the eye. He whispers: "This movie isn't so bad. It has a G or PG rating. You can't always be saying no to everyone. Don't be righteous overmuch." Then, as you slide down the slippery slope of ungodly entertainment that Satan seeks to lead you a step at a time, your conscience gradually becomes desensitized to sin.

Young people, Satan is always fishing to hook your soul on his bait. He baits his hook with lusts of the eye, but hides his hook. How many of you have become hooked on his entertainment bait-watching films that involve every imaginable sin. Some of you are hooked on watching scenes of violence or fornication. Disrespect for authority, profanity, lying, theft, and mockery of God's institutions scarcely phase you as you watch iniquity played out before your eyes. Oh, what poisonous, forbidden fruit this is!

Entertainment movies, videos, and Internet pornography represent a powerful multi-million dollar industry intent on glamorizing sin. Fornication is made to appear innocent, commonplace, and exciting. Murder is portrayed as thrilling and manly. Profanity is presented as normal, emphatic speech.

Let us not trust our own strength; we overestimate ourselves if we think we can glean good out of entertainment that embraces sin. None of us have advanced spiritually as far as the apostle Paul. Even he needed to complain against himself, "For I know that in me (that is, in my flesh,) dwelleth no good thing: for to will is present with me; but how to perform that which is good I find not. For the good that I would I do not: but the evil which I would not, that I do" (Rom. 7:18–19).

The same principles apply to television. The vast bulk of television shows are productions of an anti-Christian nature. They are positively harmful to our spiritual life and growth. Like David, let us not love the world, but make a covenant with our eyes that we will set no wicked thing before us. Let us dispense also with all wicked magazines, trashy love novels, and profane books—yes, with all printed and visual material that contradicts the Ten Commandments.

How can we pray not to be led into temptation while continuing to play with the fire of temptation? James warns us that "every man is tempted, when he is drawn away of his own lust, and enticed. Then when lust hath conceived, it bringeth forth sin: and sin, when it is finished, bringeth forth death" (James 1:14–15).

Flee the lusts of the eye. Strive for self-denial. Follow Paul who said, "Herein do I exercise myself, to have always a conscience void of offence toward God, and toward men" (Acts 24:16). "Put ye on the Lord Jesus Christ, and make not provision for the flesh, to fulfil the lusts thereof" (Rom. 13:14).

Finally, John warns against *"the pride of life."* How prevalent such pride is in our hearts by nature! George Swinnock said, "Pride is the first shirt we put on in Paradise and the last we shall take off when we die." Pride of life can include:

1. *Pride of myself and my own accomplishments.* Pride of life is at the root of our humanistic hearts. We are filled, by nature, with self-gratification, self-contentment, and self-fulfilment. We want to rule and control our own destinies. We live for ourselves, exalting our own wisdom and accomplishments.

2. *Pride of false religions.* All religions in the world that challenge Scripture, teaching that man must do or accomplish something in his own strength to find favor with God, are false and proud religions. Some form of free-will Christianity (like Arminianism) also exalt man. To assert that fallen, depraved man can do anything to contribute to his salvation oozes with pride.

3. *Pride in challenging the governing providence of God.* That includes the traditional sects such as Mormonism and Jehovah's Witnesses, as well as Masonry or secret lodges. It embraces all customs and practices related to the New Age movement and transcendental meditation. All practices related to the occult, such as fortune-telling, consulting horoscopes, ouija boards, and palm-reading are also rooted in the pride of life. All unbiblical attempts to destroy life through birth control, abortion, or euthanasia also attempt to usurp the power of divine providence.

4. *Pride in idolizing movie actors, sports heroes, government leaders, or other popular figures in church or society.* John condemns all human idolization as the pride of life.

5. *Pride in materialism.* The love of money lies at the heart of the pride of life. Loving our possessions—such as our homes or cars or clothing—more than God is idolatrous pride of life; it feeds our quest for pleasure and gratification. It provides status symbols. Dishonesty in business, tax evasion, or other illegal ways of increasing personal wealth also serve the pride of life. All covetousness or inordinate desires to become rich and increased with goods at the expense of our own and our family's spiritual welfare is rooted in pride. Pride of life is served by gambling, lotteries, and all that results in lack of stewardship in which our firstfruits must be given to the Lord.

6. *Pride in desecration of the Lord's Day and neglect of worship services.* How proud must we be to think that we don't need one day in seven to exclusively worship the Lord and that we don't need weekly spiritual food in His house to nurture us for the coming week!

Dear friends, I trust that enough has been said to show that nearly any predominant sin can be classified under one or more of these three broad paths and vivid descriptions of worldliness: the lust of the flesh, the lust of the eyes, and the pride of life. Which path are you most prone to walk down? Do you engage in holy warfare against all three of these paths? Do you walk a separate lifestyle from the world? Are you a pilgrim and stranger on the earth? My people "shall dwell alone, and shall not be reckoned among the nations," God says in Numbers 23:9. Can that be said of you? Do you love the Father or do you love the world?

Eternal consequences hinge upon your answers to these questions. John goes on to say, such worldliness is accursed of God, for "the world passeth away, and the lust thereof" (v. 17). That's the second reason John provides us for not loving the world.

3. The Curse of Worldliness

The world's best pleasures are but temporary. The world is our passage, not our portion. You and I have a unilateral appointment with death, made by God Himself. Our death-date is on His calendar. "It is appointed unto men once to die, but after this the judgment,"

Hebrews 9:27 says. You and I have no escape from death. Death knows no bail and no parole.

The world will one day be burnt up, together with all its lusts and devotees. Fill your life with the lust of the flesh, the lust of the eye, the pride of life, and what have you acquired? A worldly life that will end in eternal hell.

All these lusts for which people have sold their bodies and souls, ruined their families, and stained their own reputations—what do they have when these lusts are passed away? Nothing but a gnawing worm—a worm that can never die—and the wrath of God as an unquenchable fire. That is all that the love of the world can do for you, despite all your hard work, your daily anxiety, and your pursuit of pleasure. Charles Spurgeon said, "If you had got all the world, you would have got nothing after your coffin was screwed down but grave dust in your mouth."

Such is the end of the world. You too, my friend, you will die and meet God. And what then? Are you prepared? Do you love the Father or do you love the world? The world passes away, together with all its lusts. Death is the final extinguisher of all human hopes and pleasures.

Oh, that I could persuade everyone of you that the world is temporary, vain, and unworthy of your time and attention! The world never gives what it promises. It is a gigantic mirage, a tragic fraud, a hollow bubble. The world lacks substance.

John Trapp wrote, "Pleasure, profit, and preferment are the worldling's trinity." Long ago, Solomon discovered all three to be vanity. Read Ecclesiastes carefully, friends. Then you will understand why John Bunyan called the world Vanity Fair. No wonder James states: "Know ye not that the friendship of the world is enmity with God? Whosoever will be a friend of the world is the enemy of God" (4:4).

Thank God there is a cure for worldliness. Let's consider that in our last thought.

4. The Deliverance from Worldliness

God's deliverance of His people from worldliness can be broken down into three thoughts: *initial deliverance, continual deliverance,* and *perfected deliverance.* Let's look at each of these briefly.

Initial Deliverance

In every true work of grace in the heart of a sinner, there is without exception a fundamental and radical deliverance from attachment to the world and a pattern of worldliness. In other words, the umbilical cord that tied us to the womb of our native worldliness is cut when we are born into the kingdom of God. If our life support system is still one that flows from the womb of the world, no matter how much you know about Christ or are found among His people, you are still a worldling. If your heart is still in the world, you are like Lot's wife, notwithstanding the fact that you appear to have left Sodom. You are yet in a state of wrath and condemnation.

This is the case for two important reasons. First, because Christ died with the express intention of cutting the umbilical cord between the saved sinner and the world. Galatians 1:4 says that Christ "gave himself for our sins, that he might deliver us from this present evil world, according to the will of God and our Father." What the Father purposes, the Son purchases. Christ didn't just come as a substitute for His people to deliver them from eternal condemnation, great as that is, but it was the Father's will that He would also come to deliver them from this present evil world. All the beatings and spittings that He bore, the shame of His nakedness, and the shrouded heavens and His cry of dereliction, serve to His seeing the travail of His soul and being satisfied because He gave Himself for the sins of those whom He determined, in the application of that salvation, would be wrenched out of this present evil world and brought into the kingdom of God and into the possession of the forgiveness of their sins.

Second, because the Holy Spirit makes the Father's and Son's intention efficacious in the application of the saving virtue of the death of Christ. Paul says in Galatians 6:14, "God forbid that I should glory, save in the cross of our Lord Jesus Christ, by whom the world is crucified unto me, and I unto the world." Paul is saying that the cross of Jesus Christ was so powerful to him, by the applying work of the Spirit, that it made the world as undesirable to him as a crucified Roman felon. The world not only lost its fair colors, but became positively unattractive to Paul.

But Paul also adds that he died to the world. Before Paul came to a Spirit-wrought understanding of who Jesus of Nazareth was and the significance of the cross, he was the favored son of an entire segment of Judaism. He was the rising star of Pharasaic Judaism. He was Gamaliel's prize pupil. Paul said that he outstripped all his peers in zeal for that arrogant world of Judaism. In that context, Paul was a worldling. Not that he abandoned himself to the standards of the dishonest and cheating men of this world—for, as touching the externals of the law, he was blameless. But he lived for the pride of life in his growing stature among the Pharisees.

When Paul's eyes were opened on his Damascus journey to see that he was persecuting the Lord of glory, he immediately cried out, "Lord, what wilt thou have me to do?" (Acts 9:6). Paul felt that if Jesus is God, and He had arrested him in His grace, then he had been a fool all his life. Soon the stupendous beauty of Christ's cross conquered Paul fully, so that he now only had an eye and a heart for Christ and His glory.

Paul was then not only crucified to his world of Judaism, but the Judaizers now thought of him in a parallel manner as he thought of them. Paul was saying: "When I saw my own wretched, hell-deserving heart as a seething caldron of all kinds of sin and wickedness, and I cast all my guilt and bondage upon the crucified Savior and I found forgiveness and life in Him, and I declared boldly in the synagogue that Jesus is truly the Son of God, suddenly I was no more attractive to the Judaistic world than that Judaistic world now was to me. The world was crucified to me and I to the world. I began to live by a new set of standards. I began to live my life under the pressure of goals and longings that made me despicable in the eyes of the respected Jew."

Paul experienced a cleavage that went in both directions. That cleavage is still experienced today when God converts a sinner. That is why Jesus said, "If the world hate you, ye know that it hated me before it hated you. If ye were of the world, the world would love his own: but because ye are not of the world, but I have chosen you out of the world, therefore the world hateth you" (John 15:18–19).

What about you, my friend? Has the beauty of Christ ever de-beautified the world to you and you to the world? Has the crucified

Christ caused the world to be crucified to you? Has the love of the Father in Christ conquered within you the love of the world so that the world no longer has dominion over you?

Or do you still willingly cling to this world? Is the world to you still something handsome and attractive? Does the stroke of the world's hand still move you? Do the world's institutions and goals, its opinions and principles, its entertainment and speech still hold sway in your heart? Do you love the world more than the church? Then you love Satan more than God, and you are still under the power of the prince of this world. The cross of Christ has never been efficaciously applied to your heart by the Holy Spirit. No sinner ever received forgiveness of sin rooted in the virtue of the cross of Christ who did not have the world crucified to him. Scripture says plainly they that are Christ's "have crucified the flesh with the affections and lusts" (Gal. 5:24).

No true child of God lives dominated by the threefold cord—Satan, flesh, and the world—by which sinners are bound to the world. John says, "If any man love the world, the love of the Father is not in him." In other words, if there is a basic, predominant, and undisturbed attachment of love to the world, then God's love is not in us and we do not love God. John does not say that the love of the Father is hidden or temporarily squelched, but that His love does not exist in a worldly heart at all. The term "carnal Christian" is a heretical oxymoron; no true Christian is fundamentally carnal.

You and I are either Christians or worldlings. If we're Christians, we are of course imperfect Christians. We're not talking now about the struggles with remaining affinities or certain aspects of the world and its pleasures that may retain some allurement to the believer. That struggle will continue until our last breath. Nevertheless, a Christian is not a worldling. The world has been crucified to us and we to the world. Our goal in life is no longer to live under the dominion of the lust of the flesh (merely enjoying things), the lust of the eye (merely having things), and the pride of life (merely being someone).

On the other hand, if that which sets our standards, makes us tick, draws out our energy, and excites our emotions, habitually concerns the lust of the flesh, the lust of the eye, and the pride of life, the love of the Father is not in us. You have never known the effectual application of the death of Christ to your soul. You are still entrapped in the womb of this present, evil world. You are still marching to the beat of this world's drum. Your citizenship is still on this earth.

But if we are true Christians, we have a transplanted citizenship in heaven. Our citizenship is in heaven, from whence we await the coming of our Lord. The rules that govern us originate from where our citizenship is, and we will live by the rule and law of heaven. We do not live for this present age but for the age to come. We are pilgrims and sojourners. We have here no abiding place but we look for a city to come. Above all, we look for the King who sits enthroned in majesty and splendor and glory, for the Lamb is all the glory of Immanuel's Land.

Continued Deliverance

God's gracious deliverance works itself out continually in the believer's life. In the initial implantation of grace, the dominion of sin and the world are broken. They no longer *reign* although they *remain*. They are no longer *president* of the soul though they are yet *resident* in the soul. Sin still finds expression in the remnants of worldliness that cling to the born-again believer. The desire to have the approval of those who are living in the world—who are living by the standards and goals of the world—is not altogether dead. Believers are still tempted to conform to the world's standards—whether out of peer pressure or for economic advancement. We are tempted to have our "yea" be not quite fully "yea" in a business deal, or our "yea" may not quite be fully "yea" in our personal relationships when we may incur the frown of a worldling. How is this deliverance to be continually wrought in us when we are still so prone to compromise both our yea and our nay? We can only experience such deliverance in the power of the Holy Spirit by *doing* the will of God, John tells us (v. 17). But what does that involve?

We must believe that it is crucial to fight against worldliness. If you're not convinced that you must fight against worldliness with all your being, you will seldom make any headway. James 1:27 says, "Pure religion and undefiled before God and the Father is this, To visit the fatherless and widows in their affliction, and to keep himself unspotted from the world." The purity of our religion is in direct proportion to our commitment that we shall not allow one stain of the world to be placed upon the garments of the imparted righteousness that God has graciously granted me in His regenerating work.

James uses such vivid, antithetical language. James 4:4 says, "Ye adulterers and adulteresses, know ye not that the friendship of the world is enmity with God? Whosoever therefore will be a friend of the world is the enemy of God." He says that such people are guilty of spiritual adultery. James uses strong language because Christ died as the heavenly Bridegroom to have a chaste and spotless bride whose heart is wholly His. When you flirt with the world, you're guilty of spiritual adultery.

Teenagers, do some of you say: "I know that some of the standards in dress and modern fashion reflect a lifestyle that is not biblical, but I can't bear being out of step with the latest styles around me. I must be the world's friend." But at what price, my friend? At the price of being an enemy of God?

Or perhaps you say, "I know that the lyrics of the music I listen to are sinful and hellish, but I don't concentrate on the lyrics. Besides, if I don't know the latest hits and the latest groups, I'll look like a fool. I know too that the music is filled with repetitive noise that is born of hell where there is no order and beauty and symmetry, but my friends would mock me if I didn't listen to just enough to be able to be with it." Is all of this worth the expense of being an enemy of God?

Do you want pure religion with a pure conscience? Then you must, in dependence upon God, do the will of God by fighting to remain unspotted from the world. If I would have my heart be kept as a chaste virgin to Christ, as Paul puts, I must not let the world's smiles or frowns cause me to alter my standards, change my goals, or shape what I am convinced from the Word of God are the standards for personal dress and the use of modern entertainment. Are you jealous to retain a virgin's heart for your blessed Savior? Let us dare, friends, to be Daniels in Babylon.

We must use every God-ordained means to conquer worldliness. Use especially the Word of God. Listen repeatedly to sermons. Saturate yourself with Scripture. Meditate on the Word of God. Read good books that can make you wise to salvation. Pray without ceasing. Fellowship with believers. Sanctify the Lord's Day. Consider keeping a spiritual journal. Evangelize and serve others. Steward your time and your money.

Dear young people, the world is seeking to squeeze you into its mold, its standards, its perspectives, and its values. All the media shout at you, as do some of your peers, to live for this present, evil world. You cannot counter that onslaught without immersing yourself in the Word of God. How can you be the blessed man of Psalm 1 who meditates on the Word of God day and night if you seldom spend time with the Scriptures? Ask for grace to search, know, pray over, love, and live the Word of God.

We must continually trust our great High Priest and His Spirit. At times when the power of the world seems to invade my soul again, what comfort there is in remembering that our great High Priest prayed, "Father, I pray not that thou shouldest take them out of the world [here "world" is used in the sense of "this earth"], but that thou shouldest keep them from the evil" (John 17:15). Blessed be God that at times when every visible defense seems to be down and we are vulnerable to yielding to the foul power of the enemy of our souls, our deliverance is traceable only to the intercession of Jesus Christ and the preserving power of His Spirit. Then we cry out afterwards, "Dear Savior, were it not for Thy intercession, and blessed Spirit, for Thy preservation, in the hour of temptation, I would have been swept into evil."

Charles Spurgeon put it this way: "I thank God that when temptation is present, He removes my desire, and when desire to sin is present, He removes the temptation." That, friends, is always the gracious fruit of Jesus Christ who promises His Peters that He will pray for them in the hour of temptation that their faith will not fail (Luke 22:32).

Perfected Deliverance
Finally, dear believers, our gracious deliverance will be perfected and

consummated in the age to come, which, says John, "abideth forever!" This age is the age where worldliness is part of the burden of the overlapping of the ages. Heaven is in our hearts and in our deepest affections, dear believer, and yet the world and the devil are still at our elbow and too often penetrate our mind. But thank God that in the age to come, nothing but righteousness will dwell in the new heavens and the new earth. This *kosmos*, this *aion*, under the curse of God and the prince of the power of the air, will be no more. Satan and all his will be banished to eternal perdition. And the people of God will shine in the firmament of God's redemptive glory.

In conclusion, we all face the danger of being a present-day Demas in the midst of the world. "Demas hath forsaken me, having loved this present world," Paul lamented (2 Tim. 4:10). Demas prayed and labored with Paul. He witnessed Paul's yearnings after his fellow countrymen. He saw the tears of Paul staining the parchments when the apostle wrote his pastoral letters. At one point, Paul even called him: "Demas, my fellow-worker."

Demas forsook the godly apostle who was crucified to the world. What caused Demas to abandon Paul and everything that he stood for? The world bewitched him! Dear friends, beware of anything that has its tap roots in this world's standard of success. We must die to our success standards. Who among us will forsake the truth, having loved this present evil world? Beware of the danger of this world.

Only one thing matters: Jesus drawing near with His Word and the kisses of His own presence. Then, and may God fulfil it in us, the world will lie at our feet as dead and we dead to the world.

Chapter 37

God Is Love

God is love.
—1 JOHN 4:8

One of the Bible's most wonderful phrases is "the love of God." We find these words often in the Bible, such as in Romans 8:38–39, where Paul declares, "I am persuaded, that neither death, nor life,...nor any other creature, shall be able to separate us from the love of God, which is in Christ Jesus our Lord." Here Paul speaks of the love that lives in and proceeds from the God and Father of our Lord Jesus Christ.

The Bible also speaks about the "God of love." Consider Paul's words in 2 Corinthians 13:11: "Finally, brethren, farewell. Be perfect, be of good comfort, be of one mind, live in peace; and the God of love and peace shall be with you." Here Paul reminds his readers that they must love one another and "live in peace" if they would enjoy the presence of Him who is "the God of love and peace."

Love of God, God of love: these are three simple words of one syllable each. They are not an empty formula or mere cliché but are deep and profound.

By God's grace, I would like to bring you a message on the declaration of the apostle John that "God is love" (1 John 4:8, 16). First, we will discuss three things this text does *not* mean; secondly, three things it *does* mean; and lastly, three points of *application* for our hearts.

First, we must define what the word "love" means, especially when referencing our God and Father. As an action, to love is to glorify God and to do good to His creation, especially to people. In a world where men hate God and hate each other, it is astonishing to hear that God loves this world, that He has expressed His love by sending His Son to die for sinners, promising life and salvation to all who put their trust in Him. Such is the extent to which God loves!

1. What "God Is Love" Does Not Mean

The first thing "God is love" does not mean is that "love is God."[1] The phrases "love is God" and "God is love" are not reversible or convertible statements. There are ways of saying something that is the same back and forth in logic and grammar. For example, "a sphere is a round object" or "a round object is a sphere." Unfortunately, some people use flawed logic with "God is love." They say, "Well, if God is love, then love is God." No, that would be like saying, "An orange is round, and a baseball is round; therefore, a baseball is an orange." God is love, but not everything that goes by the name of love is God. This popular error of saying that love is God deifies the feelings of the idea of love and depersonalizes God. We find this in humanism and in the many romantic ideas of God, which approve of nearly anything that goes by the name of love. There are spurious and deceitful kinds of love, known in Scripture as "the love of the world," "the love of the flesh," "the love of pleasure," or "the love of money." These are not love but covetousness and concupiscence, an inordinate desire to possess whatever we see and use it as we will. The end of all such false love is death and destruction.

Even those who defend and promote the sin of homosexuality often use false reasoning about love, as if all forms of love are God. Homosexuals who claim to be Christians sometimes say things like, "Well, this relationship I'm in is one of love, and I like it, therefore, this must be from God." When we formulate our ideas of love from the world rather than from the Word, we will always end with a faulty or shallow view of God.

The Word of God teaches us the true idea of love. Too often, a Christian thinks of love as warm feelings oozing with sentimentality. There is a correct word for that—a Yiddish word, *schmaltz*. We say

---

1. Some thoughts in this sermon are a paraphrased or expanded version of Joel R. Beeke and Paul M. Smalley, *Reformed Systematic Theology* (Wheaton, Ill.: Crossway), 1:790-802.

something is "schmaltzy" when it is gushing with feelings of nostalgia and sentimentality. Now, there is a place for that—most of us, no doubt, are rather sentimental—but let's not confuse sentimentality with spirituality. The Bible says, "God is love." The love of God is something far other and far better than "schmaltz."

The second error is to say that God is *only* love. People who think this way say, "Well, if God is love, then that is all God is." We reduce all God's attributes to just one. We find that idea in liberal theology, and it usually eliminates holiness, justice, wrath, and other attributes of God that the unsaved find uncomfortable. It also does away with the whole idea of hell and eternal punishment. This idea that God is only love is behind phrases you may have heard, such as "My God wouldn't send anybody to hell," or "God loves everyone unconditionally." But those statements are not anywhere in the Bible. They are contrary to Scripture.

No Christian would say, "God is only love, and therefore, none of these other attributes apply to Him." But sometimes, well-meaning but misdirected and imbalanced Christians say something close to that: "God is *primarily* love." For example, they say that, among the wonderful attributes of God, the love of God stands out as the Mount Everest. He is more love than He is all His other attributes combined, they say. They may mean well, but that is immature theology, if not simply mistaken.

An important relationship exists between all the attributes of God. God is love, but He is also many other things. We dare not make any one of them primary at the expense of making others secondary. Those who consider love the main attribute of God usually downplay His holiness or justice, and it is evident in their lives. In fact, I believe that many practical errors can be traced back to a faulty view of God. So if we say that God is primarily love and we minimize His holiness, that manifests itself in a lifestyle of license and self-indulgence. If we move to the opposite extreme and say that God is mainly holiness, legalism will normally be the result. Imbalance in our view of God will result in imbalanced lives.

The truth is that God is infinite in all that He is. He is infinite in love and infinite in holiness. It is impossible for one infinity to be greater than another infinity. God is infinite love and infinite holiness. He is infinite power and wisdom. He is infinite in all that He is.

The third error is a strange one. It says that *God is not love.* This notion is easy to disprove with the following logic: if it is true to say, "God is love," it is not true to say, "God is not love." Very few people would explicitly deny that God is love, but some people come close to saying that. They sometimes overemphasize other attributes of God at the expense of God's love. As some overdo God's love, others minimize God's love. They say things like, "The essence of God is holiness; love is *merely* one of His attributes." Others will say, "Yes, God is love"; however, the way they understand it is that God is just describing Himself anthropomorphically; hence, God is not really love, for love is only a human thing. God is not a man, and therefore, it is just an illusion or figure of speech.

There is also a figure of speech called *anthropopathy,* or *anthropopathism,* which means that we attribute to God human emotions to draw some sort of analogy. Some overdo it in this area and say, "We love, so in some sense, yes, I suppose you could say that God loves, but not really." No, that's wrong, and it leads to an explicit denial of our text, "God is love." The fact that God is love and we have a kind of love doesn't mean that God is less than love. It means that He is more than love as we know it. He has perfect love in a greater way than we have love.

Then there are those who greatly minimize the love of God, even by appealing to other great biblical truths. Among those who are Calvinists, there can be a kind of "hyper-Calvinism" that says, "God loves only His elect; He does not love the non-elect or the reprobate in any way. He has no love of any kind, no goodness and no mercy to all universally. Everything positive is reserved for His elect." That is not what the Bible says, and that is not historic Calvinism. But you see, behind that error is a distorted view of God that would basically say that God is not really love but is only love in a relational way to some people.

Therefore, the Bible says that God is love. He is not *just* love, and He is not *barely* love. God is love—infinite, eternal, and unchangeable love. And now that we have set aside three things that the phrase

"God is love" does not mean, let us move on to what "God is love" does mean.

2. What "God Is Love" Does Mean

What does it mean that God is love? You see that phrase on greeting cards people send. Maybe you have a plaque on your bedroom wall reading, "God is love." It's very simple but very deep. So, let's go into the depths and see what the Bible says. Here are three things the Bible means when it says, "God is love."

1. God is love in His very essence.
The first way God is love, according to the Bible, is that God is love in His very essence. This comes from the verb in that sentence—God *is* love. In other words, love belongs to the very being or essence of God.

We find that sense in two parallel passages. The first is John 4:24, when Jesus said that God is a Spirit—purely spiritual, immortal, and invisible in His very being. He doesn't have material substance or a physical body like we do. That refers to His essence.

Second, in 1 John 1:5, we read, "God is light, and in him is no darkness at all." Here, too, the reference is to His being or essence. When John says that God is love, he is speaking about something that concerns God's essence—what He is within Himself, His internal nature—not just His external relations with His creation. God is love *in Himself*, not just *loving* to others. Way back in eternity, before anything else existed, God was love in His very being. We are speaking about His eternal substance—not what He becomes (as if He could change) and not what He is in relation to other things. God is unchangeable in all that He is; therefore, it would be legitimate to say, "God is love, God has always been love, and God always will be love." So the first point is that God is love *in His essence.*

Now, love is not some thing or some part of God. The Westminster Catechism of Faith (WCF) says that God has neither parts nor passions. We can't say, "Well, the love of God is like the arm or leg of God." That is not what it means. God has no parts; all of God is love. The love of God is simply God Himself loving. It is God who is love.

When we say that God is love in His essence, we do not mean that God is love because He meets some higher standard of love—that there is a threshold of love somewhere and God meets it, so therefore God is love. No, this runs parallel to other biblical concepts. For example, God is truth. He is not truth because He meets a higher standard of truth; He *is* the standard. It is the same thing with love. He is love by His essence, eternally. There are no other standards. He is the standard. So when God shows love, it comes from His very being, which is eternal and absolute. It comes from within Him.

God doesn't derive love from anything or anybody else; God's love is self-generated. We find a fitting illustration in the sun and moon in the sky. The light that reflects from the moon comes from the sun, but the sun doesn't reflect light. Rather, it radiates light. God is light. He is like that sun. He is love. He doesn't *reflect* it from some other source. It comes from His very being because God is love.

All the attributes of God harmonize together. God is holy and God is love, and that tells us that His holiness is a loving holiness and His love is a holy love. It is the same thing with God's infinity. The infinite God is love, and therefore, God is infinite in His love. We find this expressed in the Bible. Psalm 86:5 addresses God as "plenteous in mercy unto all them that call upon thee."

Let me give you a practical application at this point. If God is infinite in His love, this means that we can never exhaust it. There is more than enough to go around for us in our deepest valleys and certainly for all eternity. Charles Spurgeon once said, "We can no more exhaust the infinite love of God than a little fish can drink up the oceans." He said that we are like little thirsty fish. Then he went on to say, "Drink on, little fish, you will never drink the oceans dry." Dear friend, we need the love of God, and we need never fear that God will need to ration it out and make us wait in line because there is only so much to go around. He lavishes love on us and says, "Drink all you want because there is more in My infinity than you will ever be able to exhaust."

My point is that God is infinite, God is love, and therefore, He is infinite in His love. And since the love of God is a holy love, it is a pure love. When John says "God is love," that means He is absolutely pure love without even one micron of impurity. No wrong motives, wrong desires, or wrong thoughts are to be found in His infinite love. God's love is unlike our best love. Your love on your most sanctified day will still be mixed with indwelling sin, which permeates the best of us in our best thoughts, words, and actions. Only when we get to heaven will we be totally pure. But God has always had an absolutely pure love. We need to get on our hands and knees and fall on our faces and say, "God is pure love!"

Sadly, we do not know what that is like in our human experiences. Some of us have been hurt by very impure love that is really only lust masquerading as something else. Sometimes we have been wounded when someone stops loving. Or when we try to love, we find it hindered by our tainted motives. But this never happens with God. His is an absolutely pure and infinitely absolute love.

This love within God is a kind of magnetism. God is love, and God is lovable. You see, love is a heartfelt, affectionate "going-out" to another. Within God, there is a going-out among the persons of the Godhead, a magnetism that binds God to God. It binds Him to Himself without weakness, for God is *powerful* love. He is infinite in His power and in His love, so it is an omnipotent love.

So there is our first point, that God is love in His very essence.

2. Love in God is essential to the Trinity.
God is love, therefore, He has always been love. Let's go way back into eternity in our imaginations, long before creation. The Bible says, "before the world began" (Titus 1:2). What was before the world began? Eternity. And back in eternity, there was no earth, no humans, no animals, no angels, there was nothing except God—from all eternity, God from Himself and within Himself. Back then God was love. How could God be love? Since God is love in His essence, God, in His highest degree of love, loves Himself. There was no one else to love. God loves Himself. If our highest duty is to love the Lord our God—I say this with reverence—it is God's highest duty to love God, and He does.

We occasionally have problems with the idea that God loves Himself because we say, "Wait a moment, isn't self-love wrong?" Many people think nothing is wrong with self-love in us, but there is when we, by nature, love ourselves more than we love God. Hence, we become gods to ourselves and usurp God's place and deny His claims on us. Self-love in us easily becomes selfishness and greed. It results in a man-centered universe in which we forget that we are not God. But God is God, and there is nothing wrong with God loving Himself. That is His ultimate prerogative. God loves Himself. So when the Bible says that God is love, we also understand that God loves Himself.

By its very definition, love requires an object. It is a transitive verb; you love *something* or *someone*. You might say, "Yet there is only one God in eternity—no angels, people, or animals. So whom did God love?" God loved Himself. You respond, "Yes, but where is the object of God loving Himself?" Here we find that God is both subject and object, God loving Himself. There is only one God, and this therefore tells us that there is something plural within God—the Trinity. God loves Himself. This is a glorious aspect of the Trinity.

God does not merely exist as one but as one in three persons. He is a God who always exists in relationship. We are given a vision in the opening verses of John's Gospel about the reality of God: "In the beginning was the Word, and the Word was with God," and so on. There in the beginning was God with God! There was not only God in the glory of His unity and in the glory of His own uniqueness but there was also this marvelous reality of God with God. That means that in God there is always "with-ness." There is always togetherness. There is never loneliness or isolation with God. There is always love in God because from eternity God the Father loved God the Son. There was never a more loving Father, and there was never a more loved Son. And that love was reciprocated. That love is impossible for a monad, for one being that exists in undifferentiated isolation. He has nothing to love. But in God, there is with-ness. In God, there is and was always love, fellowship, and communion.

When God made man, He made him in His own image. God made him for community, for fellowship, for with-ness—for life in communion and community. And man must find that need fulfilled in his fellowship with God at one great level. God walked in the garden, and Adam came and spoke to Him. There was great familiarity between God and man before the fall. And on that vertical plain, man had fellowship with God: "This is life eternal, that they might know thee the only true God" (John 17:3)—consider the with-ness there! And then God says, "It is not good that the man should be alone; I will make him an help meet for him" (Gen. 2:18). God provided a wife for man's social needs. He provided a family to meet man's needs for togetherness with his own kind.

It is a glorious thing that when Jesus Christ became man, He had a need for fellowship in His human nature. He found marvelous fulfillment in fellowship with God, at the beginning of every day to commune with His Father and to walk with Him, while nothing separated Him and His Father. Oh, the marvelous conversations They had, the marvelous prayers He offered as His only begotten Son to His Father through the veil into the holiest place! And He went with boldness. He said, "Abba Father," and He found fellowship.

Let's examine this in a bit more detail, starting with the Father. The Bible repeatedly says that the Father loves the Son. John 3:35 reads, "The Father loveth the Son, and hath given all things into his hand." John 5:20 reads, "For the Father loveth the Son, and sheweth him all things that himself doeth."

So many verses tell us about this love of the Father for the Son. At Christ's baptism, the Father said, "This is my beloved Son, in whom I am well pleased" (Matt. 3:17). Colossians 1:13 calls Him the Father's "dear Son"—literally, the Son of His love. Consider John 17:24, where the Son of God is praying to His Father: "Father, I will that they also, whom thou hast given me, be with me where I am; that they may behold my glory, which thou hast given me: for thou lovedst me before the foundation of the world." So the love of the Father for the Son isn't just something after the incarnation. We are not talking only about incarnation love but ontological, intertrinitarian love from eternity past.

Proverbs 8:30 puts these words in the mouth of Jesus: "I was daily his delight, rejoicing always before him." God promised the Messiah in Isaiah 42:1, "Behold my servant, whom I uphold; mine elect, in whom my soul delighteth." So the Bible is replete with verses like this that say that the Father has always loved the Son within the Trinity.

There are different kinds of love, but this love is a perfect, unique love. When the Father beheld the Son, He took delight in the Son. He looked at Him and saw the essence of all beauty and all goodness.

And when He beheld the Son, He rejoiced from all eternity due to His wonderful love for the Son. Now, remember, this love is eternal. There never was a time when the Father did not love the Son, and there never was a break in this love, where the Father said, "I need to take a break for a minute and recoup my resources." No, God always had more than enough love from all eternity.

What's more, the Son loves the Father as well. Jesus faithfully delivers the commandments of His Father to His disciples, "that the world may know that I love the Father" (John 14:31). This is true in His dual nature, and Jesus had no sin. He always kept the laws of God. He kept the Great Commandment to love the Lord God.

We are going deeper than that. We are going back into eternity before Jesus became a man. God the Son loved God the Father from all eternity in His deity. As the Father eternally loved the Son, so the Son eternally received and returned that love unbroken, immediately, perfectly, and without delay, hindrance, or interruption. Infinite love is given to an infinite object and being returned perfectly for all eternity. Christ, being eternal God, has the infinite capacity to receive that infinite love and to return it in an infinite way perfectly acceptable to the Father.

God's love to God is never unrequited. Perhaps you have had a heart broken by unrequited love. You have loved somebody, and they don't return it. Or perhaps they loved you for a time but then stopped loving you. That is sad. That is an effect of sin in the world. It was never like that within God, and it never will be. God's love is never unrequited; it is never too late; it is always returned. And the Father and Son always took this eternal love and delight in each other. Jonathan Edwards put it this way:

> The infinite essential love of God is, as it were, an infinite and eternal mutual holy energy between the Father and the Son, a pure holy act whereby the Deity becomes nothing but an infinite and unchangeable act of love which proceeds from both the Father and Son. 'Tis all an holy energy consisting in that infinite flame of pure love and holy delight that there is, from all eternity, between the Father and the Son, immensely loving and delighting and rejoicing in each other.

That is great theology. Who says Calvinism is dry and emotionless? No, this is good theology for the heart—the Father loving the Son, the Son loving the Father, a self-perpetuating dynamo of holy love!

But what about the Holy Spirit? Romans 15:30 speaks of "the love of the Spirit." Here is where theologians are of one of two minds. Some say that as the Father loves the Son and the Son loves the Father, so the Spirit comes in. The Father loves the Spirit, the Spirit loves the Father, the Son loves the Spirit, the Spirit loves the Son, and so forth. That is granted. Others such as Jonathan Edwards go deeper and say, "The Spirit Himself is that bond of love between the two going back and forth."

Someone once asked Cornelius Van Til, "What is the deepest thing you meditate on?" In a flash he said, "Oh, it is the ontological eternal Trinity. You are on holy ground just to meditate on this love between the members of the Trinity."

This helps us understand the nature of God's holiness. In true love, there is always a jealousy that protects it. This jealousy is good and right between husband and wife, a jealousy that you will not share the object of your affection with another. The same thing is true within the Trinity. The Father loves the Son and the Spirit, and they love each other with holy jealousy. When anything in creation dares to intrude upon that love within and between each member of the Trinity, a holy jealousy arises within the Godhead itself.

For example, when someone comes between the Father and the Son and questions the deity of the Son or questions His perfect humanity and sinlessness, the holy jealousy of the Father rises up and says, "How dare you say that against My Son, in whom I love and delight?" The holiness of God springs like a flame issuing forth from the holy love within the Trinity. Holiness and love within God are not at loggerheads; they work together in a marvelous way. This love within the Trinity, then, is a self-perpetuating dynamo of living energy and holy glory.

3. God is love, and therefore, God displays His love.
Out of love to each other, the persons of the Holy Trinity chose to allow that love to overflow themselves so that it might be displayed outside of God Himself. The internal love of God now becomes

externalized to His creation. It began back in eternity in the covenant of redemption, which has been called the covenant of love. God predestined all things and said, "I will display this love in a variety of ways." There are different words for love as well as different flavors and degrees of love. God is the source of all true love.

First John 4:7 says, "Love is of God." Out of love, God gives good gifts to His creation. James 1:17 says, "Every good gift and every perfect gift is from above, and cometh down from the Father of lights, with whom is no variableness, neither shadow of turning." God is love; therefore God is loving and shows love to His creatures.

God so loves that He gives, and He does so in a variety of ways and degrees. There are those who say, "If God doesn't love everybody and everything equally, that is not right." God loves His creation. He loves the flowers differently than He loves the animals, yet He loves both. God loves the animals in a greater way than He does the dirt and trees. In the same way, God has a higher love for humanity and then, of course, the angels. But within humanity, it is God's sovereign prerogative to show different kinds and degrees of love. Election is His sovereign choice. God has a general love for all, but He reserves a special love for some. It all comes back to God being love; He displays the wide variety of His love. God loves all people with some love, and He loves some with all love.

Now in this display of the special ultimate love of God, God draws His elect into the special love bond within the Trinity. Look again at John 17:26, the last verse of Christ's High Priestly Prayer: "And I have declared unto them thy name, and will declare it: that the love wherewith thou hast loved me may be in them, and I in them." The elect, therefore, were created and chosen to be the love gifts between the members of the Trinity. If you are married, you men give your wives love gifts; and you wives, you love your husbands and want to show them your love. It is the same with parents to their children. The Father, Son, and Spirit within themselves in all eternity had this love, but in creating things to display it, the things they create become not only the gifts between one another but the conduits of their love. So the love from the Father to the Son flows through us, and we get to enjoy some of that love. He brings us into the bonds of the Trinity.

Now mind you, we do not become divine, but we do partake of and enjoy the love within God Himself.

The Father gives us to the Son as a gift of His love, and it goes back to the Father. That is to say, the love that is within God and is displayed within you and in His creation finds a focal point in the incarnation, in the Lord Jesus Christ. Consequently, when the Son incarnate becomes the revelation of the love of God, we can say that the Lord Jesus Christ is the love of God in human flesh. It is not just poetry; it is good theology to say, "Jesus Christ is love incarnate."

Maybe some of you have been looking for love in all the wrong places. Do you want real love? Come to Jesus. He is love in the flesh, perfect love beyond our wildest imaginations. He is better than we could ever dream. He is God's love manifest in the flesh and offered to all in the gospel.

3. Applications

Let's consider three applications of these truths:

1. The truth that God is love should move us to worship God.

God reveals His essence to us so that it might be reflected back to Him in the appropriate manner of worship. Worship is the act of acknowledging the worth of God and declaring what God means to us. Therefore, God shows His love for us and commends His love to us, and it should move us to worship Him. When we ponder that God is love, we should not just simply feel sentimental or good within ourselves, but this should move us to worship such a God who, within the Trinity, chose to display His love to us. This should move us to worship such a God as this with a holy wonder and delight, with rejoicing and singing.

2. The fact that God is love should move us to love God.

When we know how wonderful God is, what a loving God He is, that should move us to love Him in return. And that helps and enables us to keep the greatest of all the commandments, to love the Lord your God with all your soul, mind, heart, and strength.

Jonathan Edwards wrote, "If holiness in God consists chiefly in love to Himself, holiness in the creature must chiefly consist in love to Him." When we seek for true holiness without love, that is not holiness. Genuine holiness is bathed in the effectual love of God. When coupled with worship, it becomes a loving worship, a worshipful love, what the old theologians called *adoration*. We enjoy a holy, loving intimacy with God. In 1 John 4:19, we read, "We love him, because he first loved us."

3. We should love one another.
This is where we came into the text, and this is where we will go out. This is 1 John 4 over and over again. For example, it says, "Let us love one another, for love is of God." God is love. When we are moved by God, saying "God is love" is easier than to immediately love God, but the demands of love don't end there. We must also let that love He has shown us, which fills our hearts, spill over to others. Remember, God loves them too! It is not always so easy to love our fellow sinners, nor for them to love us. But the love of God makes it possible because that love flows through us. God's loving grace flowing through us even enables us to love our enemies. If we don't, then we really don't know what it means that God is love. We appreciate those three precious words best in a loving relationship with God *and* in a love for the creatures that God also loves.

All through his first epistle, John teaches that likeness is the proof of relationship. The great proof that we are truly related to the eternal God and belong to Him is that we are like Him—especially in exercising love. John says that everyone who loves has been born of God. We are naturally too sinful for such divine love. Martin Luther said that sin turns us in upon ourselves. We do not naturally reach out to others in selfless, self-sacrificing love. But when the Spirit of God breaks into our lives and we are "born of God," God shows His love for us in Christ. God plants within us the seed of a new beginning. He stirs within us a love toward those who belong to Christ.

John Owen said, "Christian love is to be as unconfined as the beams of the sun. It doesn't select on whom it will shine its beams." Our love should not shine only on those who we think deserve it, for who is deserving of God's love? Our love is to shine on everyone because God Himself so loved the world that He sent His Son to save it. Love, as much as righteousness, is part of the Christian's birthmark. God is love, says John, so we too must extend love.

"God is love." May God so work in us by His Spirit so that His love will move us to worship Him, to love Him, and to love each other!

Chapter 36

Seals Five and Six: The Persecuted Church

And when he had opened the fifth seal, I saw under the altar the souls of them that were slain for the word of God, and for the testimony which they held:

And they cried with a loud voice, saying, How long, O Lord, holy and true, dost thou not judge and avenge our blood on them that dwell on the earth? And white robes were given unto every one of them; and it was said unto them, that they should rest yet for a little season, until their fellowservants also and their brethren, that should be killed as they were, should be fulfilled.

And I beheld when he had opened the sixth seal, and, lo, there was a great earthquake; and the sun became black as sackcloth of hair, and the moon became as blood; And the stars of heaven fell unto the earth, even as a fig tree casteth her untimely figs, when she is shaken of a mighty wind. And the heaven departed as a scroll when it is rolled together; and every mountain and island were moved out of their places. And the kings of the earth, and the great men, and the rich men, and the chief captains, and the mighty men, and every bondman, and every free man, hid themselves in the dens and in the rocks of the mountains;

And said to the mountains and rocks, Fall on us, and hide us from the face of him that sitteth on the throne, and from the wrath of the Lamb: for the great day of his wrath is come; and who shall be able to stand?

—REVELATION 6:9–17

No one likes to be persecuted.[1] Yet Scripture tells us that is part of the territory that we inherit if we are godly Christians, for all who live godly in Christ Jesus shall suffer persecution (2 Tim. 3:12).

How do you handle persecution? How should you handle persecution? How should you support Christians who are persecuted around the world today much more severely than you have ever faced?

And what about future persecution? As society becomes increasingly intolerant to Christianity even as it boasts of its tolerance, would you be prepared to go to jail for Christ's sake? We can find help in addressing these questions and many more from the second part of Revelation 6.

The message of the second cycle of visions of Revelation (chapters 4–7) is that behind this world and everything in it, there is a sovereign God who works not according to whim or caprice, but according to His purpose. He carries out that plan in every detail through the crucified and risen Savior, Jesus Christ, the Lamb that was slain.

In the first cycle of visions in the book of Revelation (chapters 1–3), the Lord gives John a vision of the church in the world and Christ's relationship to it. We see things on the surface, as it were. From chapter 4 onward, John is shown what is going on behind the scenes. He sees things from God's perspective. He sees a throne, a book, and the One who alone is able to open the book and carry out the plan that is written inside it.

Revelation 6 and 7 detail the things that typically happen to us in this world before the Lord's return and what it means to be a Christian. The opening of the seven seals of the book reveals God's purposes for Christians in this world. These seven seals are not to be regarded as seven successive phases of history, but as the complete picture of what God has in store for Christians in this world.

The previous chapter addresses the opening of the first four of the seven seals, which launched the four horsemen of the apocalypse, bringing war, famine, and plague. The red horse, black horse, and

---

1. This sermon is adapted from Joel R. Beeke, *Revelation*, *The Lectio Continua* (Grand Rapids: Reformation Heritage Books, 2016), 221–33.

pale horse come to our doors as well. We live under the same kind of pressures as the Christians of John's day. But the message of the first four seals is that if we are in Christ, we will be victorious over these difficulties. All the terrible forces and influences that bear down on us like a stampede of horses will not conquer us; rather, we will conquer them in the power of Christ.

The opening of the fifth and sixth seals also brings destruction. Wherever Christ comes in the power of His gospel, the sword is bound to follow. There is antagonism, opposition, hostility, and persecution.

Let us study the second cycle of visions in Revelation under the following headings: the outrage of persecution (Rev. 6:9); the outcry of the persecuted (v. 10); and the outcome of persecution (vv. 11–17).

1. The Outrage of Persecution

When the fifth seal is opened (v. 9), John sees the souls of believers who were slain (or butchered) for the Word of God and their testimony. This seal describes something that has happened throughout the ages to God's people, wherever they have been.

Genesis 3 records the first preaching of the gospel in the garden of Eden by God Himself. He came looking for Adam, who was hiding because he had disobeyed God by eating the forbidden fruit. God asked, "Where art thou?" (v. 9). Then God preached the gospel to Adam and Eve, saying to the serpent, "I will put enmity between thee and the woman, and between thy seed and her seed; it shall bruise thy head, and thou shalt bruise his heel" (v. 15). That is the gospel. This promise foreshadowed what would happen on Calvary. Christ, as the seed of the woman, goes forth "conquering, and to conquer" (Rev. 6:2) the serpent.

But the sword is also involved. For God said, "I will put enmity between thee and the woman, and between thy seed and her seed." Hostility, hatred, antagonism, persecution, and murder follow in the wake of this enmity. Genesis 4 tells us that Cain killed his brother Abel, and Abel's blood cried out to God for vengeance. Likewise, being a Christian in this world means confronting the sword of this world and its anti-Christian agenda.

Jesus says in Matthew 10:34–39: "Think not that I am come to send peace on earth: I came not to send peace, but a sword. For I am come to set a man at variance against his father, and the daughter against her mother, and the daughter in law against her mother in law. And a man's foes shall be they of his own household. He that loveth father or mother more than me is not worthy of me: and he that loveth son or daughter more than me is not worthy of me. And he that taketh not his cross, and followeth after me, is not worthy of me. He that findeth his life shall lose it: and he that loseth his life for my sake shall find it."

Jesus is saying that true Christians will suffer persecution. All Christians must take up their crosses. They must lose their lives for Christ's sake. That may be literally true, as in physical martyrdom in some countries, but it is also true metaphorically and spiritually. To be a Christian in this world means to lose one's life for Christ's sake. It might happen in the context of an Islamic or North Korean prison, but it might also happen in a believer's own home. Mother will rise against daughter; brother against brother. This is part of what it means to be a Christian. It means suffering for Christ's sake.

Daniel certainly suffered for his faith. Though he knew he might be thrown to the lions if he didn't stop praying to his God in Babylon, Daniel did not shrink from doing his duty. He trusted in God even in the lions' den. And God preserved him. According to Daniel 6:23, "Daniel was taken up out of the den, and no manner of hurt was found upon him, because he believed in his God."

The apostle Paul viewed persecution as a constant reminder of his weakness and utter dependence on God (2 Cor. 12:9–10). The heroes of faith in Hebrews 11 learned through persecution that their focus must be on the eternal rather than the temporal (vv. 1–3). They were to trust the Lord in the midst of suffering, and they were to desire a "better country" (v. 16).

Many Christians have been martyred for their faith throughout church history. Consider the believers who were tortured to death under Roman emperors. Remember the Reformers who were driven from place to place, whipped, and then burned alive or beheaded. Today, over fifty thousand churches in 115 countries hold a special service each year commemorating the worldwide persecution of Christians. We should not ignore the plight of persecuted Christians around the world.

Millions who profess the name of Christ around the world meet secretly for worship in their homes because they are oppressed by hostile governments. If their allegiance to Christ is discovered, their homes are attacked and burned. The women and children are sold into slavery. Husbands and wives, parents and children, have their throats slit in front of each other for no other reason than refusing to deny the name of Christ. Hundreds of thousands are brutally tortured and brainwashed in an effort to force them to recant their faith. They spend years in solitary prison cells or hard labor camps. They fear daily for their lives.

Tens of thousands of believers are martyred each year for their faith. More Christians have been martyred for their faith in the past century than in the previous nineteen centuries combined.[2] Millions more face discrimination in their daily lives. Their access to education is restricted. They are forced to take the most menial jobs. They are excluded from the political and judicial processes of their societies. They are ridiculed and despised.

This is still relatively difficult to imagine in the United States. We face increasing opposition for our Christian beliefs, but not the intense persecution that millions of others suffer for the faith. The law of our land still allows us the freedom to worship. It is difficult to imagine living in constant fear that your wife, husband, or neighbor might betray you. It is hard to imagine having no legal recourse, no hope for justice, and nowhere to hide. But that is precisely what millions of Christians face in other parts of the world.

When the fifth seal is opened, John sees the souls of these martyrs under the altar. This refers to the altar of burnt offerings, as described in Leviticus. When an animal was sacrificed on the altar of burnt offerings, the blood would be caught in a basin under the altar. In his vision, John doesn't see the blood of animals under the altar, but

---

2. "Report: Christian Dies for Beliefs Every *5 Minutes*," WorldNetDaily, accessed June 21, 2016, http://www.wnd.com/2011/06/311393/#!.

rather the souls of men, women, and children who have lost their lives for Christ's sake. He sees those who did not count their lives dear for Christ's sake.

In John's vision, these saints are not being slain, but have already passed through persecution and are now in heaven, awaiting full glory. One purpose of this seal is to show that Christ controls the martyrdom of the saints, for only when Christ opens the seal do the believers who were slain cry out for vengeance.

Being a Christian means laying down your life for Christ. It requires total commitment and consecration. It means you live your life as under the altar for Christ's sake. The Christian life is marked by consecration and sacrifice.

Paul describes this life in Romans 12: "I beseech you therefore, brethren, by the mercies of God, that ye present your bodies a living sacrifice, holy, acceptable unto God, which is your reasonable service" (v. 1). He is saying: "Think of what Christ has done for you. He has poured out His soul unto death for you. Now the only reasonable thing you can do is to pour out your life as a thank offering to Him."

In 2 Corinthians 5:14–15, Paul explains what he means by "reasonable service." He says, "The love of Christ constraineth us; because we thus judge, that if one died for all, then were all dead: and that he died for all, that they which live should not henceforth live unto themselves, but unto him which died for them, and rose again." When he says, "The love of Christ constrains us," he is not talking about some sentimental feeling, but rather the love of Christ as demonstrated on the cross. Paul is saying, as it were: "When I consider Calvary, I think that if He did that for me, I can no longer live for myself. My life is not my own, but I must put it under His altar. I need to give it up to Him and live for Him. That is the reasonable thing to do."

How much of your life is under the altar? How much have you sacrificed for your faith? Do you offer the Lord only leftovers or things you no longer want? A man was once given two calves. He said, "I will give one of them to the Lord." One of the calves grew sick and died, so the farmer declared, "The Lord's calf has died." How easy it must have been, under the old covenant, to come to the Lord's house with a diseased, weak, or dying animal from the flock. But that was sacrilege. God's people were to bring Him the best of the flock and the firstfruits of their fields.

Likewise, we are to give God our best. If Christ died upon the cross, bearing God's wrath for our sin, then it is sacrilege for us to hold anything back from Him. The scandal is that people who are living not for themselves but for Christ—those whose lives are a fragrant offering to God—are often the very people hounded, persecuted, and butchered by the world.

2. The Outcry of the Persecuted

In Revelation 6:10, we read, "And they cried out with a loud voice, saying, How long, O Lord, holy and true, dost thou not judge and avenge our blood on them that dwell on the earth?" To understand this verse, we must remember that it is part of a vision, not a literal picture of heaven. There is no literal altar in heaven, just as there is no literal throne. Also, there is no unhappiness, frustration, impatience, suffering, or thirst for revenge in heaven. No matter how we understand this outcry from beneath the altar, we are not to understand it as a thirst for revenge. It is clear from verse 11 that the glorified saints here are at rest and perfectly happy. The white robes they wear signify sinlessness, happiness, and acceptance with God.

So they do not cry out for revenge; rather, they pray for the vindication of God's holy name as "Judge of the earth" (Ps. 94:2). This outcry of the martyrs is similar to the prayers in the imprecatory psalms, or "cursing psalms," in the Old Testament.

The wrong that was done to these slaughtered saints cries out to be put right. It reminds us of Abel's blood in the ground crying out to God (Gen. 4:10). We are not to understand that literally, because blood is not able to cry out. Neither are we to understand it in a sinister sort of way. The slain Abel did not become some kind of malignant force, seeking to take revenge on Cain. No, Abel is in heaven with the spirits of just men made perfect, and he is perfectly happy. He did not ask for revenge. But what happened to Abel did not go unnoticed. It was dealt with; it was put right.

The same outcome is in view in this outcry of the souls under the altar. These glorified saints are not thirsting for personal revenge. They are yearning for God's name to be vindicated and for His righteousness to be upheld.

Do you yearn for the vindication of God's holy name? Can you say with the psalmist in Psalm 119:127–28: "Therefore I love thy commandments above gold; yea, above fine gold. Therefore I esteem all thy precepts concerning all things to be right; and I hate every false way"? Stephen, the first Christian martyr, died praying, "Lord, lay not this sin to their charge" (Acts 7:60). There was no personal vindictiveness or thirst for revenge in those words. Yet what happened to Stephen and millions like him cannot go unpunished. If God is God, these crimes must be punished.

So we cry out: "LORD, how long shall the wicked, how long shall the wicked triumph? How long shall they utter and speak hard things? and all the workers of iniquity boast themselves?" (Ps. 94:3–4).

Christians are persecuted for various reasons. One is because we say there is only one way to salvation, and that is through Jesus Christ, God's Son. This exclusive claim does not fit the New Age movement. Neither does it accommodate radical Islam.

Christians are also persecuted because Satan wants to destroy the people of God. Peter thus advises believers, "Be sober, be vigilant; because your adversary the devil, as a roaring lion, walketh about, seeking whom he may devour" (1 Peter 5:8). Satan aims to swallow or destroy all believers.

Christians are persecuted so that they might be strengthened in faith. James 1:3–4 says: "The trying of your faith worketh patience. But let patience have her perfect work, that ye may be perfect and entire, wanting nothing." God tests the faith of His people to develop spiritual endurance in their walk with Him.

Persecution is also the pathway to God's gracious reward. Paul says to Timothy near the end of his life, "I have fought a good fight, I have finished my course, I have kept the faith: henceforth there is laid up for me a crown of righteousness, which the Lord, the righteous judge, shall give me at that day: and not to me only, but unto all them also that love his appearing" (2 Tim. 4:7–8).

But most of all, persecution is the way to God's kingdom of glory. The day of judgment, which follows a time of intense persecution, will make clear to the church and the entire world that Christ is holy and true, and that He represents God in His perfect justice.

The saints under the altar do not cry in vain. Everything is done to comfort them and to reassure them that the day on which God will judge the world in righteousness is not far off.

First, "white robes were given unto every one of them" (Rev. 6:11). Christians who suffer persecution will one day be adorned in white robes as they praise the triune God. White is a symbol of eternal justification by Christ's blood and acquittal by the Father. It is also a symbol of sanctification, for in heaven the saints are perfectly holy before God in Christ. And it is a symbol of their victory. Just as the rider on the white horse symbolizes Christ's victory, so the white robes given to souls under the altar symbolize that they are more than conquerors in the battle of faith. In short, white is the symbol of their perfected, glorified nature (Heb. 12:23).

Second, "it was said unto them, that they should rest yet for a little season, until their fellow-servants also and their brethren, that should be killed as they were, should be fulfilled" (Rev. 6:11). This promise is meant to reassure these souls that they have not cried out in vain. They must rest until the gathering in of all the elect, and especially the offering up of all the martyrs of God, has been accomplished. God knows all who are His, and He knows the exact number of people who will die for the faith. His timetable is also absolutely perfect. He is never one step out of sync with His glorious purposes to gather, preserve, defend and glorify His Son's church.

But we are inclined to ask: "When is Christ coming? Why does He tarry?" Peter tells us we are mistaken if we think that Christ is tarrying or delaying; rather, He is ever at work, gathering and building His church: "The Lord is not slack concerning his promise…but is longsuffering to us-ward, not willing that any should perish, but that all should come to repentance." He urges us therefore to "account that the longsuffering of our Lord is salvation," that is, salvation for all those who are ordained to eternal life through Christ (2 Peter 3:9, 15).

We have a significant responsibility to alleviate the suffering of Christians who are being persecuted for their faith. God will keep them, but we must do what lies in our power to do here on earth. Here are some ways to help persecuted Christians today:

1. *Be informed.* Write to religious liberty advocacy groups, requesting updated information on worldwide persecution.

2. *Empathize with those who are suffering for Christ.* As 1 Corinthians 12:26 says, "And whether one member suffer, all the members suffer with it; or one member be honoured, all the members rejoice with it."

3. *Pray for them.* When Peter was imprisoned, the church gathered to pray without ceasing for his release (Acts 12:5). We, too, must pray for those who are languishing in horrible conditions. We should pray also for Christians in specific countries.

For example, Afghanistan has forty-eight thousand mosques and not one church building. It has seventy unreached people groups who have never heard the gospel. Of the fifty languages spoken, the New Testament has been translated into only two, while none of the fifty has a complete Bible.

Likewise, Sudanese Christians are often forced to flee *jihad* (or Islamic holy war) into the snake-infested bush. Thousands struggle to survive by eating leaves off trees. Thousands more are killed by government-backed militias.

4. *Support them.* Speak of their faithfulness in the church. As 2 Thessalonians 1:4 says, "So that we ourselves glory in you in the churches of God for your patience and faith in all your persecutions and tribulations that ye endure." Speak of their plight to your friends. Write letters to the media. Write to your leaders in Congress and urge them to act on behalf of persecuted Christians around the world. Tell them a double crime is being committed: the crime of persecution by Communist and Islamic governments against Christians, and the crime of free nations like ours that ignore such wrongdoing out of self-interest or political cowardice.

5. *Go to them.* If we can't visit suffering Christians, we can find ways to contact them. Follow the example of Peter, who wrote to brethren scattered far and wide in his day (1 Peter 1:1). At the very least, contribute to mission groups that work among persecuted people.

When the lives of her people were in jeopardy, Esther was tempted to avoid the plight of her fellow Jews until Mordecai, her guardian, said to her: "Think not with thyself that thou shalt escape in the king's house, more than all the Jews. For if thou altogether holdest thy peace at this time, then shall there enlargement and deliverance arise to the Jews from another place; but thou and thy father's house shall be destroyed: and who knoweth whether thou art come to the kingdom for such a time as this?" (Est. 4:13–14).

Today, we are citizens of the most powerful nation in the world. Like Esther, we feel safe in the United States, secure in the possession of the freedoms of speech, religion, and assembly. But like Esther, we must speak out against the extermination of our brethren in other countries, even if it costs us something to do that. If we don't speak out, no one is safe. We may be next in line for intense persecution.

We must heed the words of Hebrews 13:3: "Remember them that are in bonds, as bound with them; and them which suffer adversity, as being yourselves also in the body."

3. The Outcome of Persecution

If evil triumphs, the world gets worse, and the wicked prosper, what is the point of being a Christian? The opening of the sixth seal (Rev. 6:12–17) answers that question. It tells us that the day of judgment is coming, when God in His almighty power will right every wrong with the world. He will shake the world and everyone in it. He will move mountains and islands, darken the sun, turn the moon into blood, and cause the stars to fall from heaven. It will be a terrifying day for those who are not right with God.

The symbols of this passage, including falling stars, the cries of the wicked, the quaking earth, and the rolling up of the sky as a scroll are all descriptive of the tremendous and terrifying upheaval that is coming on that day that God has appointed to judge the world. The opening of the sixth seal tells us about the complete overthrow of all earthly powers, rulers, movements, and systems. Every power and authority in earth and in hell will be confounded. No words could more powerfully express the total hopelessness, ruin, and despair of all earthly powers and interest.

The key figure in all of this is the Lamb. Verses 15–17 describe a dislocated universe and a terrified human race. People of all classes—kings of the earth, great and rich men, mighty men, and bondmen and free men—hide themselves in the dens and caves of the mountains and cry out, "Fall on us, and hide us from the face of him that sitteth on the throne, and from the wrath of the Lamb: for the great day of his wrath is come; and who shall be able to stand?"

These hardened men have been slaughtering Christians without a pang of guilt, yet now they cannot look into the face of the Lamb. They call upon the rocks to fall upon them and cover them. They call to the mountains to collapse upon them. They would rather perish in a nuclear holocaust than look into the face of Jesus Christ.

The wrath of the Lamb is indeed terrifying to those who have rejected Him and scorned His love. There is nothing more frightening than the face of perfect love turned against you. That is what the day of judgment is all about. When God judges the world, He will judge through the Man He has appointed, His Son, Jesus Christ. The very Jesus who went to the cross to die for sinners will be in charge on the day of judgment.

Unbelievers will plead to be delivered from the wrath of the Lamb. How horrible it will be to be damned by Him who came to save sinners! This reminds us of Psalm 130, which asks, "If thou, LORD, shouldest mark iniquities, O Lord, who shall stand?" (v. 3). But the psalm also offers this comfort: "But there is forgiveness with thee, that thou mayest be feared" (v. 4).

For many, it will be too late to repent. Before, they felt no need to repent of sin and cling to a Savior to deliver them from the wrath to come, because they thought they could get through it on their own. Now they are calling for the mountains to fall upon them. Is the Lord pleading with you even now to come to the Lamb who died to save sinners? If He is, it is comforting to know He is still speaking to you.

The next time you hear His voice, it may be too late. Then you will bear the wrath of the Lamb.

Ultimately, the only thing that matters is that we are on the right side of King Jesus. The only thing that matters is that you and I are able to look Him in the face on the day of judgment, clothed in His white robes of righteousness. Ultimately, it does not matter what kind of nest we have made for ourselves in the short time we are here on earth. The only thing that matters is how we are related to Him. Philip Doddridge puts it like this:

> Ye sinners seek His grace
> Whose wrath ye cannot bear;
> Fly to the shelter of His cross
> And find salvation there.[3]

Christ is the Lamb of God who takes away the sin of the world. God has sent forth Jesus in this day of grace to be the covering, the propitiation for sin, to hide you from His anger and righteous judgment. Let me urge you, by the grace of the Holy Spirit, to flee to Jesus as the only Savior. Hide yourself in Him today.

---

3. Phillip Doddridge, "And Will the Judge Descend," Hymnary, accessed April 12, 2024, https://hymnary.org/text/and_will_the_judge_descend.